HISTORICAL DICTIONARIES OF CITIES, STATES, AND REGIONS
Series Editor: Jon Woronoff

Historical Dictionary of New England

Peter C. Holloran

Historical Dictionaries of
Cities, States, and Regions, No. 13

The Scarecrow Press, Inc.
Lanham, Maryland, and Oxford
2003

SCARECROW PRESS, INC.

Published in the United States of America
by Scarecrow Press, Inc.
A wholly owned subsidiary of
The Rowman & Littlefield Publishing Group, Inc.
4501 Forbes Boulevard, Suite 200, Lanham, Maryland 20706
www.scarecrowpress.com

PO Box 317
Oxford
OX2 9RU, UK

British Library Cataloguing in Publication Information Available

Library of Congress Cataloging-in-Publication Data

Holloran, Peter C., 1947–
  Historical dictionary of New England / Peter C. Holloran.
    p. cm. — (Historical dictionaries of cities, states, and
regions ; no. 13)
  Includes bibliographical references and index.
  ISBN 0-8108-4861-9 (alk. paper)
  1. New England—History—Dictionaries. I. Title. II. Historical
dictionaries of cities of the world ; no. 13.
F2 .H65 2003
974'.003—dc21   2003010895

Contents

Editor's Foreword

A bit peripheral even among the thirteen colonies and much more so among today's fifty states, New England has always been central to American history. Its six relatively small states have repeatedly carried more than their weight and continue to do so in many sectors: political, economic, social, and cultural. The region was the "cradle of liberty" at the time of the American Revolution, it sparked the struggle for the abolition of slavery that culminated in the Civil War, and its sons and daughters have been engaged in important causes throughout history. New England pioneered the movements for religious freedom, women's rights and suffrage, educational and penal reform, social welfare, and health care. Economically, it led the way from agriculture to manufacturing to services, and presently boasts a disproportionately large share of dynamic, growing companies in cutting-edge sectors. Over the past few centuries, New England has supplied an endless stream of human talent, including presidents and other influential politicians, entrepreneurs and inventors, scientists, and educators.

This makes it quite appropriate that New England should be the first American region included in the series *Historical Dictionaries of Cities, States, and Regions*. This *Historical Dictionary of New England* contains information on the region as a whole, the various states that compose it, and the people who live there, both as groups and individuals. The region and states are presented in the introduction, which tells us more about them as broad entities. The dictionary then deals with specific people, places, events, institutions, and significant aspects of political, economic, social, and cultural life. The chronology follows the progression from precolonial times to the present. And the bibliography opens the way to further study on any aspects of special interest to readers.

This volume was written by Peter C. Holloran, who teaches history at Worcester State College in Massachusetts. Born in Boston, he grew up there and earned his Ph.D. at Boston University. He also wrote a book on this "hub" of the area, entitled *Boston's Wayward Children*. But Dr. Holloran is equally familiar with New England as a whole, through his travel, teaching, and writing, as well as having been director of the New England Historical Association and Northeast Popular Culture/American Culture Association. His interests are broad enough to provide a comprehensive and stimulating view of a region he fully appreciates.

Jon Woronoff
Series Editor

Preface

It is a daunting task to compile a historical dictionary of New England because this region has been the subject of more scholarly scrutiny than any other section of the United States. It is richer than many regions in history and achievement. First colonized by the French in 1604 and the British in 1607, the New England colonies were the first to secede from the British Empire and were among the first states admitted to the union. No region has claimed more presidents as native sons (seven) or produced more men and women of exceptional accomplishment.

Although not blessed with rich natural resources or strategic importance, New England has the advantage of a long, well-defined and well-documented tradition from which it derives its identity and history. As Bernard DeVoto noted, New England was the "first finished section . . . to achieve stability in the conditions of life." The Yankees of the past and the present find this sense of identity a link, a cohesive connection that distinguished them from less fortunate Americans "from away."

Each of the six states is unique but they share common traditions and distinctive virtues that set this region apart from the other 44. This dictionary deals, in alphabetical order, with many of the facts, histories, institutions, pieces of literature, names, places, topics, and words that characterize New England. It intends to be a convenient source of reliable information on all the New England states. It is selective, of course, but not random, and offers insightful raw material useful to students, visitors, and the curious reader more than the specialist or scholar. Like any dictionary, the nature of this book fragments history and covers an embarrassingly wide range of topics. Aiming to be as comprehensive as possible, the decision to include or omit items were made with a view to their usefulness to readers. Efforts were taken to explain neglected or forgotten aspects of New England that remain significant in understanding the region rather than to cover the well-known stories. I hope this book represents a rich lode to be mined at leisure and that the chronology, appendix, and selected bibliography inspire further reading.

Acknowledgments

Among the many individuals and institutions who contributed to the writing of this book, I am especially indebted for courteous and generous assistance to the Boston Public Library, the Boston University Mugar Library, the Cambridge Public Library, and the Worcester State College Library. Cooperation also has been routine and unstinting from the Connecticut Historical Society, the Maine Historical Society, the Massachusetts Historical Society, the New Hampshire Historical Society, the Rhode Island Historical Society, and the Vermont Historical Society. Worcester State College provided timely financial support. Thanks are also due to the many friends and colleagues throughout New England who have kindly furnished advice, suggestions, and insights of one kind or another. This book reflects their efforts to improve my work, but the author remains responsible for any of its deficiencies. Finally, I am most grateful as always to my wife, Kathryn Ellis Beers, for encouragement and support.

List of Abbreviations and Acronyms

ACLU	American Civil Liberties Union
AFL	American Federation of Labor
AHAC	Ancient and Honorable Artillery Company
AL	American League
APA	American Protective Association
BPL	Boston Public Library
BSE	Boston Stock Exchange
BSO	Boston Symphony Orchestra
CIA	Central Intelligence Agency
FBI	Federal Bureau of Investigation
IRL	Immigration Restriction League
IWW	Industrial Workers of the World
KKK	Ku Klux Klan
MAS	Massachusetts Audubon Society
MASS MoCA	Massachusetts Museum of Contemporary Art
MFA	Museum of Fine Arts, Boston
MHS	Massachusetts Historical Society
MHS	Massachusetts Horticultural Society
MIT	Massachusetts Institute of Technology
NAACP	National Association for the Advancement of Colored People
NBA	National Basketball Association
NCAA	National Collegiate Athletic Association
NEHA	New England Historical Association
NEHGS	New England Historic Genealogical Society
NHL	National Hockey League
PCIJ	Permanent Court of International Justice
SPCA	Society for the Prevention of Cruelty to Animals
SPNEA	Society for the Preservation of New England Antiquities
TAC	The Architects Collaborative
WHOI	Woods Hole Oceanographic Institute

New England Cities

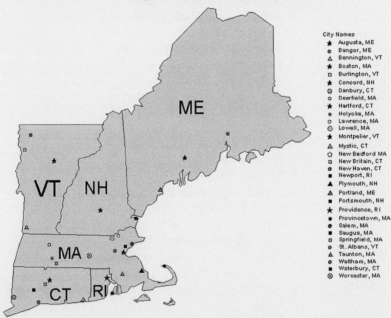

City Names

★ Augusta, ME
◉ Bangor, ME
△ Bennington, VT
★ Boston, MA
▫ Burlington, VT
★ Concord, NH
◉ Danbury, CT
○ Deerfield, MA
★ Hartford, CT
● Holyoke, MA
○ Lawrence, MA
◉ Lowell, MA
★ Montpelier, VT
△ Mystic, CT
⬠ New Bedford MA
▫ New Britain, CT
● New Haven, CT
■ Newport, RI
▲ Plymouth, NH
△ Portland, ME
■ Portsmouth, NH
★ Providence, RI
● Provincetown, MA
● Salem, MA
■ Saugus, MA
▫ Springfield, MA
● St. Albans, VT
△ Taunton, MA
◉ Waltham, MA
■ Waterbury, CT
◉ Worcester, MA

New England States and Capitals

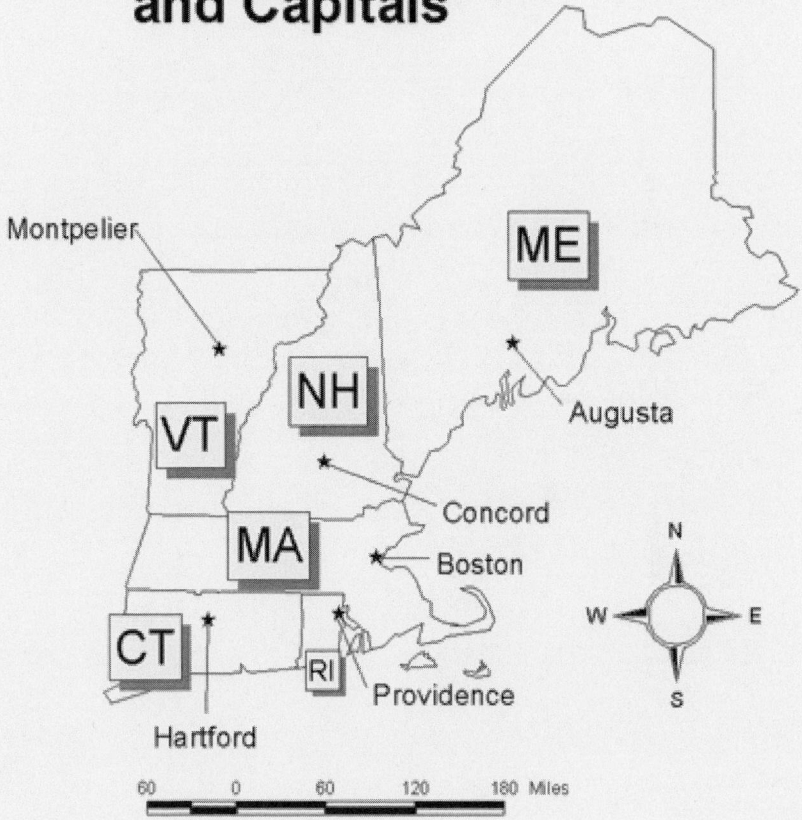

Montpelier

ME

VT

NH

Augusta

Concord

MA

Boston

CT

RI

Providence

Hartford

N

W   E

S

60   0   60   120   180 Miles

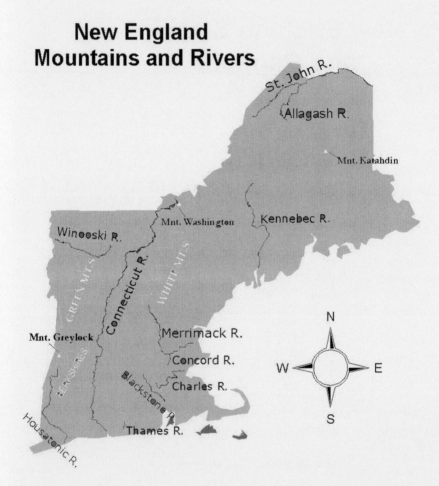

New England
Mountains and Rivers

St. John R.

Allagash R.

Mnt. Katahdin

Winooski R.

Mnt. Washington

Kennebec R.

GREEN MTS.

Connecticut R.

WHITE MTS.

Mnt. Greylock

Merrimack R.

Concord R.

BERKSHIRES

Blackstone R.

Charles R.

Housatonic R.

Thames R.

N
W   E
S

Chronology

ca. 10,000 B.C.   Last glacier in New England recedes.

ca. 9,000 B.C.   Paleo-Indians are the first humans in New England.

3000 B.C.   Native Americans build fish weirs in Boston's Back Bay.

6000 B.C.   Atlantic Ocean levels rise to cover coastal area.

3000 B.C.   Native American wigwams and pottery invented.

1000–1005 A.D.   Vikings visit New England from Newfoundland.

1497   John Cabot explores the New England coast for England.

1504   French fishing boats visit coast of Canada.

1511   Miguel Corte Real explores New England coast for Portugal.

1524   Giovanni da Verrazano explores the New England coast for France.

1525   Estevan Gomez explores New England coast for Spain.

1535   Jacques Cartier explores Canada for France.

1540   European whaling and fishing ships visit New England shore.

1602   Bartholomew Gosnold explores New England for England.

1603   Martin Pring explores New England for England.

1604   Samuel de Champlain explores the New England coast and establishes first French colony on St. Croix Island in Maine.

1605   George Waymouth explores the coast and Kennebec River for England.

1607   First English colony on the Kennebec River in Maine.

1609 Henry Hudson sails along the Massachusetts coast for England; Champlain explores Lake Champlain, Vermont.

1613 Father Pierre Biard, a French Jesuit priest, settles on Mount Desert Island.

1614 Adriaen Block sails for the Dutch up the Connecticut River and to Massachusetts Bay; John Smith maps and names New England and the Charles River.

1616–19 Native Americans suffer from European epidemics.

1620 *Mayflower* lands Pilgrims at Plymouth.

1621 Pilgrims celebrate the First Thanksgiving with the Wampanoag; Council for New England charter granted.

1622 Sir Ferdinando Gorges names Maine and sends fishing boats.

1623 Miles Standish negotiates with Native Americans; Cape Ann is settled by fishermen; first settlement in New Hampshire.

1624 Thomas Walford settles Mishawum (Charlestown), Massachusetts.

1625 Pilgrims trade for fur in Maine.

1626 Naumkeag (Salem) founded by Puritans.

1627 William Blaxton settles on Beacon Hill.

1628 Cushnoc (Augusta) trading post established in Maine; Salem settled by Puritans.

1629 900 Puritans land at Salem to found Massachusetts Bay Colony; English settlers in York and Saco, Maine.

1630 Boston founded; first colony in New Hampshire at Portsmouth; Penobscot, Maine, trading post established.

1631 York, Saco, Pemaquid, Cape Porpoise, and Kittery settlements in Maine.

1632 Direct election of Massachusetts governor by the freemen begins; French capture Castine, Maine; Portland founded.

1633 Dutch erect fort on the site of Hartford; first town meeting in New England held in Dorchester, Massachusetts; Windsor, Connecticut, founded.

1634 Anne Hutchinson emigrates to Boston; Boston Common established; Wethersfield founded in Connecticut.

1635 Boston Latin School established; Puritans settle Hartford, Connecticut.

1636 Massachusetts General Court established; Roger Williams founds Providence, Rhode Island; Harvard College opens.

1637 William Pynchon founds Springfield, Massachusetts; Pequot War begins.

1638 Anne Hutchinson settles Portsmouth, Rhode Island; John Winthrop ignores English order to surrender the charter; Roger Williams founds Baptist church in Providence; Massachusetts is first colony to legalize slavery.

1639 First printing press in North America established in Cambridge, Massachusetts; New Haven founded; Fundamental Orders of Connecticut adopted in Hartford; first free public school in Dorchester, Massachusetts; Newport founded in Rhode Island; Sir Ferdinando Gorges receives royal charter for Maine.

1640 Jesuit missionaries convert Abenaki in Maine; first book printed in America in Cambridge; town government begins in Maine.

1641 Massachusetts and Plymouth pass first slave codes.

1642 First commencement at Harvard College; Massachusetts law requires parents to educate children; Warwick founded in Rhode Island.

1643 New England Confederation established.

1645 First African slaves landed in New Hampshire.

1646 John Eliot translates the Bible into Algonquin; Father Isaac Jogues slain by Vermont Mohawks; John Winthrop, Jr. founds New London in Connecticut.

1647 Massachusetts law requires public schools in each town with 50 families; Rhode Island towns unite in the first General Assembly.

1648 Margaret Jones, first New Englander hanged as a witch, in Charlestown.

1649 Solomon Franco, the first Jew in Boston, deported.

1650 First American ironworks at Saugus; Connecticut adopts slavery and the Code of Laws.

1651 First British Navigation Act passes.

1652 First book store opens in Boston; Massachusetts annexes Maine; Providence bans slavery.

1653 First lending library in America at Boston.

1654 Massachusetts bans Irish immigrants.

1656 Quakers deported from Boston to Barbados.

1657 First English Quakers settle in Rhode Island.

1658 First Jews settle in New England at Newport, Rhode Island.

1659 Massachusetts bans Christmas and hangs four Quakers.

1661 English settle on Block Island.

1662 John Winthrop, Jr. obtains Connecticut charter; first Quakers in Maine.

1663 Rhode Island charter granted.

1665 New Haven and Connecticut colonies unite; first Native American graduates from Harvard.

1666 First French settlers in Vermont.

1669 Massachusetts annexes Maine.

1673 First mail route from Boston to New York City.

1675–77 King Philip's War.

1675 Native Americans burn Providence.

1676 Native Americans raid Falmouth, Maine; Massachusetts purchases Maine from Gorges's heirs.

1679 New Hampshire separated from Massachusetts.

1684 Massachusetts Bay colony charter revoked and royal government begins.

1686 Huguenots arrive in Massachusetts; first Anglican church in Rhode Island.

1687 Dominion of New England established under Governor Andros; Charter Oak incident; Anglican liturgy introduced.

1689–97 King William's War pits English and Iroquois against French and Abenaki.

1689 First American newspaper published in Boston; French and Indians raid Portland, Maine.

1690 Royal charter merges Plymouth Colony and Maine with Massachusetts Bay Colony.

1692 Abenaki raid York, Maine; Salem witch trials.

1696 First vice-admiralty courts try New England smugglers; first African slaves sold in Newport.

1699 First Quaker society founded in Massachusetts at New Bedford.

1700 Massachusetts bans Catholic priests; first slave ship from Newport to Africa.

1701 Yale College founded.

1702–13 Queen Anne's War.

1704 *Boston News Letter* established, first successful American newspaper; Native Americans raid Deerfield, Massachusetts.

1710 New England and British troops capture Port Royal.

1712 Nantucket whaling begins

1713 First schooner launched at Gloucester.

1716 First American lighthouse at Boston Harbor.

1717 Connecticut state house built in New Haven.

1719 First potatoes planted in the U.S. at Londonderry, New Hampshire.

1721 First smallpox vaccination introduced in Boston.

1722–27 Dummer's War.

1724 First English settlement in Vermont near Brattleboro.

1732 First Rhode Island newspaper founded by James Franklin in Newport.

1734   Great Awakening begins in Northampton, Massachusetts.

1736   First slave ship from Providence to Africa.

1741   New Hampshire separated from Massachusetts.

1742   Faneuil Hall built.

1744–48   King George's War.

1745   New England troops capture Louisbourg in Nova Scotia.

1748   Peter Harrison designs Redwood Library in Newport.

1749   Benning Wentworth grants town charters in Vermont.

1752   Boston smallpox epidemic.

1754   First settlers in Augusta, Maine.

1755   Acadians exiled by the British; first newspaper in New Haven; Cape Ann earthquake.

1756–63   French and Indian or Seven Years' War.

1756   Portsmouth, New Hampshire *Gazette* newspaper founded.

1759   Quebec captured by British; Peter Harrison designs Touro Synagogue in Newport; Crown Point Military Road built in Vermont.

1762   Bath, Maine, shipyards founded; first newspaper in Providence.

1763   France cedes all eastern American lands to Britain; first use of the name Vermont.

1764   Sugar Act extends Parliamentary imperial control; *Connecticut Courant* newspaper founded; Rhode Island College (later Brown University) begins; British revoke Vermont land grants.

1765   Stamp Act imposed; non-importation movement begins; Sons of Liberty organize in Boston.

1766   British repeal Stamp Act and reduce Sugar Act.

1767   British pass Townshend Act over Massachusetts objections.

1768   British troops arrive in Boston; Samuel Adams urges united colonial resistance; Massachusetts legislature dissolved by royal governor.

1769   Dartmouth College moves to Hanover.

1770   Boston Massacre, Townshend Act repealed.

1771   Ethan Allen forms Green Mountain Boys.

1772 *Gaspee* burned in Narragansett Bay; Boston committee of correspondence forms.

1773   British closed port after the Boston Tea Party; Burlington, Vermont, settled.

1774   Rhode Island bans slave trade; first Scots settle in Vermont; Intolerable Acts pass; first Continental Congress meets.

1775   Battle of Lexington and Concord; Bunker Hill Battle; Washington besieges General Gage in Boston; Ethan Allen defeated at Montreal; first naval battle of the Revolution off Machias; New England delegates sign the Declaration of Independence.

1776   British evacuate Boston; New Hampshire writes new constitution; British occupy Newport; Rhode Island declares independence.

1777   Battle of Bennington, Vermont declares independence, British raid Danbury, Connecticut; Springfield Armory opens.

1778   Rhode Island frees black soldiers; British expel Vermont settlers.

1779   First Universalist Church founded at Gloucester; British capture Castine, Maine, and evacuate Newport, Rhode Island; Vermont limit deer hunting.

1780   Massachusetts ratifies state constitution; Benedict Arnold attacks New London and Groton; British lead Native Americans in raid on Royalton, Vermont.

1781   First newspaper in Vermont published in Westminster; British burn Groton and New London, Connecticut.

1782   Harvard Medical School established; first Shaker commune in New England opens in Harvard, Massachusetts.

1783   Samuel Seabury founds Episcopal Church in Connecticut; Boston is first town to declare July 4 a public holiday; Massachusetts is first state to end slavery.

1784   First Massachusetts ship sails to China; law school founded in Litchfield, Connecticut; Rhode Island and Connecticut free slaves; first bridge crossed the Connecticut River at Bellows Falls, Vermont; New Hampshire ratifies state constitution; Bank of Massachusetts chartered, first commercial bank in U.S.

1785 First newspaper in Maine calls for statehood; first Unitarian church in Boston; first July 4th parade in Bristol, Rhode Island; first marble quarry in Vermont.

1786 Shays's Rebellion; Vermont abolishes slave trade.

1787 Rhode Island abolishes slave trade; first ship from Providence to China.

1788 New England states ratify U.S. Constitution and suggest a Bill of Rights; Connecticut and Massachusetts ban slave trade.

1789 President George Washington visits Boston; first abolition society in Rhode Island.

1790 Slater's mill opens in Pawtucket; Rhode Island ratifies U.S. Constitution.

1791 Vermont admitted as 14th state.

1792 Paul Revere opens his bell foundry in Boston; *Farmer's Almanac* published.

1793 Eli Whitney invents the cotton gin; Bennington pottery opens.

1794 Passamaquoddy surrender their land; first theater in Boston.

1795 First insurance company opens in Norwich, Connecticut.

1796 President John Adams elected; Penobscot surrender their land, Bulfinch builds Hartford state house; Pawtucket Canal opens in Lowell; Boston Dispensary opens.

1797 Vermont begins free town schools.

1798 Eli Whitney opens firearms factory in Connecticut.

1799 Charles Bulfinch completes the Massachusetts state house; Portsmouth Naval Shipyard founded; University of Vermont opens.

1800 Massachusetts State Prison at Charlestown opens.

1802 First U.S. canal dug at Bellows Falls, Vermont; first dinosaur tracks in U.S. discovered in South Hadley, Massachusetts.

1803 Captain Preble and the U.S. *Constitution* defeat the Tripoli pirates; Middlesex Canal links the Merrimack River with Boston; first U.S. clock factory in Connecticut.

1804 Boston Exchange Coffee House opens, the largest hotel in the nation.

1805 Montpelier becomes capital of Vermont.

1806 Noah Webster publishes first American dictionary; first African American church in Boston.

1807 President Thomas Jefferson embargoes foreign trade; Vermont state house built in Montpelier.

1808 First Catholic church in Maine; New Hampshire capital moved from Portsmouth to Concord.

1809 Hartford Fire Insurance Company founded.

1811 Merino sheep introduced to Vermont; Massachusetts General Hospital opens.

1812–15 War of 1812 stimulates New England manufacturing.

1813 First textile mill in Waltham, Massachusetts.

1814 Hartford Convention threatens to secede; Waltham textile mill opens; British capture Castine; Thomas Macdonough defeats British on Lake Champlain.

1815 *North American Review* and the Handel and Haydn Society founded; Total Abstinence Society founded in Maine; first professor of obstetrics appointed at Harvard.

1816 The year without summer; Webster argues Dartmouth College case.

1818 Connecticut approves new constitution; Boston public elementary schools open.

1819 Maine approves state constitution; first military school opened in Vermont.

1820 Maine admitted as a state in the Missouri Compromise; Town covered bridge patented.

1821 Boston opens its first public high school; first gaslights on Providence streets; first Danbury Fair in Connecticut; Massachusetts grants suffrage to adult male citizens.

1822 Rhode Island Historical Society founded; City of Boston incorporated; Rhode Island disenfranchises black voters; Maine Historical Society founded; first reenactment of the Battle of Lexington.

1823 Mill girls arrive in Lowell Mills; canal connects Lake Champlain with the Hudson River; first Catholic church built in New Hampshire.

1824 President John Quincy Adams elected; first public high school for girls in Worcester; textile workers strike in Pawtucket.

1825 American Unitarian Association established; Erie Canal diverts trade from New England; Connecticut Historical Society opens.

1826 The industrial city of Lowell, Massachusetts, founded.

1827 New state house built in Hartford, Connecticut; New England ships trade for hides in California; Massachusetts requires secondary schools in every large town.

1828 First U.S. textile worker strike by women at Dover, New Hampshire; Blackstone canal links Worcester and Pawtucket.

1829 First modern U.S. hotel opens in Boston; Boston *Pilot* founded, the oldest U.S. Catholic newspaper.

1830 Thaddeus Fairbanks invents platform scale in Vermont; first America's Cup race at Newport.

1831 William Lloyd Garrison founds *The Liberator* in Boston; City of Providence incorporated.

1832 Maine capital moved from Portland to Augusta; first state mental hospital opens in Worcester, Massachusetts; first railroad in Connecticut; Boston Lying-In Hospital opens.

1833 Massachusetts constitutional amendment separates church and state; Bath Iron Works founded; Hartford & New Haven Railroad founded; Lowell mill girls strike in Massachusetts; first Catholic church in Vermont.

1834 Boston and Worcester railroad opens; Boston mob burns convent school.

1835 Samuel Colt patents a revolver; Boston & Lowell Railroad and Boston & Providence Railroad open.

1836 Lowell Mill Girls strike; Vermont adopts bicameral legislature; Massachusetts passes first state child labor law.

1837 Mount Holyoke College founded; first state board of education established in Massachusetts; new state house opens in Montpelier; national economic depression.

1838 Earthquake shakes New England; Hartford & New Haven Railroad opens; Vermont Historical Society opens.

1839 Charles Goodyear invents vulcanized rubber in Woburn; Aroostook War in Maine; first state normal school in Massachusetts.

1840 *Amistad* trial in Hartford; Ten Hour movement begins.

1840–50 New England whaling fleet expands.

1841 First French Canadian workers settle in Lowell.

1842 Wadsworth Atheneum founded in Hartford; Webster-Ashburton Treaty settles Aroostook War; Massachusetts court recognizes unions as legal; Dorr Rebellion in Rhode Island.

1843 Bunker Hill Monument completed; Massachusetts passes child labor law; rubber invented in Connecticut.

1844 New York and New Haven Railroad chartered; William Miller predicts the end of the world; Donald McKay builds his first ships in Boston.

1845 Elias Howe invents the sewing machine in Boston; Irish potato famine sends 50,000 immigrants to New England.

1846 First use of anesthesia at Massachusetts General Hospital; first U.S. postage stamp printed in Brattleboro, Vermont; Maine passes the first statewide prohibition law.

1847 Yale University founds first agricultural experiment station; New Hampshire passes the first state 10-hour day law; Providence & Worcester Railroad opens.

1848 New York & New Haven Railroad opens; first trains in Vermont.

1849 New England ships land 25,000 men in California Gold Rush.

1850 First national Woman's Rights Convention in Worcester; Donald McKay launches his first clipper ship in Boston.

1851 First YMCA in U.S. founded in Boston; Boston Public Library opens; first collegiate sports event in New Hampshire.

1852 Massachusetts adopts a state prohibition law; Rhode Island abolishes capital punishment.

1854   Boston Back Bay filled for elite houses; Colt factory opens in Hartford; Massachusetts opens first state reform school for girls at Lancaster.

1855   Know Nothing legislature investigates Massachusetts Catholic convents and schools; Boston integrates public schools; Massachusetts ends imprisonment for debt.

1856   Republican Party controls Maine.

1857   Economic depression; *Atlantic Monthly* founded.

1860   First kindergarten opens in Boston; shoemakers strike in Lynn and Natick.

1861   6th Massachusetts Regiment mobbed in Baltimore, Maryland; Massachusetts Institute of Technology (MIT) founded; Hannibal Hamlin elected vice president; first summer camp in U.S. opens in Milford, Connecticut.

1862   Hartford opens the first Boys' Club in U.S.; Maine Central Railroad opens.

1863   Travelers Insurance founded in Hartford; Massachusetts 54th attack on Fort Wagner; first streetcar line in Rhode Island; Confederate raid on Portland, Maine; University of Massachusetts chartered; Boston draft riot.

1864   Massachusetts State Board of Charities established; Confederate raids at St. Albans, Vermont, and Calais, Maine.

1865   Child labor law passes in Massachusetts; Vermont bans deer hunting.

1866   First African-American legislators in New England elected in Massachusetts; Great Fire in Portland, Maine; Fenians raid Canada from Vermont; YWCA founded in Boston; school segregation ends in Rhode Island.

1867   Mary Baker Eddy founds Christian Science Church in Boston; Boston & Albany Railroad opens.

1868   Massachusetts Society for the Prevention of Cruelty to Animals founded; University of Maine opens; Massachusetts repeals prohibition law.

1869   First state board of health established in Massachusetts; last whaler sails from New Bedford, Massachusetts; first black man graduates Harvard Law School; National Peace Jubilee and Musical Festival in Boston.

1870 Museum of Fine Arts opens in Boston; first bananas imported to Boston; New England rural population declines rapidly.

1871 First professional baseball games in Boston; first annual New England Flower Show in Boston.

1872 Great Boston Fire; first French national Catholic church in Lewiston, Maine; *Boston Globe* newspaper founded.

1873 Arnold Arboretum founded in Boston; Hoosac Tunnels opens.

1874 Massachusetts law limits children and women to 10-hour work day; women permitted on Boston School Committee.

1875 First American Christmas cards printed in Boston; first lobster pound in Vinalhaven, Maine; first U.S. agricultural state experiment station opens in Connecticut; Hartford becomes capital of Connecticut.

1876 Alexander Graham Bell invents telephone in Boston; U.S. Coast Guard Academy founded in New London, Connecticut.

1877 Rhode Island School of Design opens in Providence.

1878 First commercial telephone exchange and telephone book in U.S. in New Haven.

1879 New State House in Hartford opens; Christian Science Church founded.

1880 First electric lights in Maine; Boston Symphony Orchestra established.

1881 University of Connecticut founded at Storrs; Vermont's last catamount shot.

1882 First female lawyer in Connecticut.

1883 Keith introduced vaudeville in Boston.

1884 First Irish mayor of Boston, Hugh O'Brien; Bath Iron Works opens; Massachusetts civil service begins for state employees.

1885 Blue Hill Meteorological Observatory opens in Milton, Massachusetts, the oldest continuous weather station in the nation.

1886 Olmsted completes the Boston Emerald Necklace parks; Rhode Island adopts prohibition.

1887 Massachusetts creates Labor Day as a holiday; Maine abolishes capital punishment.

1888 Kindergartens introduced to Boston public schools; Massachusetts adopts secret ballot.

1889 Rhode Island repeals prohibition.

1891 First basketball game played in Springfield, Massachusetts; Bangor & Aroostook Railroad serves northern Maine; Massachusetts bans sweatshops.

1892 First gasoline-powered automobile invented in Springfield; University of Rhode Island founded as a land grant college; Massachusetts adopts nine hour day for public employees; Pledge of Allegiance written in Boston.

1893 Depression causes high unemployment in New England.

1894 Boston and Maine railroad opens North Station in Boston; Bangor and Aroostook Railroad opens; Immigration Restriction League founded.

1895 W. E. B. DuBois earns Ph.D. at Harvard; first U.S. automobiles made in Springfield, Massachusetts.

1896 Massachusetts Audubon Society founded; first Fannie Farmer cookbook.

1897 First subway in U.S. opens in Boston; International Paper Company founded; first Boston Marathon; Vermont permits deer hunting.

1898 Worcester Art Museum opens in Massachusetts.

1899 Old Home Week begins in New Hampshire.

1900 First submarine built in Connecticut; Great Northern Paper mill opens in Maine; Boston Symphony Hall opens.

1901 Connecticut is first state to limit automobile speed; Boston Red Sox founded; King Gillette invents safety razor; Society for the Protection of New Hampshire Forests founded.

1903 First World Series played in Boston; Gardner Museum opens; first radio broadcast from Cape Cod to London.

1904 Fungus destroys the New England Chestnut tree forests.

1905 Treaty of Portsmouth signed.

1906   First Catholic elected Rhode Island governor.

1907   First American scientist, Albert Michelson of Worcester, wins the Nobel Prize for Physics.

1908   First French Canadian elected Rhode Island governor; Harvard Business School founded; Danbury Hatters decision by U.S. Supreme Court.

1909   Museum of Fine Arts moved to Boston's Fenway; Tercentenary celebration of Champlain's exploration of Vermont; first U.S. credit union opens in New Hampshire.

1910   U.S. Coast Guard Academy opens in New London; Green Mountain Club founded.

1911   Camp Fire Girls founded in Thetford, Vermont; Massachusetts adopts direct primary elections and eight-hour day for public employees.

1912   Lawrence textile strike; Fenway Park opens; Massachusetts passes state minimum wage law.

1914   First Catholic Massachusetts governor elected; Cape Cod canal opens.

1915–16   First New Hampshire presidential primary election; MIT moves from Boston to Cambridge; Massachusetts adopts state income tax.

1917   Yankee Division lands in France; first submarine built in Kittery, Maine; U.S. Navy submarine base founded in Groton, Connecticut; Massachusetts amends its 1780 constitution.

1918   Boston Red Sox win World Series.

1919   Boston Police Strike; Lafayette (Acadia) National Park opens; influenza epidemic reaches Massachusetts; Molasses Flood in Boston.

1920   Harvard University appoints its first woman professor; first woman elected to Vermont legislature.

1921   WBZ broadcasts as the first commercial radio station in New England; Massachusetts state police founded.

1922   Raytheon Company founded in Cambridge; first woman elected to Rhode Island legislature; Ku Klux Klan active in New England; first radio station in Vermont.

1923   President Calvin Coolidge succeeds Warren G. Harding.

1924 First women vote; President Coolidge makes first radio broadcast from the White House; first U.S. mutual fund in Boston.

1925 Last whaling voyage from New Bedford; Raytheon invents radio tube.

1926 First liquid fuel rocket launched in Auburn, Massachusetts; WNAC broadcasts first Red Sox–New York Yankees game on radio.

1927 Sacco and Vanzetti executed in Boston; Great Flood in Vermont.

1928 First nonelectronic computer invented at MIT; New Bedford textile strike.

1929 Massachusetts taxes gasoline; Long Trail completed in Vermont.

1930 Massachusetts Tercentenary celebrated; Dutch elm disease infects urban trees.

1931 Maine opens Baxter State Park; first snow train brings skiers from Boston to New Hampshire.

1933 National Guard ends Barre granite strike in Vermont.

1934 First ski tow in U.S. opens at Woodstock, Vermont; Woonsocket textile strike.

1936 Rhode Island and Harvard University celebrate Tercentenary; Connecticut River flood; Tanglewood music festival established.

1937 Lewiston-Auburn shoe strike in Maine.

1938 Hurricane and floods devastate New England.

1941 World War II begins; Quonset hut invented in Rhode Island.

1942 Cocoanut Grove fire in Boston.

1944 First automatic digital computer invented in Cambridge; Circus fire in Hartford; German submarine lands spies in Maine.

1945 World War II ends; Raytheon invents the microwave oven.

1946 Edwin Land invents the instant Polaroid camera; Old Sturbridge Village opens.

1947 Plimouth Plantation opens; Mount Desert Island forest fire; Maine Turnpike opens.

1948 WBZ broadcasts first commercial television programs in New England.

1949 First African-American professor appointed at Harvard Medical School.

1950 First Dunkin Donut shop opens in Quincy, Massachusetts; first Italian-American elected to U.S. Senate in Rhode Island; first women serve on Massachusetts juries.

1951 WGBH begins broadcasting, the first U.S. educational radio station; Lincoln Laboratory founded by MIT.

1952 New Hampshire holds its first in the nation presidential primary; Historic Deerfield founded.

1953 Last Gloucester fishing schooner sails; WAIB Maine's first television station broadcasts in Bangor, Maine; tornado devastates Worcester; wiffleball invented in Connecticut.

1954 First atomic-powered submarine built in Groton, Connecticut; Maine Native Americans first vote; Vermont elects the first woman lieutenant governor in the U.S.

1955 Construction of Interstate 95 highway begins in Rhode Island.

1956 Ivy League founded; *Peyton Place* novel shocks New Hampshire.

1957 Massachusetts Turnpike opens; first Italian-American governor elected in Massachusetts; *Mayflower II* lands at Plymouth.

1958 Strawbery Banke Museum opens in Portsmouth; first Democratic congressman in 100 years elected in Vermont.

1959 Boston (later New England) Patriots football team founded; Boston Central Artery and Southeast Expressway open.

1960 John F. Kennedy elected president; Dixville Notch begins the first in the nation presidential primary voting tradition in New Hampshire.

1961 Cape Cod National Seashore established.

1962 Boston urban renewal creates Government Center.

1963 First minicomputer manufactured in Massachusetts; U.S.S. *Thresher* nuclear submarine sinks off New Hampshire.

1964   First modern state lottery in New Hampshire.

1965   Connecticut adopts new constitution; U.S. Supreme Court rejects Connecticut birth control law; Massachusetts Turnpike opens.

1966   First Massachusetts teachers strike in Lawrence; Massachusetts passes sales tax.

1967   Massachusetts elects first African American to U.S. Senate by popular vote.

1968   Vermont bans billboards; Newport Restoration Foundation established in Rhode Island; Massachusetts assumes town welfare costs.

1969   Maine adopts state income tax; race riots in Hartford; new Boston City Hall built.

1970   Maine and Vermont adopt environmental laws.

1971   New Hampshire's Alan Shepard lands on the moon.

1972   First nuclear power plant in Maine opens; Boston Red Sox AAA team begins in Pawtucket; Massachusetts begins state lottery.

1973   U.S. Navy closes operations in Rhode Island; Boston Naval Shipyard closes.

1974   First woman elected governor of Connecticut; Boston National Historic Park created; federal court orders school busing in Boston.

1975   Final river logging drive in Maine.

1976   Quincy Market opens in Boston; first artists settle in Boston Fort Point; the original First Night celebration held in Boston.

1977   Seabrook Station nuclear plant protest in New Hampshire.

1978   Blizzard of '78 ravages New England; Narragansett reservation opens in Rhode Island; Lowell National Historical Park established.

1979   John F. Kennedy Presidential Library opens in Boston; National Guard ends mass protest at Seabrook Station.

1980   Rhode Island elects first woman to Congress; Maine settles Native American land claims; first Open Studio day at Boston Fort Point.

1981   Rhode Island repeals blue laws; 112th and final Danbury Fair in Connecticut.

1982   Interstate highway completed in Vermont.

1983   Last America's Cup Race held in Newport.

1984   Rhode Island elects first woman attorney general in the nation; Congress designates White Mountain National Forest as wilderness.

1985   First woman elected governor of Vermont.

1986   Congress establishes the Blackstone River Valley National Heritage Corridor.

1987   Rhode Island adopts new constitution.

1988   Michael S. Dukakis nominated as president; Massachusetts limits smoking.

1989   A. Bartlett Giamatti appointed major league baseball commissioner.

1990   Isabella Stewart Gardner Museum art theft; Seabrook Station nuclear power plant opens in New Hampshire.

1991   Big Dig highway project begins in Boston.

1993   Vermont declared America's Most Endangered Historic Place; Massachusetts reforms public education.

1994   Congress limits Georges Bank fishing.

1995   Fleet Bank moves to Boston from Providence.

1996   New Bedford Whaling National Historical Park opens; Asian beetle destroys sugar maple trees; 34 Boston harbor islands become a national park.

1997   First nuclear power plant in Maine closed; first woman elected governor of New Hampshire.

1998   Adams National Historical Park established.

1999   Boston Garden replaced by Fleet Center; Massachusetts Museum of Contemporary Art opens.

2000   First Jewish nominee for vice president, Joseph Lieberman; Vermont law permits same sex civil union marriage.

2001   First woman serves as Massachusetts governor.

2002   New England Patriots win Super Bowl; Cardinal Law retires.

Introduction

New England, the most clearly defined region in the United States, includes the six states of Connecticut, Maine, Massachusetts, New Hampshire, Rhode Island, and Vermont. The region was settled by Native Americans by 10,000 B.C. and the six states are home to 14 million people today, but in a larger sense New England has become home to all Americans. Europeans settled Virginia earlier, and California earlier yet, but New England has an indelible, cohesive, and complex character that endures and attracts. Not only is Boston the regional capital, but it is hailed as the cradle of liberty, the starting point of the American Revolution, so it is considered our uniquely American homeplace. Plymouth, settled a dozen years after Jamestown, is dubbed America's hometown. Like grandmother's attic, New England is a place where the past is available, a place where we can recapture the way things used to be and to understand our national origins, but it is at the same time difficult to define, slipping away like the tide. The imagined New England is distinct from the reality of New England towns, cities, people, economics, and politics. Wherever we live, New England seems familiar from the images of barns, colleges, lighthouses, lobster boats, and stone walls in schoolbooks, calendars, fiction, magazines, and movies. Indelibly imprinted on the American imagination are New England's tree-lined town commons, white steepled churches, seacoast villages, and forest hills in autumnal foliage. Tourists in search of an imagined experience of the past still find in New England sites and communities the simple rural virtues Americans cherish.

Set off from the other colonies and states by the Appalachian Mountains and lacking a river system penetrating into the hinterland, New England is geographically isolated. Its climate and environment has created the New England character, transforming into Yankees not only the English Puritans but also the immigrant Irish, Scots, French, Africans, Germans, Italians, Portuguese, Jews, Greeks, Albanians, Armenians, Poles, Chinese, Cape

Verdeans, Latinos, Vietnamese, and others. New England offered comparative advantage and economies of scale, promoting economic development and technical change. The thin, rocky, and acidic soil and hilly terrain precluded large plantations and staple crops, so New England became an area of small farms and fishing or shipping towns along the well-indented coasts with hardy, practical people intent on ways to earn a living from the soil, forest, and sea.

New England institutions—the close-knit town, Congregational church, public schools, private colleges, and New England conscience—developed in isolation, more so when the Erie Canal (1825) diverted commerce and people to New York and the western states. Yankee ingenuity and frugality promoted a wide variety of industries that demanded the cheap labor of Roman Catholic immigrants. Puritan New England became heterogenous largely due to economic development. The surplus Yankees contributed their culture by migration to New York, New Jersey, Pennsylvania, South Carolina, Ohio, Illinois, Michigan, Wisconsin, and Oregon, where New England towns were transplanted. The New England influence on the United States far exceeds its size and population.

When the American Revolution ended, visionary New Englanders made the American economy international while promoting a new national spirit. From entrepreneurial China Traders to Noah Webster's insistence on an American language, Yankees were leaders in building the new nation. Mistakenly confident that the new constitution created a national government ruled largely by consensus not unlike the New England town meeting, they overcame Shays' rebellion and the secessionist Hartford Convention to shape antebellum American society. By the 1820s New England had become the nation's spiritual capital as the young nation found legitimacy by celebrating its past.

Home to the industrialists and moral reformers more responsible than most for the coming of the Civil War, New Englanders were among the most stalwart supporters of the Union and played key roles in the taming of the western frontier. Despite a Gilded Age decline into a certain degree of provincialism, New Englanders continued to assume leadership positions in the national economy, society, and politics. By the 20th century, the region's quaint provincialism appealed to both immigrants and to other Americans in new ways giving rise to the Colonial Revival and the important tourism industry. Norman Rockwell's art using his Vermont and Massachusetts neighbors as models, and hit songs like *White Christmas* (1942) or *Moonlight in Vermont* (1944) evoked sentiment and nostalgia for an idealized New England. This region became a state of mind as well as a geographical and political region and New England qualities and traditions, real or imagined, are deeply engrained in the national psyche.

When the textile and publishing industries born in New England were relocated by the 1930s, Yankee entrepreneurs invented new industries to take their place. Recreation, electronics, defense research and development, medicine, computers, and higher education continue to support a robust economy in an economic renaissance. The greater Boston metropolitan area, 154 cities and towns that comprise the regional capital, suffered the same urban decay common in older cities of the industrial north from 1930 to 1975. Since the 1970s, however, greater Boston grew prosperous and vibrant by every measure urban statisticians employ. By 1990, employment levels rose to the highest in the nation. Boston ranks fifth in the proportion of residents with a college degree. The staid *Boston Globe* is now rated as one of the best newspapers in the country. A new diverse multicultural population halted the depopulation of New England's older cities and spread to suburban communities.

The story of New England usually begins with the arrival of the Pilgrims at Plymouth in 1620. This overlooks the previous 12,000 years of Paleo-Indian settlement and the first encounter of native Americans with European explorers, fishermen, and the earliest settlers in the territory later known as Maine and New Hampshire.

The land that is New England is best understood in its six parts, the states. An overview of each follows:

Connecticut, bordered by New York, Massachusetts, Rhode Island, and the Atlantic Ocean, was explored by the Dutch and founded by Puritans from Massachusetts in the 1630s. The Nutmeg State is the birthplace of the Yankee icon and played a leading role as the arsenal of the nation in the American Revolution. It was the home of the Industrial Revolution, and Hartford long prospered as the center of the insurance industry. The Constitution State (1788) has the nation's highest per capita income today. Like Rhode Island, Connecticut has no county government and its 169 towns and cities vary widely in wealth and municipal services. Although it looks to New York City in many ways, Connecticut is the gateway to New England.

Maine, bordered by Quebec, New Brunswick, New Hampshire, and the Atlantic Ocean, is the extreme northeastern section of the nation. It was the first part of New England settled by the French (1604) and English (1607), although permanent colonies appeared only in the 1630s. Small in population, Maine broke from Massachusetts in a great national compromise on the slavery issue (1820), but constitutes one-half of the New England area. Most of the Pine Tree State is so heavily forested that the paper, pulp, and

wood industries dominate the economy, but agriculture, especially potatoes, fishing, and tourism are very important. Maine's rocky coastline, pris-
tine lighthouses, and hardy lobster boats became downeast icons as tourist
cameras and artists captured images of the real Maine. Known as "vacationland," Maine was the most rapidly growing state on the East Coast by
1980.

Massachusetts, the most populous New England state, is bordered by
Connecticut, Rhode Island, New Hampshire, Vermont, and the Atlantic
Ocean. It was explored by European ships in the 1500s and settled by Pilgrim (1620) and Puritan (1630) dissenters from England. The church with
a white steeple on the town common, now a Bay State icon, recalls the
state's religious origins. Boston, the capital city, is the regional center of
New England. The topography varies widely, from mountains on the western border and fertile soil in the Connecticut River valley plateau to low,
sandy plains on the southern shore and rocky headlands along Cape Ann.
As in much of the region, the thin, rocky soil and forests were exhausted
quickly, which encouraged the commerce and industry dominating the state
economy since 1800. Massachusetts entered the union in 1788, was the
fourth largest state in population by 1790, was ranked 13th in 1990, and is
concentrated in 351 towns and cities. The English population dominated
until 1800 but descendants of Irish, Italian, and French Canadian immigrants are the largest ethnic groups now. The birthplace of the American
industrial revolution, the state's economy is now focused on electronics,
finance, insurance, medicine, higher education, tourism, and other service
industries.

New Hampshire, first explored by the English (1603) and French (1604),
was settled by the English colonists and Massachusetts Puritans in the
1630s and became a royal colony in 1680. The Granite State, bordered by
Massachusetts, Vermont, Maine, and Quebec, entered the union in 1788
and maintained the flinty character of its Revolutionary War slogan (Live
Free or Die). This pithy claim sums up so much of the independent Yankee
viewpoint. Best known for having the first presidential primary elections,
modern New Hampshire's rural character and industrial economy has attracted a growing population. Its short seacoast, mountains, forests, and
lakes support year-round tourism.

Rhode Island, the smallest of the fifty states, is bordered by Connecticut,
Massachusetts, and the Atlantic Ocean. The colony, known as Rhode Island
and Providence Plantations, was first explored by Europeans in 1524 and
1614. Settled as a refuge (1636) for English nonconformists, Rhode Island

continues that independent ethos so common in New England. The first state to declare independence from Britain (1776) and the 13th state in the union (1790), the Ocean State was first a leader in shipping and then in manufacturing. By 1900 it was the most ethnically diverse state in the region.

Vermont, the second largest of the New England states and the only one with no seacoast, was the last area of New England to be settled (1724) and was an independent republic for 14 years until it became the 14th state (1791). Known as the Green Mountain State, Vermont is bordered by Quebec, New York, New Hampshire, and Massachusetts. Its diversified economy, especially year-round tourism, supports a predominantly rural population.

The Dictionary

– A –

ABENAKI. "People of the sunrise," the name of the **Native American** people (also called the Wabanaki) most numerous in northern New England. The Eastern Abenaki formed a confederacy of Algonquian-speaking tribes in Maine and New Hampshire including the **Malecite, Passamaquoddy, Penobscot**, and Sokoki. The Western Abenaki in Vermont numbered as many as 10,000 people in 1600 despite friction with the **Mohawks** and others among the Iroquois, who were their chief rivals. The Abenaki hunted; fished; grew beans, squash, and **corn**; and lived in sedentary villages in birch-bark **wigwams**. European diseases killed most of the coastal people (1616–19), but French Catholic missionaries converted many Abenaki (1650) who later moved to Canada. They remained a threat to the English in **King Philip's War** and **King William's War** by raiding Falmouth, Maine (1676); Salmon Falls, New Hampshire (1690); York, Maine (1692); Haverhill (1697), **Deerfield** (1704), and Northampton, Massachusetts (1712); and many **Connecticut River** towns. The Abenaki raids may have influenced the **Salem witchcraft trials**. By the 1790s the Abenaki in Maine surrendered their land to the Americans, but they sued the state of Maine successfully and received a settlement of $81 million in federal funds (1980). Traditional brown ash and sweet grass handcrafted baskets by Abenaki and other Maine Indians, perhaps the region's oldest art form, are now collected as **art**. More than 100 Vermont places have Abenaki names, and in 1976 Vermont recognized the tribe led by Homer St. Francis (1935–2001). *See also* DEERFIELD; GREYLOCK; RASLES, SEBASTIEN; ROGERS, ROBERT.

ABOLITIONISM. Radical wing of the anti-slavery movement, firmly rooted in New England by the 1830s where social and economic conditions precluded slave labor. Although colonial New England ports profited

1

from the slave trade, the **American Revolution** ended slavery in the region. Gradual abolitionism gave way to immediate abolitionism when **William Lloyd Garrison** led the moral crusade against slavery in 1831–65. Defining slavery as a sin incompatible with the civil rights of white northerners, Garrisonians and Free Soil Party politicians seized on northern resentment of the Fugitive Slave Act and the emotional effect of anti-slavery propaganda like **Harriet Beecher Stowe's** *Uncle Tom's Cabin* as justification for the **Civil War**. This minority viewpoint spread gradually throughout New England. The Vermont Anti-Slavery Society formed in 1834 was one of 300 in the region. But abolitionist Samuel May was mobbed and prevented from speaking in **Montpelier** in 1835. Oliver Johnson, a Vermont abolitionist editor and ally of Garrison, narrowly escaped a Rhode Island mob (1832), and Garrison was rescued from a Boston mob by the mayor in 1835. Although New England's small African-American population meant that most people had little contact with slavery, prominent **Yankee** abolitionists included **John Parker Hale**, **Wendell Phillips**, **Charles Sumner**, **Lucretia Mott**, and **John Greenleaf Whittier**, who played important roles in the **Underground Railroad** and in promoting anti-slavery settlers in the West. *See also* BURNS, ANTHONY; SHADRACH; SLAVERY; WEST INDIES TRADE.

ACADIA NATIONAL PARK. Established (65 sq mi/168 sq km) at Frenchman Bay in southeastern Maine. First named Sieur de Monts National Monument (1916) and then Lafayette National Park (1919), it was renamed Acadia (1929) to reflect its exploration by **Samuel de Champlain** (1604). The site of the French **Jesuit** mission in America (1613), it was part of New France's Acadia province until 1713. The first national park in the East, Acadia comprises the forests of **Mount Desert Island** and Cadillac Mountain (1530 ft/466 m), the highest peak on the North American coast. **Mount Desert Island** includes the **Bar Harbor** resort community and palatial summer homes or Victorian cottages designed in the 1890s by **McKim**, **Mead, and White** for the Astor, Carnegie, Ford, Morgan, Rockefeller, and Vanderbilt families.

ACADIANS. French **Catholic** settlers in Nova Scotia expelled by the British (1755) to Massachusetts, Connecticut, and other colonies. Many settled later in the St. John River Valley in Maine (1785) on **Malecite** tribal land. Joined by **French Canadians** from Quebec, their cultural clubs, churches, historical societies, and museums preserve the Acadian culture today. **Henry Wadsworth Longfellow**'s poem *Evangeline* (1847) immortalized the tragic Acadian expulsion.

ACHESON, DEAN (1893–1971). Public official. Born in Middletown, Connecticut, on April 11, 1893, Dean Gooderman Acheson graduated from Yale University (1915) and **Harvard** Law School (1918). After serving in the Navy in World War I, he was clerk for Supreme Court Justice **Louis D. Brandeis** (1919–21) and practiced law in Washington, D.C. (1921–33). Acheson was under secretary of the treasury (1933), assistant secretary of state (1945–47), and secretary of state (1949–53). He was the principal author of the containment of communism policy in the Cold War. He returned to his law practice in Washington, D.C., but advised the Democratic National Committee and the Department of State on foreign policy until his death on October 21, 1971, in Maryland.

ADAMS FAMILY. A distinguished Massachusetts family that forms one of the nation's most important and enduring dynasties. It includes two presidents, writers, **railroad** executives, and historians. The family home in Quincy (formerly Braintree), birthplace of two presidents and four Adams generations, is now preserved by the National Park Service as the Adams National Historic Site (1998).

ADAMS, ABIGAIL SMITH (1744–1818). Writer and first lady. Born in Weymouth, Massachusetts, on November 11, 1744, Abigail Smith had little formal schooling but was self-educated. She married **John Adams**, a **Boston** lawyer, and they had five children. While her husband was in Philadelphia and abroad during the **American Revolution**, she raised four children, operated the family farm, and conducted business affairs. Her letters for 40 years to John Adams, her children, relatives, and friends offer a vivid picture of the homefront in Revolutionary Massachusetts and late-18th-century private and public life. She joined her husband in Paris (1784) and then in London, and during his terms as vice-president and president she lived with him in New York, Philadelphia, and Washington.

In later years, Abigail Adams was a strong supporter of her son, President **John Quincy Adams**, and her letters offered salient opinions and observations. She died at home in Quincy on October 28, 1818, one of the most admired first ladies. Her grandson, **Charles Francis Adams**, published some of her letters (1840), including the wartime correspondence between John and Abigail Adams, and other editions followed, forming a valuable source for social history. Her birthplace in Weymouth is preserved as a museum.

ADAMS, CHARLES FRANCIS (1807–1886). Congressman from Massachusetts. Born in **Boston** on August 18, 1807, Adams, the son of **John Quincy Adams**, graduated from **Harvard** College (1825). He studied law with **Daniel Webster**, practiced in Boston, wrote for the *North American Review*, and served as an anti-slavery **Whig** in the state legislature (1831, 1835–49) and in the House of Representatives as a Republican (1859–61). As U.S. minister to Great Britain (1861–68), he prevented diplomatic recognition of the Confederacy and obtained payment for damage to U.S. ships by British-built Confederate ships. Adams retired to Quincy (1872) and died in Boston on November 21, 1886.

ADAMS, CHARLES FRANCIS, JR. (1835–1915). Soldier and historian. Born in **Boston** on May 27, 1835. Adams, the son of **Charles Francis Adams**, graduated from **Harvard** College (1856) and practiced law in Boston (1858–61). He was promoted from lieutenant in the **African American 5th Massachusetts Cavalry** to general during the **Civil War**. He wrote *Chapters of Erie* (1871) and *Railroads: Their Origins and Problems* (1878), which led to his appointment to the Massachusetts Board of **Railroad** Commissioners (1869–79) and as president of the Union Pacific Railroad (1884–90). Adams built the first public library in Quincy and reorganized the public schools in his hometown. He was president of the **Massachusetts Historical Society** (1895–1915) until he died in Washington, D.C., on May 20, 1915.

ADAMS, CHARLES FRANCIS (1866–1954). Public official. Born in Quincy, Massachusetts, on August 2, 1866, Adams, the great grandson of President **John Quincy Adams**, graduated from **Harvard University** (1888) and Harvard Law School (1892). He practiced law in **Boston** and was a businessman, philanthropist, mayor of Quincy (1896–97), and the Harvard University treasurer. Until appointed secretary of the navy (1929–33) by President Herbert Hoover, Adams was the dean of American helmsmen as captain of the *Resolute* in the America's Cup Races. Adams, who was a founder of the **Woods Hole Oceanographic Institution**, died in Boston on June 10, 1954.

ADAMS, CHARLES FRANCIS (1910–1999). Businessman. Born in **Boston** on May 2, 1910, Adams, the son of **Charles Francis Adams**

(1866–1954), graduated from **Harvard University** (1932) and attended Harvard Business School. He was a Boston financier (1933–47) and served in the Navy in World War II. Adams was president of the Raytheon Corporation (1948–74) and a director of the **USS** *Constitution* Museum, **Massachusetts Historical Society**, and the **Woods Hole Oceanographic Institution.** He died in Dover, Massachusetts, on January 5, 1999.

ADAMS, HENRY BROOKS (1838–1918). Historian. Born in **Boston** on February 16, 1838, the son of **Charles Francis Adams**, Henry Adams graduated from **Harvard** College (1858). He studied in Europe and was secretary to his father who was minister to Britain (1861–68). He was a journalist in Washington, D.C. (1868–70) and editor of the *North American Review* (1870–76), and he taught history at Harvard (1870–77), introducing the seminar method. Moving to Washington, D.C. (1877–1918), Adams traveled widely and wrote biographies of *Albert Gallatin* (1879) and *John Randolph* (1882) and *History of the United States from 1801 to 1817* (1891), and *Mont-Saint-Michel and Chartres* (1904). *The Education of Henry Adams* (1906), his best known and most important work, won the Pulitzer Prize (1919). **Augustus Saint-Gaudens** designed the memorial to Adams's wife, Marian Hooper Adams, in Washington's Rock Creek Cemetery (1891). Adams died in Washington, D.C., on March 27, 1918.

ADAMS, HERBERT BAXTER (1850–1901). Historian. Born in Shutesbury, Massachusetts, on April 16, 1850, Adams graduated from Amherst College (1872) and earned a Ph.D. at the University of Heidelburg (1876). Teaching at Johns Hopkins University (1876–1901), he introduced the Teutonic school of scientific history and founded the American Historical Association (1884). His books include *The Germanic Origin of New England Towns* (1882) and *Life and Writings of Jared Sparks* (1893). Adams died in Amherst, Massachusetts, on July 30, 1901.

ADAMS, JOHN (1735–1826). President of the United States. Born in Braintree, Massachusetts, on October 19, 1735, Adams graduated from **Harvard** College (1755), taught school in **Worcester**, and practiced law in **Boston** (1758–74). His public career began (1765) when he wrote a protest against the **Stamp Act** that was used as a model by other Massachusetts towns. His series of articles in the *Boston Gazette* was published as a book (1768). Adams defended **John Hancock** in a smuggling case but also defended the British soldiers accused of murder in the **Boston**

Massacre (1770). Elected to the legislature, he opposed harsh measures imposed by Britain and was chief justice of the Massachusetts Supreme Judicial Court (1775–77).

Adams was a Massachusetts delegate to the Continental Congress (1774), where he gradually supported American independence. Serving with Thomas Jefferson and **Benjamin Franklin** on the committee that wrote the Declaration of Independence, Adams was its leading advocate in debate. Jefferson called him "our Colossus on the floor." Adams served with Franklin and Arthur Lee on a mission to France (1777) and returned home (1779) when he was elected to the Massachusetts constitutional convention, writing the first draft of the document (1780). He returned to France to negotiate secretly with the British government, signing the peace treaty (1782), serving as minister to the Netherlands and as the first U.S. minister to Great Britain (1785–88).

Adams was elected the first vice-president with George Washington (1789–97) and became the leader of the **Federalist Party** as president (1797–1801). His administration faced problems in foreign affairs as Congress called for war with France. Adams supported military defense efforts and accepted the Alien and Sedition Acts but avoided war with France. Alexander Hamilton's opposition, and public dislike of the Alien and Sedition Acts, led to Adams's defeat in the 1800 election. He retired to his Quincy home to live quietly and revived his friendship with Jefferson (1812–26) through a lengthy correspondence published as *The Adams-Jefferson Letters*. Adams died at home on July 4, 1826, on the 50th anniversary of the Declaration of Independence, a few hours after Jefferson died. He is the most underappreciated of the founding fathers and New England's greatest contribution to the new republic. In 2002 the Suffolk County courthouse in Boston was renamed in his honor. *See also* AMERICAN REVOLUTION.

ADAMS, JOHN C. (1812–1860). Hunter. Born on October 12, 1812, in Charlton, Massachusetts, Grizzly Adams was a professional hunter supplying game for California restaurants and hotels. He was most responsible for the extinction of grizzly bears in California, using bear cubs he trained on bear hunting expeditions. Adams was a colorful entertainer who toured with bears and other wild animals in **P. T. Barnum**'s circus and died in **Boston** on October 25, 1860.

ADAMS, JOHN QUINCY (1767–1848). President of the United States. Born in Braintree, Massachusetts, on July 11, 1767, the eldest son of

John and **Abigail Adams**, John Quincy Adams was educated in Europe, where he traveled with his father on diplomatic missions. He graduated from **Harvard** College (1787) and practiced law in **Boston** (1790–94). Appointed U.S. minister to the Netherlands (1794–97) and to Prussia (1797–1801), he served in the Massachusetts legislature (1802–03) and the U.S. Senate (1803–08) as a **Federalist**. His independent support of President Thomas Jefferson's embargo angered New England Federalists, who forced him to resign (1808). Adams was U.S. minister to Russia (1809) and to Great Britain (1814).

As secretary of state (1817–25), Adams signed a treaty with Great Britain (1818) extending the U.S.-Canadian border along the 49th parallel to the Rocky Mountains and arranging for arbitration of the Oregon boundary. He signed a treaty with Spain (1819) ceding Florida to the United States and wrote the Monroe Doctrine (1823). In 1824 Adams was elected the Democratic-Republican president (1825–29) by the House of Representatives in a close election. Andrew Jackson's supporters denounced the "corrupt bargain" by Adams with Henry Clay to defeat Jackson. His administration was marked by party antagonism until Jackson defeated Adams in the 1828 election.

Adams retired to Quincy, but was the only former president to return to serve in the House of Representatives (1831–48), where he was known as "Old Man Eloquent" for his support of anti-slavery petitions (1839–44). Adams successfully defended (1841) the African mutineers in the slave ship **Amistad case** and opposed annexation of Texas and the Mexican War. Adams collapsed in the U.S. House and died two days later on February 23, 1848.

ADAMS, LOUISA CATHERINE (1775–1852). First lady. Born in England on February 12, 1775, Louisa Catherine Johnson was the only first lady born outside the United States. Her mother was English and her father was from Maryland. She married **John Quincy Adams** in London (1797) and first came to New England in 1801. She served with her husband as a diplomat's wife in Berlin, St. Petersburg, Ghent, London, and Washington, D.C. As first lady (1825–29), she suffered from poor health but made the White House drawing rooms the focus of Washington social life. She retired to Quincy, Massachusetts, with her family (1829–31) but returned to Washington when the former president was elected to the House of Representatives (1831–48). Louisa Adams died in Washington on May 5, 1852, and is buried in Quincy.

ADAMS, SAMUEL (1722–1803). Governor of Massachusetts. Born in **Boston** on September 17, 1722, Sam Adams graduated from **Harvard** College (1740). After failing as a brewer and newspaper publisher, he entered politics as a Boston **selectman** and Massachusetts legislator (1765–74). As organizer of the **Sons of Liberty**, he played a key role as a polemicist for the **American Revolution** and recruited his cousin **John Adams** and **John Hancock** to the Patriot cause. Adams conceived the **Committee of Correspondence**, planned the **Boston Tea Party** (1773), and represented Massachusetts in the Continental Congress (1774–81). He signed the Declaration of Independence and supported the ratification of the U.S. Constitution, although it contradicted some of his **Whig** principles. He succeeded John Hancock as governor for four terms (1794–97) but gradually receded from public life. Sam Adams was a revolutionary with a **Puritan** character, self-disciplined, patient, ascetic, and more respected than loved when he died in Boston on October 2, 1803.

ADAMS, SHERMAN (1899–1986). Governor of New Hampshire. Born in East Dover, Vermont, on January 8, 1899, Llewelyn Sherman Adams lived in **Providence** and graduated from Dartmouth College (1920). He served in the U.S. Marine Corps (1918) and operated a **lumber** business in Vermont and New Hampshire (1921–44). He was a Republican in the New Hampshire legislature (1941–44) and in the House of Representatives (1945–47) before his election as governor (1949–53). Adams was chief of staff for President Dwight D. Eisenhower (1953–58) but resigned in a conflict of interest scandal. He was president of the Loon Mountain Corporation, one of the modern New Hampshire **ski** resort areas (1966). Sherman Adams died in Hanover on October 27, 1986.

AFRICAN AMERICANS. An early but small group in New England numbering about 1,000 in 1700 and only 16,000 in 1800. They were about 2 percent of the population in Massachusetts, and not numerous until the 1950s, but played a key (if contradictory) role in New England history. Slaves were common in seaports like New London, **Boston,** and **Portsmouth**, having been imported very early to Connecticut (1629), Massachusetts (1638), and New Hampshire (1645). William Pierce sailed from **Salem** to the West Indies (1639) to exchange **Native Americans** for black slaves, but Massachusetts was the first colony in the region to legalize slavery while forbidding capture (1640) by "unjust violence." The **New England Confederation** (1643) adopted an intercolonial agreement that magistrates may convict runaway slaves. But Judge **Samuel Sewall** wrote an anti-slavery tract, *The Selling of Joseph* (1700).

African Americans were killed in the **Deerfield Massacre** (1704), and the slave poet **Lucy Terry Prince** (1725–1821) wrote *Bars Fight* (1746) to commemorate this raid on her town. The Isaac Royall House in Medford, Massachusetts (1733), is the only house in New England with intact slave quarters. Royall owned 27 slaves, but most slave owners had only one or two slaves, and larger towns had small populations of free blacks. **Crispus Attucks**, a runaway slave from Framingham, was one of five colonists killed in the **Boston Massacre** (1770) and **Samuel Adams** refused the offer (1764) of a slave to care for his ailing wife until the woman was freed. This antislavery attitude was common in New England, leading the Continental Congress to ban the slave trade, and Rhode Island passed a law freeing all slaves brought into the colony (1774). But only a small number of New Hampshire's 656 blacks were free in 1775. Black lawbreakers were punished harshly, however, in Cambridge, Mark and Phillis were executed for petit treason (1755) for killing their master, John Codman. Phillis was burned at the stake, and Mark's body hung in chains as a public warning. New Englanders were not always consistent in their attitudes toward slavery. The Connecticut General Assembly required blacks to carry a pass from their master when leaving town (1690), banned free blacks from the state (1717), and authorized whipping slaves who defamed whites (1730) but banned the slave trade shortly before the Revolution (1774).

Many black patriots from every New England state served in the **American Revolution**. Prince Estabrook was one of eight black militiamen in the **Battle of Lexington and Concord** (1775). Black men served with the **Green Mountain Boys** in the capture of Fort Ticonderoga (1775), and Vermont was the first state to prohibit slavery in its constitution (1777). **Prince Hall**, Peter Salem, and Samuel Poor, among the 88 free and enslaved African Americans fighting at the **Battle of Bunker Hill** (1775), represented the 5,000 black soldiers who served in the Continental Army. The 1st Rhode Island Regiment was a black unit that served with distinction against the Hessians in New York (1778). Connecticut blacks joined the Bucks of Massachusetts or Rhode Island regiments when their home state refused to enlist black men. Cesar Prince and his brother, Festus Prince, born in Massachusetts, lived in Vermont, and served in the Continental Army. Cuff Smith, born a slave in Rhode Island, settled as a free man in Haddam Neck, Connecticut, and also joined the Continental Army. Prince Whipple, a slave in Portsmouth owned by General **William Whipple**, is depicted in Thomas Sully's painting of George Washington, *The Passage of the Delaware* (1819). **Lemuel Hayes** fought at Lexington and Ticonderoga.

Black residents of Fairfield County, Connecticut, sent a petition for the abolition of slavery (1779) and **Hartford** black men sent another (1780), but Governor **Jonathan Trumbull** ignored them. The Revolutionary ethos led Massachusetts courts to declare **slavery** illegal in the **Quock Walker case** (1783), and Elizabeth Freeman of Stockbridge was the first slave to be freed (1781) under the new state constitution. Rhode Island gradually abolished slavery (1784), but **Newport** blacks proposed voluntary colonization in Africa, and Captain **Paul Cuffee**, a wealthy whaler in Westport, Massachusetts, sailed with a group of free blacks to Sierra Leone (1815) and won a lawsuit for the right to vote (1783). However, **Boston**'s first minstrel show appeared (1799) and Connecticut disenfranchised blacks (1818), as did Rhode Island (1822). Despite this, black Bostonians founded the Prince Hall Grand Lodge of Masons (1784), the oldest black fraternal organization in North America.

David Walker, a black clothing merchant in Boston, published his influential anti-slavery tract (1829), and **William Lloyd Garrison** founded *The Liberator* in Boston (1831). Garrison founded the New England Anti-Slavery Society (1832), one of 300 such societies in New England. In Canterbury, Connecticut, **Prudence Crandall** was arrested for conducting a school for black girls (1833). The **African Meeting House** on Boston's **Beacon Hill**, established by a black congregation (1805), became a center for the **abolitionist** crusade. It is preserved as the Museum of Afro-American History (1963) on the **Black Heritage Trail**. The Boston School Committee denied a petition by **Prince Hall** to establish an African School (1787), but his son, Primus Hall, opened a private school for black children (1798). Charles L. Redmond, an abolitionist born in **Salem**, was the first black man to address the state legislature in 1842. Massachusetts repealed its ban on interracial marriage (1843); and when the courts upheld racial segregation in Boston public schools (1849), the legislature passed the first state school desegregation law (1855) and the first state law to permit black jurors (1860). Segregation by Negro pews in church balconies was common. **Frederick Douglass** found one in **New Bedford** (1839), but this practice disappeared in New England by 1860. Portsmouth's Negro burial ground (1705) was also no longer used by 1790. However, residential segregation was not common in David Walker's neighborhood on **Beacon Hill** (1825) but later increased in New England cities. Connecticut segregated its public schools in 1832.

The **Yankee** support for abolitionism led Rhode Island to enfranchise African Americans in 1842, as did New Hampshire and Maine in 1857. As the leading **whaling** port, New Bedford, Massachusetts, had a large population of African Americans, many runaways arriving on ships returned from seaports in the South. New Bedford **Quakers** played a key role in the abolitionist crusade. In central Massachusetts, for example, Worcester County had 769 black people in 1860 and more than 2,800 in 1900. New England soldiers and missionaries in the South encouraged some freed slaves to move to New England, as did some **Civil War** chaplains, like Horace James of the 25th Massachusetts Regiment organized in **Worcester**. Men from the 10th Connecticut Regiment joined three Massachusetts regiments in teaching "contrabands" or runaway slaves to read (1862). As a result, blacks born in Virginia and North Carolina were able to organize their own church in Worcester (1870). By 1903, George Alfred Busby was the first black man elected to the Worcester city council. New England's reputation as an abolitionist region attracted black migrants throughout the 19th century. African-American Civil War units included the **54th Massachusetts Infantry**, the 14th Rhode Island Heavy Artillery, and the 29th Connecticut Infantry. Vermont's 709 African Americans provided 152 soldiers for the Union Army. Dr. Martin R. Delaney, trained at **Harvard** Medical School (1849–52), was the first black man to received a commission in the Union Army.

Higher education offered new opportunities for New England African Americans, and Middlebury College claims the first black college graduate in the nation, Alexander Twilight (1823). He was a Vermont teacher and the first black state legislator in the nation (1836–38). Another Middlebury graduate, Martin Freeman (1826–89) of Rutland, Vermont, was the first black man to become a college president, at Avery College in Pennsylvania (1856). Edward A. Jones graduated from Amherst College (1826), and John Russworm graduated from Bowdoin College (1826). Richard T. Greener was the first black man to graduate from Harvard College (1870), and Robert Tanner Freeman graduated from Harvard Dental School (1869). Robert Taylor was the first black man to graduate from the Massachusetts Institute of Technology (1892). William Augustus Hinton, an African-American physician in Boston who developed the first syphilis test (1927), was the first black man to publish a medical textbook (1936) and to be appointed to the Harvard Medical School faculty (1949). **New Haven** native Edward Bouchet

(1852–1918) was the first black man to graduate from Yale University and to earn a Ph.D. in the United States (1876). Wilfred Johnson (1921–72), a leader of the **Hartford** Democrats in the African-American community, was the first black man elected to the Connecticut General Assembly (1958–66).

Mariah Stewart (1803–79) was the first African-American woman to give public lectures in Boston (1832) and to work as an abolitionist writer. Rebecca Lee Crumpler (1831–95) was the first African-American woman to earn a medical degree, graduating from the New England Female Medical College (1864), serving as a physician to Civil War soldiers, and later practicing in Boston. Novelist Pauline Hopkins (1856–1930) edited *The Colored American* magazine in Boston (1900–04). Eva Beatrice Dykes received a doctorate in literature at Harvard (1921), the first African-American women to earn a Ph.D. in the nation. Shirley A. Jackson was the first black woman to earn a doctorate at the Massachusetts Institute of Technology (1973). Ruth J. Simmons, the 18th president of Brown University, was the first black president of an **Ivy League** school (2001). Edmonia Lewis (1845–1911) was the African-American artist to achieve prominence, after training as a sculptor in Boston with **Anne Whitney**.

The legal profession also was an area of achievement for Yankee African Americans. New England's first black lawyer was Macon B. Allen in Boston (1845), and **George L. Ruffin** was the first black judge in Boston (1883). Walker Wolff & Brown was Boston's first black law firm (1888). Clement G. Morgan of Cambridge was the first black lawyer to argue before the Supreme Judicial Court (1901), and **William H. Lewis** was the first black U.S. assistant attorney general (1911). Blanche Woodson Braxton (1894–1939), who graduated from Portia Law School in Boston (1921), was the first black woman admitted to the Massachusetts bar (1923). Congresswoman Barbara Jordan was the first black student at Boston University Law School (1956), and Margaret Burnham was the first black female judge (1977). **Edward W. Brooke**, the first black man elected Massachusetts attorney general (1962–66), was the first black senator elected by popular vote (1967–79). Roderick L. Ireland was the first black man appointed to the Massachusetts Supreme Judicial Court (1997).

The church also provided careers in which black men achieved distinction. **Lemuel Haynes** (1753–1833), born in West Hartford, Connecticut, was the first African American ordained as a **Congregational** minister (1785), serving as pastor to white congregations in Connecticut, Massachusetts, Vermont, and New York. Born a slave in Maryland, James W. C. Pennington graduated from Yale College (1838) and was a **Congregational** minister in New Haven and Hartford and a leader in the **Amistad Case** and the **temperance** and abolitionist crusades. Despite some conflict between Irish **Catholic** immigrants and blacks, **James A. Healy** (1830–1900), the son of an **Irish immigrant** in Georgia and a slave woman, served as chancellor of the diocese of Boston (1855–75) and was the first African-American Catholic prelate as the bishop of **Portland**, Maine (1875–1901). By the 20th century, African Americans played important roles in every aspect of New England society. *See also* DOUGLASS, FREDERICK; GARRISON, WILLIAM LLOYD; NEW BEDFORD; SLAVERY; UNDERGROUND RAILROAD; WHEATLEY, PHILLIS.

AFRICAN MEETING HOUSE. Oldest African-American church in the country, founded by Thomas Paul, an **African-American** preacher from New Hampshire (1805). The congregation, led by Cato Garner, a native of Africa, built their church in 1806 on the North Slope of **Beacon Hill** in **Boston**. It was a church, school, and meeting place for black Bostonians and **abolitionists**, known as the Black Faneuil Hall. Restored to its 1855 design (1972), it is part of the National Park Service **Black Heritage Trail**.

AGASSIZ, ELIZABETH CABOT CARY (1822–1907). Educator. Born in **Boston** on December 5, 1822, Elizabeth Agassiz was the granddaughter of **Thomas H. Perkins**. She married **Louis Agassiz** (1850) and was co-author of his *A Journey to Brazil* (1867) and wrote *Louis Agassiz: His Life and Correspondence* (1885). She was a founder (1879) and first president of Radcliffe College (1882–1903). Mrs. Agassiz died in Arlington, Massachusetts, on June 27, 1907.

AGASSIZ, LOUIS (1807–1873). Geologist and educator. Born on May 28, 1807, in Switzerland, Jean Louis Rodolphe Agassiz studied in Germany and published original research on Brazil's fossil fish. He taught geology in Switzerland and was professor of natural history at **Harvard University**'s Lawrence Scientific School (1848–73). Agassiz published *Lake Superior* (1850) and four volumes on the *Contributions to the Natural History of the United States* (1857–1862). He founded Harvard's Museum of Comparative Zoology (1859) and founded the first marine biology laboratory on Penikese Island off **Cape Cod** (1873). His efforts to improve teaching methods and to stimulate interest in science were more important than much of his scientific work because of his opposition to the theory of natural selection. Agassiz was a popular and dynamic teacher at Harvard where he taught until his death on December 14, 1873, in Cambridge.

AGGANIS, HARRY (1930–1955). Athlete. Born in Lynn, Massachusetts, on April 30, 1930, Agganis was an All Star athlete at Boston University. He played first base for the **Boston Red Sox** (1953–55) until his sudden death at age 26 on June 27, 1955. Known as the Golden Greek, Harry Agganis, the son of **Greek immigrants**, was the embodiment of the American dream and is still rated as one of the finest athletes New England has ever produced.

AGRICULTURAL FAIRS. Event begun in New England when Elkanah Watson (1758–1842), the father of American county fairs, exhibited **Merino sheep** on the Pittsfield, Massachusetts, common (1807). Watson established the Berkshire Agricultural Society (1811) to improve **farming** practices and held the first agricultural fair in America at Pittsfield (1814). Essex, Hampshire, Hampden, Worcester, and Franklin counties formed agricultural societies and sponsored annual fairs by 1818. The Massachusetts writer Anthony B. Allen founded the *American Agriculturist* (1842) magazine to improve farming methods. The Massachusetts Agricultural Fairs Association formed (1920) at **Worcester** to promote county fairs, which included farm and home economics exhibits, youth participation, midway shows, commercial displays, and recreational projects. Edwin Hammond (1801–70) founded the Vermont State Agricultural Society (1851), and most states followed this example. In Connecticut, the **Danbury** Fair (1821–1981) was the largest in New England.

When the Grange organized in New England (1870), Grangers usually participated in these fairs, as did land-grant colleges, such as the University of Maine (1865), the University of Massachusetts (1867), and the University of Connecticut (1881). Modern fairs, like those in Topsfield, Massachusetts, and Rutland or Tunbridge, Vermont, are a reminder of New England's agrarian roots and serve as harvest festivals for tourists and suburban residents.

AGRICULTURE. Most common occupation in the region until 1869. It has diminished but is still an important part of the New England economy. Before the **Civil War**, a typical New England farm was about a hundred acres with chickens, milk cows, hogs, horses, and sheep and raised buckwheat, butter, cheese, **corn**, eggs, hay, honey, **maple syrup**, oats, **potatoes**, rye, and wheat. Although farming has declined, it is a more diversified industry today, in part due to the first American agricultural experiment station established at Yale University (1847) and the first state experiment station Samuel W. Johnson established at the University of Connecticut at Storrs (1875). Connecticut agriculture contributes $521 million annually to the state economy, and New London is the largest dairy-producing township in the state with 69 farms. State law (1978) encourages farmland preservation, and farm **tourism** is increasing. More than half of the dairy farms in New England are found in Vermont, and Maine ranks second.

Modern agricultural products in New England include apples, arugula, basil, beans, beets, blueberries, broccoli, cabbage, carrots, cauliflower, cheese, chives, Christmas trees, cilantro, corn, cranberries, cucumbers, dill, eggs, eggplant, garlic, kale, flowers, herbs, lettuce, livestock, maple syrup, milk, mushrooms, onions, peaches, pears, pumpkins, seafood, spinach, squash, strawberries, tobacco, tomatoes, turnips, and wool. Niche markets developed recently, and sheep, goats, bison, and llamas replaced cows on some farms for meat, soap, milk, and wool. Farm and forestland also contribute to the region's natural beauty and aid the important tourism industry. In addition to niche farming with new exotic crops, agricultural tourism (or agritourism) has increased, with farms offering bed and breakfast accommodations or attracting visitors with educational animal and farm exhibits. Tourists often pay farmers to pick their own berries or fruit. Yankee farmers may be aging and the size of farms declining, but the number of farms has increased since 1974. Moreover, 70 farms in Massachusetts have been in the same family for 100 years or more, two of these were established in 1650, nine others are more than 300 years old, and 32 are more than 200 years old. The Casey Farm (1750) and the Watson Farm (1789) are the oldest farms in Rhode Island. In New Hampshire the Tuttle farm in Dover is known as America's oldest continuously run family farm (1632). However, rural depopulation was noted by 1860 when half the towns in Vermont had population losses and about 70 percent of the state was deforested. Vermont was still the most rural state in the nation in 1945.

AIKEN, GEORGE D. (1892–1984). Senator from Vermont. Born in Dummerston, Vermont, on August 20, 1892, George David Aiken was a fruit farmer in Putney. He served as a Republican state legislator (1931–35), speaker of the house (1933–35), lieutenant governor (1935–37), and governor (1937–41). He ended the **Proctor dynasty** and served as a U.S.

senator (1941–75), defeating **Ralph A. Flanders**. Aiken, who epitomized the flinty Vermont **Yankee**, coined the term **Northeast Kingdom** for the remote northeastern corner of Vermont. He died in Putney, Vermont, on November 19, 1984.

AIKEN, HOWARD HATHAWAY (1900–1973). Scientist. Born in Hoboken, New Jersey, on March 8, 1900, Aiken earned his Ph.D. at **Harvard University** (1939). While teaching physics at Harvard (1937–61), he built the first large automatic **computer**. Funded by IBM, this device became the Mark I digital computer (1944) using punch cards and 500 miles of wire and weighing 35 tons. This was the first programmable mechanical computer used by the Navy for ballistics. After the war, Aiken started the first computer science program in the world at Harvard, launching the computer industry in New England. Aiken retired in 1961, and died in St. Louis, Missouri, on March 14, 1973.

ALBANIAN. Immigrants settled in Boston's **West End** by 1880. The first arrival was Kole Kristofor (or Nicholas Christopher), who is still remembered by Albanian Americans as a pioneer. Communities grew in Natick, Southbridge, and **Worcester**, Massachusetts; Manchester, New Hampshire; Sacco and Biddeford, Maine; and **Waterbury**, Connecticut. Most of the 15,000 immigrants who entered the country by 1911 were Orthodox Christians, settling in New York and New England, but after 1945 Albanian Roman **Catholics** and Muslims arrived. **Boston** was always the American center, with the Kafene Vatra (Hearth Coffeehouse) and the Hotel Skenderbeu and two mutual-aid associations, the Katundi Society and the Panarity Society. An Albanian picnic ground in Manchester, New Hampshire, attracted extended families from across New England to share traditional food, song, and dance. Albanians in Hudson, Massachusetts, founded the Albanian Orthodox Church (1908) in a dispute with Greek Orthodox priests. Fan S. Noli, a **Harvard University** graduate who came to the United States in 1906, founded the first Albanian Orthodox Church in the nation in Boston (1908). He became the Metropolitan bishop (1932–65) of the Boston archdiocese, which now has 13 parishes. Albanian Muslims organized in Biddeford (1915) and Waterbury (1949).

The first Albanian newspaper *Kombi* (The Nation) was published in Boston (1906–09) but *Dielli* (The Sun) also published in Boston (1909–76) and was more influential and also published textbooks for illiterate immigrants to learn their native language. Boston Albanians also published *Illyria*, a semimonthly magazine (1916–17), a monthly *The Morning Star* (1917–19), and a liberal newspaper, *Republika* (1930–32). Worcester had *The Albanian Messenger* (1934–37), but the most widely read was *Liria/Liberty*, the weekly organ of the Free Albania Organization published in South Boston (1941–70). A radio program, The Voice of Albania, began broadcasting in Boston in 1938, and Natick (1908) and Worcester offered Albanian schools and concerts.

Many of the Albanians in American exile were very interested in homeland politics. As early as 1912 they organized the Pan-Albanian Federation (or the Vatra) in Boston, with 72 branches across the country. They obtained international recognition of an independent Albania (1913) and published the *Adriatic Review* in Boston (1918–19) to lobby for their homeland. The Free Albanian Organization (1941) in South Boston united nationalists, anti-monarchists, Fascists, and radicals throughout America during World War II. After the Communist takeover of Albania, they negotiated with the government for their homeland and still offer seminars and scholarships for the 70,000 Albanian Americans in the United States today. Boston restaurateur Anthony Athanas is a leader of the Albanian community and charities.

ALBRIGHT, TENLEY (1935–). Athlete. Born in Newton, Massachusetts, on July 18, 1935, Albright graduated from Radcliffe College (1956) and **Harvard** Medical School (1960), specializing in sports medicine. She won her first figure skating title at age 12 and won a silver medal at the Winter Olympic Games (1952). She also won five consecutive national titles and was the first American woman to win a world championship (1953). After winning a gold medal at the Olympics (1956), she was the first woman to serve as an officer on the U.S. Olympic Committee (1979). Tenley Albright Blakeley, the most celebrated woman in international figure skating, lives in Brookline, Massachusetts.

ALCOTT, BRONSON (1799–1888). Writer. Born on November 29, 1799, in Wolcott, Connecticut, Amos Bronson Alcott was an eccentric teacher and writer who became a prominent **Transcendentalist** in Concord and **Boston**. His utopian commune in Harvard, Massachusetts, called **Fruitlands** (1844–45), failed but inspired **Brook Farm**. He was later superintendent of schools in Concord and founded his own Concord School of Philosophy (1859). Alcott wrote for the *Dial* magazine and *Concord Days* (1872) and *Table Talk* (1877), and he died in Boston on March 4, 1888.

ALCOTT, LOUISA MAY (1832–1888). Writer. Born in Pennsylvania on November 29, 1832, Alcott, the daughter of **Transcendentalist** philosopher **Bronson Alcott**, was raised in **Boston** and Concord, Massachusetts. Writing to support her impecunious family, by 1851 she was a prolific author producing 270 novels, plays, poems, potboilers, and short stories for magazines, including the *Atlantic Monthly*. Her letters to her family while she was a **Civil War** nurse were published as *Hospital Sketches* (1863). Although best remembered for *Little Women* (1868), Alcott was committed to social reform and was the first woman to register to vote in Concord (1879). She died in Boston on March 6, 1888, four days after her father's death. Her Concord home (1858–77), Orchard House, is a National Historic Landmark.

ALDEN, JOHN (1599–1687). Pilgrim leader. Born in England about 1599, Alden was a cooper who signed the **Mayflower Compact** and was deputy governor (1664–65, 1667) of **Plymouth Colony**. **Henry Wadsworth Longfellow**'s poem *The Courtship of Miles Standish* (1858) recounts the legend that he proposed marriage to Priscilla Mullens for his friend, **Miles Standish**. In fact, Alden married Priscilla (1622). He founded Duxbury, Massachusetts (1636), where he was the last of the **Pilgrim** leaders to die on September 12, 1687.

ALDRICH, NELSON W. (1841–1915). Senator from Rhode Island. Born in Foster, Rhode Island, on November 6, 1841, Nelson Wilmarth Aldrich served in the **Civil War**. Working in the wholesale grocery business, he served on the Providence city council (1869–74) and as a Republican state legislator (1875–76). Elected to the House of Representatives (1879–81) and the Senate (1881–1911), he dominated Rhode Island politics and became an authority on fiscal policy and the protective tariff. As one of the conservative Big Four Republican leaders, he became very wealthy from investments. Aldrich died in New York City on April 16, 1915.

ALDRICH, THOMAS BAILEY (1836–1907). Writer. Born in **Portsmouth**, New Hampshire, on November 11, 1836, Aldrich left school at age 13 and worked in New York City as a clerk, writing verse and literary reviews for the *Evening Mirror* and the *Home Journal*. He moved to Boston (1865) as editor of *Every Saturday* (1865–71). His autobiographical novel, *The Story of a Bad Boy* (1870), and other fiction won him the position as *Atlantic Monthly* editor (1881–90). Aldrich died in Boston on March 19, 1907. His boyhood home is part of the **Straw-bery Banke** museum.

ALEWIVES. Small Atlantic coast fish (*Alosa psuedoharengus*) like herring. They swim from the sea to breed in New England rivers each May. Early settlers depended on these fish as food when the winter supplies grew low. Massachusetts law (1741) required towns to do nothing to interfere with the migration, and fish ladders were built around sawmills and dams. In Maine the town of Nobleboro allotted fish to support widows (1807), and Damariscotta (an **Abenaki** word for many alewives) employed a fish herder. Alewife Brook Parkway in Cambridge and Herring Run in Weymouth, Massachusetts, were two traditional **fishing** sites, and many coastal towns still have an annual herring run when the fish are gathered in large quantities to eat or as **lobster** bait.

ALGER, HORATIO, JR. (1832–1899). Writer. Born in Revere, Massachusetts, on January 13, 1832, Alger graduated from **Harvard** College (1852) and Harvard Divinity School (1860). Unsuccessful in enlisting in the Union Army, he was a Unitarian minister in Brewster, Massachusetts (1864–66), but he resigned suddenly in a sex scandal in the church. Alger moved to New York City where he associated with **Charles Loring Brace**'s mission to slum children at the Newsboys Lodging House. Among the street urchins, Alger collected vivid material for his second novel, *Ragged Dick* (1868). This hackneyed tale of pluck, luck, and self-reliance became a successful formula for 120 novels in the rags to riches genre. The blend of social Darwinism and laissez-faire doctrine remained popular for 30 years, despite the stilted prose, **Yankee** moralism, and consistently low literary quality. Alger's melodramatic fiction suited Gilded Age beliefs that social mobility and economic enterprise reshaping the city were founded on Victorian morals. Alger retired from New York City (1895) to live in South Natick, Massachusetts, until his death on July 18, 1899.

ALGONQUIN. Largest **Native American** group on the East Coast. A loose confederation of tribes lived from Newfoundland to Carolina and to the Great Lakes. The Algonquian linguistic family included most tribes in colonial New England, who were hunters, farmers, and trappers related by geographical location, language, and culture. Each small, autonomous, semi-sedentary village had a *sachem* (leader), and political ties were based on kinship. The *shaman* (medicine man) was a religious leader and healer.

Women built the dwellings, a dome-shaped **wigwam** or round house made with wood, bark, and woven grass about eight feet high and 12 feet in diameter at the base. Men hunted and traded, and women planted **corn**, **beans**, and squash. Fish, shellfish, eels, roots, nuts, berries, and fruit supplemented the diet. By 1600 European contacts caused epidemics that drastically reduced the **Algonquin** population, but major conflict with the settlers was rare until 1637, while intertribal raids were common, especially with the **Mohawks** and **Pequots**. More than 130 **Algonquian** words in the English language include caucus, hickory, moccasin, **moose**, papoose, pecan, **podunk**, powwow, **quahog**, raccoon, skunk, squash, terrapin, tomahawk, **wampum**, wigwam, and **woodchuck**.

ALLAGASH WILDERNESS WATERWAY. Established by the U.S. Congress (1970) and the Maine legislature (1975) to preserve a continuous area of 59,000 acres and 92 miles of meandering wild water for public recreation in northern Maine. Since **Henry David Thoreau** traveled this wild river, an estimated 50,000 people canoe and fish the Allagash River each year. It became the first state-managed river in the National Wild and Scenic River system in 1970.

ALLAN, JOHN (1746–1805). Soldier. Born in Edinburgh, Scotland, on January 14, 1746, Allan came to Nova Scotia as a child (1749) when his father was posted to the British garrison at Halifax. Educated in **Boston**, Allan became a farmer, **fur trader**, and political leader in Nova Scotia but joined the New England rebels (1776). Supported by **John Adams**, Congress commissioned him a colonel in the Continental Army (1777) to defend Maine and ally with **Native Americans**. Tenacious and successful, he repulsed British troops at Machais and made the St. Croix River the U.S.-Canadian border. Compensated for his losses and service by land grants from Massachusetts (1792) and Congress (1801), Allan died in Lubec, Maine, on February 5, 1805.

ALLEN, ELISHA HUNT (1804–1883). Congressman from Maine. Born in New Salem, Massachusetts, on January 28, 1804, Allen graduated from Williams College (1823) and practiced law in Brattleboro (1825). Elected to the Maine state legislature (1835–40), he was a **Whig** in the House of Representatives (1841–43), and served again in the state legislature (1846). He practiced law in **Boston** (1847–50) and served in the Massachusetts legislature (1849) until appointed U.S. consul in Honolulu (1850). He became chief justice and regent of the Kingdom of

Hawaii and was envoy to the U.S. government (1856, 1864) and minister to the United States (1869–83). Allen, best recalled for negotiating the important reciprocity treaty (1876), died on January 1, 1883, while attending a diplomatic reception in the White House.

ALLEN, ETHAN (1738–1789). Soldier. Born in Litchfield, Connecticut, on January 10, 1738, Allen served in the **French and Indian Wars** (1757) and moved (1770) to the **New Hampshire Grants**, the disputed area between New York and New Hampshire that became Vermont. He formed the **Green Mountain Boys** (1771) with **Seth Warner** to exclude New York settlers and petitioned the British to create a new colony. As a Connecticut militia officer, Allen captured Fort Ticonderoga from the British with **Benedict Arnold** (1775) and attacked Montreal. Captured by the British, Allen was imprisoned cruelly until exchanged (1778) and returned to Vermont as a hero. But his deist philosophy in *Reason, the Only Oracle of Man* (1784) ruined his reputation. Allen died in Burlington on February 12, 1789.

ALLEN, FRED (1894–1956). Actor. Born in Somerville, Massachusetts, on May 31, 1894, John Florence Sullivan attended Boston University. In 1912 he began his career as a **vaudeville** juggler and comic as Fred Allen and joined Broadway shows, including *The Passing Show of 1922* and *The Greenwich Village Follies*. His films include *Thanks a Million* (1935), *Love Thy Neighbor* (1940), and *We're Not Married* (1952). Allen was best known as the satirical deadpan comedian on many radio programs (1932–40), his own *Fred Allen Show* (1939–49), and the television programs *Judge for Yourself* (1953–54) and *What's My Line* (1954–56). His most memorable character may have been Titus Moody, the prototypical taciturn **Yankee**. Allen wrote two autobiographies, *Treadmill to Oblivion* (1954), that **Edwin O'Connor** edited, and *Much Ado about Me* (1956) before his death in New York City on March 17, 1956.

ALLEN, HEMAN (1779–1852). Congressman from Vermont. Born in Poultney, Vermont, on February 23, 1779, Allen graduated from Dartmouth College (1795). He practiced law in Colchester, was county sheriff (1808–10) and county judge (1811–14), and was elected as a Democratic-Republican to the state legislature (1812–17) and to the House of Representatives (1817–18). He resigned to become U.S. marshal for Vermont (1818–22). Allen was U.S. minister to Chile (1823–27) and president of the Burlington branch of the United States Bank (1830–36). He practiced law in Highgate, where he died on April 7, 1852.

ALLEN, PHILIP (1785–1865). Senator from Rhode Island. Born in **Providence** on September 1, 1785, Allen graduated from Rhode Island College (later Brown University) in 1803. When shipping was suspended during the War of 1812, Allen manufactured cotton goods and printed calico in Smithfield and **Providence** with new steam engines. He was a leader of the Democrats in the state legislature (1819–21) and president of the Rhode Island branch of the United States Bank (1827–36). Elected governor (1852–53), he resigned to serve in the Senate (1853–59). Allen died in Providence on December 16, 1865.

ALLSTON, WASHINGTON (1779–1843). Painter. Born in South Carolina on November 5, 1779, Allston was educated in **Newport**, Rhode Island, and graduated from **Harvard** College (1800). He studied with Benjamin West in London, in Paris, and Italy before settling in **Boston** (1809). While in England, he was a mentor to **Samuel F. B. Morse** and painted a portrait of **Robert Rogers** (1799) and dramatic romantic landscapes. Despite poverty and poor health, Allston was a leading American painter when he lived in Cambridge (1818–43), where he died on July 9, 1843.

ALMANAC. Book containing a calendar, astronomical information, weather predictions, tide tables, planting charts, and miscellaneous useful data printed in Europe by 1457 but derived from ancient Egyptian and Greek calendars. William Pierce printed the first American almanac in Cambridge (1639), and Dr. Nathaniel Ames (1708–64) printed a very popular almanac at his Dedham **tavern** (1725–95). James Franklin published the *Rhode Island Almanac* (1728), and his brother, **Benjamin Franklin**, became famous for his *Poor Richard's Almanac* (1732–57). The Rhode Island astronomer Benjamin West published his *New England Almanack, or Lady's and Gentleman's Diary* (1763–81) in **Providence**, and the Connecticut mathematics professor and astronomer Nathan Daboll (1750–1818) published the *New England Almanack* (1773). Robert B. Thomas wrote the *Old Farmer's Almanac* (1792–present), the oldest continuously printed almanac in the nation, which is still published by **Yankee Magazine**. Dudley Leavitt published *Leavitt's Farmers' Almanac* (1797) in New Hampshire. The mixture of regional humor, poetry, prose, and recipes, in addition to practical information, made almanacs popular reading throughout New England.

AMERICAN ACADEMY OF ARTS AND SCIENCES (AAAS). Educational society. Proposed by **John Adams** (1779), the academy was incorporated in **Boston** (1780) to cultivate learning much like the American Philosophical Society in Philadelphia. Located in Cambridge (1955), the AAAS conducts interdisciplinary studies of contemporary intellectual and social issues and publishes a quarterly journal, *Daedalus,* for 3,600 elected fellows and many subscribers.

AMERICAN ANTIQUARIAN SOCIETY (AAS). Scholarly society founded in **Worcester**, Massachusetts, (1812) by **Isaiah Thomas** (1749–1831). He was the official printer for the patriots, a pioneer newspaperman, book publisher, and author of *History of Printing in America* (1810). As a consequence, the AAS contains remarkable collections of early American newspapers and printed Americana for scholarly research. It funds scholarly research based on its extensive library collections.

AMERICAN ELM. Official state tree of the Commonwealth of Massachusetts (1941). The tall, stately elms (*Ulmus americana*) long shaded **Boston Common**, **Harvard** College, and many New England towns. The **Sons of Liberty** protested the **Stamp Act** at the **Liberty Tree** (1765), a noted elm in **Boston** that the **Loyalists** cut down for firewood (1776). George Washington took command of the Continental Army under the large tree on Cambridge Common (1775) known as the Washington Elm. Dutch elm disease, a fungus spread from Europe by bark beetles, destroyed most American elms in the 1930s.

AMERICAN PROTECTIVE ASSOCIATION (APA). Secret nativist organization influential in New England politics in the 1890s. Organized in Iowa (1887) as an **anti-Catholic** society with strong ties to the Republican Party, the APA had 1 million members by 1895 and elected 20 congressmen. Public support of parochial schools and literacy tests for **immigrants** were bitter issues that led to the APA riot in **Boston** on July 4, 1895. Denounced by the Massachusetts Democratic Party (1894), the APA disappeared by 1911.

AMERICAN REVOLUTION. The Revolutionary War (1775–81) began in New England with the **Battle of Lexington and Concord** on April 19, 1775. **Ethan Allen** and **Benedict Arnold** captured Fort Ticonderoga on Lake Champlain in May while **John Adams**, **John Hancock**, and **Benjamin Franklin** led the radicals at the Second Continental Congress in Philadelphia. Following the British Pyrrhic victory in the **Battle of Bunker Hill** on June 17, 1775, George Washington assumed command of the Continental Army in July on the Cambridge common. His siege of **Boston** ended with the British evacuation of Boston on March 17, 1776. Congress appointed John Adams, Thomas Jefferson, **Roger Sherman**, Robert Livingston, and Benjamin Franklin to write the Declaration of Independence in June 1776.

The most dramatic event during the Revolution in New Hampshire was the raid by Portsmouth merchant Samuel Cutts and a patriot mob on Fort William and Mary in Portsmouth harbor (1775). This led the royal governor, John Wentworth, to flee the colony on a British warship in August 1775. In Vermont, General **John Stark**'s victory at the **Battle of Bennington** in August 1777 inspired the fledgling Continental Army, but little more warfare occurred in New England after the successful British defense in the **Battle of Newport** in August 1778. In Connecticut the British raided Stonington (1775), **Danbury** (1777), **New Haven** (1779), Groton, and New London (1781). Connecticut's state hero was the militia captain **Nathan Hale**, who the British executed as a spy (September 1776). In Maine, the first naval battle of the war was an American victory at Machais (1775), but the British navy raided Falmouth (later called **Portland**) in 1775 and Brooklin in 1778 and occupied Castine (1778–79). John Paul Jones and John Barry, the most successful commanders in the American navy, sailed from Boston, **Portsmouth**, and **Providence** with Yankee crews but could not protect the entire New England coast. Yankee privateers assisted the war effort, but the British navy raided **Martha's Vineyard** in 1778. In Vermont, the British led a **Native American** attack on Royalton in 1780, killing 22 men and taking 26 prisoners to Montreal.

Many New England **Loyalists** fled to Canada, and those who remained suffered harassment, property confiscation, or imprisonment. Some people sat out the war as neutrals, like the family of **Martha Ballard** who moved from central Massachusetts to frontier Maine after the war. New England's most infamous **Tories** include Benedict Arnold and **Robert Rogers**, who served with the British army. Arnold raided Groton and New London in the **Battle of Groton Heights**.

John Glover, the Marblehead, Massachusetts, merchant, led his sailors and soldiers to help George Washington cross the Delaware River and win the battle of Trenton (1776). **Nathanael Greene**, the Rhode Island blacksmith, was the youngest and most successful general in the Continental Army, winning key battles in the southern colonies (1780). New England also provided political leadership during the American

Revolution. New Hampshire wrote the first revolutionary constitution in 1776, Connecticut governor **Jonathan Trumbull** was the foremost supporter of the Continental Army, and **Silas Deane** negotiated a treaty with France.

AMES, ADELBERT (1835–1933). Soldier. Born in Rockland, Maine, on October 31, 1835, Ames graduated from West Point (1861). He was the colonel of the **20th Maine Regiment** succeeded by **Joshua L. Chamberlain** (1862). Major General Ames received the Congressional Medal of Honor for heroic service. After serving as military governor of Mississippi (1868–69), he was elected a **carpetbagger** Republican to the Senate from Mississippi (1870–74) and governor (1874–76). Ames retired to business in **Lowell**, Massachusetts, but served in the Spanish American War (1898). He was the last surviving **Civil War** general when he died in Florida on April 12, 1933.

AMES, FISHER (1758–1808). Congressman from Massachusetts. Born in Dedham, Massachusetts on April 9, 1758, Ames graduated from **Harvard** (1774). He served in the Revolutionary War, practiced law in Dedham (1781–89), and was a **Federalist** in the House of Representatives (1789–97). Ames was a noted orator in support of Alexander Hamilton and in opposition to **Samuel Adams** and Thomas Jefferson. He retired (1797) to live as the Federalist Sage of Dedham, where Squire Ames died on July 4, 1808.

AMES, OAKES (1804–1873). Congressman from Massachusetts. Born in North Easton, Massachusetts, on January 10, 1804, Ames was a wealthy shovel manufacturer. Elected as a Republican to the House of Representatives (1863–73), he was censured by the House (1873) for his role in the transcontinental **railroad** Credit Mobiler stock fraud (1865–72) with **Thomas C. Durant**. Protesting his innocence, Ames did not seek reelection and died in North Easton on May 8, 1873. **H. H. Richardson** designed the Oakes Ames Memorial Hall (1879) in North Easton, the Ames estate gate lodge (1881), and the town's railroad station (1881). **Augustus Saint-Gaudens** designed a memorial to Oakes Ames and his brother Oliver Ames (1807–77) in Sherman, Wyoming, the highest point of the Union Pacific Railroad they built. The Stonehill College Industrial History Center on the original Ames estate commemorates the shovel business.

AMES, OLIVER (1831–1895). Governor of Massachusetts. Born in North Easton, Massachusetts, on February 4, 1835, Oliver Ames, the son of **Oakes Ames**, studied at Brown University. He managed the Ames shovel factory (1863–90) and restored the family fortune by building 20 western **railroads** (1873–90). Elected a Republican state senator (1880–82), Ames served as lieutenant governor (1882–86) and governor (1886–90). Retiring to grand residences in **Boston** and **Martha's Vineyard**, Oliver Ames was a noted philanthropist when he died in North Easton on October 22, 1895.

AMHERST, JEFFREY (1717–1797). Soldier. Born in Kent, England, Amherst served in the British Army in European wars (1731–58). He established his reputation as an effective general by capturing the French fortress at Louisbourg in Nova Scotia (1758), Fort Ticonderoga, and Lake Champlain (1759). When he captured Montreal (1760), he was appointed governor of Virginia (1763–68) and knighted. His harsh policy toward **Native American** allies precipitated Pontiac's Rebellion (1763–66) while he was in London. Named Baron Amherst (1776), he declined commands in the **American Revolution**, urging economic blockade rather than military force. The town of Amherst (1759) in Massachusetts and Amherst College were named in his honor (1821). He died in England on August 3, 1797.

AMISTAD CASE (1839–1841). Landmark **New Haven** court decision appealed to the U.S. Supreme Court (1841) by **Roger Sherman Baldwin** and **John Quincy Adams**. When African slaves seized the Spanish ship *Amistad* carrying them from Cuba (1839), and the slaves attempted to sail to Africa, the U.S. Navy took the ship to Connecticut. After the piracy trial in New Haven, Connecticut, former president Adams and Baldwin won freedom for the slaves before the Supreme Court. The decision by Justice **Joseph Story** (1841) was an important victory for the **abolitionist** cause.

AMORY, CLEVELAND (1917–1998). Writer. Born in Nahant, Massachusetts, on September 2, 1917, Amory graduated from **Harvard University** (1940). He was a newspaperman in New Hampshire and Arizona and wrote for the *Saturday Evening Post* (1939–41). After serving in the U.S. Army in World War II, he wrote *The Proper Bostonians* (1947), a trenchant study of the **Boston Brahmins**, and a sequel, *The Last Resorts* (1952). He later became an international advocate for the humane treatment of animals. Amory died in New York City on October 14, 1998.

ANCIENT AND HONORABLE ARTILLERY COMPANY (AHAC). The nation's oldest military company and the third oldest in the world. It organized **Boston** gentlemen in the Military Company to defend Massachusetts (1637). The AHAC served in the **American Revolution**, and its armory in **Faneuil Hall** (1746) includes sabers, medals, and art works. Its members are prominent citizens who make an annual parade to the State House on **Patriot's Day** (April 18). *See also* MILITIA and TRAINING DAY.

ANDREW, JOHN ALBION (1818–1867). Governor of Massachusetts. Born in Windham, Maine, on May 31, 1818, Andrew graduated from Bowdoin College (1837). He practiced law in **Boston** (1840) and as a **Conscience Whig** was active in the **abolitionist** movement. Andrew moved to the Free Soil Party (1848) and was an organizer of the Republican Party at Worcester (1856). Elected to the Massachusetts legislature (1857), he became a prominent defender of **John Brown** after the Harper's Ferry raid. Andrew was instrumental in nominating Abraham Lincoln for president in 1860, and as governor (1861–66) Massachusetts was the first state to respond to President Lincoln's call for volunteers in April 1861. Throughout the war Andrew was a strong supporter of the Lincoln administration and persuaded the Union Army to accept the state's **54th Regiment**, the first Army unit of Northern **African-American** soldiers. To win the war, Andrew abandoned his **Know Nothing Party** sentiments and cooperated with **Irish** and **German Catholics** to organize Massachusetts units for the Army. After the 54th Regiment's heroic defeat at Fort Wagner, South Carolina, led by Colonel **Robert Gould Shaw**, Andrew authorized the Shaw Memorial bronze relief on **Boston Common**, created by **Augustus Saint-Gaudens** (1897). After five terms as governor, Andrew retired to private life and died suddenly in Boston on October 30, 1867.

ANDREWS, CHARLES MCLEAN (1863–1943). Historian. Born in Wetherfield, Connecticut, on February 22, 1863, Andrews graduated from Trinity College in **Hartford** (1884) and earned a Ph.D. at Johns Hopkins University (1889). He taught history at Bryn Mawr College (1889–1907), at Johns Hopkins University (1907–10), and at Yale University (1910–31). He was a leader of the imperial school of colonial

American history and won the Pulitzer Prize in 1935 for *The Colonial Period of American History* (1934–38). Andrews died in **New Haven** on September 9, 1943.

ANDROS, SIR EDMUND (1637–1714). Royal governor. Born in London on December 6, 1637, Andros was the royal governor of New York (1674–81). Appointed to govern the **Dominion of New England** (including New York and New Jersey), he imposed imperial government strictly but constructively (1686–89) from his **Boston** headquarters. When he demanded the return of Connecticut's 1662 royal charter, it was hidden in the **Charter Oak** in **Hartford** (1687). Governor **Walter Clarke** also refused to surrender the Rhode Island charter to Andros, who was deposed by the Massachusetts **Puritans** in the Glorious Revolution (1689). Andros returned to London but was later governor of Virginia (1692–97) and governor of Guernsey Island (1704–06). He died in England on February 27, 1714.

ANTHONY BURNS CASE. *See* BURNS, ANTHONY.

ANTHONY, SUSAN BROWNELL (1820–1906). Reformer. Born on February 15, 1820, in Adams, Massachusetts, Anthony was well educated for a **Quaker** woman of her time. She taught school in New York (1835–49) and then returned home to form a **temperance** society for women (1852) and work for the American Anti-Slavery Society (1856–65). She published a radical newspaper in New York City (1868–70) and then committed herself to the woman's suffrage movement, being repeatedly arrested for voting and refusing to pay the fines imposed. As a founder of the National Woman Suffrage Association (1869), and a leader of the National American Woman Suffrage Association (1890–1900), she lobbied ceaselessly for women's rights. She died in Rochester, New York, on March 13, 1906.

ANTI-CATHOLICISM. Deeply rooted in New England as it is throughout the nation, a legacy of the **Puritans** and the long rivalry between England and its Catholic enemies in France, Spain, Portugal, and Ireland. **Pope's Day** rituals demonstrated popular anti-Catholic attitudes, as did sermons and pamphlets on the dangers of Catholicism. **Cotton Mather** interviewed Ann Glover, a senile Irish Catholic servant in **Boston**, who was hanged as a witch in 1688. New Englanders believed French **Jesuit** missionaries encouraged Indian attacks, and the Massachusetts militia murdered Father **Sebastien Rasles** in Maine (1724).

Only Rhode Island guaranteed liberty of conscience to Catholics (1728) but withheld political privileges until 1783. However, Catholics were early and influential New Englanders. Irish Catholic coal miners and construction workers worshipped at St. Joseph Church in **Newport** (1828), the first Catholic parish in Rhode Island, and New Hampshire had a Catholic church in 1823. The Boston *Pilot* (1829) became an influential Catholic weekly newspaper across the nation, especially for Irish immigrants. But the burning of the **Ursuline Convent** in Charlestown, Massachusetts, by a nativist mob (1834), and the Broad Street Riot (1837) in **Boston** demonstrated profound distrust of Roman Catholics. **Samuel F. B. Morse** and **Lyman Beecher** were influential critics of Catholic **immigrants** in the 1830s. The Massachusetts legislature, controlled by the **Know Nothing Party** in the 1850s, passed laws limiting voting rights and naturalization and investigated Catholic convents and schools (1855).

A nativist mob attacked the school for **Irish** Catholic girls in **Lowell** (1852). In **Providence**, a Know Nothing mob threatened a Catholic convent, and Connecticut nativists were also active in the 1850s. Father **John Bapst**, a Jesuit missionary in Maine, was tarred and feathered by a mob in Ellsworth (1854). But courageous service by New England Catholics in the **Civil War**, especially Colonel **Thomas Cass** and Colonel **Patrick R. Guiney**, did much to diminish this sectarian bias. More than 200 **French-Canadian** Catholic men served with Vermont regiments in the Civil War, which also mitigated religious bigotry.

However, statements that "No Irish need apply" were common in Boston newspaper advertisements in 1868. Organized anti-Catholicism reappeared in the 1880s with the rise of the **American Protective Association**. In the 1920s the Ku Klux Klan was active in rural New England. One KKK rally and parade in Leicester, Massachusetts, on July 14, 1925, led to a riot in which the police and anti-Klan protesters were driven away by 500 hooded Klan members. The efforts of Catholic leaders to protect immigrants with parochial schools, hospitals, and asylums seemed to constitute a separatism inimical to New England values and traditions. Bishops who supported unions but resisted Progressive Era reforms aroused further mistrust. Massachusetts barred priests from state asylums until 1879 and placed Catholic foster children in Protestant families until 1905. Only loyal service in two world wars by Catholic men and women and the election of President **John F. Kennedy** (1960) signaled the decline of religious bigotry against the region's largest denomination. By 1979, few New Englanders were shocked when Pope John Paul II celebrated Mass for 1 million people on **Boston Common**. *See also* RORABACK, J. HENRY.

ANTIN, MARY (1881–1949). Writer. Born in Polotzk, Russia, on June 13, 1881, Mary Antin came to **Boston** with her **Jewish immigrant** family (1894). She studied at Barnard College and published articles in the *Atlantic Monthly* and *From Polotzk to Boston* (1899) and her autobiography, *The Promised Land* (1912). Active in the Progressive Party, Antin died in New York on May 15, 1949.

ANTINOMIANISM. Theological controversy between **Anne Hutchinson** and the Boston **Puritans** (1634–1639). The term means "against the law." Hutchinson emphasized mystical communion with God rather than doctrine or law. Because she publicly criticized salvation by works (prayer, Bible reading, church attendance), and ministers who preached this message, as antithetical to Calvinist predestination doctrine, Hutchinson was banished from Massachusetts by **John Winthrop** and other Puritan leaders. **Jonathan Edwards** revived antinomianism in 1730, denouncing the liberal Arminian doctrines of **Congregational** churches.

APPALACHIAN MOUNTAINS. Narrow mountain range that parallels the eastern coast of North America. It runs from Maine to Georgia for 1,200 miles (1,950 km). The Berkshire, Green, White, and Taconic Mountains of New England are prominent ranges in this system. They separate the coastal plain at the fall line from the piedmont and higher elevations. New Hampshire's **White Mountains** have 86 peaks, including **Mount Washington** (6,288–ft/1,917 m); and Vermont's **Green Mountains** have 80 peaks, including Mount Mansfield (4,393–ft/1,339 m). Maine has 14 peaks, including **Mount Katahdin** (5,267 ft/1,605 m), at one end of the Appalachian Trail, a hiking route (2,050 m/3,300km) established by Benton MacKaye in 1921–37 from Maine to Springer Mountain in Georgia. The Appalachian Mountain Club, founded in **Boston** (1876), is the oldest private conservation organization in the nation. Its 90,000 members maintain trails and shelters to enjoy and protect the mountains of the Northeast.

APPLES. Agricultural staple. Apples (*Malus rosaceae*) were introduced to Boston by **William Blackstone**, who lived on **Beacon Hill** before the **Puritans** arrived (1630), and Blackstone developed a new variety when he moved to Rhode Island in 1636. English apple trees flourished in New England, and colonists stored barrels of apples all winter in dry houses or used dried apples in cooking and baking or as preserves, sauce, and as apple butter and apple pandowdy. Apples were exported in the **West Indies trade** (1740), and new varieties were cultivated: the Baldwin, Jonathan, Nonesuch, Rhode Island Greening, Roxbury Russet, William, Winesap, and hundreds of others. Because inns and **taverns** served fermented apple cider or applejack more often than any other beverages, some **temperance** reformers advocated cutting down apple orchards to promote sobriety. But until 1870 cider carts sold the popular beverage on street corners in most New England cities.

Apples spread west with **John Chapman** (1774–1845), an eccentric Swedenborgian missionary from Leominster, Massachusetts, known as Johnny Appleseed. He planted apple trees and distributed seeds from cider presses to early settlers in Ohio and Indiana. Maine apple orchards can be traced to Isaac Smith, who moved from Middleborough, Massachusetts, to Monmouth, Maine (1795). His Smith's Favorite variety is still grown in many New England orchards. New England expressions, such as upsetting the apple cart (1796) and apple pie order (1813) became part of the American vernacular. Apples are still a major New England crop and the official state fruit in Vermont and Rhode Island.

APPLETON, JOHN (1815–1864). Congressman from Maine. Born in Beverly, Massachusetts, on February 11, 1815, Appleton graduated from Bowdoin College (1834). He practiced law in **Portland** (1837–38) and was editor of the *Eastern Argus* newspaper (1838). After serving as chief clerk of the Department of the Navy (1845–48) and the Department of State (1848), Appleton was U.S. minister to Bolivia (1848–49). Elected as a Democrat in the House of Representatives (1851–53), he also served as secretary to the U.S. legation in London (1855), assistant secretary of state (1857–60), and U.S. minister to Russia (1860–61). Appleton died in Portland on August 22, 1864.

APPLETON, NATHAN (1779–1861). Congressman from Massachusetts. Born in New Ipswich, New Hampshire, on October 6, 1779, Appleton studied at Dartmouth College. He was a prominent **Boston** merchant and one of **Francis Cabot Lowell's** partners in **Waltham** (1814) and **Lowell** (1824). Elected to the state legislature (1815–16, 1821–24, 1827) and to the House of Representatives as a **Cotton Whig** (1831–32, 1841–42), Appleton supported protective tariffs for the New England textile industry. He was a founder of the **Boston Atheneum** and died in Boston on July 14, 1861.

APPLETON, WILLIAM SUMNER, JR. (1874–1947). Philanthropist. Born in **Boston** on May 29, 1874, Appleton, the grandson of **Nathan Appleton**, graduated from **Harvard** College (1896). Influenced by **Charles Eliot Norton**, he studied agriculture and **architecture** at Harvard and allied with New England antiquarian organizations. Appleton led campaigns to preserve the **Paul Revere** House (1905) and the **Old State House**, prompting him to found the **Society for the Preservation of New England Antiquities** (SPNEA) in 1910, the first such group in the nation. He pioneered in historic preservation, emphasizing architectural significance and archaeological accuracy based on archival data. The SPNEA relied on Appleton's private funds and later on a wide membership. He died in Boston on November 24, 1947.

AQUACULTURE. The raising and harvesting of fresh- and saltwater plants and animals, also known as fish farming or mariculture. It has become a New England industry since 1970. **Scallops**, oysters, **clams**, mussels, **lobster**, bass, and salmon are grown by commercial hatcheries in coastal seawater on scientific principles for the consumer market. Despite environmental concerns, Maine has the fourth largest aquaculture industry in the nation, and the Maine Aquaculture Association (1977) reported a $101 million crop in 2001.

ARBELLA. First ship that brought the **Puritans** in the **Massachusetts Bay Company** to **Boston** in 1630. **John Winthrop** preached his sermon *A Model of Christian Charity* on the *Arbella* in Boston harbor.

ARCHITECTURE. Dates in New England from the **Algonquian** wigwam, a round or oblong domed-shaped hut constructed with a sapling frame covered by bark and reed mats. Northern New England tribes built a conical wigwam and longhouses were found farther west. The first European structures were wattle and daub houses with thatched roofs like those built by the **Pilgrims** (1620) and replicated at the **Plimouth Plantation** (1957). Post and beam houses with clapboard siding replaced these primitive dwellings by 1640, followed by the **saltbox house** that was ubiquitous in early New England towns (1650–1830). The **Cape Cod house**, a popular vernacular style in 1700–1850, spread across the country in the early 20th century **Colonial Revival**. America's first professional architect, **Peter Harrison**, designed splendid buildings in **Newport**, **Boston**, and Cambridge. After the **American Revolution**, **Charles Bulfinch** used the Federal style for the old state house in **Hart-**

ford (1796), the **Massachusetts State House** (1798), the **Massachusetts General Hospital** (1823), and the Maine State House (1832), and he built elegant **Beacon Hill** mansions and townhouses for prominent Bostonians. **Samuel McIntire** imitated Bulfinch's designs in graceful Federal-style and Greek Revival houses for wealthy merchants in **Salem** by 1810. **Stonewalls** are another aspect of New England vernacular architecture. **Yankee** farmers built 250,000 miles of stonewalls (1650–1850) as barn foundations or to mark meadows and fields with dry-stacked walls built without mortar.

In the **Connecticut River** valley, **Asher Benjamin**'s pattern books for housewrights made the Charles Bulfinch style popular. Benjamin's student, **Ithiel Town**, built more than 50 **covered bridges** using his patented Town lattice truss in the 1820s and designed the **Wadsworth Atheneum** (1842) in **Hartford**. William Robert Ware founded the first school of architecture in the nation at Massachusetts Institute of Technology (MIT) in 1866. His best known work is Memorial Hall (1878) at **Harvard University**. In 1889 the Boston Architectural Club began and reorganized as the Boston Architectural Center in 1944.

Henry H. Richardson, New England's best-known architect, built his Richardson Romanesque **Trinity Church** (1877) in Boston. The Boston firm **McKim, Mead and White** led the renaissance revival with their **Boston Public Library** (1892), splendid summer houses in **Bar Harbor**, Maine (1890s), and the Rhode Island State Capitol in **Providence** (1894). **Richard Morris Hunt** designed several **Newport Mansions** as part of the trend toward historical eclecticism in the 1880s.

Ralph Adams Cram was influential as a professor of architecture at MIT (1914–21) and in designing churches. Lois Lilley Howe, the first woman elected a fellow of the American Institute of Architects, trained at MIT and was influential in the Massachusetts **Colonial Revival** movement by 1880. The **Society for the Preservation of New England Antiquities** (SPNEA) began its influential role in historic preservation of significant buildings and landscapes by 1910. Walter Gropius (1883–1969) brought his Bauhaus designs from Germany as head of the school of architecture at Harvard University (1937–52). Gropius and **Benjamin C. Thompson** organized a group of young architects from the Yale University School of Architecture as The Architects Collaborative (TAC), an influential firm in Boston (1946–95). TAC designed the Harkness Commons (1950) at Harvard establishing the International style and the John F. Kennedy Federal Building (1967) in Boston. Philip Johnson graduated from Harvard University (1943) and is known for his glass-walled house in New Canaan, Connecticut (1949), and his annex for the **Boston Public Library** (1973). The Currier Gallery of Art in New Hampshire maintains the Zimmerman House (1950), the only New England residence designed by Frank Lloyd Wright. I. M. Pei, who was born in China in 1917, trained at MIT and taught at Harvard (1945–48). Pei designed notable Boston buildings, Government Center (1961), the John Hancock Tower (1976), the west wing of the **Museum of Fine Arts** (1981), and the **John F. Kennedy Library** (1979). Ben Thompson's adaptive reuse of historic buildings in the **Faneuil Hall** and Quincy Marketplace (1971–76) established a new trend. Since then, rehabilitation of New England commercial and industrial buildings for contemporary use has become common in architecture. Like **stonewalls**, New England's **lighthouses**, barns, schoolhouses, and **covered bridges** are important features of the built environment and add aesthetic and economic value to the region.

ARMENIANS. Immigrants who arrived in New England by 1867. Their numbers reached 100,000 in the nation by 1924. New England has the largest Armenian community, with many in Massachusetts or Connecticut, but Rhode Island counted 1,000 Armenian residents in 1911. By 1890 Armenia awoke to nationalist and socialist movements in Europe and an intellectual and political revival challenged the declining Ottoman Turkish government. Harsh reprisals in 1894–98, a genocidal campaign in 1915, and the annexation of the independent state of Armenia (founded in 1918) by the Soviet Union (1920) stimulated emigration to the United States. By 1910, **Providence** had 1,970 Armenians, with 1,584 in **Worcester** and 1,189 in **Boston**, and smaller numbers in Bridgewater, Chelsea, Haverhill, Middleboro, **Lowell**, and Lawrence. Massachusetts counted 4,239 Armenians in manufacturing jobs (1915), and more than 300 Armenians joined the **Lawrence Strike** (1912), but the labor movement had little appeal to most Armenian Americans.

The first Armenian Apostolic church in America was founded in Worcester (1891), but Episcopal churches also attracted Armenian worshippers. The Holy Cross Armenian Catholic Church in Cambridge, under the authority of the patriarch of Beirut, offers the Eastern-rite mass and liturgy in Armenian as well as educational, community, and recreational service.

As the immigrants assimilated and prospered, the Little Armenia neighborhoods dispersed by 1960, but **Watertown**, Massachusetts, remains the center of Armenian community life in New England. Leaving the mills, factories, and foundries for small shops, especially the carpet and rug business, Armenians retained their ethnic identity while entering mainstream society. Boston and Watertown published five Armenian newspapers (1899–1934) that supported the Republican Party, as did many Armenians. Varaztad Kazanjian (1879–1974), a pioneer in plastic surgery at **Harvard** Medical School, was a prominent leader. But Armenians often encountered prejudice and confusion with Turks, Jews, or Asians. Each year on April 24, New England Armenians commemorate Martyrs' Day in honor of the 1 million victims of the massacre by Turkey (1915). The Armenian diaspora continued after 1959 when immigration to the United States resumed.

ARNOLD ARBORETUM. Botanical garden in **Boston** founded by **Charles Sprague Sargent** and **Frederick Law Olmsted** (1872) as a research and educational institution. Named for its benefactor, James Arnold, and jointly managed by the city and **Harvard University**, the 265-acre laboratory/park contains 14,000 species of flowers, trees, shrubs, and vines from around the world.

ARNOLD, BENEDICT (1741–1801). Soldier. Born in Norwich, Connecticut, on January 14, 1741, Arnold served in the **French and Indian War** (1757). He was a merchant in **New Haven** (1762–75) and invested in the **West Indies trade**. Arnold took his militia company to **Boston** (1775) and led a successful attack on Fort Ticonderoga with **Ethan Allen**. He failed to capture Quebec (1775), but at the **Battle of Lake Champlain** (1776) he prevented a British invasion of New York. For defending **Danbury** (1777) and winning battles at Fort Stanwix and Saratoga, Congress promoted him major general. Recovering from his wounds in Philadelphia (1779), Arnold incurred heavy debts and was dissatisfied with critics in Congress. He sold military information to the British and planned the surrender of West Point when his treason was discovered. He fled to the British and became a brigadier of **Loyalist** troops in Virginia (1780) and Connecticut (1781), where he captured Groton and burned New London. After the war Arnold lived in London as a merchant in the Canada and West Indies trade. America's most notorious traitor died in England on June 14, 1801.

ARNOLD, JONATHAN (1741–1793). Congressman from Rhode Island. Born in **Providence** on December 3, 1741, Arnold was a physician who commanded a Providence militia company in the **American**

Revolution and served in the colonial legislature (1776–78). He organized a military hospital (1776–81) and was the state delegate to the Confederation Congress (1782–84), where he opposed strong central government. Arnold moved to Vermont (1784), speculating in land and planning the state university. He founded St. Johnsbury (1786) and was elected Vermont's representative to Congress (1788–89) to seek admission as a state. He served on the governor's council as a **Federalist** and was a state judge when he died in St. Johnsbury on February 1, 1793.

AROOSTOOK WAR (1838–1839). An undeclared, bloodless conflict over the boundary of Maine and New Brunswick. American and Canadian lumberjacks clashed in 1838–39 in the Aroostook River valley until President Martin Van Buren sent federal troops. General Winfield Scott persuaded both sides to withdraw until the **Webster-Ashburton Treaty** (1842) established the boundary.

ART. Began in New England with **Native American** petroglyphs and baskets like those by **Penobscot** and **Micmac** craftsmen collected by museums today. European art in the region dates from 17th century artisans working with pewter and silver in **Boston, Taunton, Newport**, and Norwich by 1700. **Puritans** discouraged art except for heraldic devices, gravestones, shop signs, or simple low-relief decorations. By 1660, unknown artists or anonymous limners painted naive portraits in English or Dutch styles, like those of prominent leaders **John Winthrop** (1629), **Edward Winslow** (1651), **John Endicott** (1665), **John Davenport** (1670), or **Increase Mather** (1688). By the 18th century more secular attitudes prevailed and **John Blackburn, John Smibert, Joseph Badger, Ralph Earle, Robert Feke**, and **John Trumbull** emerged as professional painters, usually of portraits, making Boston and Newport centers of colonial art. **Paul Revere**, best known as a silversmith, also made bells, dentures, and engravings. Carpenters, cabinetmakers, housewrights, and shipwrights produced furniture and busts.

By 1760 **John Singleton Copley** was the most accomplished of these colonial painters. **Gilbert Stuart**, like Copley, left Rhode Island in 1775 to become a leading portrait painter in London but is most famous for his portraits of George Washington. Sculpture was neglected in colonial New England, but wood carvers like **Samuel McIntire** in **Salem** or

Simeon Skillin (1716–78) in **Boston** produced some excellent shop signs, ships' figureheads, and busts as a form of folk art. New England's many slate and marble gravestones are intriguing examples of early American folk carving.

After the **American Revolution**, Boston produced **Washington Allston** and his student, **Samuel F. B. Morse**, who established a reputation for painting and science. Noted sculptors included **Thomas Ball**, **Hiram Powers**, **Horatio Greenough**, Edmonia Lewis, and **Harriet Hosmer**. George Ropes (1788–1819), a Salem painter trained by an Italian artist in Salem, Michele Felicia Corne, recorded landscapes and marine subjects while working as a sign and carriage painter. By 1860, **Eastman Johnson** was an outstanding portrait painter when he turned to genre painting. **Frederick E. Church**, Martin Heade, and **Fitz Hugh Lane** were inspired painters of the New England seacoast in the luminist form.

By the **Civil War**, Cambridge produced **Winslow Homer** and from **Lowell** the expatriate painter **James McNeill Whistler**. **William Morris Hunt** was a leading portrait painter by the 1860s, and his pupil in Newport, **John La Farge**, produced brilliant murals and stained glass in the 1870s. **John Singer Sargent** worked in England but was Boston's favorite in society portraits. **Childe Hassam** was influenced by French impressionism in some Boston city scenes. **Lilla Cabot Perry**, also an impressionist in the 1890s, was known for her portraits in Boston. **Daniel Chester French**, **Anne Whitney**, **Theo Kitson**, **Augustus Saint-Gaudens**, and **Harriet Hosmer** produced fine sculpture and notable public art. Edmonia Lewis, a student of Anne Whitney in Boston, was the first African-American sculptor to win national prominence in the 1860s.

New England art museums include the East India Maine Society (1799), now known as the **Peabody Essex Museum** (1992), in **Salem**, and the **Boston Athenaeum** art gallery (1827) that inspired Bostonians to found the **Museum of Fine Arts** (1876) and its School of Art (1877). Boston had the nation's first French Impressionist exhibition in 1883. The Boston Art Club (1855) had 800 members by 1881, and the Boston Art Students Association (1879) and the Association of Boston Artists (1880) organized annual art exhibitions. In Hartford, the **Wadsworth Atheneum** (1842), the nation's oldest public art museum, was designed by **Ithiel Town**. Despite some prudish attitudes toward nude art in the 1880s, many talented artists like Edmund C. Tarbell, Dennis Miller Bunker, and **Frank**

W. Benson, and later **Polly Thayer**, were active in New England. By the mid-20th century, expressionism replaced impressionism as the primary Boston style, especially at the DeCordova Museum (1950) in Lincoln, Massachusetts.

Richard Morris Hunt designed the building (1864) that became the Newport Art Museum, and the Rhode Island School of Design opened (1877) in **Providence**, Rhode Island. Stephen Salisbury III founded the Worcester Art Museum (1898), and the Higgins Armory Museum also opened in Worcester (1929). Guided by **Charles Eliot Norton**, the first professor of art history at Harvard (1873), and the connoisseur **Bernard Berenson**, the Renaissance Revival **Gardner Museum** opened its doors in 1903. The art collections at **Harvard University**, Yale University (1832), and Bowdoin College (1892) also did much to preserve and promote the arts. The Portland Art Museum (1882) and the Farnsworth Museum (1936) in Rockland, Maine, feature major collections by artists who worked in Maine. The Currier Gallery of Art in Manchester, New Hampshire (1929), and the **Shelburne Museum** in Vermont (1947) specialize in Americana; and the **Norman Rockwell** Museum in Stockbridge, Massachusetts (1969), attracts many **tourists** in the Berkshires each year. In North Adams, vacant factories became the Massachusetts Museum of Contemporary Art (MASS MoCA) in 1999.

Recognizing the aesthetic and economic value of the arts, Boston businessmen built the **Fenway Studios** (1905) to provide living and working space for an eclectic group of artists. By the early 20th century, New England painters included **Marsden Hartley** and later Norman Rockwell, **Frank Stella**, **Leonard Baskin**, and the Maine painters **N. C. Wyeth** and his son **Andrew Wyeth** and grandson **James Wyeth**. In 1976, the first artists settled in vacant wool and leather warehouses in Boston's Fort Point Channel area. By 1980 this unique community began an annual Open Studio day for the largest concentration of visual artists in New England. *See also* ART COLONIES.

ART COLONIES. Found throughout New England. In Lyme and Cos Cob the Bush-Holley historic site is the home of Connecticut's first art colony, where 200 artists worked (1890–1920), including American impressionists **Childe Hassam**, John H. Twachtman, Elmer Livingston MacRae, Bruce Crane, and Ernest Lawson. Weir Farm, Connecticut's only National Park, preserves the summer studio of J. Alden Weir (1852–1919), an American impressionist who hosted Albert Pinkham Ryder, **John Singer Sargent**, and Childe Hassam. Many of these painters are represented in the collections of the Yale University Art Gallery, founded in 1832 when **John Trumbull** donated 100 paintings to Yale. In the 1930s the sculptor Mahonri Young worked there.

Maine attracted artists like James Audubon (1832) and landscape painters Thomas Cole and **Frederick Church**, who summered at **Mount Desert** (1832). **Winslow Homer** worked in Prout's Neck (1884), Childe Hassam painted at the **Isles of Shoals** (1894), and Rockwell Kent lived on **Monhegan Island** (1905–10). Hamilton Easter Field organized a summer art colony at Oqunquit (1902) with George O'Keeffe and Robert Laurent. John Marin established his studio in Cape Split (1934). **Andrew Wyeth**'s painting *Christina's World* (1948) defined Maine for many. I. M. Pei (1983) designed the Payson Wing of the Portland Museum of Art (1882). In Massachusetts, Rockport's Motif #1, a waterfront building, is one of the most frequently painted sites in New England. The North Shore of Boston has long been dotted with artists' colonies at Gloucester and Rockport. New Hampshire also had art colonies in Cornish and Peterborough. The important economic contributions of these art and cultural institutions to the New England economy cannot be overlooked.

ARTHUR, CHESTER A. (1829–1886). President of the United States. Born in Fairfield, Vermont, on October 5, 1829, Chester Alan Arthur, the son of an **Irish** immigrant preacher, graduated from Union College (1848). He taught school in Vermont and practiced law in New York City (1854–71), where he was a founder of the Republican Party. He served as chief engineer of the state during the **Civil War** and collector of the port of New York (1871–78). Elected vice-president of the United States (1881), he succeeded President James A. Garfield, who was assassinated (1881). Arthur lost his campaign for renomination to **James G. Blaine** (1884) and retired to New York City, where he died on November 18, 1886.

ATHENS OF AMERICA. Term for **Boston** in the mid-19th century that is more literary and philosophical than architectural, despite Bostonians' attachment to the Greek Revival and neoclassical styles. Philanthropic merchants funded schools, colleges, libraries, museums, asylums, hospitals, and humanitarian movements.

ATLANTIC MONTHLY. Founded in **Boston** (1857) as a literary magazine. Its distinguished editors included **James Russell Lowell, James T. Fields, William Dean Howells, Thomas Bailey Aldrich**, and **Robert Manning**. Published by Ticknor and Fields at the **Old Corner Book Store**, its contributors included major writers, such as **Harriet Beecher Stowe**, Bret Harte, **Louisa May Alcott, Henry James, Oliver Wendell Holmes**, Charles W. Chestnutt, Mark Twain, and **Henry David Thoreau**. Twentieth-century contributors included John Steinbeck, Ernest Hemingway, John Dos Passos, and **John Updike**. By 1980 the magazine shifted its focus from literary to public affairs.

ATTUCKS, CRISPUS (1723–1770). Patriot. Born in Framingham, Massachusetts, in 1723 to an African-American father and a **Native American** mother, Attucks was an escaped slave (1750) and a **Boston** mariner. He was one of five patriots killed in the **Boston Massacre** on March 5, 1770, when soldiers fired into a hostile crowd assaulting British sentries. **Paul Revere**'s engraving depicted Attucks and the other rioters as patriots, and **Samuel Adams** hailed Attucks as a hero. **Augustus Saint-Gaudens** designed a statue of Attucks (1888) on **Boston Common**.

AUERBACH, RED. (1917–). Coach. Born in Brooklyn, New York, on September 20, 1917, Arnold Jacob "Red" Auerbach coached basketball in Washington, D.C. (1940–43). After serving in the U.S. Navy (1943–46), he coached the Basketball Association of America Washington Capitals and the Tri-City teams. Joining the **Boston Celtics** as coach (1950–66), he transformed the team into the most successful franchise in professional sports history. He led the Celtics to 16 National Basketball Association (NBA) championships, and his skill in picking and trading key players was legendary. Red Auerbach retired as coach (1950–66) and was president and general manager (1966–84). He was elected to the Basketball Hall of Fame (1968).

AUGUSTA. Capital of Maine. It is located in south central Maine at the head of the Kennebec River. **Pilgrims** traded there (1628) for **furs** with the **Native Americans** and to exploit the rich timberlands. The town was settled as **Fort Western** (1754) and became Augusta in 1797. It replaced **Portland** as the capital city (1832) when its economy developed with lumber, paper, shoes, textiles, and food products. Today, Augusta has a population of 22,000 people.

AUSTIN, JANE GOODWIN (1831–1894). Writer. Born in **Worcester**, Massachusetts, on February 25, 1831, Jane Goodwin was educated privately and married Loring Henry Austin in **Boston** (1850). She was a member of the Concord literary circle with **Ralph Waldo Emerson, Nathaniel Hawthorne,** and **Louisa May Alcott**. Her historical fiction about New England women and her own **Mayflower** ancestors includes *A Nameless Nobleman* (1881), *Nantucket Scraps* (1883), and *Standish of Standish* (1889). She died in **Boston** on March 30, 1894.

– B –

BABSON, ROGER (1875–1967). Businessman. Born in Gloucester, Massachusetts, on July 6, 1875, Roger Ward Babson graduated from MIT (1898). He founded the Business Statistical Organization (1904) to advise clients on stock, bond, and commodities investments and predicted the 1929 Stock Market Crash. Babson founded Babson College (1919) in Wellesley, Massachusetts, and was the Prohibition Party candidate for president (1940). He died in Florida on March 5, 1967.

BACK BAY. An elite residential district on land reclaimed from the Charles River estuary in **Boston** (1857–82). An outstanding example of American city planning, the cross streets are named for Massachusetts towns in alphabetical order from Arlington to Ipswich. Commonwealth Avenue is bisected by a mall as the centerpiece of the area's spacious and ornamental grid. The French Victorian mall and splendid architecture connect the **Boston Common** and **Boston Public Garden** to the **Emerald Necklace** designed by **Frederick Law Olmsted**. The 1,500 private houses and apartment buildings constructed in the Back Bay (1857–1917), once home to prominent financiers, industrialists, and intellectuals, and then a college student district (1950–70), have been restored in recent years.

BADGER, JOSEPH (1708–1765). Artist. Born in Charlestown, Massachusetts, on March 14, 1708, Badger was a house and sign painter who became one of the earliest American artists. Self-taught but influenced by **John Smibert**, he painted more than 150 portraits in **Boston** (1740–60) in his austere formal style. His oil portraits of New England society figures include *James Bowdoin* (1747), the *Reverend Ellis Gray* (1750), and *Hannah Minot Moody* (1758). Badger died in Boston on May 11, 1765.

BAGLEY, SARAH G. (1806–1883). Labor leader. Born in Candida, New Hampshire, on April 19, 1806, Sarah George Bagley worked in **Lowell** cotton **textile** factories (1836–45). Bagley wrote for *The Lowell Offering*, a magazine written by the **mill girls** and edited by **Harriet Farley**, who extolled the pleasures of factory life. When the Panic of 1837 led to wage cuts and speed-ups in the mills, Bagley denounced Farley (1845) as a "mouthpiece of the corporations." Advocating a 10-hour workday (1844), Bagley testified at a state legislature hearing for workers' rights (1845), but with little success. A pioneer labor leader in Massachusetts and New Hampshire, she founded the Lowell Female Labor Reform Association (1844), the first women's factory union in the nation. She was editor of the *Voice of Industry* newspaper (1846) and wrote *Factory Tracts* criticizing the "driveling cotton lords" (1845), which led the *Lowell Offering* to cease publication. Bagley became the nation's first woman telegrapher in Lowell (1846) and Springfield, married a homeopathic physician, James Durno (1851), in Albany, and disappeared from historical records in Brooklyn, New York, by 1883.

BAILEY, CONSUELO NORTHROP (1899–1976). Lieutenant governor of Vermont. Born on October 10, 1899, in Fairfield, Vermont, Consuelo Bentina graduated from the University of Vermont (1921) and Boston University Law School (1925). She served as a Burlington city and county prosecutor (1925–31) and as a Republican in the state legislature and was elected speaker of the house (1953–55). She practiced law in Burlington with her husband, Albon Bailey (1937–53), and was the first woman elected lieutenant governor in the nation (1955–57). She wrote *Leaves Before the Wind: The Autobiography of Vermont's Own Daughter* (1976) and died in South Burlington on September 9, 1976.

BAILEY, JOHN MORAN (1904–1975). Public official. Born in **Hartford**, Connecticut, on November 23, 1904, Bailey graduated from the Catholic University of America (1926) and **Harvard** Law School (1929). Practicing law in Hartford, he joined Thomas J. Spellacy's Hartford machine, becoming a lifelong Democratic Party officer (1929–75). Bailey was a judge in Hartford (1933–36, 1939–41) before he succeeded Spellacy (1946). He invigorated the party in a state that had long been dominated by Republicans by allying ethnic leaders and efficiently recruiting new candidates for governor, including **Abraham Ribicoff**, **John Dempsey**, and **Ella T. Grasso**. Bailey was an early supporter of

John F. Kennedy in 1956 and 1960. President Kennedy named him chairman of the Democratic National Committee (1961–68). Bailey, the last of the New Deal coalition state party bosses, died in Hartford on April 10, 1975. Senator **Joseph Lieberman** wrote his biography, *The Power Broker* (1966).

BAKED BEANS. Traditional New England dish in the colonial era. It became popular when **Boston** merchants imported West Indian molasses in the **triangular trade**. **Molasses** is used with salt pork and other ingredients to cook beans slowly in a beanpot. Neighborhood bakeries also provided baked beans often served with **brown bread** and **codfish** cakes on Saturday evening. Boston was dubbed **Beantown** as a result of this frugal, hearty dish, and the **Boston Braves** were known as the Bean Eaters (1883–1906). Boston's annual intercollegiate hockey series was named the *Beanpot Tournament* (1952).

BAKER, GEORGE PIERCE (1866–1935). Educator. Born in **Providence**, Rhode Island, on April 4, 1866, Baker graduated from **Harvard University** (1887) and taught English there (1888–1924). His playwriting course (1906–25) led to the formation of the influential 47 Workshop. Baker's students included talented writers **Eugene O'Neill**, Thomas Wolfe, **S. N. Behrman**, and George Abbott. He inspired practical changes in theater and dramatic arts as an academic discipline as well as the Little Theater movement. Baker, who founded the Yale University drama school and University Theater (1925–33), died in New York City on January 6, 1935.

BAKER, HARVEY HUMPHREY (1869–1915). Lawyer and judge. Born in Brookline, Massachusetts, on April 11, 1869, Baker graduated from **Harvard University** (1891) and Harvard Law School (1884). Practicing law in Brookline, he became interested in juvenile delinquency and lobbied the legislature with **James J. Storrow** and **Andrew J. Peters** to create the Boston Juvenile Court (1906). **Boston** had separate court sessions for juveniles since 1830, but Baker created one of the first juvenile courts in the nation. As the presiding justice (1906–15), Baker applied Progressive Era principles to child welfare and founded a model court clinic (later named in his honor). The Judge Baker Foundation (1917) used new child psychology methods to protect and reform "wayward" children. Judge Baker died in Brookline on April 10, 1915.

BALCH, EMILY GREENE (1867–1961). Educator. Born in **Boston** on January 8, 1867, Greene graduated from Bryn Mawr College (1889) and studied in Europe. After working with **Vida Dutton Scudder** at the Denison Settlement House, she was dismissed as a professor of economics at Wellesley College (1897–1918) for opposing World War I. She served on the Massachusetts Industrial Relations Commission (1908–09), the Massachusetts Immigration Commission (1913–14), and the Boston City Planning Board (1914–17). As a **Quaker** (1921) devoted to pacifism, she was the first secretary of the Women's International League for Peace in Geneva, Switzerland (1918–22, 1934–35). Her research and reports were the basis for the League of Nations (1920). Balch, the second woman to win the Nobel Peace Prize (1946), died in Cambridge on January 9, 1961.

BALDWIN, LOAMMI (1745–1807). Engineer. Born in Woburn, Massachusetts, on January 10, 1745, Baldwin was a cabinetmaker who attended lectures at **Harvard** College to become a civil engineer. After serving in the **American Revolution**, he was elected to the legislature and as Middlesex county sheriff. His life's work was to build the **Middlesex Canal** connecting the Charles River to the Merrimack River (1793–1803) from **Boston** to **Lowell**, opening northern Massachusetts and New Hampshire to commerce. Baldwin also was the engineer for the Boston & Lowell Railroad (1838) that superseded the canal. He cultivated the Baldwin **apple** and trained his son, Loammi Baldwin, Jr. (1780–1838), as a civil engineer and canal builder. Baldwin, the father of American civil engineering, died in Woburn on October 20, 1807.

BALDWIN, MARIA (1856–1922). Educator. Born in Cambridge, Massachusetts, on April 22, 1856, Miss Baldwin became a teacher (1882) and headmaster (1889–1922) at the Agassiz Public School in Cambridge. The first **African American** to hold such a position in New England, she managed white students, parents, and teachers with much success. Her home was popular with African-American students at **Harvard University**, including **W. E. B. Du Bois** and **William H. Lewis**. Miss Baldwin lectured widely, served on the board of the **Boston** branch of the National Association for the Advancement of Colored People (NAACP), and founded the League of Women for Community Service. She died in Boston on January 9, 1922, and the public school she administered in Cambridge was renamed in her memory in 2002.

BALDWIN, RAYMOND EARL (1893–1986). Senator from Connecticut. Born in Rye, New York, on August 31, 1893, Baldwin graduated from Wesleyan University (1916) and Yale Law School (1921). After serving in the U.S. Navy (1917–19) in World War I, he practiced law in **New Haven** and Bridgeport (1921–27). Baldwin was an assistant district attorney (1927–30) and judge (1931–33) in Stratford. He served in the state legislature as a Republican (1931–33) and as governor (1939–40, 1942–44). His election in 1938 was attributed to the death of **J. Henry Roraback** and the strong candidacy of Socialist **Jasper McLevy**. Elected to the Senate (1946–49), he became an associate justice of the state supreme court (1949–59), and then chief justice (1959–63). Baldwin died in Fairfield on October 4, 1986.

BALDWIN, ROGER NASH (1884–1981). Reformer. Born in Wellesley, Massachusetts, on January 21, 1884, Roger N. Baldwin graduated from **Harvard University** (1905). He taught sociology at Washington University (1906–09), worked in a St. Louis settlement house, and was a juvenile court probation officer there. After Baldwin went to prison as a pacifist in World War I (1918–19), he founded the American Civil Liberties Union (ACLU) with **Elizabeth Gurley Flynn**, Jane Addams, **Felix Frankfurter**, and other prominent liberal activists (1920). Baldwin was outspoken in celebrated legal controversies, including the **Sacco-Vanzetti Case**. He served as the ACLU director (1920–50) and died in New Jersey on August 26, 1981.

BALDWIN, ROGER SHERMAN (1793–1863). Senator from Connecticut. Born in **New Haven** on January 4, 1793, Baldwin, the grandson of **Roger Sherman**, graduated from Yale College (1811) and **Tapping Reeve**'s Litchfield Law School (1812–14). He practiced law in New Haven and served in the legislature (1837–38, 1840–41) and as governor (1844–46). He was a defense attorney with **John Quincy Adams** in the **Amistad Case** (1839–41) and a Whig senator (1847–51). Baldwin died in New Haven on February 19, 1863.

BALDWIN, SIMON EBEN (1840–1927). Governor of Connecticut. Born in **New Haven** on February 5, 1840, Baldwin graduated from Yale University (1861) and studied law at Yale and **Harvard**. He practiced in New Haven (1863–69) and taught at Yale University Law School (1869–1919). Baldwin was associate justice of the state supreme court

(1893–1910) and a founder (1878) and president of the American Bar Association (1890). Elected governor as a Democrat (1910–14), he was a candidate for the presidential nomination (1912). Baldwin died in New Haven on January 30, 1927.

BALL, HARVEY R. (1922–2001). Artist. Born in **Worcester**, Massachusetts, in 1922, Ball studied at the Worcester Art Museum school and served in the U.S. Army in World War II. When he designed the Smiley Face (1963) for an **insurance** company advertisement, the two black dots and upturned curve on a yellow circle became the most universally known symbol of good cheer. The ubiquitous grin is an international icon featured on a U.S. postage stamp (1999). Ball never applied for a trademark or copyright for his happy face button. He died in Worcester on April 12, 2001.

BALL, THOMAS (1819–1911). Artist. Born in Charlestown, Massachusetts, on June 3, 1819, Ball, the son of a sign painter, apprenticed with a **Boston** wood engraver and was a self-taught sculptor and portrait painter. He studied sculpting in Italy (1854–57) and worked in Florence and Boston producing fine marble busts of **Washington Allston**, Henry Ward Beecher, and **Rufus Choate** and public statues of **Charles Sumner** (1878), **Josiah Quincy** (1879), **Daniel Webster** (1886), and **P. T. Barnum** (1891). He was the first American to create large public monuments in bronze for Washington, D.C., and New York City. His best-known work is the equestrian statue of George Washington in the **Boston Public Garden** (1861). Ball was a major influence on **Daniel Chester French**, one of his students, and he died in Montclair, New Jersey, on December 11, 1911.

BALLARD, MARTHA (1735–1812). Midwife. Born in Oxford, Massachusetts, on February 20, 1735, Martha Moore settled in Hallowell, Maine (1785), with her husband. Raising her family on the northern New England frontier, her diary recorded a lifetime of work (1785–1812) as a nurse and midwife for 816 births. The diary, published as *A Midwife's Tale: The Life of Martha Ballard, Based on Her Diary, 1785–1812* (1990), was the basis for a film by the same title (1998). Her candid journal revealed the daily life of a **Yankee** frontier community until her death in **Augusta** about May 19, 1812.

BALLOU, ADIN (1803–1890). Reformer. Born in Cumberland, Rhode Island, on April 23, 1803, Ballou was a **Universalist** minister (1823). He published a reform newspaper (1840–60), and founded the Hopedale utopian commune in Milford, Massachusetts (1841). Despite his **abolitionist**, pacifist, feminist, vegetarian, and **temperance** principles, the commune failed (1856). George Draper made Hopedale a model industrial community until a bitter strike (1913). Ballou was still the Hopedale minister when he died on August 5, 1890.

BALLOU, HOSEA (1771–1852). Clergyman. Born in Richmond, New Hampshire, on April 30, 1771, Ballou was a self-educated Baptist minister in Rhode Island. Excommunicated for liberal views (1791), he became a leading **Universalist** minister (1794) in Massachusetts (1795–1803),Vermont (1803–09), and New Hampshire (1809–15). Settling in a **Boston** church (1815–52), Ballou was editor of Universalist newspapers and an influential writer on liberal theological issues. He became a key figure in moving **Universalism** toward **Unitarianism** until he died in Boston on June 7, 1852. His nephew, Hosea Ballou, was the first president of Tufts University (1852).

BALLOU, MATURIN MURRAY (1829–1895). Editor and writer. Born in **Boston**, the son of **Hosea Ballou**, he wrote for religious magazines and traveled widely to improve his health. The success of his first melodramatic dime novel, *Fanny Campbell; or, The Female Pirate, A Tale of the Revolution* (1845), led to his partnership with Frederick Gleason, a Boston printer in 1845. The firm published colorful adventure novels sold at newsstands rather than bookstores, establishing the new pulp fiction genre. Ballou founded a weekly Boston newspaper (1846) and one of the first illustrated newspapers in America (1851–59) with drawings by Frank Leslie. *Ballou's Dollar Monthly* (1855) was the first monthly paper devoted to fiction. He built a hotel in Boston, operated a dry goods firm, and was also a founder of the ***Boston Globe*** newspaper (1872). Ballou died in Boston on March 27, 1895.

BANCROFT, GEORGE (1800–1891). Historian. Born in **Worcester**, Massachusetts, on October 3, 1800, Bancroft graduated from **Harvard** College (1817) and earned a Ph.D. in Germany (1820). His 10-volume *History of the United States (1834–76)* established Bancroft as the nation's foremost historian. Appointed collector of the port of **Boston** (1838–40), he served as secretary of the navy (1845–46) and U.S. minister to Great Britain (1846–49). Bancroft was a Democrat but supported President Abraham Lincoln and was U.S. minister to Prussia (1867–74). He died in Washington, D.C., on January 17, 1891.

BANKS, NATHANIEL PRENTISS (1816–1894). Speaker of the House. Born in **Waltham,** Massachusetts, on January 30, 1816, Banks was a machinist, newspaper editor, and a lawyer in **Boston**. Elected to the state legislature (1849–52), he was a Democrat in the House of Representatives (1853–55) but was reelected by the **Know Nothing Party**. He served as speaker of the House (1856–57) and was elected as a Republican governor (1858–61). Banks served as a general in the **Civil War** and was elected to the House as a Republican (1865–73), then as an Independent (1875–79), and again as a Republican (1889–91). Banks died on September 1, 1894, in Waltham, where a statue by Henry Hudson Kitson was placed in 1908. *See also* GILMORE, PATRICK S.

BANKS, RUSSELL (1940–). Writer. Born in Newton, Massachusetts, on March 28, 1940, Banks studied at Colgate University (1958) and graduated from the University of North Carolina (1967). After publishing his first novel *Waiting to Freeze* (1967), Banks taught at the University of New Hampshire (1968–75), New England College (1977–82), and Princeton University (1981). Many of his novels explore rural New England in economic decline, including *Hamilton Stark* (1978), *The Relation of My Imprisonment* (1984), *Affliction* (1989), and *Trailerpark* (1996).

BANNED IN BOSTON. Official suppression of books, magazines, newspapers, plays, **vaudeville**, and films in **Boston** and other Massachusetts communities (1650–1967). The first literary work judged immoral and offensive, William Pynchon's *The Meritorious Price of Our Redemption* (1650), was burned by the public executioner in the Boston marketplace by order of the legislature. The Concord, Massachusetts, public library banned (1885) Mark Twain's novel, *The Adventures of Tom Sawyer* (1876). Other literary works banned as immoral were Theodore Dreiser's *American Tragedy* (1925), Sinclair Lewis's *Elmer Gantry* (1927), Upton Sinclair's *Oil* (1927), Erich Maria Remarque's *All Quiet on the Western Front* (1929), Erskine Caldwell's *God's Little Green Acre* (1950), and the underground newspaper *Avatar* (1967). Inspired by **Anthony Comstock**, the **Watch and Ward Society** was most active in suppressing "immoral" drama, dance, and literature in 1900–60 and lent the city its "puritanical" reputation. The Massachusetts state supreme court upheld this censorship in 1925. Theatrical legend claimed plays banned during a Boston tryout were more successful on Broadway, and **B. F. Keith** censored shows in his Boston vaudeville theater (1885–1930). D. W. Griffith's film *The Birth of a Nation* (1915) was banned by the mayor of Boston, and the Boston city censor demanded revisions in scripts for plays as late as 1965.

BAPST, JOHN (1815–1887). Clergyman and educator. Born in Switzerland on December 17, 1815, Father Bapst was ordained (1846) in the Society of Jesus. While serving as a **Jesuit** missionary to the **Native Americans** in Old Town, Maine (1848–59), he was tarred and feathered by a **Know Nothing** mob in Ellsworth, Maine, on October 13, 1854. Father Bapst survived to build the first **Catholic** church at Bangor (1856) and became the first president of Boston College (1863–69). He died in Maryland on November 2, 1887. *See also* ANTI-CATHOLICISM.

BAR HARBOR. Town on **Mount Desert Island** in northeast Maine founded by Massachusetts settlers (1763). It became a fashionable summer home (1870s) to many prominent families, including those of John D. Rockefeller, Andrew Carnegie, Henry Ford, and Nelson A. Rockefeller (1908–79), who was born in Bar Harbor. The town, destroyed by fire (1947), is adjacent to **Acadia National Park** (1919), on land donated by John D. Rockefeller, Jr. Bar Harbor is one of the most popular **tourist** destinations in New England today.

BARLOW, JOEL (1754–1812). Poet and diplomat. Born in Redding, Connecticut, on March 24, 1754, Barlow graduated from Yale College (1778). He served as chaplain in the **American Revolution** and practiced law in **Hartford** (1786). Barlow was a leader of the Yale literary circle known as the **Hartford Wits**. His best known poems were an epic, *Vision of Columbus* (1787), and a witty pastoral poem, *The Hasty Pudding* (1793). As U.S. consul in Algiers (1795–97), Barlow arranged the release of 100 American captive seamen. Returning to America (1805), he expanded his *Vision of Columbus,* published as *The Columbiad* (1807). While U.S. minister to France (1811–12), Barlow died in Poland on December 24, 1812, attempting to negotiate a treaty with the French during Napoleon's retreat from Moscow.

BARNARD, HENRY (1811-1900). Educator. Born in **Hartford**, Connecticut, on January 24, 1811, Barnard graduated from Yale College (1830). He was a lawyer (1835) and a Whig in the state legislature (1837-39) and wrote the law creating the state board of **education**, serving as the board's secretary (1838-42). In Rhode Island, Barnard authored the bill creating the state commissioner of schools and held that post (1843-49). He reorganized the **Connecticut Historical Society** and served as Connecticut commissioner of schools (1849), and principal of the state **normal school** in New Britain. Like **Horace Mann**, Barnard supported **lyceums**, public libraries, and public education to make good citizens. He founded and edited the *American Journal of Education* (1855-82) and was chancellor of the University of Wisconsin (1858-61) and president of St. John's College in Maryland (1866-67). When Congress established the Bureau of Education, Barnard was its first commissioner (1867-70). He retired to Hartford, where he died on July 5, 1900.

BARNUM, PHINEAS TAYLOR (1810-1891). Entrepreneur. Born in Bethel, Connecticut, on July 5, 1810, P. T. Barnum was a colorful showman. He exhibited Joice Heath, a slave (1835), who claimed to be 160 years old and George Washington's nurse. His American Museum (1842) offered a zoo, lectures, art, midgets, bearded ladies, thin men, rubber men, Siamese twins, mermaids, and other curiosities to gullible New York City audiences. His circus (1854) combined with James A. Bailey's road show to become the "greatest show on earth" (1881). Barnum served as a state legislator (1867-69) and mayor of Bridgeport (1875). When he died in Philadelphia on April 7, 1891, Barnum was one of the most famous Americans and a pioneer in mass entertainment. His circus elephant, Jumbo, was stuffed and became the Tufts University mascot (1885), and he bequeathed the Barnum Museum to the city of Bridgeport (1890). *See also* KEITH, B. F.

BARRON, CLARENCE WALKER (1855-1928). Editor. Born in **Boston** on July 2, 1855, Barron was a journalist who founded the *Boston News Bureau* (1887), a financial bulletin service. He established the *Philadelphia Financial News* (1895), took over the *Wall Street Journal* (1902), and founded *Barron's National Business and Financial Weekly* (1921). In each publication Barron created a modern interpretative style for economic journalism. He wrote books on the Boston stock exchange (1893), the Federal Reserve (1914), and *They Told Barron* (1931), on the financial leaders of his era. Barron died in Battle Creek, Michigan, on October 2, 1928.

BARRON, JENNIE L. (1891–1969). Lawyer and judge. Born in **Boston** on October 12, 1891, Jennie Loitman graduated from Boston University (1911) and Boston University Law School (1913). Practicing law in Boston with her husband, Samuel Barron, Jr. (1918–37), she served on the Boston School Committee (1925–29) and was an assistant attorney general (1934–35). Barron was the first woman to serve as an associate justice of the Boston Municipal Court (1937–59), and was the woman appointed to the Superior Court (1959–69). Known for her skill in domestic relations and juvenile delinquency cases, she was a consultant on crime to the United Nations (1955) and was named National Mother of the Year (1959). Judge Barron died in Boston on March 28, 1969.

BARTLETT, JOHN (1820–1905). Editor. Born in **Plymouth**, Massachusetts, on June 14, 1820, Bartlett operated a bookstore in Cambridge. He is best known for *Bartlett's Familiar Quotations* (1855), a booklet that became a standard reference book. He joined the publishing firm Little, Brown & Company (1863) and became the senior partner (1878). Bartlett wrote a Shakespeare concordance (1894) and died in Cambridge on December 3, 1905. The popular *Bartlett's Familiar Quotations* was revised by **Justin Kaplan** (1999).

BARTLETT, JOSIAH (1729–1795). Governor of New Hampshire. Born in Amesbury, Massachusetts, on November 21, 1729, Bartlett practiced medicine in Kingston, New Hampshire (1750), and was a leader in the colonial legislature (1765–75). He signed the Declaration of Independence as a member of the Continental Congress (1775–76, 1778). Bartlett also served with **John Stark** at the **Battle of Bennington** (1777). He was a judge and chief justice of New Hampshire superior court (1788–90) until elected governor (1790–94). The letters of his wife, Mary Bartlett, provide a unique view of the homefront during the **American Revolution**. Bartlett died in Kingston on May 19, 1795.

BARTON, CLARA (1821–1912). Reformer. Born in Oxford, Massachusetts, on December 25, 1821, Clarissa Harlowe Barton was educated at home and became a teacher at age 15. She studied at a teacher training school in New York (1851) and established a free school in New Jersey. While employed by the U.S. Patent Office in Washington, D.C. (1854–61), Barton nursed **Civil War** soldiers. The "angel of the battle-field" won permission from the Union Army to care for the wounded on a full-time basis. Following her relief work in the Franco-Prussian War (1870), she lobbied Congress to sign the Red Cross Treaty. When the United States signed the Geneva Convention (1882), Barton organized the American Red Cross (1881) and served as its president (1881–1904). Despite criticism of her management, her relief work in American calamities and disasters, in Armenia, and in Cuba (1898) was invaluable. Clara Barton retired to Maryland (1904), where she died on April 12, 1912.

BASCOM, FLORENCE (1862–1945). Geologist. Born in Williamstown, Massachusetts, on July 14, 1862, Bascom graduated from the University of Wisconsin (1882) and was the first woman to earn a Ph.D. at Johns Hopkins University (1893). She taught at Bryn Mawr College and was the first female geologist in the U.S. Geological Survey (1896). Her valuable contributions to **Appalachian Mountain** geology, as an editor of the *American Geologist* (1896–1905) and vice-president of the Geological Society of America, mark her as a pioneer in American earth science. Bascom died in Northampton, Massachusetts, on June 18, 1945.

BASKIN, LEONARD (1922–2000). Artist. Born in New Brunswick, New Jersey, on August 15, 1922, Baskin studied at Yale University (1943) and served in the U.S. Navy during World War II. While teaching **art** at Smith College (1953–74) and Hampshire College (1984–94), he founded the Gehenna Press in Northampton, a small press and a vehicle for much of his work. Baskin's sculpture, woodcuts, prints, watercolors, and lithographs are exhibited in many museums. He is best known for his monumental wood-carving *The Altar (*1977) and bas-relief at the Franklin Delano Roosevelt Memorial in Washington, D.C. Baskin died in Northampton, Massachusetts, on June 3, 2000.

BASS, ROBERT PERKINS (1873–1960). Governor of New Hampshire. Born in Chicago, Bass graduated from **Harvard University** (1896) and Harvard Law School (1898). Settling in Peterborough, New Hampshire, he managed his family farm and real estate holdings and was a Progressive Republican state legislator (1905–06). As state forestry commissioner (1906–08) and a state senator, Bass opposed corporate influence in state politics and advocated conservation policies. His major success was passing one of the first direct primary laws (1909) despite opposition from conservative Republicans and the Boston and Maine Railroad. Bass was elected governor (1910) with support from Theodore Roosevelt and served as president of the American Forestry Association (1910–13). With **Louis Brandeis** he passed the public service commission, workmen's compensation, and other reform laws. His political career ended when he supported Theodore Roosevelt's Bull Moose ticket (1912), but his public service continued on the Marine Labor Board and National Adjustment Commission during World War I. Retired to his Peterborough dairy farm (1919), he was chairman of the Brookings Institution (1946–49). Bass died in Peterborough on July 29, 1960.

BATES, KATHARINE LEE (1859–1929). Poet. Born in Falmouth, Massachusetts, on August 12, 1859, Katharine Lee Bates graduated from Wellesley College (1880), where she taught English (1885–1925). She published several volumes of poetry and travel books but is best known as the author of *America the Beautiful*. She wrote this poem (1893) on a visit to Pike's Peak in Colorado, and by 1911 it became the national hymn. Bates died in Wellesley on March 28, 1929.

BATTLE OF BENNINGTON. Victory by 1,600 colonial troops led by **Ethan Allen** and **John Stark**'s New Hampshire **Scotch-Irish** Rangers. Colonel Friedrich Baum surrendered 800 British, German, Loyalist, and **Native American** forces to General Stark on August 16, 1777. This battle promoted American morale and contributed to General John Burgoyne's defeat at the Battle of Saratoga. *See also* AMERICAN REVOLUTION.

BATTLE OF BUNKER HILL. First major battle of the **American Revolution**, occurring on June 17, 1775. Much of the battle took place on the lower **Breed's Hill**, where 1,500 New England militia were forced to retreat. General **William Howe**'s 4,000 British troops were victorious but suffered 228 dead and 826 wounded. Bunker Hill, the highest point in **Boston**'s Charlestown district, is marked by a 221-foot Quincy granite obelisk (1825–43) and is part of the Boston National Historical Park. Gridley Bryant, builder of the monument, constructed the nation's first **railroad** to carry granite from a Quincy quarry to Charlestown. *See also* BUNKER HILL DAY.

BATTLE OF GROTON HEIGHTS. A victory for British troops led by **Benedict Arnold**, who captured Fort Griswold in Groton, Connecticut, on September 6, 1781, and killed 85 patriots led by Colonel William Ledyard (1738–81). Arnold burned Groton and New London and the American ships and wharves on the Thames River. *See also* AMERICAN REVOLUTION.

BATTLE OF LAKE CHAMPLAIN. A crucial naval victory during the War of 1812 by Commodore Thomas MacDonough on September 11, 1814. He destroyed the British squadron under Captain George Downie on Lake Champlain, preventing 10,000 troops in Canada from invading New England and New York. America's first battleship, *Saratoga*, built at Vergennes, Vermont, gave America control of Lake Champlain.

BATTLE OF LEXINGTON AND CONCORD. The first major engagements of the **American Revolution**, fought in Lexington and Concord, Massachusetts, on April 19, 1775. General **Thomas Gage** sent 700 British troops led by Lieutenant Colonel Francis Smith to seize arms in Concord. Aroused by **Paul Revere**, **William Dawes**, and **Samuel Prescott**, the militia skirmished with the redcoats at Lexington and then in Concord. On the march back to Boston, 273 redcoats and 93 rebels were wounded or killed. This began the American Revolutionary War and the siege of Boston. **Patriots Day** (April 19) is a holiday in Maine and Massachusetts today.

BATTLE OF NEWPORT. An unsuccessful attack by American and French forces on the British garrison occupying **Newport**, Rhode Island, on August 15–31, 1778. General **John Sullivan** led the army with assistance from **John Hancock**'s volunteer force, but withdrawal of the French navy by Admiral Charles d'Estaing ended the battle. *See also* AMERICAN REVOLUTION; NEWPORT.

BAY PSALM BOOK. First book printed in North America. When Elizabeth Glover's printing press arrived in Massachusetts in 1639, Stephen Day installed it in Cambridge and printed 1,700 copies of *The Whole Booke of Psalmes Faithfully Translated into English Metre* (1640). Known as the Bay Psalm Book, it shows that **Puritans** and other English colonists sang with pleasure in church and at home. **John Cotton** called singing a moral duty and approved use of musical instruments. New

England singing schools, composers, and a rich tradition of music date from this book.

BAY STATE. Nickname for Massachusetts, reflecting the importance of the Massachusetts Bay and ocean in the state's history and economy. The legislature officially adopted the name Bay Staters for Massachusetts residents (1990).

BAYLEY-HAZEN MILITARY ROAD (1776–1779). Built by the Continental Army as a route to invade Canada. Begun by General Jacob Bayley and extended by General Moses Hazen, the road winds 54 miles from the **Connecticut River** on the New Hampshire border through Vermont toward Montreal. Although never used by the army, this unfinished road opened the **Northeast Kingdom** of Vermont to settlers after the **American Revolution**.

BAXTER, PERCIVAL PROCTOR (1876–1969). Governor of Maine. Born in **Portland** on November 22, 1876, Baxter graduated from Bowdoin College (1898) and **Harvard** Law School (1901). Engaged in the real estate business in Portland, he served as a Republican in the state legislature (1905–06, 1909–10, 1916–18, 1919–21) and as governor (1921–25). Baxter promoted penal reform, prohibition, conservation; signed the nation's first anti-vivisection law; and appointed many women to public offices. An active philanthropist and outdoorsman, Baxter preserved **Mount Katahdin** when he purchased 5,900 acres and donated it to the state (1931). Maine named 202,000 acres of wilderness around the mountain (1933) in his honor. Baxter died in Portland on June 12, 1969.

BEACHES. An important part of New England life from the first, providing salt marsh grass for hay, seaweed for fertilizer, driftwood for fuel, and sand for cattle bedding. Livestock grazed on the beach grass, and swine foraged for clams. Beach recreation was so common that the Massachusetts **General Court** ordered town selectmen to prevent swimming on the Sabbath (1692 and 1727). However, Methodists made Oak Bluffs on **Martha's Vineyard** a seaside vacation resort (1835). In Maine the Kennebunk beach was the site of July 4th celebrations (1828), and summer visitors found cool breezes at Maine beaches by 1833. Like many New Englanders, **John F. Fitzgerald** spent family vacations at

Ogunquit beach each summer in the 1900s. Other Bostonians enjoyed Revere Beach, designed by **Charles Eliot**, only five miles by streetcar from the city, as the first public beach and recreation area (1896) in New England.

BEACON HILL. Highest point in the city of **Boston**, named for the beacon on a pole at its summit to give notice of danger. When the **Puritans** arrived (1630), the hill was home to **William Blackstone**, an Anglican priest and hermit. The hill was lowered 60 feet (1795), and the south slope facing **Boston Common**, purchased by **Harrison Gray Otis** from **John Singleton Copley**, became the most fashionable neighborhood. **Charles Bulfinch** designed many Beacon Hill mansions, as well as the "new" State House on Beacon Street (1798). Louisburg Square, a private Greek Revival residential enclave, was built to the west (1825–45), and the North Slope was an **African-American** community (1800–1900) and home to **Irish**, **Jewish**, and **Italian immigrants** (1840–1960). *See also* BLACK HERITAGE TRAIL.

BEAN, L. L. (1872–1967). Businessman. Born in Greenwood, Maine, on October 13, 1872, Leon Leonwood Bean was an orphan who studied at Kent Hill Academy and Hebron Academy in Maine. He learned the retail business in his brother's clothing store (1892–1907) but had limited success. His unremarkable career changed when he invented his leather-top, rubber-bottom Maine Hunting Shoe (1911) and sold it by direct mail to sportsmen from "away." A lifetime of personal experience hunting, fishing, and camping in the Maine woods enabled Bean to design practical outdoors gear and to sell it to sports and **tourists** with homespun **Yankee ingenuity**. His retail store in Freeport cultivated a folksy **Downeast** image and, with an expanding mail order catalogue business, popularized high-quality clothing and equipment with a firm promise of customer satisfaction. The old-fashioned L. L. Bean store became a round-the-clock operation open every day but Christmas (1951), annually attracting millions of tourists on Maine's **Route 1** highway. As the Appalachian Trail, Baxter State Park, and **Acadia National Park** drew visitors to "Vacationland," the business became a landmark largely by a word-of-mouth reputation. After Bean's death on February 5, 1967, his grandson expanded the business to other states. The rustic specialty store Bean founded (1912) thrives as an embodiment of **Yankee** virtue and value.

BEECHER, CATHARINE (1800–1878). Educator. Born in East Hampton, New York, on September 6, 1800, Catharine Esther Beecher was the eldest child of **Lyman Beecher**. She founded the **Hartford** Female Seminary (1824), a progressive school for girls, the Western Female Institute (1832) in Cincinnati, and encouraged other colleges for women. Her most significant innovation may be introducing domestic science to school curricula. Although active in many reform movements, as a single woman whose life demonstrated personal autonomy, she opposed woman suffrage until her death in Elmira, New York, on May 12, 1878.

BEECHER, LYMAN (1775–1863). Clergyman. Born on October 12, 1775 in **New Haven,** Connecticut, Beecher graduated from Yale College (1797). Ordained by **Timothy Dwight** (1799), he was a Presbyterian pastor in East Hampton, New York (1799–1810), with a reputation for sermons railing against **Catholicism**, intemperance, and **slavery**. He served at Litchfield, Connecticut (1810–26), and in **Boston** (1826–32), where his sermons inspired the burning of the **Ursuline Convent** in 1834. As president of Lane Theological Seminary in Cincinnati (1832–50), conservatives criticized his moderate Calvinism. Beecher retired to Brooklyn, New York, where he died on January 10, 1863. His remarkable family included **Catharine Beecher**, Henry Ward Beecher, and **Harriet Beecher Stowe**. *See also* ABOLITIONISM; ANTI-CATHOLICISM.

BEERS, CLIFFORD W. (1876–1943). Reformer. Born in **New Haven**, Connecticut, on March 30, 1876, Beers graduated from Yale University (1876). While working in New York City he suffered mental illness (1906–08). His autobiography, *A Mind That Found Itself* (1908), began his campaign to improve mental hygiene. He founded state, national, and international mental hygiene commissions as a pioneer in this field of public health and was widely honored for his reforms. Beers died in **Providence**, Rhode Island, on July 9, 1943.

BEHRMAN, S. N. (1893–1973). Playwright. Born in **Worcester**, Massachusetts, on June 9, 1893, Samuel Nathaniel Behrman attended Clark, **Harvard**, and Columbia Universities. At Harvard he was a student in **George Pierce Baker**'s playwriting course. Behrman's prolific career included 21 Broadway plays, especially his successful comedies *The Second Man* (1927), *Lord Pengo* (1962), and *But for Whom Charlie* (1964). Noted for sophisticated and witty dialogue, he wrote *Biography*

(1933) and *No Time for Comedy* (1939), his most popular dramas. He also wrote 27 screenplays in Hollywood (1930–61), including *Sea Wolf* (1930), *Rebecca of Sunnybrook Farm* (1932), *Anna Karenina* (1935), *A Tale of Two Cities* (1935), *Waterloo Bridge* (1940), and *Quo Vadis* (1951). Behrman wrote two autobiographies, *The Worcester Account* (1954) and *People in a Diary* (1972), and died in New York City on September 9, 1973.

BELCHER, JONATHAN (1682–1757). Governor of Massachusetts. Born in Cambridge on January 8, 1682, Belcher graduated from **Harvard** College (1699). He was a **Boston** merchant who served several terms (1718–27) on the Governor's Council. Appointed royal governor of Massachusetts and New Hampshire (1729–41), he was accused of bribery in the states' boundary dispute. Recalled to London, he returned as governor of New Jersey (1746–57). Belcher founded the College of New Jersey (now Princeton University) in 1746. He died in New Jersey on August 31, 1757.

BELKNAP, JEREMY (1744–1798). Historian. Born in **Boston** on June 4, 1744, Belknap graduated from **Harvard** College (1762). As a **Congregational** minister in Dover, New Hampshire (1767), he traveled throughout New Hampshire collecting primary sources for his *History of New Hampshire* (1784, 1791 and 1794). While minister of the Federal Street Church in Boston, he organized the **Massachusetts Historical Society** (1791) in **Charles Bullfinch**'s Tontine Crescent on Franklin Street. As corresponding secretary, Belknap wrote to other antiquarians and historians, built the society's library, printed copies of documents, and published *American Biography* (1794 and 1798). Belknap died in Boston on June 20, 1798.

BELL, ALEXANDER GRAHAM (1847–1922). Inventor. Born in Edinburgh, Scotland, on March 3, 1847, Bell was a professor of speech at Boston University when he and **Thomas A. Watson** invented the telephone (1876). Bell founded the Bell Telephone Company and conducted research on sound transmission devices, developed new techniques for teaching the deaf, and invented the phonograph and hydroairplanes. He organized the National Geographic Society (1888) and died in Nova Scotia on August 2, 1922.

BELLAMY, EDWARD (1850–1898). Writer. Born in Chicopee Falls, Massachusetts, on March 26, 1850, Bellamy studied in Germany and practiced law (1871). He turned to journalism as an editor of the *Springfield Union* and *New York Evening Post*. His novel *Looking Backward* (1888) imagined **Boston** in 2000 as an ideal socialist society and sparked Nationalist clubs across the country. His magazine *The Nationalist* (1889–91) influenced the Populist Party, but his next magazine *The Nation* (1891–94) saw the movement decline. Bellamy died in Chicopee Falls on May 22, 1898.

BELLAMY, FRANCIS (1855–1931). Clergyman. Born in Mount Morris, New York, on May 18, 1855, Bellamy graduated from the University of Rochester (1876) and Rochester Theological Seminary (1880). He was a Baptist minister in **Boston** (1885–91) but resigned because of his support for socialism and his cousin **Edward Bellamy**'s movement. While working as an editor for the *Youth's Companion* magazine in Boston (1891–95) he wrote the Pledge of Allegiance (1982). First recited in Massachusetts public schools, the pledge caught national attention as part of the 400th anniversary of Christopher Columbus's arrival in America. Bellamy edited other magazines and led Americanization and immigration restriction movements. He died in Tampa, Florida, on August 28, 1931.

BELLAMY, SAMUEL (1689–1717). Pirate. Born in England, Black Sam Bellamy was a **Cape Cod** ship captain searching for Spanish treasure galleons wrecked in the Caribbean (1715) when he turned to piracy. By 1717 the Pirate Prince had looted 50 ships, including the *Whydah,* with rich cargoes of gold, silver, ivory, sugar, and indigo. Leading his fleet of five pirate ships in the flagship *Whydah,* Bellamy and his 140-man crew died in a storm off Cape Cod on April 26, 1717. Six of Bellamy's pirate crew were hanged in **Boston** on November 15, 1717. The *Whydah* wreck was discovered in 1985, and its cargo is exhibited now at a **Cape Cod** museum on the golden age of piracy (1680–1725).

BEMIS, SAMUEL FLAGG (1891–1973). Historian. Born in **Worcester**, Massachusetts, on October 20, 1891, Bemis graduated from **Harvard University** (1916) and taught history at Yale University (1935–70). He won the Pulitzer Prize for *Pinckney's Treaty* (1926) and for *John Quincy Adams and the Foundation of American Foreign Policy* (1949). Bemis died in Bridgeport in October 1973.

BEN AND JERRY'S. Brand name for popular ice cream products produced in Vermont. Ben Cohen and Jerry Greenfield founded Ben & Jerry's

Homemade, Inc. (1978) in a former gas station in Burlington. They soon established a national reputation for innovative flavors made from fresh Vermont milk and cream and sold across the country in supermarkets, grocery stores, restaurants, and franchised ice cream shops. The company founded the Ben & Jerry's Foundation (1985) to support conservation and projects for progressive social change by grassroots organization. Their success inspired other small, innovative food product firms in Vermont, the so-called boutique or niche **Green Mountain** industries.

BENCHLEY, ROBERT C. (1889–1945). Journalist. Born in **Worcester**, Massachusetts, on September 15, 1889, Robert Charles Benchley graduated from **Harvard University** (1912). He became a journalist for the *New York Tribune* but found a new career as a humorist and drama critic for *Life* magazine (1920–29) and the *New Yorker* (1929–40). His humorous essays were collected in *My Ten Years in a Quandary and How They Grew* (1936) and *Benchley Beside Himself* (1945). Benchley also appeared in film comedies before he died in New York City on November 21, 1945.

BENJAMIN, ASHER (1773–1845). Architect. Born in Hartland, Connecticut, on June 15, 1773, Benjamin was a carpenter and architect whose books influenced early 19th century building in New England. After designing the first circular staircase in New England for **Charles Bulfinch**'s state house in **Hartford** (1796), he won commissions in the **Connecticut River** valley, including his first brick building for **Deerfield** Academy (1798). His other buildings included the First Congregational Church in Bennington, Vermont, the Old South Meetinghouse in Windsor, Vermont (1799), and the West Church (1806) and Charles Street Meetinghouse (1807) in **Boston**. His illustrated books, *The Country Builder's Assistant* (1797), *The American Builder's Companion* (1806), and *The Elements of Architecture* (1843), promoted the neoclassical or Greek Revival style **architecture** throughout the United States. Benjamin, who trained the architect **Ithiel Town**, died in Springfield, Massachusetts, on July 26, 1845.

BENSON, FRANK WESTON (1862–1951). Artist. Born in **Salem**, Massachusetts, on March 24, 1862, Weston studied at the **Museum of Fine Arts** School in **Boston** (1880–83) and in Paris. After the successful exhibition of his painting *After the Storm* (1885) in London, he taught at the

Portland School of Art. Joining the faculty of the Museum of Fine Arts School (1889–1912), Weston made it the preeminent **art** school in the nation and became a leader of the Boston School of American Impressionism. Famous for portraits of elegant Boston ladies, as in *The Sisters* (1899), he turned to landscapes, *The Hilltop* (1903) and *Summer* (1909), and then to watercolors, *The Bowsprit* (1922) and *Boiling the Kettle* (1923). Benson was the leader of the New England art community when he died in Salem on November 14, 1951.

BENTON, WILLIAM (1900–1973). Senator from Connecticut. Born in Minneapolis on April 1, 1900, Benton graduated from Yale University (1921). Working in the advertising business in New York and Chicago (1921–29), he founded an advertising agency with **Chester Bowles** in New York City and lived in Norwalk and then Southport, Connecticut. As assistant secretary of state (1945–47), he organized the Voice of America and helped found the United Nations. Appointed to the U.S. Senate by Governor Bowles (1949), Benton was elected to the Senate as a Democrat (1949–53). He served as U.S. Ambassador to UNESCO in Paris (1963–68) and died in New York City on March 18, 1973.

BERENSON, BERNARD (1865–1959). Art historian. Born in Lithuania on June 26, 1865, Berenson was raised in Boston's **North End Jewish** neighborhood. He graduated from **Boston Latin School** and **Harvard University** (1887) and studied art at Oxford, Berlin, and Italy and advised **Isabella Stewart Gardner** on **art** collection. Settling near Florence in an 18th-century villa (1900–59), Berenson wrote *The Venetian Paintings of the Renaissance* (1894), *Drawings of the Florentine Painters* (1903), *The Italian Painters of the Renaissance* (1906), and an autobiographical trilogy. As an expert on Italian Renaissance art and one of the first to recognize Renoir and Cézanne, he was primarily a connoisseur who authenticated paintings for museums and advised private collectors. Berenson donated his Villa I Tatti near Florence to Harvard University after his death on October 6, 1959.

BERKSHIRE HILLS. A series of ridges extending from the **Green Mountains** in Vermont through western Massachusetts and Connecticut, including the Hoosac and Taconic Ranges and Connecticut's Litchfield Hills. The average elevation is 1,500 feet (1,064 m), and **Mount Greylock** is the highest peak. The **Housatonic River** (130 m/209 km) rises in the hills and flows south into Long Island Sound at Stratford, Connecticut. The Berkshires became a resort area for campers, hunters, and **tourists** and attract music lovers to the **Boston Symphony Orchestra** summer classes for students and to the Berkshire Music Festival held at **Tanglewood** since 1936 in Lenox.

BERNSTEIN, LEONARD (1918–1990). Composer. Born in Lawrence, Massachusetts, on August 25, 1918, Bernstein graduated from **Boston Latin School** and **Harvard University** (1939). He was a protégé of Serge Koussevitsky at **Tanglewood** (1940–41) and made his debut as an assistant conductor of the New York Philharmonic (1943) substituting for the ailing conductor. He composed symphonies and a New York City ballet *Fancy Free* (1944), an opera, *Trouble in Tahiti* (1950), and Broadway musicals *Wonderful Town* (1953) and *West Side Story* (1957). Bernstein was America's leading conductor, composer, pianist, and music teacher when he died in New York City on October 14, 1990.

BESTON, HENRY (1888–1968). Writer. Born in Quincy, Massachusetts, on June 1, 1888, Henry Beston Sheahan graduated from **Harvard University** (1908). After serving in World War I with the Harvard Ambulance Service, he was an *Atlantic Monthly* editor. In 1926 he lived alone for a year in a small cottage he built himself on the **Cape Cod** sand dunes in Eastham. *The Outermost House* (1928), the journal he published under his pen name, Henry Beston, became a literary classic. His dune shack was named a National Literary Landmark (1964) but was destroyed in the **Blizzard of 1978**. Beston wrote other books on nature while living on a farm in Maine, where he died on April 15, 1968.

BIG DIG. The largest, most complex public works project in the nation's history. The Central Artery Project or Big Dig replaced Interstate 93 in downtown **Boston** with an eight-mile highway/tunnel/bridge network connecting Logan International Airport to Interstates 93 and 90. This massive civil-engineering construction project (1991–2005) cost more than $14.5 billion and was so controversial and disruptive that state and federal investigations resulted. Archaeological study during the excavation revealed much about Boston history from 10,000 B.C. to the present.

BIGELOW, JABOB (1787–1879). Scientist. Born in Sudbury, Massachusetts, on February 27, 1787, Bigelow graduated form **Harvard** College

(1806) and the University of Pennsylvania medical school (1810). A life-long botanist, he wrote *Florula Bostoniensis* (1814), the standard work on New England plants, and *American Medical Botany* (1820). As an influential professor at Harvard Medical School and **Massachusetts General Hospital** staff physician, he eliminated bloodletting and drugging patients. Bigelow was a founder of **Mount Auburn Cemetery** (1831) and president of the **American Academy of Arts and Sciences** (1847–63). He died in **Boston** on January 10, 1879.

BILLINGS, FREDERICK (1823–1890). Businessman. Born in Royalton, Vermont, on September 27, 1823, Billings was raised in Woodstock. He graduated from the University of Vermont (1844), studied law, and joined the 1849 Gold Rush. He founded a San Francisco law firm (1849–64), and was the state attorney general until poor health prompted his return to Woodstock. Billings invested in the Northern Pacific **Railroad** (1866), reorganized the company (1873), and was its president (1879–81), building the line from North Dakota to Oregon. Billings was a benefactor of the University of Vermont, Amherst College, and the town of Woodstock until he died in Woodstock on September 30, 1890.

BILLINGS, WILLIAM (1746–1800). Composer. Born in **Boston** on October 7, 1746, Billings was a tanner and self-taught musician devoted to choral singing. The **Great Awakening** (1734–45) evangelical movement created interest in his church music and hymns for choral groups. Billings wrote the *New England Psalm Singer* (1770), the first collection of original sacred music composed by an American, with simple fugal pieces like *The Rose of Sharon* and *Chester*. His other popular collections of plain tunes, hymns, and anthems were *The Singing Master's Assistant* (1778), *Music in Miniature* (1779), and the *Psalm Singer's Amusement* (1781) He also trained singing masters throughout New England and wrote patriotic songs during the **American Revolution**. New England's first great composer died in poverty in Boston on September 26, 1800.

BINGHAM, HIRAM (1875–1956). Senator from Connecticut. Born in Honolulu on November 19, 1875, Bingham was the son of a missionary from Vermont. He graduated from Yale University (1898) and studied at the University of California at Berkeley and **Harvard University**. Bingham taught history at Harvard, Princeton, and Yale (1907–24) and discovered the Incan ruins at Machu Picchu in Peru (1911). He was a World War I aviator and the Republican lieutenant governor (1922–24) and governor (1924). Before his term as governor began, he was elected to the Senate (1924–33). Censured by the Senate (1929), he was the conservative director of the Loyalty Review Board (1951–53) and died in Washington, D.C., on June 6, 1956.

BIRDSEYE, CLARENCE (1886–1956). Inventor. Born in Brooklyn, New York, on December 9, 1886, Bob Birdseye studied biology at Amherst College. While working as a naturalist in the Arctic (1912), he observed **Native American** frozen fish and conceived the idea of flash freezing food for retail consumers. He patented the process in Springfield, Massachusetts (1927), and built a plant in Gloucester to make frozen fish (1925). As president of his own company (1922–34), Birdseye founded General Foods Corporation and designed low-temperature retail displays and refrigerated railroad cars to distribute his frozen food products. He expanded the seafood industry and held more than 300 patents before he died in New York on October 7, 1956.

BISHOP, ELIZABETH (1911–1979). Poet. Born in **Worcester**, Massachusetts, on February 8, 1911, Bishop graduated from Vassar College (1934). She won the Pulitzer Prize for her poetry collection, *North & South—A Cold Spring* (1955), and the National Book Award for *Complete Poems* (1969). Her poems and short stories appeared in the *New Yorker,* and she wrote two influential poetry books, *Brazil* (1967) and *Geography III* (1976). Bishop taught at **Harvard** (1970–77) and MIT (1979) and died in **Boston** on October 6, 1979.

BIXBY LETTER. A moving letter of condolence from President Abraham Lincoln to Mrs. Lydia C. Bixby of **Boston** on November 21, 1864. Massachusetts governor **John A. Andrew** suggested the president write because her five sons had been killed in the **Civil War**. The eloquent letter was printed in the *Boston Evening Transcript* and widely reprinted as evidence of Lincoln's humanity and the wartime sacrifices by New Englanders. However, Republicans were embarrassed to learn that only two sons had died, one returned home, one deserted his unit, and the other was captured, joined the Confederate army, and moved to Cuba.

BLACK HERITAGE TRAIL. A National Park Service 1.6-mile walking tour of 15 **African-American** historic sites on **Beacon Hill** in **Boston**.

BLACKBURN, JOSEPH (c.1730–c.1778). Artist. Born in England around 1730, Blackburn painted portraits in Bermuda (1752–53). Moving to **Newport** (1753) and **Boston** (1755), he found little competition. Blackburn painted 30 portraits in the Rococo style for many members of colonial New England society, especially his best work *Isaac Winslow and his Family* (1755). His portraits include *Mary Faneuil* (1755), *Andrew Oliver, Jr.* (1755), *General Jeffrey Amherst* (1758), and, in **Portsmouth**, he painted *Benning Wentworth* and *John Wentworth* (1760). His sophisticated style influenced **John Singleton Copley**, who soon surpassed him. Blackburn moved to London (1764) and Dublin (1767) but disappeared from **art** history by 1778.

BLACKSTONE CANAL. Built by Providence merchant Edward Carrington (1828) to carry cargo and passengers on barges 50 miles between **Providence**, Rhode Island, and **Worcester**, Massachusetts. **Irish** workers dug 49 granite locks that were 80 feet long and 10 feet wide. But low or frozen water on the Blackstone River delayed traffic, and the Providence and Worcester Railroad supplanted the canal (1847). Sections of the canal are preserved at the Blackstone River State Park in Lincoln, Rhode Island, and the Blackstone River and Canal Heritage Park in Uxbridge, Massachusetts. The canal expanded Worcester industries, and more so when steam power and the Providence and Worcester railroad arrived. New industries included tanneries, cotton, wire and paper mills, and tool or machine manufacturing (1830–1958).

BLACKSTONE RIVER VALLEY NATIONAL HERITAGE CORRIDOR. Established by Congress in 1986 to recognize the area's important place in American history. Part of the National Park system and cooperating private, public, and state government agencies, it includes 46 miles along the Blackstone River in 24 towns and cities from **Worcester** to **Providence**. Its roads, trails, mill villages, millponds, landscapes, and ethnic traditions reflect the changes inspired by the American industrial revolution.

BLACKSTONE, WILLIAM (1595–1675). Clergyman. Born in England on March 5, 1595, Blackstone (or Blaxton) graduated from Cambridge University (1621). He came to Massachusetts with an expedition (1623) and lived alone as missionary to the **Native Americans** on the **Shawmut** peninsula. When the **Puritans** arrived (1630), he invited them to move from Charlestown to Boston. The unorthodox Anglican priest planted the first **apple** orchards in America and then sold his land (called **Beacon Hill**) to **John Winthrop** and moved to Cumberland, Rhode Island (1634). Blackstone married a Boston widow, Sarah Stevenson (1659), and their home in Rhode Island was burned in **King Philip's War**. He died in Cumberland on May 26, 1675, and the Blackstone River, which flows 50 miles from **Worcester**, Massachusetts, to Pawtucket, Rhode Island, bears his name.

BLAINE, JAMES G. (1830–1893). Speaker of the House. Born in West Brownsville, Pennsylvania, on January 31, 1830, James Gillespie Blaine graduated from Washington College (1847). He was a teacher and studied law before moving to **Portland**, Maine (1854), where he became editor of the *Portland Advertiser* and the *Kennebec Journal.* Blaine was elected as a Republican to the state legislature (1859–62) and the House of Representatives (1863–76), serving as speaker (1869–75). He was an unsuccessful candidate for president (1876, 1880, and 1884) and served in the Senate (1876–81) and as secretary of state for President James Garfield (1881) and President Benjamin Harrison (1889–92). Known as the "Plumed Knight," Blaine moved the Republican Party to a moderate economic and business agenda after the **Civil War** and was the first president of the Pan American Congress. He died in Washington, D.C., on January 27, 1893, and his home in **Augusta** is now the governor's residence.

BLANCHARD, THOMAS (1788–1864). Inventor. Born in Sutton, Massachusetts, on June 24, 1788, Blanchard invented machines by 1802 while working in his brother's tack-making shop in Millbury. By 1819 he patented new lathes to manufacture gun barrels and gunstocks at the **Springfield Armory** in Massachusetts. His lathes also made shoe lasts, wheel spokes, and tool handles; and he built and operated steamboats on the **Connecticut River** between Springfield and **Hartford** and on the Kennebec River in Maine (1831). His mill in Burlington, Vermont, manufactured other nautical equipment. Moving to **Boston** in 1840, Blanchard became wealthy from 25 patented inventions, especially his lathes to make carriage wheels, bentwood chairs, and plow handles and to copy sculptured busts. This versatile **Yankee** inventor died in his **Beacon Hill** home on April 16, 1864.

BLIZZARD OF 1978. The worst winter storm in New England meteorological records, surpassing even the infamous blizzard of 1888. Thirty inches of snow fell on much of New England on February 6, 1978, as 92-mph winds combined with a new moon and storm-generated waves to produce a tide 14.5 feet above mean low water on the eastern Massachusetts shore. **Henry Beston**'s Outermost House in Eastham was one of hundreds of homes destroyed by waves, which reduced the Nauset sand dunes to low mounds. Thousands of New Englanders were stranded on highways for days, and normal life suspended for a week as schools, churches, stores, and offices closed and people struggled to dig out of the snow drifts. Fifty-four New Englanders died in this blizzard, and property losses exceeded $1 billion. Blizzards on March 13, 1993, and January 7, 1996, set single storm snow fall records, but the blizzard of '78 remains New England's most memorable snowstorm.

BLOCK, ADRIAEN (ca. 1585–1624?). Explorer. Block was a Dutch mariner commissioned by the New Netherlands Company to explore the North American **fur trade**. He sailed the Hudson River to Albany (1610) and explored Long Island Sound and the **Connecticut River** (1613–14). He named **Block Island** in Narragansett Bay and drew the first detailed map of the southern New England coast (1616). His reports led to the establishment of the Dutch West India Company (1621–1794) and Dutch trading posts in Rhode Island and Connecticut (1620–40) to obtain furs from the **Wampanoag**. Block commanded a Dutch **whaling** fleet (1624) and disappeared from historical records.

BLOCK ISLAND. Island 7 mi/11.2km long and 3.5 mi/5.6 km wide on Rhode Island's Atlantic Ocean coast. It was explored by **Adriaen Block** (1614) and settled by the English (1661). It is known for its fishing fleet, two **lighthouses**, and as a summer resort.

BLUE LAWS. Local regulations dating from 1650 forbidding certain secular activities on Sunday. The term may derive from Samuel A. Peter's *General History of Connecticut* (1781) that printed on blue paper the strict Sabbath regulations of **New Haven**, Connecticut. The term also may be based on 18th-century use of blue to mean morally rigid. **Puritan** communities forbade labor on Sunday, as well as public drinking, games, recreation, and travel. Like the **sumptuary laws**, municipal ordinances restricted personal behavior and dress and public conduct in gambling, sports, or shopping on Sunday. The blue laws were common in New England towns and cities, but Massachusetts voided most of them in 1977. *See also* TITHINGMAN.

BLUEBERRY. The sweet berry of various shrubs (*Vaccinium genus*) native to New England from marsh to dry upland soil. It is used as wine, jam, and jelly and in baking. The lowbush blueberry (*Vaccinium angustifolium*), a source of food and medicine for **Native Americans**, has been harvested commercially in Maine and Canada since 1900. Maine produced 100 million pounds of wild blueberries in 2000 (valued at $90 million) on 60,000 acres. New Hampshire has 1,000 acres cultivated, and Massachusetts has 500 acres. Highbush varieties have been grown commercially in other states and Canada (1916). Higher consumption of blueberries in Asia and Europe has increased the recent demand. The wild blueberry is Maine's official state berry.

BOGAN, LOUISE (1897–1970). Poet. Born in Livermore, Maine, on August 11, 1897, Louise Bogan was a poetry critic for the *New Yorker* magazine (1931–68). She held the chair in poetry at the Library of Congress (1945). Her lyrical style suited her themes on love and art, especially in *Collected Poems, 1923–53* (1954), which won the Bollingen Prize in Poetry. Her criticism was collected in *Selected Criticism: Prose, Poetry* (1955) and *A Poet's Alphabet* (1970). Bogan died on February 4, 1970.

BOLGER, RAY (1904–1987). Actor and dancer. Born in **Boston** on January 10, 1904, Raymond Wallace Bulcao was a **vaudeville** performer known as Ray Bolger. In 1924 he worked in vaudeville and by 1931 appeared in Broadway musicals as a song and dance man and comedian. As an MGM contract actor (1936–40), he gave his most famous performance as the scarecrow in *The Wizard of Oz* (1939). After 30 Hollywood films, he hosted a television series, *The Ray Bolger Show* (1953–55) and made many television and movie appearances. Bolger, elected to the Theater Hall of Fame (1980), died in Los Angeles on January 15, 1987.

BOND, WILLIAM CRANCH (1789–1859). Astronomer. Born in **Portland**, Maine, on September 9, 1789, Bond was the son of a **Boston** clockmaker and a self-taught astronomer. He became the first director of the **Harvard** College Observatory (1839–59) and made some of the first astronomical photographs with his son, George P. Bond, who succeeded him as director. Bond died in Cambridge, Massachusetts, on January 29, 1859.

BORDEN, LIZZIE (1860–1927). Alleged murderer. Born on July 19, 1860, in Fall River, Massachusetts, Lizbeth Andrew Borden was accused of murdering her father and stepmother with an ax in their Fall River home on August 4, 1892. Prosecuted by **William H. Moody**, she was found not guilty in a sensational trial in June 1893 and ostracized by the affluent community where she lived with her sister until her death on June 1, 1927. This case reflects public shock about the role of women in late Victorian Massachusetts and has inspired many books, plays, films, and folk tales.

BOSTON. The capital of Massachusetts. The city is located on the hilly **Shawmut** peninsula where the Charles River and Mystic River enter Massachusetts Bay. **John Smith** mapped Boston Harbor (1614), and **John Winthrop** led the **Puritans** to found the town (1630) for the **Massachusetts Bay Company**. The fine natural harbor made Boston the chief port in New England for transportation, shipping, fishing, and ship-building and the regional capital dubbed the **Hub** of the Solar System and the **Athens of America**. Best known for the start of the **American Revolution**, and as a cultural and educational center in the colonial era, Boston expanded by reclamation of tidal flats and annexation of neighboring towns. The narrow peninsula community doubled in size and incorporated as city (1822). Now the city population is 575,000, but the metropolitan area of 4,200 square miles in five adjoining counties of eastern Massachusetts and southern New Hampshire includes 5 million residents (2000). Greater Boston, the nation's fourth most populous metropolis, employs its residents in the financial, **insurance**, manufacturing, medical, computer, high technology, **tourism**, research, and **higher education** economy today. *See also* BOSTON ATHENEUM; BOSTON BRAHMINS; BOSTON CITY HALL; BOSTON COMMON; BOSTON GARDEN; BOSTON PUBLIC GARDEN; BOSTON PUBLIC LIBRARY; BOSTON STOCK EXCHANGE; BOSTON SYMPHONY ORCHESTRA; SUBWAY.

BOSTON ASSOCIATES. Wealthy Bostonians from the Appleton, Boott, Cabot, Dwight, Eliot, Jackson, Lawrence, Lowell, Otis, Perkins, Quincy, Sturgis, and Thorndike families who invested $600,000 in **Francis Cabot Lowell**'s textile factory in **Waltham**, Massachusetts (1814). Using his integrated Waltham System combining all cotton cloth production and marketing under one roof, and employing New England farm girls,

Lowell successfully competed with British imports. The Boston Associates expanded to **Lowell**, Massachusetts (1825), creating the first industrial city in the United States. The Associates also controlled banks, **insurance**, **railroads**, city and state government, and many philanthropies and intermarried with the **Boston Brahmins**.

BOSTON ATHENAEUM. Founded (1807) as the center of intellectual life for **Boston** gentlemen. It is the oldest independent library in North America with an **art** gallery (1827) that inspired the founding of the **Museum of Fine Arts**. By 1850 the Athenaeum was one of the five largest libraries in the nation. Today its collections emphasize Boston, New England, and local history, biography, American and English literature, and fine and decorative arts. Annual programs feature art exhibits, lectures, and concerts. The Athenaeum relocated to **Beacon Hill** (1849) at a corner of **Boston Common** adjacent to the Granary Burial Ground. The gray sandstone Renaissance villa, rebuilt by Henry Forbes Bigelow (1913), was recently expanded (2001). Proprietors are limited to 1,049 chartered shareholders, but membership is open to annual fee payers.

BOSTON BRAHMINS. The social and economic elite descended from **Puritan** settlers in Massachusetts. The term began as a witty remark by Dr. **Oliver Wendell Holmes** (1858), who compared his wealthy **Beacon Hill** neighbors to the priestly caste in India. These rich **Yankees** lived austerely despite great wealth from the **China trade**, the **Opium trade**, and **textile** industries and dominated New England politics, economics, and culture. As founders of the **Federalist Party**, and as Whigs and then Republicans, they controlled Boston and Massachusetts government until 1940 and remain influential. Their philanthropic bequests in **education**, medicine, religion, charity, and cultural institutions are a hallmark of the Boston Brahmins and their **New England conscience**.

BOSTON BRAVES (1871–1952). The only National League baseball team in New England. Also known as the Red Stockings, Beaneaters, Doves, Pilgrims, and Bees, they played at the South End Grounds (1876–1914), and at Braves Field (1915–52), before moving to Milwaukee (1953–65) and Atlanta (1965). Babe Ruth finished his career on the team (1935), and Sam Jethroe (1918–2001), Rookie of the Year in 1950, was one of the first **African-American** players in the major leagues. The **Jimmy Fund** began as the team's official charity.

BOSTON BRUINS. The first American professional ice hockey team (1924) in the National Hockey League (NHL). It was founded by a Vermont businessman, Charles Adams. The sport began in Ontario in 1855, and McGill University students played the game by 1870. Yale University players competed with other college teams (1893), and hockey became an Olympic sport in 1920, but **Walter A. Brown**, a founder of the NHL and owner of the Boston Bruins, established the team as dominant. In 1999 the team moved from the **Boston Garden** to the Fleet Center.

BOSTON CATHOLIC DIOCESE. Established (1808) to include all of New England and became an archdiocese in 1875. The **Boston** diocese created the diocese of **Hartford**, Connecticut (1843), **Portland**, Maine (1853), Burlington, Vermont (1853), Springfield, Massachusetts (1870), **Providence**, Rhode Island (1872), Manchester, New Hampshire (1884), Fall River (1904) and **Worcester**, Massachusetts (1951), and Bridgeport (1953) and Norwich, Connecticut (1953). Roman **Catholics** are the largest religious denomination in the region today. *See also* ANTI-CATHOLICISM.

BOSTON CELTICS. One of the first professional basketball teams in the newly established National Basketball League (1949). Founded (1946) by **Walter A. Brown**, the owner of the **Boston Garden** and **Boston Bruins**, the team dominated the sport when **Bob Cousy** (1950–63) and Coach **Arnold "Red" Auerbach** (1950–66) arrived. The Celtics drafted the first black player (1950), hired the first black coach, won 16 National Basketball Association (NBA) championships, and produced 28 Hall of Fame players. In 1999 the team moved from the Boston Garden to the Fleet Center.

BOSTON CITY HALL. Designed on School Street by Gridley J. F. Bryant and Arthur Gilman (1862) as the seat of city government. It is the most conspicuous example of French Second Empire architecture preserved in the city. When the "new" Boston City Hall (1969) replaced it, **Scollay Square** was renamed Government Center.

BOSTON COMMON. The oldest public park in the nation. It was originally the town pasture and militia training field. Governor **John Winthrop** purchased the 45 acres as a common or town pasture (1634) from the Reverend **William Blackstone**. The Common, enclosed (1728) to protect the grass and trees from horses, was the site of public executions, duels, promenades, winter sports, and barracks for British soldiers (1775–76). Like the common centered in most New England towns, it served many purposes, and **Beacon Hill** residents grazed cows on the Common until 1830. North America's first subway was constructed beneath the Common (1897) and later an underground parking garage (1961). Today the Boston Common is the first link in the **Emerald Necklace**, a public park in the heart of the city and the site of many civic events. *See also* BOSTON; SUBWAY.

BOSTON GARDEN (1928–1999). The home arena of the **Boston Bruins** (1928–99) and **Boston Celtics** (1946–99) as well as the city's forum for boxing, the circus, rodeo, ice shows, the Boston Beanpot Tournament, rock concerts, and political rallies with Franklin Delano Roosevelt, Winston Churchill, and **John F. Kennedy**. Its famous parquet floor, designed by Celtics founder and president **Walter A. Brown** (1946), was moved from the Boston Arena to the **Boston Garden** (1952) and then to the Fleet Center when the Boston Garden was demolished (1999).

BOSTON GLOBE. New England's leading daily newspaper founded in 1872 by **Eben Jordan** and five other **Boston** businessmen. Facing competition from Boston's 12 newspapers, the Globe's new manager, **Civil War** general Charles H. Taylor, introduced its first news illustrations, editorial cartoons, full-page advertisements, new machinery for folding and trimming (1875), and a Sunday edition (1877) and an evening edition (1878). By 1886 Taylor increased circulation to 100,000 and introduced reporters' bylines and photoengraving. His other innovations included typewriters and linotype machines (1894) and trucks (1922) to replace horse-drawn distribution vans. When Charles Taylor died (1921), his son William O. Taylor succeeded him as publisher, promising to continue the paper as a New England institution. W. Davis Taylor succeeded his father (1955) as publisher, and in 1958 the *Globe* was the last newspaper in the city to move from Newspaper Row on Washington Street to a modern plant in Dorchester.

Under editor **Thomas Winship** the *Globe* won its first Pulitzer Prize (1966), discontinued front page advertisements (1967), and was the second newspaper in the nation to oppose the Vietnam War in an editorial (1967). Tom Winship reinvigorated the staid *Globe,* and his staff won 12 Pulitzer Prizes (1972–84). The *Globe* was the first major paper to urge

President Richard M. Nixon to resign (1973), and its investigative reporters, columnists, and photographers earned more Pulitzer Prizes (1985, 1993, and 1996) for the *Globe*. The new publisher, William O. Taylor II, introduced computers (1978) and established the Globe Foundation (1982) to sponsor community programs. An era ended in New England journalism when the *New York Times* purchased the *Boston Globe* (1993) and Tom Winship died in 2002. Under publisher Benjamin B. Taylor in 1997, the *Boston Globe* is recognized as one of the best big city newspapers in the country.

BOSTON LATIN SCHOOL. The oldest public secondary school in the nation. Founded by the town of **Boston** (1635), the six-year curriculum is a college-preparatory humanities program and admission is open to all boys and (since 1972) girls in Boston based on an entrance examination. Its alumni include five signers of the Declaration of Independence, four **Harvard** College presidents, and **Wendell Phillips**, **Joseph P. Kennedy**, **Theodore White**, and **Leonard Bernstein**. *See also* EDUCATION.

BOSTON MARATHON. The world's oldest annual marathon, established in 1897 by the Boston Athletic Association (1887). Inspired by the revival of the Olympic Games (1896) at Athens, the 26.2-mile (42.195-km) road race begins on Patriots Day each April in rural Hopkinton and ends at the **Boston Public Library**. It attracted 232 runners in 1962 and 1,219 in 1972 but a field of 38,708 runners for the 100th race in 1996. Over 15,000 runners competed in 2001, including track champions from 52 countries as well as dedicated amateur men and (since 1972) women and (since 1975) wheelchair participants and uncounted unofficial runners. An estimated 650,000 spectators cheered the runners along the marathon route in 2001, generating $68 million for the Greater **Boston** economy as the world's largest single-day sporting event. With corporate sponsorship (1986), the Marathon awards cash prizes and is televised in 200 countries.

BOSTON MARRIAGE. The custom of two unmarried and unrelated women sharing an apartment or house as equal lifelong partners in 19th-century Boston. Although the relationship could have been romantic, often it was not and became a practical way for female professionals to participate in the city's social, intellectual, and cultural life. Prominent literary women in Boston marriages included **Alice James**, **Sarah Orne Jewett**, **Louise Imogene Guiney**, **Amy Lowell**, and **Katharine Lee Bates**. This custom was the subject of a play *Boston Marriage* (1999) by David Mamet.

BOSTON MASSACRE. A violent conflict between British soldiers and **Boston** workers on March 5, 1770. When a mob taunted a British sentry at the **Old State House**, Captain Thomas Preston led seven redcoats to the scene and the troops killed five citizens. **John Adams** and **Josiah Quincy**, who defended the soldiers in a Boston murder trial, won acquittal for Preston, but the jury found two soldiers guilty of manslaughter. They received minor punishment, but **Samuel Adams** convinced Lieutenant Governor **Thomas Hutchinson** to remove the troops from the city. **Paul Revere**'s inaccurate engraving of this incident aroused support for the revolution. The Boston Massacre Monument (1888) on **Boston Common** honors the five victims, Samuel Gray, Samuel Maverick, James Caldwell, **Crispus Attucks**, and Patrick Carr, who were buried in the Granary Burial Ground on Tremont Street. The massacre site is marked on State Street behind the Old State House. *See also* AMERICAN REVOLUTION.

BOSTON NATIONAL HISTORICAL PARK. Established by the National Park Service (1974). The park is composed of eight historical sites in Boston connected by the **Freedom Trail**.

BOSTON NEWS-LETTER. The first regularly published newspaper in America, founded as a weekly by John Campbell. He was a bookseller from Scotland who was the **Boston** postmaster (1704–18). The printer Bartholomew Green became the publisher (1722), and Richard Draper was the editor (1752). The newspaper had a **Loyalist** viewpoint until discontinued when the British evacuated Boston (1776). Its rivals were the *Boston Gazette* (1719) and the *New England Courant* (1721), but the *Hartford Courant* (1764) is the oldest American newspaper continuously published.

BOSTON PILOT. The first Catholic newspaper published in the United States. Founded in **Boston** in 1829 as the *Catholic Sentinel*, the publisher **Patrick Donahoe** renamed it in 1835. The weekly newspaper served as the voice of the Irish immigrant community with a national circulation under editors **John Boyle O'Reilly** and **Katherine Conway**. The *Pilot* became the official newspaper of the Catholic Archdiocese of Boston in 1908.

BOSTON POLICE STRIKE. A major labor union work stoppage in 1919 when 1,117 of the city's 1,544 policemen went on strike with support from the American Federation of Labor. Mayor **Andrew J. Peters** requested assistance from Governor **Calvin Coolidge**, whose firm response won national attention and the Republican nomination as vice-president (1920). All striking policemen were discharged after days of rioting and vandalism quelled by the National Guard and volunteers. *See also* BOSTON.

BOSTON POPS. The **Boston Symphony Orchestra**'s summer concert series of light classical music in a café setting at Boston Symphony Hall. Some free concerts are performed outdoors on the Charles River Esplanade. The Pops began as the Promenade Concerts (1885) and was transformed by conductor **Arthur Fiedler** (1930–79) into an important cultural institution. Fiedler introduced the public to classical music with a broad repertoire including popular, folk, Broadway, and Hollywood music. **WGBH** televised the concerts, *An Evening at the Pops*, making it one of the best known orchestras in the world. Seiji Ozawa was the first BSO musical director (1973–2002) to conduct the Pops on the Esplanade in 1999. *See also* BOSTON.

BOSTON POST ROAD. The major route (1673) from **Boston** to New York City. It included three roads, passing from Boston through Dedham, **Worcester**, Uxbridge, Springfield, **Providence**, **Hartford**, **New Haven**, the **Long Island Sound** shore, and Westchester County to New York City. **Taverns** and inns, such as the **Wayside Inn** (1686) in Sudbury, Massachusetts, accommodated **stage coach** passengers and travelers. Captain Levi Pease, a blacksmith from Blandford, Massachusetts, was known as the stage coach king by 1783 because so many of his lines used this road. By the 1820s about 2,000 stage coaches from 58 firms arrived each week at **Scollay Square** in Boston. The modern U.S. **Route 1** follows much of the Lower Road portion of the Boston Post Road.

BOSTON PUBLIC GARDEN. The oldest botanical garden in the nation (1837, redesigned 1859). It is best known for the Swan Boat rides (1877) and *Make Way for the Ducklings* statues (1987). The 24-acre park includes a miniature suspension bridge (1867), a replica of the Brooklyn Bridge, and statues of George Washington (1869), Thaddeus Kosciuszko (1927), **Thomas Cass** (1899), **Edward Everett Hale** (1913), **Wendell Phillips** (1915), **Charles Sumner** (1878), and **William Ellery Channing** (1902), as well as geometric flowerbeds.

BOSTON PUBLIC LIBRARY. The oldest publicly supported municipal library in the world (1848). It was expanded by the gifts of Joshua Bates and **George Ticknor** (1852). Originally located in a building designed by C. F. Kirby on Boylston Street (1858), this building was replaced by **Charles Follen McKim**'s impressive beaux-arts "palace for the people" in Copley Square (1888–95). **John Singer Sargent**, Edwin Abbey, and Pierre Puvis De Chavannes painted its murals. Known as the most distinguished architectural monument of the era, and the nation's fourth largest library, the BPL expanded with an annex designed by Philip Johnson (1973). It serves 2 million readers with 27 branches today. *See also* BOSTON.

BOSTON RED SOX. One of the first professional teams in the American Baseball League (1901). Known as the Bostons, the Americans, the Pilgrims, and the Red Stockings, *Boston Globe* publisher Charles Taylor bought the team (1904) and renamed them the Boston Red Sox (1907). The team won the first of five World Series championships (1903) at their Huntington Avenue Field and moved to the new **Fenway Park** (1912). The Taylor family sold the team to **Thomas Austin Yawkey** (1933), who rebuilt Fenway Park and adopted the **Jimmy Fund** as the team's official charity. The Red Sox remain New England's favorite sports franchise, despite the **Curse of the Bambino**, and began a new era with new owners in 2002. *See also* BOSTON.

BOSTON SHORTY. The professional name of the champion pool player Larry Johnson. Born in Cambridge, Massachusetts, Johnson (1929–2000) left high school to earn his living as a professional pool player. Known for his trademark porkpie hat, stogie, short (5'1") stature, and pronounced Boston accent, he traveled the country playing high stakes games, celebrity tournaments, or exhibitions in pool halls and resorts. Boston Shorty, who held many national and world championship titles, was inducted into the Billiards Congress of America Hall of Fame (1999). He died in Somerville, Massachusetts, on December 10, 2000.

BOSTON STOCK EXCHANGE (BSE). Founded (1834) by 13 merchants as the third stock exchange in the nation. Traded were the stocks of New England banks, insurance companies, mills, canals, and mutual funds. The capital raised would fund many mines, factories, and railroads across the country. The BSE managers meet in the **The Vault** room of the Boston Safe Deposit & Trust Company, the meeting place of **Boston** financiers who advised city and state officials (1959–80) on financial issues and redevelopment of Boston.

BOSTON STRANGLER. A serial killer who raped and murdered 13 or more women in **Boston** (1962–64). Albert DeSalvo (1931–73) confessed to some of the sensational crimes, but the police believe other killers may have been responsible. DeSalvo, who was not prosecuted for these crimes, died in a Massachusetts prison. This unsolved crime wave was the subject of a feature film *The Boston Strangler* (1968).

BOSTON SYMPHONY ORCHESTRA (BSO). Founded by **Henry Lee Higginson** (1881), a philanthropist who hired **McKim Mead and White** to design its permanent home, Symphony Hall (1900), and incorporated the BSO (1918). Its leading conductors have included George Henschel, Karl Muck, Serge Koussevitzky, Charles Munch, Erich Leinsdorf, Seiji Ozawa, John T. Williams, and Keith Lockhart. Each summer since 1885 the BSO offers light classical music in a café setting known as the **Boston Pops Orchestra** (1900). **Arthur Fiedler** conducted (1930–79) some of the concerts on the **Charles River Esplanade**. The BSO also performs at the Berkshire Music Festival (1936) known as **Tanglewood** and cooperates with the **New England Conservatory of Music** (1867). *See also* BOSTON.

BOSTON TEA PARTY. A protest by patriots on December 16, 1773, against the British Tea Act of 1773. Disguised as Native Americans, **Samuel Adams**, **Paul Revere**, and the **Sons of Liberty** dumped the cargo of India tea from three ships into **Boston** harbor to avoid paying the Townshend tax on imports. This defiance of Parliament and Governor **Thomas Hutchinson** led to the **Intolerable Acts** in 1774, closing the port and bringing the revolution to the colonies. This dramatic incident inspired similar tea party protests in Portland, Portsmouth, Providence, and New York City. *See also* AMERICAN REVOLUTION.

BOSTON TERRIER. An American breed of nonsporting dog originated (1880) by crossing English bulldogs with terriers in **Boston**,

Massachusetts. The brindle coat is short and smooth, and these lively, strong, intelligent, and gentle dogs became popular pets in 1920–40 after the American Kennel Club recognized this breed (1893). It is the official state dog in Massachusetts.

BOUTWELL, GEORGE SEWEL (1818–1905). Senator from Massachusetts. Born in Brookline, Massachusetts, on January 28, 1818, Boutwell was a merchant and lawyer in Groton. He served as a Democratic state legislator (1842–44, 1847–50) and was governor (1851–52). He was a Republican in Congress (1863–69), secretary of the treasury (1869–73), and senator (1873–77). Boutwell practiced law in Washington, D.C. (1884–1905), and was president of the Anti-Imperialist League (1898–1905) when he died in Groton on February 27, 1905.

BOWDITCH, NATHANIEL (1773–1838). Astronomer. Born in Salem, Massachusetts, on March 26, 1773, Bowditch left school (1783) to work in his father's cooperage and in a ship chandler shop. He was self-taught in mathematics and languages and at age 15 wrote an **almanac**. His sea voyages inspired his *American Practical Navigator* (1802), which became the mariner's bible with accurate information on astronomy, currents, tides, and geography. Bowditch was an insurance actuary in Boston but also published scientific papers on comets and meteors; his *Celestial Mechanics* (1829) was a landmark in American science. Much honored, he died in Boston on March 16, 1838, a figure compared to Leonardo da Vinci in the American Enlightenment.

BOWDOIN, JAMES (1726–1790). Governor of Massachusetts. Born in Boston on August 7, 1726, Bowdoin was a merchant and Revolutionary war leader, a state legislator (1753–88), and president of the state constitutional convention (1779–80). As governor (1785–87), he suppressed **Shays's Rebellion**. After Bowdoin died in Boston on November 6, 1790, Bowdoin College (1794) was named in his honor and owns a portrait (1748) of Bowdoin by **Robert Feke**. *See also* AMERICAN REVOLUTION.

BOWLES, CHESTER B. (1901–1986). Governor of Connecticut. Born in Springfield, Massachusetts, on April 5, 1901, Chester Bliss Bowles graduated from Yale University (1924). He founded an advertising agency with **William Benton** in New York City, and during World War II he served in the Office of Price Administration and Economic Stabilization

Board. Elected Democratic governor (1949–51), Bowles was ambassador to India and Nepal (1951–53) and was elected to Congress (1959–61). He served as under secretary of state (1961) and again as ambassador to India (1963–69). Bowles advised President **John F. Kennedy** on foreign policy and wrote *Promises to Keep: My Years in Public Life, 1941–1969* (1971) before he died in Essex, Connecticut, on May 25, 1986.

BOYLSTON, ZABDIEL (1679–1766). Physician. Born in Brookline, Massachusetts, on March 9, 1679, Boylston apprenticed with his father in medicine. At the urging of **Cotton Mather**, he inoculated 200 Bostonians in the smallpox epidemic (1721). Despite his success, mobs attacked his house and a pamphlet war resulted. Boylston was elected to the Royal Society (1726) and wrote *An Historical Account of the Smallpox Inoculation in New England* (1726). The smallpox epidemics that had ravaged New England (1666, 1678, 1702, 1710, 1721, 1729, 1738, and 1799) ended with inoculation. Boylston practiced in Boston until he died at his Brookline farm on March 1, 1766. Dr. **Benjamin Waterhouse** confirmed Boylston's pioneering steps by introducing safe medical smallpox vaccination in Boston (1799).

BRACE, CHARLES LORING (1826–1890). Clergyman. Born in Litchfield, Connecticut, on June 19, 1826, Brace graduated from Yale College (1846), Yale Divinity School (1847), and the Union Theological Seminary. As a **Congregational** minister in New York City, he established the New York Children's Aid Society (1853) for poor children. Brace learned about the orphan train method from the **Boston** Children's Mission (1849) and used the controversial scheme (1854–1929) to place 200,000 children in rural farm families. Brace wrote *The Dangerous Classes of New York and Twenty Years' Work Among Them* (1972) and died in Switzerland on August 11, 1890. *See also* ALGER, HORATIO.

BRADFORD, WILLIAM (1590–1657). Governor of **Plymouth Colony**. Born in England, Bradford joined **William Brewster**'s **Pilgrim** congregation (1606) and migrated with them to Holland (1609–20). He sailed on the **Mayflower** and was the colony's governor (1621–51) after **John Carver** died. His *History of Plymouth Plantation, 1620–1647* (1651) is the best source on the Pilgrims, but he died a disappointed man on May 9, 1657, because secular ideas had overcome the tolerant religious community he planned.

BRADLEE, BENJAMIN C. (1921–). Journalist and editor. Born in Boston on August 26, 1921, Benjamin Crowninshield Bradlee graduated from **Harvard University** (1942) and served in the U.S. Navy (1942–45). Born in a **Boston Brahmin** family, Bradlee was a reporter for the *Washington Post* (1948–51) and a State Department press attaché in Paris (1951–53). After stints as a *Newsweek* magazine correspondent in Paris and Washington (1953–65), he became an editor of the *Washington Post* (1965–91). Bradlee published the *Pentagon Papers* (1971) and exposed the Watergate scandals (1973). As a close friend of **John F. Kennedy**, he wrote *That Special Grace* (1964) and *Conversations with Kennedy* (1975). Ben Bradlee retired as vice-president of the *Washington Post* (1991) and wrote his memoirs, *A Good Life* (1995).

BRADLEY, MILTON (1836–1911). Manufacturer. Born in Vienna, Maine, on November 8, 1836, Bradley was a draftsman and lithographer in Springfield, Massachusetts (1856–60). During the **Civil War** he manufactured pocket games popular with soldiers (1861). His company (1864) invented other popular games, puzzles, and toys. Influenced by **Elizabeth Peabody**, he published a **kindergarten** manual and materials. Bradley died in Springfield on May 30, 1911, but his company continued and merged with the Hasbro Company in Pawtucket, Rhode Island (1984).

BRADSTREET, ANNE (1612–1672). Poet. Born in Northampton, England, in 1612, Anne Dudley Bradstreet migrated with her husband to **Boston** (1630). Her husband, **Simon Bradstreet**, was later governor of the colony. She was the first woman in America to publish a book. Her poetry, *The Tenth Muse Lately Sprung Up In America* (1650), reveals spiritual growth as a **Puritan** and domestic life in the colony. She died in Andover, Massachusetts, on September 16, 1672.

BRADSTREET, SIMON (1603–1697). Governor of Massachusetts. Born in England in March 1603, Bradstreet emigrated to **Boston** (1630) with his wife, **Anne Dudley Bradstreet**. He was an assistant in the Massachusetts Bay Colony (1630–79), and negotiated the **New England Confederation** (1634) with the **Plymouth**, **New Haven**, and Connecticut colonies. In London he persuaded King Charles II to confirm the Massachusetts charter and served as governor (1679–86, 1689–92). He died in Boston in March 1697.

BRANDEGEE, FRANK BOSWORTH (1864–1924). Senator from Connecticut. Born in New London, Connecticut, on July 8, 1864, Brandegee graduated from Yale University (1885). He practiced law in New London (1888–1902), served in the state legislature (1888, 1899), and was a Republican in the House (1902–05) and the Senate (1905–24). He is best remembered as an ally of **Henry Cabot Lodge** on the Senate Foreign Relations Committee opposed to the peace treaty ending World War I and opposed to the League of Nations. Brandegee, consistently conservative in opposition to the child labor law, woman's suffrage, the Federal Reserve System, and the income tax, died in Washington, D.C., on October 14, 1924.

BRANDEIS, LOUIS D. (1856–1941). U.S. Supreme Court justice. Born in Louisville, Kentucky, on November 13, 1856, Louis Dembitz Brandeis graduated from **Harvard** Law School (1877) and practiced law in **Boston** (1878–1916). He built a reputation as the "people's attorney" in pro bono cases using sociological and economic data to buttress his legal arguments (the Brandeis brief) and as a champion of Progressive reform. Appointed to the Supreme Court, Brandeis was the first Jew to serve on the Court (1916–39) and often was a liberal dissenter from the conservative majority. He privately encouraged **Felix Frankfurter** to criticize the **Sacco-Vanzetti Case**. His doctrine of judicial restraint and deference to the legislative branch was accepted by the Court by 1940. After retirement, he was devoted to the Zionist movement until his death in Washington, D.C., on October 5, 1941. Brandeis University in **Waltham**, Massachusetts, was named in his honor (1948).

BRASS CITY. Nickname for **Waterbury**, Connecticut.

BRAYTON, CHARLES RAY (1840–1910). Public official. Born on August 16, 1840, in Warwick, Rhode Island, Brayton attended Brown University (1859–61) and served in the **Civil War** as a general. He was the controversial Rhode Island Republican Party boss (1870–1910) who served as a U.S. Pension officer (1870–74) and the **Providence** postmaster (1874–80). After he embezzled $37,000, the U.S. Senate investigated his use of patronage and election fraud. Brayton left the state but returned as Indian inspector and postal inspector for Rhode Island as the firm ally of Senator **Nelson W. Aldrich**. The election of **James Higgins**, the first **Irish Catholic** Democratic governor (1907), ended Brayton's power. Reapportionment (1909) gave cities and immigrant Democrats more seats in the legislature, but under Brayton the Republicans still controlled the state senate and town government until he died in Providence on September 23, 1910.

BREED'S HILL. The location in Charlestown, Massachusetts, where the Battle of **Bunker Hill** took place on June 17, 1775.

BRENNAN, JOSEPH E. (1934–). Governor of Maine. Born in **Portland**, Maine, on November 2, 1934, Joseph Edward Brennan graduated from Boston College (1958) and the University of Maine Law School (1963). He served in the state legislature as a Democrat (1965–71, 1973–75) and as state attorney general (1975–77). He was elected governor (1979–87) and to the House of Representatives (1987–91).

BRETTON WOODS CONFERENCE. A meeting of the United Nations Monetary and Financial Conference at Bretton Woods, New Hampshire, on July 1–22, 1944. Experts from 44 governments designed the International Monetary Fund and World Bank to promote postwar economic recovery and stability.

BREWSTER, WILLIAM (1567–1644). Founder of **Plymouth colony**. Born in England in 1567, Brewster studied at Cambridge University and was a member of the gentry in Scrooby, Yorkshire, where he organized a **Pilgrim** congregation (1606). He financed the migration to Holland (1608) and negotiated with the Virginia Company to settle the Pilgrims in America. Brewster arrived on the *Mayflower* (1620) and was Pilgrim leader until he died in Plymouth on April 10, 1644.

BRIDGES, STYLES (1898–1961). Senator from New Hampshire. Born in West Pembroke, Maine, Bridges graduated from the University of Maine (1918) and taught at the University of New Hampshire (1921–22). He was a progressive Republican in Governor **Charles W. Tobey**'s administration but became more conservative as governor (1934–36) and as a U.S. senator (1936–61). Bridges died in **Concord**, New Hampshire, on November 26, 1961.

BRINK'S ROBBERY. Occurred on January 17, 1950, in Boston's **North End** when seven masked burglars stole $2.8 million from the Brink's Armored Car Company. This was the biggest armed robbery in American history, dubbed the crime of the century by the Federal Bureau of Investigation (FBI). In 1956 one of the thieves confessed and the gangsters were convicted and imprisoned after a sensational trial. Because the money was never recovered, this "perfect crime" became part of **Boston** legend and the subject of two popular films, *Brinks: The Great Robbery* (1976) and *The Brink's Job* (1978).

BROAD STREET RIOT. Resulted from anti-Catholic and nativist sentiments on June 11, 1837, when a **Yankee** volunteer fire company returning from a fire disrupted an **Irish Catholic** funeral procession on Broad Street in **Boston**. Thousands of spectators watched 800 men and boys battling on the streets for hours until Mayor Samuel Eliot called on the state **militia** to restore order. Three Irish **immigrants** were convicted, but all the Yankee rioters were freed, confirming in the minds of many the extent of **anti-Catholicism** and ethnic prejudice in Boston.

BROOK FARM. A utopian commune (1841–47) in West Roxbury, Massachusetts, organized by **George Ripley**, a **Unitarian** minister and Transcendentalist editor of *The Dial* magazine. Among its members were **Bronson Alcott**, **Orestes Brownson**, **Charles A. Dana**, **Ralph Waldo Emerson**, **Margaret Fuller**, **Nathaniel Hawthorne**, **Theodore Parker**, and **Elizabeth Peabody**. Hawthorne's novel *Blithedale Romance* (1852) is based on this experiment in communal living. A fire in 1846 ended the idealistic **Transcendentalist** community, and Ripley worked for 20 years to pay the debts.

BROOKE, EDWARD W. (1919–). Senator from Massachusetts. Born in Washington, D.C., on October 26, 1919, Edward William Brooke III graduated from Howard University (1941) and served in the U.S. Army (1941–45). He graduated from Boston University Law School (1948), and was elected attorney general of Massachusetts (1962–66). Brooke was elected as a Republican in the Senate (1967–79), the first **African-American** senator elected by popular vote. Brooke then practiced law in Washington, D.C.

BROOKS, PHILLIPS (1835–1893). Bishop. Born in **Boston** on December 13, 1835, Brooks graduated from Harvard College (1855) and was ordained an Episcopal priest in Virginia (1859). He earned a national reputation by his sermon at a **Harvard University** service for the **Civil War** dead (1865) and for his Christmas hymn *O Little Town of Bethlehem* (1868). Brooks was rector of **Trinity Church** in Boston (1869–91), where his moderate sermons, avoiding austere **Puritanism**, won him much respect. He was the first American clergyman to conduct services for Queen Victoria (1880), and he became bishop of Massachusetts in 1891. After his death in Boston on January 23, 1893, his statue by **Augustus Saint-Gaudens** was placed outside Trinity Church in Copley Square.

BROOKS, VAN WYCK (1886–1963). Writer. Born in Plainfield, New Jersey, Brooks graduated from **Harvard University** (1907) and began a career as a New England critic, biographer, and literary historian. His first book, *The Wine of the Puritans* (1908), attributed American cultural decline to the **Puritans**. In *America's Coming-of-Age* (1915), he argued the Puritan duality created modern high-brow and low-brow cultures. Two of his biographies blamed Puritanism for problems faced by **Mark Twain** and **Henry James**, but *The Life of Emerson* (1932) depicted **Ralph Waldo Emerson** as one American writer who accommodated life and art in his work. Brooks is best known for *The Flowering of New England, 1815–1865* (1936) and *New England: Indian Summer, 1865–1915* (1940). He died in Bridgewater, Connecticut, on May 2, 1963.

BROTHER JONATHAN. A term used for **Yankees** or all Americans in the Revolutionary War. The original Brother Jonathan, distinguished from the archetypal Englishman called John Bull, was George Washington's most reliable supporter, Governor **Jonathan Trumbull** of Connecticut. *See also* AMERICAN REVOLUTION.

BROWN BREAD. A traditional New England steamed bread made with rye flour, cornmeal, molasses, yeast, and baking powder (1830). It was often served with **baked beans** on Saturday evening and at **clambakes** as **Yankee** cuisine.

BROWN, JOHN (1736–1803). Congressman from Rhode Island. Born in **Providence** on January 27, 1736, Brown was a wealthy merchant and slave trader arrested (1775) for burning the British sloop *Gaspee* in Narragansett Bay (1772). Released through the efforts of his brother, **Moses Brown**, he served in the state legislature (1782–84) and as a **Federalist** in the House of Representatives (1799–1801). Brown's sloop the *Katy*, commissioned as the *Providence*, was the first ship in the Continental Navy (1775). Commanded by John Paul Jones, it was the most victorious ship in the American Navy, sinking or capturing 40 British ships. Brown was an early **China Trade** merchant (1787), and his elegant Georgian mansion (1786) overlooking the Providence waterfront is now part of the **Rhode Island Historical Society**. He died in Providence on September 20, 1803. *See also* AMERICAN REVOLUTION.

BROWN, JOHN (1800–1859). Abolitionist and reformer. Born in Torrington, Connecticut, on May 9, 1800, John Brown was an unsuccessful farmer, drover, tanner, and wool merchant in Springfield, Massachusetts. He conceived a violent opposition to slavery, operated an **Underground Railroad** station in Ohio, and battled proslavery settlers in Kansas with aid from prominent Massachusetts abolitionists (1855–58). Brown's small army seized the federal arsenal in Harpers Ferry, Virginia (1859), but Colonel Robert E. Lee captured the insurrectionists. Seen as a martyr by abolitionists or a fanatical traitor by others, his legal defenders included **John A. Andrew**, **Thomas Wentworth Higginson**, and **Samuel Gridley Howe**. Brown was hanged in Charles Town, West Virginia, on December 2, 1859, a dramatic step toward the **Civil War**. *See also* ABOLITIONISM.

BROWN, MOSES (1738–1836). Businessman. Born in **Providence**, Rhode Island, on September 23, 1738, Brown was a **Quaker** merchant in the **West Indies trade** with his brothers John, Joseph, and Nicholas in Providence. When his brother **John Brown** was sent to Boston (1775) for trial in the *Gaspee* incident (1772), Moses Brown obtained his release. He opposed **slavery** and established (1790) the first water-powered cotton mill in the nation with **Samuel Slater** on the Blackstone River in Pawtucket. Brown founded the Moses Brown School, a Quaker **prep school** for boys in Providence (1819). Moses Brown died in Providence on September 6, 1836.

BROWN, NICHOLAS (1769–1841). Businessman. Born in **Providence** on April 4, 1769, Brown, the nephew of **John** and **Moses Brown**, expanded the Brown family business and formed the shipping firm of Brown & Ives with his brother-in-law. His philanthropy for Rhode Island College led the trustees to rename it Brown University (1804). Nicholas Brown died in Providence on September 27, 1841. His son, John Carter Brown (1797–1874), donated his Americana collection to the Brown University Library that bears his name.

BROWN, WALTER A. (1905–1964). Sports promoter. Born in Hopkinton, Massachusetts, on February 10, 1905, Brown studied at **Boston Latin School** and graduated from the Philips Exeter **prep school** (1926). Succeeding his father as manager of the **Boston Garden** (1937), he introduced the circus, rodeo, boxing, and Ice Capades to New England audiences. He was an official for the **Boston Marathon** (1938–42), a founder of the National Basketball Association (NBA) in 1949, owner of the **Boston Celtics** (1947–64), president of the **Boston Bruins**, and an official for the Olympic Games. Elected to the Basketball Hall of Fame (1961) and the National Hockey League Hall of Fame (1962), Brown died in Hyannis, Massachusetts, on September 7, 1964.

BROWNE, GEORGE HUNTINGTON (1811–1885). Congressman from Rhode Island. Born in Gloucester, Rhode Island, on January 6, 1811, Browne graduated from Brown University (1840) and practiced law in **Providence** (1843–52). He was a Democratic state legislator (1842, 1849–52) and U.S. district attorney (1852–61). He served in the House of Representatives (1861–63) and was colonel of the 12th Rhode Island Infantry Regiment (1862–65). Browne was a state senator (1872–74) and was elected chief justice of the state supreme court (1874) but declined the office. He died in Providence on September 26, 1885.

BROWNSON, ORESTES A. (1803–1876). Reformer. Born in Stockbridge, Vermont, on September 16, 1803, Orestes Augustus Brownson was the son of a poor farmer. Ordained in the **Congregational** church, he moved to Presbyterianism (1822) and became a **Universalist** minister (1826). Brownson was the editor of the Workingmen's Party journal in Auburn, New York, and a **Unitarian** pastor in Walpole (1832–34) and Canton, Massachusetts (1834–36). In **Boston** he founded his own church and published the influential *Boston Quarterly Review* (1838–42). He broke with his **Transcendentalist** colleagues when he converted to the Roman Catholic Church (1844) but published *Brownson's Quarterly Review* (1844–75). One of the most intellectually and spiritually restless thinkers of the era, Brownson died in Detroit on April 17, 1876.

BRYANT, WILLIAM CULLEN (1794–1878). Poet. Born in Cummington, Massachusetts, on November 3, 1794, Bryant attended Williams College and practiced law in Great Barrington (1815–25). His poetry was critically acclaimed, especially *Thanatopsis* (1817) and *To a Water-fowl* (1821). He abandoned the law when he moved to New York City (1825) to become an editor. At the *New York Evening Post* (1829–78), he was an influential Jacksonian Democrat until he joined the Free Soil Party (1848) and the Republican Party (1856). Calling for the emancipation of slaves, he declared **John Brown** a martyr and continued to publish poetry but never surpassing his work in the 1820s. Bryant died in New York City on June 12, 1878.

BUCKINGHAM, WILLIAM ALFRED (1804–1875). Senator from Connecticut. Born in Lebanon, Connecticut, on May 28, 1804, Buckingham studied at Bacon Academy in Colchester. He was a merchant and mayor of Norwich, and as the Republican governor (1858–66) he zealously supported President Abraham Lincoln. Buckingham raised 54 military companies furnishing 48,000 soldiers. After the **Civil War** he resumed his business pursuits and served in the Senate (1869–75) until his death in Norwich on February 5, 1875.

BULFINCH, CHARLES (1763–1844). Architect. Born in **Boston** on August 8, 1763, Bulfinch graduated from **Harvard** College (1781) and studied in Europe (1785–87). His first major work was to design the state house in **Hartford** (1793–96) and three mansions in Boston for **Harrison Gray Otis**. He is best known for the new **Massachusetts State House** (1798) in his hallmark Federal style, dubbed by **Oliver Wendell Holmes** as the "hub of the solar system." He also designed the **Bunker Hill** monument and several New England churches and mansions in the 1790s. Bulfinch took a leading role in urban planning on the Boston board of selectmen (1791–95) and as its chairman (1799–1818). He transformed the city by elegant urban planning with street lighting, churches, banks, and coeducational public schools.

His practical, elegant neoclassical civic improvements included designing **Boston Common** and other city parks, the **Massachusetts General Hospital** (1817), Cathedral of the Holy Cross (1803), Harvard College's University Hall (1814), the **Worcester** Courthouse, and the new Maine State Capitol in **Augusta** (1831). President James Monroe invited Bulfinch to build the U.S. Capitol (1817–30). When he died in Boston on April 4, 1844, Bulfinch was America's most influential architect. *See also* ART; ARCHITECTURE; BENJAMIN, ASHER; MCINTIRE, SAMUEL.

BULKELEY, MORGAN GARDNER (1837–1922). Senator from Connecticut. Born in East Haddam, Connecticut, on December 26, 1837, Bulkeley grew up in **Hartford** and was a merchant in Brooklyn, New York (1852–72). After serving in the **Civil War**, he entered the **insurance** business in Hartford (1872) and became a banker and president of Aetna Life Insurance Company, the firm his father founded in 1853. Bulkeley was the first president of the National Baseball League (1876) and served as a Republican alderman and mayor of Hartford (1880–88) and governor (1889–93). In the Senate (1905–11) he was a vocal critic of President Theodore Roosevelt and an advocate for the Connecticut **tobacco** and insurance industries. Chiefly responsible for making Hartford a center of the insurance business, Bulkeley died in Hartford on November 6, 1922, and was inducted into the Baseball Hall of Fame (1937).

BUNDLING. A courtship practice in colonial New England as a practical way for couples to spend time together in small, dark, crowded, and often cold houses. The couple went to bed together fully dressed with a bundling board between them. No sex was permitted, but they could enjoy each other's company at night with some privacy but under the oversight of the young woman's family. Even **John Adams**, sometimes a stern parent, wrote (1761) his daughters that he approved of this traditional courtship practice. But **Jonathan Edwards** preached against bundling, which disappeared by 1800.

BUNDY, MCGEORGE (1919–1996). Public official and educator. Born in **Boston** on March 30, 1919, Bundy graduated from Yale University (1940) and studied government at **Harvard University** (1940–41). After serving in the U.S. Army in World War II, Bundy taught government at Harvard (1946–54) and was the ghostwriter of Henry L. Stimson's memoirs. He was a dean (1954–61) at Harvard when President **John F. Kennedy** named him special assistant for national security affairs (1961–63). Bundy was a pragmatic liberal in the Cold War and an architect of the Vietnam War for President Lyndon B. Johnson (1963–66). As president of the Ford Foundation (1966–79), Bundy wrote *The Strength of Government* (1968) and *Reducing Nuclear Danger* (1993). He was professor of history at New York University (1979–89) and died in Boston on September 16, 1996.

BUNDY, WILLIAM P. (1917–2000). Public official and educator. Born in Washington, D.C., on September 24, 1917, William Putnam Bundy grew up in **Boston** with his brother, **McGeorge Bundy**. He graduated from Yale University (1939) and studied history at **Harvard University** (1940). After serving in the U.S. Army (1941–45), he graduated from Harvard Law School (1947) and practiced law in Washington, D.C., before joining the Central Intelligence Agency (CIA) in 1951–60. Bundy was an adviser to President Dwight D. Eisenhower (1959–61), assistant secretary of defense (1963–64), and assistant secretary of state for Far Eastern affairs (1964–69). Bundy, one of the principal advisers on Vietnam (1964–69), was one of the "best and the brightest" advisers to President **John F. Kennedy** and President Lyndon B. Johnson. He taught at MIT (1969–72), was editor of *Foreign Affairs* (1972–84), taught at Princeton University (1984–2000), and wrote *A Tangled Web: The Making of Foreign Policy in the Nixon Presidency* (1998). Bundy died in Princeton on October 6, 2000.

BUNKER HILL DAY. A holiday in **Boston** celebrated each June with a parade in Charlestown, **militia** drills, and patriotic exercises commemorating the **Battle of Bunker Hill** on June 17, 1775.

BUNYAN, PAUL. Hero. Born in Bangor, Maine, Paul Bunyan is a mythical lumberjack giant in New England folklore. Based on oral tradition among **Irish** and **French-Canadian** lumberjacks (1860) in Maine and Canada, he first appeared as a literary character (1910) symbolizing American strength and size. Accompanied by his giant blue ox, Babe, the larger-than-life folklore hero traveled from Maine to Oregon. Rarely collected by folklorists, he is a popular legend and a literary creation of the early 20th century. A statue in Bangor (1959) celebrates this **Yankee** folk hero.

BURBANK, LUTHER (1849–1926). Horticulturist. Born in Lancaster, Massachusetts, on March 7, 1849, Burbank was raised on a farm with only an elementary education, but he developed the Russet Burbank potato in Lunenburg (1871). Moving to California (1875), he bred 800 hybrid plants and became the nation's leading horticulturalist. Burbank wrote his autobiography, *Harvest of the Years* (1927), and died in Santa Rosa on April 11, 1926.

BURLINGAME, ANSON (1820–1870). Congressman from Massachusetts. Born in New Berlin, New York, on November 14, 1820, Burlingame graduated from **Harvard** Law School (1846) and practiced law in Boston until elected to the state legislature (1852–55). He was a **Know Nothing Party** congressman (1855–59) and was reelected as a Republican (1859–61). Burlingame served as U.S. minister to China (1861–67), and when he resigned his post, China appointed him to negotiate with the United States and European nations (1867–70). He was author of the Burlingame treaty between the United States and China and died on his diplomatic mission in Russia on February 23, 1870.

BURNS, ANTHONY. Escaped slave. An incident occurred in 1854 in **Boston** when Burns was arrested under the Fugitive Slave Act (1850). An **abolitionist** mob led by **Thomas Wentworth Higginson** attempted to free him by law or by force from the federal courthouse. Guarded by the state militia and U.S. Marines from 20,000 outraged Bostonians, Burns was returned by ship on June 2, 1854, to his owner in Virginia. **Daniel Webster** and President **Franklin Pierce** were criticized for enforcing this unpopular law, and this was the last major effort to do so in New England. In 1855, a Boston abolitionist purchased Burns for $1,300 and he returned to Boston a free man. *See also* SLAVERY.

BURNSIDE, AMBROSE EVERETT (1824–1881). Senator from Rhode Island. Born in Liberty, Indiana, on May 23, 1824, Burnside graduated from West Point (1847). After serving in the U.S. Army (1847–53), he operated an arms factory in Bristol, Rhode Island (1853–57) and recruited the first Rhode Island regiment and was a general in the **Civil War** (1861–65). After the war, Burnside, for whom side-whiskers are named, was a **railroad** administrator and served three terms as Republican governor (1866–69) and in the Senate (1874–81). He died in Bristol on September 13, 1881. *See also* GILMORE, PATRICK S.

BUSH, BARBARA P. (1925–). First lady of the United States. Born in Rye, New York, on June 8, 1925, Barbara Pierce studied at Smith College (1943–45). She married **George H. W. Bush** (1945) and lived in **New Haven** (1945–48) while he completed his studies at Yale University. She raised six children in Texas and was a very popular first lady (1989–93), bringing to the White House her concern for literacy programs and humanitarian causes. She retired to Houston and the Bush family summer home in Kennebunkport, Maine. Her son, **George W. Bush**, was elected president (2000).

BUSH, GEORGE H. W. (1924–). President of the United States. Born in Milton, Massachusetts, on June 12, 1924, George Herbert Walker Bush was the son of Senator **Preston S. Bush** and the father of President **George W. Bush**. After service as a U.S. Navy pilot (1942–45), he graduated from Yale University (1948) and engaged in the Texas oil business. Like Theodore Roosevelt, Bush was an elite easterner who renewed himself in the West and was elected as a Republican to the House of Representatives (1967–71) from Houston. Bush served as U.S. representative to the United Nations (1971–73), chairman of the Republican National Committee (1972–73), chief U.S. liaison officer to China (1974–75), and director of the Central Intelligence Agency (CIA) in 1976–77. Bush was elected vice-president (1981–89) and then president (1989–93). Defeated for reelection in 1992, Bush retired to Houston and Kennebunkport, Maine.

BUSH, GEORGE W. (1946–). President of the United States. Born on July 6, 1946, in **New Haven**, Connecticut, George W. Bush, the son of **George H. W. Bush** and grandson of **Prescott S. Bush**, graduated from Yale University (1968) and **Harvard** Business School (1975). Raised in Midland, Texas, he served in the Texas Air National Guard (1968–73) and established an oil and gas exploration company (1975–86). After working in his father's presidential campaign (1987–88), he purchased the Texas Rangers baseball team (1989–93). Serving two terms as the Republican governor of Texas (1994–2000), Bush was elected president in a disputed election (2000).

BUSH, PRESCOTT S. (1895–1972). Senator from Connecticut. Born in Columbus, Ohio, on May 15, 1895, Bush graduated from Yale University (1917) and served in the Army in World War I (1917–19). He was a New York City banker before his election to the Senate as a Republican from Greenwich (1952–63). His son was President **George H. W. Bush** and his grandson was President **George W. Bush**. Prescott Bush died in New York City on October 8, 1972.

BUSH, VANNEVAR (1890–1974). Scientist. Born in Everett, Massachusetts, on March 11, 1890, Bush graduated from Tufts University (1913), and earned a Ph.D. in engineering at MIT (1916). Teaching at MIT (1919–38), he founded the Raytheon Company in Cambridge (1922), invented the radio tube (1925) and the differential analyzer **computer**

(1937), and was a pioneer in computer design. Bush was president of the Carnegie Institution (1939–55) and directed the war effort on the atomic bomb, radar, and mass production of sulfa and penicillin drugs. He formed the National Science Foundation (1950), returned to MIT (1955–71), and wrote *Modern Arms and Free Men* (1949). Bush died on June 28, 1974.

BUSHNELL, DAVID (1740–1826). Inventor. Born in West Saybrook, Connecticut, in 1740, Bushnell studied at Yale College (1771). He invented the world's first submarine (1775), the *Turtle*, and attempted to sink British war ships on the Hudson River (1776). He was appointed to the Army Corps of Engineers, and his naval mines were used successfully in the war. Bushnell practiced medicine in Georgia (1787–1826) until his death.

BUSHNELL, HORACE (1802–1876). Clergyman. Born in Bantam, Connecticut, on April 14, 1802, Bushnell graduated from Yale College (1827) and Yale Divinity School (1833). He was pastor of the North (**Congregational**) Church in **Hartford**, Connecticut (1833–59), where he became the father of American religious liberalism. Despite criticism from conservatives and accusations of heresy (1850), Bushnell advocated religious instruction for children, rejected the doctrine of original sin, and deemphasized revivals and adult conversion. He was best known for *Christian Nurture* (1847), an influential book asserting parents could raise their children as Christians without ever knowing sin. Bushnell was a flexible centrist in a time of New England evangelical fervor until his death in Hartford on February 17, 1876.

BUSING. Refers to the federal court order of Judge **W. Arthur Garrity, Jr.**, to desegregate **Boston** public schools by transferring pupils by bus from one neighborhood to another (1974–85). The court plan to achieve racial balance triggered riots and "white flight" as parents enrolled children in private, parochial, and suburban schools. National media reports contrasted the anger and violence to the reputation of Massachusetts as a center of abolitionism and liberalism.

BUTLER, BENJAMIN FRANKLIN (1818–1893). Governor of Massachusetts. Born in Deerfield, New Hampshire, on November 5, 1818, Butler graduated from Waterville (later Colby) College (1838). He practiced law in **Lowell**, Massachusetts (1840–61), and was elected as a Democrat to the legislature (1853–60), supporting labor and **immigrants**. As a general in the Union Army (1861–65) in Virginia, he freed escaped slaves as "contraband" of war. "Beast" Butler outraged New Orleans citizens (1862) by declaring women disrespectful to his soldiers would be treated as prostitutes. Butler served in the House of Representatives (1867–75, 1877–79) first as a Radical Republican and then as a Greenbacker. He managed the impeachment of President Andrew Johnson (1868) and supported President Ulysses S. Grant. Butler was governor (1883–84) and the Greenback Party nominee for president (1884). Controversial and able, Ben Butler died in Washington, D.C., on January 11, 1893. *See also* CIVIL WAR.

– C –

CABOT, GEORGE (1752–1823). Senator from Massachusetts. Born in **Salem**, Massachusetts, on December 3, 1752, Cabot attended **Harvard** College. He was a successful ship captain (1768–77), Salem merchant, and cotton mill owner in Beverly and a leader of the **Essex Junto** (1778–1823), the dominant wing of the **Federalist Party**. As U.S. senator (1791–96), Cabot introduced the first fugitive slave law (1793) and was chairman of the **Hartford Convention** (1815). He died in **Boston** on April 18, 1823.

CABOT, JOHN (1450–1499). Explorer. Born in Genoa, Cabot explored the coasts of Canada and New England (1497), claiming the land for England. Henry VII supported his second exploration (1498) of North America to find a northwest ocean route to Asia. Cabot died soon after his return to England in 1499.

CAMBODIANS. Immigrants arrived in New England by 1975 and after the civil war (1972–75) and invasion by Vietnam (1979). More than 40,000 refugees came to Massachusetts (1975–2000), settling in Attleboro, Dracut, Lawrence, Lynn, Westford, and **Worcester**. Cambodians accounted for one-fourth of the **Lowell** population (2001), many working in manufacturing and worshipping in Buddhist temples in Lowell and North Chelmsford. Chanrithy Uong, the first Cambodian-American public official in New England, was elected to the Lowell City Council (1999).

CAMBRIDGE PLATFORM. The basic document of New England **Congregationalism** (1648) defined in Cambridge, Massachusetts, to determine church government and the autonomy of congregations. Written by Richard Mather and **John Cotton**, it incorporated the Westminster Confession (1648) adopted in England for doctrine by Presbyterians.

CAMP. A New England term for a vacation home in the woods or at a pond or lake. It can be a simple cabin or a more elaborate seasonal home used for hunting, fishing, boating, and outdoor recreation (1870s).

CAMP, WALTER (1859–1925). Sportsman. Born in **New Britain**, Connecticut, on April 7, 1859, Walter Chauncey Camp graduated from Yale University (1880). As a player, coach, and adviser of the Yale football team (1876–92), he devised the rules of intercollegiate football. Camp promoted sportsmanship by books and articles and selected the first All-American teams (1889–1924). He was a **New Haven** clock manufacturer when he died in New York City on March 14, 1925. *See also* SPORTS.

CANADIANS. Excluding **French Canadians**, a migration of Canadians amounted to an estimated 500,000 people in 1860–1930. From the Maritime provinces alone (New Brunswick, Nova Scotia, and Prince Edward Island), 340,000 adults migrated to the United States in 1880–1930. Displaced by economic decline in farming, **fishing**, and shipbuilding, they found work in urban New England industries or domestic service. East Boston had a large population from Canada (20%) in 1855–1905, and many Nova Scotia immigrants settled in Cambridge, Massachusetts. These workers were sometimes criticized as "birds of passage" because they returned to Nova Scotia in the slack season when work was difficult to find in New England cities. In the **Civil War**, many men from Nova Scotia and New Brunswick served in Maine, Vermont, and Massachusetts regiments.

CANDY. A New England product since Dr. Walter Baker and **Irish immigrant** John Hannon built the Walter Baker Chocolate mill (1765–1965) on the Neponset River in Dorchester, Massachusetts. Chocolate, West Indian **molasses**, sugar, and **maple syrup** provided ingredients for candy of all types. By 1861 William Schrafft made jelly beans in **Boston** for **Civil War** soldiers and **NECCO** manufactured other confectionery products in Cambridge. By 1930 New England had 30 candy companies. *See also* WEST INDIES TRADE.

CANONICUS (1585–1647). Native American. Born at Narragansett Bay about 1585, Canonicus was a *sachem* of the **Narragansett** people in the 1630s. He negotiated peace with the **Pilgrims** (1622) and granted land to **Roger Williams** (1636) and remained friendly with the English in Rhode Island and Massachusetts during the **Pequot War** (1637).

CANUCK. A derogatory term for **French Canadians** derived from the word *Canada* and the **Algonquin** ending *uck.* Dating from 1855 in Canada and New England, it reflects the ethnic and religious prejudice immigrants from Quebec encountered. **William Loeb** undermined **Edmund Muskie**'s campaign for president in 1972 when the *Manchester Union Leader* published false claims that Muskie used this slur. *See also* ANTI-CATHOLICISM.

CAPE ANN. A rocky headland (160 sq mi) in northeastern Massachusetts settled by English fishermen (1623) and by **Roger Conant** at Naumkeag (later Salem) in 1626. **Massachusetts Bay Colony** absorbed this settlement under **John Endecott** (1628). Cape Ann experienced an earthquake in 1755 estimated to be the largest in New England history. Gloucester, Cape Ann's chief fishing port and later a summer resort, was celebrated in **Henry Wadsworth Longfellow**'s poem *The Wreck of the Hesperus* (1841) and Rudyard Kipling's novel *Captains Courageous* (1896). Leonard Craske's statue *Fisherman at the Wheel* (1925) in Gloucester commemorates the maritime tradition of scenic Cape Ann. The Rockport **quarries** provided granite, and the sandy beaches on the peninsula attracted tourists and an **art colony** (1870). Cape Ann Light was the first **lighthouse** in America to mark a danger to navigation (1771) rather than a harbor.

CAPE COD. Bounded by Nantucket Sound, Cape Cod Bay, and the Atlantic Ocean, a narrow sandy peninsula extending 65 miles (105 km) east and north into the ocean from southeastern Massachusetts. First explored by **Giovanni da Verrazano** (1524) and **Esteban Gomes** (1525), **Bartholomew Gosnold** (1602) named it for the abundant **codfish**. Here the **Pilgrims** first landed from the *Mayflower* (1620) at **Provincetown**. Early settlers farmed, fished, built ships, and hunted whales, but 19th-century tourists were attracted to beaches and sand dunes warmed by the Gulf Stream. In 1903 the Marconi station on the Wellfleet beach sent the first two-way radio message from Cape Cod to

England. Since 1970 large retirement communities have developed. **Cranberry** growing and fishing still contribute to the economy. The **Cape Cod National Seashore** was established (1961) by the National Park Service from Wellfleet to Provincetown, Massachusetts, to preserve 44,000 acres of shoreline and a 40-mile sandy beach for public recreation. Most New Englanders refer to Cape Cod as the Cape.

CAPE COD CANAL. Crosses the base of the **Cape Cod** peninsula and connects Cape Cod Bay with Buzzards Bay in southeastern Massachusetts. The artificial waterway (17.5 mi/28 km) was planned by 1870 and constructed (1909–14) with private funds to reduce (by 75 mi/120 km) the distance between **Boston** and New York City and to eliminate the often dangerous voyage around Provincetown. The U.S. Army Corps of Engineers purchased and operates the toll-free canal (1927) as part of the Atlantic Intracoastal Waterway from Boston to Key West, Florida.

CAPE COD HOUSE. A one-story, center-chimney house commonly built throughout New England (1700–1850). It was two rooms deep and often had attached farm buildings or sheds; the later two-story version of the Cape Cod included an attic and cellar. **Colonial Revival** architects made the Cape popular (1920–30), and it became common throughout the nation by 1950 in suburban housing communities. *See also* ART; CAPE COD; SALTBOX HOUSE.

CAPE VERDE ISLANDS. Immigrants arrived in New England (1810) as the crew on **New Bedford whaling** ships. Because Cape Verde is a former **Portuguese** colony and province, Cape Verdeans speak Portuguese and their own Creole language. Many descendants of Portuguese settlers and African slaves on Cape Verde cotton and sugar plantations settled in southeastern Massachusetts and Rhode Island by 1830 and number more than 100,000 in New England (2001). **Boston**, Brockton, Fall River, Cambridge, **Lowell**, and **New Bedford** communities include **immigrants** from Brazil and Portugal as well as the Cape Verde Islands. Paul Gonsalves (1920–74), the jazz saxophonist, was born in Boston and raised in Rhode Island by his parents from Cape Verde.

CAPP, AL (1909–1979). Cartoonist. Alfred Gerald Caplin was born on September 28, 1909, in **New Haven** and attended art schools in **Boston** and Connecticut. Working on the *Mutt and Jeff* cartoon strip (1930) and on the *Joe Palooka* cartoons (1933), Al Capp created his *Lil' Abner* syndicated series for newspapers (1934–77). His hillbilly characters, chunky artwork, and humorous dialogue made the satirical cartoons very popular and the basis for two movies, a Broadway musical, and an animated television series. Capp hosted a daily syndicated radio program (1970–73) and a Boston television talk show. His autobiography, *My Well-Balanced Life on a Wooden Leg: Memoirs* (1991), was published after his death in Cambridge on November 5, 1979.

CARNEY, WILLIAM H. (1840–1908). Soldier. Born a slave in Norfolk, Virginia, on February 29, 1840, William Harvey Carney and his family escaped on the **Underground Railroad** to **New Bedford** in 1856. He abandoned his studies for the ministry to enlist in the Massachusetts **54th Infantry** in New Bedford (1863). During the regiment's heroic attack on Fort Wagner in South Carolina on July 18, 1863, he carried the fallen colors in the battle despite four wounds. Sergeant Carney was the first **African American** to receive the Medal of Honor (1900). He was a lamplighter (1866–68) and letter carrier in New Bedford (1870–1901) and succeeded **Lewis Hayden** as a state legislature clerk (1901–08), working within view of the **Shaw Memorial** that depicts him. Carney died in the state house on December 8, 1908. *See also* CIVIL WAR.

CARRIGAN, BILL (1883–1969). Baseball player and manager. Born in Lewiston, Maine, on October 22, 1883, William Francis "Bill" Carrigan studied at Holy Cross College. He played for the **Boston Red Sox** (1906–16) and as manager led the team to consecutive world championships. He played in three World Series (1912, 1915, 1916) and retired to Lewiston, where he died on July 8, 1969.

CARVER, JOHN (1576–1621). Governor of **Plymouth Colony**. Born in England about 1576, Carver was a wealthy merchant who joined the **Pilgrims** in Holland (1610). He chartered the *Mayflower* to bring the Pilgrims to America (1620) and was the colony's first governor before he died in Plymouth on April 5, 1621. **William Bradford** succeeded Carver as governor (1621–56).

CASS, THOMAS (1821–1862). Soldier. Born in Ireland, Cass was an **immigrant** who became a successful businessman and member of the Boston School Committee. At the urging of Governor **John A. Andrew** and Bishop **John B. Fitzpatrick**, Cass organized an Irish regiment, the 9th Massachusetts Volunteer Infantry (1861). The nucleus of the Fighting

Ninth was the Irish Columbian Artillery disbanded by the **Know Nothing Party** (1854). Colonel Cass was fatally wounded at the Battle of Malvern Hill in Virginia and died of his wounds in **Boston** on July 12, 1862. A memorial to his heroic service was erected (1899) in the **Boston Public Garden**. *See also* CIVIL WAR; YANKEE DIVISION.

CASTLE ISLAND. Named by Governor **John Winthrop**, a peninsula in **Boston** harbor fortified by Governor **Thomas Dudley** (1634) and rebuilt by the British army (1754) as Fort William. George Washington had it repaired by **Paul Revere** and it became a prison (1795–98). President **John Adams** renamed it Fort Independence (1799) to defend Boston Harbor. Edgar Allen Poe served as a soldier there in 1827, and his story *The Cask of Amontillado* (1845) is based on a legend that a soldier was buried alive in the walls. The legend was confirmed in 1905 when a skeleton in an army uniform was discovered sealed within the walls. The great five-sided granite fort was rebuilt (1833) by **Sylvanus Thayer**. Since 1890 Castle Island has been a public park.

CATHOLICS. *See* ANTI-CATHOLICISM.

CELLUCCI, ARGEO PAUL (1949–). Governor of Massachusetts. Born in Hudson, Massachusetts, on April 24, 1949, Paul Cellucci graduated from Boston College (1970), Boston College Law School (1973), and served in the Army Reserve (1970–78). He practiced law and was a Hudson selectman (1971–77), a Republican state representative (1977–85), and state senator (1985–91). Elected lieutenant governor (1991–97), he became governor (1997) when Governor **William Weld** resigned. Cellucci was elected (1998) but later resigned (2001) when President **George W. Bush** appointed him U.S. ambassador to Canada.

CHAFEE, JOHN HUBBARD (1922–1999). Senator from Rhode Island. Born in **Providence** on October 22, 1922, Chafee graduated from Yale University (1947) and **Harvard** Law School (1950). He served in the U.S. Marines (1942–45, 1951–53) and practiced law in Providence (1950–63). He was a Republican state legislator (1957–63) and governor (1963–69). Appointed secretary of the navy (1969–72) by President Richard M. Nixon, Chafee was a U.S. senator (1976–99) until his death on October 24, 1999.

CHAFEE, LINCOLN D. (1953–). Senator from Rhode Island. Born in Warwick on March 26, 1953, Lincoln Davenport Chafee graduated from Brown University (1975). He was a Republican city councilor (1986–92) and mayor (1992–99) of Warwick. Appointed to fill the vacancy caused by the death of his father, **John H. Chafee** (1999), he was elected to that seat in 2000.

CHAMBERLAIN, JOSHUA LAWRENCE (1828–1914). Governor of Maine. Born in Brewer, Maine, on September 8, 1828, Chamberlain graduated from Bowdoin College (1852) and Bangor Theological Seminary (1855). He was a professor at Bowdoin (1855–62), Republican governor (1867–71), and president of Bowdoin College (1871–83). Chamberlain is best known as the colonel who played a key role leading the **20th Maine Infantry Regiment** at the Battle of Gettysburg (1863). Wounded six times, Chamberlain became a general in the Union Army, accepted the surrender of Robert E. Lee, and received the Congressional Medal of Honor (1893). Chamberlain died in Brunswick on February 24, 1914. *See also* CIVIL WAR.

CHAMPLAIN, SAMUEL DE (1567–1635). Explorer. Born in France in 1567, Champlain explored the St. Lawrence River in Canada (1603) for France. He visited the New England coast (1604–06), naming Oyster Harbor on **Cape Cod** and **Mount Desert Island** in Maine (1605). His men fought a bloody battle with **Native Americans** in Chatham, Massachusetts (1606), the first conflict between Europeans and Indians in New England. Champlain's voyages led Pierre du Guast Sieur de Monts to establish the first European colony in Maine at the mouth of the St. Croix River. Champlain founded Quebec (1608), explored Lake Champlain in Vermont (1609), and was commandant of New France (1612–35). His most important work was *Voyages* (1632), a book intended to attract colonists. He was captured by the British when Quebec fell (1629). Champlain allied with the **Algonquins** and Huron against the Iroquois, who supported the British. The father of Canada visited North America 12 times before his death in Quebec on December 25, 1635.

CHANDLER, WILLIAM E. (1835–1917). Senator from New Hampshire. Born in **Concord** on December 28, 1835, William Eaton Chandler graduated from **Harvard** Law School (1854), practiced law in Concord, served as a Republican state legislator (1862–64), and was solicitor of the Navy Department (1865) and assistant secretary of the Treasury (1865–67). As publisher of a Concord newspaper, he opposed railroad lobbyists who controlled the state legislature (1870–1903). Chandler was secretary of the navy (1882–85) and served in the Senate (1887–1901), after which he practiced law in Concord until he died on November 30, 1917.

CHANNING, WILLIAM ELLERY (1780–1842). Clergyman. Born in **Newport**, Rhode Island, on April 7, 1780, Channing graduated from **Harvard** College (1798) and became a **Congregational** minister in Boston (1803–42). Rejecting evangelical revivals and the Calvinist doctrine of depravity of man, he founded the **Unitarian** sect (1819) and was its most influential writer and preacher. His teachings influenced the **Transcendentalists** and many New England social reformers and literary figures. Channing died in Bennington, Vermont, on October 2, 1842.

CHARLES RIVER BRIDGE V. WARREN BRIDGE CASE (1837). A major Supreme Court decision on contracts. The Massachusetts legislature chartered the Charles River Bridge Company (1785) to connect **Boston** and Charlestown by a toll bridge. When the state chartered a rival free bridge by the Warren Bridge Company (1828), the Charles River Bridge Company sued for breach of contract. In the new economic and democratic spirit of the Jacksonian era, Chief Justice Roger Taney ruled in favor of the new free bridge, arguing that monopolies damaged the public interest. This important case stimulated economic expansion in transportation.

CHARTER OAK. A white oak tree (*Quercus alba*) in **Hartford**, Connecticut, in which Captain Joseph Wadsworth hid the colony's royal charter granted (1662) by King Charles II to **John Winthrop, Jr.** When Sir **Edmund Andros** arrived with an armed force to demand that the General Court surrender the document, the Charter was concealed in the tree (1687). The Charter Oak became a symbol of New England's love of freedom until the ancient tree fell in a storm on August 21, 1856.

CHASE, MARY ELLEN (1887–1973). Writer. Born in Blue Hill, Maine, on February 24, 1887, Chase graduated from the University of Maine (1909) and was a professor of English at Smith College (1926–55). She wrote short stories and novels about life on the Maine seacoast, including *Mary Peters* (1934), *Silas Crockett* (1935), and *Windswept* (1941). She died in Northampton, Massachusetts, on July 28, 1973.

CHASE, SALMON PORTLAND (1808–1873). Chief justice of the U.S. Supreme Court. Born in Cornish, New Hampshire, on January 13, 1808, Chase graduated from Dartmouth College (1826) and read law in Washington, D.C. Practicing in Cincinnati (1830–49), he was a prominent **abolitionist** in the Whig and Liberty parties and an organizer of the Free Soil Party (1848). Elected to the Senate as a Free Soil Democrat (1849–55), he joined the Republican Party (1854) and was elected governor of Ohio (1855–60) and to the Senate (1861). Chase was secretary of the treasury (1861–64) for President Abraham Lincoln, who appointed him chief justice of the Supreme Court (1864–73). Chase presided over the impeachment trail of President Andrew Johnson (1868) and served on the Supreme Court until his death in New York City on May 7, 1873.

CHECKLEY, JOHN (1680–1754). Clergyman. Born in **Boston** in 1680, Checkley studied at **Boston Latin School** and Oxford University. Returning to Boston (1710), he opened a bookstore and apothecary, engaging in newspaper and pamphlet disputes over **Congregational** bias against the Anglicans at **King's Chapel**. Ordained an Anglican priest in England, Checkley was sent to **Providence**, Rhode Island (1738–48), where he converted **Native Americans** and promoted the high church movement in New England. He continued to challenge the **Puritan** hegemony until he died in Providence on February 15, 1754.

CHEEVER, JOHN (1912–1982). Writer. Born in Quincy, Massachusetts, on May 27, 1912, Cheever wrote more than 100 short stories and novels, many for the *New Yorker* chronicling the life and times of the upper-middle-class Connecticut **Yankee** suburbs. He won the National Book Award for *The Wapshot Chronicle* (1957), the story of the eccentric members of an old New England family, and won the Pulitzer Prize and the National Book Critics Circle Award for *The Stories of John Cheever* (1978). Cheever died in Ossining, New York, on June 18, 1982.

CHEN, JOYCE (1917–1994). Restaurateur and chef. Born in Beijing, China, Liao-Jia-ai moved with her husband to Cambridge, Massachusetts, in 1949. Known as Joyce Chen, she opened a restaurant in Cambridge (1958) featuring northern-style Chinese food. Her unique restaurant attracted the attention of **Julia Child** and led to the *Joyce Chen Cookbook* (1962). Her influential **WGBH** television program, *Joyce Chen Cooks* (1966), gave witness that New Englanders were ready for more sophisticated cuisine. In 1971 she founded Joyce Chen

Products to manufacture Chinese kitchen utensils and food products. Mrs. Chen was a successful business leader and cultural liaison for the United States and China when she retired in 1986. She died in Cambridge on August 23, 1994.

CHEVERUS, JEAN LOUIS LEFEBVRE DE (1768–1836). Bishop. Born in France on January 28, 1768, Father Cheverus was assigned to **Boston** (1796) and was consecrated the first Roman **Catholic** bishop of Boston (1810–23). He built the first Cathedral of the Holy Cross on Franklin Street designed by **Charles Bullfinch** (1803), served missions for **Native Americans** in Maine, and cultivated prominent Protestant friends throughout New England. Bishop Cheverus transferred to France (1823) and was named archbishop of Bordeaux (1826) and a cardinal (1836) shortly before he died on July 19, 1836.

CHICKERING, JONAS (1798–1853). Businessman. Born in Mason Village, New Hampshire, on April 5, 1798, Chickering grew up in New Ipswich, where he learned music and apprenticed with a cabinetmaker. He worked for a **Boston** cabinetmaker (1818–19) and a piano maker (1819–23). By 1823 he and his partner manufactured pianos with technical improvements and imported mahogany and rosewood. Connecticut firms imported ivory from Africa for piano keys. Chickering pianos won honors at the Crystal Palace Exhibition in London (1851), and he became the most important manufacturer in the nation. After he died in his Boston factory on December 8, 1853, his three sons continued the business, winning honors at the Paris Exposition (1867), praise from leading composers and pianists, and recognition of Jonas Chickering as the father of American piano making.

CHILD, JULIA (1912–). Chef. Born in Pasadena, California, on August 15, 1912, Julia McWilliams graduated from Smith College (1934). After serving in World War II with the Office of Strategic Services in Ceylon and China, she married Paul Child and lived in Paris, where she studied at the Cordon Bleu Cooking School. With two French colleagues, she opened a cooking school and wrote *Mastering the Art of French Cooking* (1961).

When Child hosted (1963) a cooking show on **WGBH**, the PBS television station in **Boston**, *The French Chef* was an immediate success bringing continental cuisine to New England kitchens. She won an Emmy Award (1997) for *Baking with Julia* and joined Jacques Pepin (1999) for the series *Julia and Jacques Cooking at Home*. Mrs. Child received the Legion of Honor (2000) from the French government and made major contributions to American taste and culture before retiring from her Cambridge kitchen to California (2001). *See also* CHEN, JOYCE.

CHILD, LYDIA MARIA (1802–1880). Writer and reformer. Born on February 11, 1802, in a Medford, Massachusetts, **abolitionist** family, Lydia Maria Francis was educated by her brother, a professor at **Harvard** Divinity School. She studied with **Margaret Fuller** and wrote *Hobomok* (1824), describing colonial New England life and *The Rebels* (1825) on pre-Revolutionary **Boston**. Her best-selling books were *The Frugal Housewife* (1829) and *The Mother's Book* (1831). She founded the first magazine for children, *The Juvenile Miscellany* (1826), and married David Lee Child (1828). They devoted their efforts to **William Lloyd Garrison**'s abolitionist movement, and she and her husband edited the *National Anti-Slavery Standard* (1840–44), a weekly newspaper in New York City. They retired to a farm (1852) in Wayland, Massachusetts, still contributing to the abolitionist movement and influenced **William Ellery Channing, Charles Sumner**, and **Thomas Wentworth Higginson**. She wrote many books until her death in Wayland on October 20, 1880. *See also* SLAVERY.

CHINA TRADE. Began when the first New England ships sailed around Cape Horn to Asia (1784), exchanging iron tools for **furs** in Oregon and trading the furs in China for tea, silk, cotton, spices, opium, and porcelain. Major Samuel Shaw of **Boston** was the first consul general in China (1786). Federalist merchants like **Elias Hasket Derby** of **Salem** and **Thomas H. Perkins** of **Boston** accumulated enormous profits from this commerce and by 1816 in the **Opium trade** with the Dutch East Indies and China that capitalized the New England **textile** industry in the 1820s and **railroads** in the 1840s. In **Providence**, **John Brown** sent the *George Washington* to China (1787) when Rhode Island prohibited the slave trade. The China Trade made Salem the sixth largest city in the nation (1800), and wealthy merchants from the Derby, Prince, Forbes, and Crowninshield families built elegant Federal-style mansions in Salem and Boston. China Trade profits made Boston the **Athens of America**

and the **Hub of the Solar System** in the city's antebellum Augustan Age. Despite the economic depression due to the Embargo Act (1807) and the War of 1812, overseas shipping and the China Trade stimulated New England business and society. **Yankee** sea captains like **Robert Bennet Forbes**, whose Milton, Massachusetts, mansion became the China Trade Museum (1970–84), made fortunes selling opium to China and importing textiles, opium, coffee, tea, silk, and porcelain to Boston. The China Trade also stimulated westward expansion and made the United States a two-ocean nation.

CHINESE. First came to New England as a legacy of the influential **China Trade** and Yankee missionary activities in Asia and the Pacific Ocean. Although Congress excluded Chinese immigrants (1882–1943), Yung Wing (1828–1912) was the first Chinese to earn a degree from an American college. Brought to America by Samuel Robbins Brown, a New England missionary in China, he studied at Monson Academy in Massachusetts and graduated from Yale College (1854). At **Harvard**, Ko Kuen-Hau was the first Chinese faculty member (1879) at an American university.

The first Chinese residents in Massachusetts were a group brought from California as 235 strikebreakers at the C. T. Sampson Shoe Factory in North Adams (1872). They moved to **Boston**'s South Cove on Ping-On Alley (road of peace and security) near the South Station railroad center and numbered 1,200 by 1920. Because federal law excluded Chinese women, the first American Chinatowns were bachelor communities. Women composed only 2 percent of the 10,000 Chinese in the nation (1900), and the Boston census showed only 15 Chinese women in 1890. The Chinese population grew slowly in New England; Boston had 1,000 people when the Overseas Chinese School opened (1915). But the Chinese Directory of New England (1931) listed 94 Chinatown shops, as well as a Chinese monthly newspaper (1890) and the Boston Chinatown YMCA (1914). Ruby Foo (1904–50) opened the first Chinese restaurant in Boston (1929), and her exotic food attracted many sports and theatrical celebrities to Ruby Foo's Den on Hudson Street.

Connecticut had five Chinese students (1818) at the Foreign Mission School in Cornwall, and the Chinese government sent 120 Chinese to study science and technology in **Hartford** (1872–81). But secret Chinese organizations or tongs created much anxiety (1927) when rumors of gang war and revenge killing spread in Boston and Hartford. Two tong assassins, Chin Lung and See Hoo Wing, were convicted of the murder of a Chinese laundryman in Manchester, Connecticut, and hanged at the Connecticut State Prison (1927) amid an atmosphere of anti-Chinese prejudice.

Most Chinese in New England worked in the laundry, restaurant, and clothing industries until reform of **immigration** laws in 1943, 1952, and 1965 increased the Chinese population and resulted in greater economic and employment opportunities. After World War II, Asian American veterans brought their wives to America. The Boston Chinese had a Catholic mission operated by the Maryknoll Sisters (1946), an athletic club (1948), the Chinese Civic Association (1967), the Boys' Club (1970), and the Chinese Historical Society of New England (1992). Since 1970 many other immigrants from Asia, especially Korea, India, Japan, Cambodia, and Thailand, settled in New England cities, including more than 22,000 Vietnamese in Greater Boston by 2001. Prominent Chinese immigrants who found success in Boston include **Joyce Chen**, the architect I. M. Pei, who studied at MIT (1935), and the physicist, **An Wang**, who studied at Harvard (1945). By 1990 most New England cities had some residents of Chinese descent when 6.9 million Asian Americans numbered 3 percent of the U.S. population.

CHITTENDEN, THOMAS (1730–1797). Governor of Vermont. Born in East Guilford, Connecticut, on January 6, 1730, Chittenden served in the colonial legislature (1765–69) and as a militia colonel (1767–73). Moving to Williston, Vermont (1774), he drafted the declaration calling for statehood and the state constitution (1777) and was president of the **Committee of Safety** (1775–76). Elected the governor of the Republic of Vermont (1779), Chittenden was the state's first governor (1779–89, 1790–97) and held that office until his death in Williston on August 25, 1797. His son, General Martin Chittenden (1763–1840), served in the House of Representatives (1803–13) and was the last **Federalist Party** governor (1814–15) in Vermont.

CHOATE, RUFUS (1799–1859). Senator from Massachusetts. Born in Essex, Massachusetts, on October 1, 1799, Choate graduated from Dartmouth College (1819). He practiced law in Danvers and **Salem** and was a state legislator (1825–28) and an organizer of the Whig party. Choate served in the House of Representatives (1831–34) and in the Senate (1841–45). He retired to his prosperous law practice but served as the state attorney general (1853–54). Choate was the foremost orator of his day and leader of the **Boston** bar when he died in Nova Scotia on July 13, 1859.

CHURCH, FREDERICK EDWIN (1826–1900). Artist. Born in **Hartford** on May 4, 1826, Church studied **art** with Thomas Cole (1844–46) and painted in South America on an expedition with **Cyrus W. Field** (1853). A member of the Hudson River School, his panoramic paintings are noted for luminism, accuracy, and clarity of the scenery, especially *Niagara* (1857) and *Heart of the Andes* (1859). Church was forgotten when he died in Hudson, New York, on April 7, 1900.

CIVIL WAR. A national tragedy that had important ramifications in New England. The region had a long history as an anti-slavery center. Vermont was the first state to abolish slavery (1777), and Massachusetts courts declared slavery incompatible with the new state constitution (1783). **William Lloyd Garrison**, the leading **abolitionist** in the nation, was an influential **Boston** newspaper editor by 1831, and **Frederick Douglass**, a former slave and abolitionist lecturer, lived in **New Bedford** when he helped Governor **John A. Andrew** organize the **54th Massachusetts Infantry**. In fact, Andrew prepared the state for the Civil War before Fort Sumter fell and the 6th Massachusetts Regiment, the first troops sent to defend Washington, D.C., was attacked by a secessionist mob in Baltimore on April 19, 1861.

    Clara Barton, **Louisa May Alcott**, and **Dorothea Dix** volunteered to nurse wounded soldiers. Connecticut's **Gideon Welles** rebuilt the U.S. Navy and supported President Abraham Lincoln in the cabinet. **William Alfred Buckingham**, Connecticut's zealous wartime governor (1858–66), recruited 48,000 men for 54 state militia units. Rhode Island governor **William Sprague** fought at the battle of Bull Run (1861) while governor. Vermont called a special session of the legislature (1861) to prepare for war.

    Not all New Englanders were eager for the war; draft riots broke out in **Portsmouth**, New Hampshire, Rutland, Vermont, Kingfield, Maine, and Boston in 1863. **Cotton Whigs** in Boston's elite Somerset Club provoked Republican supporters of the Lincoln administration to form the rival **Union Club** in 1863. However, each New England state supported President Abraham Lincoln with soldiers and sailors and the foundries, factories, and mills produced arms, blankets, boots, uniforms, shoes, tents, and war materials of all types. Thaddeus S. C. Lowe (1823–1913), a New Hampshire inventor, directed the Union Army observation balloon corps during the war. **Winslow Homer**, an artist and war correspondent, established his reputation by his realistic painting *Prisoners from the Front* (1866).

New England also provided military leaders in the Civil War, including **Ambrose Burnside** (Rhode Island), **Joseph Hooker**, **Grenville M. Dodge**, **Benjamin Butler**, and **Nelson A. Miles** (Massachusetts), **Joshua Chamberlain**, **Oliver O. Howard**, and **Neal Dow** (Maine), **Alfred H. Terry** and **Edward W. Whitaker** (Connecticut), **Edward E. Cross** (New Hampshire), and **William Wells** (Vermont). New England provided more sailors for the Union Navy than any other region, more than 26,000 men. **Frederick Law Olmsted** directed the U.S. Sanitary Commission to support soldiers and New England women in every town and city organized committees to produce bandages, blankets, and small comforts for the soldiers.

Many women and children found new jobs in war production replacing men in uniform, especially at the federal arsenals in Watertown and Springfield, Massachusetts. But wartime inflation and loss of income from fathers, husbands, and sons increased poverty, only partly remedied by expanded state and local poor relief payments for the families of soldiers and sailors. The absence of men was also reflected in the higher incidence of delinquency and crime on the New England homefront. By 1864 the **New England Home for Little Wanderers** and the Home for Destitute Catholic Children opened in Boston to protect Civil War orphans.

The **20th Maine Infantry** played a key role in the battle of Gettysburg, and Captain John Lonegan of the 13th Vermont Regiment won the Medal of Honor at that bloody battle (1863). But the South carried the war to New England when Vermont was invaded by Confederate troops in the **St. Albans Raid** (1864), and Confederate soldiers made unsuccessful raids on **Portland** (1863) and Calais, Maine (1864). Confederate sailors disguised as passengers seized the steamer *Chesapeake* off **Cape Cod** in 1863. The ship, en route to Portland from New York City, was taken to Nova Scotia.

President Abraham Lincoln demonstrated his gentle heart in the war when he pardoned Private William Scott of Vermont from a court martial sentence of death by firing squad for sleeping on sentinel in 1861. Lincoln wrote the sympathetic **Bixby Letter** to a Boston mother in 1864. Fort Warren on George's Island in Boston Harbor was a prison for more than 1,000 Confederate soldiers. A legend claims that the Lady in Black still walks the fort's dark corridors. She is the ghost of a rebel prisoner's wife who was hanged for aiding in his escape.

Soldiers marched to war singing songs by Julia Ward Howe (*The Battle Hymn of the Republic*) and Patrick S. Gilmore (*When Johnny*

Comes Marching Home). Boston commemorated the Civil War heroes and victims with two monuments on Boston Common, the *Soldiers and Sailors Monument* (1877) by Martin Milmore and the *Shaw Memorial* by Augustus Saint-Gaudens (1890). The pair of marble lions in the Boston Public Library sculpted by Louis Saint-Gaudens also honors the Civil War dead. Daniel Chester French sculpted *Mourning Victory* (1908) at the Sleepy Hollow Cemetery in Concord, Massachusetts, and Stephen O'Kelly designed the *Soldiers and Sailors Monument* in Nashua, New Hampshire. Theo Kitson designed the *Massachusetts State Memorial* at the Vicksburg National Military Park (1903). Civil War statues and monuments are found throughout the region on town commons and city parks. Patrick S. Gilmore celebrated the victory with his mammoth National Peace Jubilee and Music Festival in Boston in 1869. Harvard University built Memorial Hall (1878) in honor of its alumni who died in the war.

During the postwar Reconstruction era (1865–77), Massachusetts senator Charles Sumner, a leader of the Radical Republicans, played a key role in asserting the power of Congress and his party after the death of Lincoln. Massachusetts congressman Benjamin Butler led the impeachment proceedings against President Andrew Johnson, although Maine senators William Pitt Fessenden and James G. Blaine had more moderate views. Vermont senator George F. Edmunds chaired the impeachment committee. Civil War veterans joined the Grand Army of the Republic (GAR) to march in victory parades in Boston and other New England cities. The dominant role of the Republican Party in New England (1860–1940) owed much to bitter feelings engendered by the Civil War.

CLAMBAKE. A seafood picnic in New England, a summer event the English settlers learned from **Native Americans** who dug clams for thousands of years as a valuable food source. Some tribes traveled to particular **beaches** each summer to dig in the clam beds. Ancient shell heaps or middens composed of soft-shell clams (*Mya arenarina*) or quahogs (*Mercenaria mercenaria*) are found on many New England shores, often near wild **blueberry** fields. The **Wampanoag** clambakes used a pit in the beach sand lined with stones heated by a slow wood fire. Clams, crabs, mussels, **lobster**, fish, and **corn** covered by seaweed baked slowly. Many of the 12,000 Atlantic coast mollusk species, including **quahog** and cherrystone (or littleneck) hard-shell clams, are edible. Soft-shell clams, also known as the longneck clam or steamer, are easily dug on New England beaches and used in broth and **New England clam chowder**. Fried clams have been a New England dish since the 1850s but were popularized (1914) by restaurateur Lawrence H. Woodman (1892–1976) in Essex, Massachusetts, and by **Howard Johnson** restaurants.

CLARKE, JOHN (1609–1676). Clergyman. Born in England in 1609, Clarke emigrated to **Boston** (1637) and supported **Anne Hutchinson** in the **Antinomian** controversy. He and **William Coddington** founded Portsmouth (1638) and **Newport** in Rhode Island (1639). Clarke was the Baptist pastor in Newport, and allied with **Roger Williams** against Coddington to unite the colonies as Rhode Island (1647). He obtained the royal charter from King Charles II in England (1663) that named the colony Rhode Island and Providence Plantations and remained the state's basic law until 1843. Clarke served in the general assembly (1664–69) and as deputy governor. He wrote *Ill News from New England* (1652) criticizing Massachusetts **Puritan** hostility to religious freedom.

CLARKE, WALTER (1638–1714). Governor of Rhode Island. Born in **Newport** in 1638, Clarke was deputy governor (1679–86, 1700–14) and Rhode Island governor three times (1676–77, 1686, 1696–98). He is best remembered for his refusal to surrender the colony's charter to **Sir Edmund Andros** (1686). Clarke died in Newport on May 23, 1714.

CLIFFORD, NATHAN (1803–1881). Associate justice of the U.S. Supreme Court. Born in Rumney, New Hampshire, on August 18, 1803, Clifford studied law in New York and practiced law in Newfield, Maine (1824–34). Elected as a Democrat to the state legislature (1830–34), he was state attorney general (1834–38) and served in the House of Representatives (1839–43). Clifford was attorney general (1846–48) and U.S. minister to Mexico (1848–49). He served as an associate justice of the Supreme Court (1858–81) until he died in Cornish, Maine, on July 25, 1881.

CLIPPER SHIPS. Long and fast sailing vessels built in New England for the **China Trade**. The Gold Rush (1849) led **Donald McKay** to build some of the most famous clipper ships in East **Boston** to carry prospectors and supplies to California. His *Flying Cloud* (1851) set a record sailing from New York City to San Francisco in 89 days and *James Baines* made a record voyage of 12 days from Boston to Liverpool and set the around-the-world record of 134 days.

Maine **shipyards** built many clippers (1850–54) until the economic depression of 1857 undermined the shipbuilders. These elegant ships, known as greyhounds of the ocean waves, were also built in Stonington and Essex, Connecticut, to carry silk, pepper, porcelain, coffee, and tea from Asia to Europe and **molasses**, **rum**, salt, iron, spices, **textiles**, and wine from New England ports around the world until the 1880s. The clipper ship era ended when the Suez Canal opened (1869) and steam ships dominated ocean transportation. Donald McKay sold his shipyard (1869), and the clipper ship era ended when a fire destroyed many of the East Boston piers (1870). The railroad, steamships, and the larger wind-jammers replaced the graceful clipper ships.

COCOANUT GROVE FIRE. Disaster on November 28, 1942, at an overcrowded nightclub on Piedmont Street in **Boston**'s Bay Village. The fire at the Cocoanut Grove killed 492 people. As a result Boston and many other cities established stricter fire codes and safety regulations concerning audience size, flammable interiors, revolving doors, building exits, and smoking in public places.

CODDINGTON, WILLIAM (1601–1678). Governor of Rhode Island. Born in England on February 4, 1601, Coddington migrated to **Boston** (1630) and was an early **Puritan** leader. His support for **Anne Hutchinson** in the **Antinomian** controversy led him to found Portsmouth in Rhode Island (1638) with **John Clarke** (1609–76). Coddington founded **Newport** (1639) and was elected governor of the Newport colony (1640–44, 1651–52) until his rival, **Roger Williams**, united all the towns with his Providence colony. Coddington resisted Williams's government, moved to Boston (1656) where he became a **Quaker** (1666), returned to Newport, and served as governor of Rhode Island (1674–75, 1678). Coddington died there on November 1, 1678.

CODFISH. Official Massachusetts state fish (1974). The *Sacred Cod* since 1784 hangs from the ceiling of the House of Representatives chamber in the State House. No single food has had more influence on New England's economic and political history. Codfish (*Gadus morhua*) fed the **Native Americans**, the **Viking** explorers, and European fishermen who brought dried cod to Europe long before the **Pilgrims** and **Puritans** arrived. Dried and salted cod was the region's principal export before the **Civil War**. Until 1870, Wellfleet and Gloucester were the chief codfish ports. Until cod stocks were depleted by overfishing in the 1970s, Massachusetts and Maine cod harvests were the highest in the nation due to increased mechanization and freezing techniques in the trawler fleet. Gloucester boats landed 32 million pounds in 1920 but only 5 million in 2000. By 2001, sportsmen on 610 Massachusetts recreational charter boats caught one-third of the cod taken in the **Gulf of Maine**, the waters from **Cape Cod** to Nova Scotia. Atlantic cod prepared in strips for cooking is known as **scrod** or served as fishcakes. Cod is a traditional New English dish, and **Boston** is known as the "home of the bean and the cod." **Clarence Birdseye**, the inventor of frozen food, established the fish stick industry in Gloucester (1925) and created new markets for the cod. *See also* BAKED BEANS; FISHING.

CODFISH ARISTOCRACY. Wealthy New Englanders whose fortunes came from **fishing** and the **West Indies trade** in the colonial era. Many of the elegant Federal-style mansions on Chestnut Street in **Salem**, Massachusetts, were built by **Samuel McIntire** for **Elias Hasket Derby** and members of the Crowninshield, Pingree, and Pierce and Nichols families, who were dubbed the codfish aristocrats.

COERCIVE ACTS (1774). Four British laws designed to punish **Boston** after the **Boston Tea Party** (1773). The Parliamentary acts were the Boston Port Bill closing the port and moving the customs house to Salem; the Administration of Justice Act providing trial in England for royal colonial officials; the Massachusetts Government Act making the colonial council and judiciary appointive and authorizing the governor to limit town meetings to one per year and to control their agendas; and the Quartering Act, which billeted troops in private homes. These harsh laws angered many Americans, who called them the **Intolerable Acts**, and led to the First Continental Congress (1774) where Dr. **Joseph Warren** wrote the **Suffolk Resolves**, declaring the Coercive Acts void. *See also* AMERICAN REVOLUTION.

COFFIN SHIPS. Overcrowded vessels carrying **immigrants** from the potato famine in Ireland (1845–50). The inhumane conditions and large number of fatalities from disease and malnutrition led Americans to label them coffin ships, like the British ship *Nestoria* that landed 630 sick and dying paupers from Galway in **Boston** on April 15, 1847. Deer Island in Boston harbor was a quarantine hospital for 4,800 **Irish** immigrants in 1847–49 and a cemetery for 800 victims of ship fever. **Herman Melville** described his voyage as a seaman on a coffin ship in his novel *Redburn*

(1849), and the *St. John*, a Boston-bound brig carrying Irish emigrants, sank off Cohasset (1849), as did 60 emigrant ships in 1847–53. Those who survived the voyage placed burdens on New England charitable institutions, leading to nativism and **anti-Catholicism**, but they also contributed important labor and skills to the region.

COHEN, WILLIAM S. (1940–). Senator from Maine. Born in Bangor on August 28, 1940, William Sebastian Cohen graduated from Bowdoin College (1962) and Boston University Law School (1965). Practicing law in Bangor (1965–68), he was a district attorney (1968–70) and mayor (1971–72). Elected as a Republican to the House of Representatives (1973–79) and the Senate (1979–97), Cohen was secretary of defense for President William Clinton (1997–2001). He wrote *Roll Call: One Year in the United States Senate* (1981) and *Men of Zeal: A Candid Inside Story of Iran-Contra Hearings* (1988) with Senator **Edmund S. Muskie**.

COLLAMER, JACOB (1791–1865). Senator from Vermont. Born in Troy, New York, on January 8, 1791, Collamer graduated from the University of Vermont (1810). He practiced law in Woodstock, Vermont, and served in the state legislature (1821–22, 1827–28) and as a superior court judge (1833–42). Collamer was a Whig in the House of Representatives (1843–49) and postmaster general (1849–50) for President Zachary Taylor. Elected as a Republican to the Senate (1855–65), Collamer was a close adviser of President Abraham Lincoln. He died in Woodstock on November 9, 1865.

COLLINS, PATRICK A. (1844–1905). Mayor of **Boston**. Born in County Cork, Ireland, on March 12, 1844, Patrick Andrew Collins came to Boston as a child (1848), graduated from **Harvard** Law School (1871), and was a lawyer in Boston (1871–83). Elected as a Democrat to the state legislature (1868–71) and to the House of Representatives (1883–89), Collins was the leading **Irish Catholic** in New England when he served as consul general in London (1893–97) and as mayor of Boston (1902–05). The self-made Irish Catholic leader was a supporter of Irish self-government when he died in Virginia on September 13, 1905. A bronze bust of Collins, designed by Henry and **Theo Kitson** (1908), is on the **Back Bay** mall.

COLONIAL REVIVAL (1880–1940). An antiquarian movement in **art** and **architecture** inspired by a respect for early American styles, first in

New England and soon across the nation. **Henry Wadsworth Longfellow** inspired the trend, and **Wallace Nutting** was influential in New England historic preservation. *See also* EARLE, ALICE MORSE; OLD HOME WEEK; SOCIETY FOR THE PRESERVATION OF NEW ENGLAND ANTIQUITIES.

COLT, SAMUEL (1814–1862). Inventor. Born in **Hartford**, Connecticut, on July 19, 1814, Colt worked in his father's **textile** factory in Ware, Massachusetts, and went to sea (1830). He patented a revolving-breech pistol (1836) and manufactured the revolvers on an assembly line with interchangeable parts. This company failed (1842), but the Mexican War created a demand for weapons by the Colt Patent Fire-Arms Company in Hartford. When Colt died in Hartford on January 10, 1862, the Colt revolver had played a key role in warfare and taming the frontier and created a New England firearms industry that continues today. His widow, Elizabeth Colt, donated her extensive art collection in his memory (1902) to the **Wadsworth Atheneum** in Hartford.

COMMITTEES OF CORRESPONDENCE. Political group organized (1764) at the **Boston** town meeting protesting British abrogation of colonial rights. They were intended to communicate Boston's views to other Massachusetts communities, but **Samuel Adams** (1772) reorganized the group with **James Otis** and **Joseph Warren**. Ten colonies followed this example leading to the first Continental Congress (1774) in Philadelphia. The **committees of safety** replaced these groups in most states (1775). *See also* AMERICAN REVOLUTION.

COMMITTEES OF SAFETY. Provided colonial government during the Revolutionary War after royal government was overthrown. They were most active in New Hampshire and Connecticut even after state governments were operating. **John Hancock** led the Massachusetts Committee of Safety (1774) to procure soldiers and weapons for the Continental Army. In 1775 **Elbridge Gerry** fled from a meeting of the Committee of Safety at the Black Horse **tavern** in Menotomy (or Arlington) when British troops returned from the **Battle of Concord**. The Second Continental Congress on July 18, 1775, recommended new committees of safety to replace the **committees of correspondence**. *See also* AMERICAN REVOLUTION.

COMMON SCHOOLS. Colonial era **pubic schools** in Massachusetts and Connecticut and gradually throughout New England. The Massachusetts legislatures required each town to maintain a free public elementary school (1642) and a Latin grammar school in towns with 50 families (1647). New Hampshire established common schools in 1649 intended to create literate people who could read the laws and the Bible. *See also* EDUCATION.

COMMONWEALTH v. HUNT. The first American court decision (1842) that workers could organize a union. Massachusetts Supreme Court Chief Justice **Lemuel Shaw** ruled the **Boston** Journeymen Bootmakers' Society strike was not an illegal conspiracy in restraint of trade, setting an important precedent for labor unions.

COMPUTERS. An important part of the New England electronics industry since **Howard H. Aiken** at **Harvard University** built the Mark I (1944), the world's first program controller calculator. At MIT, **Vannevar Bush** invented the differential analyzer (1930), an analog computer and founded the Raytheon Company (1922). His MIT colleague Jay Wright Forrester founded the Digital Computer Laboratory (1945), where he invented magnetic core memory and at the MIT **Lincoln Laboratory** (1952–56) Forrester adapted computers for military defense.

The International Business Machine (IBM) plant in Essex Junction, Vermont (1957), was an important step in diversifying New England's computer industry and is Vermont's biggest private employer. This business and academic inventors stimulated the computer, electronics, and high technology firms in Cambridge and along **Route 128** and Interstate 495 west of **Boston**. In 1951 **An Wang** founded Wang Laboratories in **Lowell**, making major contributions to practical use of business and laboratory computers. Digital Equipment Corporation, a small start-up company in a former woolen factory in Maynard, Massachusetts (1957), produced the first commercially successful minicomputer (1965) and (after IBM) became the largest computer manufacturer in the world with 121,500 employees (1988). The EMC Corporation (1979) in Newton and Data General Corporation (1968) in Westboro refined the minicomputer for office and home users. IBM Corporation computer chip manufacturing in Essex Junction also created a computer industry in Vermont. *See also* ECONOMY; YANKEE INGENUITY.

COMSTOCK, ANTHONY (1844–1915). Reformer. Born in New Canaan, Connecticut, on March 7, 1844, Comstock served in the **Civil**

War (1863–65). While working for the YMCA (1872) in New York City, he began his lifetime crusade against pornography. Comstock lobbied Congress to ban obscene material from the mail and founded the New York Society for the Suppression of Vice to prosecute writers, artists, abortionists, and anyone who violated his puritanical views. The Comstock Laws (1873) were a moral crusade that inspired the **Watch and Ward Society** in **Boston** before he died in New York City on September 21, 1915.

CONANT, JAMES BRYANT (1893–1978). Educator. Born in Dorchester, Maine, on March 26, 1893, Conant graduated from **Harvard University** (1913) and earned his Ph.D. in chemistry there (1916). He served in World War I and taught chemistry at Harvard (1919–33). Conant was the Harvard University president (1933–53) before serving as U.S. high commissioner (1953–55) and ambassador (1955–57) to West Germany. He wrote several books on science and studied American secondary **education** with Carnegie Foundation support. His influential books include *Slums and Suburbs* (1961) and *The Comprehensive High School* (1967), advocating reforms in teacher training, vocational guidance, decentralized control of schools, and increased funds for urban high schools. Conant died in Hanover, New Hampshire, on February 11, 1978.

CONANT, ROGER (1592–1679). Founder of **Salem**. Born in England in 1592, Conant immigrated to **Plymouth Colony** in Massachusetts (1623) with his wife and children and settled in Nantasket (1624). The Dorchester Company appointed him governor (1625) of their fishing settlement on **Cape Ann**, but the small colony failed so he relocated to Naumkeag, later called Salem (1626). When **John Endecott** arrived to found the town of Salem (1628), Conant and his West Country old settlers joined these **Puritans** under a New England Company patent. Conant was selectman, judge, and representative to the general court for Salem and founded a new town called Beverly (1668), where he died on November 19, 1679. Artist Henry Hudson Kitson designed a heroic bronze statue of Conant (1911) in Salem.

CONCORD. The capital of New Hampshire since 1808. The city is located on the **Merrimack River** in south central New Hampshire. Founded (1659) by English colonists, it was incorporated as Rumford, Massachusetts (1733), but after a boundary dispute (1741) with Massachusetts was settled (1762), the town was renamed Concord, New Hampshire (1765). Today the city (incorporated in 1853) has a population of 36,000 employed in **textiles**, leather, **insurance**, and granite industries as well as government and **tourism** services.

CONCORD STAGE COACH. A 9-passenger, 4- or 6-horse stage coach made in **Concord**, New Hampshire (1827–1919), by Lewis Downing and J. Stephen Abbot. This was the model for the Overland Stage carrying mail, passengers, and cargo from Missouri to California (1858–69) and also used in Australia and Africa. **Henry Wells** used 150 Concord stage coaches for his Wells, Fargo Company. Stage coach lines operated throughout New England, the first route went from **Boston** to New York (1772) and local lines, like the Brighton to Boston route (1826), were used until replaced by the omnibus and railroads. Captain Levi Pease, the New England stage coach king, founded many of the stage lines using the **Boston Post Road** from 1783 to 1824. By 1826, 58 firms sent 2,000 stages each week from **Scollay Square** in Boston. Stage coaches used many **taverns** and inns as depots or stations, such as the tavern in Kent Corners, Vermont (1837–46), on the **Montpelier** to Montreal route. The stage brought the first **tourists** through the **White Mountains** (1830). Scheduled stage coaches drove from Boston to **Concord**, New Hampshire, twice a week in 1803, a four-hour journey. Biweekly stage service between **Augusta** and Brunswick, Maine, began in 1806 and similar public transportation routes served New England until **railroads** appeared in the 1840s. **Eastman Johnson** captured the declining tradition in his painting *The Old Stage Coach* (1871). The sturdy and handsome Concord stage coach is still the trademark of the Wells Fargo Company.

CONCORD GRAPE. Fruit *(Vitis labrusca)* developed in **Concord**, Massachusetts, by Ephraim Wales Bull (1806–95) after years of cultivation of seedlings. Bull's Concord grape (1849), whose sweet, rich flavor and appearance made them popular as table grapes and grape jelly or jam, was the basis of the processed fruit juice industry by 1869. Secretary of State William Jennings Bryan startled the diplomatic corps by substituting grape juice for wine at formal receptions and Secretary of the Navy Josephus Daniels substituted grape juice (1913) for alcoholic beverages aboard U.S. Navy ships. Today, Concord grapes are grown by the Welch Company, a Concord corporation. Bull earned no profits from his grapes and his tombstone in Concord's **Sleepy Hollow Cemetery** bears the epitaph, "He sowed, others reaped."

CONGREGATIONALISTS. The largest and most influential denomination in America until 1800, derived from the **Puritans** in England. They had a more democratic form of church organization based on autonomous congregations without bishops or Presbyterian government. **John Cotton** in Boston, **Thomas Hooker** in **Hartford**, and **John Davenport** in **New Haven** were the early leaders. In a sense the **Pilgrims** or Separatists established this religious body at Plymouth (1620), and in the 1630s the Puritans in Massachusetts and Connecticut expanded the church to cooperate with the civil government in each New England colony except Rhode Island. This theocratic system ended (1690) when Britain forced the New Englanders to tolerate other denominations. The **Great Awakening** (1740–50) revived New England Congregationalism, adding many new members. But the revival led to doctrinal disagreements that contributed to the rise of other denominations (Presbyterianism and **Unitarianism**) so that the Congregationalists became a small and divided religious body. Massachusetts ended state support of the Congregational church in 1833. One contribution from the Congregationalist emphasis on a well-educated clergy was the founding of colleges such as **Harvard**, Yale, Williams, and Amherst. By 1999 Congregationalists numbered about 2 percent of New Englanders.

CONIGLIARO, TONY (1945–1990). Athlete. Born in Lynn, Massachusetts, on January 7, 1945, Anthony Conigliaro played for the **Boston Red Sox** team that won the American League championship (1967). Tony C hit 24 home runs as a rookie (1964) and was the youngest player in baseball to lead the league in home runs (32) in 1965. His career ended when he was hit by a pitch (1967), and he died in **Boston** on February 24, 1990.

CONNECTICUT COLONY. *See* NEW HAVEN COLONY.

CONNECTICUT COMPROMISE. Proposition by **Oliver Ellsworth** of Connecticut at the Constitutional Convention (1787) to solve the dispute between large and small states over representation in Congress. He suggested basing the number of representatives in the House on state population with equal representation in the Senate. This broke the deadlock and was an impetus for further compromise to complete the new Constitution.

CONNECTICUT HISTORICAL SOCIETY. Founded in **Hartford** (1825) as a nonprofit library and museum to collect, preserve, and interpret the history of the state. Reorganized by **Henry Barnard** (1844), it is the seventh oldest historical society in the nation with a diverse collection of books, prints, photographs, furniture, **art**, and artifacts. The society has the largest collection of colonial **tavern** and inn signs and offers an extensive educational program.

CONNECTICUT RIVER. Longest river (407 mi, 655 km) in New England, beginning in the Connecticut Lakes in northern New Hampshire and flowing south between New Hampshire and Vermont, across western Massachusetts and Connecticut to Long Island Sound. **Adriaen Block** was the first European to explore the river (1614), which is tidal and navigable below **Hartford**. Its valley is the region's most fertile agricultural land. Many dams provided waterpower in the 18th and 19th centuries and electricity and flood controls now. By 1900 deforestation, stream blockage, pollution of the air and water, and decline of **agriculture** accompanied the area's growth of commerce and manufacturing, prompting some early conservation reforms. *See also* MOHAWK TRAIL; RIVER GODS.

CONNOR, ROGER (1857–1931). Athlete. Born in **Waterbury**, Connecticut, on July 1, 1857, Connor played first base for the Troy Haymakers (1880–82), the New York Giants (1883–94), and the St. Louis Browns (1894–97). He was major league baseball's home run champion (132 home runs) from 1895 to 1921 when Babe Ruth surpassed him. Elected to the Baseball Hall of Fame (1976), Connor died in Waterbury on January 4, 1931. Waterbury **sports** fans located his unmarked grave in 2001.

CONSCIENCE WHIGS. Antebellum New Englanders who supported the **abolitionist** movement although it destroyed the Whig Party and heightened sectionalism. They allied with the Free Soil Party and antislavery Democrats to elect **Charles Sumner** to the U.S. Senate from Massachusetts (1851). *See also* CIVIL WAR; COTTON WHIGS.

USS *CONSTITUTION.* A 44-gun frigate built by George Claghorn in **Boston** (1797) is the oldest ship in the U.S. Navy. **Old Ironsides** served with distinction in the Tripoli War and the War of 1812. When the ship was to be scrapped, **Oliver Wendell Holmes**'s poem *Old Ironsides* (1830) aroused a public subscription that preserved the ship as a historic site. Visitors tour the ship today at the **Boston National Historical Park**.

CONSTITUTION STATE. The official name for Connecticut. It was adopted by the legislature (1959) to reflect the claim that Connecticut's **Fundamental Orders** (1638) was the first written constitution in the world.

CONTE, SILVIO (1921–1991). Congressman from Massachusetts. Born in Pittsfield, Massachusetts, on November 9, 1921, Conte served in the U.S. Navy (1942–44) and graduated from Boston College Law School (1949). He practiced in Pittsfield (1949–59) and was a Republican in the state legislature (1951–58) and in the House of Representatives (1959–91). Conte died in Bethesda, Maryland, on February 8, 1991.

CONWAY, KATHERINE E. (1853–1927). Editor and poet. Born in Rochester, New York, in 1853, Katherine Eleanor Conway was a journalist in New York City when she became a reporter for the *Boston Pilot* (1883) and the newspaper's first female editor (1904–08). She published a novel, *The Way of the World* (1900), poetry, and biographies and later edited *The Republic*, a **Boston** political weekly.

COOLIDGE, CALVIN (1872–1933). President of the United States. Born in Plymouth Notch, Vermont, on July 4, 1872, John Calvin Coolidge graduated from Amherst College (1895). He practiced law in Northampton, Massachusetts (1897–1919) where he was mayor (1910–11), a Republican state legislator (1907–08, 1912–15), lieutenant governor (1916–18), and governor (1919–21). His firm control during the **Boston Police Strike** (1919) brought him national attention and election as vice-president (1921–23). When President Warren G. Harding died, Coolidge succeeded him (1923–29). As president, "Silent Cal," as the press dubbed him for his taciturn **Yankee** ways, was conservative, and he ignored economic problems. But he manipulated the media skillfully, resolved the Harding era scandals, and managed the party machinery to win the 1924 presidential nomination and the election. He was efficient and popular in an era of prosperity when he retired to Northampton (1929). Coolidge wrote his *Autobiography* (1931) and syndicated newspaper articles. He died in Northampton on January 5, 1933.

COOLIDGE, GRACE (1879–1957). First lady of the United States. Born in Burlington, Vermont, on January 3, 1879, Grace Anna Goodhue graduated from the University of Vermont (1902). Working with deaf children in Northampton, Massachusetts, she married **Calvin Coolidge** (1905). As first lady (1923–29), she brought glamour and social grace to the White House and was noted for her personal advocacy for private charities and avid support of the **Boston Red Sox**. She introduced the first radio to the White House. Grace Coolidge died in Northampton on July 8, 1957.

COPLEY, JOHN SINGLETON (1738–1815). Artist. Born in **Boston** on July 3, 1738, in a **Loyalist** Irish family, Copley learned art in his step-father's engraving shop. Influenced by **John Smibert**, he painted portraits of leading citizens **John Hancock** (1765), **Paul Revere** (1768), and **Samuel Adams**. In London (1775–1815), he established his reputation with passionate biblical and historical canvases and portraits of American visitors (**John Adams** and **John Quincy Adams**). Copley, a member of the Royal Academy (1779), was recognized as the first great American painter. He died in London on September 9, 1815, but critical acclaim for his **art** did not come in the United States until the 20th century.

COPLEY SOCIETY. The oldest **art** association in the nation founded as the Boston Art Students Association (1879) by the alumni of the Boston Museum of Art School. It became the Copley Society of Boston (1901), open to all artists and hosting regular exhibits at its Newbury Street center in the **Back Bay** art district in **Boston**.

CORCORAN, THOMAS G. (1900–1981). Public official. Born in Pawtucket, Rhode Island, on December 29, 1900, Thomas Gardiner Corcoran graduated from Brown University (1922) and **Harvard** Law School (1925). He was a protégé of **Felix Frankfurter** and a law clerk for Justice **Oliver Wendell Holmes, Jr.** (1927–29). After working as a New York City corporate lawyer (1927–32), Corcoran worked for President Herbert Hoover (1932–33) and joined President Franklin D. Roosevelt's "brain trust" (1933–40). Known in Washington as Tommy the Cork, he drafted much New Deal legislation including the Securities Act (1933) and the Fair Labor Standards Act (1938). In private practice in Washington (1941–81), Corcoran was an influential lawyer and lobbyist and a Democratic Party adviser who urged **John F. Kennedy** to accept Lyndon Johnson as a running mate (1960). Corcoran died in Washington, D.C., on December 6, 1981.

CORN. A native American plant, also known as maize (*Zea mays*), introduced to eastern North America by 1000 B.C., became the chief food for the indigenous peoples. Requiring heavy labor to clear and plant fields, corn was grown only by the more sedentary tribes who traded corn with others. **Micmacs** raided Maine to obtain corn by 1600. Beans planted with corn grew up the sturdy cornstalks. The **Pilgrims** learned about corn (1621) from the **Wampanoag** and depended on it for food, fodder, and trade as their principal cash crop. Corn became the basis of the American diet in many forms—corn meal, **hasty pudding**, mush, **Indian pudding**, bread, **jonny cake**, or popcorn—and distilled as whiskey (1660). Fed to animals, corn provided milk, butter, cheese, eggs, meat, lard, and soap. New Englanders traded corn meal to the West Indies as food for slaves on sugar plantations.

COTTON, JOHN (1585–1652). Clergyman. Born in England on December 4, 1585, Cotton was educated at Cambridge University and was a pastor in Lincolnshire (1612–32) until he fled to Massachusetts (1633) due to his **Puritanism**. In **Boston** he became a **Congregational** pastor (1633–52). A dominant leader, Cotton opposed **Anne Hutchinson** and **Roger Williams** and other heretics who deviated from the conservative civil and religious authority he advocated. His best-known book was a children's catechism, *Milk for Babes* (1646). Cotton died in Boston on December 23, 1652.

COTTON, NORRIS (1900–1989). Senator from New Hampshire. Born in Warren, New Hampshire, on May 11, 1900, Cotton graduated from Wesleyan University (1923) and studied at George Washington University Law School, practicing in Lebanon, New Hampshire (1928–47). He was a Republican state legislator (1923, 1943, 1945) and in the House of Representatives (1947–54) and the Senate (1954–74, 1975). Cotton died in Lebanon, New Hampshire, on February 24, 1989.

COTTON WHIGS. Conservative New England Whigs who feared economic problems caused by sectionalism and the abolition of **slavery** and supported conciliation of the South until the **Civil War**. Many were **textile** manufacturers like **Amos Lawrence** whose investment in the cotton industry was threatened by the abolitionists called **Conscience Whigs** by 1850.

COUNCIL FOR NEW ENGLAND. A joint-stock company chartered by the Crown (1620) to colonize New England. Led by **Sir Ferdinando Gorges** and a group of gentry rather than merchants, it proved less successful than the **Pilgrim** and **Puritan** colonies in Massachusetts.

COUSY, BOB (1928–). Basketball player. Born in New York City on August 9, 1928, Robert J. Cousy graduated from Holy Cross College (1950) and joined the **Boston Celtics** (1950–63). He led the Celtics to six championships (1957, 1959–63), was the National Basketball Association's (NBA) most valuable player (1957), and was elected to 10 All-NBA teams. He was elected to the Basketball Hall of Fame (1970) and selected one of the NBA's 50 Greatest Players (1996). Cousy was the Boston College coach (1963–69) and Cincinnati Royals coach (1969–74) and a Boston Celtics television announcer (1974–).

COVERED BRIDGE. Design to preserve the trusses and decking of rural New England bridges crossing a stream or river. Many towns funded a covered bridge by a lottery or special tax levy and hired local millwrights or barn builders as the craftsmen. Stone and hand-hewn timber was readily obtained in the area, and hundreds of covered bridges have survived for a century or more. They were built for farmers across the country from 1785 to 1900 with pine plank siding and a singled roof. The Connecticut architect **Ithiel Town** built over 50 bridges in New England using his patented Town lattice truss (1820). Iron tension rods were added in the 1840s for greater strength. Folklore dubbed them the "kissing bridge," and many are still used, admired, and photographed by tourists and residents today. Vermont uses more than 100 covered bridges, but only four are still found in Massachusetts.

CRAM, RALPH ADAMS (1863–1942). Architect. Born in Hampton Falls, New Hampshire, on December 16, 1863, Cram apprenticed in **Boston** and opened an architectural office in 1888. Influenced by **H. H. Richardson**, his Gothic Revival designs for churches, beginning with All Saints in Boston (1891), and Massachusetts campus buildings at Wheaton College, Mount Holyoke College, Wellesley College, and Williams College established his reputation. Some of his designs were classical or colonial, but Cram's medievalism pervaded his work, writing, and lectures as professor of **architecture** at MIT (1914–21) and as chairman of the Boston city planning board (1915–22). His books include *Church Building* (1901), *The Gothic Quest* (1907), *My Life in Architecture* (1936), and *The End of Democracy* (1937). Cram died in Boston on September 22, 1942.

CRANBERRY. A Dutch name for a creeping evergreen plant (*Vaccinium macrocarpon*) native to New England marsh land whose red fruit is used for jelly, sauce, and juice. The **Pequot** on **Cape Cod** mixed cranberries with venison to make pemmican, as a dye for clothing and as a medicine. First cultivated in Harwich bogs on Cape Cod (1816), it is now grown commercially in Massachusetts, Michigan, Wisconsin, Quebec, and Europe. New England annual sales of cranberry products peaked in 1976 with over 450 small growers producing 5 million barrels of fruit, but overproduction has plagued the cranberry industry in recent years. Ocean Spray Cranberries, Inc., in Lakeville, Massachusetts, is the largest cranberry growers cooperative, and Carver, Massachusetts, is known as the cranberry capital of the world.

CRANDALL, PRUDENCE (1803–1890). Educator. Born in Hopkinton, Rhode Island, on September 3, 1803, Prudence Crandall was a **Quaker** and a Garrisonian **abolitionist** who admitted **African-American** girls to her private school in Canterbury, Connecticut (1831–34). The townspeople opposed integration so bitterly that Crandall established a new school for black girls. When the legislature passed a law banning schools for nonresident blacks students, Crandall was arrested for defying this law. Her sensational trial, in which leading abolitionists supported her, revealed the ambiguous place free blacks occupied in antebellum New England. Crandall moved (1834) to Illinois and died in Kansas on January 28, 1890.

CRANE, WINTHROP MURRAY (1853–1920). Senator from Massachusetts. Born in Dalton, Massachusetts, on April 23, 1853, Crane was a member of the Crane **paper** manufacturing family founded in Dalton (1801). He was the Republican governor (1900–02) whose settlement of a **Boston** teamsters strike served as a model for President Theodore Roosevelt's negotiation of the national coal strike. President William Howard Taft called him the "most influential member" of the Senate (1904–13), although he never made a speech or a motion. Crane broke with his party in supporting the League of Nations and died in Dalton on October 2, 1920.

CROCKETT, JAMES (1915–1979). Horticulturist. Born in Haverhill, Massachusetts, on October 9, 1915, James Underwood Crockett studied horticulture at the University of Massachusetts and Texas A & M University. After World War II service in the U.S. Navy, he established a flower shop in Lexington, Massachusetts, and published a newsletter and books on gardening. Hosting the **WGBH** television program, *Crockett's Victory Garden* (1975–79), he became the best-known gardener in the country. Jim Crockett died in **Concord**, Massachusetts, on July 11, 1979.

CROSBY, CORNELIA T. (1854–1946). Born in Phillips, Maine, in the Rangeley Lakes district, Cornelia Thurza "Fly Rod" Crosby left her job in a bank to improve her health in the outdoors. As a reporter for Lewiston and Farmington newspapers, she described her experiences hunting and fishing and advocated licensing **Maine guides** and conservation laws. Her greatest contribution was in promoting sporting **camps** and recreation as Maine's most colorful outdoorswoman in the 1890s. She dubbed Maine the "Nation's Playground" and was the first licensed **Maine guide** in 1897.

CROSS, EDWARD EPHRAIM (1832–1863). Born in Lancaster, New Hampshire, on April 22, 1832, Cross trained as a printer in Lancaster and by 1850 was a journalist in Ohio and Arizona. He was active in the **Know Nothing Party** and served as newspaper correspondent in Washington, D.C. Returning to New Hampshire, he joined the Republican Party and organized the **5th New Hampshire Regiment** in **Concord** in 1861. After many engagements, Colonel Cross died at the battle of Gettysburg on July 2, 1863. He was given a hero's funeral in Lancaster.

CROSS, WILBUR LUCIUS (1862–1948). Governor of Connecticut. Born in Mansfield, Connecticut, on April 10, 1862, Cross graduated from Yale University (1885) where he earned a Ph.D. in English (1889). Cross was a Yale University professor and dean (1894–1930). In his retirement, he was the unlikely candidate promoted by Democratic Party boss **John M. Bailey** to overcome the dominant Republican Party under conservative boss **J. Henry Roraback**. Governor Cross (1931–39) set the state on a progressive path by ending child labor and Prohibition; building highways, prisons, schools, and hospitals; establishing old age pensions; and reforming the banking and public utilities systems. His bid for a fourth term failed in 1938 because of the unexpectedly large vote for **Jasper McLevy**, the Socialist mayor of Bridgeport. Cross wrote *Connecticut Yankee: An Autobiography* (1943) and died in **New Haven** on October 5, 1948.

CROWNINSHIELD, BENJAMIN WILLIAMS (1772–1851). Congressman from Massachusetts. Born in **Salem**, Massachusetts, on December 27, 1772, Crowninshield was a member of a prosperous Salem shipping family and the **codfish aristocracy**. A painting by folk artist George Ropes, Jr., *The Crowninshield Wharf* (1806), recalls the role this family played in Salem's **China Trade**. **Crowninshield** served in the state legislature (1811–13) and as secretary of the navy (1814–18). He was again a state legislator (1821) and a **Federalist** in Congress (1823–31). Crowninshield died in **Boston** on February 3, 1851.

CUFFE, PAUL (1759–1817). Merchant. Born in Cuttyhunk, Massachusetts, on January 17, 1759, Cuffe was the son of a former African slave and his **Wampanoag** wife. He was a seaman in 1775 and then studied mathematics and navigation with **Quakers** in Westport before making his fortune in **whaling** and as a merchant and shipowner. Cuffe joined the American Colonization Society and settled 38 **African Americans** in Sierra Leone (1811–16). Captain Cuffe filed a lawsuit for the right to vote in Massachusetts (1783) and died in Westport on September 9, 1817.

CUMMINGS, E. E. (1894–1962). Poet. Born in Cambridge, Massachusetts, on October 14, 1894, Edward Estlin Cummings graduated from **Harvard University** (1915) and earned an M.A. there in 1916. He was a volunteer ambulance driver in France in 1917 and went to a French military prison for censorship violations in letters home. This experience led to his first book, *The Enormous Room* (1922). After serving briefly in the U.S. Army (1918), he devoted himself to writing and painting, producing 11 volumes of poetry as well as plays, essays, and a journal. He is best remembered for his poems in a highly individual style, for experimenting with technique and typography, and for his satire of materialism. Cummings won many awards and honors before his death in North Conway, New Hampshire, on September 3, 1962. His work is collected in *Six Nonlectures* (1953) and *Complete Poems 1913–1962* (1972).

CURLEY, JAMES MICHAEL (1874–1958). Governor of Massachusetts. Born in **Boston** on November 20, 1874, in an **Irish Catholic immigrant**

family, Curley left school at age 14, becoming a salesman and active in the local Democratic political organization. Largely self-educated in the **Boston Public Library**, he was elected to the Boston Common Council (1900), the first of a lifetime of political offices. He served in the state legislature (1902–03), as a Boston alderman (1904–09), and a Boston city councilor (1910–11) and went to the House of Representatives (1912–14), resigning to take his seat as mayor of Boston (1914–18). Defeated for reelection in 1918, he was returned in 1922, defeated in 1926, and elected mayor again in 1930. By that time he had organized his statewide political machine appealing to a broad spectrum of ethnic and working-class voters.

Curley's eloquence, wit, and irreverence charmed voters, who elected him governor in 1934. He broke with most urban Democrats to endorse Franklin D. Roosevelt over Alfred Smith (1931) and campaigned nationally for FDR. Dissatisfied with President Roosevelt's offer of an ambassadorship, Curley broke with FDR (1933), but as governor (1934–36) he fashioned his own state New Deal program of extensive and expensive public works. Defeated for the Senate (1936) and for mayor (1938 and 1942), Curley was elected to the House (1942–46) and as mayor (1946–50). Convicted of mail fraud charges, Curley served six months in **Danbury** federal prison while mayor until paroled (1947) and pardoned (1950) by President Harry Truman.

Unsuccessful in his last campaigns for mayor (1950 and 1954), the "Mayor of the Poor" retired to write his memoirs, *I'd Do It Again* (1957). **Edwin O'Connor**'s best-selling novel, *The Last Hurrah* (1956), was based on Curley's career as was **John Ford**'s film (1958) by the same title. Although suspected of graft and corruption, James Michael Curley left a modest estate when he died in Boston on November 12, 1958. His colorful and controversial career overshadows his legacy as an innovative, resourceful, and generous urban political leader. Since 1988 his Jamaica Plain home has been a city facility, and twin statues of Curley by Lloyd Lillie were erected (1980) in a park behind Boston City Hall.

CURRIER, NATHANIEL (1813–1888). Artist. Born in Roxbury, Massachusetts, on March 27, 1813, Currier apprenticed with lithographers in **Boston**, Philadelphia, and New York City before establishing his own firm (1835), joined by his partner James Merritt Ives (1824–95) in 1857. Decorative and inexpensive hand-colored prints of 7,000 19th-century American scenes made Currier & Ives a household name when Currier retired (1880). Celebrating simple **Yankee** values and homely rural virtues, the Currier & Ives prints symbolized traditional New England images. When Currier died on November 20, 1888, in New York City, the prints and the posters he designed for **P. T. Barnum** were highly prized by collectors.

CURSE OF THE BAMBINO. A baseball legend contending that the **Boston Red Sox** have not won a World Series championship since the team owner sold Babe Ruth's contract (1920) to the archrival New York Yankees. The contract was purchased by a sports memorabilia collector (1993) for $99,000, one indication how seriously New England sports fans take this legend and the loss of the Bambino, the team's greatest player.

CURTIS, BENJAMIN ROBBINS (1809–1874). U.S. Supreme Court justice. Born in Watertown, Massachusetts, on November 4, 1809, Curtis graduated from **Harvard** College (1829) and Harvard Law School (1832). He practiced in Northfield (1831–34) and **Boston** (1834–51) and served in the state legislature (1849–51). Curtis served on the Supreme Court (1851–57) and is best recalled for his dissenting opinion in the *Dred Scott* case. He was chief counsel for President Andrew Johnson in the impeachment trial. Curtis died in **Boston** on September 15, 1874.

CURTIS, CYRUS H. K. (1850–1933). Editor and publisher. Born in **Portland**, Maine, on June 18, 1850, Curtis moved to **Boston** after the **Portland Fire** (1866) and sold advertising for newspapers. He founded the weekly *People's Ledger* (1872–79) and the *Philadelphia Tribune and Farmer* (1879–83) and then his first great success, the *Ladies Home Journal* (1883). Skillful advertising and unprecedented fees attracted readers and the best writers, with a million subscribers by 1883. He purchased the *Saturday Evening Post* (1897) and the *Country Gentleman* (1911). When Curtis died in Pennsylvania on June 7, 1933, he owned the largest magazine publishing company in the world.

CURTIS, GEORGE WILLIAM (1824–1892). Editor. Born in **Providence**, Rhode Island, on February 24, 1824, Curtis was influenced by **Ralph Waldo Emerson** and **Brook Farm**. After travels in Europe and the Middle East (1846–50), he was a writer and lecturer in **Boston** and a founder of the Republican Party (1854). He is best known as an editor of

Harper's Weekly (1863–92), a genteel advocate for abolitionism, women's rights, and civil service reform. He was chairman of the Civil Service Commission (1871–92) and died on August 31, 1892, at Staten Island, New York.

CUSHING, CALEB (1800–1879). Congressman from Massachusetts. Born in Salisbury, Massachusetts, on January 17, 1800, Cushing graduated from **Harvard** College (1817). He practiced law in Newburyport (1821–35) and served in the state legislature (1825, 1827, 1833–34, 1845–46, 1850) and as a Whig in the House of Representatives (1835–43). As the first U.S. minister to China (1843–45), he negotiated opening ports for the **China Trade**. Cushing served as a general in the war with Mexico (1846–47) and was mayor of Newburyport (1851–52) and associate justice of the state Supreme Court (1852–53). He managed the nomination of **Franklin Pierce** in 1852 and served as his U.S. attorney general (1853–57). After the **Civil War** Cushing was United States counsel in the Geneva Tribunal to settle the *Alabama* claims (1871–72) and was U.S. minister to Spain (1874–77). He died in Newburyport on January 2, 1879.

CUSHING, RICHARD J. (1895–1970). Bishop. Born in South **Boston** on August 24, 1895, Richard James Cushing was educated at Boston College and St. John's Seminary. Ordained a **Catholic** priest (1921), he served in Boston and was raised to bishop (1939). He became archbishop of Boston (1944–70) and was raised to cardinal (1958). Cushing founded the Society of Saint James (1958) for missionary work in Latin America and oversaw the rapid expansion of the archdiocese to postwar suburbs. He was familiar to radio and television audiences in New England and noted for his early ecumenical efforts when he died in Boston on November 2, 1970. A public park and bust by James Rosati (1981) on Cambridge Street in Boston honor Cardinal Cushing.

CUSHING, WILLIAM (1732–1810). U.S. Supreme Court justice. Born in Scituate, Massachusetts, on March 1, 1732, Cushing graduated from **Harvard** College (1751) and practiced law in Maine (1755–59). He was a probate judge (1759–64) and represented the **Kennebec Proprietors** in local land disputes until he succeeded his father as a superior court judge in Boston (1772–80). To the dismay of **Thomas Hutchinson**, Cushing sided with the patriot cause and supported the new state constitutions (1780). As the chief justice of the state supreme judicial court (1780–89), he presided over the **Worcester** trial that ended **slavery** (1783) and court sessions during **Shays's Rebellion**, which convinced citizens that stronger central government was needed. Cushing served on the U.S. Supreme Court (1789–1810) until his death in Scituate on September 13, 1810. *See also* WALKER, QUOCK.

CUSHMAN, CHARLOTTE SAUNDERS (1816–1876). Actor. Born in **Boston** on July 23, 1816, Miss Cushman studied music and joined a Boston opera company (1825). While singing in New Orleans, she studied dramatics and began her successful career on the stage in America (1836) and England (1845–46). By 1849, Cushman was the foremost transatlantic actress of the day and began a long series of farewell performances (1857–75). She was best known in Shakespearean male and female roles until she died at her home in Boston on February 17, 1876. The Cushman Room at the **Boston Public Library** is named in her honor.

– D –

DALL, CAROLINE WELLS HEALEY (1822–1912). Writer. Born in **Boston** on June 22, 1822, Dall was educated privately and influenced by **Joseph Tuckerman** and **Margaret Fuller**. She opened an early day care nursery in the **North End** for the children of working mothers (1837–42) and organized the New England Woman's Rights Convention (1859). Dall supported herself and two children as a writer in Boston while her husband was a missionary in India (1855–86). She wrote *Historical Pictures Retouched* (1860) on women in history and *Transcendentalism in New England* (1897). *The College, the Market, and the Court: or, Woman's Relation to Education, Labor, and Law* (1867) was her most important feminist book. Dall was a founder of the American Social Science Association (1865) and died in Washington, D.C., on December 17, 1912.

DAME SCHOOL. A private nursery school operated in colonial New England towns by a matron in her own house. She prepared young children for the **public school** using the **New England Primer** and hornbook to teach boys and girls reading, writing, arithmetic, and religion.

D'AMOURS, NORMAN (1937–). Congressman from New Hampshire. Born in **Holyoke**, Massachusetts, on October 14, 1937, D'Amours graduated from Assumption College (1960) and Boston University Law School (1963). He served in the Army Reserves (1964–67) and practiced law in Manchester, New Hampshire (1964–66). He was a New Hampshire assistant attorney general (1966–69) and Manchester city prosecutor (1970–72) and was elected as a Democrat to the House of Representatives (1975–85). D'Amours practiced law in Washington, D.C., and was the first **French-Canadian** congressman from New Hampshire.

DANA, CHARLES ANDERSON (1819–1897). Journalist. Born in Hinsdale, New Hampshire, on August 8, 1819, Dana attended **Harvard** College (1839–41). After living at the **Brook Farm** commune (1841–46), he was a newspaper editor in **Boston** and then worked for **Horace Greeley**'s *New York Tribune* (1846–62). Dana edited the *New American Cyclopedia* with **George Ripley** (1858–63). During the **Civil War** Dana was an assistant secretary of war (1863–65) and wrote *Recollections of the Civil War* (1898). As the owner of the *New York Sun* (1868–97), he became one of the most influential journalists in the nation. Dana died in Glen Cove, New York, on October 17, 1897.

DANA, RICHARD HENRY (1815–1882). Writer. Born in Cambridge, Massachusetts, on August 1, 1815, Dana graduated from **Harvard** College (1837) and was a **Boston** lawyer (1840–82). He is best known for *Two Years Before the Mast* (1840), a realistic account of his voyage as a common seaman from Boston to California (1834–36). Dana specialized in marine law and advocated for seamen's rights and **abolitionism**. He helped found the Free Soil Party and was a Republican U.S. attorney in Boston. Dana died in Rome on January 6, 1882.

DANBURY. A Southwestern Connecticut community known as the **Hat City** settled in 1684 by Norwalk residents. Zadoc Benedict first manufactured beaver hats in 1780, and Danbury soon produced more hats than any other town in the nation. The British burned the town, but General **Benedict Arnold** routed the invaders at the Battle of Ridgefield (1777). Danbury hosted the state's largest **agricultural fair** (1821–1981) and incorporated as a city in 1889. It had 50 of the state's 80 hat factories in 1900, but the Danbury Hatters decision by the U.S. Supreme Court (1908) weakened the hatters' union, and changing fashions forced the last hat maker to close in 1965. Danbury extended the city limits in 1965, and the diversified industrial base now supports a population of 65,585 residents.

DARTMOUTH COLLEGE v. WOODWARD **(1819)**. A U.S. Supreme Court decision protecting contracts, which affected new business organizations. When the New Hampshire legislature amended (1816) the Dartmouth College charter, granted by George III (1769), the college trustees sued. **Daniel Webster** (class of 1801) successfully argued this case before Chief Justice John Marshall in Washington, D.C. This case enhanced Webster's reputation when the Court decided that a charter was a contract protected by the Constitution and could not be altered by unilateral action. This gave corporate contracts and economic development judicial protection from state interference.

DAVENPORT, CHARLES (1866–1944). Scientist. Born in Stamford, Connecticut, on June 1, 1866, Davenport was a zoologist who introduced statistical methods in studies of human evolution and skin pigmentation. He studied American troops in World War I to determine ethnic or racial differences and investigated body measurements and genetic factors. He was director of the Station for Experimental Evolution of the Carnegie Institute in Cold Spring Harbor, New York (1903–34), and wrote *Heredity in Relation to Eugenics* (1911). Davenport died in New York City on February 18, 1944.

DAVENPORT, JOHN (1597–1670). Clergyman. Born in April 1597 in Coventry, England, Davenport was educated at Oxford University and was an Anglican priest in London when he joined **Puritan** exiles in Amsterdam (1633–37). Emigrating with **Theophilius Eaton** to **Boston** (1637), they founded Quinnipiac (**New Haven**) in Connecticut (1638) as the nation's first planned community. Eaton was governor and Davenport was the pastor. He resisted union with the Connecticut colony and returned to **Boston** as pastor of the First Church where he died on March 15, 1670.

DAVIS, BETTE (1908–1989). Actor. Born in **Lowell**, Massachusetts, on April 5, 1908, Ruth Elizabeth studied acting in **Cape Cod** summer stock theaters (1925) and New York City (1927). She performed with the **Provincetown Players** (1928) before making her Broadway debut (1929) and began a long and distinguished Hollywood career (1931–87). She won an Oscar for her role in *Dangerous* (1935) and *Jezebel* (1938) and five nominations as best actress (1938–42) as well as the American Film Institute Life Achievement Award (1977). During her 60 years in 87 movies, the fiercely independent Davis earned

10 Oscar nominations, more than any other actress. She wrote two autobiographies, *The Lonely Life* (1962) and *This 'N That* (1987), and died in France on October 16, 1989.

DAVIS, JOHN (1787–1854). Senator from Massachusetts. Born in Northborough, Massachusetts, on January 13, 1787, Davis graduated from Yale College (1812) and practiced law in **Worcester**. He was elected to the House of Representatives (1825–34) as a National Republican supporter of **John Quincy Adams** and later allied with **Abbott Lawrence**. Elected governor (1834–35) as a **Cotton Whig**, Davis supported manufacturing interests in the state and went to the Senate (1835–41) as a conservative spokesman on financial and commercial issues. Elected again as governor (1841–43), he engaged in a bitter Whig Party conflict with **Daniel Webster** over the **Aroostook War** and **slavery**. Davis was an unsuccessful candidate for the Whig nomination for vice-president (1844) but he was elected to the Senate (1845–53), where he was one of two senators to vote against the war with Mexico (1846) and he opposed the Compromise of 1850. He retired from the Senate in 1853 and "Honest John" Davis served as president of the **American Antiquarian Society** until his death in Worcester on April 19, 1854.

DAWES, HENRY LAUREN (1816–1903). Senator from Massachusetts. Born in Cummington, Massachusetts, on October 30, 1816, Dawes graduated from Yale College (1839), edited newspapers in Greenfield, and North Adams and practiced law (1842–53). He served as a Republican legislator (1848–53) and in the House of Representatives (1857–75) and Senate (1875–93). Best remembered as the founder of the U.S. Weather Bureau and the influential chairman of the Committee on Indian Affairs, Dawes died in Pittsfield on February 5, 1903.

DAWES, WILLIAM (1745–1799). Patriot. Born in **Boston** on April 6, 1745, Dawes was one of three riders dispatched on April 18, 1775, to warn the **minutemen** that British troops were marching to Lexington and Concord. **Paul Revere** was captured, and Dawes turned back, but **Samuel Prescott** completed his ride. Dawes died in Boston on February 25, 1799, and is buried in **King's Chapel**. *See also* AMERICAN REVOLUTION.

DEANE, SILAS (1737–1789). Congressman from Connecticut. Born in Groton, Connecticut, on December 24, 1737, Deane graduated from Yale College (1758). He practiced law in Wethersfield (1761–74), was a merchant, and served in the colonial legislature (1768–75). Deane was a member of the Continental Congress (1774–76), sent to France (1776) as a secret agent, and a minister to France with **Benjamin Franklin** and Arthur Lee to negotiate a treaty with France (1778). Recalled by Congress on rumors of financial misconduct, he died on the voyage to **Boston** on September 23, 1789. Congress later voted to pay his heirs $37,000 as restitution (1842).

DEARBORN, HENRY (1751–1829). Soldier. Born in North Hampton, New Hampshire, on February 23, 1751, Dearborn practiced medicine (1771–75) until General **John Stark** took his militia company to the **Battle of Bunker Hill**. Captured during **Benedict Arnold**'s invasion of Canada, Dearborn was paroled (1777) and served with George Washington (1777–81) from Valley Forge to Yorktown. Settled in Maine (1783), he was a militia general and U.S. marshal (1789–93) until elected to the House of Representatives as a Jeffersonian Democratic-Republican (1793–97). Dearborn was secretary of war (1801–09) and collector of the port of **Boston** (1809–12). President James Madison relieved Dearborn as the senior major general in the U.S. Army when his invasion of Canada failed (1813). He served as U.S. minister to Portugal (1822–24) and retired to Roxbury, Massachusetts, where he died on June 6, 1829. *See also* AMERICAN REVOLUTION.

DEERE, JOHN (1804–1886). Inventor. Born in Rutland, Vermont, on February 7, 1804, Deere was a blacksmith in Vermont (1821–37). Moving to Illinois, he invented an iron and steel plow to suit the heavy soil of the West. Manufacturing steel plows in Decatur (1839) and Moline (1846), his company expanded rapidly and produced modern agricultural machinery. Deere, whose plow broke the Great Plains, died in Moline, Illinois, on May 17, 1886.

DEERFIELD. A town on the Deerfield River in the northwestern area of Massachusetts's **Connecticut River** valley. Twenty families from Dedham established the town (1669) on fertile land the **Pocumtuck** people had farmed since 5000 B.C. but lost in war with the **Mohawks** (1644).

The **Mohawks** raided the town in 1675 and again on February 29, 1704, when Major Jean Baptiste Hertel de Rouville, leading 47 French soldiers and 140 **Abenaki**, Mohawk, **Pennacook**, and Huron warriors, killed 56 residents, and marched 102 captives to Quebec. Only 91 captives survived the harsh journey for four weeks through Vermont to Quebec. News of the Deerfield Massacre aroused fear throughout frontier New England. In 1706, 60 captives were redeemed and brought to **Boston**. One of them, John Williams (1664–1729), the Deerfield minister, wrote a best-selling account of his ordeal, *The Redeemed Captive Returning to Zion* (1707). The Deerfield Academy (1797) is one of the oldest **prep schools** in the nation. Deerfield became the site of an early historic preservation movement (1848) and a center of the arts and crafts movement (1890). Today the Historic Deerfield Association (1952) displays baskets, quilts, and other local crafts and offers tours of 14 17th-century buildings to tourists on the **Mohawk Trail**.

DEMAR, CLARENCE (1888–1958). Athlete. Born in Madeira, Ohio, on June 7, 1888, Clarence DeMar was raised in Warwick, Rhode Island, and began his sports career with the University of Vermont cross-country team. He finished second in his first **Boston Marathon** (1910) as an unknown printer from Melrose, Massachusetts. DeMar won the race six times in seven years (1911, 1922–24, 1927, 1928, and 1930) and ran 34 times, finishing in the top 10 another 15 times. He was the oldest runner to win at age 41 (1930). DeMar raced until his late sixties and participated in three Olympic races, winning a bronze medal (1924). The Boston Marathon's first legend died in **Boston** in 1958 at age 70 and was inducted into the National Distance Running Hall of Fame (2001).

DEMARCO, TONY (1932–). Boxer. Born in **Boston** on January 14, 1932, Leonardo Liotta was a professional boxer (1948–62). He won the world welterweight championship (1955) and lost the title in the "fight of the year" (1955). His record was 58 wins, 21 losses, one draw, and 33 knockouts. Tony DeMarco retired in Boston in 1962.

DEMILLE, CECIL BLOUNT (1881–1959). Actor and film director. Born in Ashfield, Massachusetts, on August 12, 1881, DeMille began as a stage actor and operated a theatrical agency (1911) in New York City. He directed his first film and moved to Hollywood in 1913. He is considered the founder of the Hollywood film industry and defined the flamboyant image of the movie director. C. B. DeMille is best known for early silent movie westerns and for epics like *The Ten Commandments* (1924) and *The Greatest Show on Earth* (1952). He established the movie censorship office and the Hollywood anticommunist campaign. DeMille won an Academy Award (1949) and died in California on January 21, 1959.

DEMPSEY, JOHN NOEL (1915–1989). Governor of Connecticut. Born on January 3, 1915, in County Tipperary, Ireland, Dempsey was the first foreign-born governor of the state since the **American Revolution**. He came to America as a boy (1925), attended Rhode Island College (1934–35), and became an automobile dealer. He was elected to the Putnam City Council (1936–42), as mayor (1947–61), and state representative (1949–55). As Democratic lieutenant governor (1958–61), he succeeded as governor (1961–71) when **Abraham Ribicoff** joined President **John F. Kennedy**'s Cabinet. Reelected in 1962 and 1966 on a liberal New Deal platform with the active support of **John M. Bailey**, Dempsey retired in 1971 and died in Putnam, Connecticut, in 1989.

DERBY, ELIAS HASKET (1739–1799). Merchant. Born in **Salem**, Massachusetts, on August 16, 1739, Derby was an apprentice in his father's import firm. During the **French and Indian War** "King" Derby became America's first millionaire as the leading merchant in Salem, at that time the sixth largest city in the nation. His privateers captured 144 prizes in the **American Revolution**, and when peace came he sent 90 ships to Europe, the Indian Ocean, the South Seas, and the **China trade**. Derby and his wife, Elizabeth Crowninshield Derby, had a passion for building magnificent Federal-style mansions. They employed **Samuel McIntire** to build fine furniture and three townhouses in Salem before Derby died on September 8, 1799. Although the **Embargo Act** (1807–09) and the War of 1812 ended Salem's commercial prominence, Derby's son, Elias H. Derby, Jr. (1766–1826), became Salem's leading merchant and ship captain. *See also* CODFISH ARISTOCRACY.

DEVENS, CHARLES (1820–1881). U.S. attorney general. Born in **Boston** on April 4, 1820, Devens graduated **Boston Latin School**, **Harvard** College (1838), and Harvard Law School (1840). He practiced law in Greenfield, Massachusetts, and was U.S. marshall (1849–54) before he began a law practice with **George Frisbee Hoar** (1854–61) in

Worcester. Serving in the **Civil War** with the 15th Massachusetts Regiment, he was wounded three times and rose from major to major general. Devens was a Republican state senator (1848–50), a superior court judge (1867–73), and associate justice of the state supreme court (1873–77, 1881–91). He served as attorney general for President Rutherford B. Hayes (1877–81) and died in Boston on January 7, 1891. An equestrian statue by **Daniel Chester French** (1906) in Worcester and one on the **Esplanade** in Boston (1896) honor him. The Fort Devens Army base in Ayer, Massachusetts, was named for him.

DEWEY, GEORGE (1837–1917). Admiral. Born in **Montpelier**, Vermont, on December 26, 1837, Dewey attended Norwich University, graduated from the U.S. Naval Academy (1858), and served in the **Civil War**. While in Hong Kong, he was ordered to attack the Spanish fleet in Manila (1898), which he did with no losses, sinking or destroying the entire fleet. Returning to a hero's welcome, he was commended by Congress and promoted to admiral of the navy, the highest rank in history. Admiral Dewey died in Washington, D. C., on January 16, 1917.

DEWEY, JOHN (1859–1952). Educator. Born in Burlington, Vermont, on October 20, 1859, Dewey graduated from the University of Vermont (1879) and earned a Ph.D. at Johns Hopkins University (1884) as a student of **G. Stanley Hall** and **Charles S. Peirce**. He taught philosophy at the University of Michigan (1884–94) and the University of Chicago (1894–1904) and wrote *The School and Society* (1899) and *Democracy and Education* (1916). At Chicago he established the university's Laboratory School (1896), which shaped his views on progressive **education**. He was a founder of the American Association of University Professors, the American Civil Liberties Union, and the New School for Social Research. Dewey was a leading exponent of pragmatism and experimentalism in government and education when he taught at Columbia University (1904–30). He died in New York City on June 1, 1952.

DEWSON, MARY WILLIAMS (1874–1962). Public official. Born in Quincy, Massachusetts, on February 18, 1874, Mary Dewson graduated from Wellesley College (1897) and worked as an economist at the Women's Educational and Industrial Union in **Boston** and as superintendent of the Massachusetts Girls' Parole Department (1900–12). After service with the Red Cross in France (1917–19), she worked for the National Consumers' League (1919–24) and as president of the Consumers' League in New York (1925–31). She joined President Franklin D. Roosevelt's administration in 1930 and was director of the Women's Division of the Democratic National Committee and its vice-chair (1933–37). Dewson served on the Social Security Board (1937–38) and was director of the FDR Foundation until she died in Castine, Maine, on October 22, 1962.

DICKINSON, EMILY (1830–1886). Poet. Born in Amherst, Massachusetts, on December 10, 1830, Emily Elizabeth Dickinson attended Mount Holyoke Female Seminary (1847–48) but lived a reclusive life in her parents' Amherst home. In 1862 she began a 20-year correspondence with **Thomas Wentworth Higginson**, who became her mentor. He published the first volume of her poetry after her death, *Poems* (1890), winning immediate recognition as a major American poet for the "Belle of Amherst." Emily Dickinson was an eccentric who seldom left home but produced hundreds of short lyrical poems marked by metaphysical speculation and unconventional diction before her death in Amherst on May 15, 1886.

DIGHTON ROCK. An 11–foot high glacial erratic sandstone boulder on the shore of the Taunton River in southeastern Massachusetts. Covered with petroglyphs, carved designs, and words of unknown origin, it has been attributed to the Vikings from **Vinland**, **Native Americans**, and the Portuguese explorer Miguel Corte Real in 1511. **Cotton Mather** studied the mysterious rock (1677), which was removed to a museum at the Dighton Rock State Park in Berkley (1963). It is designated as the official state explorer rock (1983).

DILLINGHAM, WILLIAM PAUL (1843–1923). Senator from Vermont. Born in Waterbury, Vermont, on December 12, 1843, Dillingham studied law with his father, Paul Dillingham, the governor of Vermont, and was admitted to the bar (1867). He practiced in Waterbury and served as a Republican in the state legislature (1876–80) and as governor (1888–90). Elected to the Senate (1900–23), he was a supporter of the **Immigration Restriction League** as chairman of the U.S. Immigration Commission (1907–10), which obtained the first federal law to limit immigration by a quota system (1921). Dillingham died in **Montpelier** on July 12, 1923.

DINERS. Prefabricated restaurants designed like a **railroad** dining car. Invented by Walter Scott in **Providence**, Rhode Island (1872), 651 were manufactured by the Worcester Lunch Car Company (1906–61) in **Worcester**, Massachusetts, and the J. B. Judkins Company in Merrimac, Massachusetts (1935–42). Shipped by rail or truck across the United States, the small eatery featured hand-crafted interiors, porcelain exteriors, stainless steel panel walls, marble countertops, chrome trim, hardwood booths, and tile floors. They were popular lunch wagons on sites near factories and mills and along highways. New Englanders still enjoy regional foods at classic diners, like the Modern Diner in Pawtucket, the first diner to be placed on the National Register of Historic Places, or Vermont's Miss Bellows Falls Diner and Moody's Diner on **Route 1** in Waldoboro, Maine. The history of these culinary landmarks is preserved by the American Diner Museum in Providence (1996), and Massachusetts identified 75 diners as historical sites (2001).

DINGLEY, NELSON, JR. (1832–1899). Governor of Maine. Born in Durham, Maine, on February 15, 1832, Dingley graduated from Dartmouth College (1855). He practiced law (1856) until he became publisher of the *Lewiston Journal* (1856). He was elected as a Republican to the state legislature (1862–65, 1968, 1973) and as governor (1874–75). Dingley served in the House of Representatives (1881–99), giving his name to the high protective tariff bill, the Dingley Tariff of 1897. He died in Washington, D.C., on January 13, 1899.

DINOSAUR FOOTPRINTS. First discovered dinosaur tracks in the nation. They are located in South Hadley, Massachusetts. Found by Pliny Moody while plowing on the family farm (1802), they were called Noah's Raven until studied by the Reverend Edward Hitchcock, a geology professor at Amherst College. He collected 21,000 dinosaur (*Coelophysis*) tracks cast in sandstone. The area is now the Dinosaur Footprint State Reservation in Smiths Ferry.

DIX, DOROTHEA (1802–1887). Reformer. Born in Hampden, Maine, on April 4, 1802, Dorothea Lynde Dix lived in **Worcester** before establishing a school for girls in **Boston** (1821–35). In 1841 she discovered that mentally ill inmates at the East Cambridge jail were mistreated. Her report to the legislature on other Massachusetts institutions (1843) resulted in expansion of the state lunatic asylum in Worcester. This began her international career as the "voice for the mad" to obtain humane treatment for the insane. During the **Civil War** she was superintendent of women nurses and later published books for children. Dix was a successful lobbyist and noted humanitarian when she died on July 18, 1887, in Trenton, New Jersey, in a state hospital she founded.

DIXIE CUP. Vessel invented in **Boston** by Lawrence Luellen (1907) to dispense pure drinking water in a sanitary flat-folded paper cup. His American Water Supply Company developed a vending machine to provide a cool drink of water in an individual paper cup for a penny (1908). Luellen's brother-in-law, Hugh Moore, left his studies at **Harvard University** (1907) to join the company and led a public health campaign to banish the tin dipper from public places. Manufactured in Fitchburg, Massachusetts (1919), the Dixie Cup became universally popular when ice cream was sold in the paper cup (1923).

DODD, CHRISTOPHER J. (1944–). Senator from Connecticut. Born in Willimantic, Connecticut, on May 27, 1944, the son of Senator **Thomas J. Dodd**, Christopher Dodd graduated from Providence College (1966). After serving in the Peace Corps in the Dominican Republic (1966–68), and in the U.S. Army (1969–75), he graduated from the University of Kentucky Law School (1972). Dodd practiced law in New London (1973–81) and was elected as a Democrat to the House of Representatives (1975–81) and to the Senate (1981–).

DODD, THOMAS J. (1907–1971). Senator from Connecticut. Born in Norwich, Connecticut, on May 15, 1907, Thomas Joseph Dodd graduated from Providence College (1930) and Yale University Law School (1933). He was a Federal Bureau of Investigation (FBI) agent (1933–34), an assistant U.S. attorney general (1938–45), and chief trial counsel for the Nuremberg war crimes trials (1945–46). Dodd practiced law in **Hartford** (1947–53) until elected as a Democrat to the House of Representatives (1953–57) and to the Senate (1959–71). Censured by the Senate for financial misconduct, he was defeated for reelection (1970). Dodd died in Old Lyme on May 24, 1971.

DODGE, GRENVILLE MELLEN (1831–1916). Soldier. Born on April 12, 1831, in Danvers, Massachusetts, Dodge graduated from Norwich University in Vermont (1851). He was a civil engineer for **railroads** in

Illinois, Missouri, and Iowa until the **Civil War**. Commissioned as a colonel, he rose quickly to major general for his service in major battles and in bridge and railroad construction for the Union Army. Dodge was elected to the House of Representatives as a Republican from Iowa (1867–69) but left politics to become chief engineer for the Union Pacific Railroad (1866–70) and other lines in the Southwest. Dodge built a railroad in Cuba (1903) and directed the Dodge Commission investigating the U.S. Army in the Spanish-American War. He became a close friend of President Ulysses S. Grant and died in Council Bluffs, Iowa, on January 3, 1916.

DOMINION OF NEW ENGLAND. Formed by the British government (1686) to consolidate New York, New Jersey, and New England for better defense, administration, and commerce under royal control. But Governor **Edmund Andros** proved too unpopular. Annulment of royal charters, dismissal of representative assemblies, taxation without representation, and strict enforcement of the **Navigation Acts** united his opponents. When James II abdicated, the New England **Puritan** leaders revolted and overthrew Andros (1689).

DORCHESTER HEIGHTS. The high ground overlooking Boston Harbor. It was fortified secretly on March 4, 1776, with cannon captured by **Ethan Allen** at Fort Ticonderoga and brought to **Boston** by **Henry Knox**. This forced General **William Howe** to evacuate the British Army, Navy, and Tories from Boston to Halifax on March 17, 1776. George Washington's first major victory ended the siege of Boston and is celebrated in Boston as **Evacuation Day**. *See also* AMERICAN REVOLUTION.

DORR WAR (1840–1842). Conflict in Rhode Island led by Thomas Wilson Dorr, a state legislator and **Providence** lawyer (1834–37), whose followers demanded a new state constitution with universal manhood suffrage. Rhode Island retained property qualifications for voting; consequently, 58 percent of the state's white males could not vote in the 1840 presidential election. The **Second Great Awakening** undermined this limited franchise as undemocratic, and **Irish immigrants** saw it as nativism and **anti-Catholicism**. The legislature called a constitutional convention (1841), but the Rhode Island Suffrage Association held its own People's Convention and elected Dorr as governor. When the Dorrites twice failed to capture the Providence arsenal by force (1842), Dorr fled to New Hampshire. His followers disbanded, but a new constitution was ratified (1843) giving suffrage to all adult males and to naturalized men who owned property. Dorr was sentenced to prison for life but was released in one year (1844). Anti-Catholic and nativist sentiments continued with the election of **Know Nothing Party** legislators (1856) and a nativist mob threatening a Catholic convent in Providence.

DORY. A small boat used in the New England fisheries from 1850 to 1950. Many were built at the Lowell Boat Shop in Amesbury, Massachusetts, on the Merrimack River for the Grand Banks schooners. By 1860 Gloucester's 300 schooner fleet used 2,700 dories in a new method of **fishing** designed by Hiram Lowell. The Lowell dory, depicted in paintings by **Winslow Homer** such as *Gloucester Harbor* (1873) and *Fog Warning* (1885), is still used as a recreational row, sail, or motor boat. Dory fishing from New England schooners ended in 1953, but the Lowell Boat Shop, the nation's oldest builder of wooden boats, continues to produce the classic dory.

DOUGLASS, FREDERICK (1817–1895). Reformer. Born a slave in Tuckahoe, Maryland, Frederick Augustus Washington Bailey was apprenticed to a ship caulker in Baltimore. He escaped by ship to **New Bedford**, Massachusetts (1838), where he became known as Frederick Douglass. His extemporaneous speech in 1841 at the Massachusetts Anti-Slavery Society launched his career as an **abolitionist** lecturer. His autobiography, *Narrative of the Life of Frederick Douglass* (1845), did much to promote the antislavery movement in Great Britain and America. An ally of **William Lloyd Garrison** at first, he adopted a more moderate position while publishing a newspaper in Rochester, New York. Douglass fled to Canada when accused of supporting **John Brown** in 1859, but he returned to recruit troops for the **54th Massachusetts Regiment**, in which two of his sons served. He was appointed to the Santo Domingo Commission (1877–81) and as U.S. minister to Haiti (1889–91). Douglass died in the District of Columbia on February 20, 1895.

DOW, NEAL (1804–1897). Prohibitionist. Born in **Portland**, Maine, on March 20, 1804, Dow was a **Quaker** in the tanning business who led the prohibitionist crusade to pass the Maine Law (1851) prohibiting the sale of alcohol. Dow was mayor of Portland (1851–56). His work derived from the Total Abstinence Society founded in Portland (1815) and the American Society for the Promotion of **Temperance** founded in **Boston** (1826) and led to the Washington Movement (1840) in New England to reform alcoholics. During the **Civil War** General Dow led the 13th Maine Infantry (1861–64), known as the Prohibitionist Regiment, until he was wounded, captured, and exchanged, returning to Maine as a hero. Dow was the Prohibition Party candidate for president (1880) and died in Portland on October 2, 1897. Maine had some form of prohibition from 1851 to 1934.

DOWN EAST. A nickname for Maine because ships traveling from southern New England to Maine ports were sailing downwind. Ships called Downeasters were commercial sailing vessels built in Maine (1860–70) to carry wheat cargoes to Europe. A Downeaster also refers to a person from Maine or any New Englander. *See also* YANKEE.

DRAPER, EBEN SUMNER (1858–1914). Governor of Massachusetts. Born in Hopedale, Massachusetts, on June 17, 1858, Draper graduated from MIT (1879) and joined his family **textile** machinery company. He broke a strike led by the Industrial Workers of the World (IWW) in Milford (1913), was chairman of the state Republican Party (1893–99), and served as lieutenant governor (1906–08) and governor (1909–11). Draper died in Greenville, South Carolina, on April 9, 1914.

DRINAN, ROBERT F. (1920–). Congressman from Massachusetts. Born in **Boston** on November 15, 1920, Robert Frederick Drinan graduated from Boston College (1942) and Georgetown University Law School (1950). He was ordained a **Jesuit** priest (1953), studied theology in Rome, and taught law at Boston College (1956–70). He was elected as a Democrat to the House of Representatives (1971–81), the first **Catholic** priest to serve in Congress. Ordered by his church superiors to resign (1981), Drinan teaches law in Washington, D.C.

DU BOIS, W. E. B. (1868–1963). Historian and reformer. Born in Great Barrington, Massachusetts, on February 23, 1868, William Edward Burghardt Du Bois graduated from Fisk University (1888) and was the first **African American** to earn a Ph.D. at **Harvard University** (1895). His dissertation, *The Suppression of the African Slave Trade in the*

United States of America, 1638–1870 (1896), was the first of his 16 empirical investigations of civil rights and social justice. While teaching at Atlanta University (1897–1910, 1934–44), Du Bois became the chief critic of the conservative Booker T. Washington, arguing for liberal education in addition to vocational training. In 1909 Du Bois was a founder of the National Association for the Advancement of Colored People (NAACP) and editor of its magazine, *Crisis* (1910–34). A prolific author and eloquent speaker, Du Bois joined the Communist Party (1961) and lived in Ghana where he died on August 27, 1963. The University of Massachusetts library in Amherst is named in his honor.

DUDLEY, THOMAS (1576–1653). Governor of Massachusetts. Born in England in 1576, Dudley became a **Puritan** in John Cotton's **Boston** congregation (1620). He emigrated to Massachusetts with **John Winthrop** as deputy governor of the colony (1630). He was elected governor (1634, 1640, 1645, 1650) and was a founder of **Harvard** College (1636). His son was Governor Joseph Dudley, and his daughter was the poet **Anne Bradstreet**. Dudley died in Roxbury on July 31, 1653.

DUKAKIS, MICHAEL S. (1933–). Governor of Massachusetts. Born in Brookline, Massachusetts, on November 3, 1933, Michael Stanley Dukakis graduated from Swarthmore College (1955) and, after serving in the U.S. Army (1956–57), from **Harvard** Law School (1960). He practiced law in **Boston**, was a Democrat in the state legislature (1963–70), and hosted the **WGBH** television series *The Advocates*. Elected governor (1975–79), he was not renominated (1978) and taught at Harvard University (1979–82). Dukakis reviewed the **Sacco and Vanzetti case** (1977) and declared they were wrongfully convicted. Elected governor for two more terms (1982, 1986), he was the unsuccessful Democratic candidate for president (1988). Since 1991 Dukakis has taught government at Northeastern University in **Boston** and lobbied for public issues.

DUMMER'S WAR. An undeclared war (1722–27) between **Native Americans** and aggressively expanding colonists in Maine. Named for William Dummer, the acting governor of Massachusetts, it began when **Micmacs** captured English **fishing** boats in Maine and raided several towns. Some **Mohawk** allies fought with Massachusetts troops against the **Abenaki**, Micmacs, **Malicetes**, and **Penobscots**. The French **Jesuit** missionary, Father **Sebastien Rasles**, was killed in the Massachusetts militia attack on Norridgewock (1724) because the French were suspected of inciting the tribes to drive the English out of Maine. The Lovewell massacre, a Native American defeat of 20 militiamen at Fryeburg, Maine (1725), led to peace conferences in **Boston** (1725) and in **Portland** (1726). The war ended with the retreat of many Native Americans to Canada in 1727, but the Vermont Abenaki led by Chief **Grey Lock** remained defiant and undefeated.

DUNKIN DONUTS. An international franchise chain of 5,000 doughnut shops in 40 countries founded by William Rosenberg (1916–2002) in Quincy, Massachusetts (1950). Since the first franchise opened in **Worcester** (1955), New Englanders have patronized more than 600 Dunkin Donuts shops. The company operates as Dunkin Donuts USA in Randolph, Massachusetts, now.

DURANT, THOMAS C. (1820–1885). Businessman. Born in Lee, Massachusetts, on February 6, 1820, Durant graduated from Albany Medical College (1840) but preferred business to medicine. He invested in Wall Street **railroad** stocks and discovered a talent for railroad construction. After building lines in Michigan, Illinois, and Missouri, Durant was vice-president of the Union Pacific Railroad (1862). He attracted **Oakes Ames** and other New England investors to the corrupt Credit Mobilier scheme (1872). Despite financial and political scandals, Durant feverishly completed the transcontinental railroad (1864–69), driving the golden spike that united the tracks (1869) in Utah. Weeks later Doc Durant was ousted by the Ames faction and retired to New York where he lost his fortune in the panic of 1873 and died forgotten on October 5, 1885.

DURFEE, JOB (1790–1847). Congressman from Rhode Island. Born in Tiverton, Rhode Island, on September 20, 1790, Durfee graduated from Brown University (1813) and practiced law in **Newport** (1817–21). He was a state legislator (1816–20, 1826–29) and served in the House of Representatives (1821–25). Durfee was elected associate justice of the state supreme court (1833–35) and chief justice (1835–47). He died in Tiverton on July 26, 1847.

DURYEA, CHARLES EDGAR (1861–1938). Inventor. Born on December 15, 1861, in Canton, Illinois, Duryea was a bicycle mechanic in Springfield, Massachusetts, when he designed the first successful American gasoline automobile (1893). His brother, J. Frank Duryea (1869–1967), won the first American automobile race (1895) with this water-cooled car. The brothers formed the Duryea Motor Wagon Company in Springfield (1895) and sold the first commercial cars until the company failed (1898). Charles Duryea manufactured cars in Chicopee (1905–15) and published books and articles on automobiles until his death in Philadelphia on September 28, 1938.

DWIGHT, TIMOTHY (1752–1817). Educator. Born on May 14, 1752, in Northampton, Massachusetts, Dwight graduated from Yale College (1769). While teaching at Yale he inspired the **Hartford Wits**. After serving as a chaplain in the **American Revolution** (1777–79), he was pastor of a **Congregational** church in Greenfield Hill, Connecticut (1783–95). His epic poem *The Conquest of Canaan* (1785) and other poems, sermons, and essays reflected his Calvinist, **Federalist** views. As president of Yale (1795–1817), Dwight transformed it into a prestigious college and model for other institutions. His *Travels in New England and New York* (1822) was a vivid account of the region and introduced the term **Cape Cod House**. Dwight was an intellectual Federalist leader of New England when he died in **New Haven** on January 11, 1817.

DYER, MARY (1610–1660). Religious reformer. Born about 1610 in England, Mary Dyer migrated to **Boston** with her husband, William Dyer (1635). As a follower of **Anne Hutchinson**, she was banished by the **Massachusetts Bay Colony** (1638) and moved to Portsmouth, Rhode Island. In England she joined (1650) the Society of Friends or **Quakers**. Returning to Boston (1657), her missionary work led to imprisonment (1658, 1659) and banishment from **New Haven** and again from Boston. On her third visit, she was hanged on **Boston Common** on June 1, 1660. A statue by Sylvia Shaw Judson (1959) on the **Massachusetts State House** grounds honors this religious martyr.

– E –

EARLE, ALICE MORSE (1851–1911). Historian. Born in **Worcester**, Massachusetts, on April 27, 1851, Mary Alice Morse married Henry Earle (1874). She was a pioneer in writing about colonial New England manners and customs, including *The Sabbath in Puritan New England*

(1891), *Colonial Dames and Goodwives* (1895), and *Child Life in Colonial Days* (1899). Her books inspired the **colonial revival** movement. Earle died in Hempstead, Long Island, New York, on February 16, 1911, after surviving a **shipwreck** off **Nantucket**.

EARLE, RALPH (1751–1801). Artist. Born in Shrewsbury, Massachusetts, on May 11, 1751, Earle was a self-taught itinerant portrait painter. His **Loyalist** views prompted him to leave **New Haven** (1778) and study **art** with Benjamin West in London. By 1785 he was one of the most accomplished American artists of the day, painting *Roger Sherman* (1776) and many prominent people in New England. His monumental portrait *Oliver Ellsworth and Abigail Wolcott Ellsworth* (1792) is among his finest works. Earle painted a noted Vermont landscape, *View of Bennington* (1798), and another of his home area, *Looking East from Denny Hill* (1800), in **Worcester** before he died in Bolton, Connecticut, on August 16, 1801.

EASTMAN, JOHNSON (1824–1906). Artist. Born on July 29, 1824, in Lovell, Maine, Eastman apprenticed with a **Boston** lithographer (1840) and created portraits of **Ralph Waldo Emerson**, **Nathaniel Hawthorne**, and **Henry Wadsworth Longfellow**. He studied painting in Europe (1849–55) before settling in New York City. He is best known for painting genre scenes depicting New England rural life, especially *Sugaring Off at the Camp, Fryeburg, Maine* (1866), *The Old Stage Coach* (1871), and *Cranberry Harvest, Island of Nantucket* (1880). Eastman died in New York on April 5, 1906.

EASTERN WOODLANDS INDIANS. The members of many **Native American** peoples living in the area east of the Mississippi River from Canada to Florida. At the time of first contact with European explorers (1492–1620), these tribes spoke languages classified in three different groups: Iroquoian, Algonquian, and Siouan. The major speakers of Algonquian languages in New England were the **Abenaki**, **Mahican**, **Malecite**, **Massachusets**, **Mohegan**, **Narraganset**, **Nauset**, **Niantic**, **Nipmuc**, **Passamaquoddy**, **Pennacook**, **Penobscot**, **Pequot**, **Pocumtuck**, **Wampanoag**, and **Wappinger**. The densest populations were found on the Atlantic coast, living in the thick pine and hardwood forests, mountains, seacoast, lakeshore, and rivers where animals, berries, birds, fish, fruit, nuts, seeds, shellfish, and roots provided a food supply, clothing, and trade items.

EATON, THEOPHILUS (1590–1658). Governor of **New Haven Colony**. Born in England in 1590, Eaton was a prosperous merchant and an original member of the **Massachusetts Bay Company**. He immigrated to **Boston** (1637) with **John Davenport**, founded the New Haven colony (1638), and was its governor (1639–58). After his death on January 7, 1658, **New Haven** became part of the royal colony of Connecticut (1664).

EATON, WILLIAM (1764–1811). Soldier. Born in Woodstock, Connecticut, on February 23, 1764, Eaton served in the Continental Army (1780–81) and graduated from Dartmouth College (1790). While teaching in Windsor, Vermont, he became a U.S. Army captain and fought Indians in Ohio and Georgia. Appointed U.S. consul in Tunis (1798–1805), he negotiated a treaty to protect American ships from the Barbary pirates and led the U.S. Marines to capture Derna in the Tripolitan War (1804). Eaton served as a Massachusetts state legislator (1807–08) and died in Brimfield on June 1, 1811.

ECONOMY. Often attributed to the **Puritan** ethic that values diligence, thrift, consumption, and success, this cultural explanation may overlook government support of activities promoting the common welfare and appropriation of **Native American** land, an early trade with the Caribbean colonies, and timely capital shifts from **agriculture** to commerce and manufacturing. **Yankee** farmers, merchants, manufacturers, and shippers were in place to contribute to the post-Revolution economic development by exploiting many rapids and waterfalls to power grist and sawmills and **textile** mills. The **New England conscience** supported business enterprise in ways not common in other states. Despite the lack of endemic natural resources and with few widely demanded staples for export, Yankee entrepreneurs seized opportunities for profitable enterprises in a sophisticated manner. Capital from the **China trade** accumulated in the first American commercial bank, the Massachusetts Bank (1784), and was invested in textile mills (1790) and **railroads** in the west and the south (1840s) and in Michigan copper mines (1864). Rapid industrialization (textiles, **shoes**, arms, clocks, rubber, marble, slate, granite, metals, hardware, **shipyards**, and jewelry) in the 19th century benefited from the protective tariff, expanding domestic markets, and the supply of rural migrants and **immigrants** available as labor in new factories and mills. Military investment in armories led to the American system of manufactures and the region's machine tool industries and founded the defense industry. Industrial cities like Bridgeport played a key role in Connecticut metal industries and arms production during wartime booms.

New England experienced economic decline (1880–1940) relative to other regions' industrial growth in consumer and producer durable goods, but **Yankee ingenuity** and technology compensated by producing innovative machinery, machine tools, precision instruments, and the knowledge-based economy. Migration into the region and new **immigrants** maintained the labor supply, and wage levels remained higher than in other states. Stable political leadership has also been an important factor in promoting the regional economic expansion. Aircraft engines, electronics, radar, sonar, **computers**, and the service economy (banking, communications, **education**, finance, health services, insurance, and **tourism**) contributed to this knowledge-based economy. The Bank of Massachusetts (1784) and John Hancock Insurance Company (1862) propelled Massachusetts into the top echelon of American financial service centers. The Massachusetts Investors Trust invented the modern mutual fund (1924), initiating new financial services, which expanded dramatically when Fidelity Fund formed (1946). George Doriot, a professor at **Harvard** Business School, created the world's first venture capital firm (1946), and his greatest success was the Digital Equipment Corporation (1957). Today the Fleet Bank in Boston is the largest retail bank in New England and one of the largest banks in the nation.

New England's tradition of capital investment, **higher education**, and industrial innovation were also important factors in the region's resilient economic history, especially since revitalization in the 1950s. Innovation is constant, and the growth of high-tech businesses in the 1980s was generalized with production sites scattered widely throughout the region. By 1997 manufacturing jobs declined more sharply but the new medical device and pharmaceutical industry in Massachusetts contributed more jobs, pay, and products than the state's computer and electronics industry. Universities fostered new ideas and trained workers, fueling the region's high-tech boom by the 1980s. Academic hospitals develop and test medical devices, and venture capital is available for new and diverse high-tech companies.

Traditional agriculture and **fishing** have diminished but remain important sectors in the New England economy. New agricultural products developed recently in New England include a wide variety of items for niche markets. In addition to niche farming with new exotic crops, agricultural **tourism** (or agritourism) has increased, with farms offering bed and breakfast accommodations or attracting visitors with educational animal and farm exhibits. Tourists often pay farmers to pick their own berries or fruit. Fishing, another aspect of agriculture, has always been an important part of the New England economy; and despite federal conservation laws limiting fishing for certain species since 1984, it remains economically important. Related tourist activities, such as whale watching and sport fishing, have expanded in recent years.

Boston, the regional capital, ranked in the bottom third of all major U.S. cities in 1982 measured by unemployment, poverty, crime, and municipal debt, but a combination of government policy initiatives and economic growth improved the Boston, Massachusetts, and New England economies. Wages increased in Greater Boston despite the 1990–91 recession as the white European residents absorbed a new multicultural population.

During this time the traditional mill-based, blue-collar economy changed to a diverse knowledge-based, high-technology, financial servicee, or consulting economy. In 1950, more than one of five jobs in Greater Boston was in nondurable manufacturing, such as **textiles**, compared with one in 20 jobs in 2000. Today most jobs are in professional services in Massachusetts and generally throughout the entire region. The state's medical device industry includes 300 companies, employing 21,000 people in the nation's third largest center for these new enterprises. This is closely tied to New England's other high-tech industries in electronics, telecommunications, software, and biotechnology. Innovation in technology created new industries, such as Harold E. Edgerton's stroboscope at MIT (1931), for high-speed photography, nighttime aerial photography (1944), underwater exploration (1953), and in medicine. Charles S. Draper of MIT invented gyroscopes for World War II weapons (1942) and inertial navigation systems for ships and aircraft (1954), and MIT created the **Lincoln Laboratory** (1951), a federally funded research center in electronics, air defense, space surveillance, and communications. The Raytheon Company, the largest private-sector employer based in Massachusetts, had 87,000 workers in 2001. **Edwin Land** introduced the world's first instant camera for the Polaroid Company at the Jordan Marsh department store in Boston (1948).

Biotechnology is the most recent industry to find a home in New England, 300 new firms with 30,000 employees have been stimulated by scientific research at many universities. Academic research supported the application of new knowledge in the high-tech companies and does the same for biotechnology, contributing much to the New England economy. Walter Gilbert decoded DNA at Harvard (1977), MIT founded the Whitehead Institute (1982) for biomedical research, and the Genzyme Corporation in Boston and the Biogen Company in Cambridge (1978) built on this work. Massachusetts's 3,079 information technology companies employed 135,277 workers in 2002.

Boston's role as the economic hub for New England also changed. Its population is stable at 580,000 residents, but that comprises less than 15 percent of the state's population as suburban housing and work spaces grew dramatically. This spatial, industrial, and demographic transformation produced a new diversified economy in the city, state, and region by 2000. Examples of diversification include the contributions of cultural institutions to the regional economy. The Boston **Museum of Fine Arts** had an estimated impact of $369 million on the state's economy in 2000. Vacant shoe and textile factories in North Adams, Massachusetts, became the Massachusetts Museum of Contemporary Art (MASS MoCA) in 1999, attracting 120,000 visitors annually to the galleries and performing arts venues. Also the use of New England locations for film and television production generated $74 million for the Massachusetts economy in 2000 and $10 million for Vermont. This creative or arts sector of the economy employed 250,000 people, or 3.5 percent of the New England workforce by 2001.

Federal government investment in the public infrastructure, research and development, defense, and **higher education** played a critical role in New England economic growth until 1979 when an emphasis on deficit reduction and federal debt retirement began. Despite New England's influential political leadership in Washington, D.C., no region of the country suffered more from cutbacks than New England. In response, the region focused on urban development, housing, education, a variety of cultural and public amenities, and public investments in key industries to sustain economic growth. *See also* AGRICULTURAL FAIRS; LUMBER; MERCANTILISM; SHIPYARDS; TOURISM; WHALING.

EDDY, MARY BAKER (1821–1910). Religious leader. Born in Bow, New Hampshire, on July 16, 1821, Mary Morse Baker studied with a hypnotist (1862), who inspired her belief in natural healing. She published *Science and Health* (1875), which, with the Bible, became the major text of her new Christian Science faith. When she married Asa G.

Eddy (1877) and moved to Lynn, Massachusetts, she founded the Church of Christ, the Scientist (1879) and the Massachusetts Metaphysical College in **Boston** (1881). The daily newspaper, *Christian Science Monitor* (1908), preaches the new faith. Mrs. Eddy died in Chestnut Hill on December 3, 1910. Today the Christian Science Church guides millions of members around the world from its Boston "Mother Church."

EDDY, NELSON (1901–1967). Actor and singer. Born in **Providence**, Rhode Island, on June 29, 1901, Eddy studied opera in America and Europe before his career with the Philadelphia Civic Opera (1924). He appeared in 20 Hollywood films (1933–67), made 25 record albums, and often sang on radio, on television, and in nightclubs. Eddy died singing in Palm Beach, Florida, on March 6, 1967.

EDDY, SAMUEL (1769–1839). Congressman from Rhode Island. Born in Johnston, Rhode Island, on March 31, 1769, Eddy graduated from Brown University (1787). He practiced law in **Providence** (1790) and was clerk of the state supreme court (1790–93), secretary of state (1798–1819), and elected to the House of Representatives (1819–25). He was an associate justice of the state supreme court (1826–27) and chief justice (1827–35). Eddy died in **Providence** on February 3, 1839.

EDMUNDS, GEORGE FRANKLIN (1828–1919). Senator from Vermont. Born in Richmond, Vermont, on February 1, 1828, Edmunds studied law (1849–51) and practiced in Burlington, where he was a Republican state legislator (1854–59, 1861–62) until appointed to the U.S. Senate (1866–91). He led the impeachment trial of President Andrew Johnson and was author of the Tenure of Office Act (1867) and Civil Rights Act (1875). He led the Electoral Commission (1876), wrote the Sherman Anti-Trust Act (1890), and was an influential leader in the Senate until he resigned (1891) to practice law in Philadelphia. Edmunds retired to Pasadena, California, where he died on February 27, 1919.

EDUCATION. Began in America in New England and remains a hallmark of the region today. Massachusetts **Puritans** insisted on literacy to promote piety and discipline. Families provided some basic education and vocational training, but the **General Court** fined towns that did not teach reading (1642). **Selectmen** were ordered to hire a schoolmaster (1642), and towns with 50 families had to open a secondary (or grammar) school

(1647). Private **dame schools** taught young children the reading, writing and religion necessary to enter the free, tax-supported public schools. Boston established the first secondary school, **Boston Latin School** (1635), in North America, and New Englanders also founded many private prep schools, such as **Roxbury Latin School** (1645), the oldest in the nation. Boston opened the first public high school in the nation (1821), and Massachusetts towns provided free schools for all children in 1827 and passed the first state child labor law (1836). This created a demand for teachers, which prompted the legislatures and religious denominations to found colleges to educate teachers and ministers. **Harvard** College was the first college in North America (1636), but few of its graduates adopted teaching in public schools as a career.

The preparatory or **prep school** was created to prepare boys for the **Ivy League** colleges, but **Boston Latin School** is a free public classical high school that predates Harvard. Many New England communities established similar Latin or classical high schools that rival the prep schools. Boston English High School (1821) is the oldest public high school in the nation. Boston introduced Sunday schools (1820) and music education (1838) and was a pioneer in **kindergartens** (1860) and secondary education, which originated in the 18th-century public grammar schools. Under Horace Mann's leadership Massachusetts developed the first uniform state public school system (1838) and state **normal schools** to train teachers (1839). Connecticut did the same in 1849. As a result, by 1850, the number of female teachers, who were paid less than men, rose sharply. Integration of Boston public schools began in 1855, and other states gradually followed this example.

Massachusetts passed a truancy law (1850) and hired truant officers (1852) who sent truants and juvenile delinquents to juvenile sessions of the Boston Municipal Court (by 1830). Young lawbreakers were sent to private asylums or to the state **reform school** for boys (1848) or for girls (1856). Graduation from high school became common in New England in the 20th century, and today New Hampshire (82 percent) and Vermont (81 percent) lead the region in residents who have completed high school. *See also* COMMON SCHOOLS; HORNBOOK; MANN, HORACE; MASON, LOWELL; NEW ENGLAND PRIMER; PUBLIC SCHOOLS; SHIP SCHOOLS.

EDWARDS, JONATHAN (1703–1758). Clergyman and theologian. Born in East Windsor, Connecticut, on October 3, 1703, Edwards graduated from Yale College (1720). He joined his grandfather, **Solomon Stod-**

dard, as pastor in Northampton, Massachusetts (1726–50), where he became famous for sermons combining the principles of Isaac Newton and John Locke with his original Calvinist thinking. By 1734 he was a leader of the **Great Awakening**, but conflict with his congregation over the **Half-Way Covenant** led to his dismissal. He moved to Stockbridge in 1751 as pastor and a missionary to the **Native Americans**. His writings include *Freedom of the Will* (1754). When Edwards died on March 22, 1758, after becoming president of the College of New Jersey (now Princeton University), he was the last and greatest of the **Puritan** preachers and the leading American intellectual.

ELIOT, CHARLES W. (1834–1926). Educator. Born in **Boston** on March 20, 1834, Charles William Eliot graduated from **Harvard** College (1853). He taught chemistry at Harvard (1854–63) and MIT (1865–69) and was a reforming president of **Harvard University** (1869–1909). He transformed the provincial college to a major university, adding sciences, an elective system, written examinations, Radcliffe College (1879) for women, and new graduate schools (1890) and abolished compulsory religious worship. His writing and lectures reformed American **education** on all levels. Eliot, remembered as editor of the *Harvard Classics,* died in Maine on August 22, 1926.

ELIOT, CHARLES (1860–1897). Architect. Born in **Boston** on November 1, 1860, Eliot, son of **Harvard** president **Charles W. Eliot**, graduated from Harvard (1880) and trained in landscape architecture with **Frederick Law Olmsted**. He proposed the Boston metropolitan parkways and sinuous tree-lined roads (1892) as radiating spokes from the **Hub** along 17 miles of Charles River basin, beaches, and woodlands. Eliot died in Boston on March 25, 1897.

ELIOT, JOHN (1604–1690). Clergyman. Born in England in 1604, Eliot graduated from Cambridge University (1622). He immigrated to **Boston** (1631) as pastor in Roxbury (1632–90) and assisted Richard Mather in publishing the **Bay Psalm Book** (1640). Best known as a missionary to **Native Americans** in Massachusetts, by 1647 the "Apostle to the Indians" preached in Wopanaak, the **Wampanoag** language, with support of the Massachusetts General Court and the Society for the Propagation of the Gospel. Eliot published *A Primer or Catechism, in the Massachusetts Indian Language* (1654) and translated the Bible into Wopanaak (1663), the first Bible published in America. Eliot settled converted Native American groups (called the **Praying Indians**) in 14 towns until **King Philip's War** (1675–76) disrupted his work. He continued to minister to Natick and other Christian Indians until his death in Roxbury on May 21, 1690.

ELLERY, WILLIAM B. (1727–1820). Born in **Newport**, Rhode Island, on December 22, 1727, Ellery graduated from **Harvard** College (1747). He practiced law in Newport (1770) and was elected to the Continental Congress (1776–85) where he signed the Declaration of Independence. He was chief justice of the state (1785) and collector of the port of Newport (1790–1820). Ellery died in Newport on February 15, 1820.

ELLSWORTH, OLIVER (1745–1807). Senator from Connecticut. Born in Windsor, Connecticut, on April 29, 1745, Ellsworth graduated (1766) from the College of New Jersey (now Princeton University). He practiced law in **Hartford** (1771–77) and served in the Continental Congress (1777–84) and the Constitutional Convention (1787). Ellsworth proposed the **Connecticut Compromise** that broke the deadlock over representation in the new Congress. He was influential in Connecticut's ratification of the new Constitution as a **Federalist Party** leader. Ellsworth served in the Senate (1789–96) and as chief justice of the U.S. Supreme Court (1796–99). He retired to Windsor, where he died on November 26, 1807.

EMBARGO ACT OF 1807. Passed by Congress as President Thomas Jefferson's bold attempt to use economic coercion on Great Britain and France to stop the impressment of American seamen and restriction of neutral trade with Europe. It forbade importing British goods and then forbade all international trade to and from U.S. ports and forbade all inland water and land commerce to halt the increased trade with Canada. Enforcement of these unpopular laws was difficult, and New England merchants, shipowners, and seamen in the **West Indies trade** were outraged. It was relaxed (1809) by Congress and ended (1810) when it obviously had failed. The economic decline in New England reinvigorated the **Federalist Party**, made President Jefferson and President James Madison very unpopular, and led **John Quincy Adams** to resign from the Senate. The War of 1812 and the **Hartford Convention** (1814) were also results of the embargo.

EMERALD NECKLACE. A ribbon of green public parkland designed by **Frederick Law Olmsted** in **Boston** (1878–95). It traverses the city seven miles from the **Boston Common** to the **Public Garden**, Commonwealth Avenue Mall, Charlesgate, Fenway, Riverway, Jamaica Pond, Arborway, **Arnold Arboretum**, and Franklin Park Golf Course, ending at the Franklin Park Zoo in Dorchester. Olmsted planted trees and built rustic stone bridges and ponds, molding tidal marshes and farmland into hilly vistas and crescent meadows to create pastoral scenes. His full plan was not implemented, but his goal to create healthy, uplifting nature in the heart of the city became extraordinary landscape architecture of national significance.

EMERSON, RALPH WALDO (1803–1882). Philosopher and writer. Born in **Boston** on May 25, 1803, Emerson graduated from **Harvard** College (1821) and Harvard Divinity School (1826). He resigned as pastor of the Second (**Unitarian**) Church in Boston (1829–32) because of his religious doubts. Traveling in Europe, he was influenced by Samuel Taylor Coleridge, William Wordsworth. and Thomas Carlyle. Emerson settled in **Concord** (1834) as a lecturer and essayist, where he published *Nature* (1836), the first expression of the **Transcendental** movement he founded. His essay *The American Scholar* (1837) was influential as were his essays and poetry. Emerson avoided most reform movements but supported **John Brown** and other abolitionists. He was a great figure in American moral idealism when he died in Concord on April 27, 1882.

EMIGRANT AID COMPANY. Founded as the Massachusetts Emigrant Aid Company (1854–57), and expanded as the New England Emigrant Aid Company. Led by **Amos A. Lawrence** and **Thomas Wentworth Higginson**, it encouraged 650 antislavery settlers from New England to oppose Southerners who attempted to make Kansas Territory a slave state. By 1856 over $100,000 was raised for 1,240 Free State settlers in Lawrence and other new towns. New England clergymen were active in a convention at **Worcester** (1857), and **Charles Sumner** and **John Brown** aroused public opinion as the bitter struggle over "Bleeding Kansas" led to the **Civil War**. Rifles known as Beecher's Bibles, after the Reverend Henry Ward Beecher, were shipped secretly to the abolitionist settlers.

ENDECOTT, JOHN (1588–1655). Governor of Massachusetts. Born in England in 1588, Endecott immigrated to Massachusetts (1628) with 60 **Puritans** to absorb **Roger Conant**'s settlement at **Salem**. He also annexed the **Merrymount** colony led by Thomas Morton (1628). In a sense, Endecott was the first governor of Massachusetts until **John Winthrop** founded **Boston** (1630). As the Massachusetts militia commander he provoked the **Pequot War** (1636–37). He was a founder of **Harvard** College (1636) and governor (1644–45, 1649–50, 1651–54, and 1655) until he died in Boston on March 15, 1655.

ENDICOTT, WILLIAM CROWNINSHIELD (1826–1900). Judge. Born in **Salem** on November 19, 1826, Endicott graduated from **Harvard** College (1847) and practiced law in Boston (1850–73). He was active in Democratic politics and served as a Massachusetts Supreme Court justice (1873–83). As secretary of war (1885–89), he rebuilt many of the New England coastal fortifications. Endicott, a scion of two distinguished Salem families, died on May 6, 1900.

ESPLANADE. The parkland along the Charles River in **Boston** designed by **Charles Eliot** and Sylvester Baxter, a Boston newspaperman (1892) to preserve the wetlands and eliminate the obnoxious river basin's saltwater mudflats. The scenic area is part of the urban landscaping inspired by **Frederick Law Olsmsted**, Eliot's mentor. **James J. Storrow** proposed a dam at the river mouth and purchase of the adjacent land by **Harvard**, MIT, and Boston University or by public funds. The Esplanade (1936) and an adjacent highway (1948) were named in Storrow's honor. **Arthur Fielder** conducted the **Boston Pops** concerts on the Esplanade each summer (1930). *See also* WHITE, PAUL DUDLEY.

ESSEX JUNTO. The name **John Hancock** gave to the Essex county **Federalists** who opposed him at the Massachusetts constitutional convention (1778). This faction supported Alexander Hamilton against Thomas Jefferson and succeeded in repealing the **Embargo Act** in 1809. Led by **Timothy Pickering**, the Junto discussed secession in 1805 and called the **Hartford Convention** (1814), proposing secession during the War of 1812.

EVACUATION DAY. A holiday in Suffolk County, Massachusetts, commemorating the withdrawal of British troops and ships from **Boston** on March 17, 1776. General George Washington sent a Boston bookstore owner, Colonel **Henry Knox**, to bring captured cannon 250 miles from Fort Ticonderoga to Boston. When Knox secretly mounted the cannon on Dorchester Heights on March 17, 1776, Sir William Howe evacuated his forces from the city before his ships were bombarded. The liberation of

Boston on the **Catholic** feast day of Saint Patrick led **Irish** Bostonians to sponsor a parade on this holiday. By 1901 the city authorized an annual parade around Dorchester Heights in South Boston to celebrate this important early victory and to honor (unofficially) the patron saint of Ireland on March 17. *See also* AMERICAN REVOLUTION; KNOX, HENRY.

EVARTS, WILLIAM M. (1818–1901). Public official. Born in **Boston** on February 6, 1818, William Maxwell Evarts graduated from Yale College (1837) and studied at **Harvard** Law School. He practiced law in New York City (1841–49), served as an assistant U.S. district attorney (1849–53), and as attorney general of the United States (1868–69). He was the chief counsel for President Andrew Johnson in the impeachment trial (1868), represented President Rutherford B. Hayes in the disputed election case (1877), and was secretary of state (1877–81). Elected as a Republican senator from New York (1885–91), Evarts retired to New York City, where he died on February 28, 1901.

EVERETT, EDWARD (1794–1865). Governor of Massachusetts. Born in Dorchester, Massachusetts, on April 11, 1794, Everett graduated from **Harvard** College (1811) and studied in Germany (1815–19). Ordained a **Unitarian** minister in **Boston** (1814), he taught Greek at Harvard (1815–26) and was editor of the *North American Review* (1820–23). Everett was elected as a Whig to the House of Representatives (1825–35) and as governor (1836–40). He was U.S. minister to Great Britain (1841–45) and president of Harvard College (1846–49). Everett served as secretary of state (1852–53) and in the Senate (1853–54). He was the Constitutional-Union party candidate for vice-president of the United States (1860) and a renowned orator when he died in Boston on January 15, 1865.

– F –

FAIRBANKS, ERASTUS (1792–1864). Governor of Vermont. Born in Brimfield, Massachusetts, on October 28, 1792, Fairbanks operated an iron foundry in St. Johnsbury, Vermont (1826). He and his brother, Thaddeus Fairbanks (1796–1886), invented and manufactured the first practical platform scale in St. Johnsbury (1831). Wealthy from worldwide sales to industries, Fairbanks served as a Whig in the state legislature (1836–39), founded the Passumpic Railroad (1850), and was elected

Republican governor (1852–53, 1860–61). He organized Vermont militia units for the **Civil War** and retired to St. Johnsbury, where he died on November 20, 1864.

FAIRFIELD, JOHN (1797–1847). Senator from Maine. Born in Saco on January 30, 1797, Fairfield attended Bowdoin College. He practiced law in Saco (1826–35) and was a Democrat in the House of Representatives (1835–38) and governor (1839–41, 1842–43), resigning to enter the Senate (1843–47). Fairfield became a national hero when he ordered the state militia to expel Canadian lumberjacks from the Aroostook River (1839). The **Aroostook War** ended when General Winfield Scott negotiated a peaceful halt with the governor of New Brunswick and **Daniel Webster** and **Edward Kavanagh** signed the **Webster-Ashburton Treaty** with Great Britain (1842). Fairfield died in Washington, D.C., on December 24, 1847.

FANEUIL HALL. Designed in **Boston**'s Dock Square by **John Smibert** as a public market for the **Huguenot** merchant Peter Faneuil, who donated (1742) the marketplace and meeting hall to the town. The second-story Great Hall has been the scene of many important public meetings, earning its name as the **Cradle of Liberty**. The cupola's copper weathervane, designed by Shem Drowne as a grasshopper (1741), is a familiar landmark on the **Freedom Trail**. Faneuil Hall, rebuilt after a fire (1762) and expanded by **Charles Bulfinch** (1806), continues to serve the city today as part of the Faneuil Hall Marketplace designed by **Benjamin C. Thompson** (1971–76).

FARLEY, HARRIET (1813–1907). Writer. Born in Claremont, New Hampshire, on February 18, 1813, Farley was the well-educated daughter of a minister. She worked in the **Lowell** mills (1837–40) and was editor of the *Lowell Offering* (1840–45, 1847–50). Her genteel literary magazine avoided all labor disputes, leading **Sarah Bagley** to denounce Farley as "a mouthpiece of the corporations" (1845). Farley revived the magazine (1847–50), but it never recovered its popularity. She moved to New York City, wrote for *Godey's Lady's Book* (1850), edited by her friend **Sarah J. Hale**, and died in New York on November 12, 1907.

FARMER, FANNIE MERRITT (1857–1915). Cooking teacher. Born in **Boston** on March 23, 1857, Miss Farmer was educated in Medford and graduated from the Boston Cooking School (1889). She was the school's director (1894–1902) until she founded Miss Farmer School of Cookery (1902) for Boston society girls and young housewives interested in the culinary arts. She edited 21 editions of *The Boston Cooking School Cook Book* (1896), later published as the *Fannie Farmer Cookbook*, but she was most proud of her book *Food and Cookery for the Sick and Convalescent* (1904). Her books and monthly column in the *Woman's Home Companion* introduced Americans to standardized level measurements, written recipes for classic and traditional foods, use of modern kitchen equipment, management of the home and domestic servants, formal entertaining, etiquette, diet, and nutrition. Miss Farmer died in Boston on January 15, 1915.

FAST DAY. A holiday in New Hampshire (1680–1991) celebrated on the fourth Monday in April. It began as a day of public humiliation, fasting, and prayer in 1680 for the recovery of the governor's health. Other colonies proclaimed fast days to avert or repent for plagues, earthquakes, or other disasters. Massachusetts had its first fast day in 1670 but substituted **Patriot's Day** for it in 1894. New Hampshire made fast day a legal holiday in 1899 but abolished it in 1991. This **Puritan** tradition held before the spring planting corresponds to **Thanksgiving Day** held after the fall harvest.

FAY, JONAS (1737–1818). Public official. Born in Hardwick, Massachusetts, on January 28, 1737, Fay served in the **Seven Years' War** (1755) and studied medicine. His family moved to Bennington, where his father's Catamount **Tavern** became a center of Vermont politics (1766–81). Fay served with **Ethan Allen** at the capture of Fort Ticonderoga (1775) and as a surgeon with **Seth Warner** and the **Green Mountain Boys** (1775–77). He held leadership roles in the revolutionary government and was the Vermont delegate to Congress (1777–82). When Congress delayed admission of Vermont as a new state, Dr. Fay negotiated with New York, New Hampshire, and the British on trade, prisoners, and **Loyalist** property. He served as a state judge (1777–82), founded the state medical society (1784), and died in Bennington on March 6, 1818. *See also* AMERICAN REVOLUTION.

FEDERALIST PARTY. Organized (1787) by conservatives who found the central government under the Articles of Confederation ineffective and supported the new U.S. Constitution. This political party lost popularity by 1820 but endured in New England long after the Whig and the

Democratic parties dominated local, state, and federal politics. Adoption of the new state constitution in 1818 vanquished Connecticut Federalists. The **Hartford Convention** was one of the last efforts by New England Federalist merchants to control the national government. Although **Daniel Webster** opposed the War of 1812, his party lost its national appeal and persisted only in New England until 1830.

FEKE, ROBERT (1707–1751). Artist. Born in Oyster Bay, New York, in 1707, Feke was the first painter born in America to achieve fame for his portraits. Largely self-taught, he was a mariner in **Newport** influenced by **John Smibert**, who also painted in Newport and **Boston**. Feke's best-known painting is *Isaac Royall and His Family* (1741), and portraits of ***Benjamin Franklin*** (1746) and ***James Bowdoin*** (1748), as well as two self-portraits (1742, 1750). Often overlooked as a pioneer in American **art**, Feke died at sea in 1751.

FENIAN RAIDS. Attacks by **Irish** Republican Brotherhood (or Fenian) soldiers on Canada to promote the independence of Ireland. Samuel Spear, a Union general in the **Civil War**, led 600 Fenian troops on June 1, 1866, from St. Albans, Vermont, into Canada. They battled the Canadian militia and British troops, but the Fenians surrendered on June 15 when the U.S. Army seized their supplies in St. Albans. One Vermont woman was killed accidentally by a British soldier pursuing the Fenians into Vermont, and a U.S. Army officer was reprimanded for permitting this violation of the U.S. border. The Fenians also raided Campobello Island (1866), which was claimed by Maine and New Brunswick. Colonel John O'Neill led 200 Fenians on another raid from St. Albans into Canada (May 1870) but was repelled by the Canadian militia. These incidents led to diplomatic tension between Great Britain and the United States.

FENWAY. A public park in **Boston** winding from the Charles River along the Muddy River and passing **Fenway Park** and the **Museum of Fine Arts**. It is a central link in the **Emerald Necklace** designed by **Frederick Law Olmsted**.

FENWAY PARK. Home of the **Boston Red Sox**. It is the country's oldest and smallest major league baseball stadium (1912), shoehorned between the streets of **Boston**'s Kenmore Square and **Frederick Law Olmsted**'s

Fenway. Built by the team owner, John J. Taylor, Fenway Park was the site of Red Sox World Series victories in 1912, 1915, 1916, and 1918. The next owner, **Tom Yawkey** (1933–76), expanded the stadium, but recent plans by new owners to replace or expand Fenway Park (2002) have created much public controversy. *See also* CURSE OF THE BAMBINO; SPORTS.

FENWAY STUDIOS. Built (1905) by **Eben Jordan** and **Boston** businessmen after the ateliers of Paris as living and working space for artists. The 46 studios on Ipswich Street in the **Fenway** district, designed in the Arts and Crafts style, have 12-foot ceilings and two-story windows facing the northern light. This is the oldest building in the country designed for and used by artists, who have included **John Singer Sargent** and **Lilla Cabot Perry**. It became a resident artist's cooperative in 1981. *See also* ART.

FENWICK, BENEDICT JOSEPH (1782–1846). Bishop. Born in Maryland on September 3, 1782, Fenwick was educated at Georgetown College (1793–1805) and ordained a **Jesuit** priest (1808). He served in New York, South Carolina, and Maryland and was president of Georgetown College (1817–25) when he became the second bishop of **Boston** (1825–46). His diocese, the smallest and most feeble of the nine American dioceses, served all of New England with only two priests and eight churches. Bishop Fenwick founded a seminary, sent students to Baltimore, Rome, and Paris, and founded *The Catholic Sentinel*, one of the first **Catholic** newspapers in the nation. As **Irish** Catholic **immigrants** arrived in Massachusetts and **anti-Catholicism** increased, Bishop Fenwick founded Holy Cross College in **Worcester** (1843), built an orphan asylum (1831), and established 50 churches for 53,000 parishioners in the diocese. Bishop Fenwick died in Boston on August 11, 1846.

FERN, FANNY (1811–1872). Journalist. Born in **Portland**, Maine, on July 9, 1811, Sara Payson was educated in **Boston**, Saugus, and **Catharine Beecher**'s seminary in **Hartford**. She wrote stories for her father's magazine, *Youth's Companion*, in Boston before her marriage (1837). As a widow and divorcee, Sara Payson Willis Parton supported her family by writing under the pen name Fanny Fern for newspapers and magazines (1851–72). Her best-selling collection of stories, *Fern*

Leaves from Fanny's Port-Folio (1853), led to a job as a columnist for the *New York Ledger*, making her the country's first female—and best paid—newspaper columnist until her death in New York City on October 10, 1872.

FESSENDEN, WILLIAM PITT (1806–1869). Senator from Maine. Born in Boscawen, New Hampshire, on October 16, 1806, Fessenden graduated from Bowdoin College (1827) and practiced law in Bangor and **Portland**. He was an **abolitionist** Whig in the Maine legislature (1832, 1840, 1845–46, 1853–54) and in the House of Representatives (1841–43), but was a Republican in the Senate (1854–64, 1866–69). As secretary of the treasury (1864–65), he was a moderate opposed to a punitive Reconstruction program and the impeachment of President Andrew Johnson. Fessenden died in Portland on September 8, 1869.

FIEDLER, ARTHUR (1894–1979). Orchestra leader. Born in **Boston** on December 17, 1894, Fiedler studied music in Vienna and Berlin (1911–15) and joined the **Boston Symphony Orchestra** (BSO) in 1915–30 as a violinist. By 1930 he was the permanent conductor of the BSO's public Promenade Concerts (1885), introducing light classical music and popular tunes to the public. Fiedler's large repertoire for the (renamed) **Boston Pops** summer series attracted a large **WGBH** radio and television audience by 1970. His Fourth of July concerts with a finale of fireworks on the banks of the Charles River **Esplanade** became national events. When Fiedler died in Brookline on July 10, 1979, the maestro was the world's most successful concert and recording conductor, famous for bridging the world of classical music and contemporary entertainment and making the Boston Pops Orchestra a New England cultural institution.

FIELD, CYRUS WEST (1819–1892). Businessman. Born in Stockbridge, Massachusetts, on November 30, 1819, Cyrus W. Field became wealthy in the **paper** business (1841–54). After traveling to South America with the painter **Frederic E. Church** in 1853, he organized the company that laid the transatlantic telegraph cable with **Samuel F. B. Morse** (1857–66). Field created the rapid transit system in New York City (1877–80) but went bankrupt developing the Wabash Railroad. Field, the brother of **David Dudley Field** and **Stephen J. Field**, died in New York City on July 12, 1892.

FIELD, DAVID DUDLEY (1805–1894). Lawyer. Born in Haddam, Connecticut, on February 13, 1805, Field, the brother of **Cyrus W. Field** and **Stephen J. Field**, studied at Williams College and practiced law in New York City (1828). He was chairman of the commission that reformed the New York civil law code (1848) and the penal code (1865), and both law codes were widely imitated. As a leader of the New York bar, he represented William Marcy Tweed, Jay Gould, and **James Fisk**, as well as Samuel J. Tilden in the disputed presidential election of 1876. Field died in New York City on April 13, 1894.

FIELD, STEPHEN JOHNSON (1816–1899). U.S. Supreme Court justice. Born in Haddam, Connecticut, on November 4, 1816, Field, the brother of **Cyrus W. Field** and **David Dudley Field**, graduated from Williams College (1837). He practiced law in New York City (1841–48) and in California. He served as a Democrat in the state legislature and was chief justice of the state supreme court (1859–63). President Abraham Lincoln appointed him to the U.S. Supreme Court (1863–97). Field died in Washington, D.C., on April 9, 1899.

FIELDS, ANNIE ADAMS (1834–1915). Writer. Born in **Boston** on June 6, 1834, Annie Adams married **James T. Fields** (1854). She assisted his work, presided over a noted **Beacon Hill** literary salon, and published a novel, *Asphodel* (1866), poetry on the **Shakers**, *The Children of Lebanon* (1872), and books on **James T. Fields** (1881), **Nathaniel Hawthorne** (1899), and **Harriet Beecher Stowe** (1897). As a widow, she lived with her close friend, **Sarah Orne Jewett**, in what was known as a **Boston Marriage**. Fields, a founder of the New England Women's Club and the Associated Charities (1879), was a noted philanthropist. She died in Boston on January 5, 1915, and her portrait by **John Singer Sargent** hangs in the **Boston Atheneum**.

FIELDS, JAMES THOMAS (1817–1881). Editor and publisher. Born in Portsmouth, New Hampshire, on December 31, 1817, James T. Fields was a partner in the renowned publishing company Ticknor and Fields (1832). The firm was located above its **Old Corner Book Store** in **Boston**. Fields succeeded **James Russell Lowell** as editor of the *Atlantic Monthly* (1861–70) and wrote *Yesterdays with Authors* (1872), *Hawthorne* (1876), and *In and Out of Doors with Charles Dickens* (1876). He and his wife, **Annie Adams Fields**, created a noted literary salon on **Beacon Hill** before his death in Boston on April 24, 1881. *See also* LITERATURE; TICKNOR, WILLIAM DAVIS.

5TH MASSACHUSETTS CAVALRY. The only **African-American** cavalry regiment from Massachusetts (1863–65) during the **Civil War**. Led by white officers, including Colonel **Charles Francis Adams, Jr.**, the men suffered from the same prejudice faced by the **54th Massachusetts** and other black units, despite loyal service in Maryland, Virginia, and Texas.

5TH NEW HAMPSHIRE REGIMENT. Organized by Colonel **Edward E. Cross** (1861) and became the most celebrated of 18 New Hampshire regiments in the **Civil War**. The Fighting 5th served in 34 engagements and suffered more combat casualties (295 killed, 756 wounded) than any of the 2,000 units in the Union Army. Only 156 of the 1,183 men in the regiment returned to New Hampshire in 1863.

54TH MASSACHUSETTS REGIMENT. The first **Civil War** army unit composed of free **African Americans**. It was organized by Massachusetts governor **John A. Andrew** and **Frederick Douglass** (1863). Led by Colonel **Robert Gould Shaw** and other white officers, the 54th Regiment attacked Fort Wagner in South Carolina on July 18, 1863. **Augustus Saint-Gaudens** collaborated with the architects **McKim, Mead and White** to design a high relief bronze Shaw Memorial (1897) commemorating the gallant, futile assault. The names of the 1,357 black soldiers from 24 states were added to this **Boston Common** sculpture (1984), and the popular film *Glory* (1989) retold the story of the 54th Massachusetts.

FIG NEWTON. A cookie filled with fig jam. It is named after the city of Newton, Massachusetts (1891), where it was produced by the Kennedy Biscuit Works (later Nabisco Company). Governor **William Weld** sparked debate (1997) when he lobbied the legislature to name the Fig Newton as the official state cookie. The bill failed to pass when the legislature honored the **Toll House Cookie**.

FILENE, EDWARD A. (1860–1937). Businessman. Born in **Salem**, Massachusetts, on September 3, 1860, Edward Albert Filene was educated in the Lynn public schools and a German military academy. He built his father's dry goods store (1890) into the famous **Boston** department store William Filene's Sons. His new merchandising ideas made Filene's 56 retail stores (1998) the most innovative in New England. The Boston store, opened on Washington Street (1912), is best known for Filene's Basement, offering leftover merchandise from fashionable stores at bargain prices. Filene worked with Lincoln Steffens in civic reform, established consumer cooperatives and credit unions, and was active in **Jewish** charities. He founded the Boston Chamber of Commerce and died in Paris on September 26, 1937.

FINNS. Settled in New Jersey and Delaware by 1640 but were a very small ethnic group in New England until the 1880s. Massachusetts had 9,500 Finns by 1900 in Fitchburg **textile** factories and **Cape Ann** granite quarries. **Congregational** missionaries converted many Finns by 1889, and Gardner, Massachusetts, had a Finnish Lutheran church by 1890. Mutual-aid associations, like the Saima Aid Society in Fitchburg (1890), or a **temperance** society in **Worcester** (1892), were established by workingmen. Many of the 350 Finnish magazines and newspapers in the United States circulated in New England. The *Finska Amerikanaren* (1897), founded in Worcester and moved to Brooklyn, became the leading newspaper for 6,000 Swedish-speaking Finns subscribers in 1917. Antero F. Tanner (1868–1917) established a socialist club in Rockport (1899) and a newspaper (1900), but these efforts were short-lived. The Finnish Socialist Federation had 260 local chapters with 12,600 members by 1913, sponsoring the newspaper *Tyomies* (903) in Worcester and *Raivaaja* (1905) in Fitchburg.

Finns, who introduced log cabins and barns, cooperatives, and the sauna, became naturalized citizens by 1920, often joining the Republican Party but switching to the Democratic Party in the 1930s. World War I interrupted Finnish **immigration**, and the quota laws (1924) limited the number. Few arrived after World War II, resulting in a decline of the New England Finnish population.

FIRST NIGHT. An alternative community celebration to traditional New Year's Eve revelry, began in 1976 with a group of artists on **Boston Common**. It became a private, nonprofit organization with art, dance, music, and theater performances and exhibits in churches, museums, and theaters as well as public ice sculptures, fireworks, and a Mardi Gras–style grand procession through the downtown streets. First Night is now an international event in more than 200 cities.

1ST VERMONT CAVALRY. Organized in Burlington on November 19, 1861. It was the first regiment in the Civil War mounted entirely on **Morgan horses**, a practiced followed by the 1st Maine Cavalry, the 1st Rhode Island Cavalry, and several other Union Army units. The 1st Vermont engaged in 76 battles from the Shenandoah Valley (1862) to Gettysburg (1863) until the surrender at Appomattox (1865). The regiment enlisted 2,304 men during the war and suffered 1,428 casualties (62 percent). Four troopers earned the Medal of Honor, including Colonel **William Wells** (1837–92), who General Philip H. Sheridan called "my ideal of a cavalryman" for his courage in the Battle of Gettysburg. Statues of Wells at Gettysburg and Burlington honor the 1st Vermont Cavalry.

FISHER, DOROTHY CANFIELD (1879–1958). Writer. Born in Lawrence, Kansas, Dorothy Canfield graduated from Ohio State University (1899) and received a Ph.D. at Columbia University (1904). When she married John R. Fisher (1907), they moved to her family farm in Arlington, Vermont, where she became a writer. During World War I she and her husband worked on relief programs in France and she became a leader of the Montessori teaching method. She was a founder of the Book-of-the-Month Club (1926–50); and in addition to her novels and popular fiction, she wrote *Vermont Tradition: The Biography of an Outlook on Life* (1953), and *Memories of Arlington, Vermont* (1957). Fisher, known as the First Lady of Vermont, died in Arlington on November 9, 1958.

FISHING. A traditional and essential part of the New England economy. Since prehistoric times fishermen found food in lakes and rivers. The shallow coastal waters offered more fish and shellfish (**clams**, crabs, mussels, oysters, **scallops**, and **lobster**). Ancient shell heaps on many beaches are evidence of the importance of shellfish to **Native Americans**. The harvesting of rich Atlantic Ocean fishing in the **Gulf of Maine** off New England predates Columbus, and the **Wampanoag** traded with Basque, **Portuguese**, Spanish, and French fishing boats by 1540. Fish was the principal source of North American wealth for the British by 1700.

In Connecticut, Groton was the chief fishing port by 1650, and the **Sacred Cod** (1748) hanging in the Massachusetts General Court chamber symbolizes the important of the **codfish** industry. *The Fog Warning*

(1885) by **Winslow Homer** depicted the labor of a lone New England fisherman in his **dory**.

Gloucester was New England's major fishing port (1623–1980), and foreign competition on **Georges Bank** led the federal government to subsidize the obsolete New England fishing fleet in 1964. But declining stocks of haddock, halibut, and mackerel led to federal regulations limiting fishing and the reduction of this traditional industry by 1972. Fishermen and conservationists successfully protested oil drilling on Georges Bank in 1979, but additional federal regulations reduced the Gloucester ground fish boats from 300 in 1979 to 144 in 2002. But commercial fishing accounted for 26,000 jobs and $860 million in the Maine economy in 2002. Since 1970 **aquaculture** has become a new industry in every New England state and the number of lobster and scallop boats has increased in recent years.

Since William Underwood (1787–1864) canned lobster in Maine and oysters in **Boston** (1850), the local market for New England seafood expanded across the world. Maine also opened a sardine cannery in Eastport (1876). **Railroads** carried oysters from Guilford, Norwalk, and Milford, Connecticut, to New York City by 1850. Revenues for Northeast fisheries reached a record $1.07 billion by 1999, and the National Marine Fisheries Service reported the largest catches were for lobster, salmon, scallop, crab, goosefish, northern quahog, menhaden, squid, clams, and cod. Commercial harvesting of sea urchins began in Connecticut and Maine in 1929; and by the 1980s the Asian market for Maine purple urchins expanded to Massachusetts and New Hampshire, with over 41 million pounds landed by 1993. Edible seaweed is another marine product harvested in Maine for food, fertilizer, toothpaste, cosmetics, and pharmaceuticals. **Whaling** ended by 1929, but whale watching tours and sport fishing attract countless tourists to seaports, as do many seafood restaurants in coastal communities. Tourists have also fished in New England lakes, rivers, and streams since the 1850s. *See also* ECONOMY.

FISK, CARLTON (1947–). Athlete. Born in Bellows Falls, Vermont, on December 26, 1947, Fisk was a star athlete at the University of New Hampshire. He was the All-Star (11 times) **Boston Red Sox** catcher (1972–81) and set a major league record for catching 2,226 games. Pudge Fisk later played for the Chicago White Sox (1981–93) and was inducted into the Baseball Hall of Fame (2000).

FISK, JAMES (1834–1872). Financier. Born in Bennington, Vermont, on April 1, 1834, Jim Fisk left school at an early age and worked a variety of jobs before becoming a buyer for the **Jordan Marsh** department store in **Boston**. With Daniel Drew and Jay Gould, he became a master of Wall Street stock speculation. He was notorious for ruthless competition with Cornelius Vanderbilt to control the Erie Railroad, and his attempt to corner the gold market caused the Black Friday Panic on September 24, 1869. The **railroad** tycoon known as the Barnum of Wall Street lived an extravagant life in New York City until he was shot in a lover's quarrel on January 7, 1872.

FITCH, JOHN (1743–1798). Inventor. Born in **Hartford**, Connecticut, on January 21, 1743, Fitch was an apprentice clockmaker. He operated a brass foundry in East Windsor, served in the **American Revolution**, and managed a gun factory. Settled in Pennsylvania (1785), he invented a steamboat that he sailed on the Delaware River (1787). Fitch carried cargo and passengers from Philadelphia to Trenton (1790), but his venture failed despite his attempts to find backers in Paris. He died in Kentucky on July 2, 1798.

FITCH, THOMAS (1700–1774). Governor of Connecticut. Born in Norwalk in 1700, Fitch graduated from Yale College (1721) and practiced law in Norwalk. He served in the colonial legislature (1726–51), as deputy governor (1751–54), and as governor (1754–66). He revised the colony's law code (1750) and wrote a pamphlet (1764) against the **Stamp Act**, but his **Loyalist** views led the patriots to replace him (1766). Fitch died in Norwalk on July 18, 1774. His son, Colonel Thomas Fitch, Jr. (1724–95) and his Connecticut troops in the **French and Indian War** and at the battle at Fort Ticonderoga (1775) adopted the song "Yankee Doodle."

FITZ, REGINALD HEBER (1843–1913). Physician. Born in Chelsea, Massachusetts, on May 5, 1843, Fitz graduated from **Harvard** College (1864) and Harvard Medical School (1868). After study in Austria and Germany, he taught pathology at Harvard (1870–1913), introducing clinical use of the microscope, scientific diagnosis, and therapeutic treatment of appendicitis and pancreatitis. Fitz, who helped make Boston an international medical center, died in **Boston** on September 30, 1913.

FITZGERALD, JOHN F. (1863–1950). Mayor of **Boston**. Born in Boston on February 11, 1863, John Francis Fitzgerald was the Democratic boss of the **North End** and a newspaper publisher. Elected to the Boston Common Council (1892), state senate (1893–95), and the House of Representatives (1895–1901, 1919), Honey Fitz, as he was known for his golden voice, was the first Boston-born **Irish Catholic** mayor (1906–07, 1910–14). His daughter, **Rose Fitzgerald Kennedy**, who often campaigned with him, was the mother of President **John Fitzgerald Kennedy**. Best known as a rival to **James Michael Curley**, Fitzgerald died in Boston on October 2, 1950.

FITZPATRICK, JOHN B. (1812–1866). Bishop. Born in **Boston** on November 15, 1812, John Bernard Fitzpatrick graduated from **Boston Latin School** and was ordained a Catholic priest in Paris (1840). He served as a pastor in Cambridge and succeeded Bishop **Benedict Fenwick** as the third bishop of Boston (1846). As a native Bostonian, Fitzpatrick coped diplomatically with violent **anti-Catholicism**, obtained the election of Catholics to the Boston school committee, and appointed chaplains to state militia companies. He cooperated with Governor **John A. Andrew** to encourage Catholics to join the Union Army in the **Civil War**. During a long visit to Europe (1862–64) to improve his health, Fitzpatrick assumed the duties of the often absent American ambassador in Brussels. The diocese had prospered under his wise but cautious administration when he died in Boston on February 13, 1866.

FLANDERS, RALPH E. (1880–1970). Senator from Vermont. Born in Barnet, Vermont, on September 28, 1880, Ralph Edward Flanders lived in Rhode Island as a child. He worked in the machine tool industry in **Providence** (1897–1910) and Springfield, Vermont, making original contributions to the important industry that formed the backbone of the **Connecticut River** Valley economy. Flanders served as a Republican senator (1946–59) and was the first Republican to challenge Senator Joseph McCarthy's anticommunist crusade. Flanders died in Springfield on February 19, 1970.

FLUTIE, DOUG (1962–). Athlete. Born in Manchester, Maryland, on October 23, 1962, Flutie was a high school football star in Natick, Massachusetts, and a quarterback at Boston College (1981–85). He won the 50th Heisman Trophy (1984) and was the first collegiate quarterback to pass for more than 10,000 yards. Flutie played in the National Football League for the **New England Patriots** and in New Jersey, Chicago, Buffalo, and San Diego as well as in Canada.

FLYNN, ELIZABETH GURLEY (1890–1964). Labor leader. Born in **Concord**, New Hampshire, on August 7, 1890, Elizabeth Gurley Flynn was the daughter of socialist workers. She left high school to organize for the Industrial Workers of the World (IWW) in 1907 and began a lifelong career as a labor leader, socialist, and communist. Known as a rousing platform speaker and tireless organizer, she was prominent in the **Lawrence Strike** (1912) and in the **Sacco-Vanzetti Case** (1920s). Flynn was a founder of the American Civil Liberties Union (ACLU) in 1920, and Joe Hill wrote the IWW song *The Rebel Girl* about her. She joined the Communist Party (1937), becoming chair of the party (1961–64). Imprisoned (1955–57) for violation of the Smith Alien Registration Act, she wrote *I Speak My Own Piece: Autobiography of "The Rebel Girl"* (1955). After wining a U.S. Supreme Court case to obtain her passport, Flynn visited the USSR, where she died on September 5, 1964, honored with a state funeral in Moscow.

FLYNN, WILLIAM SMITH (1885–1966). Governor of Rhode Island. Born in **Providence** on August 14, 1885, Flynn graduated from Holy Cross College (1907) and Georgetown University Law School (1910). Practicing law in Providence (1910–23), he was a Democrat in the state legislature (1912–23), leading the effort to abolish property qualifications for voting. Elected governor (1923–25) despite Republican Party control of state government, Flynn's administration is most recalled for the violence that broke out during the Democrats' filibuster (1924) in the state senate. Conservative Republican legislators refused to agree to a constitutional convention, some senators fled to Massachusetts, and Flynn was criticized for refusing to call out the state National Guard. Although he was nominated for the U.S. Senate (1924), his political career had ended and he died in Pawtucket on April 13, 1966.

FOOT, SAMUEL AUGUSTUS (1780–1846). Senator from Connecticut. Born in Cheshire, Connecticut, on November 8, 1780, Foot graduated from Yale College (1797) and studied at the Litchfield Law School. Engaged in the **West Indies trade** in New Haven, he served as a Democrat in the state legislature (1817–18, 1821–23, 1825–26) and in the House of Representatives (1819–21, 1823–25, 1833–34). In the Senate (1827–33), he supported protective tariffs benefiting Connecticut **textile** industries and opposed the Jacksonian Democrats and slavery. Foot, an ally of **John Quincy Adams**, was the Whig governor (1834–35) and died in Cheshire on September 15, 1846.

FOOTE, ANDREW HULL (1806–1863). Naval officer. Born on September 12, 1806, in **New Haven**, Connecticut, Foote was the son of Senator **Samuel Augustus Foot**. He entered West Point (1822) but resigned to accept a commission in the U.S. Navy. He organized sailors into a temperance society and abolished the rum ration in the navy (1862). In the **Civil War**, Commodore Foote supported the Union Army in capturing Fort Henry and Fort Donelson (1862), and he opened the Mississippi River to Union forces. Wounded at Fort Donelson, Foote was promoted to rear admiral but died in New York City on June 26, 1863.

FORBES, ESTHER (1891–1967). Writer. Born in **Worcester**, Massachusetts, on June 28, 1891, Esther Forbes studied at the University of Wisconsin (1916–18) and worked in **Boston** for the Houghton Mifflin publishing firm (1919–26). She won the Pulitzer Prize for her biography *Paul Revere and the World He Lived In* (1942) and wrote a popular novel set in Revolutionary War Boston, *Johnny Tremain* (1943). She died in Worcester on August 12, 1967.

FORBES, JOHN MURRAY (1813–1898). Businessman. Born in France on February 23, 1813, Forbes was raised in Milton and apprenticed (1827–30) in **Boston** with his uncle, **Thomas H. Perkins**. He accumulated a fortune as a Boston merchant in Canton (1830–32, 1834–37), but, unlike his brother, **Robert Bennet Forbes**, he abandoned the **China trade** for **railroads** (1843), first in New York and then in the Midwest. Forbes transferred New England capital from the maritime trades to railroads, completing the Michigan Central from Detroit to Chicago (1852), connecting with the Chicago, Burlington & Quincy (1856), and serving as president of lines in Missouri, Iowa, and Nebraska. Forbes supported the **abolitionists** and the Union in the **Civil War** and was the leading conservative **Boston Brahmin** financier when he died in Milton on October 12, 1898.

FORBES, ROBERT BENNET (1804–1889). Businessman. Born in **Boston** on September 18, 1804, Forbes was a sea captain and merchant in the **China trade**. He apprenticed with his uncle, **Thomas H. Perkins**, and went to sea at age 13, earning a fortune in the **Opium trade** with China and importing silk, spices, tea, opium, and porcelain to Boston. One of the pioneers in the use of screw propellers on steamships, he retired from business (1850) but organized the Massachusetts Coast Guard and built gunboats for the U.S. Navy during the **Civil War**. Captain Forbes died in Milton on November 23, 1889, and his Greek revival house (1833) overlooking Boston harbor became the China Trade Museum (1970–84).

FORD, JOHN (1894–1973). Actor and film director. Born on February 1, 1894, in Portland, Maine, John Martin Ford was the son of **Irish Catholic immigrants**. After graduating high school in **Portland** (1913), he became an actor in Hollywood. By the 1930s Ford was one of the great directors in the golden age of movies. Ford explored a New England theme in *The Last Hurrah* (1958), a fictional account of Boston Mayor **James Michael Curley** based on **Edwin O'Connor**'s novel. John Ford died in California on August 31, 1973. The city of Portland erected a statue of John Ford in 1998.

FORT WESTERN (1754). America's oldest-surviving wooden military fortress. Built by the **Kennebec Proprietors** on the Kennebec River in **Augusta**, Maine, Captain James Howard's **Scotch Irish** militia company garrisoned the fort (1754–63) in the **French and Indian War**. General **Benedict Arnold** used the fort to stage an invasion of Canada (1775). Howard purchased the fort as a trading post, sailing his sloop to **Boston** to exchange **furs** and **lumber** for trade goods and attracting new settlers after the **American Revolution**. The fort is preserved today as a National Historic Landmark and museum of the New England frontier.

FOSTER, ABIGAIL KELLEY (1810–1887). Reformer. Born in an **Irish Quaker** family in Pelham, Massachusetts, on January 15, 1810, Abby Kelley studied at the Friends School in Rhode Island. While teaching at the Friends School in Lynn, Massachusetts, she became a disciple of **William Lloyd Garrison** (1835). She was one of the first women to give public lectures (1838) and married a radical abolitionist, Stephen Symonds Foster (1845). Their Liberty Farm in **Worcester**, Massachusetts, was an **Underground Railroad** station and where she organized the women's rights convention in Worcester (1850). Denied the right to vote, she refused to pay taxes on her farm, which was auctioned several times by the state (1870) but purchased by friends and restored to her.

Her home is a National Historic Landmark. Abby Kelley Foster was a tireless reformer until her death in Worcester on January 14, 1887.

FOSTER, FRANK KEYES (1854–1909). Labor leader. Born on December 18, 1854, in Thorndike, Massachusetts, Foster was a printer in **Hartford**. Settling in **Boston** (1880), he was a leader of the International Typographical Union, the Boston Central Trades and Labor Union, and the Knights of Labor. He was editor of the Knights' newspaper, the *Laborer,* in Haverhill (1884–87) and edited the *Labor Leader* with **George E. McNeill** in Boston (1887–97), the official organ of the Massachusetts Federation of Labor. As an advocate for pure and simple trade unionism, he influenced Samuel L. Gompers and the American Federation of Labor (AFL). Foster wrote social protest poetry and an autobiographical novel, *The Evolution of a Trade Unionist* (1901) and challenged **Harvard University** president **Charles W. Eliot** for his criticism of the trade union movement (1904). Foster died in Boston in 1909.

FRANK, BARNEY (1940–). Congressman from Massachusetts. Born in Bayonne, New Jersey, on March 31, 1940, Frank graduated from **Harvard University** (1962). While studying political science at Harvard (1962–72), he served as assistant to **Boston** mayor Kevin White and to Congressman Michael Harrington (1971–72). Elected as a Democrat to the state legislature (1973–80), Frank graduated from Harvard Law School (1977) and taught at Harvard, the University of Massachusetts-Boston, and Boston University. Elected to the House of Representatives (1981–), Frank was active in liberal issues and including civil rights for homosexuals but was censured by the House for misconduct. Despite this he became a leader of the liberal wing of the Democratic Party and wrote *Speaking Frankly* (1992).

FRANKFURTER, FELIX (1882–1965). U.S. Supreme Court justice. Born in Vienna, Austria, on November 15, 1882, Frankfurter came to New York City (1893) and graduated from the City College of New York (1902) and **Harvard** Law School (1906). He was an assistant to Henry Stimson, the U.S. attorney for New York (1906–09), and the secretary of war (1911–13). Frankfurter taught at Harvard Law School (1914–39) and advised President Woodrow Wilson at the Paris Peace Conference (1919). He and **Roger N. Baldwin** were founders of the American Civil Liberties Union (ACLU) in 1920. With private encouragement from **Louis D. Brandeis**, Frankfurter criticized the **Sacco-Vanzetti Case**. He advised Franklin D. Roosevelt as governor and president, and Roosevelt appointed Frankfurter to the Supreme Court (1939–62), the first **Jewish immigrant** to serve on the Court. Frankfurter upheld freedom of expression in *Sweezy v. New Hampshire* (1957), when a socialist college professor was subjected to a state investigation. After he retired (1962), President **John F. Kennedy** awarded him the Medal of Freedom. Frankfurter wrote *The Business of the Supreme Court* (1927), *Mr. Justice Holmes and the Supreme Court* (1938), and *The Case of Sacco and Vanzetti* (1954). He died in Washington, D.C., on February 22, 1965.

FRANKLIN, BENJAMIN (1706–1790). Public official. Born in **Boston** on January 17, 1706, Franklin was the son of a poor Calvinist candlemaker who emigrated from England. He learned the printing trade as an apprentice to his brother, James Franklin, publisher of the *New-England Courant* newspaper (1721–23). The runaway apprentice worked in Philadelphia and London (1723–26), became a prosperous printer in Philadelphia, and was famous as the author of *Poor Richard's Almanac* (1732–57). Franklin played a major role in the **American Revolution**, as a radical advocate of independence, a diplomat in Paris, and a pioneer American scientist. With **John Adams**, Robert Livingston, Thomas Jefferson, and **Roger Sherman** he wrote the Declaration of Independence in June 1776. Ben Franklin, the New England philosopher and deist, is best known from his *Autobiography* (1766) and a portrait (1789) by Charles Wilson Peale. He embodied the many facets of the American character when he died in Philadelphia on April 17, 1790. *See also* ALMANAC.

FREEDOM TRAIL. A three-mile walking tour marked by signs and red bricks embedded in **Boston** sidewalks guiding **tourists** to 16 historic sites. Suggested by William Schofield, a *Boston Herald Traveler* writer (1951), the concept was adopted by Mayor John B. Hynes and supported by the Greater Boston Chamber of Commerce, the **Boston National Historical Park**, and local historical organizations. The footpath brings 60,000 tourists and schoolchildren to Boston historic sites each year.

FREEMAN, MARY ELEANOR WILKINS (1852–1930). Writer. Born in Randolph, Massachusetts, on October 31, 1852, Mary Wilkins lived in Brattleboro, Vermont, and studied at Mount Holyoke College (1870–71). She wrote stories for **Boston** newspapers (1883) about New England **Yankees** in the local color style. She is best remembered for two collections, *A Humble Romance* (1887) and *A New England Nun* (1891). She married Charles M. Freeman and lived in New Jersey, where she died on March 13, 1930.

FRENCH AND INDIAN WARS (1689–1763). Armed conflicts between the British colonies in North America and the French and Spanish colonies, including **King Williams's War** (1689–97), **Queen Anne's War** (1702–13), and **King George's War** (1739–48). These were part of an international struggle for empire, but to New England it was a long war with periods of truce. Massachusetts governor **William Shirley** failed to seize Fort Niagara (1755), but British general James Wolfe captured Quebec. The final phase of the war, known as the Seven Years' War (1756–63), made Americans more independent, ended French control of New France, halted Indian raids on the New England frontier, and ceded Florida from Spain to Britain (1763).

FRENCH, DANIEL CHESTER (1850–1931). Sculptor. Born in Exeter, New Hampshire, on April 20, 1850, French studied at MIT and with **Thomas Ball** and **William Morris Hunt**. After traveling in Italy and France (1874–76), he worked in **Boston** and **Concord** (1878–88) creating bronze statues that became unsurpassed public monuments. His first commission was the **Minute Man** (1875) in Concord, commemorating the hundredth anniversary of the **Battle of Lexington and Concord**. He also executed busts of **Ralph Waldo Emerson** (1879) and the statue of **John Harvard** at **Harvard University** (1884). He designed the memorial to **John Boyle O'Reilly** (1896) in Boston's Fenway, the **Boston Public Library** low-relief bronze doors (1902), and the **Civil War** monument, *Mourning Victory,* (1908) in Concord's **Sleepy Hollow Cemetery**. His greatest public **art** project may be the gigantic marble Lincoln Memorial (1919) in Washington, D.C. French died at his studio in Stockbridge, Massachusetts, on October 7, 1931. *See also* ART; DEVENS, CHARLES.

FRENCH CANADIANS. One of the largest ethnic groups in New England, which represented 18 percent (or 2,352,368) of the region's 12,291,438 people in 1990. Vermont estimates 30 percent of its population today are people of French-Canadian descent, with 29 percent in New Hampshire, 27 percent in Maine, 21 percent in Rhode Island, 16 percent in Massachusetts, and 11 percent in Connecticut. The first U.S. Census (1790) listed 350 *Quebecois* in Vermont, 1,200 in Maine, and

1,000 in New Hampshire, but New England had 8,200 French Canadians by 1840 and 723,000 in 1900. The revolt in Upper Canada (1838), clashes between the *habitants* (farmers) and British-Canadian soldiers, mounting resentment over religious and cultural intolerance, and economic decline prompted the migration south. More than 900,000 emigrated from Quebec (1840–1930), finding jobs in New England mills and factories in **Lowell**, Lawrence, **New Bedford**, Fall River, **Waltham**, and **Worcester**, Massachusetts. Other centers for the *Quebecois* were Manchester, New Hampshire; Biddeford, Sacco, Lewiston, and the upper Saint John Valley in Maine; and Woonsocket and Pawtucket, Rhode Island. Many French Canadians first worked in the northern New England **quarries** or the **lumber** and **paper** industry. In Vermont, Burlington had more than 500 French Canadians in 1832 and many family farms along the border. More than 66,000 lived in New Hampshire by 1910, but Rhode Island industries employed 65,000 French Canadians in 1911, and they were 12.5 percent of the state population by 1920.

Unlike other **immigrants**, especially the **Huguenots** who settled in **Boston** and **Providence** by 1686, the French-Canadian Catholics blended slowly into the regional **Yankee** culture. Many spoke French at home or work and retained ethnic cohesion by **Catholic** parishes and schools. With the **Irish**, they made Roman Catholicism the region's largest religious denomination. The first French-Canadian Catholic parish was in Burlington, Vermont (1850), and then Springfield (1867) and Lowell (1868), Massachusetts, and **Portland**, Maine (1869).

Lowell elected the first French Canadian to public office in 1874. City Councilor Samuel P. Marin built the first tenements in a block known as Little Canada (1875). Francophone clubs, shops, and fraternal societies appeared as others moved into New England. As railroads replaced stage coaches between Quebec and Boston (1851), **Portland** (1853), and New York City (1854), migration became convenient and cheap. French Canadians assisted mill workers by establishing the first credit union in the United States in Manchester, New Hampshire (1909).

Due to the **Civil War** and migration of **Yankees** from the region, French Canadians were needed as industrial workers, numbering as many as 1.2 million from 1851–1951. By 1870, 67 percent of the **textile** workers were French Canadians, and by 1885, they were 60 percent of the shoe workers. As late as 1950, 40 percent were in factory work but only 16 percent were in white-collar jobs. This slow progress was due to the conservative nature of this group, making them reluctant to leave ethnic communities or join labor unions, accept naturalization, and assimilate. **Carroll D. Wright**, head of the Massachusetts Bureau of Statistics for Labor, expressed the prejudice French Canadians faced when he called (1881) them "the Chinese of the Eastern States." They were often criticized by the derogatory name **Canuck** for working in New England shoe or textile mills as "floaters," only to return home to Canada in the slack season. But many were here to stay, and the St. Jean Baptiste Society responded to the hostility of Irish and labor leaders by holding its first procession in Lowell (1881). At the same time a lawyer, J. H. Guillet, founded the Lowell *L'Abeille*, the first Franco-American newspaper in the country. A second Lowell newspaper, *L'Etoile,* was published in 1886.

St. Joseph Church in Lowell opened the first French-Canadian school in Massachusetts (1883), but some Yankees worried that instruction in French would not Americanize the children of immigrants. The Rhode Island State Board of Education made teaching in a foreign language a public issue (1883) owing to fears that French-Canadian children would not become loyal Americans if they did not speak English. During World War I these nativist fears resurfaced in *Providence Journal* newspaper editorials (1919). When the Republican Party and the Ku Klux Klan (KKK) in southern Rhode Island supported a state law to restrict foreign language in schools (1924), many French Canadians in New England joined the Democratic Party. In Woonsocket a dispute over use of the French language in parochial schools threatened the French-Canadian community and the Catholic Diocese of Providence. This Sentinelle Affair (1924–29) ended when moderates arranged a compromise but revealed the strong attachment of French Canadians to their religion and language as well as the rise of ethnic prejudice in New England. Connecticut also banned the use of foreign languages in public school (1918). The Ku Klux Klan in Maine and Massachusetts was openly hostile to French-Canadian residents in the 1920s.

However, friction with the Yankees and the Irish Catholics remained common in French-Canadian politics and religion. Election to local office began in Lowell (1874), but only 13 French Canadians held state legislative seats in 1890. Rhode Island elected **Aram J. Pothier** as New England's first French-Canadian governor (1908) and then sent **Louis Monast** to the House of Representatives (1926) and **Felix Hebert** to the U.S. Senate (1928). Unlike the Irish, French-Canadian voters were divided between the Republican and Democratic parties, and since 1950 many voted as Independents. Intermarriage was rare until 1940, when ethnic identification focused on the family, church, and language weakened. However, in the 1970s Franco-American organizations expanded in northern New England. The Quebec separatist movement (1968) revived ethnic pride among Quebec's French-speaking majority—80 percent of the 7 million inhabitants—and this has enhanced the self-image of New Englanders whose ancestors came from *la belle province*. The **Rhode Island Historical Society** operates the Museum of Work & Culture in Woonsocket to portray the story of the French-Canadian immigrants from the *Quebecois* farmhouse to New England mills and cities. Among the prominent New Englanders from this important ethnic group were George Albert Guertin (1869–1931), the third Catholic bishop of Manchester, New Hampshire, as well as **Rudy Vallee**, **Jack Kerouac**, and **Grace Metalious**.

FRIENDLY'S. A chain of restaurant franchises in 17 states from Maine to Florida. Founded in Springfield, Massachusetts (1935), as an ice cream shop and based in Wilbraham, Friendly's sells its New England–style food and ice cream in more than 600 roadside restaurants.

FRISBEE. A recreational game first played by Yale University students using pie plates from the Frisbie Pie Company of Bridgeport, Connecticut, in the 1970s.

FROST, ROBERT (1874–1963). Poet. Born in San Francisco on March 26, 1874, Robert Lee Frost grew up in Lawrence, Massachusetts, and attended Dartmouth College (1892) and **Harvard University** (1897–99). After working as a teacher, newspaper reporter, and farmer in Derry, New Hampshire, Frost moved to England (1912–15) where he published his first poetry volumes, *A Boy's Will* (1913) and *North of Boston* (1914). This established his reputation before he settled in Franconia, New Hampshire (1915). Frost wrote *Mountain Interval* (1916) and *New Hampshire* (1923), which won the first of his four Pulitzer Prizes (1924, 1931, 1937, 1943). He also lived in South Shaftsbury, Vermont (1920–29), and is best known for combining lyric and dramatic poetry in blank verse, both pastoral and philosophical. Frost was both a popular and a great poet when he died in **Boston** on January 29, 1963.

FRUITLANDS. A **Transcendentalist** commune (1843–44) founded by **Bronson Alcott** in Harvard, Massachusetts, on vegetarian and utopian principles. Clara Endicott Sears, an early New England preservationist, restored the house as part of the Fruitlands Museum (1914), which includes the Alcott house, a **Shaker** building (1916), the American Indian Museum (1928), and an art gallery (1941).

FULLER, ALVAN TUFTS (1878–1958). Governor of Massachusetts. Born in **Boston** on February 27, 1878, Fuller was a bicycle manufacturer and owner of the Packard Motor Car Company in Boston. He served as a Republican state legislator (1915), congressman (1917–21), lieutenant governor (1921–25), and governor (1925–29). Fuller played a key role in the **Sacco-Vanzetti Case** (1927), refusing to prevent their execution. He retired to his automobile dealership and died in Boston on April 30, 1958.

FULLER, BUCKMINSTER (1895–1983). Inventor. Born in Milton, Massachusetts, on July 12, 1895, Richard Buckminster Fuller, Jr., was educated at **Harvard University** (1913–15) and the U.S. Naval Academy (1917). After serving in the U.S. Navy in World War I, "Bucky" worked in his family **architecture** and construction firm. He moved to Chicago (1927) to develop his unorthodox design theory, which he called Dymaxion, as an original blend of engineering, mathematics, and philosophy. He built a Dymaxion house, automobile, world map, and steel igloo, which were more efficient and less expensive than conventional designs. His geodesic domes (1948) were adopted by the U.S. Air Force, and he coined the terms Spaceship Earth and synergetic while teaching architecture at Yale, Cornell, Princeton, and MIT. Fuller wrote *Operating Manual for Spaceship Earth* (1969) and *Approaching the Benign Environment* (1970). An individualist whose genius had transformed architecture, **art**, mathematics, philosophy, urban development and technology, Fuller died on July 1, 1983.

FULLER BRUSH MAN. Name given to Alfred Carl Fuller (1885–1973), who was born in Nova Scotia and sold brushes in **Boston** (1903). He founded the Fuller Brush Company in **Hartford** (1906), making wire brushes himself and selling them door-to-door. By 1913 the Fuller Brush Man was a national phenomenon and the subject of a movie, *The Fuller Brush Man* (1948). Fuller wrote his autobiography *A Foot in the Door* (1960) and died on December 4, 1973.

FULLER, MARGARET (1810–1850). Writer and social reformer. Born in Cambridge, Massachusetts. on May 23, 1810, Sarah Margaret Fuller was a precocious child extremely well educated for a woman of her time. She began a series of philosophical "conversations" or discussions (1839–44) for intellectual **Boston** women. Closely associated with **Ralph Waldo Emerson**'s **Transcendentalist** circle, she edited a literary magazine, *The Dial* (1840–42), and was a critic for the *New York Tribune* (1844–46). Her book *Woman in the Nineteenth Century* (1845) established Fuller as the leading feminist critic in the nation. While a foreign correspondent in Italy for the *Tribune*, she married the Marchese Giovanni Angelo Ossoli. Fuller died on July 19, 1850, with her husband and son in a **shipwreck** off New York.

FULLER, MELVILLE WESTON (1833–1910). Chief justice of the U.S. Supreme Court. Born in **Augusta**, Maine, on February 11, 1833, Fuller graduated from Bowdoin College (1853) and studied at **Harvard** Law School. He practiced law (1855–84) in Chicago and became chief justice (1888–1910), serving as a moderate on the Court. Fuller was a member of the arbitration commission in the boundary dispute between Great Britain and Venezuela (1897–99) and on the Permanent Court of International Justice (PCIJ) at The Hague (1900–10) until he died in Sorrento, Maine, on July 4, 1910.

FUNDAMENTAL ORDERS. Adopted (1638–39) to create the commonwealth of Connecticut and written by **Thomas Hooker** and **Roger Ludlow**. Settlers from Wethersfield and Windsor met in **Hartford** to establish the body of laws for a government independent of England. This was the first written constitution in America and the beginning of American democracy. It provided for self-government like Massachusetts except that church membership was not a qualification for voting and the legislature could convene without the governor's consent. The royal charter confirmed these laws (1662), and during the **American Revolution** the legislature adopted a resolution (1776) to eliminate from the charter all references to Britain. The Fundamental Orders were in effect until 1818 and gave Connecticut its designation as the **Constitution State**.

FUR TRADE. Influenced economic life in New England from the first, as well as its exploration, settlement, and relations with **Native Americans**, the Dutch, British, and French. European demand for bear, beaver, deer, fox, and wolf skins led settlers from the Eastern seaboard into the wilderness. The **Pilgrims** engaged in the fur trade with Native Americans, traveling as far as Maine (1625) to obtain pelts. These animals were extinct in England and scarce in Europe, where fur was prized for clothing, trimming, and felt hats. **Pequots** and other coastal tribes traded **corn** with other Native Americans for pelts to exchange with English merchants. By 1700 beaver skins were a medium of exchange and a means of reckoning daily wages. Europeans traded blankets, utensils, weapons, and **rum** for furs, revolutionizing tribal life. The **French and Indian War** (1756–63) was caused in part by British competition with the French to control the fur trade in New England, New York, and the Ohio River valley. **Boston** merchants used furs from Oregon (1790) in the profitable **China trade**, and American fur traders explored the Mississippi River to the Rocky Mountains for beaver skins until 1840.

FURCOLO, FOSTER (1911–1995). Governor of Massachusetts. Born in **New Haven** on July 29, 1911, Furcolo graduated from Yale University (1933) and Yale Law School (1936). He practiced law in Springfield (1937–41) and served in the Navy (1941–45). He was elected as a Democrat in the House of Representatives (1949–52), as state treasurer (1953–54), and as governor (1957–61). Furcolo was the first **Italian-American** governor of Massachusetts and founded the state community college system. He was an administrative law judge for the U.S. Occupational Safety and Health Review Commission (1975–95) when he died in Needham on July 5, 1995.

– G –

GAGE, THOMAS (1721–1787). Governor of Massachusetts. Born in England in 1721, Thomas Gage served in the British Army in the **French and Indian War** (1756–63) and succeeded **Thomas Hutchinson** as the last royal governor of Massachusetts (1774–75). Despite long experience in the colonies, General Gage underestimated the impact of the **Intolerable Acts** (1774) and his 4,000 British troops could not subdue the restless New Englanders. Under orders from London to restore order, he sent troops to seize rebel arms in **Concord** on April 18, 1775, precipitating the **American Revolution**. With reinforcements from Nova Scotia, Gage attacked **Bunker Hill** on June 17, 1775, winning a Pyrrhic victory that demoralized his forces. Succeeded by General **William Howe**, Gage returned to London, where he died on April 2, 1787.

GALLEN, HUGH J. (1924–1982). Governor of New Hampshire. Born in Portland, Oregon, on July 24, 1924, Gallen was raised in Medford,

Massachusetts, and came to New Hampshire in the 1940s as a Civilian Conservation Corps forestry worker. By 1948 he was a successful automobile dealer in Littleton and was the first Democrat elected by his town to the state legislature (1973–74). He won a close campaign for governor (1979–81) against former Republican governor **Meldrim Thomson** and former governor Wesley Powell, an Independent, despite much criticism by the *Manchester Union Leader*. Gallen won national publicity when he ordered the National Guard to control Clamshell Alliance protestors at the **Seabrook Station** nuclear power plant (1979). He was reelected (1980) over Thomson but lost to **John Sununu** in 1982. Gallen died in office on December 29, 1982.

GAMES. Introduced by the 17th-century settlers in New England, although the **Puritans** disliked most traditional English games and sports. In 1864 **Milton Bradley** (1836–1911), a Springfield, Massachusetts, lithographer, produced a board game called *The Checkered Game of Life* that proved very popular. He also sold kits of *Games of Soldiers*, a set of pocket-sized travel games popular with **Civil War** soldiers, as were his educational and entertaining quiz games. He made educational toys and art supplies as well as games. By 1880 Bradley added jigsaw puzzles to his company, which was the most successful manufacturer of board games in the nation. **George S. Parker** founded the Parker Brothers Company in **Salem**, Massachusetts, manufacturing many board games. James Brunot first manufactured *Scrabble* in Dodgington, Connecticut (1948), and later in Rhode Island and Vermont.

GARDNER MUSEUM. Located in **Boston** and one of the leading private collections of European **art** in America. It was founded by Isabella Stewart Gardner (1840–1924). Born in New York City on April 14, 1840, Miss Stewart married John L. Gardner (1860), and they lived in an elegant **Back Bay** townhouse. By the 1870s Mrs. Gardner shocked conservative Bostonians by her unconventional parties mingling socialites with actors, artists, athletes, and musicians. **Charles Eliot Norton** and **Bernard Berenson** advised her art collecting, and **James Whistler** painted her portrait. Mrs. Jack, as she was called, assembled one of the world's greatest private collections of Renaissance paintings housed in her new home, a 15th-century villa she imported from Italy and rebuilt (1899) on the **Fenway**. Opened to the public in 1903, it became one of New England's foremost art museums on her death in

Boston on July 17, 1924. The museum suffered a spectacular $100 million robbery in 1990.

GARRISON, WILLIAM LLOYD (1805–1879). Editor. Born in Newburyport, Massachusetts, on December 12, 1805, Garrison had little education but learned much as a printer's apprentice. As editor of the *Newburyport Free Press* (1818), he published **John Greenleaf Whittier**'s early poems. He founded the *Liberator* in **Boston** (1831–66) as a radical **abolitionist** newspaper demanding immediate emancipation. Garrison founded the New England Anti-Slavery Society (1832) and was nearly lynched by a Boston mob (1835). Although ignored by most of the clergy because of his support of woman's rights, Garrison was president of the American Anti-Slavery Society (1841–63). He became more controversial when he burned a copy of the U.S. Constitution at a **Worcester** meeting (1854), but he refused to support **John Brown**'s violence and opposed the **Civil War**. Later he supported President Abraham Lincoln and united the divided abolitionist movements (1862). Garrison was active in other reforms when he died in New York City on May 24, 1879.

GARRITY, W. ARTHUR, JR. (1920–1999). Lawyer and judge. Born in **Worcester**, Massachusetts, on June 20, 1920, Wendell Arthur Garrity, Jr., graduated from Holy Cross College (1943) and **Harvard** Law School (1946). After serving in the U.S. Army in World War II, he was an assistant U.S. attorney (1947–50) and in private practice in **Boston** (1950–61). Garrity worked in **John F. Kennedy**'s campaigns for Senate (1958) and president (1960) and served as the U.S. attorney for Massachusetts (1961–66). As a U.S. District Court judge in Boston (1966–85), his most important decision was in *Morgan v. Hennigan* (1974), ordering **busing** to desegregate Boston public schools. Riots and violence by students and parents eroded Boston's image as a liberal and tolerant community and made Judge Garrity the most reviled man in Massachusetts. Much honored by the legal community, Garrity retired (1985) and died in Wellesley on September 16, 1999.

GASPEE. A British revenue cutter patrolling Narragansett Bay that ran aground at Warwick (1772) while pursuing a smuggler. **Abraham Whipple** and **John Brown** led 60 patriots who burned the ship in the first act of outright violence against the British government. The **Sugar Act** (1764) and rigorous enforcement of customs regulations by the captain of the *Gaspee* had outraged Rhode Island merchants engaged in the **triangular trade**.

GEISEL, THEODOR SEUSS (1904–1991). Writer and illustrator. Born in Springfield, Massachusetts, on March 2, 1904, Geisel graduated from Dartmouth College in 1925, studied at Oxford, and joined an advertising agency in New York City. He wrote and illustrated three successful children's books (1937–40), but during World War II he became a political cartoonist (1940–42) and made documentary films (1943–51), which won three Oscars. In 1947 Geisel returned to children's books, earning much praise for *If I Ran the Zoo* (1950), *Scrambled Eggs Super!* (1953), *How the Grinch Stole Christmas* (1957), and many others. *The Cat in the Hat* (1957) began a series of primary reading books praised by educators for the zany characters, delightful prose, and nonsense verse. The beloved author known as Dr. Seuss died on September 24, 1991.

GENERAL COURT. The state legislature of the Commonwealth of Massachusetts. It has met annually since October 1780, exactly 150 years after the first meeting of the **Puritans'** Great and General Court. It comprises 40 senators and 160 representatives, all of whom are elected for two-year terms in the neoclassical State House designed by **Charles Bulfinch** in **Boston** on **Beacon Hill**.

GEORGES BANK. A rich fishing area 120 miles southeast of Gloucester, Massachusetts, encompassing 1,000 square miles known as the **codfish** capital of the world. Once part of the mainland, the area was submerged by the rising sea level about 6,000 years ago. Basque fishing boats visited it by 1540, and **Giovanni da Verrazano** called it Armelline Shoals, but English navigators renamed it for St. George (1605). Commercial and sport fishermen find **cod**, cusk, flounder, haddock, hake, halibut, herring, pollock, sea **scallops**, shark, swordfish, and tuna as well as porpoise, turtles, and whales. Oil and gas drilling was proposed (1980) but postponed for ecological reasons. Part of the **Gulf of Maine**, Georges Bank produces most of the $800 million northeastern fishery catch each year. Overfishing, pollution, and habitat degradation led Congress to limit fishing (1994) despite economic disruption for New England fishermen, and scientific research has been conducted on the ecosystem recovery.

GERMANS. Immigrants in New England before the **American Revolution**. Some settled Waldoboro in Maine (1748), and larger numbers came in the antebellum era. Germans worked in the glass manufactory in Sharon, New Hampshire (1780), and Chelmsford, Massachusetts (1803). Rutland County in Vermont had small German communities by 1850; some were peddlers or quarry workers. **Boston** Germans numbered only 58 in 1821, but 3,790 by 1865, and 10,739 in 1900. Many Germans worked in **taverns** or at the brewery Rudolf Haffenreffer founded (1871–1965) in Roxbury. Gottlieb Rothfuss managed the nearby American Brewing Company (1891). Other Germans found work in printing industries in Boston, Roxbury, **Lowell**, and Lawrence or in **Holyoke** paper mills. Redemptorist priests from Germany built the Mission Church (1871) for the growing German **Catholic** population in Roxbury. Many German **Jewish immigrants** also worked in Lowell by 1850.

Louis Prang, a German immigrant printer, introduced the first American Christmas cards (1875) in his Boston chromolithography firm, and Germans established the Christmas holiday (with Santa Claus and a Christmas tree) in New England. By 1836 Bishop **Benedict Fenwick** summoned five German priests to meet the needs of his German Catholic parishioners, who established Holy Trinity Church in Boston (1844). A larger church was built (1877) in the South End for the parish's 6,000 German Catholics by 1900. This parish built the first Catholic parochial school in New England, as well as an orphanage. Many Germans who arrived as political refugees in 1848 contributed to New England music as performers, orchestral and choral directors, and music teachers. During the **Civil War**, the **Massachusetts 20th Regiment** enlisted over 200 men born in Germany, who were known for their antislavery views. In World War I more than 100 Boston Germans served in the U.S. Army.

GERRY, ELBRIDGE (1744–1814). Vice-president of the United States. Born in Marblehead, Massachusetts, on July 17, 1744, Gerry graduated from **Harvard** College (1762). He was a merchant and served in the colonial legislature (1772–75) and the Massachusetts **Committee of Safety**. Gerry signed the Declaration of Independence as a member of the Continental Congress (1776–80). He served in the U.S. Congress (1789–93) and as a diplomat in Paris (1797–98). As Jeffersonian Democratic governor, (1810–12) Gerry became known for gerrymandering, the partisan redrawing of election districts (1812). He was vice-president of the United States with James Madison (1813–14) until he died in Washington, D.C., on November 23, 1814.

GIAMATTI, A. BARTLETT (1938–1989). Educator. Born in **Boston** on April 4, 1938, Angelo Bartlett Giamatti graduated from Yale University (1960) and earned his Ph.D. in literature at Yale (1964). He taught medieval and renaissance literature at Princeton University (1965–66) and Yale University (1966–78) and was the 19th president of Yale (1978–86). Bart Giamatti, although a lifelong **Boston Red Sox** fan, was the unlikely choice as president of the National League (1986–89). He died in **New Haven** on September 1, 1989, shortly after his appointment as the 7th commissioner of major league baseball.

GIBSON, CHARLES DANA (1867–1944). Artist. Born in **Boston** on September 14, 1867, Gibson studied art in New York City (1884–85) and worked as an illustrator for *Collier's Weekly*, *Scribner's*, *Harper's,* and *Life* magazines. His Victorian Gibson girl illustrations glorified the American woman and influenced fashions (1890–1914). Gibson enjoyed enormous vogue as a social satirist until World War I, and he died in New York City on December 23, 1944.

GIBSON, ERNEST WILLARD (1872–1940). Senator from Vermont. Born in Londonderry, Vermont, on December 29, 1872, Gibson graduated from Norwich University (1872) and attended the University of Michigan Law School (1899). He practiced law in Brattleboro, Vermont (1899–1908), and was a Republican state legislator (1906–09). He served in the state national guard in the Mexican border dispute and in World War I as a colonel. Gibson was a district attorney (1919–21) and vice-president of Norwich University until elected to the House of Representatives (1923–33), and then served in the Senate (1933–40). He died in Washington, D.C., on June 20, 1940, and his son succeeded him as senator.

GIBSON, ERNEST W., JR. (1901–1969). Senator from Vermont. Born in Brattleboro, Vermont, on March 6, 1901, Ernest William Gibson, Jr., graduated from Norwich University (1923) and attended George Washington University Law School. He practiced law in Brattleboro (1926–27) and was a district attorney (1927–33). Governor **George Aiken** appointed him to the U.S. Senate (1940–41) when his father, Senator **Ernest Gibson, Sr.**, died. After World War II Army service (1941–45), Gibson was elected Republican governor (1946–50), ending the **Proctor** dynasty. He resigned (1950) as governor when President

Harry Truman appointed him a federal judge. Gibson died in Brattleboro on November 4, 1969.

GILLETT, FREDERICK HUNTINGTON (1851–1935). Speaker of the House. Born in Westfield, Massachusetts, on October 16, 1851, Frederick H. Gillett graduated from Amherst College (1874) and **Harvard** Law School (1877). While practicing law in Springfield, Massachusetts, he was elected as a Republican to the state legislature (1890–93) and to the House of Representatives (1893–25). He was speaker of the House (1919–25) until elected to the Senate (1925–31). Gillett retired to Springfield in 1931, where he wrote a biography of **George Frisbee Hoar** (1934) and died on July 31, 1935.

GILLETTE, KING C. (1855–1932). Inventor. Born in Fond du Lac, Wisconsin, on January 5, 1855, King Camp Gillette was a salesman in **Boston** when he conceived the idea of a disposable steel razor blade (1895). He and MIT-trained engineer, William Emery Nickerson, introduced the Gillette safety razor to New England consumers (1901), hoping the profits would fund a utopian socialist system. Gillette retired as president of the company in 1913 and died in Los Angeles on July 9, 1932. The Gillette Company manufactures a wide variety of shaving and personal hygiene products in Massachusetts today and underwrites the **New England Patriots'** Gillette Stadium in Foxboro.

GILMAN, JOHN TAYLOR (1753–1828). Governor of New Hampshire. Born in Exeter, New Hampshire, on December 19, 1753, Gilman was a son of the New Hampshire treasurer and a prominent shipbuilder. He was a **Minuteman** in 1775 and served in the state legislature (1779, 1781) and in Congress (1782–83). Gilman was a **Federalist** governor (1794–1805, 1813–16), serving in that office longer than any governor since the Revolution. Gilman was a benefactor of Dartmouth College and the New Hampshire **prep school**, Philips Exeter Academy, when he died in Exeter on August 31, 1828.

GILMAN, NICHOLAS (1755–1814). Senator from New Hampshire. Born in Exeter, New Hampshire, on August 3, 1755, Gilman, the brother of **John Taylor Gilman**, was a clerk in his father's countinghouse. He served in the Continental Army (1775–81), participating in the British army surrender at Yorktown. Elected to the House of Representatives (1787–97), he signed the new Constitution and was a Democratic-Republican in the Senate (1805–14). He died in Philadelphia on May 2, 1814.

GILMORE, PATRICK SARSFIELD (1829–1892). Musician. Born in Ireland on December 25, 1829, Gilmore was a cornet player in Athlone before immigrating to **Boston** (1848). He played in a minstrel group and was a bandmaster in Charlestown (1852–55) and **Salem** (1855–58). Appointed by Governor **John A. Andrew** as bandmaster for the 24th Massachusetts Infantry Regiment (1861), Gilmore served with General **Ambrose E. Burnside** and General **Nathaniel P. Banks**. He earned a national reputation for large concerts and music festivals. He composed and published popular songs, especially *Freedom on the Old Plantation* (1861) and *When Johnny Comes Marching Home* (1863). In 1869 he persuaded **Eben Jordan** to fund the National Peace Jubilee and Music Festival in Boston in June 1869, a five-day celebration of the conclusion of the **Civil War**. Gilmore organized 500 musicians, 10,000 singers, and six bands to perform for 50,000 people and repeated his mammoth celebration with the World Peace Jubilee and Music Festival in Copley Square in 1872. Moving to New York City (1873), Gilmore began the New Year Eve tradition of public celebrations in Times Square (1888). His band toured the United States and Europe, and Gilmore, known as the Father of the American Band, died performing at the St. Louis Exposition on September 24, 1892.

GLOVER, JOHN (1732–1797). Soldier. Born in **Salem**, Massachusetts, on November 5, 1732, Glover was a Marblehead merchant and **militia** officer (1759). His privateer *Hannah* was the first ship in the American Navy (1775) until he led his 14th Infantry Regiment to join the Continental Army at Cambridge. Glover organized the evacuation from Long Island (1776) and ferried George Washington's troops across the Delaware River to win the battle at Trenton (1776). General Glover played a key role in the battle at Saratoga (1777) and **Newport** (1778). He served in the Massachusetts legislature and died in Marblehead on January 30, 1797. *See also* AMERICAN REVOLUTION.

GLUECK, ELEANOR T. (1898–1972) AND SHELDON GLUECK (1896–1980). Criminologists. Born in Brooklyn, New York, on April 12, 1898, Eleanor Touroff graduated from Barnard College (1920) and the New York School of Social Work (1921) and earned an Ed.D. at **Har-**

vard University (1925). While working at a Boston settlement house, she married Sheldon Glueck (1896–1980), a lawyer. He was born in Warsaw, Poland, came to Milwaukee (1903), served in the U.S. Army (1917–19), and graduated from George Washington University (1920) and the National University Law School (1920).

After he received his Ph.D. in psychology at Harvard (1924), they became a team at the Harvard Department of Social Ethics and Harvard Law School (1925–64). Their research and publications, especially *Five Hundred Criminal Careers* (1930) and *Unraveling Juvenile Delinquency* (1950), were influential in social work, education, child psychology, and juvenile justice. Eleanor Glueck died in Cambridge, Massachusetts, on September 25, 1972, and Sheldon Glueck died in Cambridge on March 10, 1980.

GODDARD, ROBERT H. (1882–1945). Scientist. Born in **Worcester** on October 5, 1882, Robert Hutchings Goddard graduated from Worcester Polytechnic Institute (1908) and earned his Ph.D. at Clark University (1911). Teaching physics at Clark (1914–44), Goddard's research on rockets and space flight was the foundation for jet propulsion. He was the first American to publish scientific work on successful space flight (1919), and in Auburn, Massachusetts (1926), he launched the first liquid-propellant rocket. Many of his 200 patents were used by aeronautic researchers at the National Aeronautics and Space Administration facility in Maryland named in his honor (1959). Goddard, the father of modern rocketry, died in Baltimore on August 10, 1945.

GOODRICH, SAMUEL GRISWOLD (1793–1860). Writer and publisher. Born in Ridgefield, Connecticut, on August 19, 1793, Goodrich served in the state **militia** in the War of 1812 and opened a publishing firm (1816) in **Hartford** and **Boston** writing textbooks and 116 books for children under the name Peter Parley. He published stories by **Nathaniel Hawthorne** and **Henry Wadsworth Longfellow** in his *Peter Parley's Magazine* (1832–44) and *Merry's Museum* (1844–54), edited by **Louisa May Alcott**. Goodrich was elected to the Massachusetts legislature (1836–38) and was consul in Paris (1851–53). He wrote *Recollections of a Lifetime* (1856) and died in New York City on May 9, 1860.

GOODRIDGE, SARAH (1788–1853). Artist. Born in Templeton, Massachusetts, on February 5, 1788, Sarah Goodridge was a self-taught portrait artist until she took some lessons while visiting **Boston** (1806). By 1812 she had learned to paint miniatures on ivory and perfected her craft as a friend of **Gilbert Stuart** in Boston (1820–24). Her miniature portraits include Stuart, **Isaiah Thomas**, **Daniel Webster**, and **Henry Knox**. Goodridge supported her family by this delicate art until she died in Boston on December 28, 1853.

GOODWIN, JOHN NOBLE (1824–1887). Congressman from Maine. Born in South Berwick, Maine, on October 18, 1824, Goodwin graduated from Dartmouth College (1844) and practiced law in South Berwick. He served in the state legislature (1854) and was a Republican in the House of Representatives (1861–63). President Abraham Lincoln appointed him chief justice of Arizona Territory (1863) and the first territorial governor (1863–65). Goodwin was elected as a Republican delegate from Arizona to Congress (1865–67), then practiced law in New York City, and died in California on April 29, 1887.

GOODYEAR, CHARLES (1800–1860). Inventor. Born in **New Haven**, Connecticut, on December 29, 1800, Goodyear worked in his father's hardware factory (1830). He discovered the vulcanization process while experimenting with rubber in Woburn, Massachusetts (1836). With **Daniel Webster** as his lawyer, he won his patent rights (1852) in court, but Goodyear never realized the profits expected. He established the rubber industry in Naugatuck, Connecticut (1843), but died in debt in New York City on July 1, 1860.

GOMEZ, ESTEVAN (c.1500–c.1533). Explorer. Born in Porto, Portugal, Gomez sailed to North America in the service of Spain. He wintered at the St. Lawrence River and explored the Maine coast (1525) in the *La Annunciada* from Nova Scotia to **Cape Cod**. Disappointed because he failed to find gold or a route to Asia, he returned to Spain with 58 **Native American** slaves. Gomez explored Bermuda and Brazil (1532) and was knighted by King Charles V for his service to Spain (1533). Portuguese Americans in **New Bedford** erected a monument in Bangor, Maine, (1999) in honor of Gomez, the first European to land there.

GORE, CHRISTOPHER (1758–1827). Senator from Massachusetts. Born in **Boston** on September 21, 1758, Gore graduated from **Harvard** College (1776). He served in the Continental Army and practiced law in Boston. He was a state legislator (1788–89, 1806–07) and a delegate to the Constitutional Convention (1788). He served as U.S. attorney for Massachusetts (1789–96) and as the chief U.S. diplomat in London (1796–1804). Gore was wealthy from investment in Continental script and new mills when he was elected governor (1809–10) and a **Federalist** senator (1813–16). Gore died at his elegant Waltham estate on March 1, 1827.

GORGES, SIR FERDINANDO (1566–1647). Colonizer. Born in Somerset, England, in 1566, Gorges was a professional soldier who obtained a royal charter (1606) for the **Plymouth Company**. He established the **Sagadahoc** colony (1607–08) at the mouth of the Kennebec River for **fishing** and **fur trading** along the New England coast. Gorges obtained another charter (1620) for the **Council for New England**, a joint-stock company with rights to all land from Pennsylvania to Nova Scotia. Although he never visited America, Gorges named Maine and issued land grants for five New England colonies in Massachusetts, New Hampshire, Maine, and Connecticut. He sent Richard Vines and Richard Gorges to the first successful settlement at Saco, Maine (1622). He divided his land grant with **John Mason**, his chief associate in New England colonization, with Gorges retaining Maine and Mason taking New Hampshire (1629). A royal charter (1639) confirmed Gorges as lord proprietor of Maine, but events in England prevented further colonization. After Gorges died in England on May 24, 1647, his grandson sold Maine (1677) to the **Massachusetts Bay Company**.

GORTON, SAMUEL (1592–1677). Clergyman. Born in Manchester, England, in 1592, Gorton emigrated to **Boston** (1637), where he was arrested for preaching against the Trinity. Banished by the **Puritans**, he joined **Anne Hutchinson** in Portsmouth, Rhode Island (1639). Gorton founded the town of Warwick on the western shore of Narragansett Bay (1643) for his own sect called Gortonites. **Roger Williams** annexed Warwick to the Rhode Island colony (1647). Gorton continued preaching until he died in 1677, but his followers established gristmills on the Pawtuxet River and were active until the 1740s.

GOSNOLD, BARTHOLOMEW (ca. 1571–1607). Explorer. Born in England around 1571, Gosnold studied at Cambridge University and sailed on the *Concord* (1602) from Falmouth to the New England coast. Astonished by the number and size of the **codfish**, he named **Cape Cod** and **Martha's Vineyard** and built a fort on Cuttyhunk Island. Trading with the **Wampanoag** for **furs**, cedar, and sassafras, Gosnold found they had met Europeans before. Gosnold died on August 22, 1607, in Jamestown, Virginia.

GOUGH, JOHN B. (1817–1886). Reformer. Born in Kent, England, in 1817, Gough came to America (1829) and became a bookbinder and an actor. At a **temperance** meeting in **Worcester** (1842), he began his international career lecturing on the evils of drinking. Gough lived on a farm in Bolyston, Massachusetts (1848–86), and was the best-known public speaker in America and Great Britain when he died in 1886.

GRAHAM, SYLVESTER (1794–1851). Reformer. Born in West Suffield, Connecticut, on July 5, 1794, Graham prepared for the ministry at Amherst Academy (1823) and was ordained a Presbyterian preacher (1830). As an agent for a Pennsylvania **temperance** society, he lectured on health and diet in the 1830s, attracting a wide following and much ridicule. His advice was simple but frequently distorted by critics, advocating temperance, vegetarianism, cold showers, fresh air, hard mattresses, light, loose clothing, and regular exercise. His chief prescription for health was whole-grain wheat flour in the form of the Graham cracker. His writing and lectures on sexual restraint to middle-class New England men were also quite controversial. Graham wrote *The Young Man's Guide to Chastity* (1834), *Treatise on Bread and Bread-Making* (1837), and *Lectures on the Science of Human Life* (1839). He died in Northampton, Massachusetts, on September 11, 1851.

GRAND BANKS. A shallow **fishing** area southeast of the continental shelf near Maine. As the cold Labrador Current crosses the banks with the warm Gulf Stream, plankton is produced to feed haddock, herring, **cod**, mackerel, and other species. One of the world's best fishing grounds, despite heavy fog, the Grand Banks have long attracted New England fishing boats.

GRANGER, GIDEON (1767–1822). Public official. Born in Suffield, Connecticut, on September 19, 1767, Granger was a Jeffersonian Democratic-Republican who served as postmaster general (1801–14) He advised President Thomas Jefferson on a key statement about the separation of church and state made to his Baptist supporters in **Danbury**, Connecticut (1802). Granger moved to Canandaigua, New York (1813), where he died on December 31, 1822.

GRANITE STATE. The nickname for New Hampshire. The Hutchinson Family Singers, celebrated antebellum entertainers from Milford, New Hampshire, made popular the song *The Old Granite State* (1843).

GRANT, WILLIAM THOMAS (1876–1972). Businessman. Born in Stevensville, Pennsylvania, on June 27, 1876, Grant was raised in Fall River, Massachusetts. After work as a peddler and in retail stores in Massachusetts and Maine, Grant opened a department store in Lynn, Massachusetts (1906), offering a variety of items for 25 cents or less. He counted on high volume sales of merchandise direct from manufacturers and economical operations to compete with the Woolworth five and ten cent stores. Grant operated 30 stores in small New England cities (1920), and 200 chain stores by 1928. Larger department stores opened in Buffalo (1939) and Houston (1940) with more expensive merchandise, and the chain expanded to 600 stores by 1950 and 1,000 by 1966. W. T. Grant died in Greenwich, Connecticut, on August 6, 1972.

GRASSO, ELLA T. (1919–1981). Governor of Connecticut. Born in Windsor Locks, Connecticut, on May 10, 1919, Ella Tambussi graduated from Mount Holyoke College (1940) and married Thomas Grasso (1942). She served in the state legislature (1953–57), as secretary of state (1958–70), and as a Democrat in the House of Representatives (1971–75). Grasso was the first woman in the nation elected governor in her own right (1975–80), but she resigned due to illness and died in **Hartford**, Connecticut, on February 5, 1981. She is remembered as one of the first **Italian**-American women to succeed in New England politics.

GRAY, HORACE (1828–1902). U.S. Supreme Court justice. Born in **Boston** on March 24, 1828, Gray graduated from **Harvard** College (1845) and Harvard Law School (1851). He practiced law in Boston and was an organizer of the Free Soil Party and the Republican Party. Gray served on the state Supreme Judicial Court (1864–73) and was its chief justice (1873–82) until appointed to the U.S. Supreme Court (1882–1902). He employed the Court's first law clerks, among them **Louis D. Brandeis**, and died in Washington, D.C., on September 15, 1902.

GREAT AWAKENING (1720–1750). A religious movement led by **Jonathan Edwards** in the **Connecticut River** valley by 1734. Itinerant evangelists preached a message of salvation by moral reform that promoted American nationality, independence, and equality. Painting vivid pictures of gloom and damnation, many New Light ministers used bombastic sermons to teach the unchurched majority that church guidance to a strict pious life was essential to avoid hell and to reach heaven. The resulting religious revivals created many new denominations, which challenged the established **Congregational** church, the educated Old Light clergy, and traditional social leaders but contributed to the democratic and egalitarian ethos of the **American Revolution**. *See also* SECOND GREAT AWAKENING.

GREAT BOSTON FIRE. Occurred on November 9, 1872, and destroyed 65 acres of downtown **Boston**, including 776 buildings, damaging $75 million of property and killing 13 people. Firemen from five New England states fought the blaze. This disaster, far more extensive than earlier Boston fires (1653, 1676, 1711, 1747, 1761, 1787, or 1794), led to the appointment of a new board of fire commissioners. The city introduced its first steam fireboat, appointed permanent district chiefs, and founded new companies fully staffed by permanent fire fighters with new communications systems for the nation's oldest paid municipal fire department (1678). The fire also created Boston's new commercial district from Washington Street to the harbor and the development of Copley Square and the **Back Bay**.

GREAT MIGRATION. The 20,000 **Puritan** men, women, and children who emigrated from England to New England in 1629–40. In contrast to the individualism and private goals of Virginia colonists, the New England colonies were settled by families from which both the church and **town meeting** arose.

GREATER BOSTON. The 154 towns and cities surrounding the City of **Boston**, the metropolitan area with Boston as its **hub**. The city population reached a peak of 801,444 residents in 1950 but declined to 589,141 in 2000 as the Greater Boston suburbs grew dramatically. Boston, the 20th largest city in the nation, has a relatively small land area (48.4 sq. mi.), and its daytime population reaches 1.2 million people.

GREEKS. Immigrants who arrived in New England in the 1890s with Greek Orthodox churches in **Boston**, Lynn, Ipswich, Peabody, Springfield, and Haverhill, Massachusetts; **Hartford**, Connecticut; and Manchester and Dover, New Hampshire. **Lowell** had Greek **textile** workers by 1891, and they founded several coffeehouses (1894) and held Greek Orthodox services at Associate Hall until the Holy Trinity Church (1906) and the Transfiguration Church were built (1924). Many Massachusetts Greeks suffered in the tuberculosis epidemic (1900–05).

Also by 1911 there were 10,000 Greek **Catholics** in Connecticut, 7,500 in Massachusetts, and 1,500 in Rhode Island, but the majority were Orthodox Greek Christians because 208,000 arrived in the United States in 1905–09. Many Greeks worked in textile mills and factories, but community leaders often owned small restaurants and coffeehouse as popular centers for **immigrants**. More emigrated to the United States by 1924, but almost half of them returned to Greece. Pushed by unemployment and political instability after World War II, about 46,000 Greeks came in 1946–60, and 142,000 more came in 1961–75. Greek Americans had a high rate of self-employment and higher **education**. The Holy Cross Seminary, founded in Pomfret, Connecticut (1937), moved to Brookline, Massachusetts (1946), and established Hellenic College (1968), which provided priests for Greek-American parishes. But Greek-born priests continue to out-number Greek-American clergy. Orthodox Greeks in Lowell founded the Holy Trinity Church (1924), one of only 32 churches in the country by 1911. Lowell was one of only four cities with Greek language parochial schools in 1970.

The leading Greek American newspaper, the weekly *Hellenic Chronicle* (1950), is published in Boston and circulates nationally. Greek radio programs broadcast in many cities keep ethnic identity strong. Brookline's **Michael S. Dukakis**, the son of Greek immigrant parents, was the first Greek governor in New England and the Democratic nominee for president (1988). Lowell's **Paul Tsongas** was the first Greek from New England to be elected to the Senate, and Nicholas Mavroules from Peabody served in Congress (1979–93). **Olympia Snowe** from Maine was the first Greek-American women elected to the House and to the Senate. **Harry Agganis**, the son of immigrants in Lynn, Massachusetts, embodied the American dream as a **Boston Red Sox** star (1953–55) until his sudden death.

GREELEY, HORACE (1811–1872). Editor. Born in Amherst, New Hampshire, on February 3, 1811, Greeley was a printer's apprentice in East Poultney, Vermont, when he moved to New York City (1834), where he founded the *New York Tribune* (1841) as a Whig newspaper, advocating **abolitionism** and other reforms reflecting his highly moral New

England values. He was soon the nation's leading journalist, a founder of the Republican Party (1854), and the Democratic candidate for president (1872). Greeley died in New York City on November 29, 1872.

GREEN, HETTY (1834–1916). Businesswoman. Born in **New Bedford**, Massachusetts, on November 21, 1834, Henrietta Howland Robinson was the daughter of a **Quaker** wealthy from **whaling** and overseas trading. She had inherited fortunes from her father and aunt when she married (1867) Edward H. Green, a wealthy **China trader** from Vermont. Known as the richest woman in the world, and the Witch of Wall Street due her litigious, eccentric, and miserly nature, she was an astute investor who predicted the stock market crash of 1907. Hetty Green left an estate valued at $100 million when she died in New York City on July 3, 1916.

GREEN MOUNTAINS. Rise from the eastern shore of the Lake Champlain lowlands and extend north to Canada and south through central Vermont to the **Berkshire Hills**, Hoosac Range, and Taconic Range in western Massachusetts and the Litchfield Hills in Connecticut. The mountain range is part of the **Appalachian Mountains** and is covered with beech, birch, maple, and spruce forests. The name originates in the French name *monts verts*. Mount Mansfield (4,393 ft/1,340 m) is the highest peak, but 32 summits are over 3,000 ft/915 m.

GREEN MOUNTAIN BOYS. A Vermont militia unit organized by **Ethan Allen** and **Seth Warner** (1771) to resist dispossession from land granted by New Hampshire but claimed by New York. The **tavern** in Bennington where they often met was decorated with a stuffed catamount, their defiant emblem. They fought for the Continental Army in the **American Revolution** and won a major victory with **Benedict Arnold** at Fort Ticonderoga on May 17, 1775, and at the **Battle of Bennington** (1777). A Vermont National Guard unit is known as the Green Mountain Boys.

GREEN MOUNTAIN STATE. The nickname for Vermont, derived from the state's defining feature, the mountain range **Samuel de Champlain** called *monts verts*. Vermont, first visited by Europeans when the French explorer Jacques Cartier arrived in 1535, was an independent republic known as the Republic of New Connecticut (1777–91) until admitted as the 14th state.

GREEN, THEODORE FRANCIS (1867–1966). Senator from Rhode Island. Born in **Providence** on October 2, 1867, Green graduated from Brown University (1887), attended **Harvard** Law School, and studied in Germany. Practicing in Providence (1892–98), he taught law at Brown University (1894–97), and he served in the U.S. Army in the Spanish-American War (1898–99) and World War I. Green was a Democrat in the state legislature (1907), and as governor (1933–36) he presided over the "Green revolution," when Democrats won control of the state government from the dominant Republicans. Elected to the U.S. Senate (1937–61), Green was the oldest man to serve in Congress at that time. He died in Providence on May 19, 1966.

GREENE, FRANK LESTER (1870–1930). Senator from Vermont. Born in St. Albans, Greene worked on the Central Vermont Railroad (1883–91) and as a newspaper reporter (1891–1912). After serving in the U.S. Army in the Spanish-American War (1898–99), he was elected as a Republican to the House of Representatives (1912–23) and to the Senate (1923–30). He died in St. Albans on December 17, 1930.

GREENE, NATHANAEL (1742–1786). Soldier. Born in a **Quaker** family in Warwick, Rhode Island, on August 7, 1742, Greene was a blacksmith. After serving as a state legislator from Coventry, he became the youngest and most successful general in the Continental Army. He commanded troops at **Boston** (1776), led battles in Rhode Island, New York, and New Jersey and defeated the British in the southern colonies (1780). Greene, who was quartermaster general (1778–80), retired to his plantation near Savannah, Georgia, where he died on June 19, 1786.

GREENOUGH, HORATIO (1805–1852). Sculptor. Born in **Boston** on September 6, 1805, Greenough studied at **Harvard** College (1825) and found patrons at the **Boston Athenaeum** and in **Washington Allston** and James Fenimore Cooper. He studied in Italy and created busts of *John Quincy Adams* (1828), *Samuel F. B. Morse* (1831) and a neoclassical marble statue of *George Washington* (1840). Greenough, the first American sculptor, settled in **Newport**, Rhode Island (1851), and died in Somerville, Massachusetts, on December 18, 1852.

GREENWOOD, CHESTER (1858–1937). Inventor. Greenwood invented earmuffs in Farmington, Maine (1873), and his other patented inventions include the folding bed, spring steel rake, shock absorber, spark plug, and wheel bearings. The Greenwood Company manufactured ear protectors (1886–1937) in Farmington until his death. The Chester Greenwood festival is celebrated each year in his hometown.

GREENWOOD, JOHN (1760–1819). Dentist. Born in **Boston** on May 17, 1760, Greenwood apprenticed with his uncle, a cabinetmaker in **Portland**, Maine (1773–75). He served at the Battle of **Bunker Hill**, Montreal, Ticonderoga, and Trenton and then on a Boston privateer. By 1785 he made nautical and mathematical instruments in New York City and became a dentist like his father and brother. Greenwood was President George Washington's dentist, adjusting or repairing his false teeth (1789–99). Greenwood died in New York City on November 16, 1819.

GREYLOCK (ca. 1690–1753). Native American leader. Greylock (or Wawamolewat, meaning Scared Ground) was a *sachem* of the **Abenaki** people who lived on the Westfield River in Massachusetts. **King Philip's War** forced his people to move to Stockbridge (1676) and to join the Western Abenaki during **Queen Anne's War** (1702) at Missisquoi Bay on Lake Champlain in Vermont. Greylock led raids with warriors from several tribes on Northampton (1712), Northfield, and Rutland, Massachusetts (1722). Allied with the French in **Dummer's War**, his attacks created much fear in the **Connecticut River** valley towns (1723). This led the Massachusetts militia to attack Abenakis at Norridgewock in Maine and murder Father **Sebastien Rasles** (1724), the French Catholic missionary. But Greylock's War (1723–27) resisted British settlement in western New England until his tribe moved to Vermont and Montreal. Greylock never accepted peace offers from the New York, New Hampshire, and Massachusetts governors. He cooperated with the French in **King George's War** (1744–48) and remained a shadowy figure, who died by 1753. The highest peak in Massachusetts was named Mount Greylock (3491 ft/1064 m) in his honor.

GRISWOLD, ROGER (1762–1812). Governor of Connecticut. Born in Lyme, Connecticut, on May 21, 1762, Griswold graduated from Yale College (1780) and practiced law in Norwich and Lyme. He was elected as a **Federalist** to the House of Representatives (1795–1805) and served as a state supreme court judge (1807–09), lieutenant governor (1809–11), and governor (1811–12). He is remembered for brawling on the floor of the House (1798) with Congressman **Matthew Lyon**

of Vermont. As governor, Griswold opposed President Thomas Jefferson, supported New England secessionists, and withheld state militia troops until the U.S. Supreme Court supported the president's authority to requisition the state militia. Griswold died in office in Norwich on October 25, 1812.

GRISWOLD V. CONNECTICUT (1965). A case in which the U.S. Supreme Court ruled that a Connecticut law (1879) forbidding use of contraception violated the Constitution. The decision also held that the right to marital privacy predates the Bill of Rights. Estelle T. Griswold, executive director of the state Planned Parenthood League, and Dr. C. Lee Buxton of Yale Medical School, had appealed their arrest in **New Haven** (1961). More importantly, this case overturned Victorian laws against contraception just as **Gregory G. Pincus** invented the birth control pill in Massachusetts.

GROTON, SAMUEL (1592–1677). Clergyman. Born in Manchester, England, in 1592, Groton came to **Boston** (1637) but was banished because of his liberal religious beliefs. He joined **Anne Hutchinson** in Portsmouth, Rhode Island, where he clashed with William Coddington (1639). He founded Warwick (1642) but was imprisoned by Massachusetts **Puritans**, who claimed that land (1643). On his release, Groton preached to the **Native Americans** and his followers in Warwick, denying the Trinity, heaven, and hell. Groton died in Warwick in 1677.

GUINEY, LOUISE IMOGEN (1861–1920). Poet. Born in **Boston** on January 7, 1861, Louise Imogene Guiney was educated at a convent school in **Providence**, Rhode Island. The daughter of Colonel **Patrick R. Guiney**, she was a member of Boston's aesthetic revival in the 1890s. Her most popular poems in *The White Sail* (1887) and *Happy Ending* (1909) were often anthologized, and she was an ambassador between Boston **Irish** and **Boston Brahmin** intellectual and artistic circles. Guiney moved to England (1901), where she died on November 2, 1920. She is best recalled for discovering the poet Kahlil Gilbran in Boston.

GUINEY, PATRICK R. (1835–1877). Soldier. Born in Ireland on January 15, 1835, Patrick Robert Guiney emigrated with his family to **Portland**, Maine, attended Holy Cross College (1854–55), and practiced law in **Boston** (1858–77). Elected to the Common Council in Roxbury, he joined Colonel **Thomas Cass** in the 9th Massachusetts Infantry (1861) as a captain and succeeded him (1862) as colonel. Recovering from his wounds in Boston, Guiney supported President Lincoln and **abolitionism** as a Republican unlike most **Irish Catholic** Democrats. He was an assistant district attorney in Boston (1865–69) and register of probate (1871–77) until he died in Boston on March 21, 1877. His daughter was the poet **Louise Guiney**. *See also* YANKEE DIVISION.

GULF OF MAINE. An extensive watershed covering 69,000 square miles from **Cape Cod** to Nova Scotia. It reaches 200 miles offshore to **Georges Bank** supporting 20,000 fishermen operating 300 Canadian and 1,350 American fishing vessels and 4,000 **lobster** boats. Rich nutrients support whales, seals, and hundreds of species of birds, fish, and shellfish, including 50 commercially harvested fish varieties. Decline in the Gulf's rich ecosystem since 1975, demonstrated by shellfish bed closures and depletion of the region's groundfish, is due to the population growth to 6.8 million people and conversion of coastal agricultural land to residential development. Approximately 1.5 million acres of coastal habitats and saltwater wetlands have been lost since 1800. **Textile** mills, **paper** mills, fish processing plants, municipal sewage, and chemical or electronic industries also produced pollution in the Gulf of Maine. Over 10 million tourists visit the Gulf of Maine each year to enjoy its natural beauty, history, and recreational opportunities.

GULICK, LUTHER (1865–1918). Educator. Born in Hawaii on December 4, 1865, Luther Gulick, the son of New England **Congregational** missionaries, graduated from Sargent School of Physical Education (now Boston University) in 1885 and New York University Medical School (1889). While teaching at the YMCA School for Christian Workers (now Springfield College), he encouraged **James Naismith** to develop the new sport called basketball (1891). Luther had distinguished career promoting physical education, the Boys Scouts, and the YMCA but is best remembered for founding the Camp Fire Girls in Thetford, Vermont (1910), with his wife Charlotte Gulick. He died in South Casco, Maine, on August 13, 1918.

– H –

HAGLER, MARVIN (1954–). Athlete. Born in Newark, New Jersey, on May 23, 1954, and raised in Brockton, Massachusetts, Marvin Nathaniel

Hagler was one of the best middleweight boxing champions in history. He defended his world title 12 times (1981–87) and won 62 professional bouts. Marvelous Marvin Hagler lost his title in 1987, retired, and became a movie actor. He was elected to the International Boxing Hall of Fame (1993).

HALE, EDWARD EVERETT (1822–1909). Clergyman and writer. Born in **Boston** on April 3, 1822, Hale graduated from **Harvard** College (1839) and was ordained in **Worcester**, Massachusetts (1842). While a **Unitarian** pastor in Boston (1846), he wrote 150 books and tracts for many causes. His short story *The Man Without a Country* (1863) in the *Atlantic Monthly* was his best known work, but he also wrote *The Ingham Papers* (1869), *Franklin in France* (1888), and *A New England Boyhood* (1893). Hale was a leader of the Social Gospel movement and was chaplain of the U.S. Senate (1903–09). He died in Roxbury, Massachusetts, on June 10, 1909.

HALE, EUGENE (1836–1918). Senator from Maine. Born in Turner, Maine, on June 9, 1836, Hale studied law in **Portland** and practiced in Ellsworth (1857–58). He was a county prosecutor (1858–66), and a Republican state legislator (1867–68, 1879–80), and served in the House of Representatives (1869–79). Elected to the Senate (1881–1911), Hale became one of the most influential senators known as the Big Five. He was a conservative but opposed U.S. imperialism following the Spanish-American War. Hale died in Washington, D.C., on October 27, 1918.

HALE, JOHN PARKER (1806–1873). Senator from New Hampshire. Born in Rochester, New Hampshire, on March 31, 1806, Hale graduated from Bowdoin College (1827). He practiced law in Dover (1830–34), and served as a Democrat in the state legislature (1832–34), as U.S. attorney (1834–41), and in the House of Representatives (1843–45). Breaking with his party over the annexation of Texas, Hale was elected as the first great antebellum Whig **abolitionist** in the Senate (1847–53). The Free Soil Party elected Hale to the Senate (1847–53, 1855–57) and nominated him for president (1852), but he organized the Republican Party in New Hampshire and returned to the Senate (1857–65). Accused of unethical business contracts with the U.S. Navy by Secretary of the Navy **Gideon Welles**, Hale left the Senate to become minister to Spain (1865–69) but was recalled for irregularities in Madrid. Hale died in Dover on November 19, 1873.

HALE, NATHAN (1755–1776). Soldier. Born in Coventry, Connecticut, on June 6, 1755, Hale graduated from Yale College (1773) and taught school in East Haddam and New London. As a militia officer he served in the **American Revolution** at the siege of **Boston** and New York campaigns. Captain Hale gathered information about British troops on Long Island disguised as a **Loyalist** schoolteacher but was captured and hanged as a spy on September 22, 1776. His last words were, "I only regret that I have but one life to lose for my country." Hale became a **Yankee** hero, a fort at **New Haven** was named for him in 1812, and a bronze statue of Hale was placed in 1886 at the capitol in **Hartford**.

HALE, SARAH J. (1788–1879). Editor. Born in Newport, New Hampshire, on October 24, 1788, Sarah Josepha Buell Hale was the widow of a lawyer (1822) who supported her five children as a writer. She was editor of *Ladies' Magazine* in **Boston** (1828–37) and in Philadelphia when it became *Godey's Lady's Book* (1837–77). Hale was an influential writer on a variety of patriotic, progressive issues and an arbiter of national taste with 150,000 subscribers (1860). She is best remembered for her poem *Mary Had a Little Lamb* and her campaign to make **Thanksgiving Day** a national holiday. Hale died in Philadelphia on April 30, 1879.

HALF-WAY COVENANT. A term describing the doctrine approved by a synod of **Congregational** churches in Massachusetts (1662) and Connecticut (1669). It permitted church membership without testimony of a conversion experience. Adults baptized as children could have their children baptized, but they and their children were only half-way members, ineligible to vote on church affairs or take communion. This was an attempt by New Englanders to cope with a serious religious crisis in many towns but weakened **Puritan** control of society.

HALL, DONALD (1928–). Poet. Born in **New Haven**, Connecticut, on September 20, 1928, Hall graduated from **Harvard University** (1951) and Oxford University (1953). After teaching at the University of Michigan (1957–75), he was a writer and editor of poetry anthologies. He is best known as a lyric poet for *Exiles and Marriages* (1955), *The Happy Man* (1986), and *The Museum of Clear Ideas* (1993). Hall was the poet laureate of New Hampshire (1984–89) and lives in his ancestral home in New Hampshire.

HALL, G. STANLEY (1844–1924). Educator and psychologist. Born in Ashfield, Massachusetts, on February 1, 1844, Granville Stanley Hall graduated from Williams College (1867) and studied at the Union Theological Seminary (1867–68). After study in Germany (1868–72), Hall earned his doctorate at **Harvard University** with **William James** (1878), where he taught educational psychology (1880–81). While teaching at Johns Hopkins University (1881–88), he founded (1883) one of the first psychological laboratories and established the American Psychological Association (1891). Hall launched the new field of child psychology with his major work, *Adolescence* (1904). As president of Clark University (1888–1920) in **Worcester**, Massachusetts, Hall hosted conferences with Sigmund Freud and Carl Jung (1909). He died in Worcester on April 24, 1924.

HALL, PRINCE (1735–1807). Reformer. Born in **Boston** in 1735, Prince Hall was freed from **slavery** by his master, William Hall (1770). Hall was a peddler, caterer, and leather dresser listed as a voter, taxpayer, and property owner. After joining a British army lodge of Masons in Boston, he founded the African Lodge No. 1 (1776), the world's first lodge of black Freemasonry. He served in the Revolutionary army and as Grand Master Hall obtained a permanent charter (1787) and sponsored a second lodge in **Providence**, Rhode Island (1797). Hall petitioned the state legislature to colonize **African Americans** in Africa (1787) and lobbied to end the slave trade (1788). Hall sponsored Boston's first public school for black children in his home (1800–06) and was a leader of the African-American community when he died in Boston on December 11, 1807.

HAMILL, DOROTHY (1956–). Athlete. Born in Chicago on July 26, 1956, Dorothy Stuart Hamill was raised in Riverside, Connecticut. She won three U.S. championship figure skating titles (1974–76), a silver medal in the world championships (1974), and the Winter Olympic gold medal (1976). Hamill performed in the Ice Capades (1977–94) and as the world professional champion (1983–87). Elected to the U.S. Figure Skating Hall of Fame (1991), she retired to Riverside in 1995.

HAMLIN, HANNIBAL (1809–1891). Vice-president of the United States. Born in Paris, Maine, on August 27, 1809, Hamlin practiced law in Hampden (1833–48). He was a Democrat in the state legislature (1836–41) until his election to the House of Representatives (1843–47) and to the Senate

(1848–57). Hamlin served as Maine's first Republican governor (1857), returned to the Senate (1857–61), and was vice-president (1861–65) in President Abraham Lincoln's first term. He later served as collector of the port of **Boston** (1865–66) and in the Senate (1869–81). Hamlin was U.S. minister to Spain (1881–82) and died in Bangor, Maine, on July 4, 1891.

HANCOCK, JOHN (1737–1793). Governor of Massachusetts. Born in Quincy, Massachusetts, on January 12, 1737, Hancock graduated from **Harvard** College (1754). He inherited his uncle's **Boston** mercantile business (1764) and protested the **Stamp Act** (1765) as an ally of **Samuel Adams** in the Massachusetts **General Court** (1766–74). His **Beacon Hill** mansion (1737) was Boston's first stone building and the site of the "new" State House. As president of the Continental Congress (1775–77), he was the first to sign the Declaration of Independence on July 4, 1776. Hancock was elected the first governor of Massachusetts (1780–85), served in Congress (1785–86), and was in his ninth term as governor (1787–93) when he died in Quincy on October 8, 1793.

HANDEL AND HAYDN SOCIETY (1815). Founded by **Boston** merchants to bring orchestral and choral music of the highest quality to the city. The first concert took place at **King's Chapel** on Christmas Eve in 1815 with a chorus of 100 men and women from church choirs. Professional singers and musicians replaced the amateurs by 1845. This inspired similar oratorio societies in other New England towns and remains the oldest performing arts organization in the nation. *See also* MASON, LOWELL.

HARD TACK. A biscuit or cracker baked in New England seaports for use on sailing ships. Known as ship's biscuit or pilot bread, it is a hard, unleavened, unsweetened, plain, flat rectangular wheat cracker. John Pearson baked hard tack in Newburyport, Massachusetts, and packed it in barrels and boxes for sailing ships (1792). When his bakery merged with the National Biscuit Company (1898), the Crown Pilot Cracker became a popular consumer product sold only in New England. When Nabisco discontinued this product (1996), Maine consumers persuaded the company to return the pilot cracker to grocery shelves (1997). Josiah Bent (1771–1836) popularized his hand-baked crackers in Milton, Massachusetts, as another type of hard tack for New England households. Since 1801 **Yankees** have eaten hard tack in **clam chowder** or crumbled in milk as breakfast food for children or the sick. The similar Medford cracker was as necessary for New England mariners as Medford **rum**. In the **Civil War** soldiers ate hard tack, as did generations of Yankee sailors and fishermen, who consumed hard tack with salt **cod** on long voyages.

HARDWARE CITY. A nickname for **New Britain**, Connecticut.

HARRISON, PETER (1716–1775). Architect. Born in York, England, on June 14, 1716, Harrison settled in **Newport**, Rhode Island (1740), as a merchant. Although untrained, he made maps and built fortifications and designed the **Redwood Library** (1748), Brick Market (1772), and **Touro Synagogue** (1763) in Newport; **King's Chapel** (1758) in **Boston**; and Christ Church (1761) in Cambridge. His **architecture** is exceptional for its monumental qualities and pure design, creating a distinctive colonial New England style. Harrison, America's first architect, moved to **Hartford**, Connecticut (1761), where his **Loyalist** views were tolerated. He died there on April 30, 1775.

HARTFORD. The state capital of Connecticut. At the head of navigation of the **Connecticut River**, it was founded as a Dutch trading post (1633) and was settled by **Puritans** from Cambridge, Massachusetts (1635). The town joined nearby settlements as the Connecticut Colony and adopted a written constitution (1639) known as the **Fundamental Orders**. **Hartford** was the joint capital with **New Haven** of the colony and the state (1664–1875). Known as the **insurance city**, Hartford incorporated in 1784 and is the second largest city in Connecticut with 140,000 residents and 700,000 people in its metropolitan area.

HARTFORD CONVENTION. A secret discussion in **Hartford**, Connecticut, about national political issues arising from **Federalist Party** opposition to the War of 1812, which ruined New England commerce. The Massachusetts legislature called 26 delegates from Connecticut, Massachusetts, New Hampshire, Rhode Island, and Vermont. They met from December 15, 1814, to January 4, 1815, to consider secession from the Union, but most delegates preferred moderate solutions. Proposed constitutional amendments would limit the power of Southern states and the Democratic Party, limit the power of Congress to declare war and to restrict commerce, or to admit new states, also prohibit the election of foreign-born citizens to Congress, and make the president ineligible for reelection. The Boston merchant **Thomas H. Perkins** was nominated to propose these measures to Congress, but the conclusion of the war ended this protest and led to the demise of the **Federalist Party**.

HARTFORD COURANT. The nation's oldest newspaper in continuous publication. Founded by Thomas Green in 1764 as a weekly paper, Ebenezer Watson published the paper until he died in 1777. His widow operated the paper during the **American Revolution** as one of the first women publishers in the country. She supported the Revolution and increased circulation despite the **Tories**, who burned her paper mill twice. In 1837 the paper became a daily with a weekly edition for rural subscribers and added a tri-weekly edition (1896–1913). Since Abraham Lincoln visited **Hartford** in 1859, the *Courant* was closely identified with the Republican Party. The Sunday edition was added in 1913, and modern production methods were added in the 1930s. The Times Mirror Company purchased the *Courant* in 1979, and the paper won Pulitzer Prizes in 1992 and 1999. The *Courant* and its parent company, Times Mirror, was purchased by the Tribune Company in 2000, and daily circulation increased to 200,000. The newspaper apologized in 2000 for its complicity in the West Indies slave trade and **slavery** in colonial Connecticut.

HARTFORD, GEORGE HUNTINGTON (1833–1917). Businessman. Born in **Augusta**, Maine, on September 5, 1833, Hartford worked in a **Boston** dry goods firm and founded the Great Atlantic and Pacific Tea Company (1859) in New York City. By 1878 the popular A & P was the nation's first grocery chain and operated 1,600 cash and carry stores (1913). Managed by his sons, John and George, the chain grew to 13,961 stores (1925) and was the forerunner of the modern supermarket. Hartford died in New Jersey on August 29, 1917.

HARTFORD WITS (OR CONNECTICUT WITS). A literary group of Yale graduates in **Hartford** (1770–90), including **Joel Barlow**, Lemuel Hopkins, **Timothy Dwight**, Richard Alsop, David Humphreys, and **John Trumbull**. As **Federalists**, they favored a strong central government, a national literature independent of Europe, and college **education** reform. They collectively wrote *The Anarchiad* (1786–87), an anonymous satirical poem published in installments and *The Echo* (1791–1807).

HARTLEY, MARSDEN (1877–1943). Painter. Born in Lewiston, Maine, on January 4, 1877, Edmund Marsden Hartley studied **art** in Cleveland

and New York. By 1907 he became one of the most accomplished American modernist painters in **Boston**. Moving to New York City (1909) he was an important figure in Alfred Stieglitz's avant-garde circle but spent each summer in Maine declaring (1937) he was "the painter from Maine" and a "Maine-ac." He lived in Paris and Berlin but returned to New England in 1915. His later paintings depict Maine people and seascapes, especially *Mount Katahdin* (1939), *The Wave* (1940), and *Log Jam, Penobscot Bay* (1941). Marsden died in Ellsworth, Maine, on September 2, 1943.

HARVARD, JOHN (1607–1638). Clergyman. Born in London in 1607, John Harvard studied at Cambridge University. He immigrated to Massachusetts in 1637 and was a minister in Charlestown. His bequest of 300 books and half of his estate to the college in New Towne (later Cambridge) led the Massachusetts **General Court** to name the school **Harvard** College in 1639. A statue of John Harvard designed by **Daniel Chester French** (1884) presides over Harvard Yard.

HARVARD UNIVERSITY. Oldest institution of higher education in the United States, began as a college training **Puritan** ministers in New Towne (now Cambridge), Massachusetts, in 1636. Renamed Harvard College by the **General Court** (1639) in honor of an early benefactor, the Reverend **John Harvard**, the college attracted male students from every American colony. By 1780 Massachusetts chartered Harvard as a university with much autonomy and a private endowment that grew to be the largest in the world, $18 billion (2001). Harvard added graduate schools in medicine (1783), divinity (1811), law (1817), science and engineering (1847), arts and sciences (1872), business (1908), dental medicine (1908), **education** (1920), public health (1922), and public administration (1936). However, Harvard was actually a small provincial college until 1876 when it adopted the model used by universities in Germany and granted its first doctorate (1873). The Annex for women (1879) became Radcliffe College (1894), which merged with Harvard University in 1999.

Despite many distinguished alumni, including **Increase** and **Cotton Mather**, **John Adams**, **Ralph Waldo Emerson**, **Henry David Thoreau**, **James Russell Lowell**, **Oliver Wendell Holmes**, and **John F. Kennedy**, Harvard's reputation for academic excellence and a superior faculty dates from the presidency of **Charles W. Eliot** (1869–1909). Physical expansion and reorganization under **Abbott Lowell** (1909–33) created the modern university campus in Cambridge and **Boston**, especially with Harvard Stadium (1902) and Widener Library (1913). Seven U.S. presidents have attended Harvard, and countless other men and (since 1963) women of achievement. It was a founder of the **Ivy League** (1956) and created the modern general education curriculum adopted by most American colleges in 1945 and 1979. Harvard University enrolls 18,000 students with 2,000 professors and 10,000 staff members (2002) and is governed by the oldest corporation in the nation. *See also* HIGHER EDUCATION.

HARVARD REGIMENT. A nickname for the **20th Massachusetts Infantry Regiment** in the **Civil War** (1861–65) because so many officers had been **Harvard** College students.

HARVEY, GEORGE BRINTON MCCLELLAN (1864–1928). Editor. Born in Peacham, Vermont, on February 16, 1864, Harvey began his career as a reporter for the *Springfield Republican* and was a protégé of Joseph Pulitzer on the *New York World* (1890–93). After earning a fortune building electric **railroads**, he was editor and publisher of the *North American Review* (1899), president of Harper and Brothers publishing firm, and editor of *Harper's Weekly* (1901–13). Once a firm supporter of President Woodrow Wilson, he became a conservative critic of the administration's foreign policy. Harvey was U.S. ambassador to Great Britain (1921–23) and wrote *Henry Clay Frick, the Man* (1928). He retired to Dublin, New Hampshire, where he died on August 20, 1928.

HASSAM, CHILDE (1859–1935). Painter. Born in **Boston** on October 17, 1859, Frederick Childe Hassam was an engraver and illustrator in Boston. After studying **art** in Paris (1883, 1885–89), he became the leading American Impressionist painter. His New England seascapes, like *Surf, Isles of Shoals* (1913), as well as *Rainy Day in Boston* (1885) or *Boston Common at Twilight* (1886), are among his best works. Hassam spent summers in the 1890s on Appledore Island, one of the **Isle of Shoals**, where he painted *Celia Thaxter's Garden* (1890). By 1900 he visited summer art colonies in Old Lyme and Cos Cob, Connecticut, and died in East Hampton, New York, on August 27, 1935.

HASTY PUDDING. A **corn** meal mush that became a traditional **Yankee** dish. It was often served at **Harvard** College, where it became the name of the oldest collegiate dramatic society in the nation, the Hasty Pudding Club (1795). **Joel Barlow** wrote a poem, *The Hasty Pudding* (1793).

HAT CITY. A nickname for **Danbury**, Connecticut.

HAWTHORNE, NATHANIEL (1804–1864). Writer. Born in **Salem**, Massachusetts, on July 4, 1804, Hawthorne graduated from Bowdoin College (1825). He wrote *Twice-Told Tales* (1837) and supported his family by hack writing and a patronage position in the **Boston** customhouse (1839–41). Hawthorne lived briefly at the **Brook Farm** commune and joined the **Concord** literary circle (1842), where he wrote *Mosses from an Old Manse* (1846) and his masterpiece, *The Scarlet Letter* (1850). While living in Lenox, he wrote *The House of the Seven Gables* (1851) and *The Blithedale Romance* (1852). After seven years in Europe, he returned to Concord to write *The Marble Faun* (1860) and *Our Old Home* (1863). When Hawthorne died in Plymouth, New Hampshire, on May 19, 1864, he had produced great fiction, bridging the **Puritan** heritage and the **Transcendentalist** optimism.

HAYDEN, LEWIS (1816–1889). Public official. Born a slave in Lexington, Kentucky, Hayden escaped on the **Underground Railroad** to **Boston**. His **West End** clothing shop became a center for abolitionists and his home on the north slope of **Beacon Hill** was an Underground Railroad station. **Harriet Beecher Stowe** visited his house when she was writing *Uncle Tom's Cabin*. Hayden was a recruiter for the **54th Massachusetts Regiment**, was elected as a Republican state legislator (1873–75), and worked as a state house clerk (1859–89). Hayden died in Boston in 1889.

HAYNES, JOHN (1594–1654). Governor of Massachusetts and Connecticut. Born in England in 1594, Haynes immigrated to **Boston** (1633) and was elected governor of **Massachusetts Bay Colony** (1635). He banished **Roger Williams** (1635) and moved to **Hartford** (1637), where he was elected the first governor (1639) under the **Fundamental Orders**. Haynes supported union of the Connecticut colonies and served as Connecticut delegate to the **New England Confederation**. He served as governor on alternate years until his death in January 1654.

HAYNES, LEMUEL (1753–1833). Clergyman. Born in West Hartford, Connecticut, to an African-American father and the daughter of a prominent white family, Haynes grew up as an indentured servant in Middle Granville, Massachusetts. He served in the **militia** and fought with **Benedict Arnold** and **Ethan Allen** at Ticonderoga (1775). He was the first **African American** ordained a **Congregational** minister (1785), serving white congregations in Torrington, Connecticut (1785–87), Rutland (1787–1818) and Manchester, Vermont (1818–22), and in New York (1822–33). He wrote *The Nature and Importance of True Republicanism* (1801) and received an honorary degree from Middlebury College (1804). Haynes died in New York in 1833.

HEAD OF THE CHARLES REGATTA. An annual international rowing competition on the Charles River in **Boston** since 1964. The October 2002 race attracted 7,000 athletes representing 1,500 colleges or clubs in 20 races over three miles of Boston-Cambridge riverfront. With 300,000 spectators, this race is the world's largest two-day rowing competition. *See also* SPORTS.

HEALY, JAMES AUGUSTINE (1830–1900). Bishop. Born in Clinton, Georgia, on April 6, 1830, James A. Healy was the son an **Irish immigrant** and his **African-American** wife, who was a slave. Healy graduated from Holy Cross College in **Worcester** (1849) and was ordained in Paris (1854), the first African-American Catholic priest. He served as chancellor of the diocese of Massachusetts (1855–66) for Bishop **John Fitzpatrick** and as pastor of St. James Church in **Boston** (1866–75). Healy became the second bishop (1875–1900) of **Portland**, Maine, the first African-American Catholic bishop in the United States, serving with much success until he died in Portland on August 5, 1900.

HEBERT, FELIX (1874–1969). Senator from Rhode Island. Born in Quebec on December 11, 1874, Hebert came to Coventry, Rhode Island, with his parents (1890). He worked as a **railroad** clerk (1893–96) and deputy **insurance** commissioner, practiced law in **Providence** (1907–08), and was a state court judge (1908–28). Elected as a Republican to the U.S. Senate (1929–35), Hebert was the first **French Canadian** in the Senate. He died in Warwick on December 14, 1969.

HECKLER, MARGARET M. (1931–). Congresswoman from Massachusetts. Born in New York City on June 21, 1931, Margaret Mary

O'Shaughnessy graduated from Albertus Magnus College (1953) and Boston College Law School (1956). She married John M. Heckler (1953–85), practiced law in Wellesley (1956–62), and was elected as a Republican to the Governor's Council (1962–66) and to the House of Representatives (1967–83). Mrs. Heckler served as secretary of health and human services (1983–85) and ambassador to Ireland (1985–89) and retired to Wellesley.

HENTOFF, NAT (1925–). Writer. Born in **Boston** on June 10, 1925, Nathan Irving Hentoff graduated from Northeastern University (1945) and studied at **Harvard University** (1946) and the Sorbonne (1950). He was a Boston radio announcer and became an influential jazz critic for *Downbeat* (1953–57). Hentoff wrote *The Jazz Makers* (1957) and was editor of *Jazz Review* magazine (1958–61). His memoir *Boston Boy* (1986) reveals the anti-Semitism during his youth in Boston. Hentoff writes on social reform and music as a columnist for the *Village Voice* and the *Washington Post*.

HEPBURN, KATHARINE (1907– 2003). Actor. Born in **Hartford**, Connecticut, on May 12, 1907, Katherine Houghton Hepburn graduated from Bryn Mawr College (1928). After her Broadway debut (1928), she began a long career in Hollywood (1932–81) and won the first of four Oscars (and eight nominations for that award) for her part in *Morning Glory* (1933). During the 1950s she was investigated by the House Un-American Activities Committee, and her career suffered for a time. However, she remained one of the great movie actors in more than 40 films until she retired to Connecticut (1981). She died on June 29, 2003.

HERTER, CHRISTIAN ARCHIBALD (1895–1966). Governor of Massachusetts. Born in Paris on March 28, 1895, Herter graduated from **Harvard University** (1915) and was a diplomat in Europe and in the Department of State and Department of Commerce in Washington, D.C. (1916–24). He was a Republican state legislator (1931–43) and served in the House (1943–53) and as governor (1953–57). Herter was under secretary of state (1957–59) and secretary of state (1959–61). He died in Washington, D.C., on December 30, 1966.

HICKS, LOUISE DAY (1923–). Congresswoman from Massachusetts. Born in **Boston** on October 16, 1923, Ann Louise Day graduated from Wheelock College (1938), Boston University School of Education

(1955), and Boston University Law School (1958). Practicing law in Boston, she married John Hicks and was elected to the Boston City Council (1969–71) and as a Democrat to the House of Representatives (1971–73). She is best recalled as the leading opponent of the school **busing** orders of Judge **W. Arthur Garrity, Jr.** (1974).

HIGGINS, GEORGE V. (1939–1999). Writer. Born in Brockton, Massachusetts, on November 13, 1939, Higgins graduated from Boston College (1961) and Stanford University (1965). He was a newspaper reporter in **Providence**, Springfield, and **Boston** (1962–66) and graduated from Boston College Law School (1967). After terms as an assistant attorney general (1967–70) in Boston and an assistant U.S. attorney (1970–74) in Boston, he was in private practice. His clients included the Watergate conspirator G. Gordon Liddy and the Black Panther Eldridge Cleaver. Higgins taught at Boston College Law School (1973–74, 1978–79) and taught creative writing at Boston University. His first novel, *The Friends of Eddie Coyle* (1972), was followed by a series of acclaimed crime novels noted for Boston underworld locations and crisp dialogue. Higgins's nonfiction includes *Style versus Substance: Boston, Kevin White, and the Politics of Illusion* (1984). He died in Milton, Massachusetts, on November 6, 1999.

HIGGINS, JAMES HENRY (1876–1927). Governor of Rhode Island. Born in Lincoln on January 22, 1876, Higgins graduated from Brown University (1898) and Georgetown University Law School (1900). He practiced law in Pawtucket, served in the state legislature (1901–02) and as mayor (1902–07), and became the state's youngest and first **Irish Catholic** governor (1907–09). The Bourn Amendment (1888) to the state constitution (1843) abolished the property restriction in statewide elections for naturalized citizens, enfranchising 15,000 Democratic voters who supported Higgins. His liberal reform program ended Republican Party control of the state under **Charles R. Brayton**. Higgins died in Pawtucket on September 16, 1927.

HIGGINSON, HENRY LEE (1834–1919). Businessman. Born in New York City on November 18, 1834, Higginson attended **Harvard** College and studied music in Europe. In the **Civil War** he served in the 1st Massachusetts Cavalry (1861–65) and became president (1868–1919) of **Boston**'s leading banking firm, Lee, Higginson & Company founded by his father (1848). His firm invested in Western **railroads**, the American

Telephone and Telegraph Company, and the General Electric Company as pioneer State Street venture capitalists. His profitable investments in the Calumet and Hecla copper mines in Michigan (1868) enriched **Boston Brahmins** as the **China trade** and **textile** mills had done for earlier generations. Colonel Higginson founded the **Boston Symphony Orchestra** (1881) and built Symphony Hall (1900). He died in Boston on November 14, 1919.

HIGGINSON, THOMAS WENTWORTH (1823–1911). Soldier, reformer, and writer. Born in Cambridge, Massachusetts, on December 22, 1823, Higginson graduated from **Harvard** College (1841) and from Harvard Divinity School (1847). As a pastor in Newburyport, he engaged in so many reform movements that his congregation dismissed him. Moving to a **Worcester** church (1852–61), Higginson led the **Boston** mob that freed a runaway slave, **Anthony Burns**, from the courthouse (1854) and supported **John Brown** in Kansas. Colonel Higginson led the 1st South Carolina Regiment, one of the first **African-American** units in the Union Army (1862). After the **Civil War**, he wrote *Army Life in a Black Regiment* (1870), contributed to the *Atlantic Monthly* and the *North American Review,* and wrote biographies of **Henry Wadsworth Longfellow**, **John Greenleaf Whittier**, and **Margaret Fuller**. Higginson, who encouraged **Helen Hunt Jackson** and **Emily Dickinson** to write, died in Cambridge on May 9, 1911.

HIGHER EDUCATION. Began in the United States in New England and remains a hallmark of the region today. The **Puritans** insisted on literacy to promote piety and discipline; and although families provided some basic education and vocational training, the Massachusetts **General Court** ordered **selectmen** to hire a schoolmaster (1642) and to open a secondary (or grammar) school (1647). **Boston** established the first secondary school, **Boston Latin School** (1635), in North America, and New Englanders also founded many private **prep schools**, such as **Roxbury Latin School** (1645), the oldest in the nation. This led legislatures and religious denominations to found colleges to educate teachers and ministers. The Massachusetts General Court founded **Harvard** College (1636) in Cambridge to prepare Puritan clergymen in the first college in North America. When Harvard seemed too liberal, conservative **Congregationalists** founded Yale College (1701) in Connecticut. Baptists founded Rhode Island College (1764) in **Providence** (renamed Brown University in 1804). Dartmouth College, founded in Hanover, New Hampshire, to train Congregational missionaries

(1769) to the **Native Americans**, was the last college established before the **American Revolution**.

New England also pioneered in women's education with Wheaton College (1834), Vermont College (1834), Mount Holyoke College (1837), Colby-Sawyer College (1837), Wellesley College (1870), Smith College (1871), Radcliffe College (1879), Wheelock College (1888), Simmons College (1899), Lesley College (1909), Connecticut College (1911), Emmanuel College (1919), Albertus Magnus College (1925), and Bennington College (1932). The elite **Seven Sisters** colleges also began in New England.

By 2002 these institutions of higher education would number 154 private and 41 public colleges and universities in New England. Connecticut has 20 private and 6 public institutions of higher education, as well as 12/8 in Maine, 82/15 in Massachusetts, 15/5 in New Hampshire, 9/2 in Rhode Island, and 16/5 in Vermont. Greater Boston is home to 62 private and 6 public colleges enrolling 250,000 students in 2002. The large number of private institutions throughout New England is unique: 79 percent of the colleges and universities in Massachusetts are private schools, compared with 62 percent nationally. Similarly, 58 percent of the state's college students attend independent schools, in contrast to only 24 percent of the college students in the United States. This reflects the competition between religious denominations after the **American Revolution** as well as the **Yankee** respect for learning. Public colleges began with the first **normal schools** in Massachusetts and Connecticut in 1839 and by land grant state colleges and universities after 1862.

The primacy of private institutions increases the cost of high education in New England but created a major industry enrolling 800,000 students each year and contributing $15 billion annually to the regional economy as well as stimulating the arts, sciences, and culture. However, the New England states compare unfavorably with other states in public funding of higher education: New Hampshire ranks 50th, Massachusetts, 49th, Vermont, 48th, Connecticut, 46th, Rhode Island, 43rd, and Maine, 35th. But federal funding to New England colleges and universities, which increased from $152 million in 2000 to $180 million in 2001, is an additional economic stimulus. The number of students attending the 270 (junior, community, and four-year) colleges in New England has declined since 1990. In Massachusetts, for example, more than 50 percent of high school graduates entered college, and 66 percent earned a bachelor's degree within five years. Moreover more than 5 percent of all college students in the United States attended New England schools in

2000, and many of these graduates find employment in this region, creating a brain drain from other states and nations. New England has one of the largest concentrations of international students in the nation, and in 1999–2000 Massachusetts ranked fourth in the nation, with 28,192 foreign students who contributed more than $1 billion to the state economy. Based on a measure of the economic and social benefits the region receives from having well-educated residents, this contributed to New England in countless ways. Massachusetts is the most educated state in the nation today, and 1 in 3 adults has a bachelor's degree and 14.3 percent of adults in Massachusetts and 14 percent in Connecticut have a graduate degree. In 2001 about 46 percent of the Greater Boston work force were college graduates, a higher proportion than any other U.S. metropolitan area. The number of New Englanders with a college diploma rose rapidly in recent years from 1,425,114 in 1980 to 2,871,195, or 29 percent of the adult population, in 2001. This demand for education is related to the regional economic prosperity and also fueled an expansion of colleges and universities. *See also* ECONOMY; EDUCATION; HARVARD, JOHN; SPORTS; YALE, ELIHU.

HISPANICS. Immigrants who first came to New England from Puerto Rico and Columbia as agricultural migrant workers by the 1950s. They harvested **apples**, **cranberries**, and **tobacco** but some remained to work in **Lowell** and **Lawrence shoe** and **textile** factories and also in Rhode Island and New Hampshire by the 1960s. Changes in federal laws permitted immigration from Jamaica and Trinidad by 1965 to ease the region's labor shortage. Political and economic instability prompted more **immigrants** to move from Central America, Haiti, and the Dominican Republic by 1970. The demographic revolution in Greater **Boston** since 1960 increased the Hispanic population to 4 percent and is part of still-evolving social and economic changes throughout New England. Felix D. Arroyo was the first Latino to serve on the Boston City Council in 2002.

HITCHCOCK CHAIR. Designed by Lambert H. Hitchcock (1795–1852) in his Riverton, Connecticut, furniture factory. Using the assembly line method, more than a hundred workers produced the popular chair of simple turned legs, rungs, and back posts with a wood or rush seat (1818–28). Despite bankruptcy in 1829, the firm expanded with other types of traditional New England furniture, and the factory was revived (1946) as the Hitchcock Chair Company. **Newport**, Rhode Island (1740), and Gardner, Massachusetts (1870), were also important furniture centers.

HITCHCOCK, EDWARD (1793–1864). Scientist. Born in **Deerfield**, Massachusetts, on May 24, 1793, Hitchcock was a **Congregational** minister (1821–25) who taught natural science at Amherst College (1825–64) and Mount Holyoke College (1836–64). He served as the Amherst president (1845–54) and as state geologist for Massachusetts (1830) and Vermont (1857–61). His pioneer research on fossil dinosaur footprints, geology, paleontology, and glaciology made him the father of American ichnology. Hitchcock died in Amherst on February 27, 1864.

HITCHCOCK, HENRY-RUSSELL (1903–1987). Historian. Born in **Boston** on June 3, 1903, Hitchcock graduated from **Harvard University** (1927). He taught at Wesleyan University (1929–41) and Smith College (1948–68) and wrote *Modern Architecture* (1929), *The Architecture of H. H. Richardson and His Times* (1936), and *Rhode Island Architecture* (1939). Hitchcock coined the term International Style for his seminal exhibition at the Museum of Modern Art (1932) and played a leading role in the Society of Architectural Historians. He died in New York City on February 19, 1987.

HOAR, GEORGE FRISBEE (1826–1904). Senator from Massachusetts. Born in **Concord** on August 29, 1826, Hoar graduated from **Harvard** College (1846) and Harvard Law School (1849). Practicing law in **Worcester**, he served in the state legislature (1852–57) and as a Republican in the House (1869–77) and the Senate (1877–1904). He opposed **immigration** restriction and was a crusader for civil service reform and an anti-imperialist. Hoar was the son of Samuel Hoar, the brother of Ebenezer R. Hoar, and the father of Rockwood Hoar, all members of Congress. George Frisbee Hoar wrote *Autobiography of Seventy Years* (1903) and died in Worcester on September 30, 1904.

HOFF, PHILIP HENDERSON (1924–). Governor of Vermont. Born in Turners Falls, Massachusetts, on June 29, 1924, Philip H. Hoff served in the U.S. Navy (1941–45) and graduated from Williams College (1948) and Cornell University Law School (1951). He practiced law in Burlington, Vermont (1951–62), and served in the state legislature (1961–62). Hoff was the first Democratic governor of Vermont in 100 years (1962–69) and an unsuccessful candidate for the Senate (1970).

HOFFMAN, ABBIE (1936–1989). Activist. Born in **Worcester**, Massachusetts, on November 30, 1936, Abbott Hoffman graduated from

Brandeis University (1959) and the University of California, Berkeley (1960). He joined civil rights workers in the South, was an activist for minority youths in Worcester (1960–66), ran a theater in New York City, and organized the East Village community. At Chicago antiwar demonstrations (1968), he became a prominent Youth International Party leader and was acquitted in the Chicago Seven trial (1969). Arrested on a drug charge (1974), Hoffman went underground (1974–80), worked as an environmental activist in New York, and resurfaced on national television (1980). He went to prison for a year but returned to activism. Hoffman wrote *Revolution for the Hell of It* (1968), *Steal This Book* (1971) and *To America with Love: Letters from the Underground* (1976) and died in Pennsylvania on April 12, 1989.

HOLMES, OLIVER WENDELL (1809–1894). Physician and writer. Born in Cambridge, Massachusetts, on August 29, 1809, Holmes graduated from **Harvard** College (1829) and Harvard Medical School (1836), where he was professor of anatomy (1847–82) His medical work was impressive but he is best known for his poetry (*Poetry,* 1836), essays (*The Autocrat at the Breakfast Table*, 1858), biographies (*Emerson*, 1885) and a novel (*Elsie Venner*, 1861). As **Boston**'s best known man of letters, wit, and poet laureate, Holmes coined the term **Boston Brahmins**, and his poem *Old Ironsides* (1830) saved the **USS** *Constitution*. Boston's literary golden age, the Augustan Age of Beacon Street wit, died with Dr. Holmes on October 7, 1894.

HOLMES, OLIVER WENDELL, JR. (1841–1935). United States Supreme Court Justice. Born in **Boston** on March 8, 1841, Holmes was the son of Dr. **Oliver Wendell Holmes**. Graduating from **Harvard** (College (1861), he served in the **20th Massachusetts Regiment** in the **Civil War** (1861–64). After graduating from Harvard Law School (1866), he practiced law in Boston and produced influential legal scholarship in the *American Law Review* (1870–73) and *The Common Law* (1881) as a Harvard Law School professor. After 19 years on the state Supreme Judicial Court (1882–1902), Holmes was appointed to the U.S. Supreme Court (1902–32). As an outspoken advocate of judicial restraint and federalism, the Great Dissenter ranks as one of the greatest members of the Court. Holmes's career was the subject of a Hollywood film, *The Magnificent Yankee* (1950), after he died in Washington, D.C., on December 6, 1935.

HOLMES, PEHR GUSTAF (1881–1952). Congressman from Massachusetts. Born in Sweden on April 9, 1881, Holmes immigrated to **Worcester** with his parents (1886). He was employed in the banking and insurance business when he was elected as a Republican to the Worcester Common Council (1908–11), board of aldermen (1913–16), and as mayor (1917–19). Elected to the governor's council (1925–28) and to the House of Representatives (1931–47), for many years Holmes was the most prominent Swedish American in New England. He died in Venice, Florida, on December 19, 1952. *See also* SWEDES.

HOMER, WINSLOW (1836–1910). Artist. Born in **Boston** on February 24, 1836, Homer grew up in the small Cambridge village surrounding **Harvard** College. Apprenticed (1855–57) with a lithographer, he became a popular commercial artist in New York City (1857–75), depicting simple rustic American scenes in a naturalistic style. During the **Civil War**, Homer drew realistic and emotional scenes of Army life for *Harper's Weekly* (1861–65). After visiting France (1866–67), he painted landscapes and in the 1870s he lived on the Gloucester and Maine coast. There he painted watercolors and oils of the New England forests and coast and later scenes in Florida, Bermuda, and Cuba (*The Gulf Stream*). His **art** was in great demand during his lifetime, and he is compared to the greatest French Impressionists. Homer died at Prouts Neck, Maine, on September 29, 1910.

HONEYMAN, JAMES (1675–1750). Clergyman. Born in Scotland in 1675, Honeyman was an Anglican chaplain in the Royal Navy. Sent as a missionary to Long Island, New York (1704), he moved to **Newport** as pastor of the Trinity Church (1704–50). Honeyman built an elegant new church (1726) as his congregation expanded and obtained much support from England for the church, its school, and missionary work. When he died in **Newport** on July 2, 1750, the Anglican church in Rhode Island had thrived under his tactful leadership despite considerable resistance from dissenters in New England.

HOOD, HARVEY PERLEY (1821–1900). Businessman. Born in Chelsea, Vermont, Harvey P. Hood founded a one-man milk company (1846), making daily deliveries to **Boston** homes. Hood created the first milk train (1854) from his dairy farm in Derry, New Hampshire, to Boston retailers. His sons made the H. P. Hood Company the largest dairy company in New England by 1890 with retail sales on 152 routes and 15 milk plants from Maine to Connecticut. Because New England farmers switched from **sheep** to dairy cows by 1860 and used selective breeding, more milk was produced for central creameries. The milk, cream, butter, and cheese were shipped by **railroads** to cities. The Hood milkman delivered these dairy products to millions of New England consumers and introduced pasteurized milk (1895) in sanitary glass milk bottles (1896). Since 1915 the Hoodsie, a prepackaged cup of ice cream, has become a New England tradition. The Hood Company, based in Chelsea, Massachusetts, is still the second largest dairy processing business in the region.

HOOKER, ISABELLA BEECHER (1822–1907). Reformer. Born in Litchfield, Connecticut on February 22, 1822, the daughter of the Reverend **Lyman Beecher**, Isabella studied at **Catherine Beecher**'s Hartford Female Seminary. Married on feminist principles to John Hooker (1841), a **Hartford** lawyer, she advocated reform of legal rights of women and wrote *Womanhood: Its Sanctities and Fidelities* (1873). Hooker was a leader of the National Woman Suffrage Association in New England but was ostracized by her family when she accepted public charges that her famous brother, the Reverend Henry Ward Beecher, was an adulterer. She drafted the state's married women's property law (1877) and was president of the Connecticut Woman Suffrage Association until 1905. She and her husband supported Mary Hall, who was the first woman admitted to the Connecticut bar (1882). Isabella Hooker died in Hartford on January 25, 1907.

HOOKER, JOSEPH (1814–1879). Soldier. Born in Hadley, Massachusetts, on November 13, 1814, Hooker graduated from West Point (1837) and served in the Seminole War and the Mexican War. He rejoined the army as a general in the **Civil War**. Hooker replaced **Ambrose E. Burnside** (1863) but, unable to defeat General Robert E. Lee in Virginia, General George Meade replaced him. Hooker retired as a major general (1868) and died in New York City on October 31, 1879. An equestrian statue by **Daniel Chester French** (1903) on the Massachusetts State House grounds honors "Fighting Joe" Hooker.

HOOKER, THOMAS (1586–1647). Clergyman. Born in Leicestershire, England, on July 7, 1586, Hooker graduated from Cambridge University (1608) and was a pastor (1620–30) in Essex until he fled to Holland because of his **Puritanism**. Hooker sailed with **John Cotton** to Massachusetts

(1633) and led his parishioners to found **Hartford**, Connecticut (1636). He wrote Connecticut's **Fundamental Orders** (1638–39) and joined his Massachusetts colleagues in defending **Congregationalism** against Presbyterianism and other heresies in the **New England Confederation** and was an author of the **Cambridge Platform** (1648). Hooker was a Hartford pastor until his death on July 7, 1647.

HOOSAC TUNNEL. Proposed in 1819 to open the Great Lakes to New England commerce. It was the longest **railroad** tunnel in the nation (1851–73). One of the great engineering feats of the 19th century, the tunnel began in Florida, Massachusetts, and cost $21 million and the lives of 195 workers. Nitroglycerine and compressed air rock drills were used for the first time to blast five miles (8 km) of granite beneath the Hoosac Mountain range. The Boston and Maine Railroad expanded the tunnel (1951, 1997), but it never produced the economic benefits intended.

HOPKINS, MARK (1802–1887). Educator. Born in Stockbridge, Massachusetts, on February 4, 1802, Hopkins graduated from Williams College (1824) and Berkshire Medical School (1829). He returned to Williams as an influential professor of philosophy (1830–87) and as president (1836–72). Ordained in the **Congregational** Church (1836), he served as president of the American Board of Commissioners for Foreign Missions (1857–87). Hopkins died in Williamstown on June 17, 1887.

HOPKINS, SAMUEL (1721–1803). Clergyman. Born in **Waterbury**, Connecticut, on September 17, 1721, Hopkins graduated from Yale College (1741). He studied with **Jonathan Edwards** and was the **Congregational** minister in Great Barrington, Massachusetts (1743–69). His writings formed a major school in Congregationalism called Hopkinsianism. As a pastor in **Newport**, Rhode Island (1769–1803), Hopkins was the first Congregationalist to denounce **slavery** (1776) and raise funds to free slaves. He died in Newport on December 20, 1803.

HOPKINS, STEPHEN (1707–1785). Governor of Rhode Island. Born in **Providence** on March 7, 1707, Hopkins was a surveyor and merchant. He served in the legislature (1732–52, 1770–75), as chief justice, and as governor for 10 terms (1755–67). As a member of the Continental Congress (1774–76, 1778), he signed the Declaration of Independence. Hopkins, an outspoken **Quaker abolitionist**, died in Providence on July 13, 1785.

HORNBOOK. A child's primer consisting of sheets of parchment paper covered by transparent sheet made from a cow's horn. Pupils brought their hornbook to the **dame school** or **common school** in colonial New England.

HOSMER, HARRIET (1830–1908). Artist. Born in Watertown, Massachusetts, on October 9, 1830, Harriet Goodhue Hosmer was educated by her father and at schools in Lenox, **Boston**, and St. Louis. She traveled with **Charlotte Cushman** to study **art** in Italy (1852–57) and became the best-known American sculptor of her era. Her *Puck* (1856) was very popular, and her *Zenobia* (1859) was a neoclassical depiction of the ancient warrior queen captured by the Romans. Hosmer's colossal bronze of *Thomas Hart Benton* (1868) in St. Louis is her best-known statue. She died in Watertown on February 21, 1908.

HOUGHTON, HENRY OSCAR (1823–1895). Editor and publisher. Born in Sutton, Vermont, on April 30, 1823, Houghton was an apprentice printer (1836) at the *Burlington Free Press* and graduated from the University of Vermont (1846). He was a **Boston** newspaper reporter and founded the H. O. Houghton Publishing Company in Cambridge (1880), which became the Riverside Press. Merging with the firm created in 1832 by James R. Osgood, **William Davis Ticknor,** and **James T. Fields**, and forming a partnership with George H. Mifflin, the Houghton Mifflin Company published the works of distinguished New England writers, including **Ralph Waldo Emerson**, **Nathaniel Hawthorne**, **Oliver Wendell Holmes**, **Henry Wadsworth Longfellow**, **James Russell Lowell,** and **John Greenleaf Whittier**. Houghton was the mayor of Cambridge (1872) and died in North Andover on August 25, 1895. Houghton Mifflin Company, the last large independent publisher in the country, was sold to a French firm, Vivendi Universal (2001), ending the era of Boston as a major publishing and literary center.

HOUSATONIC RIVER. Connecticut's longest river. It flows 150 mi/240 km from Pittsfield, Massachusetts to Canaan, Connecticut, and winds its way to enter **Long Island Sound** at Stratford. It powered colonial mills and modern hydroelectric plants and offers fly-fishing, kayak, and canoe recreational areas.

HOUSE OF THE SEVEN GABLES. A 17th-century house in **Salem**, Massachusetts, said to have inspired **Nathaniel Hawthorne**'s 1851 novel by that name. Built in 1668 and restored in 1910, the building carries a curse on the owners from the **Salem witchcraft trials**. Despite this, it is the most famous site in historic Salem and attracts numerous students of **literature** and **Yankee** folklore each day.

HOWARD ATHENAEUM. The first theater in **Boston** (1845–1962) with cushioned seats. Once a fashionable venue for opera and drama, when the **West End** and **Scollay Square** district declined (1870), the theater offered **vaudeville** and later burlesque. Despite the scrutiny of the **Watch and Ward Society** and the city censor's **banned in Boston** tradition, generations of rowdy **Harvard** students, soldiers, and sailors (since 1915) patronized the well-known theater known as the Old Howard. Demolished in 1962 to make way for the new Government Center, the Old Howard was evidence of the improper Bostonians.

HOWARD, ADA LYDIA (1829–1907). Educator. Born in Temple, New Hampshire, on December 19, 1829, Howard graduated from Mt. Holyoke College (1853). After teaching in Ohio, Illinois, and New Jersey, she became the first president of Wellesley College (1875–81) and the first woman in the world to serve as a college president. She died in Brooklyn, New York, on March 3, 1907, and is buried on the Wellesley College campus.

HOWARD, OLIVER OTIS (1830–1909). Soldier. Born in Leeds, Maine, on November 8, 1830, Howard graduated from Bowdoin College (1850) and from West Point (1854). He commanded the 3rd Maine Regiment in the **Civil War** and rose to major general, losing an arm (1862) and earning the Congressional Medal of Honor. Known as the Christian soldier, he headed the Freedmen's Bureau (1865–72) and was founder (1867) and president of Howard University (1869–74). Howard served in the Indian Wars (1874–77) and as superintendent of West Point (1880–82). He wrote biographies of Chief Joseph (1881), Zachary Taylor (1892), and his *Autobiography* (1907) and died in Burlington, Vermont, on October 26, 1909.

HOWE, ELIAS (1819–1867). Inventor. Born in Spencer, Massachusetts, on July 9, 1819, Howe was an apprentice in machine-tool shops and while working for a **Boston** watchmaker he patented the first practical sewing machine (1846) but could not sell his device. After a trip to England, he sued (1849) Isaac Singer and other inventors who infringed on his patent and won the suit (1854). Howe raised and served with a Connecticut regiment in the **Civil War** and opened a factory in Bridgeport to manufacture sewing machines. His invention made possible American mass-produced clothing before his death in Brooklyn on October 3, 1867.

HOWE, JULIA WARD (1819–1910). Poet. Born in New York City on May 27, 1818, Julia Ward married the Boston reformer **Samuel Gridley Howe** (1843) and published her first poetry volume *Passion Flowers* (1854). The *Atlantic Monthly* published her poem *The Battle Hymn of the Republic* (1862), which was set to music and inspired the Union Army. She was president of the New England Woman Suffrage Association (1869), a leader in the international peace movement (1871), and founded Mother's Day (1972). She published poetry, essays, travel books, and a biography of **Margaret Fuller**. Her daughter Laura Howe Richards (1850–1943) was a popular children's writer in Maine. Mrs. Howe died in **Newport** on October 17, 1910.

HOWE, MARK ANTONY DEWOLFE (1864–1960). Writer. Born in Bristol, Rhode Island, on August 23, 1864, Howe graduated from Lehigh University (1886) and **Harvard University** (1888). He was an editor in **Boston** for the *Youth's Companion* magazine (1888–93, 1899–1913), and an editor for *Atlantic Monthly* (1893–95). Howe was best known for 15 biographies, many of **Boston Brahmins** he knew well, including **Phillips Brooks** (1899), **George Bancroft** (1908), **Charles Eliot Norton** (1913), **Annie Adams Fields** (1922), Moorfield Storey (1932), and **Oliver Wendell Holmes** (1939). He won the Pulitzer Prize (1924) for *Barrett Wendell and His Letters*. Known as the dean of Boston's literary world, he was an indefatigable clubman, trustee, and spokesman for the Boston genteel tradition until he died in Cambridge, Massachusetts, on December 6, 1960.

HOWE, SAMUEL GRIDLEY (1801–1876). Reformer. Born in **Boston** on November 10, 1801, Howe graduated from Brown University (1821) and **Harvard** Medical School (1824). He was a surgeon in the Greek war for independence from Turkey (1825–31) and directed the Perkins School for the Blind in Boston (1832–45). Howe was active in prison, public school, and mental asylum reforms, edited an **abolitionist** newspaper with his wife **Julia Ward Howe**, and served as chairman of the Massachusetts Board of State Charities (1865–74). Their **Beacon Hill**

home was a center for reformers of many types. Howe died in Boston on January 19, 1876.

HOWE, WILLIAM (1729–1814). Soldier. Born in England on August 10, 1729, Howe served with the British Army in the **French and Indian War** (1758–60) and won the costly **Battle of Bunker Hill**. Forced to evacuate **Boston** in 1776, General Howe retreated to Halifax as commander in chief in the colonies, captured New York and Philadelphia, but failed to defeat the Continental Army. Howe was succeeded by General Henry Clinton (1778) and died in England on July 12, 1814.

THE HUB (OR THE HUB OF THE SOLAR SYSTEM). A popular reference to **Boston**, a term originally used by **Oliver Wendell Holmes** in *The Autocrat of the Breakfast Table* (1858). The witty Dr. Holmes remarked that the Massachusetts State House is "the hub of the solar system." It reflected the pompous **Boston Brahmin** belief that their city was not only the regional capital but the most important city in the nation or the world.

HUGUENOTS. French Protestants who followed the teaching of John Calvin. The colony they attempted in Canada failed (1541), but the first permanent French colony in North America, Port Royal, Nova Scotia, was a Huguenot success (1604). To avoid religious persecution by **Catholics** in France (1572–1685), many Huguenots fled to **Boston** and **Salem**. The wealthy Huguenot **West Indies trader** Philip English (or L'Anglois) came to Salem from the Channel Island of Jersey. He was an Anglican who assisted the Huguenots until he was imprisoned as a witch in 1692. The 14,000 refugees arriving in North America before the **American Revolution** were largely the urban bourgeoisie. Many prospered in America but reinforced **anti-Catholicism**. George Bernon came to **Boston** in 1688, prospered in the naval stores business, and built an Anglican church in **Providence**, where he died in 1736. Huguenots also settled in **Newport** and **Hartford** and founded Oxford, Massachusetts (1686) and Dresden, Maine (1751). The best-known Huguenot in Boston was Peter Faneuil, but **Paul Revere**'s paternal grandfather was one of these émigrés, as were the ancestors of **James Bowdoin**, **Richard Henry Dana**, **George Dewey**, **J. Pierpont Morgan**, **Henry Wadsworth Longfellow**, **Henry David Thoreau**, and **John Greenleaf Whittier**.

HULL, ISAAC (1773–1843). Naval officer. Born in Derby, Connecticut, on March 9, 1773, Hull grew up in Newton, Massachusetts, and went to sea (1787) as a cabin boy. He was captain of a merchantman (1793) and a U.S. Navy officer (1798). Hull became famous for cutting out a French privateer in Santo Domingo and served in the Tripolitan War (1803–06). As captain of the *Constitution* (1810), he captured the British frigate *Guerriere* (1812) off New Jersey, the first U.S. naval victory in the War of 1812, earning the nickname **Old Ironsides** for his ship. He commanded the **Boston** Navy Yard and rebuilt the Portsmouth Navy Yard (1814). Commodore Hull died in Philadelphia on February 13, 1843.

HUNT, RICHARD MORRIS (1827–1895). Architect. Born in Brattleboro, Vermont, on October 31, 1827, Hunt graduated from **Boston Latin School** (1843) and studied art in Geneva and Paris (1843–54). Returning in 1854, he supervised the additions to the U.S. Capitol and settled in New York City, where he designed the Lenox Library, the Tribune Building (1873), the Statue of Liberty base, and Metropolitan Museum of Art facade, as well as the Princeton University library and chapel and the Yale Divinity School. He is best known for the Marble House (1888) and Breakers (1892) **Newport Mansions** in Rhode Island using his eclectic Beaux-Arts style. Hunt trained a new generation of architects, founded the American Institute of Architects, and was the dean of American architects when he died in **Newport** on July 31, 1895. His brother, **William Morris Hunt**, was a prominent painter in **Boston**.

HUNT, WILLIAM MORRIS (1824–1879). Artist. Born in Brattleboro, Vermont, on March 31, 1824, Hunt attended **Harvard** College and studied painting in Paris. He introduced the Barbizon school of **art** to **Boston** (1855) and was commissioned to paint portraits of well-known New Englanders. Much of his work was lost in the **Boston Fire** (1872) and he was an influence on **John La Farge** and **Henry James**. Hunt, the brother of **William Morris Hunt**, died on the **Isles of Shoals** in New Hampshire on September 8, 1879.

HUNTINGTON, SAMUEL (1731–1796). Governor of Connecticut. Born in Windham on July 3, 1731, Huntington was a farmer but practiced law in Windham (1754–60) and Norwich (1760–73). He served in the colonial legislature (1764) and on the state superior court

(1773–76). Huntington signed the Declaration of Independence as a member of Congress (1776–81, 1782–84) and was president of the Continental Congress (1779–84). Elected as **Federalist** lieutenant governor (1785–86) and as governor (1786–96), he built the new state house in **Hartford** designed by **Charles Bulfinch**. Huntington died in office on January 5, 1796, at Norwich.

HURLEY, ROBERT A. (1895–1968). Governor of Connecticut. Born in Bridgeport on August 25, 1895, Hurley graduated from Lehigh University (1916). He served in the Navy (1917–19) and was a civil engineer. Hurley was a Democrat appointed by Governor **Wilbur Cross** as assistant state director of the Works Progress Administration and later as commissioner of public works (1937–40). Hurley was elected as the state's first Catholic governor (1941–43) and died in West Hartford on May 3, 1968.

HURRICANES. Wind and rain storms from June to November that often cause natural disasters in New England. The name is used only in the Atlantic; western Pacific storms are called typhoons. Wind velocity may reach 180 mph/300 kmh, but the tides and waves generated by the hurricane cause the most damage.

Few weather forecasts were proven wrong as dramatically as the hurricane on September 21, 1938. The 180-mph winds crossed Long Island Sound to devastate New England, flooding **Providence** and the Connecticut coast, inundating **New Bedford**, and felling 16,000 trees in Springfield. During New England's worst weather disaster 700 people died, 63,000 were homeless, and 275 million trees were felled. Despite U.S. Weather Service use of radio technology and reconnaissance aircraft, the Great Atlantic Hurricane on September 9, 1944, killed 390 people in New England. In 1954 Hurricane Carol devastated New England, and Hurricane Donna on September 10, 1960, brought 13-foot waves to the New England coast and 138-mph winds in Massachusetts. National Weather Service meteorological observations and satellite data have improved the accuracy and range of forecasts since 1970, but hurricanes continue to damage New England. However, environmentalists now see hurricane winds and floods as natural occurrences that uproot exotic species, giving native plants the chance to thrive and scour sediments from coastal streams, improving habitat for fish.

HUTCHINSON, ANNE (1591–1643). Puritan leader. Born in England in 1591, Anne Marbury was educated at home by her father, a clergyman, and married William Hutchinson (1612). They followed **John Cotton** to **Boston** (1634), where she became an influential religious teacher and midwife. Her theological views contrary to the Puritan orthodoxy and her covenant of grace were the focus of the Antinomian controversy. When Governor **John Winthrop** and the General Court banished her from the colony (1638), Mrs. Hutchinson and her family moved to Rhode Island. After the death of her husband, she moved to Long Island, where Indians killed her and five of her children. The Hutchinson River and Hutchinson River Parkway in New York are named in her honor, and a statue of her by Cyrus E. Dallin (1922) was placed on the Massachusetts State House grounds.

HUTCHINSON, THOMAS (1711–1780). Governor of Massachusetts. Born in **Boston** on September 9, 1711, Hutchinson graduated from **Harvard** College (1727). As a prosperous merchant he was a town selectman and legislator (1737–49), serving as lieutenant governor (1758–71) and chief justice of the state Supreme Judicial Court (1761–69). His conservative **Loyalist** views and support of the **Stamp Act** (1765) led a **Boston** mob to destroy his house. Hutchinson was appointed governor (1771–74), but he provoked the **Boston Tea Party**. Replaced by General **Thomas Gage**, Hutchinson moved to London where he died on June 3, 1780.

– I –

IMMIGRANTS. Those who arrived in New England after the **Mayflower**. They came by ship until **railroads** reached Canada (1840). An unknown number of **Irish** and **Scottish** immigrants came to Massachusetts as transported convicts, kidnapped children, or **indentured servants** from 1650 to 1750. French **Huguenot** émigrés also settled in New England by 1680. Sailing ships bringing American raw materials to Europe often returned with immigrants traveling in cheap and crowded accommodations. During the Irish Potato Famine (1845–50), some of these **Irish** exiles traveled on disease-ridden **coffin ships**. The Cunard line (1839), carrying mail from Great Britain to North America, established scheduled voyages for passengers by steam ships. By 1847 ships made a fast voyage from Liverpool to Halifax, Quebec, or **Boston** in 14 days.

Uncounted immigrants entered New England by crossing the unde-fended Canadian border or by packet ships from Nova Scotia. Migration from Canada increased when the Grand Trunk Railway connected with **Portland** and **Boston** (1853), and House Island in Portland harbor be-came a U.S. Immigration Quarantine Station (1900–20). Immigrants were responsible for the growth of Boston from 250,000 residents in 1880 to more than 500,000 in 1890. One-third of the city residents were immigrants, a majority of them from Ireland, and one-third were the chil-dren of immigrants in 1890. By 1920, 24 percent of the Massachusetts population was foreign born.

By 1880, **Italian**, **Polish**, **Albanian**, **Lithuanian**, **Swedish**, **Welsh**, **Syrian**, **Portuguese**, and Russian **Jewish** immigrants joined the earlier Irish, **German**, and **French Canadian** or Maritime Province immigrants in Boston and other New England cities. Although they provided a much-needed workforce and fueled economic growth, nativist fears were expressed in the **Know Nothing Party**, **American Protective Associa-tion**, and the **Immigration Restriction League**. Prejudice against French Canadians and other immigrants made the Ku Klux Klan influ-ential in Maine politics in the 1920s when more than one-third of Maine residents were immigrants or the children of immigrants. In Connecticut, industrial cities attracted greater numbers of immigrants like Bridgeport whose population was 73 percent foreign stock by 1920.

More recent labor shortages prompted **Lowell textile** companies to re-cruit **Hispanic immigrant** worker from Puerto Rico (1960) and Colom-bia (1969), and since 1970 immigrants from other areas of Latin Amer-ica have arrived. By 2002 Rhode Island's 92,000 Latinos composed 11 percent of the state population and 9,600 Latinos in Maine were the state's largest minority group. Maria C. Sanchez (1926–89), a native of Puerto Rico and founder of **Hartford**'s annual Puerto Rican parade (1964), was the first Hispanic woman elected to the Connecticut legisla-ture (1988) and Eddie Perez was elected Hartford's first Hispanic mayor in 2001. Boston voters elected Marie St. Fleur in 2000, the first Haitian ever elected to a state legislature in the nation, and the first Hispanics were elected to the Boston City Council and to the state senate in 2002. Greater Boston also had 50,000 Salvadoran immigrants by 2000. Immi-grants from Southeast Asia joined them, and Lowell had 10,000 **Cam-bodian** residents (2001), who built its first Buddhist temple in 1985.

Boston minority groups accounted for 51 percent of the city popula-tion (2000), 14.4 percent Latinos, 7.5 percent Asians, and 3.1 percent multiracial, as well as 23.8 percent **African Americans**. Across the state

1,150,738 people, or 18.1 percent of the population, were from one or more minority groups in 2002. Increased immigration to New England by 355,000 foreign workers stimulated the Massachusetts economic boom in the 1990s. The state's high-tech industries benefited from 44,000 skilled workers from India, and immigrants from Latin America, Africa, and the West Indies had a great impact on New England's African-American community, which is now one-third foreign born. By 2001 about 8.5 percent of the Rhode Island population did not speak English fluently compared with 7.7 percent in Massachusetts, 7.4 percent in Connecticut, 2.4 percent in New Hampshire, and 2 percent in Maine.

IMMIGRATION RESTRICTION LEAGUE (IRL). Founded in **Boston** (1894) by **Henry Cabot Lodge**, Prescott Hall, A. Lawrence Lowell, Robert DeCourcey Ward, **Francis A. Walker**, and other prominent Bostonians. The organization was concerned that "new immigrants" from southern, eastern, and central Europe and Asia, who arrived in America in large numbers after 1880, were inferior and would cause social and political problems. They advocated literacy tests and other methods to limit immigration to more acceptable people from northern and western Europe. Lodge persuaded the U.S. Senate to appoint Vermont senator **William P. Dillingham** as chair of a commission to study immigration, and the 42-volume report (1910–11) proposed strict limits to exclude the undesirables. Racial prejudice, religious bias, and white supremacist views were evident in the IRL and the Dillingham Report.

IMPRESSMENT. The enlistment of seamen into the British Navy by force. Press gangs of sailors led by a Royal Navy officer, usually with the assistance of the governor and sheriff, searched New England waterfronts for suitable mariners. The unlucky men were taken by force to the ship for an indefinite period of service. This provoked much discontent and deprived **whaling**, merchant, and **fishing** ships of trained crews. Riots in **Boston** (1741, 1747), Casco Bay (1764), and **Newport** (1765) did little to halt the press gangs until the **American Revolution**. Impressment of **Yankee** seamen by British captains was an important cause for the War of 1812.

INDENTURED SERVANTS. Common labor system in colonial New England in which British or **German immigrants** came to America by selling their labor in a legal contract, articles of indenture binding them to a period of unpaid labor, usually two to seven years. Ship owners sold their indentures at public auction in **Boston** or other American ports. It is estimated that one-third to one-half of all European colonists came as indentured servants. Many New England parents indentured their children to craftsmen as a form of vocational **education**. New England town **selectmen** also indentured orphans, bastards, or delinquents and some adult lawbreakers to respectable farmers. Uncounted **Irish** children were kidnapped and sold as indentured servants in New England from 1650 to 1750, so great was the need for labor. In 1749 Irish women from Belfast jails were transported as convicts to become servants in Massachusetts. After the Battle of Dunbar (1650), more than 150 Scottish prisoners of war were transported to Boston, some to work at the **Saugus Iron Works**. At the end of the indentured labor period, masters were required to give land, tools, clothing, or money to their workers. Abuses were common but servants appealed to selectmen and courts that often ruled in their favor. This system of labor exchange came to resemble binding out homeless children or formal apprenticeship in some communities before it disappeared in the antebellum era.

INDIAN PUDDING. A traditional New England baked dish made with milk, **corn** meal, butter, eggs, and **molasses**. Recipes date from 1743, but **Pilgrims** and **Puritans** ate it in the 17th century and it is still served today.

INDIAN MOTORCYCLES. Manufactured (1901–53) in Springfield, Massachusetts, by George M. Hendee, a high wheel bicycle champion, and Carl Oscar Hedstrom, a **Swedish** machinist. The company manufactured bicycles, airplane engines, outboard motors, air conditioners, and other items, but it was best known for the fast and reliable Indian Motorcycles. This was the first commercially marketed gasoline powered motorcycle company and the largest in the world. Its Blackhawk Chief model, used by many police departments in 1922–53, is considered a classic vehicle now. The company museum in Springfield attracts many motorcycle aficionados each year.

INGERSOLL, RALPH ISAACS (1789–1872). Congressman from Connecticut. Born in **New Haven** on February 8, 1789, Ingersoll graduated from Yale College (1808). He practiced law in New Haven (1810–25, 1848–72) and served in the state legislature (1820–25). Elected to the House of Representatives (1825–33), he was the U.S. minister to Russia (1846–48) and mayor of New Haven (1851). Ingersoll died in New Haven on August 26, 1872.

INSURANCE. A new industry in London when Moses Michael Hays (1738–1805) first sold marine insurance in **Boston** (1780). Rhode Island incorporated the Providence Insurance Company in 1799. Connecticut had the Mutual Assistance Company (1795) and **Hartford**, an important seaport on the **Connecticut River**, was known as the **Insurance City** because so many insurance companies were founded there. These firms included the Hartford Fire Insurance Company (1810), Aetna Insurance Company (1819), Mutual Insurance Company (1831), Connecticut Mutual Life Insurance Company (1846), Phoenix Mutual Insurance Company (1851), Travelers Insurance (1864), and Connecticut General life Insurance Company (1865). This profitable business accumulated much capital to invest in New England industries, and the Connecticut abolitionist and mathematician, **Elizur Wright** (1804–85), introduced important reforms as the Massachusetts Insurance Commissioner (1858–66). *See also* BULKELEY, MORGAN GARDNER.

INSURANCE CITY. A nickname for **Hartford**, Connecticut.

INTOLERABLE ACTS. Another term for the **Coercive Acts** (1774) passed by the British Parliament to punish the colonies after the **Boston Tea Party**.

IRISH FAMINE MEMORIAL. A public park with sculpture by Robert Shure (1998) on Washington Street in downtown **Boston** to commemorate the 150th anniversary of the famine migration from Ireland (1845–50). As a consequence of this disaster, more than 100,000 **Irish** refugees emigrated to Boston, transforming the antebellum city and providing the labor force for extensive public works and manufacturing enterprises throughout New England. The City of Cambridge also erected a sculpture (1997) on the Cambridge Common in memory of the Irish potato famine refugees who fled to New England.

IRISH. Immigrants who arrived quite early in America. By 1660 the American colonies numbered 10,000 Irish immigrants. Religious and cultural differences prompted the Massachusetts **General Court** to ban Irish immigrants in 1654. **Cotton Mather** investigated Anne Glover, an old Irish woman hanged as a witch in Boston (1688). When five ships arrived in **Boston** (1718) with 200 emigrants from Ulster, the Massachusetts legislature passed an ordinance (1720) directing that "certain families recently arrived from Ireland be warned to move off" and later ordered

(1723) them to register. But the need for labor and the profit in selling indentured servants overcame **Puritan** prejudice, and the *Boston News-Letter* advertised an auction of Irish boys recently landed in 1730. Irish women transported as convicts from Belfast were sold in Boston in 1749, and some were sold to other colonies.

Irish Protestants established the Charitable Irish Society in Boston (1737) when 10 ships arrived with 1,000 Irish emigrants, and by 1750 Irish Catholics joined the society. William Molineux, who was born in Dublin, was an ally of **Samuel Adams** and participated in the **Boston Tea Party**. These early immigrants gave Irish names to Antrim, Derry, Dublin, Kilkenny, and Sullivan in New Hampshire and Belfast, Keegan, and Limerick in Maine. Two signers of the Declaration of Independence from New Hampshire, **Matthew Thorton**, and **William Whipple**, were Irish, as was General **John Stark**, whose Rangers were Irishmen. General **Henry Knox** and General **John Sullivan** were the sons of Irish immigrants. Sailing a Machias lumber schooner, the *Liberty,* Jeremiah O'Brien, son of an Irish immigrant in Maine, captured the British schooner, *Margaretta* (1775), the first American Navy victory of the **American Revolution**.

Irish Catholic soldiers in the British garrison outraged Bostonians by celebrating St. Patrick's Day with Hibernian enthusiasm (1775). Many Irish rebels fled to New England (1798) despite nativist and **anti-Catholic** prejudice. By 1820 the Irish immigrants made public works projects possible and provided the labor force for economic development throughout New England. Irish workers built the **Blackstone Canal** (1828) and Vermont's first railroads (1847). The *Catholic Sentinel* (1829), the first Catholic newspaper published in the United States, was intended for Irish immigrants in New England. Publisher Patrick Donohoe renamed it the *Boston Pilot* (1835), and by 1850 it served local and national interests of Irish immigrants. Under editors **John Boyle O'Reilly** and **Katherine E. Conway** the *Pilot* had a national circulation and became the voice of the Catholic Archdiocese of Boston in 1908.

Immigrants who fled the Potato Famine (1845–50) and their sons served loyally in many New England **Civil War** units, especially the **9th Massachusetts** and the 15th, 19th, and 28th Regiments. These men were the immigrants or their sons who arrived in waves, 17,000 landed in Boston between 1836 and 1840, and 113,000 from 1846 to 1850. There were 181,000 Irish in Massachusetts in 1855 and 235,000 in 1875. Many men moved into forestry work in Maine and iron mines in

Vermont, and Irish women dominated the **Lowell** mills and domestic service by 1850.

These numbers account for the legendary success of the Irish in New England politics. **Matthew Lyon** was a congressman from Vermont (1797), **John Sullivan** was governor of New Hampshire (1786), his brother **James Sullivan** was governor of Massachusetts (1807), and **Edward Kavanagh** was governor of Maine (1843). John J. Donovan was the first Irishman elected mayor of Lowell (1882), as was **Hugh O'Brien** in Boston (1885–88), and Cornelius Driscoll in **New Haven** (1899). **David I. Walsh** was the first Irish Catholic elected governor of Massachusetts (1914–16) and U.S. senator (1919–25, 1926–47). Irish immigration to New England increased sharply in the 1980s due to a chronic labor shortage. By 1900 a majority of Bostonians were Irish, and today the city's population is 17 percent Irish (93,000 residents), higher than other Irish-American cities such as Chicago, New York City, Philadelphia, or San Francisco. Massachusetts has a larger population of Irish and Irish-American residents (23 percent or 1.4 million) than any state, with 21 percent in New Hampshire and Rhode Island in 2000. The Irish contribution to New England has never been adequately described.

ISLES OF SHOALS. Nine small rocky islands six miles southeast of Portsmouth and straddling the New Hampshire and Maine border. Mapped by **John Smith** (1614), the rich **fishing** attracted 600 English colonists by 1645. The poet **Celia Laighton Thaxter** lived in the **lighthouse** cottage with her family (1839), and her father's hotel on Appledore Island attracted many artists and literary visitors (1890–1910). **Childe Hassam**'s summer sojourns there are reflected in his paintings *Celia Thaxter's Garden (1890)* and *Surf, Isle of Shoals* (1913). Star Island hosted many **Unitarian** conferences (1914) and later a marine biology laboratory. The pirate treasure said to be buried on the Isles of Shoals has never been discovered.

ITALIANS. Immigrants who settled in Rhode Island and Connecticut by 1700, and after the **American Revolution** a few northern Italian artists, musicians, and teachers worked in **Boston**. But Massachusetts counted only 196 Italians in 1850, although large numbers of southern Italians arrived in southern New England by the 1880s, finding work in the clothing, **fishing**, construction, and wholesale food industries. Boston's **North End** had some Italian families from Genoa living on Ferry Street (1860), and the Little Italy gradually expanded as men found work as fishermen and on the nearby wharves. By 1880 Boston had 1,277 Italians among its 350,000 residents, and this grew to 7,700 in 1895 and 36,300 in 1930, or 5 percent of the city population. Despite ethnic and religious prejudice, most Italians settled into New England life. William Draper, the American ambassador in Italy, recruited 75 Italian workers for his family's machine factory in Hopedale, Massachusetts (1900), but the model company town was the scene of a bitter strike by the immigrants (1913).

Skilled stone-cutters from Italy found work in the Barre, Vermont, granite **quarries** by 1880, and about 10 percent (13,000 people) of the **New Haven**, Connecticut, population was Italian by 1910. Many of these were women working in the needle trades and corset factories. Bridgeport counted 8,700 Italian residents by 1920. Rhode Island counted 40,000 Italian residents in 1911. Boston's **North End**, once the home of elite Bostonians and then Irish and **Jewish** immigrants, became an Italian district by 1890, much like Federal Hill in **Providence**, Rhode Island. St. Stephen's Church in the North End, designed by **Charles Bulfinch** (1804), became a **Catholic** church (1862) for Irish immigrants but the parish was largely Italian by 1870. Nearby St. Leonard's Church (1873) was the first of 13 Italian Catholic parishes in Massachusetts (1873–1927). The Boston Italian community grew from 264 people in 1870 to 31,380 by 1910.

World War I and the Immigration Restriction Act (1924) reduced the numbers of newcomers, and the **Sacco-Vanzetti Case** (1921–27) demonstrated the prejudice Italians encountered. The **Immigration Restriction League**, founded in Boston (1894), feared that Italians could never be assimilated into American society. Luigi Storti, an Italian immigrant, was the first person executed by the electric chair in Massachusetts (1901). Nonetheless, prosperity of the 1920s benefited Italians and their offspring, dispersing them into skilled jobs and professions in many New England communities. Prohibition and World War II provided opportunities for some Italian Americans in organized crime and concerns about the loyalty of immigrants became a public issue in the 1940s. But only 228 people were interned, and half a million Italian Americans served the United States loyally in the war. The Northeast had 2.9 million of the nation's 4.2 million Italian Americans by 1970, from whom came new political leaders in New England. Rhode Island's **John O. Pastore** became the first Italian American elected governor of a state (1945) and the first to be elected to the Senate (1950). **Foster Furcolo** was the first Italian American elected to the House (1949) and as governor (1956) in Massachusetts. **Ella T. Grasso** was the first Italian American and first woman elected governor of Connecticut (1975), and Antonina P. Uccello of **Hartford** was the first woman elected mayor in Connecticut (1968–70). Thomas A. Menino was the first Italian-American mayor of **Boston** (1993), and Massachusetts had 890,000 residents (14.5 percent) of Italian origin in 2000.

IVES, CHARLES (1874–1954). Composer. Born in **Danbury**, Connecticut, on October 20, 1874, Charles Edward Ives graduated from Yale University (1898). While working in the New York City **insurance** business (1898–1930), he composed his best work but was little known until he received the Pulitzer Prize (1947) for his *Third Symphony* (1913). His *Second Symphony* was first performed in 1952 and his *Fourth Symphony in* 1965. Much of his work includes popular melodies, march music, and hymns from his **Transcendentalist** background. Ives also composed piano and violin sonatas (*Concord* sonata, 1939) and chamber music at his West Redding, Connecticut, farm. Ives, Connecticut's official state composer, died in New York City on May 19, 1954.

IVY LEAGUE. A group of American colleges and universities regarded as academically and socially elite, including **Harvard University** (1636), Yale (1701), Pennsylvania (1740), Princeton (1746), Columbia (1754), Brown (1764), Dartmouth (1769), and Cornell (1865). They are members of an intercollegiate athletic conference (1870), which dominated college sports until 1920. The first Harvard-Yale football game played in New Haven in 1875 set an example for Christian gentlemen who were scholars and athletes. Since 1956 administrators met to discuss common issues in sports, admissions, and financial aid. The **Seven Sisters** association of elite northeastern colleges for women was modeled on the Ivy League.

– J –

JACKSON, HELEN HUNT (1830–1885). Writer. Born in Amherst, Massachusetts, on October 18, 1830, Helen Maria Fiske was a neighbor and close friend of **Emily Dickinson**. She married Edward Hunt (1852) and began writing as a widow in **Newport**. **Thomas Wentworth Higginson**

encouraged her to write. Living in Colorado with her second husband, William Jackson (1875), she became interested in **Native Americans** and is best known for *A Century of Dishonor* (1881) and her novel *Ramona* (1884), both indictments of U.S. government mistreatment of Indians. Mrs. Jackson died in San Francisco on August 12, 1885.

JAMES, HENRY (1843–1916). Writer. Born in New York City on April 15, 1843, Henry James was educated at private schools in America and Europe. He lived in **Newport**, Rhode Island, and Cambridge, Massachusetts, and attended **Harvard** Law School (1862). James published reviews and stories (1864) and his first novel *Watch and Ward* in 1871. Living as an expatriate in Paris and London inspired *Roderick Hudson* (1876), *The American* (1877), *Daisy Miller* (1879), *The Portrait of a Lady* (1881), and *The Bostonians* (1886). He was the brother of **William James** and died in London on February 28, 1916.

JAMES, WILLIAM (1842–1910). Philosopher and psychologist. Born in New York City on January 11, 1842, the brother of **Henry James**, he studied art in **Newport** with **William Morris Hunt** and graduated from **Harvard** Medical School (1869). James created the nation's first psychology laboratory (1876) at Harvard, where he taught philosophy (1872–1907). His books introduced Americans to pragmatism, especially *The Principles of Psychology* (1890) and *Pragmatism* (1907). James died in Chocorua, New Hampshire, on August 26, 1910.

JEFFORDS, JAMES MERRILL (1934–). Senator from Vermont. Born in Rutland, Vermont, on May 11, 1934, Jeffords graduated from Yale University (1956) and served in the U.S. Navy (1956–59). After graduating from **Harvard** Law School (1962), Jeffords practiced in Rutland and was a Republican in the state senate (1967–68) and state attorney general (1969–73). Elected to the House (1975–89) and to the Senate (1989–), Jeffords became an independent (2001), which caused the Senate to change from Republican to Democratic leadership.

JESUITS. Members of the Society of Jesus. The Jesuits played an important role in New England history as missionaries to **Native Americans**, Catholic clergymen, and educators. The first Jesuit in New England was Father Pierre Briard (1567–1622), who established a mission for the **Abenaki** at Port Royal in Nova Scotia (1611) and on **Mount Desert Is-**

land (1613). His reports on the land and the people in *The Jesuit Relations* encouraged colonization in Maine. Father Gabriel Druillettes (1610–1681) was the first European to travel the Native American route from Quebec to Moosehead Lake and the Kennebec River to **Augusta** and by sea to his mission with the Abenaki on the Penobscot River (1646). Despite pronounced **anti-Catholicism** by the **Puritans**, he was sent by the governor of New France as a diplomat to **Boston** and **Plymouth** (1650) and **New Haven** (1651) to negotiate a commercial treaty and a joint expedition against the Iroquois.

Father **Sebastien Rasles** succeeded Father Druillettes as missionary at Norridgewock, Maine, and he had compiled an Abenaki dictionary when Massachusetts military forces (1724) killed him. Other notable Jesuits include **Benedict J. Fenwick**, the second bishop of Boston and Father Virgil Horace Barber, who built the first Catholic church in New Hampshire (1823). Father **John Bapst** was tarred and feathered by a **Know Nothing Party** mob in Ellsworth, Maine (1854), and became the first president of Boston College (1863). Jesuits founded the College of the Holy Cross in **Worcester** (1843) and Fairfield University in Connecticut (1942). **Robert F. Drinan**, a Jesuit priest, was dean of the Boston College Law School and a Democrat from Massachusetts in the House of Representatives (1971–81). *See also* ANTI-CATHOLICISM.

JEWETT, SARAH ORNE (1849–1909). Writer. Born in South Berwick, Maine, on September 3, 1849, Jewett was largely self-educated when she published local color stories of New England towns in the *Atlantic Monthly* (1870). She wrote *Deephaven* (1877) and *The Country of the Pointed Firs* (1896) in the regional style depicting life on the declining Maine seacoast. She lived part of each year in a **Beacon Hill** literary salon with her close friend **Annie Adams Fields** in what was called a **Boston Marriage**. Miss Jewett died in South Berwick on June 24, 1909.

JEWISH. Immigrants who arrived in New England long before the **American Revolution**, unlike cities in Europe they were free to live where they chose. **Harvard** scholars even learned Hebrew (1636). Solomon Franco, a Dutch Jewish merchant, was warned to leave Massachusetts (1649). But a **Portuguese** Jew, Rowland Gideon, traded in **Boston** (1674), and Isaac Lopez was a prominent merchant in the city (1716).

Judah Monis, an **Italian** Jew, received a Master of Arts degree at Harvard College for his Hebrew grammar and joined the faculty, after his conversion (1722). Isaac Solomon and Michael Asher built a snuff mill in Boston (1734). But these pioneers were not part of an established Jewish community, which came after the Revolution.

Rhode Island granted liberty of conscience to Jews in 1684, and **Newport** had a Jewish population by 1730. Newport's **Touro Synagogue** (1763), designed by **Peter Harrison**, is the nation's oldest Jewish synagogue. Some Jews migrated from Rhode Island to Boston's **North End**, creating the city's first Jewish neighborhood from 1780 to 1910. It was home to the wealthy merchant Moses Michael Hays (1738–1805), the first marine **insurance** agent in Boston and founder of the first bank. Hays was a benefactor of Harvard College and a Mason. His nephew Abraham Touro (1774–1822) contributed funds to establish **Massachusetts General Hospital**. Portuguese Jews had a synagogue in Boston (1816), and 1,000 **German** Jews built another (1842). Massachusetts admitted Jews as citizens (1821), a Jewish cemetery began in East Boston (1844), and more German Jews settled in Boston and **Lowell** (1850). The Massachusetts community of Portuguese, Dutch, and German Jews, numbering 2,000 in 1860, expanded when Eastern European Orthodox Jews arrived in the 1880s. The North End of Boston (1880s) had 6,200 Jews among its 23,000 residents in 1895, and Jews lived in the South End and West End. The Vilna Shul (1919–85), the last intact example of Boston's 50 immigrant synagogues, has been restored as an historic site on **Beacon Hill**. East Boston had the largest Jewish community in New England (1905) with five synagogues (1892–1900). As Boston's Jewish population expanded to 40,000 (1900), Jews moved to the suburbs of Chelsea, Dorchester, Roxbury, and Mattapan (1910–60). Cambridge had 5,000 Jewish residents (1875–1925).

New Haven had the first synagogue in Connecticut (1839) before the state granted civil rights to Jews in 1843. New Haven had 7,900 Jewish residents by 1910, about 16 percent of the city population, and many worked in the needle trades and corset factories. New Haven elected the state's first Jewish mayor, Samuel Campner (1915), a Republican lawyer born in Russia who graduated from Yale. German Jewish businessmen established **Hartford**'s first synagogue (1843), and the city's East Side was a thriving Jewish neighborhood by 1880. The Broadway star **Sophie Tucker** called **Hartford** her home. By 1933 Connecticut elected its first

Jewish congressman, **Herman P. Koppleman**, and **Abraham Ribicoff** was the state's first Jewish governor (1954) and senator (1963).

Some Boston Jews who worked as peddlers in rural New England settled in New Hampshire, Vermont, and Maine as merchants. Vermont's first synagogue opened in Burlington in 1875. **Portland** opened the first elementary Hebrew school in Maine (1884) and another in 1908. But most Jewish immigrants preferred urban life and adjusted rapidly to modern America. Boston city councilor Isaac Rosnosky and Congressman **Leopold Morse** were progressive Jewish leaders in the 1880s. **Bernard Berenson**, a North End Jewish immigrant, graduated from Harvard University (1887) and became a prominent art critic. **Louis D. Brandeis**, a Jewish lawyer in Boston, became the first Jew on the U.S. Supreme Court (1916), and Harvard Law School professor **Felix Frankfurter** was the second (1939). **Edward A. Filene**, the Boston department store magnate, played a leading role in civic affairs and philanthropy. Louis E. Kirstein (1867–1942), vice-president of Filene's stores, built the downtown branch of the **Boston Public Library** for the business community (1930). Boston banker Abraham Ratshesky served as the U.S. ambassador to Czechoslovakia (1930).

Springfield had its first synagogue (1898), as did Northampton (1905) with 25 Jewish families in the city. **Worcester** counted 8,000 Jews in the city in 1915, many in the garment and needle trades and well represented in labor and socialist organizations. However, prejudice was common, so Lowell Jews established a cemetery in Pelham, New Hampshire (1893), when denied a permit in Lowell. But they opened three new synagogues (1897, 1899, 1902) and a Yiddish-speaking Lowell Workmen's Club (1900). Although New Hampshire had a small Jewish population, Bethlehem, a resort town in the **White Mountains**, had 34 summer hotels for Hasidic Jews by 1890, and this tradition continues today.

Harvard and other **Ivy League** colleges imposed a quota for Jewish students in the 1920s, but other New England universities welcomed growing numbers of Jewish students. American Jews founded Brandeis University (1948) in **Waltham**, Massachusetts, partly in reaction to this anti-Semitism. By 2001 about 8.5 percent of New Englanders were Jewish, and 200, 000 Jews lived in Greater Boston.

JIMMY FUND. A charity supported by **Billy Sullivan** and the **Boston Braves** (1948–53) and since then by **Thomas Yawkey** and the **Boston**

Red Sox. This annual fund-raising campaign for the Dana-Farber Cancer Institute in Boston became New England's favorite charity to aid children suffering from cancer.

JOHNSON, EASTMAN (1824–1906). Artist. Born in Lovell, Maine, on July 29, 1824, Jonathan Eastman Johnson apprenticed with a **Boston** lithographic draftsman (1840–45). He was a crayon portraitist in Washington, D.C. (1845–51), drawing **Daniel Webster** (1846) and **John Quincy Adams** (1846). After study in Dusseldorf and The Hague, he was known in Boston as the American Rembrandt. His best **art** includes portraits of **Ralph Waldo Emerson**, **Nathaniel Hawthorne**, **Henry Wadsworth Longfellow**, and **Charles Sumner**. His genre landscapes integrate rustic New England figures with light and color, as in *Cornhusking* (1860), *Sugaring Off* (1861), *The Old Stage Coach* (1871), and, after settling on Nantucket, *The Cranberry Harvest* (1880). He later turned from genre painting to portraiture. Johnson died on April 5, 1906.

JOHNSON, HOWARD (1905–1972). Restaurateur. Born in Quincy, Massachusetts, in 1905, Howard Dearing Johnson created 28 flavors of ice cream for his Quincy drugstore (1926) and Wollaston beachfront stand. Johnson's restaurants introduced Americans (1928) to traditional New England food: **baked beans**, **brown bread**, **clam chowder**, **clams**, salt water taffy, and, of course, ice cream. Johnson sold his first franchise (1935) in Orleans on **Cape Cod** and had 200 roadside restaurants (1941), each with his trade mark orange roof, weathervane, white clapboards, and Simple Simon and Pie Man road signs. He insisted on high standards of cleanliness, quality food, and friendly service as the "host of the highway," but the Great Depression, and wartime gas and food rationing, limited his expansion. Howard B. Johnson, his son and successor (1959), added 500 Howard Johnson motor lodges and 1,000 restaurants in 42 states. The growth of fast-food chains in the 1980s led to the decline of the ubiquitous HoJo. The last restaurant in Massachusetts closed in 2002, but some are found in Maine and Vermont.

JOHNSON, SAMUEL (1696–1772). Clergyman. Born in Guilford, Connecticut, on October 14, 1696, Johnson graduated from Yale College (1714). He was a **Congregational** minister in West Haven (1720) but was ordained in England as an Episcopal priest (1723). Johnson returned as a missionary in Stratford and established churches in Connecticut, Rhode Island, and New York (1724–54). He trained **Samuel Seabury** for the ministry and was a pioneer of the Episcopal Church in America. As president (1754–63) of King's College (now Columbia University), Johnson expanded the curriculum and avoided sectarianism. He wrote an influential text, *Introduction to Philosophy* (1731), and retired to his Stratford pastorate (1763), where he died on January 6, 1772.

JOHNSON, WILLIAM SAMUEL (1727–1819). Senator from Connecticut. Born in Stratford, Connecticut, on October 7, 1727, Johnson graduated from Yale College (1744) and **Harvard** College (1747). He practiced law in Stratford and served in the Connecticut legislature (1761, 1765–66, 1771–75). He was a delegate to the **Stamp Act** Congress (1765) and the Connecticut agent in London (1767–71), where he was a member of the Royal Society. Johnson was a state judge (1772–74) and was elected to the House of Representatives (1785–87) and to the Senate (1789–91). He followed his father, **Samuel Johnson**, as president of Columbia College (1792–1810) and died in Stratford on November 14, 1819.

JONNY CAKE. A **Yankee** dish similar to **corn** bread but sweetened with **maple syrup**, sugar, or **molasses**. It was served traditionally to guests after a long journey.

JORDAN, EBEN DYER (1822–1895). Businessman. Born in Danville, Maine, Eben D. Jordan moved to **Boston** (1836) and founded the Jordan Marsh department store (1841). He combined his name with that of his partner, Benjamin L. Marsh, and adopted a **Yankee** merchant as the store logo. Jordan financed **Patrick Gilmore**'s National Peace Jubilee and Musical Festival in Boston (1869) and was a founder of the *Boston Globe* (1872). He died in Boston on November 15, 1895, but his son, Eben Dyer Jordan, Jr. (1857–1916), modernized the store. He was the first to offer credit to retail customers and introduced annual Christmas displays that attracted customers from all over New England. He also founded the city's best concert venue, Jordan Hall at the **New England Conservatory of Music** (1903). When the store merged with the Macy department store chain (1996), the familiar name Jordan Marsh disappeared from New England.

– K –

KAPLAN, JUSTIN (1925–). Writer. Born in New York City on September 5, 1925, Kaplan graduated from **Harvard University** (1944). He was an editor for the Simon and Schuster publishing company but moved to Cambridge, Massachusetts (1959), to write. Kaplan won the National Book Award and the Pulitzer Prize for his biography *Mr. Clemens and Mark Twain* (1966). He wrote *Lincoln Steffens* (1974) and *Walt Whitman: A Life* (1980) and was editor of a new edition of **John Bartlett**'s *Familiar Quotations* (1992).

KAVANAGH, EDWARD (1795–1844). Governor of Maine. Born in Newcastle, Maine, on April 27, 1795, Kavanagh graduated from St. Mary's College in Baltimore (1813). He practiced law in Damariscotta (1815–31) and was a Democrat in the state legislature (1827–28) and in the House of Representatives (1831–35). After serving as chargé d'affaires in Portugal (1835–41), he was a commissioner with **Daniel Webster** to negotiate the **Webster-Ashburton Treaty** (1842). As president of the state senate (1842–43), Kavanagh became governor (1843–44) when Governor **John Fairfield** resigned to enter the U.S. Senate. He was the first **Irish Catholic** governor of Maine and died in Newcastle on January 22, 1844.

KEITH, BENJAMIN FRANKLIN (1846–1914). Businessman. Born in Hillsboro, New Hampshire, on January 26, 1846, B. F. Keith was a circus concessionaire with **P. T. Barnum.** He opened America's first continuous performance vaudeville theater in **Boston** (1883) and later formed a partnership with Edward Franklin Albee (1857–1930), a circus manager from Machias, Maine. Keith coined the term **vaudeville** for his continuous variety shows in ornate theaters available to the average person. Aware of the **banned in Boston** tradition, Keith censored the acts to attract more respectable audiences. The Keith-Albee circuit offered "Sunday School" shows in Fall River, Lawrence, **Lowell**, Pawtucket, **Portland, Providence**, and Woonsocket and had a chain of 400 vaudeville theaters (1914). Keith died in Palm Beach, Florida, on March 16, 1914, and Albee sold the firm to **Joseph P. Kennedy** (1928). Albee died in Palm Beach on March 11, 1930.

KELLEY, JOHN A. (1908–). Athlete. Born in Arlington, Massachusetts, in 1908, Johnny Kelley ran the **Boston Marathon** in 1928 and ran his last Boston Marathon at age 85, finishing in 5 hours and 58 minutes. He won the marathon twice (1935, 1945). Kelley became a beloved figure in New England sports and still participates in road and track events.

KENNEBEC PROPRIETORS. Boston investors in frontier Maine selling the land granted to the **Puritans** in the 17th century. As unpopular absentee landlords they were represented in many lawsuits by **William Cushing**, who was later a U.S. Supreme Court justice.

KENNEDY FAMILY. Rivals the **Adams** family as New England's most famous political dynasty. Patrick Kennedy (1823–58), an Irish **immigrant** from County Wexford, fled the potato famine and arrived in **Boston** (1848), where he became a cooper in East Boston. His son, Patrick J. Kennedy (1858–1929), was an East Boston tavern-keeper, state senator, bank president, and Democratic ward boss. His son, **Joseph P. Kennedy**, was a Boston banker, Wall Street investor and chairman of the Securities and Exchange Commission, and U.S. ambassador in London. Three of Joseph P.'s sons, **John F. Kennedy**, **Robert F. Kennedy**, and **Edward M. Kennedy**, served in the U.S. Senate, and John F. Kennedy was elected president. Two of his grandsons served in the House of Representatives, **Joseph P. Kennedy II** and **Patrick J. Kennedy**, and his granddaughter **Kathleen Kennedy Townsend** (1951–) was the first woman elected lieutenant governor of Maryland (1995–2002). Other members of the Kennedy family have been leaders in charitable, environmental, and civic causes.

KENNEDY, EDWARD MOORE (1932–). Senator from Massachusetts. Born in **Boston** on February 22, 1932, Ted Kennedy graduated from **Harvard University** (1956) and the University of Virginia Law School (1959). After serving in the U.S. Army (1951–53), he succeeded his brother, **John F. Kennedy**, in the Senate (1962–). He declined the nomination for president (1972) and became a leader of the liberal wing of the Democratic Party.

KENNEDY, JACQUELINE LEE BOUVIER (1929–1994). First lady of the United States. Born in East Hampton, New York, on July 28, 1929,

Jackie Bouvier attended Miss Porter's School in Farmington, Connecticut, Vassar College, and George Washington University (1951). She was a photojournalist in Washington when she married **John F. Kennedy** at her family estate in **Newport** (1953). As first lady (1961–63), her elegant and sophisticated official social life dubbed the Kennedy White House as Camelot. She is best remembered for her historic preservation of the White House and as the widow of the assassinated president. Jackie Bouvier Kennedy married Aristotle Onassis (1968) and was a publisher's editor (1975–94) when she died in New York City on May 19, 1994.

KENNEDY, JOHN FITZGERALD KENNEDY (1917–1963). President of the United States. Born in Brookline, Massachusetts, on May 29, 1917, Jack Kennedy graduated from **Harvard University** (1940). After heroic service in the U.S. Navy (1941–45), he was elected in **Boston** as a Democrat to the House of Representatives (1947–53) and the Senate (1953–60). JFK, the youngest man and first Roman Catholic elected president (1961–63), was assassinated in Dallas on November 22, 1963. The Kennedy Presidential Library, designed by I. M. Pei in 1979, overlooks **Boston** harbor, and a statue of JFK by Isabel McIlvain was placed on the State House grounds (1990).

KENNEDY, JOSEPH PATRICK (1888–1969). Businessman. Born in **Boston** on September 6, 1888, Joseph Patrick Kennedy graduated from **Boston Latin School** and **Harvard University** (1912). He was a banker, Wall Street investor, movie executive (1926–30), the first Securities and Exchange Commission chairman (1934–37), and U.S. ambassador in London (1938–40). Joe Kennedy married (1914) Rose Fitzgerald (1890–1995), daughter of **John Francis Fitzgerald** (1863–1950). He died at the family home in Hyannisport, Massachusetts, on November 18, 1969.

KENNEDY, JOSEPH PATRICK II (1952–). Congressman from Massachusetts. Born in **Boston** on September 24, 1952, Joe Kennedy, the son of **Robert F. Kennedy**, graduated from the University of Massachusetts at Boston (1976) and served as a Democrat in the House of Representatives (1987–99).

KENNEDY, PATRICK JOSEPH (1967–). Congressman from Rhode Island. Born in **Boston** on July 14, 1967, Patrick Kennedy, the son of **Edward M. Kennedy**, graduated from Providence College (1991). He served in the Rhode Island legislature (1988–94) and was elected as a Democrat to the House of Representatives (1995–).

KENNEDY, ROBERT FRANCIS (1925–1968). Senator from New York. Born in **Boston** on November 20, 1925, Bobby Kennedy, the son of **Joseph** and **Rose Kennedy**, graduated from **Harvard University** (1948) and the University of Virginia Law School (1951). After serving in the U.S. Navy in World War II (1944–46), he was a Department of Justice attorney (1951–52) and staff attorney for U.S. Senate committees (1953–60). After serving as U.S. attorney general (1961–64), he was elected to the Senate from New York (1965–68) and was assassinated in Los Angeles on June 6, 1968, while campaigning for the Democratic presidential nomination.

KENNEDY, ROSE FITZGERALD (1890–1995). Born in **Boston** on July 22, 1890, Rose Fitzgerald, the daughter of **John F. Fitzgerald**, was educated at Catholic schools in Massachusetts and Holland. Active in her father's political campaigns, she married **Joseph P. Kennedy** (1914) and was the mother of President **John F. Kennedy** and matriarch of the large Kennedy family. She died in Hyannisport on January 22, 1995.

KENNELLY, BARBARA BAILEY (1936–). Congresswoman from Connecticut. Born in **Hartford** on July 10, 1936, the daughter of **John M. Bailey**, Barbara Bailey graduated from Trinity College in Washington, D.C. (1958), and studied at **Harvard** Business School (1959) and Trinity College in Hartford (1971). She was elected secretary of state (1979–82) and as a Democrat in the House of Representatives (1982–99).

KEROUAC, JACK (1922–1969). Writer. Born in **Lowell**, Massachusetts, on March 12, 1922, Jean Louis Kerouac studied at Columbia University (1940–42) and served in the Merchant Marine (1942–43) and the U.S. Navy (1943). Living in New York City Bohemian circles, Jack Kerouac wrote *On the Road* (1957), a semiautobiographical account of cross-country journeys that established his reputation. He became a spokesman for the Beat Generation, and his beatnik novels include *The Dharma Bums* (1958), *Lonesome Traveler* (1960), and *Big Sur* (1962). Kerouac, always conflicted about his **French-Canadian** roots, lived in Lowell and St. Petersburg, Florida, where he died on October 21, 1969.

KERRIGAN, NANCY (1969–). Athlete. Born in Woburn, Massachusetts, on October 13, 1969, Nancy Kerrigan graduated from Emmanuel College in **Boston** (1991). She won an Olympic bronze medal (1992) and a silver medal (1994) and was the U.S. women's champion (1993). Kerrigan became a professional figure skater in 1995.

KERRY, JOHN FORBES (1943–). Senator from Massachusetts. Born in Denver on December 11, 1943, Kerry graduated from Yale University (1966). After serving in the Navy in the Vietnam War (1966–69), he graduated from Boston College Law School (1976) and was a Middlesex County district attorney (1977–82). Kerry served as lieutenant governor (1982–84) and was elected as a Democrat to the Senate (1985–).

KINDERGARTENS. Introduced to America by **Elizabeth Peabody** who conducted the first kindergarten in **Boston** (1860–67). She taught in **Bronson Alcott**'s Boston school (1834) and was active in progressive **education** as the sister-in-law of **Horace Mann**. Miss Peabody studied the kindergarten methods of Friedrich Froebel in Germany and published the magazine *Kindergarten Messenger* (1873–75). **Lucy Wheelock**, a graduate of Peabody's Kindergarten Training School (1879), expanded the movement and founded the teacher training school that became Wheelock College. *See also* BRADLEY, MILTON.

KING, CLARENCE (1842–1901). Scientist. Born in **Newport**, Rhode Island, on January 6, 1842, King graduated from the Sheffield Scientific School at Yale University (1862). He directed the U.S. government survey of Arizona, Colorado, and California (1870–80) and organized the first U.S. Geological Survey (1879–81). King wrote *Mountaineering in the Sierra Nevada* (1872) and *Systematic Geology* (1878). He was a pioneer in western geology and mining engineering when he died in Phoenix, Arizona, on December 24, 1901.

KING, JOHN W. (1918–1996). Governor of New Hampshire. Born in Manchester, New Hampshire, on October 10, 1918, John William King graduated from **Harvard University** (1938) and Columbia University Law School (1943). He practiced law in New York City (1943–48) and in Manchester (1948–62). After serving in the state legislature (1954–62), he was the first Democrat elected governor of the state in the 20th century (1962). King was reelected in 1964 and for an unprecedented third term in 1966. He signed the law creating the nation's first modern state lottery

(1963) and served as a judge (1969–79) and chief justice of the state supreme court (1981–86). King died in Manchester on August 9, 1996.

KING, RUFUS (1755–1827). Senator from New York. Born in Scarborough, Maine, on March 24, 1755, King graduated from **Harvard** College (1777). After serving in the **American Revolution**, he studied law with **Theophilus Parsons** and practiced in **Salem** (1780–88). He was a **Federalist** in the state legislature (1783–85), in the Continental Congress (1784–87), and at the Constitutional Convention (1787). Moving to New York City, he was elected to the state legislature and to the U.S. Senate (1789–96). King was the U.S. minister to Great Britain (1796–1803) and an unsuccessful candidate for vice-president (1804, 1808) and was elected again to the Senate (1813–25). He ran for president (1816) and was again U.S. minister to Great Britain (1825–26). King died in Jamaica, New York, on April 29, 1827.

KING, STEPHEN (1947–). Writer. Born in **Portland**, Maine, on September 21, 1947, Stephen Edwin King graduated from the University of Maine (1970) and wrote a series of popular supernatural horror novels. Several novels and short stories have become films, including *Carrie* (1974), *The Shining* (1977), *Firestarter* (1984), and *Misery* (1987). King set many stories in small **Yankee** towns, and he is known as a philanthropist for many New England charities.

KING, WILLIAM (1768–1852). Governor of Maine. Born in Scarborough, Maine, on February 9, 1768, King worked in sawmills in Sacco and Topsham, Maine (1781). As a militia general in the War of 1812, King resisted British occupation of Penobscot Bay when Massachusetts **Federalist** leaders refused to help. King was Maine's leading shipbuilder (1800), founded the first bank in Bath, and opened Maine's first cotton mill in Brunswick (1809). Elected to the Massachusetts legislature as a Democratic-Republican (1795–19), King campaigned for statehood and founded the *Eastern Argus* newspaper in **Portland** to promote this cause. Elected as the state's first governor (1820–21), he resigned when his public improvement plan was rejected by the legislature. King died in Bath on June 17, 1852.

KING'S CHAPEL. The first Anglican church in New England (1688). It was built on the orders of Governor **Edmund Andros** (1689) for **Boston**'s 400 Anglicans over the protests of the Congregational majority.

Rebuilt by **Peter Harrison** (1749), the adjacent Burial Ground includes the grave of **John Winthrop** and **William Dawes**. After its **Loyalist** congregation was exiled (1776), the elegant Georgian stone building became the first **Unitarian** church in the nation (1787), with the largest church bell ever cast by **Paul Revere**.

KING GEORGE'S WAR (1744–1748). The American phase of the War of Austrian Succession (1739–48) when England, Holland, and Austria battled France, Spain, and Prussia. **William Pepperrell** led a small New England force to capture the French fortress Louisbourg in Nova Scotia (1745). Aided by Sir Peter Warren's British ships and armed merchantmen, Pepperrell captured the fort from which French privateers had preyed on New England **fishing** boats. He was knighted for his efforts, but Louisbourg was returned to France in the peace treaty (1748). **Abenaki** and other **Native American** allies of the French raided many western New England towns during this war.

KING PHILIP'S WAR (1675–1676). The bloodiest war in New England history. **Metacom**, the successor of his father, **Massasoit**, the **Wampanoag** *sachem,* was known as King Philip (ca.1638–76) in Massachusetts. Resenting English expansion and the missionary efforts of **John Eliot**, Metacom led his people with **Narragansett** and **Nipmuc** allies in attacks on Swansea (June 1675), and 52 of the 90 towns in New England. The **Native American** warriors burned 12 towns and killed or captured 1,000 colonists. Plymouth, Massachusetts, and Connecticut military forces and their Indian allies, including the **Mohegan** *sachem* Uncas (1588–1682), killed 3,000 Indians in the war. Metacom was shot on August 12, 1676, and his head was displayed on a pole at Plymouth. Many of his warriors died from smallpox and influenza, and others were executed. Deer Island in **Boston** harbor was a prison camp for 500 Native Americans; many were buried there or sold into West Indies **slavery**. The pan-tribal alliance included **Abenakis** in Maine, and its conclusion marked the end of Native American independence in New England but retarded English settlement for decades.

KING WILLIAM'S WAR (1689–1697). The first of the **French and Indian Wars**, the American phase of an international conflict. New England frontier towns were attacked, and **Sir William Phips** captured Port Royal in Nova Scotia (1690) with a New England force. The peace treaty (1697) settled little, and in 1702 England and Holland resumed war with France and Spain.

KITSON, THEO (1876–1932). Artist. Born in Brookline, Massachusetts, in 1876 Theo Alice Ruggles studied sculpting with Henry Hudson Kitson (1863–1947), who she married in 1893. They executed several public **art** projects, including a bust of *Patrick Collins* on the Commonwealth Avenue mall in **Boston** (1908) and a statue of Sir *Richard Saltonstall* in Watertown (1926). Theo Kitson is best known for *The Minuteman*, a blacksmith militia soldier in Framingham (1905), and a statue of *Thaddeus Kosciuszko* in the **Boston Public Garden** (1927) and the *Massachusetts State Memorial* (1903) at the Vicksburg National Military Park. She was one of the most prolific female sculptors in the nation when she died in Massachusetts in 1932.

KNIGHT, SARAH KEMBLE (1666–1727). Diarist. Born in **Boston** on April 19, 1666, Sarah Kemble married Richard Knight, a Boston bricklayer, and had one child, a daughter (1689). When she traveled by horseback from Boston to **New Haven** and back (1704), her witty and insightful journal described the bad roads, crude **taverns**, poor food, and rural people on her journey. It became a classic account of travel and manners in colonial New England when first published as *The Journal of Madame Knight* (1825). Widowed in 1706, Mrs. Knight moved near her married daughter in New London (1713), where she was an innkeeper and land speculator until her death on September 25, 1727.

KNOW NOTHING PARTY. Formed (1843) when several nativist, patriotic, **anti-Catholic** organizations combined as the secretive national political party. Its members in New England, New York, and other states answered "I know nothing" when questioned about the party, dubbing themselves Know Nothings. The new party dominated the Massachusetts government (1854), electing the governor, all but two seats in the legislature, all the congressional seats, and two mayors of Boston. State laws abolished **Irish** militia companies and limited naturalization and voting rights for **immigrants**. Reading the King James Bible became mandatory in Massachusetts public schools, and the legislature appointed a joint committee to investigate Catholic convents and schools (1855).

The **Dorr War** demonstrated the threat Roman Catholics posed to some Rhode Islanders and William T. Minor was the Know Nothing governor of

Connecticut (1855–57). But the party disappeared when industry recognized its need for **immigrant** labor and the issue of **slavery** in Kansas, the success of the Free Soil party, and the attack on **Charles Sumner** on the Senate floor drew support away from the nativist party by 1857.

KNOX, HENRY (1750–1806). Soldier. Born in **Boston** on July 25, 1750, Knox was a bookseller who served as a militia and Continental Army artillery officer. General George Washington ordered Colonel Knox to bring 55 cannons, captured by **Ethan Allen** at Fort Ticonderoga, to Boston (1775). Under difficult winter conditions, he transported the artillery pieces 250 miles overland to lift the siege of Boston on March 17, 1776. This day is celebrated in Suffolk County as **Evacuation Day**. Knox was a close adviser to Washington throughout the war, organized the Army's first artillery school, and commanded West Point (1782–84). He founded the Society of the Cincinnati (1783) and as secretary of war (1785–94, 1789–95) established the U.S. Navy. General Knox retired to Thomaston, Maine, where he died on October 25, 1806. *See also* AMERICAN REVOLUTION; EVACUATION DAY.

KOPPLEMAN, HERMAN PAUL (1880–1957). Congressman from Connecticut. Born in Odessa, Russia, on May 1, 1880, Koppleman settled in **Hartford** with his parents (1882). He was a publishers' agent for newspapers and magazines (1894) when he was elected as a Democrat to the Hartford City Council (1804–12) and state senate (1917–20). He was the first **Jewish** congressman from Connecticut (1933–39, 1941–43, 1945–47). Koppleman died in Hartford on August 11, 1957.

KUNIN, MADELEINE M. (1933–). Governor of Vermont. Born in Switzerland on September 28, 1933, Madeleine May Kunin moved to Pittsfield, Massachusetts (1940), and graduated from the University of Massachusetts (1957). After earning a master's degree in journalism at Columbia University and a master's degree in literature at the University of Vermont, she was a reporter for the *Burlington Free Press*. Elected as a Democrat to the Vermont legislature (1973–78), Kunin served as lieutenant governor (1979–82) and three terms as governor (1985–93). She was the first woman elected governor of Vermont, the second women to be governor in New England after **Ella Grasso**, and only the third Democratic governor in 130 years of Vermont history. She served as deputy secretary of education (1993–96) and ambassador to Switzerland (1996–99).

– L –

LA FARGE, JOHN (1835–1910). Artist. Born in New York City on March 31, 1835, La Farge graduated from Mount Saint Mary's College (1853). He studied painting with **William Morris Hunt** in **Newport**, Rhode Island (1859), and became recognized for landscapes and murals. **Henry H. Richardson** invited him to decorate the **Trinity Church** interior in **Boston** (1876). This led to commissions at Bowdoin College, the Crane Memorial Library in Quincy, Massachusetts, and church murals and stained glass windows. La Farge's stained glass influenced **Louis Tiffany**, but he painted watercolors after travel with **Henry Adams** in Japan (1886) and the South Seas (1890). He died in **Providence**, Rhode Island, on November 14, 1910.

LALLEMENT, PIERRE (1843–1891). Inventor. Born in France, Lallement immigrated to Ansonia, Connecticut, where he invented the bicycle (1865). His patent for the first pedal-powered two-wheeler (1866) started a cycling **sport** craze in New England. Lallement worked for Colonel **Albert A. Pope**, who first manufactured bicycles in **Hartford** and **Boston** and founded the League of American Wheelmen (1880). Improved road paving, bike races, and greater freedom for women were unexpected results of Lallement's invention. **Harvard University** students (1878) held the first American bike race. David Wilson invented the recumbent bicycle at MIT (1970), creating a new fad as interest in bikes reached unprecedented levels. The sturdy, lightweight mountain bike became common in rural New England (1990). Lallement, forgotten when he died in Boston, is remembered by a new Boston bicycle path named for him (1993).

LAND, EDWIN HERBERT (1909–1991). Inventor. Born in Bridgeport, Connecticut, on May 7, 1909, Edwin H. Land studied at **Harvard University** (1928–30). While an undergraduate he invented the first modern polarizers for light (1929). Land is best remembered for the instant-photo film and camera (1947) and instant color photography (1963) produced by his Polaroid Corporation (1937) in Cambridge, Massachusetts. Land spent a lifetime in research and development of optical devices for the U.S. government and private industry. He had 500 patents when he died in Cambridge on March 1, 1991.

LANE, FITZ HUGH (1804–1865). Artist. Born in Gloucester, Massachusetts, on December 19, 1804, Nathaniel Rogers Lane apprenticed in a

Boston lithography shop (1832–37), where he was influenced by English and Dutch marine paintings at the **Boston Athenaeum** annual **art** exhibitions. Returning to Gloucester in the 1840s, he became America's foremost maritime painter and the leading figure in American luminism. His canvases of Massachusetts and Maine ships and coastal panoramas, such as *Castine Harbor and Town* (1851) and *Owl's Head, Penobscot Bay* (1862), project shimmering intensity and serenity compared to **transcendentalism**. Fitz Hugh Lane died in Gloucester on August 14, 1865.

LANE, GERTRUDE BATTLES (1874–1941). Editor. Born in Saco, Maine, on December 21, 1874, Lane attended Burdett College in **Boston** and was an editor for the Cyclopedia Publishing Company (1896–1902). She became an editor for the *Woman's Home Companion* magazine in New York (1902), rising to editor in chief (1912–41). Her innovations included practical service departments, fiction (by Edna Ferber, Sinclair Lewis, Willa Cather, Pearl Buck, **Booth Tarkington**, Sherwood Anderson), and feature articles on maternal and infant health, child labor, psychology, careers, and politics, which greatly increased subscriptions and advertising revenue by 1940. She lived in Harwinton, Connecticut, and died in New York City on September 25, 1941.

LANGDELL, CHRISTOPHER COLUMBUS (1826–1906). Lawyer and educator. Born in New Boston, New Hampshire, on May 22, 1826, Langdell attended **Harvard** College (1848–49) and graduated from Harvard Law School (1854). He practiced law in New York City (1854–70) until Harvard president **Charles W. Eliot** appointed him professor of law and dean of the law school (1870–95). He introduced the case-study method and raised the quality of legal training. Langdell retired as dean (1895) but taught until he died in Cambridge on July 9, 1906.

LANGDON, JOHN (1741–1819). Governor of New Hampshire. Langdon was born on June 26, 1741, in **Portsmouth** and became a merchant, shipbuilder, and Revolutionary War leader. He was a state legislator (1775, 1777–81, 1784–87, 1801–05), led the **Committee of Correspondence**, and served in the Continental Congress (1775–76, 1787). Langdon built two ships for the U.S. Navy, the *Raleigh* and *Ranger* at Portsmouth, and became wealthy as a privateer. He served at the **Battle of Bennington** and at Saratoga (1777). He was governor (1785, 1788, 1805–09, 1810–12) and served as a Democratic-Republican in the House of Representatives (1784) and in the Senate (1789–1801). Governor

Langdon signed laws making **Concord** the state capital and prohibiting the importation of slaves into the state. His brother, **Woodbury Langdon**, was also a member of Congress. Langdon's elegant Portsmouth home built in 1784 was remodeled by **McKim, Mead and White** (1890). In his later years he founded the New Hampshire Bible Society, and he died in his Portsmouth mansion on September 18, 1819.

LANGDON, WOODBURY (1739–1805). Congressman from New Hampshire. Born in **Portsmouth**, New Hampshire, in 1739, Langdon was a prosperous merchant and revolutionary leader. He served in the state legislature (1774–75, 1780–82) and in the Continental Congress (1779). He was a state superior court judge (1782, 1786–91) and was appointed (1790) as a commissioner to settle Revolutionary War claims. Langdon, the brother of **John Langdon**, died in Portsmouth on January 13, 1805.

LANGFORD, SAM (1883–1956). Boxer. Born in Weymouth Falls, Nova Scotia, on March 4, 1883, Langford ran away from home (1895) to **Boston** where he became a boxer (1899). Known as the "Boston Tar Baby," he won 137 and lost 23 of his 252 professional bouts from lightweight to heavyweight but never fought a title match (1902–26). The popular **African-American** fighter did win the heavyweight title in Great Britain, Mexico, and Spain (1923) but retired blind and poor. His fans established a trust fund (1944) to support him until he died in Cambridge, Massachusetts, on January 12, 1956. Langford was the first non-champion elected to the Boxing Hall of Fame (1955) and to the International Boxing Hall of Fame (1990).

LARCOM, LUCY (1824–1893). Writer. Born in Beverly, Massachusetts, on March 5, 1824, Lucy Larcom worked in the **Lowell** mills for 10 years (1836–46). Her books offer rare views of the new **textile** industry in *Among Lowell Mill-Girls: A Reminiscence* (1881), *An Idyll of Work* (1875) and *A New England Girlhood* (1889). She was later a teacher in Illinois, wrote poetry in Beverly, taught at Wheaton College (1854–62), contributed to the *Atlantic Monthly*, and edited a children's magazine (1865–73). Larcom died in **Boston** on April 17, 1893.

LAW, BERNARD F. (1931–). Bishop. Born on November 4, 1931, in Mexico, Bernard Francis Law graduated from **Harvard University** (1953) and was ordained a Catholic priest in Ohio (1961). He was a

Catholic newspaper editor and pastor in Mississippi (1961–73) and bishop of Springfield–Cape Giradeau, Missouri (1973–84). In 1984 he became archbishop of **Boston** (1984–2002) and an influential cardinal (1985). Cardinal Law resigned as archbishop on December 13, 2002.

LAWRENCE, ABBOTT (1792–1855). Congressman from Massachusetts. Born in Groton, Massachusetts, on December 16, 1792, Lawrence was **Boston**'s leading **textile** merchant and importer with the **Boston Associates**. Elected as a Whig to the House of Representatives (1835–37, 1839–40), he was a commissioner to settle the U.S.-Canada boundary (1842) and was U.S. minister to Great Britain (1849–52). He founded the Lawrence Scientific School at **Harvard** (1847), promoted the Boston and Albany Railroad (1835), and founded the cotton **textile** city, Lawrence, Massachusetts (1845) with his brother **Amos Lawrence**. Abbott Lawrence died in Boston on August 18, 1855.

LAWRENCE, AMOS (1786–1852). Businessman. Born in Groton, Massachusetts, on April 22, 1786, Lawrence was a **textile** importer in **Boston** with his brother **Abbott Lawrence**. The A. & A. Lawrence firm (1814) imported textiles from Europe and founded the largest cotton manufacturing firms in Massachusetts at Lawrence (1845). Amos Lawrence was a benefactor of Williams College (1845) and well known as a **Unitarian** Whig and philanthropist when he died in Boston on December 31, 1852.

LAWRENCE, AMOS ADAMS (1814–1886). Businessman. Born in **Boston** on July 31, 1814, Amos Adams Lawrence graduated from Harvard College (1835). He was the son of **Amos Lawrence** and a wealthy Boston commission merchant and **textile** manufacturer. He funded the **New England Emigrant Aid Company** and aided **John Brown** to make Kansas a free state. His interest in philanthropy led him to found Lawrence University in Appleton, Wisconsin (1847), and a college in Lawrence, Kansas, that became the University of Kansas (1866). Lawrence was a benefactor to **Harvard University** and the Episcopal Theological School in Cambridge. He died in Nahant on August 22, 1886, and his son, Bishop **William Appleton Lawrence**, wrote his biography.

LAWRENCE, WILLIAM APPLETON (1850–1941). Bishop. Born in **Boston** on May 30, 1850, Lawrence, the son of **Amos Adams Lawrence**, graduated from **Harvard University** (1871) and was ordained an Episcopal minister (1876). He taught theology at the Episcopal Theological School in Cambridge (1884–93) and was the seventh bishop of Massachusetts (1893–27). He wrote biographies of **Roger Wolcott**, **Phillips Brooks**, and **Henry Cabot Lodge** and also of his father. Lawrence died in Milton, Massachusetts, on November 6, 1941.

LAWRENCE STRIKE (1912) . An epic confrontation between labor and capital in Lawrence, Massachusetts, when 30,000 **textile** workers protested unsafe working conditions and wage cuts. Organized by the radical Industrial Workers of the World (IWW) union under the leadership of **Elizabeth Gurley Flynn**, the poet Arturo Giovannitti, and labor leader Joseph Ettor, the ethnically diverse workers were assaulted by police and state militia and three workers were killed on January 29, 1912. Public outrage led to congressional hearings and widespread sympathy and support for the "Bread and Roses" workers, until the mill owners relented.

LEAF PEEPING. A major tourist attraction throughout New England as visitors arrive each autumn to view the region's colorful foliage. Since 1914 state **tourism** agencies and the media have advised visitors when and where the fall color has reached a peak. This natural phenomenon, the result of the regional climate and diversity of tree species, is a major economic activity. The millions of visitors (7 million in 2001) create important revenue for scenic **railroads**, hotels, motels, inns, and restaurants as well as traffic congestion at scenic locations.

LEGAL SEA FOODS. A chain of seafood restaurants founded in Cambridge, Massachusetts (1950), by George Berkowitz. Born in Cambridge on December 30, 1924, Berkowitz served in the U.S. Marine Corps in World War II and attended Dartmouth College. His neighborhood fish market became a popular restaurant in 1968 and grew to a chain of 20 restaurants from Massachusetts and Rhode Island to Florida. He wrote *The Legal Sea Foods Cookbook* (1988) with Jane Doefer. Legal Sea Foods' **New England clam chowder** has been served at every presidential inauguration since 1981.

LEWIS, WILLIAM HENRY (1868–1949). Public official. Born in Virginia on November 28, 1868, William H. Lewis graduated from Amherst College (1892) and **Harvard** Law School (1895). He was a football star at Amherst and Harvard, was the first **African American** named to the All-Star team, and coached football for Harvard. Lewis practiced law in

Cambridge, served on the Cambridge Common Council (1899–1901), and was a Republican state legislator (1901–02). With **W. E. B. Du Bois**, he founded the Niagara Movement, the forerunner of the National Association for the Advancement of Colored People (NAACP), but he later joined the conservative Booker T. Washington organization. Lewis was an assistant U.S. attorney in Boston (1903–06) and an assistant attorney general (1911–13) in Washington, the highest position held by an African American at that time. Lewis was active in the civil rights movement and practiced law in **Boston** (1913–49), where he died on January 1, 1949.

LIBERATOR **(1831–1865).** The most influential antislavery weekly newspaper in the antebellum era. It was published in **Boston** by **William Lloyd Garrison** (1805–79), a self-educated printer and **abolitionist** reformer from Newburyport, who demanded the immediate emancipation of millions of **African-American** slaves in the United States and opposed African colonization or moderate reform of the "peculiar institution."

LIBERTY TREE. An elm tree in **Boston** that became the focus of patriotic protests and celebrations from 1765 to 1776. The **Sons of Liberty** hanged the **Stamp Act** commissioner in effigy on the tree in August 1765 and organized annual celebrations under the tree to commemorate the event. **Loyalists** and British soldiers chopped down the tree for firewood in 1776, but it remained a patriotic symbol long after the **American Revolution**.

LICHT, FRANK A. (1916–1987). Governor of Rhode Island. Born on March 13, 1916, in **Providence**, Licht graduated from Brown University (1938) and **Harvard** Law School (1941). He practiced law in Providence (1943–56) and was a Democrat in the state senate (1949–56). Appointed a superior court judge (1956–68), he was elected governor (1969–73), Rhode Island's first **Jewish** chief executive. Licht died on May 30, 1987.

LIEBERMAN, JOSEPH I. (1942–). Senator from Connecticut. Born in Stamford, Connecticut, on February 24, 1942, Lieberman graduated from Yale University (1964) and Yale Law School (1967). His political mentors were **John M. Bailey** and **Abraham Ribicoff** before he served as a Democratic state senator (1970–80), state attorney general (1983, 1986–88), and U.S. senator (1989–). He was the candidate for vice-president of the United States in 2000, the first Jewish nominee for that office. After that close and disputed election, Lieberman returned to the Senate. He wrote *The Power Broker* (1966) and *The Legacy: Connecticut Politics, 1930–1980* (1981).

LIGGETT, LOUIS K. (1875–1946). Businessman. Born in Detroit, Michigan, on April 4, 1875, Louis Kroh Liggett was a patent medicine salesman in **Boston** (1897–1903). He founded the United Drug Company (1903), which became the Liggett Rexall Drug Store chain with 25,000 drugstore franchises (1950), the largest pharmaceutical firm in the nation. He provided **tonics**, patent medicines, over-the-counter products, and innovative retailing methods to pharmacies across the country. As a Republican national committeeman (1928–32) from Newton, Massachusetts, Liggett introduced modern advertising to political campaigns and founded the Republican League of Young Men (1914). He died in Washington, D.C., on June 5, 1946.

LIGHTHOUSES. Important navigation guides on the New England coast since the **Boston** Light was built (1716) on Little Brewster Island in Boston harbor, where it still operates as the only manned lighthouse in the nation. The twin **Cape Ann** Light (1771), the last constructed in the colonial era, was the first to mark a dangerous site rather than a harbor. Each New England state had lighthouses by 1858, even landlocked Vermont's Lake Champlain (1871). Massachusetts built some in 1785 to revive the **whaling** industry, but the U.S. Lighthouse Department (1789) assumed control of 169 New England lighthouses. In Maine, the **Portland** Head Light was completed in 1791 and Winslow Lewis (1770–1850), a Massachusetts sea captain, patented an efficient whale oil lamp (1810) and installed them in all 49 American lighthouses (1815). By 1840, Lewis constructed 100 new lighthouses. Most used candles or oil until electricity was introduced in the 1890s, and all were automated by 1998 except for the Boston Light. Lighthouses, which are exposed to the seas, require expensive maintenance. A public lottery built the New London Harbor Lighthouse (1760). It was rebuilt in 1801, 1863, and 1900 and automated in 1912.

The 150 lighthouses in New England today are preserved by the U.S. Coast Guard as historic sites or leased to the American Lighthouse Foundation. **Cape Cod**'s Highland Light in Truro (1797), one of the more picturesque on the high ocean bluff, is the first lighthouse seen by ships coming from Europe to America. Despite these efforts, more than 3,000 **shipwrecks** have occurred on the New England coast since 1626. The

Massachusetts Humane Society (1786), which evolved into the Life-Saving Service (1872) and became part of the U.S. Coast Guard (1915), worked closely with lighthouse keepers to save lives from shipwrecks. The first U.S. lightship was stationed off **Nantucket** (1856). Still considered one of New England's most scenic locations, the lighthouse on Isle au Haut in Maine now operates as a unique inn.

LINCOLN, BENJAMIN (1733–1810). Soldier. Born in Hingham, Massachusetts, on January 24, 1733, Lincoln was a general in the **American Revolution**. He served with distinction in New York City and at the Battle of Saratoga (1777) but was forced to surrender to the British in South Carolina (1780). Lincoln was secretary of war (1781–83) and commanded the Massachusetts troops that suppressed **Shays's Rebellion** (1787). He died in Hingham on May 9, 1810.

LINCOLN, ENOCH (1788–1829). Governor of Maine. Born in **Worcester**, Massachusetts, on December 28, 1788, Lincoln graduated from **Harvard** College (1807) and practiced law in **Salem**, Massachusetts, and Paris, Maine. Elected as a Massachusetts Democratic-Republican to Congress (1818–21), he also served as a congressman from the new state of Maine (1821–26) and was governor of the state (1827–29). Lincoln, a mentor to **Hannibal Hamlin**, died in **Augusta** on October 8, 1829. His father, **Levi Lincoln**, and his brother. **Levin Lincoln, Jr.**, were both governors of Massachusetts.

LINCOLN, LEVI (1749–1820). Governor of Massachusetts. Born in Hingham on May 15, 1749, Lincoln graduated from **Harvard** College (1772), served in the **American Revolution**, and practiced law in **Worceste**r (1775–98). He was a state legislator (1796–98) and a Democratic-Republican in Congress (1800–01). As attorney general (1801–05), he advised President Thomas Jefferson on his public statement about the separation of church and state (1802) made to his Baptist supporters in Danbury, Connecticut. Lincoln cautioned that New Englanders cherished traditional public fasts and **Thanksgiving Day** holidays. Lincoln was governor (1808–09) and died in Worcester on April 14, 1820. His son **Enoch Lincoln** was governor of Maine.

LINCOLN, LEVI, JR. (1782–1868). Governor of Massachusetts. Born in **Worcester** on October 25, 1782, Lincoln graduated from **Harvard** College (1802) and practiced law in Worcester (1805–22). He served in the state legislature (1812–22), as lieutenant governor (1823), as a justice of the state supreme court (1824–25), and as governor (1825–34). Elected as an Anti-Jacksonian to Congress, he joined the Whig Party (1834–41) and was collector of the port of **Boston** (1841–43), a state senator (1844–45), and the first mayor of Worcester (1848) and a Republican when he died in Worcester on May 29, 1868. His father, **Levi Lincoln**, was governor of Massachusetts and his brother, **Enoch Lincoln**, was governor of Maine.

LINCOLN LABORATORY. A federally funded research and development center founded in 1951 by the Massachusetts Institute of Technology in Lexington, Massachusetts, makes major contributions in high technology. Its most successful projects have been for the Department of Defense and other federal agencies, especially lasers, **computers**, communications satellites, and missile defense and air traffic control systems, many of which stimulated the New England electronics industry.

LITERATURE. Began in America with the first book published in New England, the *Bay Psalm Book* (1640), printed by Stephen Day on his press in Cambridge, Massachusetts. **Michael Wigglesworth**'s popular Puritan poem, "Day of Doom" (1662) and the poetry of **Anne Bradstreet** (1650) express the Puritan theology. But the diaries of **Samuel Sewall** (1623–1729) and **Sarah Kemble Knight** (1704) reveal daily life in colonial New England. **Mary Rowlandson**'s *Captivity and Restoration* (1682) describes a uniquely American experience, her capture by Native Americans, the first and best known of this genre. **Cotton Mather** represents the Puritan literary ideal in *Magnalia Christi Americana* (1702), as does New England's leading intellectual, **Jonathan Edwards**, in *Freedom of the Will* (1754). Boston's multitalented **Benjamin Franklin** personified **Yankee** common sense in *Poor Richard's Almanack* (1733–58), but his posthumous *Autobiography* (1867) reveals a more rational philosophy.

The era of the **American Revolution** prompted fiery sermons by **Jonathan Mayhew** and pamphlets by **James Otis** and **John Adams** (1765). **John Trumbull** satirized **Loyalists** in *M'Fingal* (1775), but **Phillis Wheatley**, an African-American slave in Boston, wrote more religious poetry (1773). In the letters of **Abigail Adams** we view the Massachusetts homefront during the Revolutionary War. After the war, **Royall Tyler** introduced **Brother Jonathan**, the original stage **Yankee**, in his comedy *The Contrast* (1787). New England writers continued their contributions to American literature in the early national period with the **Hartford Wits'** poetry.

The region's unusual literary productivity included influential magazines, *Youth's Companion* (1827), *Dial* (1839), and *The Arena* (1889). **William Davis Ticknor** and **James T. Fields** published the prestigious *North American Review* (1863) and *Atlantic Monthly* (1857–64) at their **Old Corner Bookstore**, a literary mecca in Boston. The Ticknor and Fields firm was the first American publisher to deal honorably with authors. This all contributed to Boston's reputation as a literary center, as did the antebellum era poet **William Cullen Bryant**, whose poetry linked New England literature to English Romanticism in the 1820s. But **Noah Webster**'s *An American Dictionary* (1828) argued for literary nationalism, as did **William Ellery Channing**, **Edward Everett**, and, especially, **Ralph Waldo Emerson**'s *The American Scholar* (1837). New England writers in the antebellum era who declared America's intellectual independence of Europe include **Henry Wadsworth Longfellow** ("Hiawatha," 1855 and "The Courtship of Miles Standish," 1858) and **John Greenleaf Whittier** and **Oliver Wendell Holmes** ("Old Ironsides," 1830).

The New England Renaissance, a romantic movement in 1830–60, included **Transcendentalist** writers such as **Bronson Alcott**, **Margaret Fuller**, and **Henry David Thoreau** who were indebted to **Ralph Waldo Emerson**. The poet **James Russell Lowell** satirized the war with Mexico in his *Biglow Papers* (1848), and **John Greenleaf Whittier** attacked slavery and Daniel Webster ("Ichabod," 1850) but is best remembered for idealizing Yankees ("Barefoot Boy," 1856 and "Snowbound," 1866). The short stories and novels of **Nathaniel Hawthorne** (*Twice-Told Tales* [1837] and *The Blithedale Romance* [1852]) probed the Puritans and Transcendentalism for original insights. **Herman Melville**, in contrast, used his experiences as a seaman to create a masterpiece, *Moby Dick* (1851), which was unrecognized until 1920. **Richard Henry Dana, Jr.**, also recounted his brief career at sea in *Two Years Before the Mast* (1840).

At a time when history was a form of literature, New England produced the historians **George Bancroft**, **Francis Parkman**, **William H. Prescott**, and **John L. Motley**. Foreshadowing the sectional conflict, **Harriet Beecher Stowe** wrote her best-selling novel *Uncle Tom's Cabin* (1852), the book President Abraham Lincoln said had started the **Civil War**. **Frederick Law Olmsted**'s *The Cotton Kingdom* (1856) also explained the South to American readers.

Postwar writers in New England include **Mark Twain**, a transplanted Connecticut Yankee, who captured the region's industrial age in *A Connecticut Yankee in King Arthur's Court* (1889). **William Dean Howells** captured the Gilded Age ethos in *The Rise of Silas Lapham* (1885), his realistic portrait of a Vermont paint manufacturer seeking social respectability in Victorian Boston. In contrast, **Henry James** departed from provincial New England with his novels about expatriate Yankees, *The Europeans* (1878) and *The Bostonians* (1886).

Local color writers who found themes in New England include **Mary Wilkins Freeman** (*A New England Nun* [1891]) and **Sarah Orne Jewett** (*The Country of the Pointed Firs* [1896]). In the 20th century, **Henry Adams** turned from history and biography to analyze American power (*The Education of Henry Adams* [1907]). Modern New England produced the best-known and best-loved poet, **Robert Frost**, as well as **E. E. Cummings, Robert Lowell, Sylvia Plath, David McCord, Anne Sexton**, and **Elizabeth Bishop**. The playwright **Eugene O'Neill** and the novelist **Edwin O'Connor** and **W. E. B. Du Bois** were other celebrated writers. Contemporary New England writers include **Russell Banks, John Cheever, Nat Hentoff, George V. Higgins, Justin Kaplan**, and **Robert B. Parker**.

LITHUANIANS. Immigrants who arrived in the United States due to a famine (1867–68) but did not settle in New England until 1900. Lawrence, Massachusetts, numbered 1,324 immigrants or their children in 1904, and New Hampshire had 1,500 immigrants by 1910. Lithuanian communities were established in Brockton and **Worcester** by 1890, as well as **Waterbury, New Britain**, and **Hartford** in Connecticut. **Boston** had the largest community in New England, including many workers in tailor shops. But most of the 600,000 Lithuanian immigrants who arrived by 1912 settled in New York, Pennsylvania, Ohio, and Illinois.

Many of the community leaders in Boston were shopkeepers or tailors, and disputes between **Irish** American Catholic priests and immigrants led to schismatic Polish National Church parishes (1900–20) in Worcester and Lawrence. Socialists and freethinkers also avoided the Catholic leadership. One independent socialist weekly newspaper, *Kelevis* (The Traveler), was published in Boston (1905) to express liberal nationalist and anticlerical attitudes. The radical Industrial Workers of the World (IWW) organized some Lithuanian workers in Massachusetts **textile** and shoe factories by 1910, and the Amalgamated Clothing Workers of American unionized some Boston tailoring workers by 1914. New England had more than 50

Lithuanian Citizens' clubs by 1900, mutual-benefit organizations allied with the local Democratic or Republican parties. But Lithuanians had a lower rate of naturalization than other ethnic groups by 1930 until the New Deal created a strong attachment to the Democrats. World heavyweight boxing champion **Jack Sharkey**, the son of immigrants from Lithuania, was a popular hero when he lived in Boston and New Hampshire.

Still, most Lithuanian Americans in New England were rather conservative and used churches, schools, clubs, and unions to adjust to America while retaining ethnic identity. They gradually accepted religious leadership by the Irish Catholic clergy and bishops, and parishes with a majority of Lithuanians often built parochial schools, one of which opened in South Boston's large Lithuanian community. The grammar schools, high schools, and academies were staffed by Lithuanian Sisters from three teaching orders. The Marian Fathers, a Lithuanian community of missionary priests, who came to America in 1913, established Marianapolis College in Thompsonville, Connecticut (1931).

World War I ended immigration from Lithuania but heightened interest in the politics and independence of their homeland. Lithuanian Americans lobbied for U.S. recognition of the new Baltic nation, which came in 1922 and prompted 10,000 Lithuanians to return to their homeland. Political instability and hostility by Poland (1920s) and the Soviet Union occupation (1940) aroused anticommunism in Lithuanian-American communities. After World War II about 30,000 Lithuanian immigrants arrived under the Displaced Persons Act (1948), many settling in New England with the assistance of Catholic organizations.

LITTLE, ARTHUR D., INC. (ADL). The first research and development organization or private consulting firm in the world. Founded by a chemical engineer, Arthur Dehon Little (1886), in Cambridge, Massachusetts, ADL became an international consulting firm for scientific research and product development with offices and laboratories in 30 countries. The ADL think tank closed in bankruptcy in 2002.

LIVERMORE, SAMUEL (1732–1803). Senator from New Hampshire. Born in **Waltham**, Massachusetts, on May 14, 1732, Livermore graduated from the College of New Jersey (1752). He practiced law in Waltham, **Portsmouth**, and Londonderry, New Hampshire; served in the state legislature (1768–69); and was attorney general (1769–74) for Governor **Benning Wentworth** and for the new state (1776–79). Elected to the Continental Congress (1780–82, 1785–86), he served as chief justice of the state supreme court and in the House (1789–93) and Senate (1793–1801) as a **Federalist**. He died in Holderness, New Hampshire, on May 18, 1803.

LOBSTER. Marine crustacean *(Homarus americanus)* found on the ocean floor from Labrador to Virginia. Caught in baited cages called lobster traps or pots, its white meat has been prized as a delicacy, but before the **railroads** came to New England, there was no market for lobsters. Fishermen used lobster for bait until 1850 when the first Gloucester smacks carried lobster to **Boston**. When William Underwood opened a lobster cannery in Harpswell, Maine, and Vinalhaven, Maine, began the first lobster pound (1875), lobstering became a New England commercial industry.

In Connecticut, Noank was the port for more than 40 lobster boats (1875–1900). The Noank sloops landed 500 lobsters a day for the New London and New York restaurants. Lobster populations declined and conservation measures imposed in Maine (1900) spread to the other states, but as New England fisheries declined in the 1980s, many fishermen turned to lobstering. The 1999 New England harvest rose to 78.4 million pounds, valued at $300 million. This was 30 percent of all fishery revenues, and Maine was the nation's leading producer with 53.5 million pounds, followed by Massachusetts with 15.5 million pounds. Maine lobstermen set 1.5 million traps in 1982 and 2.7 million in 1997, and a statue called *The Lobsterman* in Portland pays tribute to the important crustacean. *See also* FISHING.

LODGE, HENRY CABOT (1850–1924). Senator from Massachusetts. Born in **Boston** on May 12, 1850, Lodge graduated from **Harvard University** (1871) and Harvard Law School (1875). He was an editor of the *North American Review* (1873–76), and earned a Ph.D. in political science at Harvard (1876), where he taught history (1876–79). Lodge was a Republican state legislator (1880–81), U.S. congressman (1887–93) and U.S. senator (1893–1924). He founded the **Immigration Restriction League** in Boston (1894) and prevented ratification of the League of Nations (1919). He wrote the biographies *Alexander Hamilton* (1882), *Daniel Webster* (1883), and *George Washington* (1889). Lodge died in Boston on November 9, 1924.

LODGE, HENRY CABOT LODGE, JR. (1902–1985). Senator from Massachusetts. Born in Nahant, Massachusetts, on July 5, 1902, he was the grandson of **Henry Cabot Lodge**. Lodge graduated from **Harvard**

University (1924) and wrote for the *Boston Transcript* and *New York Herald Tribune*. He was a Republican state legislator (1933–36) and U.S. senator (1937–44), and served in the U.S. Army in World War II (1944–45). He returned to the Senate (1947–53) but lost his seat to **John F. Kennedy** (1953). Lodge was the U.S. ambassador to the United Nations (1953–60) and an unsuccessful candidate for vice-president (1960). He was ambassador to South Vietnam (1963–64, 1965–67), ambassador to Germany (1968–69), chief U.S. negotiator at the Paris peace talks on Vietnam (1969), and special envoy to the Vatican (1970–77). Lodge died in Beverly, Massachusetts, on February 27, 1985.

LODGE, JOHN DAVIS (1903–1985). Governor of Connecticut. Born in Washington, D.C., on October 20, 1903, Lodge, the brother of **Henry Cabot Lodge, Jr.**, graduated from **Harvard University** (1925) and Harvard Law School (1929). He appeared in 26 Hollywood movies (1933–89) and practiced law in New York City (1932–42). Lodge served in the U.S. Navy (1942–46) and was a Republican U.S. congressman (1947–51), governor (1951–55), and U.S. ambassador to Spain (1955–61), Argentina (1969–74), and Switzerland (1983–85). Lodge lived in Westport, Connecticut, and died in New York City on October 29, 1985.

LOEB, WILLIAM (1905–1981). Editor and publisher. Loeb was born on December 26, 1905, in Washington, D.C., and raised in Oyster Bay, New York. He graduated from Williams College (1927) and attended **Harvard** Law School (1929–30). Although he lived in Reno, Nevada, and Prides Crossing, Massachusetts, for 35 years Loeb was a major influence in New Hampshire and national politics as owner and publisher of the *Manchester Union Leader,* the only statewide newspaper in New Hampshire (1946–81). He also owned Massachusetts, Vermont, and Connecticut newspapers. After his marriage to Nackey Scripps Gallowhur (1952), heiress of the Scripps newspaper family, Loeb made the *Union Leader* the primary outlet for his conservative Republican views. His colloquial front-page editorials denounced liberals, mourned Joseph McCarthy, and criticized President Dwight D. Eisenhower and **Sherman Adams**. He opposed President Richard Nixon's visit to China (1972) and castigated Gerald Ford, Henry Kissinger, and **Edmund S. Muskie** (1972). Loeb supported **Meldrim Thomson**, Ronald Reagan (1976, 1980, 1984), and **George H. W. Bush** (1988). When Loeb died on September 13, 1981, his wife, Nackey S. Loeb (1924–2000), succeeded him as publisher, continuing the newspaper's controversial, conservative tradition.

LOGAN INTERNATIONAL AIRPORT (1922). New England's largest airport and the fifth busiest in the nation. Established as the **Boston** municipal airport (1922), it was named in honor of General Edward L. Logan, a World War I **Yankee Division** commander from South Boston. Despite expansion into **Boston** harbor on Bird, Apple, and Governor's Islands, the airport became congested. Regional airports in Bedford and **Worcester**, as well as Rhode Island, Connecticut, and New Hampshire were redesigned to serve some of this aircraft traffic.

LOGUE, EDWARD J. (1921–2000). Public official. Born in Philadelphia on February 7, 1921, Logue graduated from Yale University (1942), served in the U.S. Army Air Corps (1942–45), and graduated from Yale Law School (1947). He was an aide to Governor **Chester Bowles** in **Hartford** (1947–52) and India (1952–54) and directed the **New Haven** urban renewal project for Mayor Richard Lee (1955–60). Logue directed the **Boston** Redevelopment Authority (1960–67) for Mayor John F. Collins, transforming the city with major urban renewal projects in Government Center, Prudential Center, **Faneuil Hall**, and Quincy Market. He ran for mayor of Boston (1967) and directed urban redevelopment projects in New York. Logue died in West Tisbury, Massachusetts, on January 27, 2000.

LOMASNEY, MARTIN M. (1859–1933). Public official. Born in **Boston** on December 3, 1859, Lomasney, the orphan son of **Irish immigrants**, left school at age 11. He ran errands for a **West End** politician and worked as a city lamplighter before he founded the Hendricks Club (1885) for the Democratic voters of Ward 8. From his office above the club in Bowdoin Square, Lomasney, known as the Mahatma, provided jobs, aid, and advice to his neighbors in exchange for votes on Election Day. He served as an alderman and state legislator for 20 years but was more influential as the West End ward boss. He was widely respected as an honest power broker between the rival factions of **James Michael Curley** and **John F. Fitzgerald**. An abstemious bachelor and devout Catholic, Lomasney died in Boston on August 12, 1933, bequeathing his modest estate to Catholic charities.

LONG ISLAND SOUND. The Atlantic Ocean area bounded by Connecticut and New York. The sound, approximately 90 mi/145 km long and 3 to 20 mi/5 to 32 km wide, is important for fishing, **tourism**, and shipping to the Connecticut ports of Bridgeport, New London, and **New Haven**.

The **Connecticut**, Thames, Quinnipiac, and **Housatonic** rivers flow into Long Island Sound.

LONG TRAIL. A 261-mile recreational hiking route over the **Green Mountains** from Williamstown, Massachusetts, to the Canadian border, including 126 miles of side trails. The scenic route through the **Green Mountain** National Forest's 630,000 acres was constructed in Vermont by James P. Taylor and the Green Mountain Club (1910–29), who maintain the trail with the U.S. Forest Service.

LONG, JOHN DAVIS (1836–1915). Governor of Massachusetts. Born in Buckfield, Maine, on October 27, 1836, Long graduated from **Harvard** College (1857) and attended Harvard Law School. He practiced law in Maine (1861–63) and **Boston** (1863–69). Elected from Hingham as a Republican in the Massachusetts legislature (1875–78), he served as lieutenant governor (1879) and governor (1880–82). Long was elected to the U.S. House of Representatives (1883–89) and was secretary of the navy (1897–1902). He died in Hingham on August 28, 1915.

LONGFELLOW, HENRY WADSWORTH (1807–1882). Poet. Born in **Portland**, Maine, on February 27, 1807, Longfellow graduated from Bowdoin College (1825) and returned to Bowdoin as professor of modern languages (1829–35). He was a noted poet, critic, and translator when he taught at **Harvard** College (1836–54). His poetry, often reflecting New England history, gained great popularity by the 1850s, especially "The Wreck of the Hesperus" (1841), "The Arsenal at Springfield" (1846), "The Song of Hiawatha" (1855), "The Courtship of Miles Standish" (1858), and "Tales of a Wayside Inn" (1863). His home in Cambridge was a center for Boston intellectuals (1837–82). Longfellow, America's greatest Romantic writer and best-known poet, died in Cambridge on March 24, 1882. His work drew on colonial history and New England scenes for his best-loved poems, and he was the first American to be honored with a bust in Poet's Corner of Westminster Abbey (1884). *See also* LITERATURE.

LORING, GEORGE BAILEY (1817–1891). Congressman from Massachusetts. Born in North Andover on November 8, 1817, Loring was a physician who reformed the U.S. marine hospitals (1849). He founded the New England Agricultural Society (1849) to improve stock breeding and served as a Republican state legislator (1866–67, 1873–76) and in the House of Representatives (1877–90). Loring was U.S. commissioner of agriculture (1881–85) and minister to Portugal (1889–90). He died in **Salem** on September 13, 1891.

LOWELL. The **Spindle City**, founded in northeastern Massachusetts on the Concord and Merrimack rivers (1826) as a **textile** center. Designed by the **Boston Associates** as the nation's first industrial city, the Lowell textile mills and factories attracted Charles Dickens, Davey Crockett, and many other distinguished visitors. The population grew with the arrival of the Yankee **mill girls** and **Irish**, **German**, **French-Canadian**, **Jewish**, **Portuguese**, **Polish**, **Hispanic**, and Asian **immigrants**. The city, named in memory of **Francis Cabot Lowell**, suffered with the decline of the textile and **shoe** industry by 1930, but chemical, plastics, and electronic firms support the current population of 104,000.

LOWELL, ABBOTT LAWRENCE (1856–1943). Educator. Born in **Boston** on December 13, 1856, Lowell graduated from **Harvard University** (1877) and Harvard Law School (1880). He practiced law in Boston (1880–97) and was a professor of political science at Harvard (1897–1909), and president of the university (1909–33). To avoid specialization in college education, he introduced an elective system (1914), general examinations for the bachelor's degree (1917), and the tutorial system for undergraduates. His new residence houses along the Charles River, modeled on the English university, were the most striking physical expansion of the university. Lowell was a strong proponent of academic freedom and the League of Nations but also was vice-president of the **Immigration Restriction League**. His books include *Public Opinion* and *Popular Government* (1913) and *Biography of Percival Lowell* (1935). Lowell died in Boston on January 6, 1943. *See also* HARVARD UNIVERSITY.

LOWELL, AMY (1874–1925). Poet. Born in Brookline, Massachusetts, on February 9, 1874, Amy Lowell was the sister of **Abbott Lawrence Lowell**. Privately educated, Miss Lowell was the leading exponent of the modernist movement in American poetry, influenced by Ezra Pound and an advocate of imagism. Her books include *Sword Blades* and *Poppy Seed* (1914), *Men, Women, and Ghosts* (1916), and a biography of John Keats (1925). Brilliant and unconventional, she was a defiant figure in literary **Boston** when she died in Brookline on May 12, 1925. Her book *What's O'Clock* was posthumously awarded the Pulitzer Prize (1926).

LOWELL, FRANCIS CABOT (1775–1817). Businessman. Born in Newburyport, Massachusetts, on April 7, 1775, Lowell graduated from **Harvard** College (1793). He entered his uncle's importing firm, but during a tour of England he became interested in **textile** machines. His Boston Manufacturing Company built the nation's first cotton textile factory (1813) in **Waltham**. After his death in **Boston** on August 10, 1817, Lowell's partners founded the great textile city (1826) on the Merrimack River named in his memory. Known as the **Spindle City**, **Lowell** was the prototype for early American industrialization and used the **Waltham System** Lowell devised to manage the mechanized cotton factory.

LOWELL, JAMES RUSSELL (1819–1891). Writer and editor. Born in Cambridge, Massachusetts, on February 22, 1819, Lowell graduated from **Harvard** College (1838) and Harvard Law School (1840). He gave up his law practice (1843) to write for the abolitionist crusade and other reforms. Lowell succeeded **Henry Wadsworth Longfellow** as the Harvard professor of modern languages (1855–76) and was the first editor of the *Atlantic Monthly* (1857–61) and co-editor of the *North American Review* (1863–72). He served as minister to Spain (1877–80) and Great Britain (1880–85) but was best known for **Yankee** dialect satire in *The Biglow Papers* (1848). Lowell, who produced many poems and critical essays, was the nation's leading man of letters when he died in Cambridge on August 12, 1891.

LOWELL, JOSEPHINE SHAW (1843–1905). Reformer. Born in **Boston** on December 16, 1843, Josephine Shaw, the sister of **Robert Gould Shaw**, was the widow of Charles Russell Lowell, a **Boston Brahmin** officer in the **Civil War**. After working with the U.S. Sanitary Commission to aid **Civil War** soldiers and freed slaves, she founded the New York City Charity Organization Society (1882) and was its director for 25 years. Lowell died on October 12, 1905.

LOWELL, RALPH (1890–1978). Philanthropist. Born in Chestnut Hill, Massachusetts, on July 23, 1890, Ralph Emerson Lowell graduated from **Harvard University** (1912) and served in the U.S. Army (1917–18). Lowell was a prominent **Boston** banker but is best recalled as a pioneer in educational radio and television (1946) and founder of **WGBH** (1951). He endowed the Boston Arts Festival held each spring in the **Boston Public Garden** (1960) and was a model **Boston Brahmin**, active in civic and cultural institutions. Lowell was a trustee of the **Mu-**

seum of Fine Arts, **Massachusetts General Hospital**, the Lowell Institute, and an overseer for Harvard University. As chairman of the Boston Safe Deposit and Trust Company, he organized the Coordinating Committee known as the **Vault** (1959) to promote urban renewal in Boston. Known as Mr. Boston, Lowell died in Boston on May 15, 1978.

LOWELL, ROBERT (1917–1977). Poet. Born in **Boston** on March 1, 1917, Robert Traill Spence Lowell, a descendant of **James Russell Lowell**, attended **Harvard University** (1935–37). He graduated from Kenyon College (1940) and studied at Louisiana State University and served a prison term in World War II as a conscientious objector. Lowell wrote "Land of Unkindness" (1943) and "Lord Weary's Castle" (1946), which won the Pulitzer Prize for Poetry (1947). He wrote "The Mills of the Kavanaughs" (1951) and, despite suffering mental illness, he wrote *Life Studies* (1959), which won the National Book Award. Some of his other volumes, in the confessional style he made famous, include *For the Union Dead* (1964), *Near the Ocean* (1967), and *The Dolphin* (1974), for which he won his second Pulitzer Prize. His last book, *Day by Day* (1977) appeared shortly before his death on September 12, 1977, in New York City.

LOWELL INSTITUTE. Founded by John Lowell, the son of **Francis Cabot Lowell**, in 1836 to support free public lectures. Its purpose was to extend New England's cultural renaissance to the citizens of Boston by an annual series of lectures by distinguished scholars. By 1862 these included free courses at the Massachusetts Institute of Technology and later the University Extension school at **Harvard** University and the **WGBH** educational television station in 1953. *See also* LYCEUM.

LOWELL OFFERING. Literary magazine published (1840–45, 1847–50) in Lowell, Massachusetts, started with funds from **Amos Lawrence** and other **textile** factory owners. The first editor was Abel C. Thomas, a **Universalist** minister who published uplifting and positive articles written by the **mill girls**. The other editors, Harriet F. Curtis and **Harriet Farley**, reflected the paternalism of the **Boston Associates** and the fascination of many New Englanders with the world's first modern industrial city. **Sarah Bagley**, who wrote on the "Pleasures of Factory Life" (1840), later was a severe critic of the genteel magazine (1845) and deteriorating factory conditions. Her speeches and articles led the *Lowell Offering* to cease publication (1845), and a revival (1847–50) proved unsuccessful as labor disputes rose and **immigrants** replaced the **Yankee** mill girls.

LOYALISTS (OR TORIES). Americans who were loyal to Britain during the **American Revolution**. About 1 in 10 New Englanders were Loyalists, mostly royal officials, Anglicans, and wealthy merchants. Disenfranchised by the Patriots or **Whigs**, they were often jailed, whipped, or fined, lost their property, or were banished. About 1,000 Tories fled to Nova Scotia when the British evacuated Boston (1776). Loyalists were shunned by **selectmen** in towns such as Newbury, Vermont (1783), but David Redding was hanged as a traitor and spy in Bennington (1778) and Moses Dunbar was hanged in Connecticut (1777). Prominent New England Loyalists include **Benedict Arnold**, **Thomas Hutchinson**, **Robert Rogers**, and **Samuel Seabury**.

LUCE, CLAIRE BOOTHE (1903–1987). Congresswoman from Connecticut. Born in New York City on April 10, 1903, Claire Boothe was an editor for *Vanity Fair* and other magazines (1929–34) before her marriage to Henry R. Luce, the publisher of *Vogue* (1935). She wrote plays including *The Women* (1936), *Kiss the Boys Goodbye* (1938), and *Margin for Error* (1939) and published *Stuffed Shirts* (1931) and *Europe in the Spring* (1940). She was elected to the U.S. House of Representatives as a Republican from Connecticut (1943–47) and was ambassador to Italy (1953–57) and to Brazil (1959). She was the first woman ambassador to a major nation, but she soon resigned after winning a bitter confirmation battle in the Senate. Mrs. Luce died in Washington, D.C., on October 9, 1987.

LUDLOW, ROGER (1590–1664). Judge. Born in England on March 4, 1590, Ludlow migrated to **Boston** (1630), where he founded Dorchester and was the deputy governor (1634). He moved to Connecticut to organize the new colony at Windsor (1635) and Fairfield (1639). Ludlow presided over the first court and drafted the **Fundamental Orders**, the colony's constitution (1638–1818), and he wrote the Code of 1650, a compilation of the colony's laws. Ludlow went to Ireland with Oliver Cromwell's army in 1654, where he later died in 1664.

LUMBER. A major resource in the New England economy. It was the first cargo the **Pilgrims** shipped to England. Cutting, hauling, and milling wood became the economic lifeblood for many New Englanders when

Berwick, Maine, opened the first sawmill (1631). Northern New England operated 50 water-powered sawmills (1675), producing board lumber and barrel staves. Colonists resented the British law (1699), which reserved the most valuable trees (or mast trees) marked with an arrow for Royal Navy masts and spars. When the British surveyor-general, Daniel Dunbar, investigated timber poaching in Exeter, New Hampshire (1734), an armed mob drove his men away in the Mast Tree Riot. The legislature apologized to Lieutenant Governor Dunbar, but the poaching continued because New Englanders saw the forests as their most important natural resource. Farmers cut trees to create pasture and burned them as firewood and to make potash.

After the **American Revolution** Maine became the lumber center, and by 1850 Bangor was the busiest lumber port in the world. **Fitz Hugh Lane**'s painting *Lumber Schooners at Evening on Penobscot Bay* (1863) depicts this important trade. Located on the Penobscot River, Bangor expanded as a commercial and industrial center when the Great Northern Company opened the first **paper** mill in Millinocket (1899). Rapid developments in the new pulp and paper industry (1885–1915) harvested millions of prime trees in northern Maine by river log drives to mills in Berlin and Rumford. Annual spring log drives in New Hampshire were hazardous work for lumberjacks on the **Connecticut River** until 1900 and in Maine until 1975.

Concerned citizens formed the Society for the Protection of New Hampshire Forests (1901). **Maine guides**' sporting camps for visiting hunters and fishermen in Maine's upper Androscoggin River and Rangeley Lakes area were a by-product of this economic interest in the northern woods. The lumber industry still dominates the Maine economy and is a major employer throughout northern New England despite fears for exhaustion of New England timber resources. To keep some of the woods forever free, Maine governor **Percival Baxter** purchased 200,000 acres around **Mount Katahdin** (1919) as a state park. The Lumberman's Museum in Patten recalls the saga of the lumberjack era. Congress responded to intense lobbying by New England conservation groups by creating the White Mountain National Forest (1911).

The impact on the environment was overlooked; by 1850 only one-third of the Massachusetts forest remained. **Mount Greylock** was deforested by 1900 to provide pine for barrels and boxes (1880–1920). Steam-powered sawmills (1860) and portable sawmills (1880) harvested the remote woodlands. Concern escalated when lumberjacks wielded new chainsaws (1950) and the skidder extended the logging season (1960).

The spruce budworm epidemic (1970) promoted clear cutting, the removal of all trees in an area to save the forests. By 1904 a fungus blighted most of the region's chestnut trees, but researchers in Hamden, Connecticut, in 1930 produced a new variety of chestnut tree resistant to the disease.

The New England Forestry Foundation (1945) promotes scientific management of the forests, which have increased since 1945 and continue to produce pulpwood, softwood logs and lumber, hardwood logs, plywood, poles, posts, rails, Christmas trees and wreaths, sawdust, cooperage, railroad ties, shingles, pilings, and maple syrup. The autumn foliage season is a major tourist attraction for **leaf peeping** as the leaves change into brilliant colors. Rural depopulation, however, increased the forest as farms were abandoned after the **Civil War**. The **Paul Bunyan** logging era, represented by a statue of the giant lumberjack in Bangor (1959), ended when the river log drives were banned (1975) and corporations built extensive logging roads to transport timber by trucks. Since 1996 Maine voters considered various referenda restricting logging operations, which continue despite international competition. Leisure activities in the woods—**tourism**, hiking, fishing, hunting, camping, canoeing, boating, whitewater rafting, snowshoeing, cross-country skiing, snowmobiling, and other recreation—now may be incompatible with the environmental impact of logging and more profitable. New England forests have increased dramatically; Vermont, for example was 30 percent forest in 1800 and 63 percent in 1948 but 78 percent forest in 2001. Most of these 4.7 million acres are private land today.

LUSCOMB, FLORENCE HOPE (1887–1985). Reformer. Born in **Lowell**, Massachusetts, on February 6, 1887, Florence H. Luscomb was among the first women to graduate from the Massachusetts Institute of Technology with a degree in **architecture** (1909). She was a partner in a woman-owned firm in **Boston** (1909–17) but soon joined the suffrage movement and campaigned to amend the Massachusetts constitution (1915). She was a leader of the League of Women Voters and the Massachusetts branch of the Women's International League for Peace and Freedom. In the 1920s she served on the National Association for the Advancement of Colored People (NAACP) and Massachusetts Civil Liberties Union boards and was a Progressive Party candidate for Boston City Council (1922), Congress (1936, 1950), and governor (1952). Opposed to McCarthyism and the Vietnam War, she was a "foremother" of the feminist movement (1970–85) and a lifelong radical until her death in Watertown on October 27, 1985.

LYCEUM. An educational movement founded in Millbury, Massachusetts (1826), by Josiah Holbrook (1788–1854) to provide literary and scientific knowledge to New England towns and villages. The lyceum was a town civic association that often built a lyceum hall for public lectures, concerts, and debates to entertain and instruct. Local audiences heard luminaries like **Daniel Webster**, **Henry David Thoreau**, **Charles Sumner**, and **Oliver Wendell Holmes**. Sometimes the lyceum established a town public or free library (1850), as in Gloucester (1830). **Ralph Waldo Emerson**'s Concord Lyceum popularized **Transcendentalism**. Named for the school where Aristotle taught the Athenians, the lyceum movement spread across America until **vaudeville**, movies, and radio appeared.

LYME DISEASE. A bacterial infection transmitted to humans by deer ticks *(Ixodes dammini)*. Named for Old Lyme, Connecticut, where it was first identified by Dr. Allen Steere (1975), the disease infected more than 145,000 people by 2001. The potentially fatal disease occurs from Maine to Maryland, often affecting people in **agriculture**, forestry, and other outdoor activities.

LYON, MARY (1797–1849). Educator. Born in Buckland, Massachusetts, on February 28, 1797, Mary Mason Lyon studied at Amherst Academy and a ladies seminary in Byfield. Supporting herself from age 17 as a teacher, Miss Lyon founded Mt. Holyoke Female Seminary (1837) in South Hadley, Massachusetts. Enrollment rose quickly as Miss Lyon developed a well-rounded liberal arts college emphasizing service to others, and the **education** of American women entered a new era. After she retired as principal (1849), Mt. Holyoke College became a leading private college for women. She died at the college on March 5, 1849.

LYON, MATTHEW (1749–1822). Congressman from Vermont. Born in Ireland on July 14, 1749, Lyon came to Connecticut (1765) as an indentured servant. He joined Ethan Allen's **Green Mountain Boys** and served as an officer in the Continental Army (1775–78). The fiery Anti-Federalist founded Fair Haven, Vermont (1783), operated a paper mill, and was a state legislator (1779–83, 1786–96) and a Jeffersonian Democratic U.S. congressman (1797–1801). Lyon was jailed under the Sedition Act (1798) for four months for criticism in a newspaper of President **John Adams**. Lyon was denounced in the House of Representatives for brawling with a fellow member on the floor of Congress (1798). As a presidential elector his decisive vote elected Thomas Jefferson over Aaron Burr (1800). Lyon led settlers to Kentucky (1801), where he was elected to the U.S. House (1803–11). He served as U.S. agent to the Cherokee nation (1820–22) until his death in Spadra Bluff, Arkansas, on August 1, 1822.

– M –

MCCALL, SAMUEL WALKER (1851–1923). Governor of Massachusetts. Born in East Providence, Pennsylvania, on February 28, 1851, McCall graduated from Dartmouth College (1874). While practicing law in **Boston** (1875), he was a Republican state legislator (1887–89, 1892–93). McCall was editor and co-owner of the *Boston Daily Advertiser* until elected to the House of Representatives (1893–1913), where he was independent and a Progressive anti-imperialist. As governor (1916–18) for three terms, the state constitutional convention (1917) was the highpoint of his administration. Considered disloyal by Republican conservatives, his political career ended in 1918. McCall wrote for the *Atlantic Monthly*, published biographies of Thaddeus Stevens (1899) and **Thomas B. Reed** (1914), and died in Winchester on November 4, 1923.

MCCARRON, CHRISTOPHER (1955–). Athlete. Born in **Boston** in 1955, Chris McCarron set records for wins in a season (546) as a rookie jockey in 1974. He won the Kentucky Derby (1987, 1994), the Preakness (1987, 1992), and the Belmont races (1986, 1997). McCarron, elected to the Racing Hall of Fame (1989), began his career at the Suffolk Downs track in Boston and retired as the leading jockey in North America in 2002.

MCCLOSKEY, ROBERT (1914–2003). Artist. Born in Hamilton, Ohio, on September 15, 1914, McCloskey studied **art** in **Boston**, New York City, and Rome before serving in the U.S. Army in World War II. Working on **Cape Cod**, he wrote and illustrated the classic children's book, *Make Way for Ducklings* (1941), the story of a family of ducks living in the **Boston Public Garden** lagoon. In commemoration of the park's 150th anniversary (1987), the city installed a bronze sculpture by Nancy Shon, *Mrs. Mallard and Her Eight Ducklings,* at the Public Garden. His later books were set in coastal Maine, especially *Blueberries for Sal* (1949), *One Morning in Maine* (1953), and *Time of Wonder* (1958), for which he won a second Caldecott Prize. McCloskey retired to Scott Island, Maine, and died on June 30, 2003.

MCCORD, DAVID (1897–1997). Poet. Born in New York City, David Thompson Watson McCord graduated from **Harvard University** (1921) and never left. He was director of the Harvard College Fund for 38 years, raising more than $15 million, and editor of the *Harvard Alumni Bulletin* (1940–46) and received Harvard's first honorary degree as doctor of humane letters (1956). McCord wrote prose and poetry, and most of his 550 poems were for children. His books include *Oddly Enough* (1926), *What Cheer* (1945), *About Boston* (1948), *Far and Few* (1952), *All Day Long* (1966), and *One at a Time* (1978). He retired to the Harvard Club in **Boston** (1963), was named one of seven Grand Bostonians by the city (1973), and died on April 13, 1997. *See also* LITERATURE.

MCCORMACK, JOHN W. (1891–1980). Speaker of the House. Born in **Boston** on December 21, 1891, John William McCormack studied law privately and was admitted to the Massachusetts bar (1913). After U.S. Army service (1917–19), he was elected as a Democrat from South Boston to the state legislature (1920–26) and to the House of Representatives (1929–71) and was majority leader (1940–47, 1949–53, 1955–62) and speaker of the House (1962–71). McCormack was a New Deal liberal and anticommunist until he retired in 1971. The Federal Building in Boston's Post Office Square was renamed in his honor (1972). McCormack, a formidable ally of President **John F. Kennedy** and a mentor to **Thomas P. O'Neill, Jr.**, died in Dedham on November 22, 1980.

MCCULLOCH, HUGH (1808–1895). Public official. Born in Kennebunk, Maine, on December 7, 1808, McCulloch was a banker in Indiana appointed comptroller of the currency (1861–65) and secretary of the treasury (1865–69) by President Abraham Lincoln and President Andrew Johnson. He restored financial stability after the **Civil War** by reducing the national debt and collecting tax revenue in the Southern states. He was secretary of the treasury (1884–85) for President Chester A. Arthur. McCulloch wrote *Men and Measures of Half a Century* (1888) and died on May 24, 1895.

MACDOWELL, EDWARD ALEXANDER (1861–1908). Composer. Born in New York City on December 18, 1861, MacDowell studied in Paris and Germany. Performing his own piano sonatas with considerable success, he taught music and composed in **Boston** (1888–96) and at Columbia University. MacDowell drew on American historic themes for some of his finest compositions, *Indian Suite* (1892), *Woodland Sketches* (1896), and *New England Idylls* (1902). He transformed his farm in Peterborough, New Hampshire (1906) into a summer **art colony** for creative artists. After his death on January 23, 1908, in New York, his wife, Marian Nevins McDowell, continued the MacDowell Colony in Peterborough as a summer retreat for musicians, artists, and writers, which operates today.

MCGRATH, JAMES HOWARD (1903–1966). Senator from Rhode Island. Born in Woonsocket on November 28, 1903, McGrath graduated from Providence College (1926) and Boston University Law School (1929). He was city solicitor for Central Falls and U.S. district attorney for Rhode Island (1934–40). Elected governor as a Democrat (1941–45) for three terms, McGrath established the state's first juvenile court and presided at the state's first constitutional convention. He served as solicitor general (1945–46) and was elected to the Senate (1947–49). President Harry Truman named him Democratic national chairman (1947–49) and attorney general (1949–52). McGrath practiced law in Washington and was a banker in Rhode Island until he died in Narragansett on September 2, 1966.

MCINTIRE, SAMUEL (1757–1811). Architect. Born in **Salem**, Massachusetts, on January 16, 1757, McIntire was a housewright and self-taught architect. Employed by Salem's **codfish aristocracy**, especially the merchant prince, **Elias Hasket Derby**, McIntire built and remodeled several elegant Georgian and Federal houses in Salem. He adapted the neoclassical style of the Scottish architect Robert Adams that **Charles Bulfinch** popularized in New England. He also carved a portrait bust of Governor **John Winthrop**, figureheads for ships, furniture, and ornamental interior woodwork. Several of his buildings survive as Salem Maritime National Historic sites, including the Georgian-style Hawkes House (1780), the Federal-style Gardner-Pingree House (1810), and South Congregational Church (1805). McIntire died in Salem on February 6, 1811.

MCKAY, DONALD (1810–1880). Shipbuilder. Born in Nova Scotia on September 4, 1810, McKay studied shipbuilding in New York City, Wiscasset, Maine, and Newburyport, Massachusetts. By 1844 he established his own **shipyard** in **Boston**. His first **clipper ship** the *Stag Hound* (1850) established his reputation for large, fast, elegant vessels like *Flying Cloud* (1851) and *Sovereign of the Seas* (1852) in the Gold Rush and **China trade**. McKay suffered financial losses in the 1857 panic and died in Hamilton, Massachusetts, on September 20, 1880. A monument at **Castle Island** overlooking Boston harbor honors McKay and his clippers.

MCKIM, MEAD AND WHITE. A prominent architectural firm founded by **William Rutherford Mead** and Charles Follen McKim in New York City (1878). After Stanford White (1880) joined the firm, they designed many New England structures, including the Rhode Island State Capitol (1894), **Boston Public Library** (1892), the **Shaw Memorial** (1897), summer cottages in **Bar Harbor** (1890s), **Boston Symphony Hall** (1900), and the **Plymouth Rock** canopy (1921).

MCKINNEY, LUTHER FRANKLIN (1841–1922). Congressman from New Hampshire. Born in Newark, Ohio, on April 25, 1841, McKinney served in the Union Army (1861–63) and graduated from St. Lawrence University (1870). Ordained pastor of the **Universalist** Church in Bridgton, Maine (1871), he held pulpits in Newfields (1873) and Manchester, New Hampshire (1875). McKinney was a Democrat in the House of Representatives (1887–89, 1891–93) and U.S. minister to Colombia (1893–97). He served as pastor in Bridgton (1897–1922) and in the Maine state legislature (1907–09) and died in Bridgton on July 30, 1922.

MACLEISH, ARCHIBALD (1892–1982). Poet. Born in Glencoe, Illinois, on May 7, 1892, MacLeish graduated from Yale University (1915) and **Harvard** Law School (1919). He served in the U.S. Army in World War I (1917–18) and was a **Boston** lawyer (1920–23) but moved to France, where he wrote acclaimed books of poetry *The Happy Marriage* (1924), *The Pot of Earth* (1925), and *Conquistador*, which won the Pulitzer Prize (1932). MacLeish was librarian of Congress (1939–44) but also worked in the Department of War as an assistant secretary of state for cultural affairs (1944–45) and as chair of the UNESCO conference in Paris. Known as the "poet laureate of the New Deal," he taught at Harvard University (1949–62) and won a second Pulitzer Prize for *Collected Poems* (1952) and a third for his Broadway verse play, *J.B.* (1958). MacLeish won an Oscar for his screenplay *The Eleanor Roosevelt Story* (1965) and died in Boston on April 20, 1982.

MCLEVY, JASPER (1878–1962). Public official. Born in Bridgeport, Connecticut, in 1878, McLevy left school at age 14, operated his own roofing business in Bridgeport, and was a leader in city and state labor organizations. As the Socialist Party perennial candidate for mayor (1911–57) and for governor (1932–57), he championed the ethnic workers' antibusiness and reform views. His candidacy for governor resulted in the defeat of **Wilbur Cross** by **Raymond E. Baldwin** in 1938. Honest Jasper McLevy, mayor of Bridgeport for 12 terms (1933–57), was known for his fiscal prudence and anticorruption practices. He died in Bridgeport on November 20, 1962.

MCMAHON, BRIEN (1903–1952). Senator from Connecticut. Born in Norwalk on October 6, 1903, James O'Brien McMahon graduated from Fordham University (1924) and Yale University Law School (1927). He changed his name to Brien McMahon and practiced law in Norwalk (1927–33), where he was a city court judge (1933). McMahon served as special assistant to the U.S. attorney general (1933–35) and assistant attorney general (1935–39). He practiced law in Washington, D.C., and Norwalk (1939–44) until elected as a Democrat to the U.S. Senate (1944–52), where he wrote the law creating the Atomic Energy Commission. McMahon died in office in Washington, D.C., on July 28, 1952.

MCNEILL, GEORGE EDWIN (1837–1906). Labor leader. Born in Amesbury, Massachusetts, on August 4, 1837, McNeill worked in a local woolen mill and **shoe** factory as a boy. Moving to **Boston** (1856), he edited labor newspapers and was known as the father of the eight-hour movement. As president of the Workingmen's Institute (1867–69) and the Boston Eight-Hour League (1869–74), McNeill lobbied to pass state laws for an eight-hour day, but when they were not enforced he turned to trade unionism. With **Wendell Phillips**, he founded the New England Labor Reform League (1869) and was a director of the nation's first Bureau of Labor Statistics. The idealistic reformer organized for the Knights of Labor (1883), mediated the bitter Boston horsecar strike (1885), edited the *Labor Leader* newspaper, and ran for mayor of Boston. He was a spokesman for the American Federation of Labor (AFL) in 1886–1906 and vice-president of the American Anti-imperialist League (1898) and wrote the first history of American labor, *The Labor Movement: The Problem of Today* (1887). McNeill died in Somerville, Massachusetts, on May 19, 1906.

MAHICAN (OR MOHICAN). An **Algonquian**-speaking **Native American** people who lived in the **Housatonic River** valley in Connecticut and Massachusetts until the **Mohawks**, Dutch, and English forced them into Vermont (1650). Some moved to Stockbridge, Massachusetts (1664), where they were known as the **Stockbridge Indians**. Although living at a **Puritan** mission (1736), they preserved their culture, unlike other Mahicans, who scattered and merged with other tribes. More than a dozen Vermont place names are Machican. They live in Wisconsin today and are best known from James Fenimore Cooper's novel *The Last of the Mohicans* (1826).

MAHONEY, MARY (1845–1926). Nurse. Born in Dorchester, Massachusetts, on May 7, 1845, Mary Mahoney was the first **African American** to graduate from the New England Hospital for Women nursing school (1878). She was the first black member of the American Nurses Association and addressed the National Association of Colored Graduate Nurses at its first annual convention in **Boston** (1909). Mahoney, one of the first women to register to vote in Boston (1920), died in Boston on January 4, 1926. She was named to the Nursing Hall of Fame (1976) and to the National Women's Hall of Fame (1993).

MAINE COON CAT. One of the nation's oldest breeds, a long-haired cat descended from Angora cats brought to colonial New England seaports by sailors. This is a large domestic cat (30 lb/13.5 kg) with a long coat in several colors with broad paws and often a striped tail like a raccoon. First identified in 1861, one of these cats won the Best Cat prize at the Madison Square Garden Cat Show (1895), and today the Maine Coon Breeders and Fanciers Association (1968) includes more than 200 breeders. It is the official state cat in Maine.

MAINE GUIDES. Persons registered (1897) and licensed by the state (1975) to accompany visiting sportsmen hunting or fishing in the Maine woods, lakes, and streams. Some famous guides were **Penobscots**, Joseph Aitteon and Joe Polis, who took **Henry David Thoreau** to **Mount Katahdin** (1846) and **James Russell Lowell** to Moosehead Lake (1853). Wealthy sportsmen like **Thomas Wentworth Higginson** hired guides (1855) to lead parties of **Boston** literary ladies and gentlemen on a Maine camping and fishing vacation. Some sportsmen took annual vacations at permanent sporting camps the professional guides operated for the **summer people** "from away." By 1890 **tourists** who enjoyed roughing it in the woods found the Maine **railroad** magazines advertised guides, who provided equipment, canoes, and woods lore (1895). Unlike fashionable resorts, the Maine **camps** were seen as a natural and wholesome experience for city people and were popularized by Maine writers like **Cornelia T. ("Fly Rod") Crosby.**

MAINE HISTORICAL SOCIETY. The nation's third oldest state historical society, founded in **Portland** in 1822 by leaders of the Maine statehood movement. Stephen Longfellow, Prentiss Mellen, and other gentlemen intended to document the state's history separate from that of Massachusetts. First located at Bowdoin College in Brunswick, the society moved to the Portland Public Library and to the **Henry Wadsworth Longfellow** House in Portland in 1907. The society offers a research library, museum, tours of Longfellow's birthplace, and a variety of educational exhibits and programs on Maine's history and culture.

MALECITE (OR MALISEET). An **Alqonquian**-speaking **Native American** people who lived in northeastern Maine and Canada in a confederacy with the **Abenaki**. They traded with European explorers and fishermen before **Samuel de Champlain** met them (1604). By 1700, many of the Malecite intermarried with the French along the St. John River in New Brunswick, and they had many land disputes with the British (1763–76) until land was reserved for them (1790). By 1880 some Malecite men were professional **Maine guides** for **tourists** who hunted and fished in Maine.

MANN, HORACE (1796–1859). Educator. Born in Franklin, Massachusetts, on May 4, 1796, Mann graduated from Brown University (1819) and studied at **Tapping Reeve**'s Litchfield Law School (1821–23). He practiced law in Dedham (1823–33) and served in the state legislature (1827–33, 1835–37). As the first secretary of the new state board of education (1837–48), Mann founded the nation's first **normal school** and reorganized the **public schools** on a nonsectarian professional basis that profoundly influenced American **education**. He was a Whig in the House of Representatives (1848–53) and president of Antioch College (1852–59) until he died in Ohio on August 2, 1859.

MAPLE SYRUP. A **Native American** food adopted by New England colonists. Each spring sugar maple trees *(Acer saccharum)* are tapped for sap, which is boiled to a sticky syrup used as a sweetener. Forty gallons of sap yield one gallon of syrup used in place of honey or as sugar. Samuel Robinson of Bennington was the first Vermonter to make maple sugar (1752), and now 2,400 Vermont farmers tap an average of 1,000 trees each in the early spring sugaring season. By **town meeting** day, the first Tuesday in March, millions of gallons of sap are gathered from sugar maple and black maple trees and boiled in sugarhouses across the region. **Eastman Johnson** depicted this rural economy in *Sugaring Off* (1861). Vermont produces 500,000 gallons, more than any state, because the sugar maple tree is the most common species in the state, about one-fifth of the 4.7 million acres of forestland in 2001. The $9 million maple syrup industry is common across New England, New York, Canada, and parts of the Midwest.

MARCIANO, ROCKY (1923–1969). Athlete. Born in Brockton, Massachusetts, on September 1, 1923, Rocco Marchegiano served in the U.S. Army (1943–46) and became a professional heavyweight boxer (1947–56). "The Brockton Blockbuster" became the heavyweight champion of the world when he defeated Jersey Joe Walcott in 1952. His record of 49 consecutive professional victories has never been surpassed, and he defended his title six times before retiring undefeated. Rocky Marciano died on August 31, 1969.

MARK TWAIN HOUSE. In **Hartford**, Connecticut, the home of Samuel Langhorne Clemens (1835–1910) from 1874 to 1891. Twain died on April 21, 1910, in Redding, Connecticut. The ornate Victorian mansion, decorated by **Charles** and **Louis Comfort Tiffany**, reminded Twain of the steamboats of his youth and was the site of his most productive writing. The house, and the adjacent home of **Harriet Beecher Stowe**, has been a literary and historic landmark since 1929.

MARQUAND, J. P. (1893–1960). Writer. Born in Wilmington, Delaware, on November 10, 1893, John Phillips Marquand graduated from **Harvard University** (1915). As a popular novelist, his best subject was **Boston Brahmin** society. Descended from elite New Englanders, he won the Pulitzer Prize for his subtle satire of a **Beacon Hill** family *The Late George Apley* (1937) and a play by the same title (1945). Marquand died in Newburyport, Massachusetts, on July 16, 1960.

MARSH, CHARLES (1765–1849). Congressman from Vermont. Born in Lebanon, Connecticut, on July 10, 1765, Marsh graduated from Dartmouth

College (1786) and studied law with **Tapping Reeve** in Litchfield, Connecticut. He practiced law in Woodstock, Vermont (1788–97) until President George Washington named him U.S. district attorney for Vermont (1797–1801). He was a **Federalist** in the House of Representatives (1815–17) and founded the American Colonization Society in Washington. Marsh practiced law in Woodstock until his death on January 11, 1849. His son, **George P. Marsh**, was also a congressman from Vermont.

MARSH, GEORGE P. (1801–1882). Congressman from Vermont. Born in Woodstock, Vermont, on March 15, 1801, George Perkins Marsh graduated from Dartmouth College (1820), and practiced law in Burlington (1825–43). Elected as a Whig to the House of Representatives (1844–49), he was U.S. minister to Turkey (1849–53) and the first U.S. minister to Italy (1861–82), where he served until his death on July 23, 1882. The versatile Marsh wrote 20 books, including *Man and Nature* (1864), an early argument for conservation.

MARSHALL, MARGARET H. (1945–). Lawyer and judge. Born in South Africa in 1945, Marshall graduated from the University of Witwatersrand in Johannesburg (1966) and Yale University Law School (1976). After practicing law in **Boston**, she was a vice-president and general counsel at **Harvard University** and president of the Boston Bar Association (1991). She was the second woman to serve on the Massachusetts Supreme Judicial Court in its over-300-year history (1996) and the first woman to serve as its chief justice (1999).

MARTHA'S VINEYARD. An island (108 sq mi/280 sq km) four miles southwest of **Cape Cod**, Massachusetts. Explored and named by **Bartholomew Gosnold** (1602), the Reverend **Thomas Mayhew** brought the first English settlers to the island (1642). Mayhew was the island's governor (1642–82), living in peace with the **Wampanoag** people. Salt, bricks, fish, **sheep**, butter, and cheese were the chief exports by 1720. When the Vineyarders captured a British ship in 1775, the British Navy looted the island (1778). It was a **whaling** center (1750–1850), and annual Methodist camp meetings (1835) made the island a popular summer resort. The population included many deaf people by 1700, as well as **Wampanoag** people and **African Americans** who worked in the island's whaling and **fishing** fleet. The painters who spent summer vacations at Chilmark in the 1920s attracted writers, intellectuals, and tourists, who still enjoy the island and its five picturesque **lighthouses**, dunes, and **beaches**. The Wampanoag reclaimed ancestral land at Gay Head (1980), now called Aquinah. The island, 20 miles long and 10 miles wide, includes a state forest and a thriving **tourism** economy.

MARTIN, JOSEPH W., JR. (1884–1968). Speaker of the House. Born in North Attleboro, Massachusetts, on November 3, 1884, Joseph William Martin, Jr. was a reporter for the *Attleboro Sun* and *Providence Journal* (1902–08) and publisher of the *North Attleboro Evening Chronicle* (1908–68) and *Franklin Sentinel.* Elected as a Republican to the state legislature (1912–17) and to the House of Representatives (1925–67), Martin became a conservative anti–New Deal speaker of the House (1947–49, 1952–54). Joe Martin retired to North Attleboro and died in Florida on March 6, 1968.

MASON, JOHN (1586–1635). Founder of New Hampshire. Born in England in 1586, Captain John Mason was the governor of Newfoundland (1615–21) and **Sir Ferdinando Gorges**'s chief lieutenant in New England colonization. They received a land grant for the **Council for New England** (1620) and divided it (1629). Mason called his portion New Hampshire, and his Laconia Company (1629–32) developed the **fishing** and **fur trade** at **Strawbery Banke** (later called **Portsmouth**) on the Piscataqua River. Mason died in London in December 1635, and his heirs sold New Hampshire, which became a royal colony (1679), to a group of Portsmouth men called the Masonian Proprietors (1691).

MASON, JOHN (1600–1672). Soldier. Born in England in 1600, Mason was an army officer who emigrated to Massachusetts (1630) and moved to Windsor, Connecticut (1635). He led the colonial militia in the **Pequot War** (1637) and virtually destroyed the tribe. Major Mason declared it was a divine blessing when 600 Pequot were massacred at Mystic. Mason wrote *A Brief History of the Pequot War* (published in 1736) and became deputy governor (1660–70) and died in Norwich on January 30, 1672. His statue at the site of the 1637 Pequot massacre in Mystic (1889) was relocated to Windsor, Connecticut, in 1996.

MASON, LOWELL (1792–1872). Composer and educator. Born in Medfield, Massachusetts, on January 8, 1792, Mason was the son of a musician and a musical prodigy in his youth. While working in a bank in Georgia (1812–27), the success of his first collection, *The Boston Handel and Haydn Society Collection of Church Music* (1822), established his reputation. Returning to **Boston** as president of the **Handel and Haydn Society** (1827–32), he introduced music to churches and **public schools** and influenced American **education** by training music teachers. He wrote many hymns, including "Nearer, My God to Thee," and assisted in composing "America," which begins with the words "My country, 'tis of thee" and was first performed in Boston on July 4, 1831. Mason willed his extensive musical library to Yale University and died in Orange, New Jersey, on August 11, 1872.

MASSACHUSET. The **Algonquin** name, meaning great hill range, for 3,000 **Native Americans** living in 20 villages around **Boston** and along the Charles and Neponset River valleys in 1614. Diseases introduced by European traders and fishermen (1617) reduced their numbers to 500 when the **Puritans** arrived in 1630. No organized groups survived by 1800, but the Puritans borrowed their name for the new colony. **John Eliot** converted many of the Massachuset people to Christianity at Natick and 13 other villages of **Praying Indians** by 1660.

USS *MASSACHUSETTS* **(BB 59).** A battleship built in Quincy, Massachusetts (1939–42). "Big Mamie" served in the North African invasion (1942) and South Pacific (1943–45) and fired the last 16-inch shells in World War II combat on Japan (August 9, 1945). After earning 11 battle stars for heroic service, the ship was decommissioned (1947) and became the Bay State memorial to World War II veterans at Fall River (1965).

MASSACHUSETTS AUDUBON SOCIETY. The first state Audubon Society in the United States, founded (1896) by **Boston** reformers and philanthropists Harriet Lawrence Hemenway (1858–1960) and Minna Hall (1851–1941). Concerned that the women's hat industry threatened many birds native to North America, they persuaded the state legislature to prohibit the trade in wild bird feathers (1897). The society, affiliated with the National Audubon Society (1886), cooperates with Audubon societies for species and habitat conservation in Connecticut (1897), Maine (1922), Rhode Island (1897), New Hampshire, and Vermont. The MAS is now the largest conservation organization in New England, with 29,000 acres in 41 wildlife sanctuaries open to the public and educational groups.

MASSACHUSETTS BAY COMPANY. An English chartered joint-stock company (1628). It took over the **Dorchester Company** and established a fishing colony on **Cape Ann** (1623). The **Council for New England** granted the company leader, **John Endecott**, the land between the Merrimack and Charles Rivers (1628). The Massachusetts Bay Company organized the New England Company (1628) to establish a colony under a royal charter (1629). The stockholders purchased the Massachusetts Bay Company (1629) and sent **John Winthrop** with 1,000 **Puritans** to settle in **Salem**, then in Charlestown, and finally in **Boston** (1630). Thereafter the Massachusetts Bay Company and the colony were identical, and the only English colony in North America not controlled by a board of governors in England. Despite attempts by the Council for New England, led by Sir **Ferdinando Gorges**, to annul the Puritan land claims, the Massachusetts Bay Company prospered until its charter was withdrawn (1684) and a new charter (1691) made Massachusetts a royal colony including **Plymouth** and Maine.

MASSACHUSETTS GENERAL HOSPITAL (MGH). Founded in 1821 as a private, nonsectarian medical center by **Thomas H. Perkins** and other philanthropic **Boston** gentlemen. It is the third oldest general hospital in the nation and the first and largest in New England. The MGH, as it is known, is the oldest and largest teaching hospital of **Harvard** Medical School (1782), and conducts the largest hospital research program in the country. Richard C. Cabot (1868–1939) introduced medical social work there and advocated prepaid medical group practice (1913). This institution, like Boston Children's Hospital (1869) and Tufts University Medical School (1893), did much to establish Boston as an international center for medical care and research. *See also* MORTON, WILLIAM T. G.

MASSACHUSETTS HISTORICAL SOCIETY (MHS). Founded (1791) by Jeremy Belknap (1744–98), a **Congregational** minister in New Hampshire and **Boston**. The society incorporated (1794) and moved to **Charles Bulfinch**'s Tontine Crescent on Franklin Street in Boston. It was the first institution to publish American history documents. The MHS, relocated in a Renaissance-revival mansion in the **Fenway** (1899), is open to members and scholarly researchers.

MASSACHUSETTS HORTICULTURAL SOCIETY. Founded in **Boston** (1829) by the **Salem** pomologist Robert Manning (1784–1842). Its first members imported fruit trees, established an extensive library, and have sponsored the annual New England Spring Flower Show since 1871. Located in the splendid Horticultural Hall in the **Back Bay**

(1901–91) and, since 1996, at the Elm Bank Reservation in Dover, the society offers educational and environmental program for children and adults.

MASSACHUSETTS SOCIETY FOR THE PREVENTION OF CRU- ELTY TO ANIMALS (MSPCA). Founded in **Boston** (1868) by George Thorndike Angell (1823–1909) and Emily Appleton. Promoting the humane treatment of animals, the MSPCA published a magazine *Our Dumb Animals* (1868) and distributed Anna Sewell's novel *Black Beauty* (1877) to children organized in the American Band of Mercy (1882). The MSPCA lobbied for state humane laws, was a founder of the American Humane Society (1889), and established the Angell Memorial Animal Hospital (1915) in Boston and animal shelters or veterinary hospitals throughout New England.

MASSACHUSETTS STATE HOUSE. Designed (1795–98) by **Charles Bulfinch** on **Beacon Hill** at the former site of **John Hancock**'s mansion. As the Commonwealth of Massachusetts seat of government, it replaced the Old State House on Washington Street. Its neoclassical style in red brick with a golden dome was widely imitated, and **Paul Revere** clad the dome with copper (1802). The golden dome overlooking **Boston Common** since 1874 defined the political center of the state and New England until skyscrapers rose around it in the 1960s. The Brigham annex on the north and the east and west wings (1914) expanded the building, and the first restoration of the original Bulfinch building was completed in 2002.

MASSACHUSETTS TURNPIKE. The 135-mile state toll road built from West Stockbridge near the New York State line to **Boston** (1955– 65). It is a monument to the importance of motor vehicle traffic in New England. William F. Callahan (1891–1964), commissioner of the state department of public works and the chairman of the Massachusetts Turnpike Authority, built this highway to stimulate the stagnant economy. It also has encouraged suburban development, commuter traffic, **tourism,** and the new **computer** industry on **Route 128**. The Mass Pike connected with the **Big Dig** highways in 2001.

MASSASOIT (1590–1661). Native American leader. Born in Rhode Island, Massasoit (or Ousamequin) was a sachem of the **Wampanoag** tribe in Rhode Island and Massachusetts. His treaty with the **Pilgrims** in

March 1621, which **Samoset** helped negotiate, maintained friendly relations with the Pilgrims and **Puritans** throughout his life, prompted by Wampanoag fear of the **Narragansett** tribes to the south. Massasoit negotiated with **Edward Winslow**, **William Bradford**, **John Winthrop**, and **Roger Williams**, and the Wampanoag were neutral during the **Pequot War** in 1636. When he died in Bristol, Rhode Island, in 1661, his son, **Metacom**, succeeded Massasoit and became the militant leader in **King Philip's War** (1675–76). Since 1921 a bronze statue of Massasoit by Cyrus E. Dallin overlooks the **Plymouth Rock** memorial.

MATHER, COTTON (1663–1728). Clergyman. Born in **Boston** on February 12, 1663, Cotton Mather, the son of **Increase Mather**, graduated from **Harvard** College (1678). Ordained a minister (1685), he preached in his father's Boston church for the rest of his life. The author of more than 450 works, his scientific writing contributed to the **Salem witchcraft** hysteria (1692), although he deplored the irrational excesses. He led the struggle for smallpox inoculation in Massachusetts (1721) and was the first American-born member of the Royal Society. A founder of Yale College, Mather was the best known of the American **Puritan** divines at his death in Boston on February 13, 1728.

MATHER, INCREASE (1639–1723). Clergyman. Born in Dorchester, Massachusetts, on June 21, 1639, Increase Mather graduated from **Harvard** College (1656) and Trinity College in Dublin (1658). He served in his father's church in Dorchester (1661–64) and in **Boston**'s Second Church (1664–1723). As president of Harvard College (1685–1701), he led the struggle against revocation of the colony charter by **Sir Edmund Andros**. He obtained a new charter from William III (1691) uniting **Plymouth Colony** and **Massachusetts Bay Colony**. His support for Governor **William Phips** led to his dismissal from Harvard. Mather played a key role in ending the **Salem witchcraft trials** (1692) and was the leader of New England **Congregationalism** when he died in Boston on August 23, 1723.

MAYFLOWER. Three-masted merchant ship of 180 tons chartered to bring 102 English **Pilgrims** to New England. After sailing 66 days, the *Mayflower* anchored at **Cape Cod** near the future **Provincetown** (1620). The men signed the **Mayflower Compact** and elected **John Carver** as the first governor of Plymouth Colony. By December they settled in Plymouth, and the ship returned to England in April 1621. Although half of the colonists died in the harsh winter of 1620–21, the small colony survived. A replica, the *Mayflower II*, sailed from England to Plymouth, Massachusetts (1957). It is part of the **Plimouth Plantation** museum.

MAYFLOWER COMPACT. Document signed by 41 **Pilgrim** men on the *Mayflower* on November 21, 1620. Modeled on the Separatist church covenant to create a civil body politic, it established a democratic government with law-making powers for elected officials. This was the first written constitution in America (1620–30) and the model for all later New England colonial governments.

MAYHEW, JONATHAN (1720–1766). Clergyman. Born on **Martha's Vineyard** on October 8, 1720, Mayhew graduated from **Harvard** College (1744) and was pastor of the West Church in **Boston** (1747–66). The Mayhew family governed **Martha's Vineyard** for generations and provided diligent missionaries to the Indians. By 1750 Jonathan Mayhew preached against unpopular laws imposed by Britain and began the doctrinal movement toward **Unitarianism**. His sermons, pamphlets, and letters to newspapers opposed the **Stamp Act** and made him an influential leader when he died in Boston on July 9, 1766.

MAYHEW, THOMAS (1593–1682). Clergyman. Born in England in March 1593, Mayhew purchased **Martha's Vineyard**, the Elizabeth Islands, and **Nantucket** from the **Native American** and English landholders (1642). He was the governor of Martha's Vineyard (1671–82) and converted most of the **Wampanoag** on the island before he died there on March 25, 1682.

MEAD, WILLIAM RUTHERFORD (1846–1928). Architect. Born in Brattleboro, Vermont, on August 20, 1846, Mead attended Norwich University and graduated from Amherst College (1867). After study in Italy, Mead established a partnership with Charles Follen McKim in New York City (1878). Stanford White soon joined the firm (1880), known as **McKim, Mead and White**. By 1900 the firm was the largest architectural office in the world and designed the **Boston Public Library** (1892), the Rhode Island State Capitol (1894), **Boston Symphony Hall** (1900), and palatial summer cottages at **Bar Harbor** (1890s) on **Mount Desert Island** in Maine. Mead was most famous for his classicism and innovative use of new materials and construction technology. He died in Paris on June 30, 1928.

MEDEIROS, HUMBERTO S. (1915–1983). Bishop. Born in the Azores on October 6, 1915, Humberto Sousa Medeiros immigrated to Fall River (1931), graduated from the Catholic University of America (1942), and was ordained in Washington, D.C. (1946). After serving as a priest in Fall River, Massachusetts (1946–50), he studied in Rome and was bishop of Brownsville, Texas (1966–70). As the archbishop of **Boston** (1970–83) and cardinal (1973), he was the spiritual leader for more than 2 million Catholics. Cardinal Medeiros coped skillfully with racial, ethnic, and social tensions, the decline of parochial schools, and increasing church debt until his death on September 17, 1983.

MELVILLE, HERMAN (1819–1891). Writer. Born in New York City on August 1, 1819, Melville was the grandson of Thomas Melvill, a Scottish **immigrant** and wealthy Boston merchant. Melville went to sea (1837), jumped ship from a whaler in the South Seas (1842), and served in the U.S. Navy. These experiences were the basis for his novels *Typee* (1846), *Omoo* (1847), and *Redburn* (1849). Settling in Pittsfield, Massachusetts (1850–63), he was a close friend of **Nathaniel Hawthorne** and wrote his saga of a **New Bedford whaling** ship, *Moby Dick* (1851), which was not recognized as a literary masterpiece until 1920. His novel *Billy Budd* (1890) was unpublished until 1924. Melville wrote some of his best books in Pittsfield, but he died forgotten in New York City on September 28, 1891.

MERCANTILISM. An economic doctrine adopted by Great Britain and European nation-states (1650–1849). From the New England viewpoint, it imposed taxes on colonists who were not represented in Parliament, restricted their trade to British ports, and hindered economic development. The **Navigation Acts** (1650–1765), implementing mercantilism, were a cause of the **American Revolution.** *See also* MOLASSES; TRIANGULAR TRADE; WEST INDIES TRADE.

MERRIMACK RIVER. Flows south (110 mi/177 km) from the **White Mountains** and Lake Winnepesaukee through New Hampshire into Massachusetts. It enters the Atlantic Ocean at Newburyport. The river attracted settlers (1638) and supplied waterpower for many mills and factories in **Concord**, Manchester, and Nashua, New Hampshire, and **Lowell** and Lawrence, Massachusetts, by the 1820s.

MERRYMOUNT. A colony established by the Wollaston Company on Mount Wollaston in Quincy, Massachusetts (1624). When most of the settlers moved to Virginia, it was governed by Thomas Morton (1579–1647), a lawyer and merchant, who renamed the settlement Merry-mount. As an Anglican and one of the most picturesque New England pio-neers, Morton scandalized his **Pilgrim** neighbors by boisterous revels and selling firearms to the Indians to monopolize the **fur trade**. Governor **William Bradford** ordered **Miles Standish** to arrest Morton and exiled him to the **Isles of Shoals** (1628), from which he fled to England. When he returned (1629), Merrymount was abandoned and Morton was arrested and his property confiscated. Morton went to England (1630), where he wrote *New English Canaan* (1637), satirizing the New Englanders, and attempted to have the Massachusetts charter revoked. He returned to **Plymouth** (1643) but was exiled to Maine, where he died in 1647. **Nathaniel Hawthorne** featured Morton in *The Maypole of Merrymount* (1836), and **John Lothrop Motley** wrote two novels about Morton.

METACOM OR KING PHILIP (1638–1676). Native American leader. Metacom was the son of **Massasoit** and a **Wampanoag** sachem who ended 40 years of peaceful relations with the **Pilgrims** and **Puritans** when he attacked Swansea, Massachusetts, in June 1675. The English colonists in Plymouth, Massachusetts, and in Connecticut reacted bru-tally against the Wampanoags and their **Abenaki**, **Nipmuc**, and **Narra-gansett** allies. Over 300 Native Americans died in the Great Swamp bat-tle near Kingston, Rhode Island, in November 1675. **King Philip's War** continued after Metacom was killed on August 12, 1676, until the Indi-ans surrendered or fled New England. When peace returned in 1676, 52 of the 90 Puritan towns had been attacked and 12 destroyed. As many as 1,000 colonists died, about 5 percent of the white male population. Thou-sands of Native Americans were killed or sold into West Indies **slavery**. Prejudice against the Native Americans weakened Christian missionary efforts and no serious resistance to the whites was possible.

METALIOUS, GRACE (1924–1964). Writer. Born in Manchester, New Hampshire, on September 8, 1924, Grace DeRepentigny grew up in a **French-Canadian** family. After her marriage to George Metalious, she raised two children in Gilmanton, New Hampshire, the small town that inspired her best-selling novel *Peyton Place* (1956). The book and a film (1957) and melodramatic television series (1965–69, 1972–74) by the same title shocked readers by revealing the secrets and sex scandals in the dark underside of a picturesque New Hampshire town. The *Man-chester Union Leader* publisher **William Loeb** denounced the book in a front-page editorial in 1957, but critics praised the novel as a realistic feminist assessment of domestic issues. Grace Metalious published three other novels with less success and died in **Boston** on February 25, 1964.

METROPOLITAN PARK COMMISSION. Established by the Massachusetts legislature (1893) to maintain scenic and historic parks around **Boston**. Renamed the Metropolitan District Commission (1919), it was the first regional organization of public open space in the nation and is an international model for multijurisdictional parks. **Charles Eliot** (1860–97), a student of **Frederick Law Olmsted**, and Sylvester Baxter, a *Boston Daily Advertiser* reporter, designed the system of 20,000 acres of beaches, city parks, wetlands, woodlands, and recreational areas for 2.5 million residents of 34 cities and towns in eastern Massachusetts.

MICMAC. An **Algonquian**-speaking **Native American** people, associated with the **Abenaki**, who ranged from Maine to Newfoundland. They were the first tribe to encounter Europeans in Maine and eastern Canada, encountering the **Vikings** (A.D. 1000), **John Cabot** (1497), and European fishermen. Maine recognized the tribe (1973), and Congress passed the Aroostook Band of Micmacs Settlement Act (1991), recognizing the tribe and granting $900,000 to purchase 5,000 acres of ancestral land in northern Maine. Some worked as woodsmen, as guides, and in sawmills by 1870, and in the 1960s many were high-steel construction workers in **Boston**. The surviving 8,500 Micmacs still produce baskets woven from split-ash that are often collected as **art** today.

MIDDLESEX CANAL. Connected **Boston** and the Merrimack River at **Lowell**, carrying passengers and cargo 27 miles (1803–53) until superseded by the Boston & Lowell Railroad. Incorporated by the Massachusetts legislature and Governor **John Hancock** (1793) for **James Sullivan**, the canal made continuous water passage possible from Boston Harbor to **Concord**, New Hampshire, with 20 locks and eight aqueducts. The canal boats or rafts drawn by horses or oxen were cheap and convenient transportation, and passengers rode comfortable packet boats at 4 mph. Stage coaches connected with the terminal in Charlestown and Lowell. Constructed by **Loammi Baldwin**, this canal was an engineering triumph and a model for the Erie Canal.

MILES, NELSON APPLETON (1839–1925). Soldier. Born in Westminster, Massachusetts, on August 8, 1839, Miles served in the 22nd

Massachusetts Regiment (1861) and rose to major general (1865). After the **Civil War**, Miles was a colonel in the regular Army campaigns against the Plains Indian tribes (1869–90). His reputation was damaged by the Army's massacre of Sioux women and children at Wounded Knee (1890), but he became the U.S. Army commander in chief (1895–1903). Miles published his autobiography and died in Washington, D.C., on May 15, 1925.

MILITIA. Companies organized in each colonial New England town for self-defense. The **Massachusetts Bay Company** charter (1628) required them. They numbered about 100 men, and any able bachelor or lower-class male older than age 18 could be required to serve. Public officials, the elderly or infirm, gentlemen, and **Harvard** students were exempted by the county court. Diminishing military need made the militia a social institution, weekly drills (1631) were reduced to eight per year (1660), but **training day** was held four times a year for muster and drill and those absent were fined. This was a secular holiday with pageantry and parades, and target practice made local heroes of the best marksmen. The local gentry, elected by the company or appointed by the governor or legislature, displayed their authority as militia officers. The **Ancient and Honorable Artillery Company** of **Boston** (1638) and military academies trained some officers. The **Peabody Essex Museum** dedicated (2002) a park in **Salem**, Massachusetts, to mark the birthplace of the National Guard in 1637.

MILK SHAKES. A popular beverage in the United States, composed of milk, ice cream, and flavoring shaken or whipped until foamy. But in Rhode Island this drink is called a cabinet and in Boston it is a frappe.

MILL GIRLS. Rural workers employed by **Francis Cabot Lowell** in his Waltham textile factory (1813–17). His agents recruited young single women (ages 10–30) from New England farms to work in the factory and live in chaperoned boarding houses operated by the company. This paternal management system was necessary to attract workers and was continued in Lowell (1824–45). Most mill girls worked for a few years before returning home to marry. When factory conditions deteriorated and the paternalism proved unprofitable, **Irish** and **French-Canadian immigrants** replaced the **Yankee** girls by 1847. The *Lowell Offering*, a magazine published by the owners with literary contributions from the mill girls, offers insights into factory life.

MILLAY, EDNA ST. VINCENT (1892–1950). Poet. Born in Rockland, Maine, on February 22, 1892, Millay graduated from Vassar College (1917). While writing poetry in New York's Greenwich Village, she acted with the **Provincetown Players** and wrote skits for them. She won the Pulitzer Prize for *The Harper-Weaver and Other Poems* (1923). Her opera, *The King's Henchman* (1927), was very popular, and she wrote a poem protesting the execution of **Sacco and Vanzetti** (1927). Millay died in Austerlitz, New York, on October 19, 1950.

MILLER, WILLIAM (1782–1849). Clergyman. Born in Pittsfield, Massachusetts, on February 15, 1782, Miller was a farmer in Poultney, Vermont, and served in the War of 1812. He became a Baptist preacher (1833), wrote *Evidences from Scripture* and *History of the Second Coming of Christ, About the Year 1843* (1836), and converted 100,000 to his Millerite or Adventist church (1843). The movement declined in 1844, but Miller continued preaching until his death in Low Hampton, New York, on December 20, 1849. His millennial sect revived (1863) as the Seventh Day Adventist Church (1849).

MINUTEMEN. Members of the colonial **militia** force authorized by the Continental Congress (1775) but common in New England towns by 1774. They were intended to be a special unit of local militia who would respond to an alarm within one minute. **Daniel Chester French** designed the *Minuteman* statue in Concord (1875), a citizen soldier with one hand on his plow and in the other his musket. This is a symbol of American readiness to defend freedom from the **American Revolution** to the contemporary National Guard. On Lexington Green stands Henry Hudson Kitson's bronze statue *The Minuteman* (1899); and **Theo Kitson**'s *Minuteman* (1905), a blacksmith leaving his forge to fight for freedom, stands on the Framingham militia drill grounds. *See also* BATTLE OF LEXINGTON AND CONCORD.

MITCHELL, GEORGE J. (1933–). Senator from Maine. Born in Waterville on August 20, 1933, George John Mitchell graduated from Bowdoin College (1954) and Georgetown University Law Center (1960). After serving in the U.S. Army (1954–56), he practiced law in **Portland** (1965–67) and was a district attorney (1971), the U.S. attorney (1977–79), and U.S. district judge in Maine (1979–80). Appointed to succeed **Edmund S. Muskie** as a Democrat in the Senate (1980–95), Mitchell became majority leader (1989–95) and wrote *World on Fire: Saving an Endangered*

Earth (1991). Mitchell was a special adviser to President William J. Clinton on Northern Ireland (1995–99) and the Middle East (2000) and then practiced law in Washington, D.C., and Portland.

MITCHELL, MARIA (1818–1889). Astronomer. Born in **Nantucket**, Massachusetts. on August 1, 1818, Miss Mitchell was self-educated as the first woman astronomer in America. She discovered the orbit of a new comet (1847). which earned her election to the **American Academy of Arts and Sciences**, the first women so honored. After a trip to Europe (1858), she was the first professor of astronomy and director of the Vassar College observatory (1865–88). Mitchell earned an international reputation in sciences when she died in Lynn on June 28, 1889.

MOAKLEY, JOHN JOSEPH (1927–2001). Congressman from Massachusetts. Born in South Boston on April 27, 1927, Moakley served in the U.S. Navy (1943–46), attended the University of Miami (1950–51), and graduated from Suffolk University Law School (1956) in **Boston**. He served as a Democrat in the state legislature (1953–63, 1965–71) and the Boston City Council (1971–73). Elected to the House of Representatives (1972–2001) as an Independent, Moakley joined the Democratic Party leadership under his mentor Speaker **Thomas P. O'Neill**. Joe Moakley played a major role in allocating federal funds to New England and on human rights and Latin American issues. Before he died on April 28, 2001, the new federal courthouse in Boston was named in his honor.

MOHAWK. An Iroquoian-speaking tribe in eastern New York and Vermont who were often at war with New England **Algonquins**. The Mohawk sachem **Hiawatha** founded the Iroquois League (1575) and inspired **Henry Wadsworth Longfellow**'s fictional **Native American** in *The Song of Hiawatha* (1855). The tribe fought for the English in **King Philip's War** at the urging of Governor **Edmund Andros** and raided **Deerfield** in 1693, 1695, 1696, and 1704. Mohawks supported the British in the **American Revolution**. Led by Joseph Brant (1742–1807) they settled in Ontario. More than 50 place names in Vermont are Mohawk.

MOHAWK TRAIL. Route used by several **Native American** tribes in western Massachusetts through the Berkshire Hills and Connecticut River valley to the Great Lakes. Settlers made it an ox road (1753) and the first toll-free road, or shunpike, through the **Appalachian Moun-**

tains (1786). Massachusetts rebuilt the road (1914) and designated it as a scenic 63-mile auto route in recognition of the growing importance of **tourism** and **leaf peeping** in the New England **economy**. The highway connected **Boston** with resort hotels in the **Berkshires**.

MOHEGAN. An **Algonquian**-speaking **Native American** people living on the Thames River in Connecticut, and in Massachusetts and Rhode Island. They were dominated by the **Pequot** leader Sassacus (1560–1637) until the **Pequot War** (1637). The Mohegan sachem Uncas (1588–1682) allied with the English colonists in both the Pequot War and **King Philip's War** (1676), and for a time the Mohegan were the only important tribe in southern New England. They took land from the **Narragansett**, **Niantic**, and **Nipmuc**, but the population gradually declined from 2,300. Many scattered to New York (1788) and Wisconsin, but some intermarried with whites in Norwich, Connecticut. Fidelia Hoscott Fielding (1827–1908), the last native speaker of the Mohegan language, died in Connecticut. But the 1,300 Mohegans who opened the Mohegan Sun Casino (1996) in Montville, Connecticut, have revived their culture.

MOLASSES. Syrup derived from refining the Asian sugar cane plant grown in the West Indies. It was imported by New Englanders (1640) and distilled as **rum**. It was a sweetener less expensive than **maple syrup** in cooking and baking. Plentiful and inexpensive, it was used with salt to preserve meat and to brew beer. The molasses industry stimulated the **triangular trade** in rum and slaves with profits capitalizing much of the New England economy. Molasses and sugar were also essential for more than 30 **candy** manufacturers in Massachusetts by 1930. In **Boston** the William Schrafft candy company used sugar to produce jelly beans (1861) for soldiers in the **Civil War**. *See also* CANDY; SLAVERY; WEST INDIES TRADE.

MOLASSES FLOOD. Occurred in **Boston** on January 15, 1919, when a 50-foot high waterfront storage tank in the **North End** exploded, releasing 2.5 million gallons of molasses (used as a sweetener in **brown bread**, **baked beans**, candy, cookies, and cake and for **rum**). The 14,000 tons erupted in waves 8 to 15 feet high at 35 miles per hour in a sticky flood down Commercial Street. It killed 21 people, injured 150, and destroyed automobiles, buildings, and elevated train trestles. Horses stuck in the deep ooze were shot. The fire department used seawater to clean Causeway and Commercial Streets for months and the Purity Distilling

Company paid $1,000,000 in damages. A plaque at the waterfront Langone Park marks the disaster site today.

MONAST, LOUIS (1863–1936). Congressman from Rhode Island. Born in Quebec on July 1, 1863, Monast came to Pawtucket with his father (1865) and worked in **textile** mills (1872–82), as a bricklayer, plasterer, and carpenter (1882–92), and in the building construction and real estate business. Elected to the state legislature as a Republican (1909–11), he served in the House of Representatives (1927–29) and resumed his real estate business. He died in Pawtucket on April 16, 1936. Monast was the first **French-Canadian** congressman from Rhode Island.

MONHEGAN ISLAND. Located 10 miles off Port Clyde in Maine. This island was visited by European **codfish** boats before **John Cabot** explored it (1498). Settled by the English (1626), it became an **art colony** and summer resort in the 1870s. The **lighthouse** built in 1824 was replaced in 1850 and 1959.

MONKIEWICZ, BOLESLAUS J. (1898–1971). Congressman from Connecticut. Born in Syracuse, New York, on August 8, 1898, Monkiewicz moved to New Britain, Connecticut, with his family (1899) and served in the U.S. Navy (1918). He graduated from Fordham University Law School (1921) and practiced law in New York and New Britain (1933–37). Monkiewicz was clerk of the New Britain court (1932–33) and a prosecuting attorney (1937–39). He was elected as a Republican to the House of Representatives (1939–41) and resumed the practice of law in New Britain. He was the first **Polish** American elected to Congress in New England and served as a circuit court judge (1961–68). Monkiewicz died in New Britain on July 2, 1971.

MONTPELIER. State capital of Vermont. It is located on the Winooski River in the **Green Mountains** and was founded by settlers from New Hampshire and Connecticut (1787). It replaced Windsor as the state capital (1805) when the first state house was built (1808). The nearby **granite** industry stimulated growth of the city. Montpelier was incorporated as a city in 1895 and now has a diverse population of 9,000.

MOODY, DWIGHT LYMAN (1837–1899). Clergyman. Born in East Northfield, Massachusetts, on February 5, 1837, Moody was a shoe store clerk in **Boston** when he joined the **Congregational** church (1856).

Working in Chicago, he organized a Sunday school for poor children (1858) and a mission for **Civil War** soldiers. As president of the Chicago YMCA (1866), Moody became a spellbinding evangelist, touring England, Scotland, and Ireland (1873–75) with the organist and composer Ira D. Sankey. From his headquarters in Northfield, he was a conservative evangelist (1875–99) popular throughout the nation. Moody's income from the hymn collections he published with Sankey endowed the two schools he founded, Northfield Seminary for girls (1879) and Mount Hermon School for boys (1881). They later merged as a coeducational **prep school**. Moody died in Northfield on December 22, 1899.

MOODY, WILLIAM HENRY (1853–1917). U.S. Supreme Court justice. Born in Newbury, Massachusetts, on December 23, 1853, Moody graduated from **Harvard** College (1876), attended Harvard Law School, and studied with **Richard Henry Dana** in **Boston**. He practiced in Haverhill (1878–88) and was prosecutor in the **Lizzie Borden** case (1893). Moody was a Republican in the House of Representatives (1895–1902) and served as secretary of the navy (1902–04) and attorney general (1904–06) before he served on the Supreme Court (1906–10). Moody wrote some famous dissents, later adopted by the Court, and died in Haverhill on July 2, 1917.

MOOSE. Largest member of the deer family *(Alces alces)* and the largest animal in New England forests. The name is an **Algonquin** word for the massive animal hunted from eastern Canada and New England to Alaska in ash, birch, poplar, and willow forests and lake shores. Rarely seen after 1900, the moose population has risen from 3,000 (1900) to 40,000 (2001) because hunting was prohibited, many farms are reforested, and no natural predators exist in New England. The spruce budworm outbreak (1960) killed much old-growth forest and modern clear-cutting methods created new food sources for moose. Highway salt in the winter also provides sodium necessary for the moose but leads to more than 2,000 traffic accidents each year. Maine reported 29,000 moose, but they are now common in New Hampshire (7,000), Vermont (3,500), Massachusetts (700), and Connecticut (20). Maine allowed moose hunting in 1980, and the state issued 3,000 permits in 2001. Vermont permitted limited fall hunting in 1993. Moose create wildlife management problems when they enter suburban neighborhoods and have even been seen in **Boston** and Rhode Island. The moose is the official state animal in Maine.

MORGAN, J. P. (1837–1913). Businessman. Born in **Hartford**, Connecticut, on April 17, 1837, John Pierpont Morgan studied at the University of Gottingen (1854–56) and worked as a banker in London (1856–57) and New York City (1871–95). His firm, J. P. Morgan and Company (1895), was one of the world's most influential banks. He defeated **Jim Fisk** for control of one **railroad** (1869) and reorganized banks, mines, railroads, shipping lines, and insurance companies. Morgan prevented financial panics (1873, 1895 and 1907) and created the U.S. Steel Corporation (1901). Investigated by Congress for creating illegal monopolies (1912), Morgan became an **art** collector and philanthropist before he died in Rome on March 31, 1913. *See also* PIERPONT, JAMES L.

MORGAN HORSE. A compact, muscular horse used for riding, steeplechases, and as a coach or light draft horse. First bred by **Justin Morgan** (1748–98) in Randolph, Vermont (1789), Morgans became famous for their beauty, strength, speed, stamina, and gentle disposition throughout the Connecticut River valley. They set world-trotting records in the 1830s when the harness racing sport began, and Colonel **William Wells** mounted his **1st Vermont Cavalry** entirely on Morgans during the **Civil War**. This unique American breed registry established by Colonel Joseph Battell in Vermont in 1894, lists more than 147,000 Morgan horses throughout the world today. The Morgan became Vermont's official state animal in 1961 and the state horse in Massachusetts.

MORISON, SAMUEL ELIOT (1887–1976). Historian. Born in **Boston** on July 9, 1887, Morison graduated from **Harvard University** (1908). He earned a Ph.D. (1913) at Harvard, where he taught history for 40 years (1915–55). Morison served in the Navy Reserve (1942–51), retiring as a rear admiral. His love of sailing is evident in *Admiral of the Ocean Sea* (1942) and *John Paul Jones* (1959), both of which won the Pulitzer Prize. Morison was a prolific writer of vivid prose, combining meticulous research with an eloquent narrative style. His 25 books investigated **Harrison Gray Otis**, Harvard College, Massachusetts maritime history, **Matthew C. Perry**, the European exploration of America, and the U.S. Navy in World War II. After his death in Boston on May 15, 1976, a statue of this **Boston Brahmin** sailor and scholar was placed on the **Back Bay** mall in 1982.

MORRILL, JUSTIN SMITH (1810–1898). Senator from Vermont. Born in Strafford, Vermont, on April 14, 1810, Morrill was a merchant and farmer in Strafford. He was elected as a Whig to the House of Representatives (1855–67) and then as a Republican congressman and senator (1867–98). He is best known for the land-grant law, the Morrill Act (1862), which funded 70 agricultural and mechanical colleges in the United States, including Massachusetts Institute of Technology, the University of Massachusetts, the University of Rhode Island, and the University of Connecticut. Morrill was also author of the protectionist Tariff Act of 1861. He died in Washington, D.C., on December 28, 1898.

MORSE, JEDIDIAH (1761–1826). Clergyman. Born in Woodstock, Connecticut, on August 23, 1761, Morse graduated from Yale College (1783) and studied theology at Yale (1783–85). He was a **Congregational** minister in Charlestown, Massachusetts (1789–1819), and a conservative **Federalist** who founded the *Panoplist* newspaper (1805–10) and the Andover Theological Seminary to defend the orthodox church against **Unitarianism**. Morse wrote the first and most influential textbooks on geography, New England history, and **Native Americans**. He died in **New Haven** on June 9, 1826.

MORSE, LEOPOLD (1831–1892). Congressman from Massachusetts. Born in Germany on August 15, 1831, Morse immigrated to New Hampshire (1849) and worked in a **Boston** printing business he later purchased. Morse was the first **Jewish** member of the House of Representatives, elected as a Democrat (1877–85, 1887–89). Well known as a philanthropist, he died in Boston on December 15, 1892.

MORSE, SAMUEL F. B. (1791–1872). Inventor and artist. Born in Charlestown, Massachusetts, on April 27, 1791, Samuel Finley Breese Morse, the son of **Jedidiah Morse**, graduated from Yale College (1810). He studied art with **Washington Allston** and in London (1811–15) and painted portraits in **Boston**, Charleston, and New York City. His "Old House of Representatives" (1822) and "Marquis de Lafayette" (1826) are his best works. Morse turned to electrical inventions (1832) and **anti-Catholicism**, publishing a tract (1835) on the "dangers" **Irish** and **German immigrants** posed. He demonstrated his telegraph (1844) by sending the first message in Morse code over wires from Baltimore to Washington, D.C. Later, Morse worked on **Cyrus W. Field**'s transatlantic cable (1858) and was a founder of Vassar College (1861). He died in New York City on April 2, 1872.

MORTON, LEVI PARSONS (1824–1920). Vice-president of the United States. Born in Shoreham, Vermont, on May 16, 1824, Morton was in business in Hanover, New Hampshire, and **Boston** and established one of the nation's largest banks in New York City. Elected to the House of Representatives as a Republican (1879–81), he was U.S. minister to France (1881–85) and served as vice-president with President Benjamin Harrison (1889–93) and as governor of New York (1895–96). Morton founded the Morton Trust Company (1899), retired in 1909, and died in Rhinebeck, New York, on May 16, 1920.

MORTON, MARCUS (1784–1864). Governor of Massachusetts. Born in Freetown, Massachusetts, on February 19, 1784, Morton graduated from Brown University (1804) and from **Tapping Reeve**'s Litchfield Law School. He practiced law in **Taunton** (1807–64) and was a Jeffersonian Republican in the House of Representatives (1817–21) and served on the Massachusetts Executive Council (1823–24). As lieutenant governor (1824–25), he became governor (1825) when Governor **William Eustis** died. While serving on the state supreme court (1825–40), Morton was elected governor in 1839 and in 1843 on a liberal Jacksonian Democratic platform. He was collector of the port of **Boston** (1845–48) but refused the nomination for vice-president (1848). Morton joined the Free Soil Party (1852), was elected to the state legislature (1858), and supported President Abraham Lincoln during the **Civil War** until he died in Taunton on February 6, 1864.

MORTON, WILLIAM T. G. (1819–1868). Inventor. Born in Charlton, Massachusetts, on August 9, 1819, William Thomas Green Morton practiced as a dentist in Connecticut. After moving to **Boston** (1842), Dr. Morton used ether as a painkiller for his patients (1844) and demonstrated the inhalation of sulfuric ether gas (1846) at **Massachusetts General Hospital** (1846). By successfully rendering a surgical patient unconscious and oblivious to pain, surgery rapidly increased. Dr. **Oliver Wendell Holmes** named this medical gift to humanity "anesthesia." Morton failed to profit from his invention, and others claimed credit for the discovery. Morton testified for the defense in the **John White Webster** murder trial (1850), the first use of dental evidence in a trial. He died in poverty in New York City on July 15, 1868.

MOSHER, HOWARD FRANK (1943–). Writer. Born in New York in 1943, Mosher graduated from Syracuse University (1964). After graduate studies at the University of Vermont, he was a **public school** teacher and social worker in Vermont. Mosher won fellowships from the National Endowment for the Arts and the Guggenheim Foundation for his fiction, vivid historical portraits of independent-minded Vermonters in the **Northeast Kingdom**. His best-known novel *Disappearances* (1977) describes whiskey smugglers in the 1920s. He also wrote *Where the Rivers Flow North* (1978), and *A Stranger in the Kingdom* (1989). All three books were the basis for films of the same titles. Mosher also wrote *Northern Borders* (1994) and *North Country: A Personal Journey through the Borderland* (1997) and now lives and writes in Irasburg, Vermont.

MOTLEY, JOHN LOTHROP (1814–1877). Historian. Born in Dorchester, Massachusetts, on April 15, 1814, Motley graduated from **Harvard** College (1831) and studied and traveled in Europe. Returning to **Boston** (1835), he wrote two novels about Thomas Morton's **Merrymount** colony and was a U.S. diplomat in Russia, but he quickly turned to a career as an historian. His most popular work was *The Rise of the Dutch Republic* (1856). He was U.S. minister to Austria (1861–67), and Great Britain (1869–70) and wrote *The History of the United Netherlands, 1584–1609* (1860–67). Motley died in England on May 29, 1877.

MOTT, LUCRETIA COFFIN (1793–1880). Reformer. Born on January 3, 1793, on **Nantucket** Island in a **Quaker** family, Lucretia Coffin married James Mott (1811) and moved to Philadelphia. Mott was a leader in the Society of Friends (1828) and joined the **temperance**, peace, and abolitionist movements. When she was denied her seat as a delegate to the World Anti-Slavery Convention in London (1840), she and **Elizabeth Cady Stanton** organized the first woman's rights convention at Seneca Falls, New York (1848). Mott addressed the convention, which her husband moderated, and continued to write, speak, and lobby for abolition and woman's rights. Active in the secret **Underground Railroad** in the 1850s, she died in Philadelphia on November 11, 1880.

MOUNT AUBURN CEMETERY. Founded in Cambridge, Massachusetts (1831), by **Joseph Story** and **Jacob Bigelow**. Their purpose was to create a tranquil, natural setting for the commemoration of the dead and the consolation of the living. This was the first garden cemetery in the nation and inspired the American rural cemetery movement. It remains an active, nonsectarian cemetery (174 acres) as well as a premier arboretum, bird sanctuary, and an outdoor museum of 19th- and 20th-century architecture and sculpture. Its graves include a large number of prominent New Englanders and **Boston Brahmins**.

MOUNT DESERT ISLAND. Largest island off the Maine coast (100 sq mi/260 sq km). Separated from the mainland by Frenchman Bay, it has a chain of rounded granite peaks dominated by Cadillac Mountain (1,532 ft/467 m) named by **Samuel de Champlain** (1604). French **Jesuits** built the first **Catholic** mission in North America (1613), and English settlers arrived in 1762. The island became a fashionable summer resort after the **Civil War**, despite a devastating forest fire (1947), and has been part of **Acadia National Park** since 1919 and a very popular **tourist** destination.

MOUNT KATAHDIN. A monolith (5,268 ft/1,605 m) rising abruptly from the flat lake country of central Maine. Governor **Percival Baxter** purchased the land and donated Baxter State Park to Maine, to be kept forever in a wilderness state. **Native Americans** saw the mountain as the home of their god Pamola. **Henry David Thoreau** described climbing the peak (1846) in his book *Maine* (1864), and **Thomas Wentworth Higginson** (1855) led **Boston** ladies and gentlemen in a camping party to the summit. Today it is the terminus of the 2,143 mile **Appalachian Trail**.

MOUNT WASHINGTON. The highest mountain in New England (6,288 ft/1,917 m) located 25 miles south of Berlin, New Hampshire, in the **Presidential Range** of the **White Mountains**. Darby Field was the first settler to climb the mountain (1642), but an eight-mile road ascends to the peak (1861), and a unique cog railroad (1869) carries **tourists** to the summit each summer. Completion of the railroad (1875) began the era of grand hotels in the area. Hikers find the arduous ascent popular despite Mount Washington's harsh and changeable weather conditions. The Mount Washington Observatory (1932), a scientific and educational station at the summit, recorded the world's highest wind speed (231 mph) on April 12, 1934. It is in the White Mountain National Forest and is the watershed of the Androscoggin, Sacco, and **Connecticut Rivers**. *See also* TOURISM.

MOXIE. The first mass-marketed American soft drink invented by Dr. Augustin Thompson in **Lowell**, Massachusetts (1884) as a patent medicine or tart tonic for a variety of ills. Because Moxie was promoted creatively by the manufacturer, Frank Archer, as a healthy tonic, the word **tonic** is still used in the **Boston** area for all carbonated soft drinks. Although popular first in New England, Moxie was a national favorite until 1960. The word "moxie" entered the language by 1939 meaning nerve or boldness. The Moxie Festival in Lisbon Falls, Maine, an annual event inspired by Frank Potter's book *The Moxie Mystique* (1981), attracts Moxie fans from across the nation.

MUD SEASON. The early spring period when many rural New England unpaved roads are impassable. As the snow melts, the frozen earth thaws by day and freezes by night. Roads become quagmires, cars and trucks sink axle-deep into the sticky muck, and mud coats everything. Never one to romanticize rural New England, **Robert Frost** wrote "Two Tramps at Mud Time" (1936). With more paved roads, mud season is now confined to northern New England in March and April, which **Yankees** call the fifth season.

MUNSEY, FRANK ANDREW (1854–1925). Editor and publisher. Born in Mercer, Maine, on August 21, 1854, Munsey founded *Munsey's Magazine* in New York (1889), the nation's first illustrated general circulation periodical (1889). He bought several major newspapers, including the *New York Star* (1891), *Baltimore News* (1908), and the *New York Daily News* (1901). He was a freewheeling Republican publisher when he died in New York City on December 22, 1925.

MURPHY, FRANCIS PARNELL (1877–1958). Governor of New Hampshire. Born in Winchester, New Hampshire, on August 16, 1877, Murphy graduated high school in Hudson, Massachusetts and worked his way up from packing shoe crates to owning the J. F. McElwain Shoe Company (1922), which became New Hampshire's largest employer with 12 factories (1936). Murphy was a Republican state legislator (1931) and served on the Governor's Executive Council (1933–36) before he was the first Catholic elected governor (1937–41). Murphy supported the New Deal, built the Cannon Mountain Tramway and Hampton State Beach to promote recreation and **tourism**, and established the state police. He became a Democrat but was an unsuccessful candidate for the U.S. Senate (1942). Murphy retired from politics, operated a radio station, and was active in philanthropy until he died in Newport, New Hampshire, on December 19, 1958.

MURPHY, MICHAEL CHARLES (1861–1913). Athletic coach. Born in Westborough, Massachusetts, on February 28, 1861, Murphy was a pioneer in collegiate **sports** training. After earning success in track events, he established a popular training camp in Westborough (1880). His progressive methods made him a track and football coach at Yale University (1887–89, 1892–96, 1900–05) and the University of Pennsylvania (1896–1900, 1905–13). Noted for innovations, such as the crouch start for sprinters and his skill in motivating young athletes, Murphy coached U.S. Olympic teams (1908, 1912) with much success. He was responsible for the acceptance of sports as an extracurricular program in American **education** when he died in Philadelphia on June 4, 1913.

MURRAY, JOHN (1741–1815). Clergyman. Born in England on December 10, 1741, and raised in Ireland, Murray came to **Boston** as an evangelist (1774). He founded the first **Universalist** church in America at Gloucester (1779) and served as a chaplain with Rhode Island troops during the **American Revolution**. He married **Judith Sargent Stevens Murray** (1788) and was a minister in Boston's **North End** (1793–1809). Murray died in Boston on September 3, 1815.

MURRAY, JUDITH SARGENT STEVENS (1751–1820). Writer. Born in Gloucester, Massachusetts, on May 1, 1751, Judith Sargent, the daughter of a prosperous **Cape Ann** merchant, married John Stevens, a sea captain (1769). She wrote verse and essays (1770) for **Boston** magazines as the **American Revolution** aroused interest in women's rights. Widowed in 1786, she married **John Murray** (1788) in Gloucester. Her poem "On the Equality of the Sexes" (1790) appeared in the *Massachusetts Magazine* as well as a column on public issues. She wrote plays *Virtue Triumphant* (1795) and *The Traveller Returned* (1796) for the Federal Street Theater in Boston and a biography of her husband (1816). She died in Natchez, Mississippi, on July 6, 1820.

MUSEUM OF FINE ARTS (MFA). Opened in **Boston** (1876) at Copley Square and relocated to a larger building that R. Clipston Sturgis and Guy Lowell designed in the **Fenway** (1909). **John Singer Sargent** painted murals in the entryway, rotunda, and stairway (1916–25). The collections include art from Egypt, Greece, Rome, the Near East, China, Japan, India, medieval, renaissance, modern Europe, and the Americas, and the museum operates an art school. The MFA, equaled only by the Metropolitan Museum of Art in New York City, expanded with a wing designed by architect I. M. Pei (1981), and a new wing opens in 2007.

MUSEUM OF SCIENCE. Began in **Boston** as the Museum of Natural History (1830). Located in the **Back Bay** (1863–1949), the renamed Museum of Science moved to the Charles River shore (1949) and became an important **tourist** attraction and regional educational center.

MUSKIE, EDMUND S. (1914–1996). Senator from Maine. Born in Rumford, Maine, on March 28, 1914, Edmund Sixtus Muskie graduated from Bates College (1936) and Cornell University Law School (1939). He practiced law in Waterville (1940–42) and served in the U.S. Navy (1942–45). He was a Democrat in the state legislature (1947–51) and governor (1955–59) until his election to the U.S. Senate (1959–80). Muskie was an unsuccessful candidate for vice-president (1968) and for president (1972) and later was secretary of state (1980–81). He practiced law in Washington, D.C., until his death on March 26, 1996. *See also* CANUCK.

MYSTIC SEAPORT. An outdoor maritime history museum established in Mystic, Connecticut, on the Mystic River. It began as the Marine Historical Association at the former Greenman **shipyard** (1929) and includes the *Charles W. Morgan,* the only surviving American wooden **whaling** ship (1841), the *Joseph Conrad* (1882), a square-rigged training ship, and the *L. A. Dunton* (1921), a **fishing** schooner. Educational programs and exhibits about the 600 vessels launched in Mystic (1784–1919) attract 1 million **tourists**, students, and scholars each year. *See also* WHALING.

–N–

NADER, RALPH (1934–). Lawyer. Born in Winsted, Connecticut, on February 27, 1934, Nader graduated from Princeton University (1955) and **Harvard** Law School (1958). Practicing law in **Hartford**, his bestselling book, *Unsafe at Any Speed* (1965) launched Nader's career as a consumer advocate. Congress passed laws (1966) that forced the automobile industry to design safer cars. Nader founded the Center for Study of Responsive Laws (dubbed Nader's Raiders) to protect consumers, workers, taxpayers, and the environment from corporate abuse. He also directed Public Citizen (1971–80), a consumer protection agency, and assumed a leading role as a social critic. Nader was the Green Party candidate for U.S. president in 2000 and lives in Washington, D.C.

NAISMITH, JAMES (1861–1939). Inventor of basketball. Born in Almonte, Ontario, on November 6, 1861, Naismith was educated at McGill University and Presbyterian College in Montreal. While teaching physical **education** at the YMCA Training School (now Springfield College) in Springfield, Massachusetts, Naismith invented basketball (1891), at the suggestion of **Luther Gulick**, as an indoor activity for his students during the winter. Naismith was director of physical education at the University of Kansas (1898–1937) and died in Lawrence, Kansas, on November 28, 1939. He was elected to the Basketball Hall of Fame (1959), which was renamed in his honor in Springfield. *See also* BOSTON CELTICS; SPORTS.

NANTUCKET. An island (45 sq mi/120 sq km) 25 miles south of **Cape Cod**, the southernmost point of Massachusetts. **Bartholomew Gosnold** explored the island (1602), later claimed by New York (1660–92), and settled by English **Quakers** (1659), who displaced the **Native American** community. Nantucket became a major **whaling** port (1750–1869) when more than 2,200 Nantucket men served on 150 Atlantic and Pacific Ocean whalers. Nantucket also produced wool and mutton, with 16,000 **sheep** by 1800. The island's historic buildings, cobblestone streets, sandy **beaches**, and resort facilities made the town of Nantucket (1687) a popular **tourist** center by 1870. The first U.S. lightship (1856) was located near the island.

NANTUCKET SLEIGH RIDE. Term used when a harpooned whale surfaced and swam at 20 miles per hour, pulling the whaleboat across the ocean. This humorous **Yankee** term disguised the dangerous situation for the **whaling** crew whose boat might be towed under the waves, overturned, or lost, unless the whale tired and the harpooner killed the whale.

NARRAGANSETT. A **Native American** tribe in Rhode Island. These **Algonquian**-speaking horticultural people were unaffected by the epidemics (1617–19) that decimated other New England tribes. This permitted them to expand their territory; and two sachems, Miantonomo (1600–43) and **Canonicus**, welcomed **Roger Williams** to Rhode Island (1636). They enjoyed friendly relations with **William Coddington** and the Massachusetts **Puritans** in the **Pequot War** (1637) and numbered more than 5,000 people until **King Philip's War** (1675) when 1,000 of the 5,000 Narragansetts died in a battle at Kingston. **John Winthrop** permitted his **Mohegan** ally, Uncas, to execute Miantonomi, causing many Narragansetts to flee to Canada or join the **Mahican** and **Abenaki** tribes. Some of the survivors settled with the **Niantic** people on a reservation at Charleston, Rhode Island (1682–1970), where their numbers declined to 400, and many intermarried with whites or **African Americans**. The Narragansett were not recognized as a tribe by Rhode Island (1880) but won a lawsuit (1978) to regain their Charlestown reservation. The federal government later recognized the tribe (1983).

NATIVE AMERICANS. First encountered by Europeans by 1540 when **whaling** and **fishing** boats from Spain, Portugal, and France visited the coast. Fishermen landed for water and fuel and to dry or salt **codfish** before sailing home. In trading with coastal tribes, they transmitted diseases common in Europe but unknown in America. As many as three-fourths of some tribes died of smallpox, influenza, and measles introduced by fishermen and explorers by 1620. The epidemic of 1616–19 inadvertently cleared land for the **Pilgrims** in 1620. Early explorers kidnapped some Native Americans, like **Squanto** who translated for the **Wampanoag** and Pilgrims in 1621. The dominant **Pequot** tribe was devastated by the **Pequot War** (1637–38), after which the **Puritans** sold the prisoners as slaves. By 1676 the costly **King Philip's War** marked the end of tribal life in southern New England.

Efforts to bring Native Americans into New England culture include those of missionaries like **John Eliot** and **Jonathan Edwards**, as well as a provision in the **Harvard** College charter (1650) for the education of Native Americans. Caleb Cheeshateaumuck was the first Native American to graduate from Harvard (1665), and Daniel Simmons was the first at Dartmouth College (1777). The **Jesuit** missionary Father **Sebastien Rasles** compiled an **Abenaki** dictionary before he died, and John Eliot published the Bible in the **Wampanoag** language in 1663.

The federal government recognized 11 tribes in New England: the Paugusset, **Mohegan**, and Pequot in Connecticut; the **Maliseet**, **Micmac**, **Passamaquoddy**, and **Penobscot** in Maine; the **Nipmuc** and **Wampanoag** in Massachusetts; the **Narragansett** in Rhode Island; and the **Abenaki** in Vermont. Connecticut also recognized the Pequot and the **Schaghticoke** people. *See also* KING PHILIP'S WAR; MASSASOIT; SAMOSET.

NAUSET. An **Algonquian**-speaking **Native American** people on **Cape Cod** who encountered **Samuel de Champlain** (1606) and the **Pilgrims** (1620). Like many New England tribes, they moved seasonally, cultivated corn and beans, hunted, and fished. Although initially hostile to the **Plymouth** settlers, they traded **corn** with the starving colonists in 1622. By 1675 many had converted and allied with the English during **King Philip's War** and organized church congregations. Decimated by an epidemic (1710), their numbers were restored when other Indians who lost their lands joined the surviving Nauset (1800).

NAVIGATION ACTS. Laws passed by the British parliament (1651–1765) to implement **mercantilism** in the American colonies. Despite some advantages for Americans, they restricted colonial merchants, hindered manufacturing, raised taxes, and stimulated smuggling in New England ports, especially the Molasses Act (1733) and the **Sugar Act** (1764). These laws caused resistance and protests that led to the **American Revolution** and compelled New England merchants to find non-British markets in Europe, Latin America, and the **China trade** after the Revolution.

NECCO. New England's oldest and best-known **candy** company, founded in **Boston** by Oliver R. Chase (1847), a natural outgrowth from the New England **molasses** trade. Chase invented a machine for pulverizing sugar (1850) and a lozenge-printing machine (1866). The Chase Company grew (1901) into the New England Confectionery Company (NECCO) and moved to Cambridge in 1926, where it was one of 32 candy manufacturers. NECCO invented the first candy bars (1917) distributed to American soldiers in World War I, increasing consumer demand for candy in the 1920s. The company introduced chocolate candy in a box as a popular gift (1938), and NECCO brand candy is still manufactured in Revere, Massachusetts.

NELL, WILLIAM COOPER (1816–1874). Reformer and writer. Born in **Boston** on December 22, 1816, Nell was educated in Boston's segregated public schools and worked with **William Lloyd Garrison** and **Frederick Douglass** for the abolition of slavery and with the **Underground Railroad**. Nell published *Services of Colored Americans in the Wars of 1776–1812* (1851) and *Colored Patriots of the American Revolution* (1855) and lobbied to commemorate **Crispus Attucks** in the **Boston Massacre**. He was the first black man appointed to a federal office (1861–74) in New England and died in Boston on May 25, 1874.

NEW BEDFORD. One of the largest cities in Massachusetts located where the Acushnet River enters Buzzards Bay. Settled in 1640 by **Quakers**, it was incorporated in 1787 and its economy focused on **whaling** (1750–1869) and **fishing**. During the **American Revolution** many privateers sailed from New Bedford and fought a battle with British general Charles Grey, who burned the town in 1778. The city had a large **African-American** population by 1860 due to the influence of Quaker abolitionists and the **Underground Railroad**.

Its Seamen's Bethel (1832) was described in **Herman Melville**'s novel *Moby Dick* (1851) and is remembered in the **New Bedford Whaling National Historical Park** (1996). **Textile** mills employed the large immigrant population (1850–1930), and at present the metropolitan population of 175,000 residents still includes a large **Portuguese** population.

NEW BEDFORD WHALING NATIONAL HISTORICAL PARK. Established by the National Park Service (1996) in **New Bedford**, Massachusetts. It commemorates the world capital of the **whaling** industry on 34 acres in 13 city blocks, including historic buildings, museum collections, archives, and ships.

NEW BRITAIN. Known as the **Hardware City** and settled in central Connecticut in 1686. Its many sawmills, grist mills, blacksmith shops, and New England's first tinsmith industries led Frederick T. Stanley to manufacture (1843) bolts, hinges, and various hardware items. The Stanley Works grew into a major manufacturer of woodworking tools. This international firm and similar companies produce 300 kinds of hardware, making New Britain the nation's largest hardware center. **Frederick Law Olmsted** designed the city park, and New Britain has a population of 75,491 residents now.

NEW CONNECTICUT. *See* NEW HAMPSHIRE GRANTS.

NEW ENGLAND. The region named by Captain **John Smith** (1614) that became the six states of the northeastern United States: Connecticut, Maine, Massachusetts, New Hampshire, Rhode Island, and Vermont. The region is bordered on the north by Canada, on the west by New York, on the east by the Atlantic Ocean, and on the south by **Long Island Sound**. The **Appalachian Mountains** rise in the north and west, and the coast has always been the most populated and economically important area, first for **fishing**, farming, **whaling,** and shipping and by industry and **tourism** in the 20th century.

NEW ENGLAND ANTI-SLAVERY SOCIETY. Founded in **Boston** by **William Lloyd Garrison** (1832) and 12 men who favored the immediate abolition of **slavery**. *The Liberator* (1831–65) was the society's organ, publishing its increasingly radical views (racial equality, woman's rights, nonviolence, civil disobedience, opposition to colonization) derived from **Puritan**, **Unitarian** and **Quaker** theology and Enlightenment rationalism. The group expanded as the Massachusetts Anti-Slavery Society, but the Garrisonian **abolitionists** split the American Anti-Slavery Society when Garrison denounced the U.S. Constitution as sinful (1844) and led a moral crusade that culminated in the **Civil War**.

NEW ENGLAND BOILED DINNER. A popular traditional meal in this region consisting of beef cooked in a large pot with carrots, turnip, potatoes, onions, and cabbage. This dish reflects austere New England food ways derived from the **Puritan** preference for simple food, East Anglian tastes, and conditions in early New England. **John Winthrop**, and other **Puritan** leaders, suspected that indulgence in rich food led to spiritual ruin.

NEW ENGLAND CLAM CHOWDER. A popular dish that came to the region with the **Acadians**, the Catholic **French Canadians** from Nova Scotia. Chowder derives from the French word for kettle or cauldron, *chaudière*. A mixture of minced clams, milk, onions, and diced potatoes, it was well-known **Yankee** fare by 1750. Unlike its culinary cousin in Manhattan, it never contains tomatoes. This regional food was introduced to many Americans in the 1930s by the **Howard Johnson** roadside restaurants and today by the **Legal Sea Foods** restaurants.

NEW ENGLAND CONFEDERATION. A mutual defense union formed in Boston by Connecticut, **New Haven**, **Massachusetts Bay**, and **Plymouth** colonies (1643) as the United Colonies of New England. Influenced by **Simon Bradstreet**, it settled boundary disputes but failed to resolve petty rivalries. Maine and Rhode Island settlements were denied admission, and Massachusetts refused to join a war with the Dutch (1653). The confederation revived in **King Philip's War** (1675–76) but dissolved when the Massachusetts charter was revoked (1684). It was the first experiment in federation in America based on a written constitution and compromise.

NEW ENGLAND CONSCIENCE. The regional propensity for a somber and serious view of life derived from the **Pilgrims** and **Puritans**. Even wealthy and sophisticated New England **Yankees** lived austerely and did not build great estates or entertain lavishly. Their egalitarian traditions precluded conspicuous display of wealth and required civic-minded public service. These values were expressed in private charitable institutions like those founded, funded, and managed by **Boston Brahmins** for public benefit and were transmitted to **immigrants**.

NEW ENGLAND CONSERVATORY OF MUSIC. Oldest independent music school in the nation, founded in **Boston** by Eben Tourjee (1867). Its undergraduate and graduate students are taught by members of the **Boston Symphony Orchestra** (BSO) and often join the BSO, and a close relationship has resulted since 1881. **Eben D. Jordan** was a principal supporter of the school and his son Eben D. Jordan, Jr., built the school's concert auditorium, Jordan Hall (1903) in Boston. Today the school is one of the nation's preeminent schools of music, enrolling 800 student in its college and 1,600 preparatory and continuing education students.

NEW ENGLAND EMIGRANT AID COMPANY. Founded by **Eli Thayer** in **Worcester**, Massachusetts, to encourage antislavery settlers in Kansas (1854). The Free Soil Party and New England abolitionists raised funds to promote settlement of the territory of Kansas by antislavery voters. **Amos Adams Lawrence** and others sent 1,500 settlers to "Bleeding" Kansas to prevent the expansion of **slavery** in the western territories. Thayer accomplished little in Kansas, but increased **abolitionist** propaganda contributed to the coming of the **Civil War**. The company later sent women to Oregon (1864) and settlers to Florida (1866) before disbanding in 1907.

NEW ENGLAND FREEDMAN'S AID SOCIETY. Organized (1862) to provide food, clothing, medicine, and **education** to former slaves in the South during the **Civil War**. New Englanders responded to newspaper appeals from Union Army chaplains and civilian missionaries by sending hundreds of men and women to the occupied Southern states as teachers. **Yankee** soldiers in the 15th, 23rd, 25th, and 27th Massachusetts and 10th

Connecticut Regiments taught in makeshift schools in Virginia and North Carolina (1862), and some invited freedmen to come home with them. As a result, thousands of "contrabands" (as the former slaves were called) migrated to New England by 1900.

NEW ENGLAND HISTORIC GENEALOGICAL SOCIETY (NEHGS). Founded in **Boston** (1845) as a private, nonprofit center collecting, preserving, and publishing New England family history from the colonial era to the present. Its heart has always been the research library in the **Back Bay**, containing 200,000 volumes for 19,000 members and visiting researchers. Publications, conferences, tours, and educational programs make it a venerable institution renowned for family history. The NEHGS was the first scholarly institution in the region to admit women to membership (1898).

NEW ENGLAND HISTORICAL ASSOCIATION (NEHA). Founded in 1965 by historians in Connecticut, Rhode Island, and Massachusetts as a scholarly regional society for professional and avocational historians throughout New England. The first president, Professor Frank Friedel of **Harvard University**, sponsored annual academic conferences, and today the NEHA has more than 900 members and holds a conference each fall and spring at locations around New England. Its programs support all areas of historical research, writing, and teaching.

NEW ENGLAND HOME FOR LITTLE WANDERERS. Founded in the **North End** by **Boston** Methodists (1865) as an orphanage for the children of **Civil War** veterans. Relocating to the South End, and later to Jamaica Plain, the Home accepted orphans and homeless children from all parts of New England, and some **African-American** children from the South. Children who could not return to their relatives were placed out as domestic servants or foster children or adopted. Orphan trains carried groups of children to rural families in northern New England and to the Midwest (1867–1920). Satellite branches in **Salem** and Pittsfield, Massachusetts, and Caribou and Waterville, Maine, provided child welfare services; and the Boston asylum became a pioneer in child psychology by 1920. The children's choir and fundraising publications made the Home for Little Wanderers a beloved **Yankee** charity. Merging with the Boston Children's Services (1999), the Home for Little Wanderers continues its work for children and families today.

NEW ENGLAND PATRIOTS. A professional football team founded (1959) by William H. "Billy" Sullivan, Jr., as the **Boston** Patriots in the American Football League. Their first home was Boston University's Nickerson Field, the former home of the **Boston Braves**, but some games were played at Harvard Stadium, Boston College, and **Fenway Park**. The renamed New England Patriots moved to the Schaefer Stadium in Foxboro, Massachusetts (1971), which was named Sullivan Stadium in 1982. When **Billy Sullivan** sold the team (1988), the home field was renamed Foxboro Stadium (1990), and, after winning the 36th Super Bowl (2002), the team built the new **Gillette** Stadium in Foxboro.

NEW ENGLAND PRIMER. Book published (1690) in **Boston** by Benjamin Harris. It was the book from which **Puritan** children in the **Dame School** or at home learned to read using woodcut illustrations and rhyming couplets from the Old Testament texts ("In Adam's fall, we sinned all").

NEW HAMPSHIRE GRANTS (1749–1777). An area between New York and New Hampshire claimed by both colonies. Governor **Benning Wentworth** made 140 land grants (1747–60), and **Ethan Allen** and **Seth Warner** organized the **Green Mountain Boys** to expel the New Yorkers. Allen petitioned the British government to declare the area a new colony, but Vermonters declared independence as **New Connecticut** (1777). Renamed Vermont (1777), it became the 14th state in the Union on March 4, 1791.

NEW HAMPSHIRE HISTORICAL SOCIETY. Founded in **Concord** in 1823 as an independent, nonprofit educational organization to preserve the history of the state. Its exhibits, library, and museum serve 50,000 students, scholars, and visitors each year. The society is governed by 22 trustees and operates with a staff of 44 professional archivists, librarians, and historians.

NEW HAMPSHIRE PRESIDENTIAL PRIMARY. Political primary first held in 1916. It became a tradition (1920–96) for the state to hold the first primary in the nation. Often held on **town meeting** day, the second Tuesday in March, this gave the state much influence in national politics and increased revenue from **tourism**. Since 1960, Dixville Notch, a remote village in the **White Mountains**, has been the first town in the nation to vote in presidential elections. Its 29 voters gather at midnight on primary election day to cast and count the ballots.

NEW HAVEN. A Connecticut seaport on **Long Island Sound** at the mouth of the **Quinnipiac** River founded by **Puritans** (1638). The first planned community in America, New Haven was the capital of **New Haven Colony** (1643–64) until it joined the **Connecticut Colony** and served as joint capital with **Hartford** (1701–1875). The city is best known as the home of Yale University and for its pioneering urban renewal programs since 1957. Today New Haven has a population of 130,000 and is the center of an expanding metropolitan community with firearms, hardware, clothing, chemical, and rubber industries.

NEW HAVEN COLONY. Located at the mouth of the **Quinnipiac** River in south central Connecticut and founded (1638–64) by **John Davenport** and **Theophilus Eaton**. By 1643 it was the chief town of the colony's six settlements, Guilford, Branford, Stamford, Southold, and Milford. **New Haven** joined the **New England Confederation** (1643) and was annexed by **John Winthrop** of **Hartford** to form the Connecticut Colony (1664). Colonial New Haven was a thriving port on **Long Island Sound** and a center for firearms, hardware, and transportation by 1820 as well as the home of Yale University.

NEWPORT. Chief seaport in Rhode Island, founded at the mouth of the Narragansett Bay in 1639 by **William Coddington** and dissenters from Massachusetts. Despite Coddington's rivalry with **Roger Williams**, Newport united with Portsmouth (1640) and **Providence** and Warwick (1654). The colonial town became known for its fine cabinetmaking (1740–1810) and **Peter Harrison**'s architecture, especially the **Redwood Library** (1750), Brick Market (1761), and **Touro Synagogue** (1763). Shipping and the slave trade made Newport prosperous until the British occupation (1776–79) during the **American Revolution**. The **Battle of Newport** (1778) was an unsuccessful effort to liberate the town, which was the state's joint capital with Providence until 1900.

Newport became a fashionable summer resort by 1760 for southern planters, and 400 colonial buildings have survived. After the **Civil War** wealthy summer residents built opulent **Newport Mansions** and enjoyed tennis, yacht racing, and the cool ocean breezes. Newport, a shipbuilding center by 1646, is home to the Naval War College (1884), but the economy suffered when the U.S. Navy base closed in 1973. Newport is best known as the home of the America's Cup Race (1930–83) and summer jazz (1954) and folk music (1959) festivals. The city employs many of its 28,277 residents in **tourism**, electrical manufacturing, and service industries.

NEWPORT FOLK FESTIVAL. An annual summer music event attracting large audiences for two days to Fort Adams State Park in **Newport**, Rhode Island. Many celebrated singers, musicians, and composers have appeared since 1959. Among the notable performances was that by Bob Dylan, who introduced an electric guitar with his poetic folk songs in 1965. This began folk rock, a synthesis of folk revival music and rock 'n roll. Since 1989 **Ben and Jerry's** ice cream company has sponsored this nonprofit festival.

NEWPORT JAZZ FESTIVAL. A summer music festival in **Newport**, Rhode Island. Organized in 1954 by George Wein, the owner of the Storyville Club in **Boston**, this annual three-day event features most of the great American and international jazz musicians and crossover popular music artists. The program includes discussions by jazz critics and historians. When riots caused performance cancellations (1960, 1969, and 1971), the festival moved to New York City (1972–86), but it later returned to Fort Adams State Park in Newport.

NEWPORT MANSIONS. A dozen lavish summer houses built in **Newport**, Rhode Island, after the **Civil War** when the small seaport's scenic location and temperate climate attracted wealthy summer visitors. **Richard Morris Hunt** designed several mansions (known as cottages), including Marble House (1893) and The Breakers (1895), an Italian Renaissance-style mansion built for Cornelius Vanderbilt. Elite summer residents made lawn tennis and yachting popular, and the America's Cup race attracted international yachtsmen to the East Passage of Narragansett Bay. By 1870 socially prominent families, including the Astors and Vanderbilts, found refuge in Newport's ocean breezes and sea bathing in the Gilded Age (1865–90). Tobacco heiress Doris Duke, a lifelong summer resident, established the Newport Restoration Foundation (1968) to preserve local historic sites.

NIANTIC. An **Algonquin**-speaking **Native American** people living on the coast of Rhode Island and Connecticut. The migration of the **Pequot** divided them into two tribes. The Eastern Niantic were neutral in **King Philip's War** (1675–76) and merged with the **Narragansett** (1677). The Western Niantic, who lived near New London and on the Connecticut River, were nearly destroyed by the **Pequot War** (1637) and merged with the **Mohegan** people. **Puritans** sold some Niantic women and children as slaves in Virginia, Bermuda, and the West Indies.

NICHOLS, ROSE STANDISH (1872–1960). Landscape architect. Born in **Boston**, Rose Standish Nichols was encouraged by her uncle, **Augustus Saint-Gaudens**, to study landscape architecture at his Cornish, New Hampshire, studio, at MIT, and in Paris. She was her uncle's confidante and author of *English Pleasure Gardens* (1902). Her home in Boston, designed by **Charles Bulfinch** (1804), is the only house on **Beacon Hill** open to the public as a museum. In 1998 her summer home in Cornish, Mastlands, opened as a museum.

9TH MASSACHUSETTS REGIMENT. Organized in **Boston** in 1862 by Colonel **Thomas Cass**, former commander of the Irish Columbian Artillery disbanded in the **Know Nothing Party** hysteria in 1855. Governor **John A. Andrew**, Bishop **John Fitzpatrick**, and the editor of the *Boston Pilot*, Patrick Donohue, raised funds for the Irish Catholic recruits. When Cass was wounded in battle, Colonel **Patrick R. Guiney** succeeded him.

NIPMUC. An **Algonquin** name for 3,000 **Native Americans** living in 40 villages on the central Massachusetts plateau, in Rhode Island, and in Connecticut (1620–50). Subject to **Pequot** control until 1637, they fought with the Pequots in **King Philip's War** (1675–76), but only 1,000 Nipmucs were counted in the 1680 census. Some Nipmucs migrated to Quebec, New York, and New Jersey tribes. Others became **Praying Indians** under **Puritan** missionary influence. The Massachusetts legislature granted the Nipmucs citizenship in 1869. Federal government recognition of 1,600 Nipmucs in central Massachusetts and in northeast Connecticut revived the tribe (2001).

NORMAL SCHOOL. A teaching training college for women first established by **Horace Mann** in Lexington and Westfield (1839) and Bridgewater, Massachusetts (1840). This was intended to professionalize public **education** along with Mann's program to raise teachers' salaries, building new public schools on a nonsectarian, tax-supported basis. By 1848, when Mann resigned as the first secretary of the state board of education to enter the House of Representatives, higher education for schoolteachers was well established and a majority of New England teachers were females. Vermont established the first private normal school in Concord (1829), and many states followed the Massachusetts and Connecticut (1849) example. By 1970, most normal schools became coeducational state colleges or universities.

NORTHEAST KINGDOM. An area of Vermont named by Senator **George Aiken** (1949). It is the state's most rural and lake-spotted corner, encompassing 2,000 square miles in three northeastern counties. With Jay Peak as its high point and Burke Mountain at its heart, the humped hills, rolling farmland, and forests attract adventuresome tourists, hunters, fishermen, and skiers to an underdeveloped and beautiful last frontier in northern New England. *See also* MOSHER, HOWARD FRANK.

NORTHEASTER. A storm in New England with cold gale winds coming from the northeast, a term used since 1774. From the first the **Pilgrims** and **Puritans** were astonished by the harsh weather, and later colonists were misled by accounts of the mild climate in Virginia and expected similar weather in New England. The cold and heavy snowfall led early New Englanders to coin such terms as snowshoes (1664), flurry (1686), snowstorm (1771), cold snap (1776), and snow plow (1792).

NORTH AMERICAN REVIEW. Magazine founded in Boston (1815–1940) and published by the Ticknor and Fields firm by 1863. **Richard Henry Dana**, **Jared Sparks**, **Edward Everett**, **James Russell Lowell**, **Charles Eliot Norton**, **Henry Adams**, **Henry Cabot Lodge**, and **George Brinton McClellan Harvey** were among the distinguished editors of this influential national magazine.

NORTH END. The oldest **Boston** neighborhood, located between **Faneuil Hall** and the waterfront. Before the **American Revolution** it was home to many of Boston's wealthiest residents, as well as a small **African-American** community. As the buildings deteriorated in the 1820s, the North End became an **Irish immigrant** district and then a new home for **Jews** (1890–1920) and **Italians** (1920–90). More recently its restaurants, shops, food stores, and tourists visiting the Old North Church and the **Paul Revere** House have gentrified the North End and supplanted the Italian-American community.

NORTON, CHARLES ELIOT (1827–1908). Writer and critic. Born in Cambridge, Massachusetts, on November 16, 1827, Norton graduated from **Harvard** College (1846). After traveling to India, Egypt, and Europe, he founded an importing firm in **Boston**. In 1855 Norton began his career as a man of letters, contributing to the *Atlantic Monthly*, joining **James Russell Lowell** as co-editor of the *North American Review*

(1864–68), and helping found *The Nation* (1865). Norton, the first professor of art history at Harvard (1873–97), inspired **Isabella Stewart Gardner**, the new **Museum of Fine Arts**, the **Society for the Preservation of New England Antiquities**, and the American arts and crafts movement. When he died in Cambridge on October 21, 1908, Norton exerted a profound influence on American **art**, **literature**, and **architecture**.

NORUMBEGA. A site on the Charles River in Newton, Massachusetts, said to be a settlement by Leif Eriksson's **Vikings** about A.D. 1000. **Eben Norton Horsford**, the **Harvard University** chemistry professor who researched this legend in 1889, built a stone tower on the Weston bank of the river. From 1897 to 1964 Norumbega was a popular amusement park with the Totem Pole ballroom in the 1930s.

NOYES, JOHN HUMPHREY (1811–1886). Reformer. Born in Brattleboro, Vermont, on September 3, 1811, Noyes graduated from Dartmouth College (1830) and studied at Andover Theological Seminary and Yale (1832–34). He preached that perfection was possible at his Putney, Vermont, Bible commune founded on free love doctrines (1837). Fleeing to Oneida, New York (1847), he adopted complex marriage, male continence, and eugenics policies. This was the most successful of the antebellum communes and inspired a branch in Wallingford, Connecticut (1850–80), but Noyes moved to Canada to avoid arrest (1879). He wrote *History of American Socialisms* (1870), *Scientific Propagation* (1873), and other radical works. Noyes reorganized the Oneida Community as a cooperative, later famous for manufacturing silver flatware, before the **Yankee** saint died in Niagara Falls, Ontario, on April 13, 1886.

NUTMEG STATE. A nickname for Connecticut, known officially as the **Constitution State**. This name refers to folklore about dishonest Connecticut peddlers who sold nutmegs carved from wood rather than the costly spice imported in the **China trade** from the East Indies. Ground nutmeg, the fruit of the tropical evergreen tree *(Myristica fragrans),* was used in colonial-era cooking and for punch.

NUTTING, WALLACE (1861–1941). Antiquarian photographer. Born in Marlborough, Massachusetts, on November 17, 1861, Nutting grew up in Maine, graduated from **Harvard** College (1883), and was a **Congregational** minister (1888). When he retired as a pastor in **Providence**, Rhode Island (1894–1902), he published his photographs of

New England landscapes, houses, and antiques in popular magazines. His Framingham, Massachusetts, studio employed 100 photographic print colorists (1912–25) and published influential books on colonial decorative arts. His factory also reproduced colonial furniture, and he restored the **Saugus Ironworks** (1916). Nutting's photographs, lectures, books, house tours, and furniture reproductions stimulated the **colonial revival** in American decorative arts. His antiques became the core of the **Wadsworth Atheneum** collection after his death on July 19, 1941.

– O –

O'BRIEN, HUGH (1827–1895). Mayor of **Boston**. Born in Ireland on July 13, 1827, O'Brien came to Boston (1832), left school at age 12 to work in a newspaper, and became a successful publisher. Self-educated in the public library, he was a Boston alderman (1875–83), and the first **Irish** mayor of Boston (1885–88) for four terms. He hired **Frederick Law Olmsted** to design the **Emerald Necklace** (1875) parklands and laid the cornerstone for the new **Boston Public Library** (1888). His election marked the end of the **Yankee** plutocracy and encouraged other Irish Catholic Democrats to seek public office. O'Brien, widely respected as an efficient and able administrator, died in Boston in 1895. A bust of O'Brien by John Donoghue was placed in the Boston Public Library he fostered.

OCEAN STATE. The nickname for Rhode Island, the smallest of the 50 states (1,214 sq mi). The name refers to its seacoast crowded with **fishing**, shipping, and U.S. Navy facilities and resorts noted for beach and boating recreation. Narragansett Bay is famous for sailing, and **Newport** was home to the America's Cup race (1930–83).

O'CONNELL, WILLIAM HENRY (1859–1944). Bishop. Born in **Lowell** on December 8, 1859, William H. O'Connell graduated from Boston College (1881) and the American College in Rome, where he was ordained (1884). He served as a parish priest in **Boston** (1886–95) and then as rector of the American College. He became bishop of **Portland**, Maine (1901–07), and was named archbishop of Boston (1907–44) and the first New England cardinal (1911). Cardinal O'Connell was both militant and modern in his administration, reorganizing Catholic charities and winning respect for the now dominant Catholic majority in New England, especially when he relocated archdiocesan offices to his Italian Renaissance residence adjacent to Boston College (1926). He was irreverently dubbed "Gangplank Bill" as a result of newspaper photographs showing the princely prelate disembarking from annual vacations in the Bahamas. When he died in Boston on April 22, 1944, Cardinal O'Connell oversaw one of the largest and most active Catholic communities in the nation. *See also* ANTI-CATHOLICISM.

O'CONNOR, EDWIN (1918–1968). Writer. Born on July 29, 1918, in **Providence**, Rhode Island, Edwin Greene O'Connor graduated from the University of Notre Dame (1939). After serving in the U.S. Coast Guard in **Boston** (1942–45), he was a journalist and radio announcer in **Hartford**, **Providence**, and Boston and an editor at the *Atlantic Monthly*. He wrote three novels exploring the history of **Irish** Catholics in Boston, including *The Edge of Sadness* (1961), for which he won a Pulitzer Prize, and *All in the Family* (1966). The career of Massachusetts governor **James Michael Curley** is the basis for his most successful novel, *The Last Hurrah* (1956). O'Connor died in Boston on March 23, 1968.

OLD CORNER BOOKSTORE. The oldest brick building in **Boston**, built (1712) as an apothecary shop on the site of **Anne Hutchinson**'s home. Timothy Carter opened the first bookshop (1829) that housed the publishing firm founded by **William Davis Ticknor** and **James T. Fields** (1832) and the office of the *Atlantic Monthly* magazine (1861) and the *North American Review* (1863). The bookstore became a literary mecca known as Parnassus Corner at School and Washington Streets on Boston's Newspaper Row. Historic Boston Inc. has operated the Old Corner Bookstore since 1960.

OLD HOME WEEK. A summer festival celebrating the history and tradition of New England towns by former residents who return for parades, pageants, picnics, bonfires, speeches, and family reunions. New Hampshire governor Frank W. Rollins developed Old Home Week in 1899, hoping summer visitors would promote **tourism**, historic preservation, and economic development. The custom spread quickly to other states and Canada and continues today.

OLD HOWARD. *See* HOWARD ATHENEUM.

OLD IRONSIDES. The nickname for the USS *Constitution* (1797), the oldest commissioned ship in the U.S. Navy. Built in **Boston** by the **New Bedford** shipwright George Claghorn, the frigate was intended for the Tripoli War. Docked in Charlestown at the **Boston National Historical Park**, it is a popular **tourist** site. *See also* HOLMES, OLIVER WENDELL.

OLD MAN OF THE MOUNTAIN. A natural rock ledge on Profile Mountain in Franconia Notch, New Hampshire. The craggy face of the **White Mountains**, noted by travelers since 1805 and celebrated by **Nathaniel Hawthorne** in *The Great Stone Face* (1850), is the symbol of New Hampshire and was a popular **tourist** attraction for many years. After a considerable amount of effort to keep it intact, however, the formation collapsed in May 2003.

OLD SOUTH MEETING HOUSE. Built in 1729 to replace the Cedar Meeting House. It was the church of **Phillis Wheatley** and **Benjamin Franklin**. It is best remembered as the site of tax protests that led to the **Boston Tea Party** in 1773. Plans to demolish the brick building on **Boston**'s Washington Street in 1876 prompted the first instance of successful historic preservation in New England. The Old South is a popular site on the **Freedom Trail** today.

OLD STATE HOUSE. The oldest surviving public building in **Boston**, designed (1713) as the headquarters of the **Massachusetts Bay Colony**. Built on the site of the first Boston Town House (1658), it contained a merchants exchange, the **Massachusetts General Court** (or legislature), the royal governor's council chamber, the Suffolk county courts, and the supreme judicial court. Official proclamations were read on the east end balcony, above the site of the **Boston Massacre**, and the legislature sat there (1780–98) until **Charles Bulfinch** completed the "new" **Massachusetts State House** on **Beacon Hill** (1798). It was the Boston City Hall (1830–41), and commercial property until preserved by the Bostonian Society (1881). Since 1974 the Old State House has been part of the **Boston National Historical Park**.

OLD STURBRIDGE VILLAGE. A living history museum established in Sturbridge, Massachusetts, by the Wells family (1946). An authentic recreation of a composite New England town, the village includes 40 exhibits staffed by well-trained interpreters who plow fields, make hay, shear sheep, stitch leather, bake traditional **Yankee** food, and explain 100,000 artifacts to visitors each day. The farms, shops, sawmill, houses, school, and church present the story of a rural town in the 1790–1840 period. Nonprofit, educational programs and agricultural exhibits are also offered.

OLMSTED, FREDERICK LAW (1822–1903). Landscape architect. Born in **Hartford**, Connecticut, on April 27, 1822, Olmsted studied engineering and scientific agriculture (1844–50). He designed Central Park (1858) in New York City as the "lungs of the city" and planned Brooklyn's Prospect Park, Philadelphia's Fairmount Park, the Stanford University campus, the Capitol grounds in Washington, D.C., and the **New Britain** park in Connecticut. His **Emerald Necklace** (1875) is a series of six public parks from **Boston Common** to the Franklin Park Zoo. He founded the profession of landscape **architecture** in the United States and was the foremost park maker. Olmsted established his office and home (1883) in Brookline, Massachusetts, where he retired (1895) until his death on August 28, 1903.

OLNEY, RICHARD (1835–1917). Public official. Born in Oxford, Massachusetts, on September 15, 1835, Olney studied at Brown University and graduated from **Harvard** Law School (1858). Practicing law in **Boston**, he served as a Democrat in the state legislature (1873) but had little success in politics. As U.S. attorney general (1893–95), his bias in favor of **railroad** corporations was obvious in the Pullman strike (1894). Olney became secretary of state (1895–97) and retired to his law firm in Boston, where he died on April 8, 1917.

OLSON, CHARLES (1910–1970). Poet. Born in **Worcester**, Massachusetts, on December 27, 1910, Charles John Olson graduated from Wesleyan University (1932) and studied at **Harvard University** (1933–39). A leading avant-garde poet and literary theorist, he was an influential teacher at Black Mountain College (1948–57) and the State University of New York at Buffalo (1963–65). His prose works include *Call Me Ishmael* (1947) and *The Special View of History* (1957), but he is best remembered for the three volumes of poetry set in **Cape Ann**, *The Maximus Poems* (1960, 1968, 1975). Olson died in New York City on January 10, 1970.

ONASSIS, JACQUELINE KENNEDY. *See* KENNEDY, JACQUELINE LEE BOUVIER.

O'NEILL, EUGENE (1888–1953). Playwright. Born in New York City on October 16, 1888, Eugene Gladstone O'Neill grew up in the theater as the son of an actor. His family lived in New London, Connecticut, and he studied at Princeton University (1906–07) and worked as a merchant seaman, longshoreman, and then a reporter in New London. After he studied at **Harvard University**'s 47 Workshop (1914–15), the **Provincetown Players** produced his first play (1916). His successful plays in New York included *Long Voyage Home* (1917) and *Beyond the Horizon* (1920), which won the first of his four Pulitzer prizes. O'Neill set new standards for American drama in his long career and was the first American playwright to receive the Nobel Prize for Literature (1936). He died in **Boston** on November 27, 1953.

O'NEILL, THOMAS P. (1912–1994). Speaker of the House. Born in Cambridge, Massachusetts, on December 9, 1912, Thomas Phillip O'Neill, Jr., graduated from Boston College (1936). He served in the state legislature (1936–52) and was the first Democrat and first Catholic elected speaker of the house (1949–52) in Massachusetts. Elected to the House of Representatives (1953–87), Tip O'Neill's career as an urban New Deal Democrat was shaped by the minority status of **Irish** Catholics in Massachusetts, by the Great Depression, and by the moderate ideology of his party. As Speaker of the House (1977–87), he broke with President Lyndon B. Johnson to oppose the Vietnam War (1967) and adroitly resisted the rise of neo-conservatism during President Ronald Reagan's administration. When O'Neill retired to **Cape Cod** (1987), he was the most popular, effective, and accomplished Speaker in 40 years. He wrote his memoirs, *Man of the House* (1987), and died in **Boston** on January 5, 1994.

OPIUM TRADE. Part of the New England **China trade** from the first. The British East India Company ships in the **Boston Tea Party** carried opium from India as part of the cargo. Like many New England merchants, **Thomas H. Perkins** imported opium (1816) as well as tea, porcelain, and textiles from Asia to Boston. **Fitz Hugh Lane** painted the *Brig Antelope in Boston Harbor* (1863), showing a ship built by **Robert Bennet Forbes** in **Boston** to import opium from India and Turkey to China and the United States. Although physicians used opium as a painkiller, by 1871 the Massachusetts State Board of Health annual report warned of the opium addiction in many New England cities.

O'REILLY, JOHN BOYLE (1844–1890). Poet and editor. Born in Ireland on June 24, 1844, O'Reilly, a printer who joined the British army (1863–66), was sentenced to the Australian penal colony by a Dublin court martial for his role in a Fenian conspiracy. O'Reilly escaped to **Boston** on a **New Bedford** whaler (1869) and became editor of the *Boston Pilot* (1870–76) and proprietor of this weekly **Irish** Catholic newspaper (1876–90). His poetry collections, *Songs from the Southern Seas* (1873) and *Songs, Legends and Ballads* (1878) established his reputation as a man of letters at home in Hibernian and **Boston Brahmin** literary circles. O'Reilly bridged the **Yankee** Protestant and Irish Catholic communities and was an influential leader of the new multicultural Boston when he died on August 10, 1890. A memorial on the **Fenway** by **Daniel Chester French** (1896) commemorates his memory.

ORR, BOBBY (1948–). Athlete. Born in Parry Sound, Ontario, on March 20, 1948, Robert Gordon Orr was an outstanding defenseman for the **Boston Bruins** National Hockey League (NHL) team (1966–76) and the Chicago Black Hawks (1976–79). His speed, creativity, grace, and puck-handling skills revitalized his team and changed the nature of professional hockey, winning the Stanley Cup championship with the Bruins (1970, 1972). He won eight consecutive Norris trophies (1968–75) as the best defenseman and three Hart trophies as the NHL most valuable player (1970–72) and set records for goals and assists. When Orr retired on January 9, 1979, at the **Boston Garden** arena, the "great Number Four" was a New England hero and sports legend. Orr was the youngest player elected to the Hockey Hall of Fame (1979) and began a banking and philanthropic career in Massachusetts.

O'SULLIVAN, MARY KENNEY (1864–1943). Labor organizer. Born in Hannibal, Missouri, on January 8, 1864, Mary Kenney left school at age 14 and became a bookbinder. She moved to Chicago (1888) to organize women in the printing trades and was the first salaried organizer for the American Federation of Labor (AFL) in 1892 in New York City. After marrying John O'Sullivan, a *Boston Globe* labor editor (1893), they lived in a **Boston** settlement house while organizing shoe, rubber, garment, and laundry workers. She founded the National Women's Trade Union League (1903) to promote minimum wage laws and trade unionism and was a leader of Massachusetts reform movements for woman suffrage, prohibition, pacifism, housing, and child labor laws. When Massachusetts passed a factory inspection law, Mary Kenney O'Sullivan was one of the inspectors for 20 years. She died in Medford, Massachusetts, on January 18, 1943.

OTIS, ELISHA GRAVES (1811–1861). Inventor. Born in Halifax, Vermont, Otis was building a factory in Yonkers, New York, when he invented a mechanical elevator with a new safety device (1852). When New York City firms asked for the new freight elevator, Otis manufactured them in Yonkers and demonstrated its safety at the American Institute Fair (1854). He installed the first passenger elevator in New York City (1857), causing a revolution in **architecture**. Otis patented his steam elevator (1861) which made the skyscraper practical, before he died in Yonkers on April 8, 1861.

OTIS, HARRISON GRAY (1765–1848). Mayor of **Boston**. Born in Boston on October 8, 1765, Otis graduated from **Harvard** College (1783). He practiced law in Boston (1786–96), and served in the legislature (1794–96, 1802–17). Otis was the U.S. attorney for Massachusetts (1796–97, 1801–02), and a **Federalist** in the House of Representatives (1797–1801), and the Senate (1817–22). He was a delegate to the **Hartford Convention** and lived in three mansions designed by **Charles Bullfinch**. Otis was the third mayor of Boston (1829–32) and died in Boston on October 28, 1848.

OTIS, JAMES (1725–1783). Public Official. Born in West Barnstable, Massachusetts, on February 5, 1725, Otis graduated from **Harvard** College (1743). He practiced law in **Boston** and was advocate general of the vice-admiralty court until he resigned to defend Boston merchants against the **writs of assistance** (1760). Using natural law and common law, he opposed the writs, the **Navigation Acts** (1761), and the **Stamp Act** (1765). Otis served in the legislature (1762–69) as the leading patriot famous for his fiery oratory and political pamphlets opposing unconstitutional parliamentary government. Mentally unstable after a scuffle with a royal officer in a **tavern**, his public career ended (1769) and Otis died in Andover, Massachusetts, on May 23, 1783.

OUIMET, FRANCIS (1893–1967). Athlete. Born in Brookline, Massachusetts, on May 8, 1893, Ouimet was a caddie at the Country Club in Brookline who won the 1913 U.S. Open tournament in golf's greatest upset, ending the British domination of the sport. He was the first amateur to win the U.S. Open, and his success drew new players to the sport. He won the U.S. Amateur Championship (1914, 1931) and the Walker Cup eight times. Elected to golf's Hall of Fame (1944), his statue on the first tee of the Brookline course honors his victory, and a postage stamp was issued in his honor. Ouimet was a stockbroker and a golf champion in his long amateur career before he died on September 3, 1967.

OVERSEERS OF THE POOR. Town **selectmen** responsible for public welfare. This included binding out orphan or bastard children and the insane, indigent, and elderly. Those "going on the town" were sometimes "auctioned off" at the **town meeting** to any householder who bid lowest for their care. The town paid householders to care for these paupers, and the overseers supervised the care provided. Nonresident paupers or vagabonds were **warned out** of town by the constable and ordered to return to the town where they were born to receive public welfare. By 1760 many towns also built an almshouse or workhouse and the 1880s the town welfare department replaced the overseers.

OWEN, MARIBEL YERXA VINSON (1911–1961). Athlete. Born in Winchester, Massachusetts, on October 12, 1911, Owen graduated from Radcliffe College (1933). The daughter of a competitive skater, she won her first championship at the Cambridge Skating Club (1922), and won nine U.S. ladies' senior single championship titles (1928–33), and three others (1935–37). She competed in the Olympic Games (1928, 1936) and won the silver medal at the World Championships (1929) and the bronze medal (1930). Owen became a professional skater (1937), coached her daughters and **Tenley Albright** to championships, and was a sportswriter for the *New York Times* (1933). Owen died in Belgium on February 15, 1961, en route to the World Figure Skating Championships in Prague. She was elected to the U.S. Figure Skating Association Hall of Fame (1976).

– P –

PAINE, JOHN KNOWLES (1839–1906). Composer. Born in **Portland**, Maine, on January 9, 1839, Paine studied music in Europe (1858–61) and was an organist in **Boston** (1861). He was the nation's first professor of music at **Harvard University** (1862–1900) and a pioneer in music as an academic discipline. Paine was the first American composer of an oratorio (*St. Peter*, 1872), a symphony (*Second Symphony*, 1880), choral works, an opera, chamber music, songs, and piano pieces. Paine died in Cambridge on April 25, 1906.

PAINE, ROBERT TREAT (1731–1814). Congressman from Massachusetts. Born in **Boston** on March 11, 1731, Paine graduated from **Harvard** College (1749), studied theology, and practiced law in **Portland**, Maine, and **Taunton**, Massachusetts (1757–70). He was a delegate to the Continental Congress (1774–76), where he signed the Declaration of Independence and served in the state legislature (1777). Paine was the state's first attorney general (1777–90), having prosecuted the British troops in the **Boston Massacre** case, and was active in suppressing **Shays's Rebellion**. He was a state supreme court justice (1790–1804) and died in Boston on May 11, 1814.

PALEO-INDIANS (9000–7000 B.C.). Migrated from the north and west to New England as the Wisconsin glaciers, the last of the region's Pleistocene glaciers, melted and the tundra grassland developed into conifer forests with the caribou and mastodon. Archaeological evidence, for example at the Bull Brook site in Ipswich, Massachusetts, shows these ancient **Native Americans** traveled seasonally in groups of 30 people but sometimes gathered in groups as large as 200 people to trade or marry. As the climate warmed and the deciduous hardwood forests spread, the Archaic Period Indians (7000–500 B.C.) migrated into New England, replacing or intermarrying with the Paleo-Indians.

PALMER, NATHANIEL BROWN (1799–1877). Explorer. Born in Stonington, Connecticut, on August 8, 1799, Palmer went to sea (1813) as a sailor on a blockade runner in the War of 1812. As captain of the schooner *Galina* (1818) he hunted seals in the South Seas, and on the sloop *Hero* he explored the western Antarctica coast (1819–20), which is named for him, Palmer Land. Captain Palmer later designed ships for the **China trade** and died in San Francisco on June 21, 1877. His house is now the Stonington Historical Society.

PAPER. An important product in New England since Norwich, Connecticut, opened the state's first paper mill (1766). The Dexter Paper Company in Windsor Locks, Connecticut (1769), is the oldest company listed on the New York Stock Exchange. In Massachusetts, a paper mill opened on the Neponset River in the Hyde Park section of **Boston**

(1773) that is the oldest continuously operated paper-manufacturing site in the nation. Zenas Crane founded the Crane Company in Dalton (1801) using rags to manufacture the first bond paper (1850) and the paper for U.S. currency. The Holyoke Paper Company (1857) was the first of seven new paper mills that named the city of **Holyoke** as the **Paper City** (1880), dominating the paper industry in the United States until 1950. **Irish**, **German**, **French-Canadian**, and **Polish immigrants** provided 1,900 workers by 1880 for these water-powered paper mills using wood-pulp and rag-scrap from nearby cotton mills. Alvah Crocker (1801–74) established a large paper company in Fitchburg. **Worcester** began envelope production in Massachusetts when Russell Hawes invented new paper machines (1852).

In New Hampshire the Brown Company in Berlin is one of the largest paper mills in the world, and Hinsdale is also a center of paper production. Millions of acres of New Hampshire pine and spruce trees were harvested by **Yankee** and French-Canadian woodsmen to make paper, floating the logs down the Androscoggin River to Berlin by 1821. In Maine the Samuel Dennis Warren Company employed workers in three 8-hour shifts at papermills in Westbrook, Yarmouth, and Gardiner (1887). When the Great Northern Paper Company built a dam on the Penobscot River (1907), East Millinocket, Maine, became a major paper production center. Hugh Chisholm (1847–1912) merged small firms as the International Paper Company (1897) with 20 sites in Maine, Massachusetts, New Hampshire, Vermont, and New York. This became the world's largest manufacturer of paper and paper production continues today.

PARKER HOUSE. The oldest continuously operating hotel in the nation was founded in **Boston** (1855) by Harvey D. Parker. Its chefs created the Boston cream pie, the Parker House dinner rolls, and **scrod**. The hotel was the first in the country to serve à la carte meals all day and had the first hot running water and elevator in New England. It was the meeting place in the 1850s for the Saturday Club, a monthly gathering of prominent men of letters, including **Ralph Waldo Emerson**, **Nathaniel Hawthorne**, **Oliver Wendell Holmes**, **Henry Wadsworth Longfellow**, **James Russell Lowell**, **John Greenleaf Whittier**, and others. Charles Dickens first read *A Christmas Carol* (1843) to an audience at the hotel, and **John F. Kennedy** launched his political career there.

PARKER, GEORGE SWINNERTON (1866–1952). Manufacturer. Born in **Salem**, Massachusetts, on December 12, 1866, George S. Parker invented his first board game in 1883. The Parker Brothers Company produced over 30 popular games by 1888. Parker's *Monopoly* game (1934) saved his declining Massachusetts firm, selling 2 million games in two years. Parker died in **Boston** on September 26, 1952, and his company merged with General Mills Corporation (1968) and then with Hasbro, Inc., in Pawtucket, Rhode Island (1991).

PARKER, ISAAC (1768–1830). Lawyer. Born in **Boston** on June 17, 1768, Parker graduated from **Harvard** College (1786) and practiced law in Castine, Maine (1787–97). Elected to the House of Representatives as a **Federalist** (1797–99), he was U.S. marshal for Maine (1799–1803) and was a Massachusetts Supreme Judicial Court justice (1806–30) and chief justice (1814–30). Parker is best remembered as the founder of the Harvard Law School (1817), where he taught (1815–27) and was a Harvard overseer. Parker was president of the state constitutional convention (1820) and died in Boston on July 25, 1830.

PARKER, ROBERT B. (1932–). Writer. Born in Springfield, Massachusetts, in 1932, Robert Brown Parker graduated from Colby College (1954) and served in the U.S. Army in Korea. He earned his doctorate in English at Boston University (1971) and taught at Northeastern University (1971–79). Parker wrote a series of 30 detective novels set in **Boston**. The ABC television series (1985–88) *Spenser for Hire* was based on this detective saga. Parker won the Edgar Allan Poe Award (1976) for *Promised Land*.

PARKER, THEODORE (1810–1860). Reformer. Born in Lexington, Massachusetts, on August 24, 1810, Parker graduated from **Harvard** Divinity School (1836). He was a **Unitarian** minister in West Roxbury closely associated with the **Transcendentalists**. Parker resigned his pulpit (1845) but attracted large numbers to his 28th **Congregational** Society in **Boston** (1845–57). He was influential in many reform movements, especially **John Brown**'s violent **abolitionism**. Parker's health failed, and he died in Italy on May 10, 1860.

PARKMAN, FRANCIS (1823–1893). Historian. Born in **Boston** on September 16, 1823, Parkman graduated from **Harvard** College (1846). His journey on the Great Plains became the subject of a popular book, *The Oregon Trail* (1849), but he is best known as the author of *France and England in the New World* (8 volumes, 1865–84). Parkman established new standards for historical scholarship based on archival research and vivid prose. He was professor of horticulture at Harvard (1871) but was primarily a **Boston Brahmin** gentleman scholar until he died at his **Beacon Hill** home on November 8, 1893.

PARSONS, THEOPHILUS (1750–1813). Lawyer and judge. Born in Byfield, Massachusetts, in 1750, Parsons graduated from **Harvard** College (1769). He practiced law (1774–1806) and was a leading member of the **Essex Junto**. He wrote *The Essex Result* (1778) that **John Adams** used to draft the new state constitution (1780) and promoted ratification of the U.S. Constitution (1788). Parsons was chief justice of the Massachusetts Supreme Judicial Court (1806–13) and a conservative leader in the **Federalist Party** until he died in **Boston** on October 30, 1813.

PASSAMAQUODDY. An **Algonquian**-speaking **Native American** people in coastal Maine in the **Abenaki** confederacy. They hunted, fished, and lived in conical wigwams in palisaded villages as French allies until Maine was settled by Massachusetts **Puritans** (1652). They supported the Americans in the Revolution but lost much of their land by 1794. Some Passamaquoddy men served in the **Civil War** and were known for their fine basketmaking. Their population was reduced to 1,500 people by 1970 when the tribe joined the **Penobscot** and **Malecite** in a lawsuit against the state of Maine (1977–80) and used the $81 million settlement to purchase land and for business investments. The tribe sends a representative to the Maine legislature from two reservations.

PASTORE, JOHN ORLANDO (1907–2000). Senator from Rhode Island. Born in **Providence** on March 17, 1907, Pastore graduated from Northeastern University Law School (1931) and practiced law in Providence (1932–37). He was a Democrat in the state legislature (1935–37), assistant attorney general (1937–38, 1940–44), and lieutenant governor (1945). Pastore became governor when J. Howard McGrath resigned and was the first **Italian-American** elected governor in the country (1946–50) and to the U.S. Senate (1950–76). No one in Rhode Island history dominated state politics as long as Pastore, and in the Senate he was influential in ratification of the Limited Nuclear Test Ban Treaty (1963) and the Nuclear Non-Proliferation Treaty (1969) and was the conscience of the television industry as chair of the Senate Communications Subcommittee. Pastore retired (1977) to Cranston until his death on July 15, 2000.

PATRIOTS DAY. State holiday in Massachusetts and Maine since 1894 to commemorate the start of the **American Revolution** on April 19, 1775, with the **Battle of Lexington and Concord**. It is celebrated by parades, pageantry, and reenactments of **Paul Revere**'s ride. Massachusetts named the holiday in 1938 and moved it to the third Monday in April in 1968. It now coincides with the **Boston Marathon**. *See also* FAST DAY.

PATTERSON, JAMES WILLIS (1823–1893). Senator from New Hampshire. Born in Henniker, New Hampshire, on July 2, 1823, Patterson graduated from Dartmouth College (1848) and studied at the Theological Seminary in **New Haven**. He was a professor of mathematics at Dartmouth (1854–65), served in the state legislature, and was a Republican in the House of Representatives (1863–67) and Senate (1867–73). Patterson's reputation was damaged by his role with **Oakes Ames** in the Credit Mobilier **railroad** scandal (1872). He returned to the state legislature (1877–78) and was state superintendent of public instruction until his death in Hanover on May 4, 1893.

PEABODY, ELIZABETH PALMER (1804–1894). Educator. Born in Billerica, Massachusetts, on May 16, 1804, Elizabeth Palmer Peabody was secretary to **William Ellery Channing** and taught in **Bronson Alcott**'s school (1834–36) in **Boston**. She was active in **Salem** literary and reform movements as the sister-in-law of **Nathaniel Hawthorne** and **Horace Mann**. Her bookshop in Boston became a **Transcendentalist** center (1839–44), but Miss Peabody supported herself as a writer, lecturer, and the nation's first female publisher. She is best recalled for introducing progressive **German kindergartens** to Boston (1860), where she died on January 3, 1894. A **West End** settlement house in 1896 was named in her honor.

PEABODY, ENDICOTT (1857–1944). Educator. Born in **Salem**, Massachusetts, on May 30, 1857, Peabody studied at a public school in England, Cambridge University, and the Episcopal Divinity School. Ordained an Episcopal priest (1884), he founded Groton School, an elite **prep school** for boys in Groton, Massachusetts (1884). As headmaster (1884–1940), Dr. Peabody was the influential teacher of many prominent men until he died at Groton School on November 17, 1944.

PEABODY, ENDICOTT (1920–1987). Governor of Massachusetts. Born in Lawrence on February 15, 1920, Peabody graduated from **Harvard**

University (1942) and Harvard Law School (1948). After serving in the U.S. Navy (1942–46), he was a Democrat on the Governor's Council (1954–56) and governor (1963–65). Chub Peabody was an unsuccessful candidate for the Senate (1966), practiced law in **Boston**, and retired to New Hampshire, where he died on December 1, 1987.

PEABODY ESSEX MUSEUM. America's longest operating museum founded (1799) as the East India Marine Society by merchants and shipmasters, who collected 2 million documents and **art** objects from Africa, Asia, the Pacific Islands, and New England to study and display in **Salem**, Massachusetts. The society merged (1992) with the Peabody Academy of Science and the **China Trade** Museum. Its collections include 50,000 marine paintings, drawings, and prints, representing 300 years of New England decorative art, folk art, and costume, as well as the Phillips Library historic research archives. Today the National Park Service maritime history district surrounds the museum on the Salem waterfront.

PEIRCE, CHARLES SANDERS (1839–1914). Scientist. Born in Cambridge, Massachusetts, on September 10, 1839, the son of a **Harvard** College mathematics professor, Saunders graduated from Harvard (1859). He worked with the U.S. Coast Survey (1859–91) as a mathematician and taught at Harvard (1864–70) and Johns Hopkins University (1879–84). Best known as a founder of pragmatism with **William James**, Peirce wrote *Photometric Researches* (1878) and died in Milford, Pennsylvania, on April 19, 1914.

PELL, CLAIBORNE (1918–). Senator from Rhode Island. Born in New York City on November 22, 1918, Pell graduated from Princeton University (1940) and Columbia University (1946). He served in the U.S. Coast Guard (1941–45) and was a State Department officer in Europe (1945–52). Pell was a Democratic senator (1961–97), best remembered for writing the bill creating the National Foundation for the Arts and Humanities. He was later the U.S. delegate to the United Nations (1997).

PENDER, PAUL (1930–2003). Athlete. Born in Brookline, Massachusetts, on June 20, 1930, Paul Pender was the New England amateur welterweight champion when he became a professional boxer (1949). Fighting in the 1950s golden age of boxing, the Brookline firefighter retired (1953) to serve in the U.S. Marine Corps but returned to the ring in 1954.

Pender twice defeated the legendary Sugar Ray Robinson for the middleweight world championship (1960 and 1962). Known as a thinking man's fighter who used the European style to outbox his opponents, his record was 40–6–2 when he retired as champion (1963). He later graduated from Boston State College and was a coach at a Massachusetts prison and the University of Massachusetts in **Boston**. The often-overlooked champ died in Bedford on January 12, 2003.

PENNACOOK. An **Algonquian**-speaking **Native American** people living in northeastern Massachusetts, New Hampshire, eastern Vermont, and Maine. Like other New England tribes, they hunted; fished; cultivated **corn**, beans, and squash; and were semi-sedentary. When **Puritans** founded the town of Chelmsford on their land along the Merrimack and Concord Rivers (1655), some conflict developed, although the *sachem* Passaconaway swore allegiance to the English (1644). During **King Philip's War** (1675), they moved to New Hampshire and their *sachem,* Wannalancit, sold their tribal lands to Chelmsford (1686). When smallpox and other European diseases killed half of the Pennacook population (1600–74), the 1,200 survivors moved to Canada and New York. Led by Kancamagus, the Pennacook raided Dover, New Hampshire (1689), to retaliate against the enslavement of 200 of their people (1676). They allied with the French (1690s) before migrating with the **Abenaki** to Quebec. The tribe numbered about 1,400 people in 1990. The city of **Lowell** was built on Pennacook land (1824).

PENOBSCOT. An **Algonquian**-speaking **Native American** people living in coastal Maine along the Penobscot River who joined the **Abenaki** confederacy. They encountered the English explorer **David Ingram**, who described the Penobscot land as the mythical city of **Norumbega** (1569), and **Martin Pring** (1603) and **Samuel de Champlain** (1604). After French **Jesuit** missionaries converted some Penobscot (1688), they were allies against the British. Their treaty with Britain (1749) permitted them to remain in Maine when most Indians in the Abenaki confederacy moved to Canada. Louis Francis Sockalexis (1871–1913), a Penobscot from Old Town, was the first Native American to play major league baseball as an outfielder for the Cleveland Nationals (1897–99). Penobscots often sold handcrafted baskets to **tourists** at **Bar Harbor** in the 1890s. Today the Penobscot send a representative to the Maine legislature and settled a lawsuit against the state for $81.5 million (1980) to recover lands lost in a 1794 treaty with Massachusetts. Today 500 of the 2,000 members of the tribe live on Indian Island in Old Town, Maine.

PEP, WILLIE (1922–). Athlete. Born in Middletown, Connecticut, on September 19, 1922, Guiglermo Papelo was the world featherweight boxing champion. Dubbed the "Will o' the Wisp" because of his dazzling footwork and speed, he boxed as Willie Pep (1940–66), winning 230 of 242 bouts, with 1 draw, 11 losses, and 65 knockouts. He was undefeated in his first 54 bouts and became the youngest featherweight champion (1942–50). Pep, who began his career as state amateur champion (1938), served in the U.S. Navy in World War II. He is considered New England's greatest fighter from the lighter weight divisions. Pep retired to Connecticut (1966) and was elected to the International Boxing Hall of Fame (1990).

PEPPERIDGE FARM. Company that began with a **Yankee** bread-baking recipe on the Fairfield, Connecticut, farm of Margaret Fogarty Rudkin (1898–1967). When her healthy bread attracted local interest, Mrs. Rudkin opened a bakery in Norwalk (1947) that grew into a national firm famous for New England–style bread and cookies. The popular *Margaret Rudkin Pepperidge Farm Cookbook* (1963) and an advertising campaign (1958–70) featuring a flinty New England character, Titus Moody, driving a horse-drawn bakery wagon, contributed to the firm's success.

PEPPERRELL, SIR WILLIAM (1696–1759). Soldier. Born on June 27, 1696, in Kittery, Maine, Pepperrell was the richest merchant and shipbuilder in New England. He was a colonel in the Maine militia and served in the Massachusetts legislature and the governor's council (1726–29). Pepperrell commanded the New England forces that captured the French fortress at Louisbourg in Nova Scotia (1745). For this victory he was made a baronet (1746), a title never before awarded to an American. During the **French and Indian War** (1756–63), he was the general commanding all troops in Massachusetts. Pepperrell, painted by **John Smibert**, was chief justice of Massachusetts (1730–59) and died in Kittery on July 6, 1759.

PEQUOT. An **Algonquin** name (meaning destroyers) for the 8,000 **Native American** people living in Connecticut and Rhode Island in 1620. A smallpox epidemic (1634) reduced the tribe to 3,000 people, who continued to trade with the Dutch despite their treaty with the **Massachusetts Bay Colony**. When the **Pequot War** broke out (1637–38), **John Mason** led the Connecticut and Massachusetts militia with **Mohegan** and **Narragansett** allies. They killed half of the warriors and 500 Pequot died in a battle at Mystic, Connecticut. The **Puritans** sold the survivors as slaves in the West Indies and made servants of the women and children. Once dominant in Connecticut, the surviving Pequots in Mystic took refuge with the Mohegans (1637) but were so badly treated that the Puritans settled them on two reservations (1666 and 1683).

William Apes, a Pequot born in Colrain, Massachusetts, was a Methodist minister who defended the Native Americans on **Cape Ann** (1833) and wrote four books about them. There were only 140 Pequots in New England by 1762 and about 320 when they opened the successful Foxwoods Casino (1992) on their Ledyard, Connecticut, reservation. The Mashantucket Pequot Museum (1998) in Ledyard preserves their culture.

PEQUOT WAR. *See* PEQUOT.

PERKINS, FRANCES (1880–1965). Public official. Born in **Boston** on April 10, 1880, Frances Perkins was raised in **Worcester** and graduated from Mt. Holyoke College (1902). After teaching and working as a social worker, she earned a master's degree in social economics at Columbia University (1910) and was director of the Consumers' League of New York (1910–12) and the New York State Industrial Commission (1919–33). President Franklin D. Roosevelt named her secretary of labor (1933–45), the first woman in a cabinet position. Perkins was a member of the U.S. Civil Service Commission (1946–63), taught at Cornell University (1957–65), and died in New York City on May 14, 1965.

PERKINS, THOMAS HANDASYD (1764–1854). Merchant and philanthropist. Born in **Boston** on December 15, 1764, Thomas H. Perkins grew up amid the sights and sounds of the **Boston Massacre** and the **American Revolution**. Prevented from entering **Harvard** College by the war, he apprenticed in a Boston countinghouse and by 1786 engaged in the lucrative **West Indies trade** with his brother, James. The J. & T. H. Perkins firm was among the first to send ships from Boston to the Dutch East Indies and China, opening the profitable **China trade** (1789) and the **Opium trade** (1816). Economic growth, philanthropy, and civic improvements by Perkins and other antebellum merchants dubbed Boston the **Hub of the Solar System** and the **Athens of America**. Colonel Perkins was a leader of the state militia, a **Federalist Party** state senator, a delegate to the **Hartford Convention**, and a pioneer in **Lowell textile** factories, the United States Bank, and the Quincy granite quarry

railroad. He founded a Boston fire-fighting company and the **Massachusetts General Hospital** and promoted the **Bunker Hill** Monument, modern landscaping, and private art collections. He died in Boston on January 11, 1854, and the Perkins School for Blind Children (1832) was named in his honor. A portrait of Perkins by Thomas Sully hangs in the **Boston Atheneum** he founded.

PERRY, LILLA CABOT (1848–1933). Artist. Born in **Boston** on January 13, 1848, Lilla Cabot was educated at elite private schools and studied **art** in Boston and France (1880s). She married Thomas Sargeant Perry (1874) but did not paint professionally until 1884. Living near Claude Monet in France each summer (1889–1907), Perry became a leading American impressionist and introduced Monet's art to Boston (1889). While her husband taught literature in Tokyo (1898–1901), Perry introduced impressionism to Japan. Returning to Boston's **Back Bay**, Perry blended several cultures and was known for her portraits of **Boston Brahmin** women (*The Trio, Alice, Edith and Margaret Perry*, 1898) and her landscapes. She died in Hancock, New Hampshire, in 1933.

PERRY, MATTHEW CALBRAITH (1794–1858). U.S. Navy officer. Born in South Kingston, Rhode Island on April 10, 1794, Perry was the brother of **Oliver Hazard Perry** and joined the U.S. Navy in 1809, serving in the War of 1812 and the war with the Tripoli pirates. He reformed the system to train seamen and the curriculum at the U.S. Naval Academy in Annapolis. Commanding the navy's first steamship, he introduced gunnery schools (1839), suppressed the African slave trade, and served with distinction in the war with Mexico (1846–47). He is best remembered for his diplomacy compelling Japan to end its isolationism by signing a treaty with the United States (1854). Commodore Perry died in New York City on March 4, 1858.

PERRY, OLIVER HAZARD (1785–1819). U.S. Navy officer. Born in South Kingston, Rhode Island, on August 23, 1785, Perry, the brother of **Matthew C. Perry**, joined the U.S. Navy (1799–1819) and served in the Quasi-War with France (1798–1800), the Tripolitan War (1802–06), and the War of 1812. His victory over the British fleet in the Battle of Lake Erie (1813) made him a national hero. Captain Perry died in service at Trinidad on August 23, 1819.

PETERS, ANDREW JAMES (1872–1938). Mayor of **Boston**. Born in Boston on April 3, 1872, Peters graduated from **Harvard University**

(1895) and Harvard Law School (1898). He practiced law in Boston (1898–1907) and served as a Democratic state legislator (1902–07) and in the House of Representatives (1907–15). He was an assistant secretary of the treasury (1914–17), mayor of Boston (1918–22), and president of the Boston Chamber of Commerce (1926–28). Peters, best remembered as the **Yankee** Democratic mayor during the **Boston Police Strike**, died in Boston on June 26, 1938.

PHILLIPS, WENDELL (1811–1884). Social reformer. Born in **Boston** on November 29, 1811, Phillips, the son of Boston's first mayor, John Phillips, graduated from **Boston Latin School**, **Harvard** College (1831), and Harvard Law School (1834). He abandoned his law practice (1836) to speak across the nation for **abolitionism**, prohibition, woman suffrage, penal reform, labor unions, and other reforms. Allied with **William Lloyd Garrison**, Phillips was an eloquent and witty orator known as "abolitionism's golden trumpet," until the radical **Boston Brahmin** died in Boston on February 2, 1884. A statue of Phillips by **Daniel Chester French** was placed on the **Boston Public Garden** in 1915.

PHIPS, SIR WILLIAM (1651–1695). Governor of Massachusetts. Born in Woolwich, Maine, on February 2, 1651, Phips settled in **Boston** as a shipbuilder. He became one of the colony's wealthiest citizens (1686) by recovering sunken Spanish treasure ships in the Caribbean. Knighted (1697) through the patronage of his London partners, the rough-hewn sea captain commanded the Massachusetts expedition that captured Port Royal in **King William's War** (1690). Phips was appointed the first royal governor of Massachusetts (1691–95), and with **Increase Mather** he ended the **Salem witchcraft trials**. Conflict with the legislature led to his recall to London, where he died on February 18, 1695.

PICKERING, TIMOTHY (1745–1829). Senator from Massachusetts. Born in **Salem**, Massachusetts, on July 17, 1745, Pickering graduated from **Harvard** College (1763). He practiced law in Salem (1768–77) and was a member of the **Committee of Correspondence** (1774–75) and a state legislator (1776). He served as quartermaster general of the U.S. Army (1780–90), postmaster general (1791–95), secretary of war (1795), and secretary of state (1795–1800). When President **John Adams** dismissed him, Pickering became a judge in Massachusetts until elected to the Senate as a **Federalist** (1803–11) and to the House of Representatives

(1813–17) as an opponent of the War of 1812. Pickering died in Salem on January 29, 1829.

PIERCE, FRANKLIN (1804–1869). President of the United States. Born in Hillsborough, New Hampshire, on November 23, 1804, Franklin Pierce graduated from Bowdoin College (1824) and was admitted to the bar in 1827. He served as a Democrat in the state legislature (1829–33) and in the House of Representatives (1833–37) and Senate (1837–42). During the war with Mexico, Pierce was a brigadier general. Elected president as a dark horse or compromise candidate (1852), his adminis- tration (1853–57) failed to maintain harmony between the Northern and Southern Democrats on the issue of **slavery**. Not renominated by his party in 1856, Pierce opposed President Abraham Lincoln's conduct of the **Civil War**. He returned to practice law in **Concord**, New Hampshire, where he died on October 8, 1869. *See also* CUSHING, CALEB.

PIERCE, JANE (1806–1863). First lady of the United States. Born in New Hampshire on March 12, 1806, Jane Means Appleton married **Franklin Pierce** (1834). Uninterested in politics, she encouraged Pierce to retire from the U.S. Senate (1842) and live in **Concord**, New Hamp- shire, as a lawyer. She was so depressed by poor health and the death of her son Benny in a **railroad** accident (1853) that President Pierce did not hold an inaugural ball. Mrs. Pierce could meet few of her social obliga- tions as first lady (1853–57) and died in **Concord** on December 2, 1863.

PIERPONT, JAMES L. (1822–1893). Musician. Born in Medford, Mass- achusetts, the son of the town's abolitionist **Unitarian** minister, Pierpont wrote many songs, the most famous of which was *Jingle Bells* (1857). While living in Savannah, Georgia, Pierpont served in the Confederate Army (1861–65) and died in poverty in Florida before his song became a popular Christmas classic. His nephew was the financier **J. Pierpont Morgan**.

PIERSALL, JAMES (1929–). Athlete. Born in **Waterbury**, Connecti- cut, on November 14, 1929, Jimmy Piersall played baseball for the **Boston Red Sox** (1948–58). He was voted an all-star team rightfielder (1954, 1956) and won the Gold Glove award (1958, 1961). Despite hospitalization for mental illness (1952), he resumed his professional career with Boston, Cleveland, Washington, Los Angeles, and the New York Mets. His autobiography, *Fear Strikes Out* (1955), was the basis of a film (1957) by the same title. Piersall was a colorful and controversial player until 1967 and was a coach, manager, and sports broadcaster.

PILGRIMS (OR SEPARATISTS). The first colonists in New England, a dissenting Protestant group who favored separation from the Church of England. After 10 years of exile in Holland, the Pilgrims obtained a patent from the London Company to settle in America. Sailing on the *Mayflower* they landed on **Cape Cod** and settled on December 21, 1620, in **Plymouth**, Massachusetts, governed by their own **Mayflower Compact**. Half of the 102 colonists died the first winter from malnutrition and disease but aided by friendly **Native Americans**, **Squanto**, **Samoset**, and **Massasoit**, they learned to adapt to the new environment under governors **John Carver** and **William Brewster**.

PILLSBURY, CHARLES ALFRED (1842–1899). Businessman. Born in Warner, New Hampshire, on December 3, 1842, Charles A. Pillsbury graduated from Dartmouth College (1863). He worked in a Montreal store and moved to Minneapolis, where he purchased a small flour mill (1869). Although he knew nothing about milling, Pillsbury and his brother, John Sargent Pillsbury (1828–1901), invested in modern machinery and methods to process Northwestern spring wheat for high quality flour. Pillsbury & Company was the largest flour mill in the world when Charles Pillsbury died in Minneapolis on September 17, 1899.

PINCUS, GREGORY GOODWIN (1903–1967). Biologist. Born in Woodbine, New Jersey, on April 9, 1903, Pincus graduated from Cornell University (1924) and earned a doctorate at **Harvard University** (1927). Teaching at Boston University (1950–67), he and his colleague, Dr. John Rock, a professor of obstetrics at Harvard Medical School, developed the first effective oral contraceptive (1955). The Enovid birth control pill was approved by the U.S. Food and Drug Administration (1960) after field tests on women in Brookline, Massachusetts, and developed in Shrewsbury. The new drug benefited from the *Griswold v. Connecticut* case (1965), in which the U.S. Supreme Court overturned the law prohibiting the use of birth control devices. This led Massachusetts to repeal its anti–birth control law (1972). Dr. Pincus, honored for his pioneering research, was elected to the National Academy of Sciences (1965) before he died on August 22, 1967.

PINE TREE SHILLING. A 12-penny silver coin minted in **Boston** by John Hull (1624–83), the first Massachusetts mint master. This was a colonial solution for the shortage of gold and silver British coins in New England. The coins were made with a pine tree emblem from 1652 to 1682, but all the coins were dated 1652 because British law forbade private colonial coinage. Dutch guilders, French livres, Portuguese crusados, and Spanish doubloons also circulated in New England as currency.

PINE TREE STATE. The nickname for Maine, derived from the vast forest of white pines (*Pinus strobus*) and the important role the **lumber** industry plays in the New England **economy**. More than 17.7 million acres or 90 percent of the land area in Maine today is forest, much of it white, red, pitch, and jack pine trees. The many long-lived white pines 125 feet high with a diameter of 4 to 6 feet impressed the early colonists. The white pine is displayed on the state seal (1820) and was designated the state tree (1945).

PINKHAM, LYDIA ESTES (1819–1883). Businesswoman. Born in Lynn, Massachusetts, on February 9, 1819, Lydia Estes was a **Quaker** schoolteacher active in many reform movements. She married Isaac Pinkham (1843) and when the Panic of 1873 threatened the family finances, she used her skills as a herbalist to manufacture home remedies for "female complaints." This cottage industry became the profitable Lydia E. Pinkham Medicine Company (1875). Her picture on the label attracted hundreds of letters daily from women seeking Mrs. Pinkham's advice, which her all-female Department of Advice answered. The vegetable compound was a harmless **tonic** but ineffective despite its therapeutic claims and 18 percent alcohol content. She also published a facts-of-life manual for women at no charge, recommending exercise, cleanliness, and proper diet. Known as the "savior of her sex," Lydia Pinkham was the most successful businesswoman in New England when she died in Lynn on May 17, 1883.

PIONEER VALLEY. An area of western Massachusetts in Hampshire, Hampden, and Franklin counties settled by **Connecticut River** valley colonists at Springfield (1636), Northampton (1656), Hadley (1656), **Deerfield** (1669), and Greenfield (1686). The region between the Westfield, Green, and Deerfield Rivers bears this name popularized by **tourism** agencies in the 1940s.

PIRACY. A serious crime for New England merchants in the golden age of piracy (1650–1725). Dixie Bull, a **fur trader** in the Penobscot Bay area of Maine (1623), may have been New England's first pirate and was never captured, although Massachusetts governor **John Winthrop** dispatched a naval expedition (1632) to find him. Thomas Cromwell's pirate crew spent a month in **Plymouth** in 1646. Thomas Tew, born in Rhode Island, was a notorious pirate plundering Arab and Indian ships in the Red Sea when he died in battle (1695). One **Cape Cod** sea captain, **Samuel Bellamy** (1689–1717), became the prince of pirates in 1715. Bellamy allegedly buried treasure on the banks of the Machias River near his pirate republic in Maine, and six of his pirate crew were hanged in **Boston** on November 15, 1717.

New England's most infamous pirate, Captain William Kidd (1645–1701) from Scotland, was hired by Massachusetts governor Bellomont to capture the pirate Blackbeard (1698). Kidd was said to have buried treasure on Jewell Island in Casco Bay before he was arrested in Boston and sent to England to be hanged for piracy. Edward Teach, known as Captain Blackbeard, buried treasure and abandoned his bride on the **Isles of Shoals** in New Hampshire before he died in a battle in 1718. Legend says his widow still haunts the shore in her wedding gown. Governor Joseph Dudley commissioned the brigantine *Charles* (1703) to suppress pirates. Rhode Island hanged 26 pirates at **Newport** in 1723.

Rachel Wall, New England's only female pirate, was a **Beacon Hill** maid married to a **Boston** fisherman, George Wall. She and her husband captured many ships off the Isles of Shoals by feigning distress at sea. She confessed her pirate crimes before hanging in Boston on October 8, 1789. Federal courts in Boston, Newport, and **Portland** hanged 77 men for piracy (1673–1858), although the crimes were usually committed on the high seas, many involved New England ships and seamen.

PLATH, SYLVIA (1932–1963). Poet. Born in **Boston** on October 27, 1932, Sylvia Plath graduated from Smith College (1955) and studied at the University of Cambridge. She published her first book, *The Colossus* (1960), in London, followed by an autobiographical novel in the confessional style, *The Bell Jar* (1963). *Ariel* (1965) may be her best work reflecting self-absorbed concern with death. Plath killed herself on February 11, 1963, but her poetry, letters, and journals were published posthumously to much popular and critical acclaim, including *Crossing* *the Water* (1971), *Winter Trees* (1972), *Letters Home* (1975), and *The Collected Poems* (1981), which won a Pulitzer Prize.

PLATT, ORVILLE HITCHCOCK (1827–1905). Senator from Connecticut. Born in Washington, Connecticut, on July 19, 1827, Orville H. Platt studied at the Litchfield Law School and practiced in Meriden (1850–77). He was an **abolitionist** Whig and then joined the Free Soil Party and was chair of the Connecticut **Know Nothing Party** (1855–56) before joining the new Republican Party. He was elected a probate judge (1853–56), secretary of state (1857–58), a state legislator (1861–62, 1864, 1869), and **New Haven** County district attorney (1877–79). Elected to the U.S. Senate (1879–1905), Platt became one of the most influential senators known as the "Big Five" and was the author of the Platt Amendment (1901), making Cuba a quasi-protectorate of the United States (1901–34). Platt died on April 21, 1905, in Washington, Connecticut.

PLIMOUTH PLANTATION. A living history museum established in **Plymouth**, Massachusetts (1947). Many tourists, students, and scholars visit the 1627 **Pilgrim** Village, the **Wampanoag** site called Hobbamock's Village, and the *Mayflower II* (1957), as well as the crafts center and research center.

PLUMLEY, FRANK (1844–1924). Congressman from Vermont. Born in Eden, Vermont, on December 17, 1844, Plumley studied law at the University of Michigan and practiced in Northfield, Vermont (1869–76). He was a district attorney (1876–80), Republican state legislator (1882), U.S. attorney for Vermont (1889–94), state senator (1894), and chief justice of the state supreme court (1904–08). President Theodore Roosevelt appointed him to the Venezuela Commission (1903) and to the French-Venezuela Commission (1905). Plumley was elected to the House of Representatives (1909–15), resumed his law practice in Northfield, and served as a U.S. delegate to the Interparliamentary Union of the World in Geneva (1912). He died in Northfield on April 30, 1924.

PLYMOUTH COLONY. Settled by 100 **Pilgrims** (1620) who arrived on the *Mayflower* with a patent from the Virginia Company in London. The 41 men signed the **Mayflower Compact**, an unprecedented agreement for self-government, before landing on **Cape Cod**. The colony had a patent (1621) from the **Council for New England** giving legal status to their lands. Property was held in common until 1626, and the Pilgrims purchased the title to the colony from the London merchants (1627). The robust colonists founded 20 towns by 1687, and each town was self-governed and sent a representative to the colony's general court in Plymouth until **Massachusetts Bay Colony** annexed Plymouth, the "Old Colony" (1691), and its 7,500 inhabitants under a royal charter.

PLYMOUTH COMPANY. A joint-stock company also known as the Virginia Company of Plymouth. Chartered by the Crown (1606), the investors were men from Plymouth, Bristol, and Exeter who intended to trade and colonize the East Coast of North America. The **Sagadahoc** settlement at the mouth of the Kennebec River in Maine (1607) lasted one year, and the Plymouth Company, led by **Sir Ferdinando Gorges**, reorganized as the **Council for New England** (1620).

PLYMOUTH ROCK. Identified (1741) by Thomas Faunce, who was born in Plymouth, Massachusetts, in 1650, as the stepping-stone onto which the **Pilgrims** landed from the *Mayflower* on December 21, 1620. Although no evidence exits for this legend, the massive stone, an erratic glacial boulder of Dedham granite, was moved (1774) to the town square; by 1889 it reposed under a classical canopy. For the Tercentenary celebration, **McKim, Mead and White** designed a granite portico (1921) with four columns and an ornamental fence to shelter Plymouth Rock. It attracts countless **tourists** each day to "America's hometown" and is the official state rock.

POCUMTUCK. An **Algonquian**-speaking **Native American** people living in western Massachusetts, Vermont, and Connecticut numbering 1,200 in 1600. They were defeated by the **Mohawks** at the Deerfield River (1667) but joined the **Pequots** in **King Philip's War** (1675–76). The survivors fled to New York and later (1754) to Canada. The fertile land along the Deerfield River was the center of the Pocumtuck **corn**, squash, bean, pumpkin, and **tobacco** cultivation by 5000 B.C. The first **Puritan** colonists displaced the Pocumtuck in 1669.

PODUNK. A **Native American** people, one of seven **Connecticut River** tribes, who lived in South Windsor when the first English settlers arrived (1636). The name means swamp, but in the 19th century the village of Podunk in **New Haven** county came to mean a rustic, out-of-the-way community (1841). Massachusetts, Vermont, and New York each have communities named Podunk.

POLISH. Immigrants who arrived in New England in large numbers in the 1890s, creating eight Polish **Catholic** parishes in Massachusetts by 1910. Western Massachusetts farmers, in need of farm workers, paid agents at Ellis Island to recruit men, and by this means Polish immigrants came to pick onions in Sunderland (1888). By 1910 about 5,000 Poles purchased **Connecticut River** valley land abandoned by **Yankees** who had moved to the city or to western states. Massachusetts agriculture revived in Hadley, Hatfield, Easthampton, and South Deerfield as Polish Americans grew onions, **tobacco**, squash, potatoes, tomatoes, lettuce, cucumbers, hay, strawberries, **corn**, peppers, and asparagus. Although most of the 3 million Poles who emigrated to the United States by 1900 went from New York to Pennsylvania, Illinois, Michigan, and Wisconsin, many of the 29,000 Poles in Massachusetts (1900) found jobs in Connecticut River Valley industries and in **Lowell**, Fall River, **Salem**, and Cambridge. There were 39,000 Poles in Connecticut by 1911, with 5,000 in New Hampshire, 8,000 in Rhode Island, and 1,600 in Maine. Bridgeport, home of many Connecticut metal, arms, and corset factories, attracted 3,600 Polish immigrants by 1930.

A statue sculpted by **Theo Kitson** in the **Boston Public Garden** honors the great Polish hero of the **American Revolution** *Tadeusz Kosciuszko* (1927). Prominent Poles in Massachusetts included MIT professor Edmund Louis Zalinski, who served with General **Nelson Miles** in the **Civil War**, and Dr. **Maria Zakrzewska**, who founded a hospital for women in Boston. Connecticut elected three Polish Americans to Congress, the Republican **Boleslaus J. Monkiewicz** (1939–41, 1943–45) and Democrats Frank Kowalski (1959–63) and Bernard F. Grabowski (1963–67).

POMEROY, JESSE HARDING (1860–1932). Criminal. Born in **Boston** in 1860, Jesse H. Pomeroy was sent to the Massachusetts state **reform school** in Westborough (1872–73) and released after 14 months. Arrested (1874) by Boston police, he admitted murdering and mutilating 29 children. Declared sane, he was sentenced to death, but the court commuted his sentence to life in prison. Pomeroy spent 41 years in solitary confinement. Despite repeated suicide and escape attempts, the "Boston Boy Fiend" and America's youngest serial killer died in the prison at Bridgewater on September 29, 1932.

PONZI, CHARLES (1882–1949). Criminal. Born in Lugo, Italy, on March 3, 1882, Ponzi emigrated to **Boston** in 1903. Although he served a prison term in Montreal (1908) for forgery and was arrested in New York for smuggling aliens into the United States (1910), this flamboyant swindler attracted thousands of eager investors in the 1920s to his Ponzi Plan, a pyramid investment scheme. Ponzi cheated thousands of people, including many **Italian immigrants**, throughout New England who invested $9 million in his confidence game, which promised 50 percent interest every 45 days. Rumors that he was bankrupt led mobs to his downtown Boston office, but Ponzi blandly denied any wrongdoing and welcomed reporters to his Lexington mansion. The federal court in Boston sentenced him to prison (1920) for misuse of the mails, and on his release a Massachusetts court sentenced him to prison (1927) for larceny. While awaiting trial, Ponzi was arrested in Florida (1926) for real estate fraud. Fleeing the country disguised as a waiter on an Italian ship, Ponzi was kidnapped in New Orleans by a Texas policeman. From jail in Houston (1926) the irrepressible crook appealed to President **Calvin Coolidge** for help. After his release from a Massachusetts prison, New England's most notorious con man was deported to Italy (1934). Ponzi emigrated to Brazil (1939) where he died in poverty on January 15, 1949.

POPE, ALBERT AUGUSTUS (1843–1909). Businessman. Born in **Boston** on May 20, 1843, Pope served in the **Civil War** (1862–65) and founded a successful shoe company in Boston. After visiting bicycle manufacturers in England, Colonel Pope imported bicycles to New England (1877). He manufactured his new Columbia Safety Bicycle at five factories in **Hartford** and Boston by 1898. His magazine, *The Wheelman* (1882), promoted the new sport by bicycle races, and his lobbying for better roads led to the creation of the Massachusetts Highway Commission. He also founded the League of American Wheelmen (1880) to promote bicycling. Pope employed **Pierre Lallement**, an immigrant from France, who invented the modern bicycle in 1865. When the biking craze diminished, Pope produced automobiles at his Hartford factory in 1896 but with little success. He died in Cohasset, Massachusetts, on August 10, 1909. *See also* SPORTS; TAYLOR, MARSHALL.

POPE'S DAY. An **anti-Catholic** celebration in New England on November 5 also known as Guy Fawkes Day or Gunpowder Plot Day. First celebrated in **Plymouth** (1623) by rowdy sailors, it became an annual holiday in **Boston**, **Salem**, Newburyport, Marblehead, **Newport**, **Portsmouth**, and New York City until suppressed by General George Washington (1775). The July 4th holiday replaced Pope's Day by 1776.

In Boston, gangs of working-class boys and men in 1720–74 paraded effigies of the pope and satan on floats through the streets and burned them on Copps Hill or at the gallows on Boston Neck. En route the boys rang bells and sang No Popery ballards at the houses of rich men to demand funds for bonfires, feasting, and drinking on threat of broken windows. Rivals gangs from the South End and **North End** often battled with sticks and stones in the streets. Four apprentice printers drowned in Boston in 1735, a boy was killed in 1764, and a sailor was beaten to death by the antiauthority, antielite mummers in 1775. Although town **selectmen** tried to restrain the mobs, this holiday created working-class leaders for the **American Revolution**. *See also* ANTI-CATHOLICISM.

POPHAM COLONY. The first English settlement in New England (1607–08) established on the Kennebec River. The **Plymouth Company** sent 120 colonists under Sir Raleigh Gilbert on the *Mary and John* and George Popham (1550–1608) on the *Gift of God* to this colony at **Sagadahoc** (now Phippsburg), Maine (1607). **Martin Pring** and **George Waymouth** selected the site for the colony in 1606. Only 45 men remained for the harsh winter, but they built the first ship in North America, the *Virginia*, sailing it to England with a cargo of **furs** and sassafras. When Popham died, Gilbert abandoned the colony and returned all the settlers to England (1608). The English did not settle Maine in large numbers until the **Massachusetts Bay Colony** assumed authority (1652).

PORTER, DAVID (1780–1843). U.S. Navy officer. Born in **Boston** in 1780, Porter went to sea with his father, a Revolutionary War privateer captain, and entered the U.S. Navy as a midshipman (1798). He served in the war with Tripoli and captured several British ships in the War of 1812 as commander of the *Essex*. After suppressing **pirates** in the West Indies, he was court-martialed for offending officials in Puerto Rico (1824). Porter resigned and commanded the Mexican navy (1826–29), and served as U.S. consul in Algiers (1830) and as U.S. minister in Constantinople (1831–43) until his death.

PORTER, SARAH (1813–1900). Educator. Born in Farmington, Connecticut, on August 16, 1813, Sarah Porter was educated at home and by her brother, Noah Porter (1811–92), a professor and later the president of Yale University. She was an experienced teacher when she founded Miss Porter's School in Farmington (1843), which became one of the leading

prep schools for girls. Porter was socially conservative, her private progressive school with a classical curriculum attracted young women from elite families. She died in Farmington on February 17, 1900. *See also* EDUCATION.

PORTLAND. Located on Casco Bay between two peninsulas is Maine's chief deepwater port and economic center. English **fur traders** arrived in 1623 and George Cleeve (1586–1666) landed in Maine in 1630 and founded the town (1633) known as Falmouth. Massachusetts annexed Maine (1652). Falmouth was attacked by the **Abenaki** (1676) and by the French (1690) and abandoned until 1716. Burned by the British (1775), Falmouth was renamed Portland (1786) and was the state capital (1820–32). This important New England seaport, second only to **Boston**, is now the state's largest city with 215,000 metropolitan residents. *See also* PORTLAND FIRE; PORTLAND RIOTS.

PORTLAND FIRE. Fire that consumed much of the city of **Portland**, Maine, on July 4, 1866. So many buildings were destroyed that most new buildings were constructed of stone or brick with slate roofs. Lincoln Park, the city's first public park (1866), was built on a burned-over section as open space to prevent the spread of future fires.

PORTLAND RIOTS (1825). A series of three mob actions in **Portland**, Maine, against waterfront brothels. Twice crowds of workers, truckmen, and boys collected in the evening and tore the buildings to the ground. When the prostitutes relocated, a third riot on November 10, 1825, broke out. One brothel on Crabtree's Wharf was set on fire, and the house of a black barber named Gray was attacked. Gray shot into the crowd, one man was killed, and eight others were wounded. Similar whorehouse riots in **Boston** (1737, 1825) and New York City (1793, 1799) demonstrated that moral outrage could lead to violence against commercial sex. In contrast, public, church, and U.S. Navy officials in **Portsmouth**, New Hampshire, closed the city's red light district near the waterfront and Navy Yard without violence in 1912.

PORTSMOUTH. The chief seaport in New Hampshire was founded as a trading and fishing post by English colonists sent by **John Mason**. Known as **Strawbery Banke** (1630–53), the town was annexed by Massachusetts (1641–79), renamed Portsmouth (1653), and became a royal colony in 1679. Its natural harbor at the mouth of the Piscataqua

River and prosperous shipping and **shipbuilding** economy made it New Hampshire's capital until 1808. Before the **American Revolution**, Portsmouth merchants engaged in **whaling** and the **slave trade**. Today the metropolis has a population of 224,000 employed in **tourism**, in light industry, and at the Portsmouth Naval Shipyard.

PORTSMOUTH PEACE CONFERENCE (1905). A meeting held by President Theodore Roosevelt in **Portsmouth**, New Hampshire, with representatives of Russia and Japan to settle the Russo-Japanese War. The Treaty of Portsmouth, signed on September 5, 1905, established Japan as the dominant power in Manchuria and a major naval power in the Pacific. Roosevelt won the Nobel Peace Prize (1906) for his mediation role.

PORTUGUESE. Immigrants who came to New England from the Azores by 1800, learning about the rich **fishing** in **Provincetown** and **New Bedford** from **Yankee whaling** ships resupplied in the Azores and **Cape Verde Islands**. Many Portuguese settled in Stonington, Connecticut, on **Cape Cod**, in southeastern Massachusetts, or in Gloucester. The U.S. Immigration Service recorded 35 immigrants in 1820, but the numbers grew steadily to 16,978 in 1881–90, and 29,994 in 1921–30, and 75,717 in 1971–77. **Lowell** had a Portuguese boarding house (1862) and a Catholic church (1901), and many found jobs at **textile** mills in Lawrence, Ludlow, **New Bedford**, and Fall River, Massachusetts. Rhode Island counted 10,000 Portuguese residents by 1911. Cape Verdean Creoles encountered some racial prejudice, and all Portuguese experienced **anti-Catholicism** in New England. Massachusetts had 21 Portuguese Roman Catholic parishes (1869–1976), with 8 in Rhode Island, and 3 in Connecticut, but fewer parochial schools than the **Irish**, **Italians**, or **French Canadians** established. Portuguese social clubs, mutual-aid societies, restaurants, credit unions, newspapers, and radio programs contribute to the region's music, cuisine, and maritime traditions. New England's Portuguese in recent years have celebrated Miguel Corte Real who explored the northeast coast for Portugal in 1501–11. The Portuguese remain a small but stable part of New England's population, 2 percent in Massachusetts, 3.8 percent in Rhode Island, and .5 percent in Connecticut by 1970.

POTATO. Vegetable that arrived in New England with **Scotch-Irish immigrants** in Londonderry, New Hampshire (1719). The white, or Irish, potato became the principal crop grown in Maine by 1860 for food and starch. The South American tuber is a very nutritious food that grows easily in a variety of soils. The potato crop blight in Europe caused the devastating potato famine (1845–50) and sent 1.5 million Irish immigrants to the United States. Maine ranks fourth in U.S. potato production, harvesting 20 varieties valued at $566,400,000 in 1999 from 65,000 acres on 480 farms. Since Joseph Houlton introduced potatoes to Aroostook County (1807), "The County" has produced 90 percent of Maine's potato crop, and high schools still close for the fall harvest. The annual Potato Blossom Festival in Fort Fairfield, Maine, celebrates the important crop.

POTHIER, ARAM (1854–1928). Governor of Rhode Island. Born in Philimene, Quebec, on July 28, 1854, Pothier graduated from Nicolet College (1872) in Quebec and emigrated to join his family in Woonsocket. Entering a Woonsocket bank as a clerk, he rose to bank president (1875–89) and was elected a Republican state legislator (1887–94), mayor (1894–96), lieutenant governor (1897–99), and governor (1909–15, 1925–28). Like many **French Canadians** in New England, Pothier preferred the more conservative Republican Party to the **Irish**-dominated Democratic Party. As governor he signed a workmen's compensation law and labor laws for women and minors. He returned to his position as bank president (1915–25) until drafted as governor again in the 1925 Republican sweep of state elections. Pothier, the first **French-Canadian** governor in New England, died in office on February 4, 1928.

POWERS, HIRAM (1805–1873). Artist. Born in Woodstock, Vermont, on July 29, 1805, Powers learned to model wax working in a Cincinnati museum (1829–34). He sculpted marble busts in Washington, D.C., of *Andrew Jackson* (1835), *John Marshall* (1835), and *John Quincy Adams* (1837). In Florence, Italy, he became recognized for his neoclassical marble *The Greek Slave* (1843) and *The Last of the Tribe* (1872). His busts of *Benjamin Franklin* (1862) and Thomas Jefferson (1863) are in the U.S. Capitol, and a statue of *Daniel Webster* (1859) stands on the State House grounds in **Boston**. Powers was America's most famous neoclassical sculptor when he died in Florence on June 27, 1873.

PRANG, LOUIS (1824–1909). Artist. Born in Breslau, Poland, on March 12, 1824, Prang's father was a French **Huguenot** and his mother was **German**. He was a printer before immigrating to **Boston** in 1850, where he joined a lithographic firm (1856). Prang prospered by making portraits, maps, and scenes of **Civil War** battle sites and introduced Christmas cards to Americans (1874). By 1882 he promoted art **education** in public schools by publishing art texts and popular reproductions of fine art by **Winslow Homer** and **Eastman Johnson**. Prang & Company (1860–97) also produced high-quality color pictures of New England scenes that stimulated **tourism**. Prang increased popular appreciation of fine art, and his textbooks influenced public school drawing classes. Much admired in Boston, Prang retired in 1899 and died in California on June 14, 1909.

PRATT, FRANCIS ASBURY (1827–1902). Inventor. Born in Woodstock, Vermont, on February 15, 1827, Pratt was a toolmaker who invented machine tools with interchangeable parts. He founded the Pratt & Whitney Company in **Hartford**, Connecticut, with Amos Whitney (1865) to manufacture machinery and engines. Pratt died in Hartford on February 10, 1902.

PRAYING INDIANS. Native Americans converted by **John Eliot** and other **Congregational** missionaries, who settled in 14 Massachusetts towns (1651–74). Natick, Massachusetts, was the largest community. Eliot insisted the Indians adopt English religion and culture. After conquest of the **Pequot** and **Narragansett** people was complete (1643), missionaries went to the weaker **Algonquin** tribes. The Massachusetts **General Court** passed laws prohibiting Indian religious practices, appointed a superintendent of Indian affairs, and imposed fines on traditional Indian customs. Eliot's missionary efforts ended with **King Philip's War** (1675–76) when a 1677 law restricted all Native Americans to the remaining four Praying Towns.

PREBLE, EDWARD (1761–1807). U.S. Navy officer. Born in Falmouth (now **Portland**), Maine, on August 15, 1761, Preble served in the Massachusetts navy in the **American Revolution** and in the U.S. Navy (1798–1805). As commander of the USS *Constitution*, he led the Mediterranean squadron in the war against Tripoli (1803–05) but with little success in suppressing the Barbary Coast pirates. Preble died on August 25, 1807.

PRECISION VALLEY. A nickname for the area of southern Vermont known for its history of precision manufacturing. The series of waterfalls in Springfield, on the Black River, a tributary of the **Connecticut River**, provided water power (1840) and later hydroelectric power for precision tool and machine tool plants. The American Precision Museum in Windsor, housed in the original Robbins & Lawrence Armory and Machine Shop (1848), has the largest collection of historic precision machine tools in the nation.

PREP SCHOOLS. Developed in New England to educate the sons of elite families. Some of the most prestigious boarding schools include Philips Academy (1778), Deerfield Academy (1799), St. Mark's School (1865), Groton School (1884), Milton Academy (1884), and Middlesex School (1901) in Massachusetts; Phillips Exeter Academy (1781) and St. Paul's School (1856) in New Hampshire; St. George's School (1896) in Rhode Island; and Taft School (1890), Hotchkiss School (1892), Choate School (1896), and Kent School (1906) in Connecticut. These private preparatory schools were dubbed prep schools because they prepared pupils for **Ivy League** colleges and intended to foster highbred manliness in the United States. The rector of Groton School, the Reverend **Endicott Peabody**, was considered the model of the **Yankee** schoolmaster devoted to educating perfect Christian gentlemen for public service rather than as leisurely dilettantes. For 56 years he guided boys to manhood at Groton, he based on the English public school he attended. Similar prep schools for girls in New England include Miss Porter's School in Farmington, Connecticut (1843), and Dana Hall School in Wellesley, Massachusetts (1881). New England boarding schools educated elite children from every state and some other countries. *See also* EDUCATION; PORTER, SARAH.

PRESCOTT, SAMUEL (1751–1777). Patriot. Born in Concord, Massachusetts, on August 19, 1751, Prescott was a physician in Concord whom **Paul Revere** met on his famous ride on April 18, 1775. He joined Revere and **William Dawes** in warning the **Minutemen** that British troops were marching to Concord and was the only one of the three to complete his ride. Prescott served in the Continental Army but was captured at Ticonderoga (1776) and died in prison in Halifax (1777). *See also* AMERICAN REVOLUTION; BATTLE OF LEXINGTON AND CONCORD.

PRESCOTT, WILLIAM (1726–1795). Soldier. Born in Groton, Massachusetts, on February 20, 1726, Prescott served in the **French and Indian War**, was a farmer in Pepperell, and was the colonel of a militia company at Concord on April 19, 1775. Ordered to fortify Bunker Hill, he decided his troops were in better position on Breed's Hill. Prescott was the major American hero in the **Battle of Bunker Hill** on June 17, 1775. He served in the New York (1776) and Saratoga (1777) campaigns but retired in poor health (1777) and died at his Pepperell farm on October 13, 1795. *See also* BATTLE OF LEXINGTON AND CONCORD.

PRESCOTT, WILLIAM HICKLING (1796–1859). Historian. Born in **Salem**, Massachusetts, on May 4, 1796, Prescott, the grandson of **William Prescott**, graduated from **Harvard** College (1814) despite partial blindness. His first book, *History of the Reign of Ferdinand and Isabella the Catholic* (1837), established his reputation as an historian. He continued with *History of the Conquest of Mexico* (1843) and *History of the Conquest of Peru* (1847), both popular dramatic works of his vivid historical imagination at a time when history was a form of literature. Prescott had not completed his *History of the Reign of Philip II, King of Spain* (1855–58) when he died in **Boston** on January 29, 1859.

PRESIDENTIAL RANGE. A ridgeline in the **White Mountains** of New Hampshire named for eight U.S. presidents: Mount Adams, Mount John Quincy Adams, Mount Eisenhower, Mount Jefferson, Mount Madison, Mount Monroe, Mount Pierce, and **Mount Washington**. The range is popular for day hikers and long-distance backpackers on the **Appalachian Trail**, although the weather can be dangerous for **tourists** even in the summer. Since the first fatality in 1849, many people have died climbing these mountains.

PRINCE, LUCY TERRY (1724–1821). Poet. Born in West Africa, Lucy Terry came to Massachusetts as a child and was a slave in **Deerfield**, where she married (1756) a free **African-American** farmer, Abijah Prince. She was the first American black woman to write poetry; her ballad *Bars Fight* (1746) commemorates a Native American raid on Deerfield. She moved with her family to Guilford, Vermont, and used her eloquence to argue for the admission of her son to Williams College and for her own successful land case before the Vermont Supreme Court.

PRING, MARTIN (1580–1626). Explorer. Born in Devonshire, Captain Pring sailed for Bristol merchants with two ships, *Speedwell* and *Discoverer*, to the New England coast (1603). He explored the Piscataqua River in New Hampshire and the Penobscot River in Maine and traded with **Native Americans** for sassafras in **Plymouth**. His maps, charts, and reports on the land and the rich **fishing** encouraged further exploration and colonization. Pring sailed for London merchants to Virginia (1606) and died in Bristol about 1626.

PROCTOR, REDFIELD (1831–1908). Senator from Vermont. Born in Proctorsville, Vermont, on June 1, 1831, Proctor graduated from Dartmouth College (1851) and Albany Law School (1859). He practiced law in **Boston** (1860–61) and served in the Union Army (1861–63). Returning to Vermont to practice law, he founded the Vermont Marble Company in Rutland (1863) and served as a Republican state legislator (1867–68, 1874–75, 1888), lieutenant governor (1876–78), governor (1878–80), secretary of war (1889–91), and senator (1891–1908). His son, Fletcher Proctor, was governor (1923), as was his grandson, Mortimer Proctor (1945), in a dynasty that split the state's dominant Republican Party into pro-Proctor and anti-Proctor factions long after Redfield Proctor died in Washington, D.C., on March 4, 1908.

PROUTY, WINSTON LEWIS (1906–1971). Senator from Vermont. Born in Newport, Vermont, on September 1, 1906, Prouty attended Lafayette College and was mayor of Newport (1938–41) and operated a **lumber** business. He was a Republican state representative (1941, 1945, 1947) and served in the House of Representatives (1951–59) and in the Senate (1958–71) until his death on September 10, 1971, in **Boston**.

PROVIDENCE. Capital of Rhode Island. Located on the Providence River at the head of Narragansett Bay in northeastern Rhode Island, it has been the state capital since 1900. Founded (1636) by **Roger Williams**, on land he purchased from the **Narragansett** people, the town was a refuge for Massachusetts exiles and religious dissenters but was burned during **King Philip's War** (1676). Colonial Providence flourished as a center for the **molasses**, **rum**, and slave trade and later as a pioneer in the industrial revolution (1790). The Gorham Manufacturing Company (1863) produced fine-art silverware and jewelry. Best known as the home of Brown University, Providence is the state's largest city, with 160,000 residents. The metropolitan population of 900,000 makes it New England's second largest urban center after **Boston**.

PROVIDENCE PLANTATIONS. The name for four Rhode Island towns—**Providence**, Portsmouth, Warwick, and **Newport**—settled by

Puritan dissenters (1634–39). **Roger Williams** obtained the royal patent in London (1644) over the objections of Massachusetts **Puritans**. Charles II granted Williams a new royal charter (1663) for the colony of Rhode Island and Providence Plantations, which annexed the original four towns. Roger Williams had purchased land from the **Narragansett** people (1636) for the town of Providence and formed local and colonial government by 1637 with separation of church and state.

PROVINCETOWN. The *Mayflower*'s (1620) first landing place at the tip of **Cape Cod** in Massachusetts. Settled by 1700 and incorporated in 1727, the town was a **fishing**, **whaling,** and salt-making center captured by the British navy in the **American Revolution** and War of 1812. During the **Civil War** the town became a major fishing port, and **Portuguese** seamen from **Cape Verde** settled there. By the 1890s it was a popular resort center with a bohemian character associated with the **Provincetown Players** and an artistic and literary community. Provincetown is still a commercial fishing port and popular vacation resort adjacent to the **Cape Cod National Seashore** with a population of 4,000 residents.

PROVINCETOWN PLAYERS. An influential summer theater founded (1915–29) by the Greenwich Village writers George Cram Cook and his wife Susan Glaspell in a converted fish warehouse in **Provincetown**, Massachusetts. **Eugene O'Neill** launched his career with the group (1916), which established the experimental Playwright's Theatre in New York City.

PROVIDENT INSTITUTION FOR SAVINGS. The first savings bank in the nation (1816–1966). Chartered by Massachusetts as a secure depository for ordinary Bostonians, it promoted **Yankee** thrift and capital formation for local real estate mortgages and small business loans. This mutual savings bank, owned by depositors, was modeled on British banks and inspired 1,000 other banks in New England and the Middle Atlantic states.

PUBLIC GARDEN. A park designed by George Meacham (1860) on Charles Street in **Boston**. More formal and elegant than the adjacent **Boston Common**, it features an equestrian statue of George Washington by **Thomas Ball** (1869) and a statue of **William Ellery Channing** (1902), as well as a miniature replica of the Brooklyn Bridge. Since 1877 the swan boats have carried generations of children and **tourists** around a small pond used for skating in the winter. **Robert McCloskey**'s book *Make Way for Ducklings* (1941) has made this small park a mecca for children. The bronze sculpture called *Make Way for Ducklings* by Nancy Schon was added in 1987.

PUBLIC SCHOOLS. Required by law in Massachusetts (1642). Specifically, parents and masters of apprentices were to make sure their children learned to read the Bible and understand the laws of the commonwealth. Home schooling was common, and private **dame schools** conducted by matrons in many towns educated young children with the **hornbook** and **New England Primer**. In time these practices led the **Puritans** to establish free tax-supported town or common schools. The **selectmen** could remove uneducated or wayward children from the home if necessary. Massachusetts law (1647) required towns of 50 families to hire a schoolmaster to teach children reading and writing, and towns of 100 families had to have a grammar school to prepare boys for **Harvard** College. This **education** model became common throughout colonial New England, in contrast to other English colonies. *See also* COMMON SCHOOLS; EDUCATION.

PUCKERBRUSH. Unused New England farmland naturally returning to forest. The first stage is the reseeding of meadows or pasture by weeds, grasses, bushes, and trees. This was common after the **Civil War** when rural depopulation permitted abandoned farms to return to a natural state. The **woodchuck**, a derogatory term for the rural poor or **Swamp Yankee**, is one who lives in the woods or puckerbrush. *See also* TROUSE.

PURITANS. Extreme Protestants in 16th-century England who insisted on purifying the Church of England of all traces of Roman **Catholicism**. Their Calvinist leaders were usually Cambridge University graduates and ministers. Some Puritan dissenters, called **Pilgrims** or Separatists, migrated to Holland in 1607 and then founded **Plymouth Colony** (1620) in northern Virginia, now called Massachusetts in New England. A larger group of Puritans founded **Massachusetts Bay Colony** in **Boston** (1630) and annexed **Plymouth** (1689) and sent dissenters to other parts of New England. **John Winthrop** led 11 ships to found Massachusetts Bay Colony at Boston (1630), and the **Great Migration** (1630–40) brought 20,000 Puritans to join him.

The Restoration of the Stuart monarchy (1660), the liberal **Half-Way Covenant** (1660), population growth and expansion to the frontier, new commercial enterprises, and revocation of the Massachusetts charter (1684) weakened Puritan control and gave New England secular government. Puritans were later known as **Congregationalists**, the largest denomination in America until 1790, and for two centuries or more this church was supported by public funds in Connecticut (1818) and Massachusetts (1833). As a theological movement, Puritanism created a theocracy in New England, but each church had some autonomy that promoted democracy over time. Puritan or Calvinist values developed the **New England conscience** and a foundation for social, intellectual, and economic innovation. **Augustus Saint-Gaudens**'s statue *The Puritan* (1887) in Springfield, Massachusetts, is a portrait of Deacon Samuel Chapin, a founder of the town, as well as a representation of the Puritanism that was a single, but not the only, defining feature of early New England.

PUTNAM, ISRAEL (1718–1790). Soldier. Born in **Salem** Village, Massachusetts, on January 7, 1718, Putnam was a farmer in Pomfret, Connecticut (1740). Known for heroic deeds while serving with **Robert Rogers**'s rangers (1756–58), Putnam served at the **Battles of Lexington, Concord,** and **Bunker Hill**. He was a Connecticut state legislator and founded the Connecticut **Sons of Liberty**. Putnam was a major general under George Washington in New York until invalided (1779). The colorful scout died in Pomfret on May 29, 1790.

– Q –

QUABBIN RESERVOIR. Provides water to 2.5 million residents in 44 metropolitan **Boston** communities. Built (1928–46) to bring water from the Swift and Ware Rivers, the state project submerged the towns of Dana, Enfield, Greenwich, and Prescott (1939) and created the largest (39 sq. mi.) man-made reservoir in the country. Quabbin Reservoir became a major wildlife refuge and recreational area for 500,000 visitors each year to western Massachusetts.

QUAHOG. A hard-shell clam common on the East Coast of the United States. Immature quahogs, called cherrystone or littleneck clams, are eaten raw on the half shell. Larger quahogs are used in **New England Clam Chowder**. *See also* CLAMBAKE; FISHING.

QUAKERS. The Society of Friends, began in England (1647). Members were deported from **Boston** to Barbados (1656) and persecuted until 1689. **Puritans** expelled or punished Quakers, but a statue on the State House grounds honors Mary Dwyer, a Quaker hanged on **Boston Common** (1660). **Roger Williams** welcomed Quakers to Rhode Island (1657) and passed the first conscientious objectors law to respect Quaker pacifism (1673). **Cape Cod** had the first Quaker meetinghouse in Massachusetts at Sandwich (1672), and Quakers settled North Adams (1737). Quakers visited Maine in 1662 and established their first meetinghouse at Kittery (1730). On **Nantucket Island** the Quaker settlers included the family of **Lucretia Coffin Mott** and many whalers, who are remembered in **Robert Lowell**'s poem *The Quaker Graveyard at Nantucket* (1946). Prominent New England Quakers include the poet **John Greenleaf Whittier**, the Rhode Island missionary Jemina Wilkerson (1752–1819), and **Moses Brown**, as well as the reformers **Abigail Kelley Foster** and **Susan B. Anthony**, **Neal Dow**, and **Paul Cuffe**, and the educator **Emily Greene Balch**. Many Quakers were **abolitionists** and active in the **Underground Railroad**.

QUARRIES. An important industry throughout New England, for example, Chelmsford and Medford had granite quarries (1790), and Rockport opened granite quarries close to the sea for Massachusetts shipping (1850–1929). Quincy built the first horse-drawn railway in the nation (1824) to transport granite for the **Bunker Hill** monument. **Henry H. Richardson** quarried **Roxbury puddingstone** in **Boston** for many significant buildings, including the **Trinity Church** (1877). Isaac Underhill opened America's first commercial marble quarry in Dorset, Vermont, in 1785; and, in Massachusetts, marble was also quarried in North Adams (1810–1947).

In New Hampshire **Concord** white granite was used for the Library of Congress and many other public buildings. Soapstone for sinks, stoves, and water pipes was quarried in Francestown, New Hampshire. Eben Judd opened a marble quarry in Middlebury, Vermont (1802), and marble quarries operated at Proctorsville, producing 62 percent of the nation's marble by 1890. Granite quarries opened at Hardwick and Bethel by 1868. Six quarries in Barre and **Montpelier** (1815) still provide granite for buildings, tombstones, and curbstones around the country, attracting skilled stonecutters from Scotland and Italy in the 1880s. Vermont also had talc quarries, asbestos in Eden, and 67 **slate** quarries by 1885, all worked by **immigrants** from Scotland, Ireland, Wales, and Italy. In

Maine the first granite was quarried in **Augusta** in 1808 and the Stonington and Vinalhaven quarries (1826–1920) provided stone for the **Museum of Fine Arts** in Boston and the New York City Stock Exchange. William Farnsworth quarried limestone in Rockland, Maine, by 1850. The Westerly, Rhode Island, granite quarries operated by 1850; and in Connecticut the Guilford quarry provided granite for the Brooklyn Bridge (1870) and the Statue of Liberty (1885). Sand and gravel are related mineral resources from New England quarries to make bricks, mortar, and cement. Pink feldspar was used for ceramics, quartz for glass, barite for paint, graphite for pencils, talc for lubricants, and iron oxide for steel.

QUEBEC ACT (1774). A law passed by Parliament to govern the French **Catholic** residents of Canada, but it coincided with the four **Intolerable** or **Coercive Acts** (1774) designed to punish rebellious New Englanders for the **Boston Tea Party**. Americans saw the Quebec Act as an intrusion on their rights and united to declare independence.

QUEEN ANNE'S WAR (1702–1713). The American phase of the War of the Spanish Succession. New England forces twice failed to capture Port Royal (1704–07) in Nova Scotia from the French but succeeded in 1710. Indian raids encouraged by the French in Canada endangered many New England towns, notably in **Deerfield** (1704). England, Holland, and Austria waged war with France and Spain to prevent Louis XIV of France from inheriting the Spanish Empire. This war ended with the Treaty of Utrecht (1713), which awarded Nova Scotia, Newfoundland, and Hudson's Bay to England from France.

QUINCY, JOSIAH (1772–1864). Mayor of **Boston**. Born in Boston on February 4, 1772, Quincy graduated from **Harvard** College (1790). He practiced law in Boston (1793–1805) and served in the state legislature (1804–05, 1813–20, 1821–22). Elected to the House of Representatives (1805–13), Quincy abandoned his **Federalist Party** and served in the state legislature (1813–22) and as a Boston municipal court judge (1822–23). Elected the second mayor of the City of Boston (1823–29), Quincy expanded city services and public works projects. As president of **Harvard University** (1829–45), he reformed the law school and wrote a history of Harvard, and a biography of his father, Josiah Quincy (1744–75), a Revolutionary War leader. Josiah Quincy died in Quincy, Massachusetts, on July 1, 1864.

QUINNIPIAC (OR LONG WATER PEOPLE). An **Algonquin**-speaking **Native American** people living on the southern Connecticut coast when **Adriaen Block** and the first Dutch traders arrived (1614). The tribe suffered devastating epidemics (1633–34), and their population was so reduced that they welcomed 500 **Puritans** from **Boston** led by **Theophilus Eaton** to Quinnipiac land (1638), hoping an alliance with the English would protect them from the **Mohawks** and **Pequots**. They sold **New Haven** by treaty with Eaton and **John Davenport** (1638), and allied with the colonists against the **Wampanoag** and **Narragansetts** in **King Philip's War** (1675). As the Quinnipiac population declined, the Connecticut legislature permitted the town of New Haven to sell the tribal land. By 1740 only 20 Quinnipiac families lived in New Haven and none existed in the state by 1850.

QUOCK WALKER CASE. *See* WALKER, QUOCK.

QUONSET HUTS. First built for the U.S. Navy at Quonset Point, Rhode Island, in 1941. Corrugated sheet metal sections were laid on a skeleton of semi-circular steel ribs to create a self-supporting building 20 feet wide and 48 feet long with 720 square feet of floor space. They were inexpensive to ship and easy to assemble on remote locations. In World War II 170,000 Quonset huts were used as military barracks, hospitals, and warehouses; and after the war they became college dormitories, churches, businesses, and garages. Some are still in use on the Boston College athletic fields and by Vermont highway departments.

– R –

RAILROADS. First appeared in New England in 1827 when a small horse-drawn line transported granite from Quincy, Massachusetts, for the construction of the **Bunker Hill** Monument. Connecticut's first railroad connected **Boston**, Norwich, and New London (1832) and then **New Haven** and **Hartford** (1838). Construction of the Boston & Worcester line (1834) stimulated industry in central Massachusetts and more so when the Boston & Lowell (1835), Boston & Providence (1835), and Hartford & New Haven (1838) lines reached Springfield (1844). The Providence & Worcester line (1847) replaced the **Blackstone Canal** and made **Worcester** a vital industrial city with reliable transportation to the sea. By 1849 the Rutland Railroad (1843) and the Vermont Central Railroad (1845) connected Boston and Burlington, Vermont. Maine's first railroad connected Bangor and Oldtown (1836), and **Portland** lines linked with Canada's Grand Trunk Railway (1853). The Main Central and the Boston & Maine also connected Portland with Montreal and Boston (1853). By 1875 railroads in New Hampshire brought **tourists** to grand hotels in the **White Mountains**. In the 1880s the New York & New Haven Railroad (1848) combined several smaller New England lines.

By 1840 Massachusetts had 285 miles of tracks extending into New Hampshire, Rhode Island, and Connecticut. By 1850 there were 1,037 miles of track and 421 miles in the other states, and by 1870 Massachusetts had 1,439 miles of tracks connecting with 688 miles of tracks in every New England state. Vermont had 290 miles of tracks in 1870 and 614 miles by 1890. Considerable economic development resulted, for example, the Boston & Maine line (1850) stimulated the Maine **lumber** and **lobster** industries. The consolidated Boston & Albany (1867) and the **Hoosac Tunnel** (1851–73) completed the statewide railroad network to the West.

John Murray Forbes invested his profits from the **China trade** in Midwestern railroads in the 1840s and the Boston firm **Lee, Higginson & Company** was a major investor in Western railroads such as the Chicago, Burlington and Quincy and the Atchison, Topeka and Santa Fe (1848–1900). **Grenville M. Dodge** left Massachusetts and Vermont to construct the Union Pacific Railroad and other lines in the Midwest and Southwest before and after the **Civil War**. Massachusetts established the first state commission (1869) to regulate railroads and hear complaints, but New Englanders involved in the transcontinental railroad's Credit Mobilier scandal (1872) included **Oakes Ames**, **James W. Patterson**, and **Thomas Durant**. Despite this, raw materials imported by train moved to the South and the West as New England's manufactured goods flowed from factories and mills. One-fourth of Quebec's rural population migrated by train to New England in 1870–90, providing an important labor force. By 1899 Boston opened South Station to consolidate increasing passenger and freight train services.

The Old Colony Railroad (1854) served **Cape Cod**, as did the New York, New Haven and Hartford Railroad (1865), which reached **Provincetown** by 1873 but was abandoned in 1920. This short Cape Cod & Old Colony line attracted tourists as well as writers, artists, and actors to Provincetown. The railroad bed is now a bicycle path. Winter sports also benefited from the **snow train** from Boston to the White Mountains carrying pioneer skiers (1931) to New Hampshire ski lodges. Although most passenger service declined on New England railroads by 1960, since 1990 passenger traffic has expanded to New York City, Montreal, and Portland. Scenic railroad tours in the **Green Mountains**, on **Mount Washington**, in Cape Cod, and in Essex, Connecticut, attract many **leaf-peeping** tourists each autumn.

RASLES, SEBASTIEN (1652–1724). Clergyman. Born in Besançon, France, on January 27, 1652, Sebastien Rasles joined the Society of Jesus (1675) and was ordained a Catholic priest. He came to New France (1689) as a **Jesuit** missionary to the **Native Americans**. For 30 years he lived with the **Abenaki** people on the Kennebec River in Norridgewock (now Madison), Maine (1694–1724), and wrote a dictionary of their language (1721). During **Dummer's War**, the Massachusetts **militia** killed Father Rasles in a raid on Norridgewock on August 23, 1724. **Anti-Catholicism** had increased owing to suspicion that the French urged the Indians to drive the English out of Vermont and Maine. Father Rasles's dictionary was sent to **Harvard** College and published in 1833.

REDMOND, SARAH PARKER (1826–1894). Social reformer. Born in **Salem**, Massachusetts, on June 6, 1826, Redmond attended the Salem **public schools** only after her father convinced the town to integrate them in 1841. She and her **African-American** family joined the **abolitionist** crusade and hid runaway slaves on the **Underground Railroad**. By 1856 Sarah became famous as an antislavery lecturer in America and Great Britain. In 1866 she studied medicine in Italy, where she remained in self-imposed exile until her death in Florence on December 13, 1894.

REDWOOD LIBRARY. Founded by Abraham Redwood in **Newport**, Rhode Island (1747), on land donated by the merchant and philanthropist Henry Collins. Designed by **Peter Harrison** (1748), it is the oldest lending library and library building in the nation. Renamed the Redwood Library and Athenaeum (1833), its rare books, **art** collections, and landscaped grounds are open to the public.

REED, THOMAS BRACKETT (1839–1902). Speaker of the House. Born in **Portland**, Maine, on October 18, 1839, Reed graduated from Bowdoin College (1860). He served in the U.S. Navy (1864–65), practiced law in Portland (1865–70), and was a Republican state legislator

(1868–70) and attorney general of Maine (1870–72). Reed served in the House of Representatives (1877–99) and as Speaker of the House (1889–91, 1895–99). Known as Czar Reed for his strict control of legislation by the rules of parliamentary procedure he devised, Reed resigned in disagreement with Republican expansionist policies and the war against Filipino guerrillas. Reed practiced law in New York City (1899–1902) and died in Washington, D.C., on December 7, 1902. Massachusetts governor **Samuel W. McCall** wrote Reed's biography (1914).

REEVE, TAPPING (1744–1823). Lawyer and educator. Born in Brookhaven, New York, in October 1744, Reeve graduated from the College of New Jersey (1763) and studied law in **Hartford**. Practicing in Litchfield, Connecticut (1772–84), he founded the Litchfield Law School, the first and most prestigious law school in America (1784–1833). Reeve was the sole professor until appointed to the state superior court (1798–1814) and as chief justice of the state supreme court (1814–16). Among his many prominent students were **Roger Sherman Baldwin**, Aaron Burr, and **Horace Mann**. Judge Reeve left the school in 1820, but it continued until 1833. Reeve died in Litchfield on December 13, 1823.

REFORM SCHOOLS. Introduced to North America by Theodore Lyman, the mayor of **Boston**, who contributed $85,000 to found the state reform school for boys in Westborough, Massachusetts (1846). This state reformatory for "young culprits," the first in North America, was later named for Lyman. A similar public institution for girls opened in Lancaster (1854). Both institutions were examples of the antebellum romantic reform movement based on European model schools to rescue children from delinquency and crime. The concept spread to other states after the **Civil War**, but later these industrial reform schools resembled prisons rather than schools. Charges of abuse and ineffective methods and deinstitutionalization policies closed both institutions by 1970.

REVERE, PAUL (1735–1818). Hero and silversmith. Born in **Boston** on January 1, 1735, Paul Revere, the son of **Huguenot** émigrés, was a master craftsman whose engraving of the **Boston Massacre** (1770) depicted the British as murderers of innocent citizens. He was a leader of the **Boston Tea Party** and a courier for the Massachusetts Provincial Congress to the Second Continental Congress. On April 18, 1775, he carried news of the British army march on Lexington and Concord. Revere designed the official seal of Massachusetts, printed Continental currency, and manufactured arms for the patriots. After the war, his foundry armed *Old Ironsides*, cast the bell for **King's Chapel**, covered the new State House dome with copper (1802), and provided the copper boilers for Robert Fulton's first steamboat. **Henry Wadsworth Longfellow**'s poem *Paul Revere's Ride* (1861) immortalized his heroism. His **North End** house, the only example of Boston 17th-century domestic architecture, became the city's most popular **tourist** site when it opened to the public (1908). Paul Revere died in Boston on May 10, 1818. *See also* AMERICAN REVOLUTION; DAWES, WILLIAM; HUGUENOTS.

RHODE ISLAND HISTORICAL SOCIETY. Founded in **Providence** in 1822 as a private, nonprofit educational and cultural organization. Funds from an 1837 lottery paid for the society's Greek temple building on Waterman Street (1844). The society moved into the historic **John Brown** House in 1941 where books, documents, artifacts, and **art** from **Roger Williams**, **Moses Brown**, **Nathanael Greene**, and other historic figures are preserved. As the fourth oldest private historical society in the nation, the society maintains a research library, museum of state history, public lectures, and publications in Providence and the Museum of Work and Culture in Woonsocket for its 2,500 members and visitors.

RHODE ISLAND INDEPENDENCE DAY. Celebrated since 1884 on May 4 because the legislature voted on May 4, 1776, to renounce the colony's allegiance to the English king.

RIBICOFF, ABRAHAM A. (1910–1998). Senator from Connecticut. Born in **New Britain**, Connecticut, on April 9, 1910, Abraham Alexander Ribicoff graduated from the University of Chicago Law School (1933). He practiced in Kensington and **Hartford** and served in the state legislature (1938–41) and as a Hartford judge (1941–43, 1945–47). Ribicoff was a Democrat in the House of Representatives (1949–53), governor (1955–61), and secretary of health, education and welfare (1961–62). He was elected to the Senate (1963–81), retired to private practice in New York City, and lived in Cornwall Bridge, Connecticut, until his death in New York City on February 22, 1998. Abraham Ribicoff is remembered as a pragmatic liberal and one of the most influential **Jewish** political leaders in New England.

RICHARDS, ELLEN SWALLOW (1842–1911). Chemist. Born in Dunstable, Massachusetts, on December 3, 1842, Ellen Richards graduated from Vassar College (1870). She was the first woman to graduate from MIT (1873) and taught chemistry there (1876–1902). The first sanitary engineer to study public health, she set state standards for water, sewage, and environmental quality. Richards coined the term *home economics,* founded the American Home Economics Association (1908), promoted school lunch programs, and developed inexpensive, nutritious diets. Her home in Jamaica Plain was the laboratory for the Center for Right Living, and she wrote *The Cost of Living* (1899) on household management. Richards died in **Boston** on March 30, 1911.

RICHARDSON, ELLIOT LEE (1920–1999). Lawyer. Born in **Boston** on July 20, 1920, Richardson graduated from **Harvard University** (1941) and Harvard Law School (1947). He served in the U.S. Army in World War II (1941–45) and was a law clerk for Justice Learned Hand (1947–48) and Justice **Felix Frankfurter** (1948–49) before joining a Boston law firm (1949–57). After serving as assistant secretary of health, education and welfare (1954–59) and U.S. attorney for Massachusetts (1959–61), he was elected Republican lieutenant governor (1965–67) and attorney general (1967–69). Richardson was undersecretary of state (1969–70), secretary of health, education and welfare (1970–73), secretary of defense (1973), and U.S. attorney general (1973). He resigned when President Richard Nixon ordered him to fire special prosecutor Archibald Cox (1973). President Gerald Ford appointed him ambassador to Great Britain (1975–76) and secretary of commerce (1976–77), making him the first person to hold four different cabinet seats. President Jimmy Carter appointed him ambassador-at-large (1977–80). Richardson, an archetypal **Boston Brahmin**, received the Presidential Medal of Freedom (1998) for his integrity in public service, retired from his Washington, D.C., law practice (1992), and died in Boston on December 30, 1999.

RICHARDSON, HENRY HOBSON (1838–1886). Architect. Born in Louisiana on September 28, 1838, Richardson graduated from **Harvard** College (1859) and studied in Paris (1859–65). His New York City firm won competitions for the First **Unitarian** Church (1866) in Springfield, Massachusetts, and the Grace Church in Medford, Massachusetts (1869). He is best known for the granite and red sandstone Italian Romanesque **Trinity Church** (1877) in **Boston**, where he moved his office (1874). His shingled Stoughton house (1883) in Cambridge was widely imitated, and he influenced Charles F. McKim and **Augustus Saint Gaudens**, who both worked with him. Two buildings at **Harvard University** and office buildings in Boston are among his best designs in the well-engineered style called Richardsonian Romanesque. Richardson, who often collaborated with **Frederick Law Olmsted**, died in Boston on April 27, 1886. *See also* AMES, OAKES; ARCHITECTURE.

RIPLEY, GEORGE (1802–1880). Reformer. Born in Greenfield, Massachusetts, on October 3, 1802, Ripley graduated from **Harvard** Divinity School (1826). He was a **Unitarian** minister in **Boston** (1826–41), editor of the **Transcendentalist** magazine *The Dial* (1840–44), and founder of **Brook Farm** (1841–47). When the commune went bankrupt, he worked as a literary critic for Horace Greeley's *New York Tribune* (1849–80). Ripley founded *Harper's Monthly* magazine (1850) and published the *New American Cyclopedia* (1862), a popular reference book. He died in New York City on July 4, 1880.

RIVER GODS. A name for the wealthy families who dominated society, politics, and the economy of the **Connecticut River** towns in colonial Massachusetts. Their religious leader was **Solomon Stoddard** in Northampton. Members of the Dwight, Pyncheon, and Williams families controlled political offices until the **American Revolution**.

***ROBERTS v. BOSTON* (1850).** A decision by Massachusetts chief justice **Lemuel Shaw** that Sarah Roberts, an **African-American** pupil in **Boston**, was not entitled to attend a desegregated public school. This case proposed the separate but equal doctrine extended by the U.S. Supreme Court (1896), but it prompted the legislature to pass the first state law prohibiting school segregation (1855). Desegregation was slowly accepted in New England, although **New Haven**, Connecticut, followed this example in 1869.

ROBERTS, KENNETH (1885–1957). Writer. Kenneth Lewis Roberts was born in Kennebunk, Maine, on December 8, 1885, and graduated from Cornell University (1908). After serving in the U.S. Marine Corps in World War I, he wrote for the *Saturday Evening Post* but turned to historical novels at the suggestion of his neighbor, Booth Tarkington. His novels chronicle New England in the **American Revolution**, including *Arundel* (1930) and *Rabble in Arms* (1933). *Northwest Passage* (1937) is a colorful account of Major **Robert Rogers**. Roberts won a Pulitzer Prize (1957) for inspiring public interest in early American history and died in Kennebunkport on July 21, 1957.

ROBINSON, EDWIN ARLINGTON (1869–1935). Poet. Born in Head Tide, Maine, on December 22, 1869, Robinson studied at **Harvard University** (1891–93). He grew up in Gardiner, immortalized in his poetry as Tilbury Town, and is most recognized for his collection, *The Town Down the River* (1910). Robinson spent summers at the **MacDowell Colony** but was often destitute. His early poems about disappointed people, his relatives and neighbors, such as *Richard Cory* and *Miniver Cheever*, are most popular for ironic detachment and shrewd insight into small-town life in Maine. Robinson won Pulitzer Prizes for *Collected Poems* (1922), *The Man Who Died Twice* (1924), and *Tristram* (1927). He died in New York City on April 6, 1935.

ROBINSON, HARRIET H. (1825–1911). Writer. Born in **Boston** on February 8, 1825, Harriet Jane Hanson Robinson was a **textile** factory operative in **Lowell** (1834–48). She wrote for the *Lowell Offering* and her memoir *Loom and Spindle* (1898) recounted the Lowell **mill girls** strike (1836). Robinson married William Stevens Robinson (1813–76), a founder of the Free Soil Party and crusading editor of the *Lowell Courier*. She founded the General Federation of Women's Clubs (1890) and wrote *Massachusetts in the Woman Suffrage Movement* (1881). Harriet Robinson died in Malden, Massachusetts, on December 22, 1911.

ROCKWELL, NORMAN (1894–1978). Artist. Born in New York City on February 3, 1894, Norman Percevel Rockwell studied art in New York (1908–10) and Paris (1923). His success was assured in 1916 when he drew his first cover for the *Saturday Evening Post*, the first of 321 covers over 47 years. Moving to Arlington, Vermont (1939–53), his magazine and book illustrations, posters, advertisements, and other artwork idealized the New England town and **Yankee** values, a theme he continued when he moved to Stockbridge, Massachusetts (1953–78). Rockwell was the most popular painter and illustrator in the nation when he died in Stockbridge on November 8, 1978.

RODGERS, BILL (1947–). Athlete. Born in **Hartford**, Connecticut, on December 23, 1947, William Henry Rodgers graduated from Wesleyan University (1970) and Boston College (M. Ed., 1975). He won the **Boston Marathon** (1975, 1978, 1979, 1980) and the New York Marathon (1976, 1979). Rodgers also held world and U.S. records in other track races and was elected to the National Distance Running Hall of Fame (1997). He competed in the 100th Boston Marathon, continues to race, and is a media commentator on track events.

ROGERS, EDITH NOURSE (1881–1960). Congresswoman from Massachusetts. Born in Saco, Maine, on March 19, 1881, Edith Nourse Rogers worked with the Red Cross in World War I (1917–22) and assisted disabled veterans (1922–33). Elected as a Republican from **Lowell**, Massachusetts, to fill the vacancy created by the death of her husband, John J. Rogers (1881–1925), she was the state's first congresswoman and became the longest-serving woman in the history of the House of Representatives (1925–60). Her major accomplishments were creating the G. I. Bill (1944) and establishing the Women's Army Corps (WACS). Mrs. Rogers died in **Boston** on September 19, 1960.

ROGERS, ROBERT (1731–1795). Soldier. Born on November 7, 1731, in Methuen, Massachusetts, Rogers volunteered for a New Hampshire expedition in the **French and Indian War** (1754–63). Earning a commission in the British army for his daring raids (1758) against the **Abenaki** in Canada, Major Rogers organized nine scouting units known as Rogers's Rangers. After the war he held frontier appointments, but his own misadministration, illicit trade with **Native Americans**, and debts forced him into exile in England, where he published his *Journals* and his *Concise Account of North America* in 1765. Arrested for debt in London, he returned to America, where George Washington arrested him as a spy (1776), but he escaped to organize two **Loyalist** ranger units. Rogers died in London on May 18, 1795. His guerrilla warfare was depicted in **Kenneth Roberts**'s novel *Northwest Passage* and in a popular movie (1940) by the same title.

RORABACK, J. HENRY (1870–1937). Businessman and politician. Born in Sheffield, Massachusetts, on April 5, 1870, John Henry Roraback studied law in North Canaan, Connecticut, with his brother. He practiced law in **Hartford** (1892–1907), representing the New York, New Haven and Hartford Railroad and several public utility companies. In 1905 he reorganized small electric companies and was the founder (1917) and president (1925–37) of the Connecticut Power and Light Company. Roraback is best remembered as the state's Republican Party boss, serving as chairman of the Connecticut state party (1912–37) and directing politics from his office at the Hartford Hotel. Old Guard Republicans controlled the state from 1858 to 1930, dominating the governor's office, state legislature, and congressional delegation. Cultivating both industrialists and rural **Yankee** farmers, Roraback's program was to reduce taxes to attract business to the state and to avoid liberal laws on work-ing conditions, minimum wages, pensions, and benefits. He crafted his party's message to appeal both to the state's Ku Klux Klan members and to many Irish Catholic voters in the 1920s. Only Democrat **Simon Baldwin**'s terms as governor (1910–14) interrupted Republican control of the governor's office until **Wilbur Cross** was elected (1930). During Governor Cross's fourth term, Roraback died on May 19, 1937, in Harwinton.

ROUTE 1. The nation's oldest highway from Fort Kent, Maine, to Key West, Florida. Known as U.S. Highway 1, the route is the gateway to the wilderness and recreation areas of northern Maine. Traveling to the south, it passes through New Hampshire's short coastline to **Boston**'s North Shore and along the **Long Island Sound** coast of Connecticut. Maine author **E. B. White** claimed he learned to spell the word "moccasin" while driving Route 1 from New York to **Bar Harbor**.

ROUTE 128. The 65-mile highway built (1951) as a ring around metropolitan **Boston**. It is known as America's technology highway because of its many high-tech and pioneer **computer** industries. Officially designated as the Great Northern Circumferential Highway, it eliminated traffic congestion by traveling around rather than through suburban town centers and opened recreational areas north and south of Boston as one of the first expressways in the country. Stimulated by university research projects like MIT's **Lincoln Laboratory** in Lexington, more than 169 defense-related and high-tech firms relocated along Route 128 (1953–61), building unique industrial parks on abandoned farmland for 24,000 employees. Suburban housing and economic development were unforeseen consequences of this highway. *See also* MASSACHUSETTS TURNPIKE.

ROWLANDSON, MARY (1636–1711). Writer. Born in England in 1636, Mary White emigrated with her family (1639) to **Salem**, Massachusetts, where she married a minister, Joseph Rowlandson (1656). While living in Lancaster, Massachusetts, she was captured by the **Wampanoag** and marched 150 miles with them to Connecticut, where she met **King Philip** (or **Metacom**) and then to New Hampshire. After she was re-deemed, she wrote a memoir, *Narrative* (1682) with the assistance of **In-**

crease **Mather**, who hoped captivity tales would demonstrate the power of **Puritan** faith. Mrs. Rowlandson lived in Wethersfield, Connecticut, until her death on January 5, 1711. Her book became a classic account in the body of New England captivity literature.

ROXBURY LATIN SCHOOL (1645). The oldest continuously operating school in North America. Founded by **John Eliot** in the town of Roxbury, the elite private **prep school** relocated to West Roxbury. Major General **Joseph Warren** and **Harvard University** president **James B. Conant** are among the independent school's prominent graduates.

ROXBURY PUDDINGSTONE. The official state rock of Massachusetts is a brown and gray stone common in eastern Massachusetts. **Henry H. Richardson** used it for Trinity Church (1877) and the Old South Church in **Boston**'s Copley Square and for the Chestnut Hill Reservoir Pumping Station. This conglomerate of shale, sandstone, and volcanic rock was celebrated in Dr. **Oliver Wendell Holmes**'s poem *The Dorchester Giant* (1830), imagining it was like plums in a pudding.

RUDMAN, WARREN BRUCE (1930–). Senator from New Hampshire. Born in **Boston** on May 18, 1930, Rudman graduated from Syracuse University (1952). He served in the U.S. Army (1952–54), graduated from Boston College Law School (1960), and practiced law in Manchester, New Hampshire (1976–80). Rudman was elected as a Republican to the Senate (1980–93). He practiced law in Washington, D.C., and founded the Concord Coalition to promote ethics in government.

RUFFIN, GEORGE LEWIS (1834–1886). Lawyer and judge. Born in Richmond, Virginia, on December 16, 1834, Ruffin moved with his free parents to **Boston** (1853). He attended **public schools** and was active in the Republican Party and the **abolitionist** movement with **William Lloyd Garrison**. He married **Josephine St. Pierre** and moved to England (1858) after the Dred Scott Case but returned in six months. Ruffin was the first black graduate of **Harvard** Law School (1869), practicing law with white and black clients. Elected to the state legislature (1869–70), he was the first **African American** on the Boston Common Council (1876–77). Governor **Benjamin F. Butler** appointed Ruffin as a municipal judge in Charlestown (1883–86), the first African-American judge in New England. Ruffin died in Boston on November 20, 1886.

RUFFIN, JOSEPHINE ST. PIERRE (1842–1924). Reformer. Born in **Boston** on August 31, 1842, Josephine St. Pierre was educated at integrated schools in **Salem** and married **George Lewis Ruffin** (1858). Josephine and George Ruffin were active supporters of the abolitionist movement, the **Civil War**, and reform organizations while living on **Beacon Hill.** Mrs. Ruffin served on the board of the Massachusetts Moral Education Association and the Massachusetts School Suffrage Association. She was a key link for the black community with the Boston elite while working with **Julia Ward Howe** and **Lucy Stone** in the New England Women's Club (1868). She founded the first newspaper for black women, the *Women's Era*, and organized the Women's Era Club (1893), one of the first clubs for **African-American** women in the nation. She organized the Boston conference in 1895 that led to the National Federation of Afro-American Women, merging it (1896) with the National Association of Colored Women and serving as its first vice-president. Mrs. Ruffin was also a founder of the Boston branch of the National Association for Colored People and an influential leader of the black community when she died in Boston on March 13, 1924.

RUM. An alcoholic beverage distilled from **molasses**, the syrup that is a by-product of refining sugar cane. The fermented molasses is distilled and aged in oak casks to form the rum. New Englanders used rum in the **fur trade** (1633) and exchanged **lumber**, horses, fish, and cider for molasses or sugar in the **West Indies trade** (1640) to make rum. It became such a popular drink that the Massachusetts **General Court** passed a law regulating the sale of rum (1657) and **Increase Mather** deplored the drunkenness due to cheap rum in 1686. Merchants traded rum, produced by 63 distilleries in Massachusetts and 22 in Rhode Island (1763), for English manufactured goods and for West African slaves in the **triangular trade**. Rum became more popular than beer, ale, and cider in New England and other American colonies. Revenue from local excise taxes on rum increased rapidly and prompted new laws (1690) to control drunkenness. The rum trade flourished because the Molasses Act (1733) was not enforced, but the stricter **Sugar Act** (1764) led to colonial protests. John Hall produced one very popular brand in Medford, Massachusetts (1715–1905), where schooners built at Mystic River **shipyards** (1635–1873) carried his Old Medford Rum around the world. The profits from rum provided much capital for regional commercial and industrial enterprises. *See also* TEMPERANCE.

RUMFORD, COUNT. *See* THOMPSON, BENJAMIN.

RUSSELL, WILLIAM E. (1857–1896). Governor of Massachusetts. Born in Cambridge on January 6, 1857, William Eustis Russell graduated from **Harvard University** (1877) and Boston University Law School (1879). He practiced law in Cambridge and was elected mayor (1884–87). Billy Russell was elected governor for three terms (1891–94), the first Democrat elected governor since the **Civil War**, which ended Republican domination of the state. Russell was a pro-labor Gold Democrat and died on July 16, 1896, in Canada shortly after addressing the Democratic national convention.

– S –

SACCO-VANZETTI CASE. A controversial murder trial in Massachusetts reflecting social and political issues of the 1920s. Two men were murdered in Braintree on April 15, 1920, during a robbery. Nicola Sacco, a fish peddler, and Bartolomeo Vanzetti, a factory worker, were arrested. Both men had emigrated from Italy to America in 1908 and were known as anarchists opposed to World War I. Tried in Braintree, they were sentenced to death in 1921. Their execution (1927) was an international cause célèbre as leftists and intellectuals questioned the justice of the police and courts. **Felix Frankfurter**, a professor at Harvard Law School, was an influential critic of the trial, privately encouraged by Supreme Court Justice **Louis D. Brandeis**. Nevertheless, Governor **Alvan T. Fuller** ordered the execution on August 22, 1927, after a commission headed by the presidents of MIT and **Harvard University** supported the court verdict. Controversy about this case led Governor **Michael Dukakis** to sign an executive order (1977) regretting the execution. Governor **Paul Cellucci** and **Boston** mayor Thomas Menino unveiled a memorial in the **Boston Public Library** (1997). The case remains a disputed symbol of conservative nativism in the 1920s.

SACRED COD. A wooden replica of the **codfish** hanging from the ceiling of the Massachusetts House of Representatives since 1748. It symbolizes the important role **fishing** plays in New England history. The first millionaires in New England, dubbed the **codfish aristocracy**, earned their wealth from commercial fishing.

SAGADAHOC. A settlement on the mouth of the Kennebec River in Maine (1607–08) established by the **Plymouth Company**. It failed due to the harsh winter and led **Sir Ferdinando Gorges** to reorganize the joint-stock company as the **Council for New England** (1620).

ST. ALBANS RAID. An attack by 20 Confederate troops from Canada on St. Albans, Vermont, on October 19, 1864. After robbing three banks and killing one citizen, the Confederates were arrested in Canada but not extradited, and most of the money was returned. Secretary of State William H. Seward protested this violation of neutrality to the British government and threatened to terminate the Rush-Bagot disarmament agreement of 1817. Despite the vigilance of Canadian officials, some Americans demanded retaliatory attacks in Canada or annexation of Canada. The dispute dissipated with the creation of the Dominion of Canada (1867). *The Raid* (1954) is a Hollywood film based on this northernmost engagement of the **Civil War**. Confederate raids in **Portland** harbor (1863) and at Calais, Maine (1864), also failed.

SAINT BOTOLPH (610–680). Patron Saint of **Boston**. Born in England, Saint Botolph was a monk in Ireland who founded the monastery around which the East Anglia town of Boston (named for him) developed (654). His feast day is June 17, and he is the patron saint of shipbuilders.

SAINT-GAUDENS, AUGUSTUS (1848–1907). Sculptor. Born in Dublin, Ireland, on March 1, 1848, Saint-Gaudens lived with his parents in **Boston** and New York City (1848). He apprenticed with a cameo cutter and studied at Cooper Union and in Paris and Rome (1867–72). His major works include *The Puritan* (1886) in Springfield, Massachusetts, the memorial to Mrs. **Henry Adams** (1891) in Washington, D.C., and the **Shaw Memorial** (1897) on **Boston Common**. Saint-Gaudens lived and worked in Cornish, New Hampshire (1885–1907), until his death there on August 3, 1907. His studio was the focus a prominent **art colony** and is now a national historic site.

ST. GERMAIN, FERNAND JOSEPH. (1928–). Congressman from Rhode Island. Born in Blackstone, Massachusetts, on January 9, 1928, St. Germain was raised in Woonsocket, Rhode Island. He graduated from Providence College (1948) and Boston University Law School (1955), served in the U.S. Army (1949–52), and practiced law in Woonsocket (1956–61). The popular **French-Canadian** lawyer was elected as a Democrat to the state legislature (1953–61) and to the House of Representatives (1961–89).

SALEM. A town on **Cape Ann** 15 miles northeast of **Boston**. It was settled by **Roger Conant** (1626) and **John Endecott** (1628), the first governor of the **Massachusetts Bay Colony**. Although **John Winthrop** moved the capital to Boston (1630), Salem became a major port for **fishing** and international trade. The Salem Maritime Historic Park and the **Peabody Essex Museum** preserve its history today. *See also* CODFISH ARISTOCRACY; DERBY, ELIAS H.; HOUSE OF SEVEN GABLES; MCINTIRE, SAMUEL; SALEM WITCHCRAFT TRIALS.

SALEM WITCHCRAFT TRIALS. Occurred in 1692 and ended witchcraft persecution in New England that began in Charlestown (1648), **Boston** (1655), Northampton (1674), and Newbury (1680). Arising from the hysterical and exhibitionistic accusations of adolescent girls in **Salem**, Massachusetts, 20 people were executed by the courts for consorting with the devil. Sometimes áttributed to community tensions over landholding or **Abenaki** raids, this frightening episode soon had a sobering effect on public opinion. Judge **Samuel Sewell**, one of 10 judges presiding in the trials, publicly repented (1696) for his errors in the hysteria, and one of the girls confessed her accusations were false. A memorial to the 20 victims was dedicated in Salem (1992), but at least 44 women and 5 men were executed for witchcraft in 10 New England towns (1648–92).

SALTBOX. A colonial-style house common in New England (1650–1830) with two stories in front and one story in the rear. The gable roof has a rear slope longer than the front slope and a center chimney. The hand-hewn, timber frame was covered by shingles or clapboards. The National Park Service preserves the birthplace of **John Adams** in Quincy, Massachusetts (1650–1927) as an example of the vernacular saltbox house. *See also* ARCHITECTURE.

SALTONSTALL, LEVERETT (1892–1979). Senator from Massachusetts. Born in Chestnut Hill, Massachusetts, on September 1, 1892, Saltonstall graduated from **Harvard University** (1914) and Harvard Law School (1917). After serving in the U.S. Army in World War I, he was an alderman in Newton (1920–22) and a Middlesex county assistant district attorney (1921–22) and served as a Republican state legislator

(1923–36). Saltonstall defeated **James Michael Curley** for election as governor (1939–45) and was a U.S. senator (1945–67). Although a **Boston Brahmin**, he was unerringly popular with Democratic voters, who called him Salty. He died in Dover on June 17, 1979.

SAMOSET (1590–1663). Native American leader. Little is known of his birth, but Samoset was the Pemaquid *sachem* known as Osamoset who greeted the **Pilgrims** at **Plymouth** in March 1621. Having learned English from fishermen in Maine (1614), he introduced the **Wampanoag** leaders **Massasoit** and **Squanto** to the Pilgrims. Samoset signed the first deed transferring 12,000 acres in Maine to the English (1625). He signed another deed (1653) to English colonists and was buried in his village in Bristol, Maine.

SAMSON, DEBORAH (1760–1827). Hero. Born in **Plymouth**, Massachusetts, on December 17, 1760, Deborah Samson was an **indentured servant** who enlisted in the 4th Massachusetts Regiment (1778) as Robert Shurtleff. She served for three years in several battles, suffering sword and musket wounds, until her identity was discovered by army surgeons. Discharged after the **American Revolution** (1783), she married a Massachusetts farmer, Benjamin Gannett, in 1794. By 1802 she was one of the first American women to lecture professionally, dressed in a soldier's uniform. Deborah Samson died in Sharon, Massachusetts, on April 29, 1827, but Congress awarded a full military pension (1838) to her heirs. The legislature named her the official state heroine (1983).

SAMUELSON, JOAN BENOIT (1957–). Athlete. Born on May 16, 1957, in **Portland**, Maine, Joan Benoit Samuelson graduated from Bowdoin College (1979). She won the **Boston Marathon** (1979) and broke the world record (1983). She won a gold medal in the first women's Olympic marathon (1984) and received the Sullivan Award as the outstanding U.S. amateur athlete (1985). She still holds many track records and is a television sports commentator.

SANDERS, BERNARD (1941–). Congressman from Vermont. Born in Brooklyn, New York, on September 8, 1941, Sanders graduated from the University of Chicago (1964). After teaching at **Harvard University** (1989) and Hamilton College (1990), he moved to Vermont as a freelance writer and was an independent candidate for the U.S. Senate (1972, 1974) and governor (1972, 1976, 1986). Sanders was elected mayor of Burlington (1981–89) and to the House of Representatives (1991–present). He is the only socialist and independent in Congress and votes with the Democratic Party.

SAN SOUCI, EMERY JOHN (1857–1936). Governor of Rhode Island. Born in Saco, Maine, on July 24, 1857, San Souci was a shoe salesman who founded a successful department store in **Providence** (1888–1919). He served on the Providence Common Council (1901–07), as lieutenant governor (1915–19), and as Republican governor (1921–23). Although the son of **French-Canadian** immigrants, Sans Souci became unpopular for using the state **militia** to end a bitter **textile** workers' strike (1922). He served as collector of the port of Providence (1923–35) and died in **Hartford**, Connecticut, on August 10, 1936.

SANTAYANA, GEORGE (1863–1952). Writer. Born in Spain on December 16, 1863, Santayana was raised in **Boston** and graduated from **Boston Latin School** and **Harvard University** (1886). After study in Germany, he earned his Ph.D. at Harvard University (1888) and taught philosophy there (1888–1912). Retiring in Europe, he wrote *The Life of Reason* (1906) and *The Realms of Being* (1927–40) on his own theory of philosophical naturalism. Coining the term "genteel tradition" to describe New England literature in the Gilded Age, he wrote poetry, literary criticism, and a novel, *The Last Puritan* (1935). Santayana died in Rome on September 26, 1952.

SARGENT, CHARLES SPRAGUE (1841–1927). Educator. Born in **Boston** on April 24, 1841, Sargent graduated from **Harvard** College (1862). After serving in the Union Army (1862–65), he taught at Harvard (1872–1927) and founded and directed the **Arnold Arboretum** (1873–1927). In addition to developing its unique horticultural collections, he was a leader in the conservation and National Park movements, wrote *Manual of the Trees of North American* (1905), and edited the magazine *Garden and Forest*. Sargent died in Brookline on March 22, 1927.

SARGENT, JOHN SINGER (1856–1925). Artist. Born to American parents in Florence on January 12, 1856, Sargent studied art in Italy, France, and Germany. He visited the United States for the first time in 1876, and after a major exhibition in **Boston** (1887) he became the leading portrait artist in London and Paris. Sargent is most often associated with Boston by his portraits of *Henry James* (1913), *Bishop William Lawrence* (1916), *Abbott Lawrence Lowell* (1923), *Mrs. William Crowninshield Endicott* (1902), and *The Daughters of Edward Darley Boit* (1882). He also painted murals at the **Boston Public Library** (1895–1919), the **Museum of Fine Arts** (1916–25), and **Harvard University**'s Widener Library (1921–22). Sargent, the van Dyck of his times, died in London on April 15, 1925.

SARTON, MAY (1912–1995). Writer. Born in Belgium on May 3, 1912, Eleanore Marie Sarton grew up in Cambridge, Massachusetts (1916–29). She published her first poetry in *Encounter in April* (1937) and a novel, *The Bridge of Years* (1946). Moving to New Hampshire (1958), Sarton wrote novels, memoirs, and another volume of poetry, *As Does New Hampshire* (1967). Settling in York, Maine (1973), she published *Journal of a Solitude* (1973), her most influential book, establishing her as a major feminist author. Her letters and several critical works on her career were published after her death in York on July 16, 1995.

SAUGUS IRON WORKS. The site of the first integrated ironworks in North America, established in Saugus, Massachusetts (1646–68) with a blast furnace, forge, rolling mill, and water wheel on the Saugus River. Robert Bridges, the Lynn magistrate, also mined bog iron ore and operated an ironworks (1646–83). This forerunner of American industry produced wrought iron nails, wagon wheels, hoes, hinges, shovels, andirons, latches, and tongs. Most ironworkers were English and Welsh **indentured servants**, but 62 **Scottish** prisoners of war arrived (1651) from the Battle of Dunbar to work in Saugus. **Wallace Nutting** restored the ironworks (1916), and it became a National Park Service historic site (1968).

SAYBROOK PLATFORM (1708). Created county associations of ministers with authority over congregations and permitted the **Half-Way Covenant** in Connecticut **Congregational** churches. Written by 12 ministers and four laymen delegates in Saybrook, it was enacted by the Connecticut legislature but could be rejected by any congregation. This was a more conservative centralized form of church government than prescribed by the **Cambridge Platform** (1648).

SCALLOP. A bivalve living on the sea bottom in underwater grass beds, using jet propulsion to swim and eating algae and plankton. The bay scallop *(Aequipecten irradians)* is found from Canada to Florida but numerous and easy to harvest by hand dredging in New England shallow bays. The adductor muscle of the deep-sea scallop *(Placopecten magellanicus)* is also edible. Scallop **fishing** produces a traditional New England seafood, baked, broiled, fried, or in a pie, and the industry has increased since conservation laws (1994) limited **cod** fishing. **Aquaculture**, a new industry in New England (1970s), also produces scallops for restaurants. Conservationists fear dredging, by mobile fishing gear (a large chain bag) pulled by trawlers over the seabed, harms sensitive marine habitats on **Georges Bank**.

SCHAGHTICOKE. A **Native American** people who lived in the **Housatonic River** valley in Connecticut when they encountered English colonists in 1699. When the *sachem* Gideon Mauwee sold land to colonists (1729) the tribe numbered 600 people. Moravian missionaries arrived in 1743, and the colonial general assembly created a reservation in 1752. Schaghticoke warriors served in the **American Revolution**, but the tribe declined to a hundred people by 1800 at Kent, Connecticut. Although recognized by the state, the federal government had not accepted tribal claims by the 300 surviving Schaghticoke people by 2002.

SCOLLAY SQUARE. An area in **Boston** adjacent to **Faneuil Hall** owned by William Scollay (1795) and named for him (1838). Once the site of elegant hotels and restaurants, it became a commercial center (1860) as the city's elite moved to the **Back Bay** away from **Irish immigrants** in the **North End** and **West End**. The **Howard Athenaeum** Theater (1845–1961), featured Shakespearean actors Junius Booth and Edmund Kean in the 1850s but declined with minstrel and burlesque shows (1869–61). By 1915 the theater was known as the **Old Howard**, attracting rowdy **Harvard** students, soldiers, and sailors to Scollay Square in World Wars I and II. The **banned in Boston** tradition of censorship and urban renewal closed the Scollay Square tattoo parlors, **taverns**, hot dog stands, and Old Howard Theater (1962).

SCOTS. Early **immigrants** to New England. David Thomson settled on a 6,000 acre land grant in Little Harbor, New Hampshire (1623), but soon moved to the **Boston** harbor island that bears his name. One hundred and fifty prisoners of war from the Battle of Dunbar (1651) were sent from Scotland to Massachusetts as **indentured servants**. Later Scottish immigrants include John Campbell (1653–1728), publisher of the *Boston Newsletter* (1704–22), and Thomas Melvill, a Boston merchant, who was the grandfather of **Herman Melville**, and the father of **Gilbert Stuart**, who operated the first water-powered snuff mill in Rhode Island (1755). James Thomas was the father of the Connecticut clockmaker **Seth Thomas**.

Boston's Scots Charitable Society (1657) is the oldest private charity in the nation. Scots settled Barnet (1763), Craftsbury, and Ryegate, Vermont, and named Caledonia County (1792) after the Roman term for Scotland. After the **French and Indian War** (1763), Maine attracted Scots to the Kennebec River area at **Augusta**. The first U.S. census (1790) counted 260,000 Americans of Scottish origin. The economic problems and the potato famine of the 1840s sent more Scots to America, Gaelic-speaking **Catholics** from the Highlands and Presbyterian or Anglican Lowland Scots. Some immigrated to Canada and then entered the United States by foot, **stage coach**, or packet ships, numbering about 478,000 people (1852–1910). Economic depression sent 391,000 Scots to America from 1921 to 1931.

Although most immigrants were found in New York and Pennsylvania, the Massachusetts population in 1855 was 9.5 percent Scottish and 1 percent in Connecticut. After the **Civil War**, skilled workers from Scotland found **textile** jobs in Pawtucket, Rhode Island, and Thompsonville, Connecticut. New England **quarries** also employed many Scots. **Samuel Seabury**, who studied medicine in Edinburgh, was consecrated an Episcopal bishop in Scotland (1794), and the Episcopal Church and the Presbyterian Church in New England were strongly influenced by the Scots. Scottish Halloween and New Year's Eve traditions and the Highland clans (lodges) and games were introduced to New England by 1880. Although some Scots had been **Loyalists** in the **American Revolution**, they blended easily with the **Yankee** majority by the Civil War. **Alexander Graham Bell** was the most famous Scotsman in New England.

SCOTCH-IRISH. The descendants of 200,000 Lowland Presbyterians from Scotland who migrated to Ulster in northern Ireland in the 17th century. They were an influential ethnic group throughout New England. About 250,000 of these **immigrants** arrived in the United States from 1695 to 1775 and over 2 million by 1920. They adopted the name Americans applied to them in the 1840s to distinguish themselves from the **Irish Catholic** immigrants. Many came as **indentured servants**, and by 1718 Scotch-Irish families settled on the New England frontier from Connecticut and western Massachusetts to coastal Maine. Towns named

Antrim, Bangor, Belfast, Colrain, Derry, and Orange reflect Ulster origins. These hardy immigrants introduced flax and the **potato** to New England when settling in Londonderry, New Hampshire, in 1719.

Religious conflict was common, and **Congregationalists** destroyed a newly built Scotch-Irish church in **Worcester** (1734) and a **Boston** mob prevented Belfast and Londonderry immigrants from landing (1729). Fear that these Presbyterians would add to the poor relief costs and the incidence of crime were major concerns in Massachusetts. But they shared with the New England **Yankees** a high literacy rate and a love of learning and were commonly found in **militia** companies by 1775. But the Scotch-Irish members of the Loyal Irish Volunteers in Boston (1777) proved that not all New Englanders supported the **American Revolution**. Many Scotch-Irish played a role in **Shays's Rebellion**.

Emigration from Ulster resumed after the Revolution (1781), but with fewer indentured servants. Two hundred Scotch-Irish immigrants landed in New York to take up farms in Connecticut (1794), and the failed Irish revolution (1798) sent many more to New England. **Harrison Gray Otis**, the Boston **Federalist**, supported the Naturalization Act (1798) because the Scotch-Irish tended to become Jeffersonian Democrats and later followed their countryman, Andrew Jackson. Discontent with the British government, overpopulation, economic decline, and famine prompted 500,000 more to emigrate from Ulster to North America (1815–45), and British records show 1,075,000 Ulster emigrants went to the United States (1851–99).

Anti-Catholicism caused many Scotch-Irishmen to join the Whig Party (1830) and the Republican Party (1854) because most Irish Catholics joined the Democrats. The Scotch-Irish also joined the **Know Nothing Party** and the **American Protective Association**, and their Orange Society alienated Irish Catholics after the **Civil War**. About one in five emigrants from Ireland were Scotch-Irish in the 1880–1914 era and were absorbed as Yankees more easily than the Irish Catholic immigrants.

SCRIMSHAW. An art form developed by men on New England **whaling** ships who carved designs and objects on whalebones and teeth on voyages that often lasted three years. The objects included bracelets, canes, dominoes, doorknobs, rings, tools, and pictures.

SCROD. A New England term for young cod or haddock that is split and boned for cooking. This simple dish, first served at the **Parker House**

hotel in **Boston**, is another example of the austere **Yankee** food ways derived from the **Puritan** distrust of fine foods and the abundance of fresh **codfish**.

SCUDDER, VIDA DUTTON (1861–1954). Writer. Born in India on December 15, 1861, Julia Vida Scudder was the daughter of **Congregational** missionaries. She graduated from Smith College (1884) and studied at Oxford University (1885). While teaching English at Wellesley College (1887–1928), she founded the Denison House Settlement in **Boston** (1888) and the Women's Trade Union League (1903). Newspapers criticized her support of the **textile** workers in the **Lawrence Strike** (1912), but Wellesley College defended her academic freedom. Her books include *Socialism and Character* (1912) and her autobiography *On Journey* (1937). Scudder, the genteel **Back Bay** reformer, died in Wellesley on October 9, 1954.

SEABROOK STATION. Nuclear power generation plant built (1976–90) in Seabury, New Hampshire. Despite delays and much public controversy led by the Clamshell Alliance, an environmental coalition, Seabrook provides 7 percent of New England's electricity. *See also* GALLEN, HUGH J.

SEABURY, SAMUEL (1729–1796). Bishop. Born in Groton, Connecticut, on November 30, 1729, Seabury graduated from Yale College (1748). Influenced by **Samuel Johnson**, he studied at the University of Edinburgh and was ordained an Anglican priest in London (1753). Serving in New York, he wrote **Loyalist** tracts, which led to his imprisonment (1775). Although he aided the British, after the **American Revolution** Seabury was consecrated in Scotland (1784) as the first Episcopal bishop of Connecticut and Rhode Island (1784–96). He unified the English and **Scottish** factions of his church (1789) as bishop and rector of St. James Protestant Episcopal Church in New London, where he died on February 25, 1796.

SECOND GREAT AWAKENING (1800–1840). An evangelical religious revival on the frontier led by Baptists, Methodists, **Universalists**, and Presbyterians. Camp meetings attracted large crowds to hear emotional sermons by itinerant, female, and lay preachers declaring salvation was open to all who repented their sins and rejected the Calvinist doctrine of predestination. In New England the established **Congregational** Church, supported by tax revenues until 1833, was disestablished in the wake of this democratic movement, and church membership became voluntary. Rather than draw new converts into existing churches, the movement had a centrifugal effect, creating non-Calvinist churches. More women than men responded to this egalitarian revival, and many new charitable and missionary organizations were founded. *See also* GREAT AWAKENING.

SEDGWICK, CATHARINE MARIA (1789–1867). Writer. Born in Stockbridge, Massachusetts, on December 28, 1789, the daughter of Pamela Dwight and **Theodore Sedgwick**, Maria became the most popular novelist in America. Her best known novels capture the manners and character of New England, including *A New England Tale* (1822), *Redwood* (1824), and *Hope Leslie* (1827). Her novel *Married or Single?* (1857) defended the right of women to refuse to marry. She died in Roxbury, Massachusetts, on July 31, 1867.

SEDGWICK, THEODORE (1746–1813). Speaker of the House. Born in West Hartford, Connecticut, on May 9, 1746, Sedgwick attended Yale College and practiced law in Great Barrington and Sheffield, Massachusetts (1766–76). After serving in the **American Revolution** and in the Massachusetts legislature (1780–88), Sedgwick was elected to the Continental Congress (1785–86, 1788). He was a **Federalist** in the House of Representatives (1789–96) and in the Senate (1796–99) and served as speaker of the house (1799–1801). Sedgwick was a Massachusetts Supreme Court justice (1802–13) until his death in **Boston** on January 23, 1813.

SELECTMAN. A town official who governs the community in between **town meetings**. Because New England county government is limited to courts, jails, and highways, the board of selectmen exercises considerable authority in local issues. Since the first board of selectmen sat in Charlestown, Massachusetts, in 1634, they have been elected annually from among the most respected and experienced residents in the town. *See also* BLUE LAWS; TITHINGMAN.

SEVEN SISTERS. The seven most prestigious private American colleges for women: Barnard (1889), Bryn Mawr (1885), Mount Holyoke (1837), Radcliffe (1879), Smith (1875), Vassar (1861), and Wellesley (1870). Like the **Ivy League**, this elite consortium was organized (1915) to improve fund-raising efforts and discuss common goals.

SEWELL, SAMUEL (1652–1730). Judge. Born in England on March 28, 1652, Sewell emigrated to Newbury, Massachusetts (1661), and graduated from **Harvard** College (1671). He was a **Salem** minister, merchant, and a publisher (1681–91) and served on the Governor's Council (1691–1725). Sewell was a judge in the **Salem witchcraft trials** (1692) but later repented publicly (1696). He served as chief justice of the Massachusetts Supreme Judicial Court (1718–28) but is best known for his *Diary, 1674–1729*, a lively and engaging view of **Puritan** society. Sewell wrote *The Selling of Joseph* (1700), the first antislavery pamphlet in New England, and he died in **Boston** on January 1, 1730.

SEXTON, ANNE (1928–1974). Poet. Born in Newton, Massachusetts, on November 9, 1928, Anne Harvey Sexton attended Garland College and worked as a model in **Boston**. Despite her mental illness, she studied with **Robert Lowell** at Boston University and wrote *To Bedlam and Back* (1960) and *All My Pretty Ones* (1962). She won the Pulitzer Prize for her collection *Live or Die* (1966) and taught at Boston University (1969–74). Associated with Lowell and **Sylvia Plath** as a self-revelatory poet, Sexton's *The Awful Rowing toward God* (1975) was published after her death on October 4, 1974.

SHADRACH CASE. An **abolitionist** victory at the federal court in **Boston** (1851). Federal marshals arrested a waiter at the elegant Cornhill Coffee House to return him to his owner in Virginia under the Fugitive Slave Law (1850). The escaped slave, Shadrach Minkins, was freed from the courthouse by an **African-American** mob led by **Lewis Hayden**. Unlike **Anthony Burns**, Minkins escaped on the **Underground Railroad** to Montreal. This incident outraged Southerners and frustrated the presidential aspirations of **Daniel Webster**. *See also* SLAVERY.

SHAHEEN, JEANNE (1947–). Governor of New Hampshire. Born in St. Charles, Missouri, on January 28, 1947, Jeanne Bowers Shaheen graduated from Shippensburg University (1969) and earned a master's degree in political science at the University of Mississippi (1973). She taught high school in New Hampshire and was in business before she was elected as a Democrat to the state senate (1991–96). Shaheen was the first woman elected governor of New Hampshire (1997–2003).

SHAKERS. Members of a religious community founded in England by Ann Lee (1736–1784). She immigrated to New York (1774), establishing the

United Society of Believers in Christ's Second Appearing on a farm near Albany. Her sect broke away from the **Quakers** and were known as Shakers. Mother Lee won many converts in New England while living at Harvard, Massachusetts, in a celibate commune (1782). She was assaulted by a mob in Petersham as an accused witch and persecuted while preaching in Connecticut. After her death, 20 Shaker communities expanded with as many as 6,000 members in Shirley (1793) and Hancock, Massachusetts (1783–1959); Enfield, Connecticut (1780–1915); Canterbury, New Hampshire (1792); Sabbathday Lake, Maine (1783); and other states. Widows, abused women, and orphans were welcomed as members, and orphanages such as the **New England Home for Little Wanderers** placed children in perfectionist, pacifist Shaker communities. Best remembered for finely crafted furniture, vocal music, and utilitarian inventions (clothespins, packaged garden seeds, square brooms, round barns), Shaker numbers declined by 1900. The Canterbury, Enfield, and Hancock communes are now museums, but the last surviving five Shakers still lived at Sabbathday Lake in New Gloucester, Maine, in 2003.

SHARKEY, JACK (1902–1994). Boxer. Born in Binghamton, New York, on October 26, 1902, Joseph Paul Zukauskas, the son of Lithuanian **immigrants**, became a professional boxer in **Boston** in 1924. After serving in the U.S. Navy in New England, he boxed as Jack Sharkey (1924–36), winning 38 of 55 bouts including the world heavyweight championship in 1932. After Sharkey retired, he operated a bar and restaurant in Boston and lived in Epping, New Hampshire. He died in Beverly, Massachusetts, on August 17, 1994.

SHATTUCK, GEORGE CHEYNE (1813–1893). Physician. Born in **Boston** on July 22, 1813, George C. Shattuck attended **Boston Latin School** and graduated **Harvard College** (1831). After one year at Harvard Law School he graduated Harvard Medical School (1835) and studied in Europe. Practicing medicine in Boston with his father, he founded the Boston Society for Medical Observation and taught at Harvard Medical School (1855–73). Shattuck founded St. Paul's School, an Episcopal Church **prep school** in Concord, New Hampshire (1856). A distinguished member of a prominent medical family, he died in Boston on March 22, 1893.

SHAW, LEMUEL (1781–1861). Lawyer and judge. Born in Barnstable, Massachusetts, on January 9, 1781, Shaw graduated from **Harvard**

College (1800). He was the leader of the **Boston** bar (1804–30), a state legislator (1811–16, 1821–22, 1828–29), wrote Boston's first city charter (1822–1913), and served as chief justice of the state Supreme Judicial Court (1830–60). His decisions of national significance included *Commonwealth v. Hunt* (1842), which ruled labor unions were not a conspiracy in restraint of trade. In *Roberts v. Boston* (1850), he made the first separate but equal ruling later accepted by the U.S. Supreme Court (1896). His ruling, however, prompted the legislature to pass the first state school desegregation law in the nation (1855). Shaw, the father-in-law of **Herman Melville**, died in Boston on March 30, 1861.

SHAW, ROBERT GOULD (1837–1863). Soldier. Born in **Boston** on October 10, 1837, Shaw attended **Harvard** College (1856–59) and joined the Union Army in 1861. Governor **John A. Andrew**, a friend of Shaw's **Boston Brahmin abolitionist** family, appointed him colonel of the **54th Massachusetts Regiment**, the first Army unit of free **African Americans** in the North. Shaw and many of his men were killed in an attack on Fort Wagner in South Carolina on July 18, 1863. Shaw was buried with his men in an unmarked grave, but the Shaw Memorial on **Boston Common**, designed by **Augustus Saint-Gaudens** (1897), commemorates the heroic 54th Infantry Regiment. *See also* CIVIL WAR.

SHAWMUT. The **Algonquin** name (land of living waters) for the peninsula with three hills or trimount/Tremont—Mount Vernon, **Beacon Hill**, and Pemberton Hill—that the **Puritans** named **Boston** (1630) for **St. Botolph**, the patron saint of shipbuilders, and the town of Boston in England. A narrow neck of land (now called Washington Street) connected Shawmut to Roxbury on the south.

SHAYS'S REBELLION (1786–1787). An armed protest by Massachusetts and New Hampshire farmers against the state legislature's hard money policy, high taxes, and depression that impoverished debtors and led to foreclosures. Led by Captain Daniel Shays (1747–1825), a Revolutionary War hero from Pelham, Massachusetts, angry farmers closed Hampshire and **Worcester** County courts in August 1786. His 600 men battled 500 state militiamen led by General William Shepherd at Springfield. Shepherd defended the Springfield Armory from Shays's attack on January 25, 1787, and routed the insurgents at Petersham on February 4. Governor **James Bowdoin** sent General **Benjamin Lincoln** with a large force to end the insurrection. The legislature responded by reforming the courts and tax laws and pardoned the rebels and Shays (1788), who fled to Vermont and settled in Scottsburg, New York. This rebellion by 4,000 central and western Massachusetts men against the eastern elite brought George Washington out of retirement and convinced Americans that a new U.S. Constitution should replace the Articles of Confederation.

SHEEP. First raised in New England by 1624 when Edward Winslow imported English sheep for meat, cheese, and wool. **Puritans** grazed sheep on **Boston** harbor islands free from wolf depredation, and the colony's laws (1648) decreed it was lawful to keep sheep on the town common. Another law (1684) ordered towns to teach women to spin and weave wool for clothing. Wool was the chief export on **Nantucket** until 1675, and the British army commandeered 10,000 sheep from **Martha's Vineyard** in General Grey's raid (1776). Farm stocks declined during the **American Revolution**, but William Jarvis and Edwin Hammond introduced Merino sheep from Spain to the United States at Weathersfield, Vermont (1811). Among the 450 domesticated breeds, this northwestern Spanish breed, noted for fine, soft fleece and high lanolin oil content, was used for cosmetics. The merino exhibit at the Berkshire County Fair (1812) led to a merino mania until 1840 when overproduction of sheep, the end of the protective tariff (1846), the Erie Canal (1825), and **railroads** (1840s) reduced the price of wool by half. But the northern New England population tripled (1850) as hill country farmers improved their livestock and agricultural practices. Sheep raising became such an important occupation that Vermont had 1.6 million sheep by 1840 and exported them to the western states and Australia. The New England Agricultural Society (1849) improved animal husbandry and **agricultural fairs** award prizes for the best sheep. Before the **Civil War** woolen mills were found in many towns throughout New England, but Vermont's flocks declined by 60 percent (1870) and Massachusetts had only 500 farms raising 9,000 sheep in 2001.

SHELBURNE MUSEUM. Established (1947) by Electra Havenmeyer Webb on her estate in Shelburne, Vermont, to house her collection of Americana. The museum is a major repository of **art**, **architecture**, and New England artifacts, including a Vermont **stage coach** inn (1783), **railroad** station, and the Lake Champlain **lighthouse** (1871).

SHELDON, WILLIAM HERBERT (1898–1977). Scientist. Born in Warwick, Rhode Island, on November 17, 1898, Sheldon graduated from

Brown University (1918). He earned a master's degree in psychology at the University of Colorado (1923) and a Ph.D. in psychology (1926) and M.D. at the University of Chicago (1934). Influenced by his godfather, **William James**, Sheldon developed the somatotype system for rating human physique by anthropometric techniques while teaching at the University of Chicago (1924–27) and the University of Wisconsin (1927–30). He studied child psychology in Europe (1934–36), and his research at **Harvard University** led to *The Varieties of Human Physique* (1940), *The Varieties of Temperament* (1942), and *Varieties of Delinquent Youth* (1949). Adopted by criminologists and physicians, but received with skepticism by social scientists, Sheldon argued eugenics proved the biological superiority of Anglo-Saxons, and his book *Atlas of Men* (1954) resulted in much controversy. Sheldon founded the Biological Humanics Foundation in Cambridge, Massachusetts, where he died on September 16, 1977.

SHEPARD, ALAN BARTLETT, JR. (1923–1998). Astronaut. Born in East Derry, New Hampshire, on November 15, 1923, Shepard graduated from the U.S. Naval Academy (1944). He served in World War II and as a U.S. Navy test pilot (1950–61). In the NASA space program Project Mercury (1961), he became the first American astronaut in space. His suborbital flight in the *Freedom 7* capsule traveled 302 miles to a height of 115 miles. Shepard commanded the *Apollo 14* lunar landing (1971). Admiral Shepard retired from the navy (1974) and wrote *Moon Shot: The Inside Story of America's Race to the Moon* (1994). Shepard died in California on July 21, 1998.

SHERMAN, ROGER (1721–1793). Senator from Connecticut. Born in Newton, Massachusetts, on April 19, 1721, Sherman was a shoemaker in New Milford, Connecticut (1743). He practiced law (1754–61) and served in the legislature (1755–85) and as a superior court judge. Sherman was the only member of the Continental Congress (1774–81, 1783–84) who signed the Declaration of Independence, Articles of Confederation, and U.S. Constitution. Sherman was the first mayor of **New Haven**, Connecticut (1784–93), and served as a **Federalist** in the House of Representatives (1789–91) and the Senate (1791–93) until he died in New Haven on July 23, 1793. **Ralph Earle**'s stark portrait of Roger Sherman (1776) is considered the archetypal image of the reserved **Yankee**.

SHIP SCHOOLS. Operated in **Boston** and **New Bedford**, Massachusetts (1859–71), by the state board of charities to train boys as seamen for the

New England maritime industries. They diverted more than 1,000 homeless boys, young lawbreakers, and **Civil War** orphans from the orphanage or the prison. Officially known as the Massachusetts Nautical **Reform School**, this innovative vocational education experiment closed due to the postwar economic decline in maritime industries. *See also* EDUCATION; REFORM SCHOOLS.

SHIPYARDS. A New England tradition from the earliest times. The first English colonists in Maine built the *Virginia* (1608), which made transatlantic voyages from Virginia to England, and the **Pilgrims** built a shallop (1621). Massachusetts **Puritans** in Medford built an oceangoing ship, the *Blessing of the Bay* (1631), and employed 1,000 men on the Mystic River shipyard at its peak (1855). The **fishing** industry stimulated colonial-era shipbuilding, and **Boston** built its first ship, the *Trial*, in 1643, and had the first drydock in North America at the Charlestown shipyard (1678). The first wharf (1639) to unload cargoes was joined by 15 private wharves by 1645, vying with church steeples as town landmarks. The cargo included barrel staves, cattle, clapboards, cloth, **corn**, crockery, fish, **furs**, indigo, **lumber**, iron, **molasses**, peas, pork, rum, slaves, sugar, spirits, tar, **tobacco**, whale-oil, wheat, and wine. Rich merchants who traded with great hazard to Europe and the West Indies demanded their own trading vessels. Governor **William Phips**, a shipbuilder from Maine, encouraged the English merchant Thomas Coram (1668–1751), who opened shipyards in Boston (1694) and **Taunton** (1698). The shipyards in Essex, Massachusetts, built 4,000 two-masted fishing schooners, more than any port in the nation. Fairhaven, Massachusetts, the **whaling** port that sent **Herman Melville** to sea, also had a thriving shipbuilding industry. Gloucester launched the first New England fishing schooner in 1713 and became the largest fishing port in the world by 1862. But its last great schooner, *The Adventure*, sailed on its final voyage in 1953.

Ships have been constructed in Maine since 1762 on the Kennebec River in Bath, the "birthplace of American shipbuilding." The city's riverbanks once held more shipyards than any place in the world. The Percy & Small Shipyard is the only intact shipyard in the country where large wooden sailing vessels were built, 41 from 1897 to 1920, huge four- to six-masted schooners carrying coal, lumber, and other coastal cargo. The Bath Iron Works (1833) employed shipbuilders for luxury steam yachts and navy vessels by 1889, with 12,000 workers in 1990 and 7,600 in 2000. Owned by General Dynamics Corporation, it is Maine's largest employer, building naval vessels and ships of all types.

In the age of sail most ships were built in small yards by a master shipwright and a few others, perhaps farmers in the off season before specialists—carpenters, joiners, caulkers, sailmakers, blacksmiths, and rope makers—finished the ship. John Paul Jones's ship, *Ranger* (1777), launched in Kittery, was the first ship to fly the American flag. The nearby **Portsmouth** Naval Shipyard (1800) was a shipbuilding site by 1690 when the *Falkland* was launched for the Royal Navy, and the *Raleigh* (1776), *Ranger* (1778), and *America* (1782) for the **American Revolution**. The Portsmouth Yard later built (1917–71) and serviced submarines. In Connecticut, Essex built 500 ships (1720–1860), including the *Oliver Cromwell* (1776), the first Connecticut ship in the Continental Navy; the British raided Essex in 1814. Nearby New London on the Thames River was home port for many privateers, whose success prompted the **Battle of Groton Heights** (1781) and the burning of New London. This was the site of the U.S. Navy Submarine School (1917) and home of the U.S. Coast Guard Academy (1876). Rhode Island shipyards launched many ships for the **triangular trade**, and Bristol was the chief American slave trade port. The Naval War College (1884) is in Newport, and the U.S. Navy Base in **Newport** was a major employer until 1974.

Donald McKay built elegant and speedy **clipper ships** in his East Boston shipyard (1845). Sailing ships carried figureheads on the bow carved by professional artists like **Samuel McIntire** in **Salem** and Simeon Skillin (1716–78) of Boston and his son John Skillin (1747–1800). George Claghorn and Boston shipwrights built *Old Ironsides* (1797), and the Charlestown Navy Yard (1800) employed 47,000 workers in World War II. The U.S. Naval Shipbuilding Museum in Quincy, Massachusetts, preserves the memory of ships built on the Fore River in World War I and World War II. Also a new shipyard in Hingham, Massachusetts, launched navy ships during World War II. Groton and New London are the center of shipbuilding in Connecticut, and during World War I the Groton Iron Works in Noank built merchant ships for the Emergency Fleet Corporation (1917). The *Nautilus*, the first nuclear submarine, was launched at the New London Naval Base (1954) on the Thames River. The legacy of the age of sail is preserved at **Mystic Seaport** in Mystic, Connecticut, as well as at the **Peabody Essex Museum** in Salem, Massachusetts, and the **New Bedford Whaling National Historical Park**. The Herreshoff Marine Museum in Bristol, Rhode Island, birthplace of eight America's Cup defenders (1893–1934), recalls the golden age of yachting in New England.

SHIPWRECKS. Common disasters on the New England coast despite the construction of many **lighthouses**. A French trading vessel was the first recorded shipwreck in **Boston** harbor (1614), and the *Warwick*, a 10-gun English bark, sank at the mouth of the Neponset River (1636). Scavengers on **Nantucket** used timbers from many wrecks on the beach to build the Old Mill (1746). The 74-gun French warship *Magnifique* wrecked on Lovell's Island in Boston Harbor (1782), and the paddle-wheel steamboat *Lexington* sank on a routine trip from Bridgeport, Connecticut, to New York City (1840) in another of many memorable disasters. When the brig *Saint John* went down in a storm off Cohasset, 99 **Irish immigrants** drowned (1849). **Margaret Fuller** died in a shipwreck (1850) off Fire Island, and the *Lizzie Carr* went down in a storm off Rye, New Hampshire (1905), only to wash ashore in 2000.

Shipwrecks and the dangers of the sea inspired **Henry Wadsworth Longfellow**'s poem *The Wreck of the Hesperus* (1841), based on an actual disaster in the Great Blizzard of 1839. **Winslow Homer**'s paintings *Life Line* (1894), *Gulf Stream* (1899), and *Early Morning after a Storm at Sea* (1902) depict the struggle of mariners against nature's fury on the ocean. Fog, formed as the warm Gulf Stream meets the cold Atlantic seas off the New England coast, causes more shipwrecks than storms. Despite **lighthouses** and the efforts of the U.S. Coast Guard, modern shipwrecks continue to occur in New England waters. More than 192 people died when the luxury steamship *Portland* disappeared in a snowstorm gale on **Stellwagen Bank** (1898), a mystery until researchers discovered the wreck (2002). The liner *Larchmont* went down off Watch Hill in Rhode Island (1907), and 52 people died when the Italian ocean liner *Andrea Doria* collided with the *Stockholm* and sank off **Nantucket** (1956). The tanker *Chester Poling* sank off **Cape Ann** (1971). More often commercial fishing vessels are lost at sea. Gloucester, Massachusetts, alone has lost 5,368 ships since 1716, and 249 fishermen perished in one tragic season (1879). The popular film *The Perfect Storm* (2000) depicted the loss of one Gloucester swordfish boat in an extraordinary 1991 gale.

SHIRLEY, WILLIAM (1694–1771). Governor of Massachusetts. Born in England on December 2, 1694, Shirley graduated from Cambridge University (1715). He practiced law in London until he immigrated to Massachusetts (1731), where he became an admiralty judge (1733). As Massachusetts governor (1741–49, 1753–56), Shirley improved the colony's currency and defenses and raised 4,000 volunteers to capture Louisbourg on Cape Breton from the French in **King George's War**

(1745). **Peter Harrison**, imprisoned at the Louisbourg fortress in 1745, provided plans of the fort to Shirley. After diplomatic duties in Paris, he returned to **Boston** (1754) and became commander of all British armed forces in North America in the last phase of the **French and Indian War** (known as the **Seven Years' War** in Europe, 1756–63). Shirley expelled French **Acadian** settlers from Nova Scotia to Louisiana, Connecticut, Massachusetts, and other British colonies. Military failure at Fort Niagara led to his recall to London, but he served as royal governor of the Bahamas (1758–67). Shirley died in Roxbury, Massachusetts, on March 24, 1771.

SHOEMAKING. Began in New England in **Salem**, Massachusetts, in 1629 and became an important industry in Lynn, Massachusetts, by 1781. Ebenezer Breed persuaded Congress to tax imported shoes (1789), stimulating shoemaking throughout New England, with 40 factories on the Assabet River in Hudson, Massachusetts (1816–94). Lyman Reed Blake invented machines to sew shoes (1858), which expanded the modern shoe industry to Brockton and Whitman. Governor William L. Douglas operated one of the largest shoe factories in the nation in Brockton. Waterpower made shoemaking possible in many New England towns like Weare (1823) and Farmington, New Hampshire (1835), and Holbrook, Massachusetts. Using **Charles Goodyear**'s vulcanization process, Leverett Candee made rubber shoes in Hamden and Hartford, Connecticut (1842).

The shoe industry transformed some towns; for example, Haverhill, Massachusetts, was a regional cattle market in 1800, but it produced 20,000 pairs of shoes in 1811 and 1.5 million in 1830. Haverhill employed 11,000 people in 200 factories by 1890. Sidney Wilmont Winslow (1854–1917), publisher of the *Boston Herald* newspaper, organized the United Shoe Machinery Company in Beverly (1899), controlling most of the shoe machinery production and distribution in the nation from its Art Deco–style skyscraper in Boston (1930). The shoe industry was second only to textiles in Massachusetts by 1929 in value of products and the number of employees, but bitter union strikes in **Boston**, Lynn, Chelsea, and **Salem** prompted many companies to relocate to New Hampshire and Maine and outside New England. Shoe workers in Lewiston and Auburn, Maine, waged a costly strike in 1937.

In 1930 shoemaking firms were the largest employers in **Lowell**, but the last major shoe factory closed in 1985. The industry benefited from many inventions, including shoemaking machinery patented by Margaret

Knight of Boston. Keds sneakers, the first rubber-soled shoes with canvas tops designed for basketball, were introduced in Malden, Massachusetts (1917). Recreational shoes are still produced in Dexter, Maine, and in Canton and Marlborough, Massachusetts (2002).

SILLIMAN, BENJAMIN (1779–1864). Scientist. Born in Trumbull, Connecticut, on August 8, 1779, Silliman graduated from Yale College (1796). He was Yale's first professor of chemistry (1802–53), studying with natural scientists in the United States and Europe and founding the Yale Medical School (1813) and the Sheffield Scientific School (1847). His *American Journal of Science and the Arts* (1818) was a leading scientific periodical. Silliman died in **New Haven**, Connecticut, on November 24, 1864.

SILLIMAN, BENJAMIN, JR. (1816–1885). Scientist. Born in **New Haven**, Connecticut, on December 4, 1816, Silliman graduated from Yale College (1837) and assisted his father, **Benjamin Silliman**, as editor of the *American Journal of Science and the Arts* (1818–85). He was professor of chemistry at Yale (1846–70) and published a pioneer work on petroleum, *Report on the Rock Oil* (1855), that led to the Pennsylvania oil industry. Silliman died in New Haven on January 14, 1885.

SILVER CITY. Nickname for **Taunton**, Massachusetts.

SIRICA, JOHN J. (1904–1992). Judge. Born in **Waterbury**, Connecticut, on March 19, 1904, John Joseph Sirica graduated from Georgetown University Law School (1926). After practicing in Washington, D.C., he served as U.S. assistant district attorney (1930–34), entered private practice, and was general counsel to the House Select Committee to Investigate the Federal Communications Commission (1944). Sirica was active in Republican Party politics before his appointment as a judge of the U.S. District Court for the District of Columbia (1957–74). He came to national attention as presiding judge in the Watergate trials (1973–74). He wrote *To Set the Record Straight: The Break-In, The Tapes, the Conspirators, the Pardon* (1979) to express dissatisfaction with the pardon for President Richard M. Nixon. Sirica retired (1986) as an American folk hero and died in Washington, D.C., on August 14, 1992.

SKIING. Began in New England when Norwegians and **Swedes** organized the first American ski club in Berlin, New Hampshire (1882). Dartmouth

College had a ski club (1909) as did Williams College (1915), both skiing at the first winter carnival in Newport, New Hampshire (1917). By 1914 skiers ascended **Mount Washington** and Tuckerman Ravine. Dartmouth hired an Austrian ski instructor and introduced the first U.S. slalom set (1923). Franconia, New Hampshire, opened the first U.S. ski school (1929), and the first snow train brought skiers from **Boston** to Warner, New Hampshire (1931). The third Winter Olympics at Lake Placid, New York (1932), inspired more interest in the sport, and the first rope tow opened in Woodstock, Vermont (1934). New Hampshire had the first chair lift at Belnap (1937) and the first ski trail (1931) and the first U.S. aerial tramway at Cannon Mountain (1938). **Swedish immigrants** introduced cross-country skiing in Maine by 1900, and the Poland Springs resort offered winter sports in 1916.

Snow trains brought skiers from Boston and from New York City to Norfolk, Connecticut, and Pittsfield, Massachusetts, when Amherst College students introduced the sport to the Berkshires (1935). By 1935 snow trains carried 40,000 skiers on one-day trips to New Hampshire. Tuckerman Ravine on **Mount Washington** had races (1933), and **Mount Greylock** ski races drew 6,000 enthusiasts in 1938. C. Minot Dole of Vermont created the first National Ski Patrol (1938). Austrian ski instructors designed the first groomed slope at Mount Cranmore (1939). The first national women's downhill and slalom championships at Mount Mansfield (1939) made Stowe the most fashionable ski resort. The Pico Peak ski lodge in Rutland, Vermont, opened the first alpine lift (or T bar) in 1940.

The exploits of the U.S. Army 10th Mountain Division and the 87th Mountain Regiment in World War II did much to make skiing more popular by the 1950s. The sport appealed to more women when Gretchen Fraser was the first American to win a gold medal at the 1948 Winter Olympics. New England skiers have represented the United States in every Olympic Games since 1942, and Penny Pitou, a young downhill racer from New Hampshire, was the first American to win two silver medals at the 1960 Winter Olympics. This broadened the appeal of skiing and more luxurious ski resorts opened at Mount Mansfield and Mad River Glen (1949) and the Trapp Family Lodge in Stowe, Vermont (1950). Winter sports contributed $10 million to the Vermont economy, a new and expanding recreation and **tourist** industry.

John Jay (1916–2000), a Williamstown, Massachusetts, filmmaker, won an Academy Award for his short subject documentary *Alpine Safari* (1952), and he was inducted into the U.S. Ski Hall of Fame (1981).

When the National Collegiate Athletic Association (NCAA) recognized skiing as an intercollegiate sport (1954), the sport attracted a wider range of skiers. The popular film *The Sound of Music* (1959) made Vermont the Switzerland of America. Bromley Mountain in Vermont introduced New England's first snowmaking system in the 1960s, a method imitated by most New England ski resorts. In the 1990s, Jake Burton, the godfather of snowboarding in Vermont, introduced a new sport to the New England ski areas: 5 in Connecticut, 17 in Maine, 14 in Massachusetts, 18 in New Hampshire, 20 in Vermont, and 1 in Rhode Island. Skiing, enhanced by completion of the interstate highway linking Vermont and New Hampshire (1982), has significantly stimulated the New England economy. New Hampshire adopted skiing as its state sport in 1998.

SLATE. A metamorphic rock found in southwestern Vermont formed by compacting clay, silt, or mud. By 1839 slate was quarried in Fair Haven, and Colonel Alonson Allen (1803–78) opened commercial slate **quarries** in western Vermont's Slate Valley by 1845. Vermont colored slate from 67 quarries provided roofs for 3,000 buildings a year by 1885, often worked by **Welsh** craftsmen and **immigrants** from Scotland, Ireland, Hungary, and Italy. Blackboards, headstones, sidewalks, hearths, mantelpieces, bathtubs, and architectural tiles were made from Vermont and Maine slate. Asbestos and talc mining in Johnson (1951) and Eden (1954) were also important industries in Vermont.

SLATER, SAMUEL (1768–1835). Manufacturer. Born in England on June 9, 1768, Slater brought new British **textile** machinery designs to Rhode Island (1789). Financed by the **Quaker** merchant **Moses Brown** in **Providence**, Rhode Island, Slater built the first cotton-spinning mill on the **Blackstone River** in Pawtucket (1790). This textile mill started the New England textile industry. He founded 12 factories by 1812 and erected the first steam mill (1827) at Providence. Slater died in Webster, Massachusetts, on April 21, 1835. Slater's Mill is now a National Park Service historic site in Pawtucket.

SLAVERY. A feature of New England economic history since 1638 when Massachusetts became the first colony to legalize slavery. But **Native Americans** were enslaved by 1606, and survivors of **King Philips' War** were shipped to the West Indies in 1676. African slaves were auctioned in **Boston**, **Salem**, Medford, **Portsmouth**, Bristol, and **Newport** by 1650. Connecticut also legalized slavery in 1650. Most seaports engaged in the slave trade, but Rhode Island merchants controlled much of the American slave trade (1725–1807). African slaves were 11 percent of Rhode Island's population by 1755. Bristol was the chief New England seaport engaged in the **triangular trade** from Africa to the West Indies to New England, exchanging **rum** for 100,000 slaves by 1808. In 1999 the Hartford Life Insurance Company, Aetna Insurance Company, the Providence Bank, and the *Hartford Courant* newspaper acknowledged their role in the slave trade.

Although **John Winthrop**, **Cotton Mather**, and **John Eliot** expressed doubts about slavery, many New England ministers owned slaves, including **Jonathan Edwards** and many Quakers. Lifetime servitude with a Christian master was considered beneficial for Africans, and Puritans often converted their slaves. **Phyllis Wheatley** came to **Boston** as a slave (1761) and rose to fame as a pious poet. The spirit of the **American Revolution** led **Quakers** in Newport in 1773 to manumit their slaves. **Moses Brown**, a leading **Quaker** merchant, became an **abolitionist**, unlike his brother, **John Brown**, the **Providence** ship owner who was a prominent slave trader. **African-American** patriots fought in Rhode Island's **Battle of Portsmouth** (1778) and served in their Black Regiment (1777–83) with the promise of freedom after the war. The importation of slaves was prohibited first in Connecticut and Rhode Island (1774), and slavery ended in 1787. Vermont is the only state that never permitted slavery (1777). By court decision, Massachusetts was the first state to end slavery (1783), and New Hampshire (1784), Rhode Island, and Connecticut passed gradual emancipation laws (1784). However, **Eli Whitney**'s cotton gin and the New England **textile** industry stimulated the demand for slavery (1793).

Because New England lacked the economic and social need for slavery once the international slave trade was prohibited in the United States (1808), antislavery opinion developed and led to the more radical abolitionist crusade in the 1830s. The **Amistad case** (1839) gave former president **John Quincy Adams** a prominent role in **abolitionism** but only a small number of New Englanders were adamantly opposed to slavery before the **Civil War**. Like many Americans, **Yankees** were conflicted about slavery, Connecticut law barred black children from private schools (1833) but state law prohibited slavery (1848). *See also* ABOLITIONISM; AFRICAN AMERICANS; ANTHONY BURNS CASE; DOUGLASS, FREDERICK; SHADRACH CASE; WALKER, DAVID; WALKER, QUOCK.

SLEEPY HOLLOW CEMETERY. Established (1855) in Concord, Massachusetts, and is the final resting place of prominent New Englander writers, including **Henry David Thoreau**, **Nathaniel Hawthorne**, **Bronson Alcott**, **Louisa May Alcott**, and **Ralph Waldo Emerson** buried on Authors' Ridge. **Daniel Chester French** sculpted the cemetery's **Civil War** monument, *Mourning Victory* (1908).

SLOCUM, JOSHUA (1844–1909). Writer. Born in Wilmot, Nova Scotia, on February 20, 1844, and raised in Westport, Massachusetts, Slocum went to sea in 1860. The master of sailing vessels in the Pacific (1869–84), Captain Slocum lived in **Boston** and wrote about his adventures, *The Voyage of the Liberdad* (1890) and *Voyage of the Destroyer* (1894). He was the first man to sail alone around the world, departing Boston on April 24, 1895, and returning to **Newport**, Rhode Island, on June 27, 1898. He recounted his 46,000-mile voyage on the 37-foot sloop *Spray* in *Sailing Alone Around the World* (1900). Slocum lived on **Martha's Vineyard** but was lost at sea on a solo voyage in the *Spray* to South America (1909).

SMIBERT, JOHN (1688–1751). Artist. Born in Edinburgh, Scotland, on March 24, 1688, Smibert studied **art** in London and Italy before settling in **Newport**, Rhode Island (1729). Moving to **Boston** (1730), he painted 250 portraits, including ones of Peter Faneuil and **William Pepperrell** (1745). One of his few landscapes is *View of Boston*, and he designed **Faneuil Hall** (1742). Smibert influenced the paintings of **Robert Feke** and **John Singleton Copley** before he died in Boston on April 2, 1751.

SMITH, ELIZABETH OAKES (1806–1893). Writer. Born in North Yarmouth, Maine, on August 12, 1806, Elizabeth Oakes married **Seba Smith** (1823). She edited his **Portland** newspaper and published poems and fiction in magazines as well as the best-selling novel *Bald Eagle* (1867). She lectured widely on women's rights and was the first woman to climb **Mount Katahdin** (1849). Smith died in North Carolina on November 15, 1893.

SMITH, JEREMIAH (1759–1842). Congressman from New Hampshire. Born in Petersboro, New Hampshire, on November 29, 1759, Smith attended **Harvard** College and graduated from Queen's (later Rutgers) College (1780). He served under General **John Stark** at the **Battle of Bennington** and practiced law in Petersboro (1786–91). He served as a

Federalist state legislator (1788–91) and in the House of Representatives (1791–97). Smith was U.S. attorney for New Hampshire (1797–1800) and a probate judge (1800–02). He served as a U.S. circuit court judge (1801–02) and was chief justice of the state superior court (1802–09) until elected governor (1809–10). Smith was chief justice of the state supreme court (1813–16) and practiced law until he retired (1820). He was treasurer of the most renowned **prep school** in New Hampshire, Phillips Exeter Academy, when he died in Dover on September 21, 1842.

SMITH, JOHN (1580–1631). Explorer. Born in 1580 in England, Captain John Smith was a mercenary solider in Europe (1599–1604) who became one of the Virginia colony's seven councilors (1606). He led the first English settlement to Jamestown, Virginia, in May 1607, was captured by the **Native American** leader Powhatan and saved from death by Pocahontas. Smith returned to England (1609), but he made a voyage to **New England** (1614) and published an accurate map in his book *Description of New England* that named this region. Smith died in London on June 21, 1631.

SMITH, JOHN J. (1820–1906). Public official. Born free in Richmond, Virginia, on November 2, 1820, Smith moved to **Boston** (1848). After an unrewarding adventure in the Gold Rush (1849), he opened a barbershop on Beacon Hill that became a center for **Charles Sumner** and other **abolitionists**. Smith was a recruiter for the all-black **5th Massachusetts Cavalry**. Elected as a Republican to the Massachusetts legislature (1868–72) and the Boston Common Council (1878), Smith was the most prominent **African-American** politician in New England. His house on **Beacon Hill** is a site on the **Black Freedom Trail**. Smith died in Boston on November 4, 1906.

SMITH, JOSEPH (1805–1844). Clergyman. Born in Sharon, Vermont, on December 23, 1805. Joseph Smith moved to New York (1816), where his religious experiences led him to found the Church of Jesus Christ of the Latter Day Saints (1830). He published *The Book of Mormon* (1830), the bible of his new faith reflecting the religious, social, and political ferment common in antebellum New England and New York. Despite his limited education, Smith led his expanding congregation to Ohio (1831), Missouri (1838), and Illinois (1838), but the Mormons had considerable friction with other settlers, owing to their practice of polygamy and communalism. The sect numbered 18,000 when Smith was shot by a mob in Carthage, Illinois (1844). **Brigham Young**, who was also born in Vermont, led most of Smith's followers to Utah in 1846.

SMITH, MARGARET CHASE (1897–1995). Senator from Maine. Born in Skowhegan, Maine, on December 14, 1897, Margaret Madeline Chase taught school in Skowhegan and worked for the telephone company and for a weekly newspaper. When her husband, Clyde Harold Smith, died, she succeeded him as a Republican in the House of Representatives (1940–49) and the Senate (1949–73). Mrs. Smith was the first women to serve in both houses of Congress and won national attention by early criticism of Senator Joseph R. McCarthy (1950). She was known for her support of national defense, for never missing a roll-call vote, and for her independence as the "Conscience of the Senate." Chase was the only woman in the Senate for a decade and was the first woman nominated for president at a major party convention (1964). She died in Skowhegan on May 29, 1995.

SMITH, SEBA (1792–1869). Editor. Born in Buckfield, Maine, on September 14, 1792, Seba Smith graduated from Bowdoin College (1818) and founded the *Portland Courier* (1829), Maine's first daily newspaper. His wife, **Elizabeth Oakes Smith**, wrote and edited the newspaper in her husband's absence. For 20 years he wrote a column in the form of satirical letters to the editor by a fictional writer, Major Jack Downing, who represented the quintessential **Yankee** wit, commenting on Jacksonian-era politics. Smith published two collections of these monologues, *The Life and Writings of Major Jack Downing of Downingville* (1833) and *My Thirty Years Out of the Senate* (1847). He died in New York on July 28, 1869.

SNOW, CHARLES WILBERT (1884–1977). Governor of Connecticut. Born on White Head Island in Maine on April 6, 1884, Snow graduated from Bowdoin College (1907) and Columbia University (1910). He served in the U.S. Army in World War I and taught English at Wesleyan College for 31 years. He is best remembered for his poetry, especially *Maine Coast* (1923), *Downeast* (1932), *Maine Tides* (1940), and *The Collected Poems of Wilbert Snow* (1963). Always active in politics, Wilbert Snow was elected the Democratic lieutenant governor of Connecticut (1945–46). He served the state's shortest term as governor, for 13 days in 1946–47 when Governor William Baldwin resigned to enter the U.S.

Senate. Snow lectured for the U.S. Department of State in Europe and the Near East (1951–62) and died in Maine on September 28, 1977.

SNOWE, OLYMPIA J. (1947–). Senator from Maine. Born in **Augusta**, Maine, on February 21, 1947, Olympia Jean Bouchles Snowe graduated from the University of Maine at Orono (1969). She was elected as a Republican to the state legislature seat (1973–78) vacated by the death of her first husband. Snowe was the first Greek-American woman elected to the House of Representatives (1978–94) and to the Senate (1994–).

SOCIETY FOR THE PRESERVATION OF NEW ENGLAND ANTIQUITIES (SPNEA). A nonprofit private organization established (1910) by **William Sumner Appleton, Jr**. Located in Boston's **West End** in the Federal-style mansion designed by **Charles Bullfinch** for **Harrison Gray Otis**, SPNEA is an international leader in historic preservation. It manages 35 house museums, historic landscapes, and countless objects and documents for public and scholarly use throughout New England.

SONS OF LIBERTY. A loose coalition of patriot organizations formed in 1765 to protest the **Stamp Act** in **Boston**, Portsmouth, **Newport**, and other seaports where the British law had greatest effect. The members were mostly urban workers led by gentlemen like **Samuel Adams** in **Boston**, Samuel Cutts in Portsmouth, and John Durkee in **Hartford**, who were eager to broaden the opposition and arouse hostility to the law. The Sons of Liberty denounced the Stamp Act as an unconstitutional internal tax levied without their consent. They used intimidation and violence to force local stamp officers to resign or leave the colonies until Parliament repealed the law in 1766. **Paul Revere** led them in the **Boston Tea Party** (1773). *See also* AMERICAN REVOLUTION; LIBERTY TREE.

SOUTER, DAVID H. (1939–). U.S. Supreme Court justice. Born in Melrose, Massachusetts, on September 17,1939, David Hackett Souter graduated from **Harvard University** (1961), was a Rhodes Scholar at Oxford University (1963), and graduated from Harvard Law School (1966). He practiced law in **Concord**, New Hampshire (1966–68), and was a state assistant attorney general (1968–71), deputy state attorney general (1971–76), and New Hampshire attorney general (1976–78). He served as associate justice of the New Hampshire superior court (1978–83) and associate justice of the state supreme court (1983–90). President **George H. W. Bush** appointed Souter a judge on the U.S. Court of Appeals and to the U.S. Supreme Court (1990), where his opinions proved to be less conservative than expected and more in the centrist tradition.

SPARKS, JARED (1789–1866). Historian. Born in Willington, Connecticut, on May 10, 1789, Sparks graduated from **Harvard** College (1815) and Harvard Divinity School (1819). He was a **Unitarian** minister in Baltimore, Maryland (1819–23), and editor of the *North American Review* (1824–30), making it the nation's leading literary magazine. Sparks, who sat for a portrait by **Gilbert Stuart** (1828), wrote books on George Washington, **Benjamin Franklin**, and the **American Revolution** that fostered a new interest in history. He was McLean Professor of History (1838–49) at Harvard College, the first such chair in the nation. Sparks was president of Harvard College (1849–53), and he died in Cambridge on March 14, 1866.

SPENCER, PERCY L. (1894–1970). Inventor. Born in Howland, Maine, on July 19, 1894, Spencer was an orphan with limited formal education. But he became a senior vice-president of the Raytheon Company with 120 patents in his career. While working in Cambridge, Massachusetts, on a more efficient way to manufacture magnetrons for radar, he created a device to cook food using microwave radiation (1945). Raytheon sold the popular microwave ovens by 1947. Spencer received the U.S. Navy Distinguished Service Medal and died on September 8, 1970.

SPENDTHRIFT TRUST. A legal device to preserve New England family fortunes. By the 18th century, wealthy families placed their money in irrevocable trusts for their less experienced or more profligate heirs who might spend their inheritance unwisely. Supported by the courts and the legislature, this created a class of financial managers, the Boston trustee, like **Henry Lee Shattuck**, who shrewdly invested and dispersed funds for generations of **Boston Brahmins**. The children and grandchildren of **China Traders** and pioneer industrialists lived on the interest not the principal under the watchful eyes of prudent trustees and were free to enter prestigious but less remunerative professions, the arts, public service, or administering private philanthropies. Dr. **Oliver Wendell Holmes** recommended the frugal trust in *The Autocrat of the Breakfast Table* (1858).

SPINDLE CITY. Nickname for the textile center **Lowell**, Massachusetts.

SPOCK, BENJAMIN (1903–1998). Physician. Born in **New Haven**, Connecticut, on May 2, 1903, Benjamin McLane Spock graduated from Yale

University (1924) and Columbia University Medical School (1929). Trained in pediatrics and psychiatry, he practiced as a pediatrician in New York City (1933–44). After serving in the U.S. Navy (1944–46), he published *Baby and Child Care* (1946), a best-selling guide for parents in the postwar baby boom. Employing psychiatric principles and a permissive attitude toward child-rearing, Spock became so influential he was criticized for the child-centeredness and permissiveness said to produce the youthful rebellion of the 1960s. Feminists blamed him for producing guilt-ridden, homebound mothers. In any case, his book continues to be a popular guide. Dr. Spock retired (1967) and was a leader in the peace movement. He died in San Diego, California, on March 15, 1998.

SPORTS. Arrived with the first New England colonists, who hunted, raced horses, bowled, enjoyed foot races, and dogs fighting bears or rats. Many **Puritans** played ball games at **taverns** on holidays and market days. Despite fear of profaning the Sabbath, children and adults played with hoops and marbles, swam, wrestled, skated, sledded, and danced.

Dr. **Sylvester Graham** promoted healthy exercise (1830), and boxing was popular though illegal. The crew race by **Harvard** and Yale students on Lake Winnepesaukee on August 3, 1852, was the first college sporting event in America. Dr. **Oliver Wendell Holmes, Sr.**, rowed on the Charles River and advocated harness racing as a useful, democratic sport. **Thomas Wentworth Higginson** and other New England clergymen advocated sports for muscular Christians (1850s), and summer resorts made billiards, bowling, golf, swimming, and tennis popular (1880s). **Boston**'s YWCA, the first in the nation (1866), opened the first gymnasium for women (1884) with the first YWCA swimming pool (1927), recognizing new interest in athletics for women.

John L. Sullivan, the Boston boxer, was the first U.S. heavyweight champion (1892) when prizefighting became a national sport and popular entertainment. By 1890 college students played football, and the annual Harvard-Yale game on **Thanksgiving Day** attracted the upper class to parades, parties, and balls. **Walter Camp** devised the rules for intercollegiate football at Yale University (1880).

Baseball began as a working-class game in the 1840s, but the **Civil War** made it the national pastime, and the first major league double header was played between the **Providence** and **Worcester** teams (1883). The **Boston Red Sox**, organized in 1901, built **Fenway Park** (1912) to accommodate urban fans. **Irish immigrants** contributed their own affinity for handball and other sports when they arrived in New England. David N. Mullany invented **wiffleball** in Connecticut in 1953.

Basketball was invented at the Springfield, Massachusetts, YMCA (1891), and New England college women and men soon enjoyed this game and bicycling, as well as the volleyball game invented in **Holyoke** (1895) by William Morgan. Senda Berenson Abbott, the mother of women's basketball, introduced the intercollegiate game at Smith College (1893), and her rules were used until 1960. Nahant, Massachusetts, and **Newport**, Rhode Island, built the first tennis courts in the nation (1875), and Newport held the first national men's tennis championship (1881–1915) in the stately Newport Casino, designed by Stanford White. The Casino houses the International Tennis Hall of Fame and the oldest tennis court in the country. The first national meeting of bicyclists in Newport (1880) led to the organization of the influential League of American Wheelmen. Polo was also introduced to America at Newport (1876).

Newport also made yachting popular and hosted the most prestigious race, the America's Cup (1930–83). Newport also was the site of the first U.S. Golf Association men's championship (1895). The Brookline, Massachusetts, golfer **Francis Ouimet** became a national hero (1913) as the first amateur to win the U.S. Open. The annual Harvard-Yale boat race is held on the Thames River at New London, and the annual **Head of the Charles Regatta** on the Charles River has become an international event (1964).

Motorcycle races, promoted by the **Indian Motorcycle** Manufacturing Company in Springfield, Massachusetts (1901–53), began in New England. However, misgivings about wasteful leisure activities prompted many sports advocates to defend amateur athletic contests by associating them with manly virtue or muscular Christianity by 1900. New England's many Canadians introduced hockey by 1870. Yale students first played hockey in 1893, and it became an Olympic sport in 1920. The **Boston Bruins** was the first professional team in the new National Hockey League (1924).

James B. Connolly, a **Harvard University** student, won the first gold medal in the modern Olympic Games in Athens (1896), and many New England athletes like **Tenley Albright** (1952, 1956) and **Bill Cleary** (1956, 1960) have been Olympic champions. **Luther Gulick**, an early advocate of basketball, physical education, camping, and the YMCA in Springfield, was an Olympic Games official (1906–98). The Sports Museum of New England, established in **Lowell**, Massachusetts (1999), celebrates the region's long athletic tradition. Since 1950, white water rafters, canoeists, and kayakers have enjoyed rivers and lakes throughout New England. By 1990 country bicycle touring and mountain bikers were popular with **Yankees** and **tourists**. *See also* BOSTON BRUINS; BOSTON CELTICS; BOSTON MARATHON; BOSTON RED SOX; HEAD OF THE CHARLES REGATTA; NEW ENGLAND PATRIOTS; SKIING; SULLIVAN, BILLY.

SPRAGUE, WILLIAM (1830–1915). Senator from Rhode Island. Born in Cranston, Rhode Island, on September 12, 1830, Sprague was a **textile** and locomotive manufacturer. Elected the Republican governor of Rhode Island (1860–63), he organized the 1st Rhode Island Regiment, one of the first state militia units to arrive in Washington, D.C. Colonel Sprague fought at the battle of Bull Run on July 21, 1861, while governor. After the **Civil War** he served in the Senate (1863–75) and married the daughter of **Salmon P. Chase**, whose political career he financed. Sprague retired to his farm at Narragansett Pier and died in Paris on September 11, 1915.

SPRINGFIELD ARMORY (1777–1968). Founded by General **Henry Knox** in Springfield, Massachusetts, to manufacture weapons for the Continental Army. By 1780 it was the nation's major arsenal and was attacked in **Shays's Rebellion** (1787). President George Washington named it the first U.S. Arsenal (1794) to manufacture flintlock muskets for the army. It became a center for technology where **Thomas Blanchard** developed a new lathe for the mass production of interchangeable rifle stocks (1819). The new percussion system replaced the flintlocks (1840), a breech-loading design replaced the muzzle-loading rifle (1865), and the armory became the army's laboratory for development of small arms (1891), especially the Springfield Model 1903 rifles, the M1 rifle (1936), and M14 rifle (1957). **Henry Wadsworth Longfellow** celebrated this "organ of muskets" in his poem *The Arsenal at Springfield*. When the armory closed (1968), it became a museum and the Springfield Armory National Historic Site (1978) to commemorate New England's technological history in the Connecticut River's **Precision Valley**.

SQUANTO (1580–1622). Native American leader. Born in the Pawtuxet tribe in Massachusetts, Squanto (Tisquantum) lived on **Cape Cod** until the English captain **George Waymouth** (1605) kidnapped him. Sold as a slave in Spain, he was taken to England but returned to New England with Captain **John Smith** (1614). He went to England again with Captain Thomas Hunt (1615) and returned to find his tribe wiped out by a smallpox epidemic (1619). Squanto lived with the **Wampanoag** and was an interpreter for the **Pilgrims** (1621–22). He taught the English to plant **corn**, attended the first **Thanksgiving** celebration, and assisted in the treaty signed by **Massasoit** and Governor **William Bradford** shortly before he died in Chatham in November 1622.

STAMP ACT (1765). A law designed by the British Parliament to pay military costs in the American colonies. Tax stamps required for **almanacs**, public documents, newspapers, and licenses outraged Americans as unconstitutional taxation without representation. The **Sons of Liberty** led popular and official protests, sent petitions and lobbyists to London, and persuaded American merchants not to import British goods. In Boston the Stamp Act commissioner was hanged in effigy by rioters at the **Liberty Tree**, which became the focus for annual celebrations to commemorate this event. In **New Haven** John Durkee led the Sons of Liberty who forced Jared Ingersoll to resign as Stamp Act commissioner. The law was repealed (1766) but had inspired intercolonial cooperation and consciousness that resurfaced in the **American Revolution**.

STANDISH, MILES (1584–1656). Soldier. Born in 1584 in England, Standish was a mercenary in Holland where he joined the **Pilgrims** on the **Mayflower** (1620). As their military leader, he negotiated 50 years of peaceful relations with the **Native Americans**, whose language he learned. He was one of the colonists who went to England (1625–26) to buy out the London merchants, enabling the Pilgrims to own their land. Standish arrested **Thomas Morton** (1628) and founded Duxbury (1632), where he died on October 3, 1656, as one of New England's most influential and wealthy pioneers. He is best known from **Henry Wadsworth Longfellow**'s poem *The Courtship of Miles Standish* (1858).

STANLEY, FRANCIS EDGAR (1849–1918). Inventor. Born in Kingfield, Maine, on June 1, 1849, Stanley graduated from the state **normal school** in Farmington (1871). As a portrait photographer in Lewiston, he invented a process for manufacturing photographic dry plates (1883) with his twin brother, Freelan O. Stanley (1849–1940). The Stanley brothers invented a steam-powered automobile (1897), the popular Stanley Steamer (1902–18), they produced until Francis died in an automobile accident on July 31, 1918. Freelan Stanley died in **Boston** on October 2, 1940.

STARK, JOHN (1728–1822). Soldier. Born in Londonderry, New Hampshire, on August 28, 1728, and raised in Manchester, Stark served with Major **Robert Rogers**'s rangers in the **French and Indian War** (1758). He was a New Hampshire militia colonel from the **Battle of Bunker Hill** (1775) to the end of the **American Revolution**. General Stark won the decisive **Battle of Bennington** (1777) and played a key role in the surrender of the British general John Burgoyne. Stark's slogan, "Live Free or Die," became the state motto. After the war he declined public office and retired to Manchester, New Hampshire, where he died on May 8, 1822.

STELLA, FRANK (1936–). Artist. Born in Malden, Massachusetts, on May 12, 1936, Frank Philip Stella graduated from Princeton University (1958). He was a Minimalist painter using irregularly shaped canvas and color in decorative motifs in the 1960s, as in *The Marriage of Squalor and Reason* (1959) and *Hyena Stomp* (1960). His reputation grew after his work was exhibited at the Museum of Modern Art (1959) and **Harvard University**'s Fogg Museum (1965). Stella's dense three-dimensional abstract sculptures of stainless steel and bronze in the 1990s are exhibited in major **art** museums and collections around the world. The Museum of Modern Art retrospective exhibitions of his work in 1970 and 1987 were rare honors for an American artist in his lifetime.

STELLWAGEN BANK. A shallow, submarine platform 20 miles north of **Cape Cod** and south of **Cape Ann** formed by receding glaciers 18,000 years ago. It provides an 842-square mile feeding and nursery ground for 17 species of whales, porpoises, and dolphins as well as birds and fish. Congress created the Stellwagen Bank National Marine Sanctuary in 1993. Recent researchers have discovered many **shipwrecks** on the muddy ocean floor.

STEVENS, THADDEUS (1792–1868). Congressman from Pennsylvania. Born in Danville, Vermont, on April 4, 1792, Stevens attended the University of Vermont and graduated from Dartmouth College (1814). Moving to Pennsylvania, he practiced law in Gettysburg, York, and Lancaster, served in the state legislature (1833–35, 1837, 1841) and was elected as a Whig to the House of Representatives (1849–53) and then as a Republican (1859–68). Known as the Great Commoner, he was a leader of the Radical Republicans who insisted on harsh treatment of the former Confederate states. Stevens was chairman of the House committee to conduct the impeachment of President Andrew Johnson and died in Washington, D.C., on August 11, 1868.

STEVENS, WALLACE (1879–1955). Poet. Born in Reading, Pennsylvania, on October 2, 1879, Stevens attended **Harvard University** (1897–1900) and graduated from New York University Law School (1903). He was a lawyer in New York City and an **insurance** company executive in **Hartford**, Connecticut (1916–55). Stevens published his first lyric poetry in 1914 and his first book of lyric poems, *Harmonium,* in 1923. He won the Pulitzer Prize and the National Book Award for *Collected Poems* (1954) and wrote an essay collection, *The Necessary Angel* (1951). Stevens was recognized as a major American poet when he died in Hartford on August 2, 1955.

STEWARD, IRA (1831–1883). Labor leader. Born in New London, Connecticut, on March 10, 1831, Steward was raised in **Boston** and apprenticed as a machinist in **Providence**, Rhode Island (1850). Allied with the radical Boston **abolitionists**, he was president of the International Union of Machinists and led the Boston Eight-Hour League and the National Ten-Hour League (1863). Steward was one of the first to lobby the state legislature on labor issues, and Massachusetts was the first state to pass a 10-hour law for women and children (1874). A self-taught political economist, he foresaw that a higher standard of living for the working class would benefit democratic society. Steward, a mentor to **George E. McNeill**, was one of the most influential **Yankee** labor leaders. He moved to Illinois (1880), where he died on March 13, 1883.

STOCKBRIDGE INDIANS. Members of the **Machian** people who lived on the **Housatonic River** in Massachusetts. Converted to Christianity, they moved to a mission at Stockbridge, Massachusetts (1736). **John Eliot** and **Jonathan Edwards** (1751–55) preached to them and the 200 surviving **Algonquins** who lived with them. Most of the Stockbridge Indians later moved to Wisconsin in 1850.

STODDARD, SOLOMON (1643–1729). Clergyman. Born in **Boston** on September 27, 1643, Stoddard graduated from Harvard College (1670) and was a pastor at Northampton, Massachusetts (1670) for 59 years. As the most influential minister in western New England and a leader of the **River Gods**, he was known as the **Puritan** pope of the **Connecticut**

River valley. Stoddard died on February 11, 1729, and was succeeded by his grandson **Jonathan Edwards**.

STONE, HARLAN FISKE (1872–1946). Chief justice of the U.S. Supreme Court. Born in Chesterfield, New Hampshire, on October 11, 1872, Stone graduated from Amherst College (1894) and Columbia University Law School (1898). Practicing law in New York City (1899–1924), and teaching law at Columbia (1899–1924), Stone advocated simpler law statutes and an improved law curriculum. President **Calvin Coolidge** appointed him attorney general (1924–25) and to the U.S. Supreme Court (1925). Although a moderate Republican, he voted with the liberal wing of the Court on constitutional issues and to uphold New Deal laws. President Franklin D. Roosevelt appointed him the 11th chief justice (1941–46). Stone presided during a period of sharp division on the Court, and he died in Washington, D.C., on April 22, 1946.

STONE, LUCY (1818–1893). Reformer. Born in West Brookfield, Massachusetts, on August 13, 1818, Lucy Stone was the first Massachusetts woman to graduate from college (1847). She worked to pay for her education at Oberlin College over her family's objections. As an **abolitionist**, **temperance**, and woman's suffrage advocate, she attended the national woman's rights conference in Worcester (1850). In 1855 she married Henry Brown Blackwell, an Ohio abolitionist, but lived as Mrs. Stone. She moved to **Boston** (1866) to work for the New England Woman Suffrage Association and formed the American Woman Suffrage Association. She founded (1870) the suffrage movement's leading magazine, *Woman's Journal,* which she and her husband edited (1872–93). In conflict with her old friends **Susan B. Anthony** and Elizabeth Cady Stanton, Mrs. Stone led the moderate wing of the movement. Her daughter, **Alice Stone Blackwell** (1857–1950), continued this work. Lucy Stone died at her Dorchester, Massachusetts, home on October 18, 1893.

STONEWALLS. An important aspect of New England vernacular architecture. Farmers built 240,000 miles of stonewalls (1750–1870). Geothermal forces formed these stones, tectonic movements brought them to the surface, and glaciers broke them apart. Thrifty Yankees dragged them on ox- or horse-drawn sleds to build foundations, cemetery walls, or mill dams or to mark meadows and fields with dry-stacked walls built without mortar. Over-clearing forests made stone walls practical until barbed wire appeared in 1874. Many stonewalls are in disrepair now, but more are still in use or can be found in abandoned farmland that has become forest. These walls link the natural history and human history of New England and are cherished today, like **covered bridges** and barns, as an antique regional hallmark.

STORROW, JAMES J. (1864–1926). Public official. Born in **Boston** on January 20, 1864, James Jackson Storrow graduated from **Harvard University** (1885) and Harvard Law School (1888). A prominent Boston banker, his public career included terms as president of the Boston Chamber of Commerce, president of General Motors (1910), and president of the National Council of Boy Scouts (1925–26). Elected as a Democrat to the Boston School Committee (1901–07), Storrow was instrumental in establishing the Boston Juvenile Court (1906) and was the Good Government Association candidate for mayor (1910), losing narrowly to **John F. Fitzgerald**. He also served as commissioner of the Metropolitan District Commission, arbitrated the **Boston Police Strike** (1919), founded the West End House, one of the nation's first Boys Clubs, and was elected to the Boston City Council (1915–17). Because he was the driving force for the construction of the Charles River Dam and Esplanade, the adjacent highway was named in his honor (1952). Storrow died in New York City on March 13, 1926.

STORY, JOSEPH (1779–1845). U.S. Supreme Court justice. Born in Marblehead, Massachusetts, on September 18, 1779, Story graduated from **Harvard** College (1798). He practiced law in **Salem** (1801–11) and served as a Jeffersonian Democrat in the state legislature (1805–07) and in the House of Representatives (1808–09). He returned to the state legislature until appointed to the U.S. Supreme Court (1811–45). Assigned to the New England federal court circuit, his decisions shaped constitutional law, as did his teaching at Harvard Law School (1829–45), which he helped found. Story was an ally of **Daniel Webster** and a nationalist whose decisions often concurred with the **Federalist Party**, including the **Amistad Case** (1841). Known for his influential text *Commentaries on the Constitution* (1833), Story founded **Mount Auburn Cemetery** (1831) and died in Cambridge on September 10, 1845.

STOWE, HARRIET BEECHER (1811–1896). Writer. Born in Litchfield, Connecticut, in June 1811, Harriet Beecher was the daughter of the influential **Boston** preacher **Lyman Beecher** and the sister of **Catharine Beecher**. Harriet Beecher married Calvin Ellis Stowe (1836), an abolitionist and Bowdoin College professor, and while living in Brunswick, Maine, she wrote *Uncle Tom's Cabin* (1852), a popular and influential exposé of slavery. Her local color stories appeared in the *Atlantic Monthly* and as popular novels. She was an early New England regionalist writer and among the first New Englanders to spend winter vacations (1872) in Florida. She lived next to the **Mark Twain House** in **Hartford**, where she died on July 1, 1896.

STRAWBERY BANKE. A living history museum established (1958) on 30 acres in Portsmouth, New Hampshire, on the Piscataqua River. The name comes from the original name for Portsmouth (until 1653). Colonial merchants and prosperous sea captains built 40 handsome houses in the neighborhood, visited by **John Hancock**, George Washington, and the Marquis de Lafayette and home to John Paul Jones and **Thomas Bailey Aldrich**. The town was New Hampshire's capital until 1808. Now the museum role players interpret daily life for tourists in an urban maritime Portsmouth neighborhood from the 17th to the mid-20th centuries.

STUART, GILBERT (1755–1828). Artist. Born in North Kingston, Rhode Island, on December 3, 1755, Stuart studied with Cosimo Alexander, a Scottish painter visiting Newport, and with Benjamin West in London (1777–82). He settled in **Boston** (1805), where he was the most celebrated painter of the era. He is best known for three portraits of George Washington, the third of these (1796) was used on the U.S. one-dollar bill. Stuart, the father of American portraiture, painted 1,000 portraits, including those of **John Singleton Copley** (1784), **John Adams** (1800), and **Abigail Smith Adams** (1815). He died in Boston on July 9, 1828.

SUBWAY. The nation's first subway, and the fourth subway in the world, opened in **Boston** on September 1, 1897. The Tremont Street Subway ran under the **Boston Common** powered by electricity and carried passengers one block from Park Street to Boylston Street. It was an immediate success with the public by reducing the traffic congestion caused by private electric trolley cars. Soon additional subway lines connected to Roxbury (1901), East Boston (1904), and Cambridge (1912) as the public Metropolitan Transit Authority, now called the Massachusetts Bay Transit Authority and known as the T.

SUCCOTASH. A Native American dish with **corn** *(Zea mays)* and **beans** *(Phaseolus vulgaris)* cooked together. This food was adopted by the early New England settlers from the **Pequots**.

SUFFOLK RESOLVES. Radical resolutions from **Boston**, or Suffolk County, declaring the **Coercive Acts** void and urging Massachusetts to form a government, collect and withhold taxes, arm the people, and impose economic sanctions against Britain until Parliament repealed the acts. The First Continental Congress (1774) adopted these resolutions written by Dr. **Joseph Warren** and offered by **Paul Revere**.

SUGAR ACT (1764). Passed by the British Parliament to defray the costs of the **French and Indian War** in North America. Unlike the **Molasses Act** (1733), it was enforced strictly and raised much revenue but caused resistance and protests in New England that led to the **American Revolution**. Sugar and molasses were staples in New England, especially to distill the **rum** consumed widely and in the **triangular trade** to obtain slaves.

SULLIVAN, ANNE (1866–1936). Educator. Born in Feeding Hills, Massachusetts, on April 14, 1866, Joanna (Anne) Sullivan was a blind child in the Tewksbury Poorhouse. At the Perkins School for the Blind in Boston (1880–86) she recovered her sight and learned to teach the blind. Employed to care for Helen Keller (1887), a deaf, mute, and blind girl in Alabama, Sullivan developed new methods for educating handicapped children. She married John Macy (1905), worked for the American Foundation for the Blind, and wrote her biography (1933). Anne Sullivan Macy died in New York on October 20, 1936.

SULLIVAN, BILLY (1915–1998). Sportsman. Born in Lowell, Massachusetts, in 1915, William H. Sullivan, Jr., was a publicity director for Boston College and the **Boston Braves** (1946–52) and worked in the oil business until he founded the American Football League **Boston Patriots** (1959–88). He was a founder of the **Jimmy Fund** (1948), arranging for baseball stars to visit children treated for leukemia in Boston hospitals until the **Boston Red Sox** adopted this charity. Billy Sullivan died in Florida on February 23, 1998.

SULLIVAN, GEORGE (1771–1838). Congressman from New Hampshire. Born in Durham, New Hampshire, on August 29, 1771, Sullivan, the son of Governor **John Sullivan**, graduated from **Harvard** College (1790) and practiced law in Exeter (1793–1811). He served in the state legislature (1805, 1813–15) and as attorney general (1805–06, 1815–35) and was a **Federalist** in the House of Representatives (1811–13) strongly opposed to the War of 1812. Sullivan, a leader of the bar, opposed **Daniel Webster** in the famous *Dartmouth College v. Woodward* case (1819). He died in Exeter on April 14, 1838.

SULLIVAN, JAMES (1744–1808). Governor of Massachusetts. Born in Berwick, Maine, on April 2, 1744, Sullivan was the son of **Irish immigrants** who settled in Maine (1723). He practiced law in Biddeford (1782–88) and was a leader in the Revolutionary movement. He was a member of the provincial congress (1774–75) and legislature (1775–76) and was elected to (but did not attend) the Continental Congress (1782–83). Sullivan was a judge in **Boston**, state attorney general (1790–1807), and Democratic-Republican governor (1807–08) and died in Boston on December 10, 1808. His brother was **John Sullivan**, governor of New Hampshire.

SULLIVAN, JOHN (1740–1795). Governor of New Hampshire. Born in Somersworth, New Hampshire, on February 17, 1740, Sullivan was the son of **Irish immigrants** to Maine (1723). His brother was **James Sullivan**, governor of Massachusetts. He practiced law in Berwick, Maine (1760), and Durham, New Hampshire (1764), and served as a **militia** officer. He was a delegate to the Continental Congress (1774–75, 1780–81) and a general in the **American Revolution** (1775–79). Elected state attorney general (1782–86) and governor (1786–87, 1789–90), he was a federal judge (1789–95) in New Hampshire until his death in Durham on January 23, 1795.

SULLIVAN, JOHN L. (1858–1918). Boxer. Born in **Boston** on October 15, 1858, Sullivan attended Boston College before turning to boxing (1877) and won the world heavyweight championship (1882). The "Great John L" held the bare-knuckle title for a decade, attracting wide popularity as a folk hero and spending his fortune in lavish style. The "Boston Strong Boy" lost the title to James J. Corbett in the first U.S. title fight (1892) using gloves under the Marquis of Queensberry rules. Thereafter the **Irish-American Catholic** sports hero toured in theaters and **vaudeville**. John Lawrence Sullivan died in Abington, Massachusetts, on February 2, 1918, and was inducted into the Boxing Hall of Fame (1954).

SUMMER PEOPLE. A New England term for vacationers to the **White Mountains** in New Hampshire, the **Green Mountains** in Vermont, the

Berkshire Hills in Massachusetts, and the seacoast of Connecticut, Maine, Rhode Island, or **Cape Cod**. The extravagant way of life in **Newport** mansions ended with the Stock Market Crash (1929), but middle-class summer vacations in the mountains, lakes, or seacoast gained popularity. Splendid views of nature, a respite from city life, and entertainment and fine food provided by new hotels or resorts made York and Kennebunk, Rye and Salisbury, and Hyannis and **Provincetown** or Lake Champlain popular summertime destinations for **tourists**. Summer theater companies, founded in New Hampshire by 1931, entertain visitors, and historic sites are an added attraction and a new industry for the region. Summer people, often called flatlanders in Vermont or people "from away" in Maine, have sent their children to New England's many summer camps since 1861. *See also* MAINE GUIDES.

SUMNER, CHARLES (1811–1874). Senator from Massachusetts. Born in **Boston** on January 6, 1811, Sumner graduated from **Harvard** College (1830) and Harvard Law School (1833). After practicing law in Boston, Sumner traveled in Europe (1837–40) before returning to teach law at Harvard and to found the Free Soil Party (1848). Elected as a Free Soiler to the Senate (1851–57) and as a Republican (1857–74), Sumner was a vituperative opponent of **slavery**. Assaulted at his desk in the Senate by a South Carolina congressman (1856), Sumner was incapacitated for three years but reelected despite his illness. He was a leading Radical Republican opponent of the lenient reconstruction policy and led the impeachment trial against President Andrew Johnson. Sumner opposed President Uly..es S. Grant's foreign policies and died in Washington, D.C., on March 11, 1874. **Anne Whitney**'s bronze statue of Sumner (1900) presides over Harvard Square.

SUMNER, WILLIAM GRAHAM (1840–1910). Educator. Born in Paterson, New Jersey, on October 30, 1840, Sumner was raised in **Hartford**, Connecticut, and graduated from Yale College (1863). After study in Europe, he was ordained an Episcopal minister (1869), but joined the Yale faculty as a professor of political economy (1872–1910). An outstanding teacher, he was nationally known as a social Darwinist and laissez-faire economist. Sumner wrote *A History of American Currency* (1874), *American Finance* (1875), and *Folkways* (1906). He served on the Connecticut state board of education (1882–1910) and was president of the American Sociological Association (1910) when he died in **New Haven** on April 12, 1910.

SUMPTUARY LAWS. Known in Asia and Europe and used by **Puritans** to regulate personal behavior through the **blue laws**. Colonial New England emphasized status and deference to social superiors, so these laws defined social class and prevented anyone from assuming the appearance of a higher status. **Boston** forbade (1634) the purchase or wearing of silk, linen, or woolen garments with silver, silk, gold, or thread lace. The **Massachusetts General Court** (1651) permitted those of higher status (with an estate worth £200) and magistrates to wear silk and lace, but the common people could not. Only the gentry could wear a sword or be addressed as Mister (or Mistress), others were known as Goodman (or Goodwife) until the **American Revolution** made egalitarianism widespread. *See also* SELECTMAN; TITHINGMAN.

SUNUNU, JOHN HENRY (1939–). Governor of New Hampshire. Born in Havana, Cuba, on July 2, 1939, Sununu graduated from MIT (1960), where he earned a Ph.D. in mechanical engineering (1966). He was a professor and dean at Tufts University (1966–73). Sununu served as a Republican legislator (1973–74) and governor (1983–89). He was chief of staff for President **George H. W. Bush** (1989–91) and later a television commentator.

SWAMP YANKEE. A nickname for the descendents of the early English settlers who lived on less desirable rural land, often wetlands and marshes or in the **puckerbrush**. The jocular term now refers to all nonelite New Englanders descended from early English colonists. *See also* WOODCHUCK; YANKEE.

SWEDES. Settled in America by 1638 at the New Sweden colony on the Delaware River, but large numbers of immigrants did not arrive until the 1850–1920 era. The U.S. consul in Sweden, W. W. Thomas, a native of Maine, invited Swedish farmers to settle in northern Maine (1870), and by 1930 over 4,000 Swedes lived in Maine towns named New Sweden, Stockholm, Jemtland, and Westmanland. Swedes introduced cross-country skiing at New Sweden and manufactured the skis many Maine children used to get to school in the winter.

Attleboro, Massachusetts, **Providence**, Rhode Island, and **New Haven**, Connecticut, had Swedish communities by 1890. Most New England Swedes voted Republican by 1860, electing **Pehr Gustaf Holmes** the mayor of **Worcester** (1917–19) and as a member of the

House of Representatives (1931–47). Worcester metal trades attracted many Swedes, who accounted for 20 percent of the city population (1935). **Lowell** had a Swedish Methodist Church in 1892, and Swedish-American craftsmen dominated the jewelry industry in Rhode Island and Massachusetts.

SWIFT, JANE M. (1965–). Governor of Massachusetts. Born on February 24, 1965, in North Adams, Massachusetts, Jane Maria Swift graduated from Trinity College in **Hartford**, Connecticut (1987). She was the youngest woman ever elected to the Massachusetts state senate (1991–96). Elected as the Republican lieutenant governor (1999–01), she became acting governor (2001–2002) when **Paul Cellucci** became U.S. ambassador to Canada. Swift was the first woman to be governor of Massachusetts, and the first chief executive in American history to give birth while in office (2001).

SWIFT, MORRISON (1856–1946). Labor leader. Born in Ravenna, Ohio, in 1856, Morrison Isaac Swift graduated from Williams College (1879), earned a Ph.D. at Johns Hopkins University (1885), and studied in Germany. Scorning an academic career, he organized meetings of unemployed workers on **Boston Common** (1893–94) with the Socialist Labor Party, led marches, and wrote petitions for shorter hours, public works, nationalization of **railroads**, mines, and the telegraph, and government relief and reform. Swift led thousands of **Boston** men to the State House where he delivered a petition and persuaded the governor to address the crowd on the lawn (1894). As a result the legislature approved a public works program and created a state commission to study the problem of unemployment. Swift led 60 New England Industrial delegates to join Coxey's Army in Washington, D.C. (1894), greeted by large crowds en route in Rhode Island and Connecticut. Returning to **Boston** (1907), he lectured and published tracts on rent reduction and the minimum wage law and led marches on city hall, the state house, and into the genteel **Trinity Church** (1908), where collection funds were distributed to the unemployed. He led a demonstration to the Boston Chamber of Commerce and the elite Algonquin Club in the **Back Bay** (1914) and met with Governor **David I. Walsh**. Swift continued writing on labor issues and eugenics when he settled in Newton, Massachusetts (1917), where he died in 1946, the year Congress passed an Employment Act making the federal government responsible for promoting full employment.

SWIFT, WILLIAM HENRY (1800–1879). Soldier. Born in **Taunton**, Massachusetts, on November 6, 1800, Swift graduated from West Point (1819) and spent much of his military career as an engineer for canals, coastal defenses, post roads, and **railroads**. He supervised river and harbor improvements in New England, traveled in Europe on military assignments (1837–42), and was a construction engineer for the Massachusetts Western Railway. Swift designed **lighthouses** at Black Rock Harbor in Connecticut and Minot's Ledge in Massachusetts. Resigning from the army (1849), he was president of the Massachusetts Western Railroad and wrote *Massachusetts Railroads, 1842 to 1855* (1856). Swift died in New York City on April 7, 1879.

SYRIANS. Immigrants who arrived in New England by 1854. The first Syrian family entered the United States in 1878, and a **Boston** community appeared by 1880. The poet Khalil Gibran (1883–1931) lived in the South End in 1895. After New York City, Boston had the largest Syrian community on the East Coast (1910); about 3,150 lived in the South Cove and South End. Many were peddlers traveling rural New England; others operated coffeehouses, restaurants, and shops or worked in **textile** factories. Most Syrians were Eastern-rite Christians, and immigrant clergy served churches in urban centers, like Our Lady of the Cedars of Lebanon Church for Maronite Christians in Boston (1893). Lawrence had a Maronite church (1896) and a Melkite church (1905), whose parishioners played a major role in the **Lawrence Strike** (1912). Lowell had St. George's Antiochian Orthodox Church (1919).

Towflek Maloof established the Syrian American Federation of New England (1932) in Boston as a regional association of local Syrian organizations in Quincy, Worcester, Lawrence, and **Lowell**, Massachusetts; Pawtucket and Central Falls, Rhode Island; and New London, Connecticut. Massachusetts had 25,000 Syrian-Americans by 1926. Boston's Judge Elias Shamon, the first Syrian-Lebanese judge in America, and other American-born, English-speaking leaders, guided other regional federations to unite the community by an interest in Arabic culture, food, music, and dance. When the modern state of Lebanon came into existence (1946), these immigrants and their children responded with charitable activities. But the **immigration** of 100,000 Islamic Arabs from other Middle Eastern countries in 1945–80 overshadowed the Syrian pioneers in New England.

– T –

TANGLEWOOD. The popular name for the **Boston Symphony Orchestra**'s Berkshire Music Festival held each summer on the Tanglewood estate in Lenox, Massachusetts, since 1936. Its program includes a training school, recitals, and a concert series featuring well-known musicians and conductors performing in the Tanglewood Music Shed designed by Eero Saarinen and Joseph Franz (1938).

TAPPAN, ARTHUR (1786–1865). Reformer. Born in Northampton, Massachusetts, on May 22, 1786, Tappan was a **Boston** dry goods merchant. He established silk-importing firms in **Portland** (1807) and Montreal before relocating in New York City (1826–37) with his brother, Lewis Tappan (1788–1873). They founded a newspaper (1827–31) and the nation's first commercial credit rating agency (1849). The Tappan brothers used their fortune to support the **Amistad Case**, the **abolitionist** crusade, and the **Underground Railroad**. Arthur retired to **New Haven**, Connecticut, where he died on July 23, 1865. Lewis died in Brooklyn on June 21, 1873.

TAPPAN, MASON WEARE (1817–1886). Congressman from New Hampshire. Born in Newport, New Hampshire, on October 20, 1817, Tappan practiced law in Bradford (1841–55). He served in the state legislature (1853–55) and was elected as a **Know Nothing Party** candidate to the House of Representatives (1855–57) and reelected as a Republican (1857–61). During the **Civil War** he was colonel of the 1st New Hampshire Infantry Regiment and served in the state legislature (1860–61). Tappan was state attorney general (1876–86) until he died in Bradford on October 25, 1886.

TAUNTON. A community founded in southeastern Massachusetts (1638) known as the **Silver City**. Located on the Taunton River, the silverware industry was developed there early and remains important, as are the city's jewelry, clothing, leather, **textiles**, and plastics firms for the 49,832 residents. In 1824 Isaac Babbitt (1799–1862) created a new metal alloy called Britannia metal as a substitute for silver. Henry G. Reed and Charles E. Barton purchased the firm, which became Reed & Barton (1840), one of the most famous silverware manufacturers in the nation. Using new electroplate technology and silver mined in the West, several

Taunton firms produced fine sterling silver, silver plate, and flatware products. Companies in this area and Rhode Island still produce a wide variety of jewelry today. Thomas Danforth, born in Taunton in 1703, developed the related pewter industry in Norwich, Connecticut, in 1733, and Meriden is also known for its fine pewter and silverware.

TAVERNS. An English institution imported by 17th-century colonists that offered food, drink, and beds to travelers. Local residents bought beverages on a take-out basis in their own bottles. Respectable widows were often licensed by **selectmen** to keep a tavern or inn like Cole's Tavern in Boston (1634). The **General Court** passed regulations enforced by the town **tithingmen** against selling cakes or buns (1637) except for a wedding or funeral and banned drinking toasts (1639), playing shuffleboard (1647), bowling (1650), and singing (1664). Massachusetts designated Richard Fairbanks's tavern in Boston as the depository for overseas mail (1639).

James Wilson, the Boston town crier, founded the oldest operating tavern in the city, the Bell in Hand (1794), and **Samuel Adams** planned the **Boston Tea Party** in the Green Dragon Tavern (1712). Robert Long's family operated a tavern (or ordinary) known as the Three Cranes Tavern (1635) in Charlestown until it was burned in the **Battle of Bunker Hill** (1775). During the **Big Dig** highway project (1999–2003), urban archaeologists excavated its wine cellar and brewery.

Located on main roads from Boston about eight miles apart, travelers found warmth and refreshment in celebrated inns or taverns like the **Toll House** Inn (1709) in Whitman, Massachusetts. Despite legislators' efforts to promote **temperance** by restrictions on innkeepers, taverns were a focus for news, gossip, and mail delivery, with broadsides and notices posted on the walls and newspapers available to read. During the **American Revolution**, the **Sons of Liberty**, the Masons, and the **Committees of Correspondence** met at taverns, which offered locally produced beer, wine, and cider or coffee and tea. Rhode Island patriots met at James Sabin's tavern in **Providence** before burning the *Gaspee* (1772). New England's most famous tavern may be the Wright Tavern (1747) in Lexington, which was the British army command post on April 19, 1775. The Golden Ball on the **Boston Post Road** in Weston, a **Loyalist** tavern (1775), lost its license during the Revolution and is now a museum. Despite regulations against loitering and idleness, townspeople found companionship in 18th-century New England taverns. Some taverns, like the William Pitt Tavern (1766) in **Portsmouth**, New Hampshire, auctioned slaves and imported merchandise. In Vermont, **Ethan Allen** and the

Green Mountain Boys met at the Landlord Faye's tavern in Bennington. They decorated the tavern with their emblem, a stuffed catamount.

After the Revolution some taverns became restaurants, like Boston's Union Oyster House (1826), a favorite of **Daniel Webster**, and the nation's oldest restaurant, or Durgin-Park (1827) at the **Faneuil Hall** marketplace, both popular with **tourists** today. The **Wayside Inn**, a **Yankee** restaurant in Sudbury, which **Henry Wadsworth Longfellow** celebrated, began as a tavern (1702) on the **Boston Post Road**. The elegant Jared Coffin House (1847) in **Nantucket** still operates as an inn and restaurant. Boston's elite Locke-Ober restaurant (1875) began as Locke's New England Tavern. New Hampshire's oldest inn still in operation, the Hancock Inn (1789), was famous for its food and ballroom dances. The first public inn at **Augusta**, Maine (1784), was authorized as a house of entertainment for travelers.

The Griswold Inn in Essex, Connecticut, has operated since 1776, and the Elms Inn in Ridgefield dates from 1800. The state's oldest tavern may be the Old Babcock Tavern (1720) in Tolland, or the Curtis House (1754) in South Woodbury. Some Connecticut taverns or inns served as **stage coach** depots, like the Old Riverton Inn (1796) on the **Hartford** to Albany Post Road in Riverton or the Madison Beach Hotel on the Boston Post Road. The Old Rowley Inn in North Waterford, Maine (1790), was also a stage coach tavern, as was the Red Lion Inn (1773) in Stockbridge, Massachusetts, and the Black Lantern Inn (1799) in Montgomery, Vermont, or the Golden Stage Inn (1796) in Proctorsville and the Kent Tavern in Kent Corners, Vermont (1837). Most taverns had little competition, but Nathaniel Ames, who operated the Inn at the Sign of the Sun in Dedham, Massachusetts, advertised his establishment in the **almanac** he published (1725–64). *See also* STAGE COACH; TEMPERANCE.

TAYLOR, EDWARD T. (1793–1871). Clergyman. Born in Richmond, Virginia, on December 25, 1793, Edward Thompson Taylor was an orphan who spent his childhood as a cabin boy on merchant ships. After a religious conversion in **Boston**, he became a Methodist preacher (1819) in Massachusetts. "Father" Taylor was chaplain of the Seamen's Bethel in Boston (1829–71), a popular, colorful preacher. **Herman Melville** modeled Father Mapple in *Moby Dick* on Taylor, who died in Boston on April 5, 1871.

TAYLOR, MARSHALL WATER (1878–1932). Athlete. Born in Indianapolis, Indiana, on November 26, 1878, Marshall W. Taylor lived in

Worcester, Massachusetts (1895–1930). By 1898 he held seven world records in bicycle races and was the U.S. Champion. Known as Major Taylor or the Worcester Whirlwind, he became World Champion at Montreal (1899), one of the first **African-American** athletes to become a popular star and an international champion in any sport. Taylor's career was limited by racial prejudice, which led him to race on outdoor tracks and indoor velodromes in New England, Europe, and Australia, and he died impoverished and forgotten in Chicago on June 21, 1932. The League of American Wheelmen honored him (1999), and a bicycle path in Worcester was named in his honor. *See also* POPE, ALEXANDER AUGUSTUS; SPORTS.

TEMPERANCE. An American social reform movement with deep roots in New England. Colonial towns regulated **taverns** and discouraged public drinking. The Massachusetts **General Court** passed a law regulating the salc of strong liquors by 1657 and **Increase Mather** deplored the drunkenness associated with cheap rum in 1686. The American Society for the Promotion of Temperance founded in **Boston** (1826) had state and local chapters across New England. The Washingtonian Movement (1840) in Boston tried to cure people addicted to alcohol, drawing large audiences to its colorful lectures by reformed drunkards. **Neal Dow**, the mayor of **Portland**, Maine, led the crusade against intemperance, and prohibition was a major issue in New England politics throughout the 19th century. James Appleton (1785–1862), a Beverly, Massachusetts, temperance reformer, was also a leader in the movement in Maine, which passed the first statewide prohibition law in 1846. Massachusetts enacted prohibition laws (1852–68, 1869–75), but they were unpopular and widely evaded. City liquor commissions or license boards were ineffective until state control began in 1885, and by 1896 about 80 percent of liquor dealers in Boston were hotels and restaurants rather than **taverns** or saloons. Rhode Island prohibition laws (1886–89) were also unsuccessful. National prohibition (1920–33) proved very unpopular in New England, and much liquor was smuggled from Canada into Vermont, New Hampshire, and Maine. *See also* GRAHAM, SYLVESTER.

TERRY, ALFRED HOWE (1827–1890). Soldier. Born in **Hartford**, Connecticut, on November 10, 1827, Terry studied law at Yale University Law School (1848–49) and practiced in **New Haven**. He served as colonel of the 2nd Connecticut Regiment (1854–62) and was promoted to general (1862). After the **Civil War**, Terry commanded the army in

Dakota Territory (1865–86) during the campaigns against the Plains Indians. Major General Terry retired in 1888 to New Haven, where he died on December 16, 1890.

TEXTILES. An important New England industry since the first woolen mill opened in Rowley, Massachusetts (1643). Watertown had the first water-powered wool mill (1794), but cotton textile production began with **Samuel Slater** and **Moses Brown**. They opened the first American cotton-spinning mill in Pawtucket, Rhode Island (1790), and others in Connecticut and Massachusetts. **Eli Whitney**'s cotton gin (1793) increased cotton production, and **Francis Cabot Lowell** expanded the cotton textile industry at **Waltham**, Massachusetts (1813), with water-powered looms spinning yarn and weaving cloth. Employing young unmarried **Yankee** farm girls and women, he drew upon large capital investment and professional managers. His success inspired **Providence**, Rhode Island, merchants to open 170 mills (1815); and his investors, the **Boston Associates**, founded **Lowell**, Massachusetts (1826), America's first industrial city on the Merrimack River. **Irish** and **French-Canadian** immigrants replaced the **mill girls** by 1850. The Stevens Mill in Dudley, Massachusetts (1846), the first linen mill in the nation, also employed Irish, **German**, and **Polish** immigrants. Lowell had 10 textile corporations with 32 mills by 1840. James De Wolf built the first cotton factory in Rhode Island (1812) at Coventry. Tariff protection, cheap southern cotton, and expanding domestic markets created great profits that **Boston Brahmin** families invested in banks, real estate, **railroads**, shipping, **insurance**, and **lumber** firms, as well as schools, colleges, and charities.

Erastus Bigelow (1814–79) invented the first loom for lace manufacture (1837), and founded the Bigelow Carpet Mill in Clinton. Hezekiah Conant (1827–1902) invented machines for his important Conant Thread Company in Dudley, Massachusetts. **Elias Howe**'s sewing machine (1846) created the ready-to-wear clothing industry. Lawrence, Fall River, **New Bedford**, and Hopedale, Massachusetts; **Providence**, Rhode Island; Saco, Maine; and Manchester, New Hampshire were other cotton, wool, and linen textile cities, but the substandard, unsafe, and unhealthy working conditions led to much labor unrest.

The Amoskeag Manufacturing Company (1809–1935) in Manchester, New Hampshire, was the largest cotton textile mill in the world by 1880. In Connecticut, the Cheney Silk Mill at Manchester was the largest silk weaving company in the nation. Frank Cheney (1817–1904) patented a machine for making silk thread (1847) and traveled to China and Japan for materials. **New Haven** also had nine corset firms by 1890 employing 3,000 **Italian** and **Jewish** immigrant women. After the **Civil War** textile manufacturing expanded in Rhode Island, and the workers were often women and children, especially recent immigrants, working and living in brutal conditions unregulated by the state. Lillie Chace Wyman, the daughter of a Rhode Island manufacturer, wrote articles in the *Atlantic Monthly* (1877–88) exposing the conditions and impoverished lives of factory operatives, and this led to some reform laws (1894).

The Industrial Workers of the World (IWW) led the bitter **Lawrence Strike** (1912) to win improved wages and working conditions for the city's multiethnic work force. Sara Agnes McLaughlin Conboy (1870–1928), a **Boston** labor organizer, was a pioneer leader of the United Textile Workers. But in 1920–40 many textile factories, facing competition from rayon and silk, closed or relocated to the South to avoid labor unions and high costs. New England textile mills, large red-brick structures on rivers or smaller wood-framed buildings on streams, survive today as apartment buildings, **computer** firms, offices, restaurants, and artist lofts. The Digital Equipment Corporation started (1957) in a converted woolen mill in Maynard, Massachusetts, that had produced blankets and uniforms for the **Civil War**.

THANKSGIVING DAY. Began as a traditional New England holiday when Governor **William Bradford** proclaimed a day of prayer and feasting on December 13, 1621. The 52 **Pilgrims** fired a cannon in salute, marched in solemn procession to the Meetinghouse to hear **William Brewster's** sermon, and enjoyed a feast of turkey and venison provided by **Massasoit** and 90 **Wampanoag** guests. The harvest holiday lasted three days with **sports**, games, psalm singing, Indian dances, and militia drills by Captain **Miles Standish**'s company. This became an annual holiday, perhaps an alternative to the "Popish mummery" of the English Christmas, celebrated throughout New England by 1684. General George Washington proclaimed it a holiday for the Continental Army (1777); and at the urging of Congress (1789), President Washington declared it a national holiday on November 26, 1789. Most presidents and state governors followed the custom, but a campaign by **Sarah J. Hale**, editor of *Godey's Lady's Book* (1859), made it a national event. President Abraham Lincoln standardized the date as the last Thursday in November (1863), and by the 1870s Thanksgiving dinner, parades, shooting matches, social calls, and open houses rivaled church services as the focus of the day. The Thanksgiving holiday attracted over 4,000 **tourists** to

Plymouth in 2000. Since 1970 **Native Americans** convene at **Plymouth Rock** each Thanksgiving Day for a national day of mourning for the millions of North American Indians killed by epidemics and wars. *See also* FAST DAY.

THAXTER, CELIA LAIGHTON (1835–1894). Poet. Born in **Portsmouth**, New Hampshire, on June 29, 1835, Thaxter's father was a **lighthouse** keeper and innkeeper on the **Isles of Shoals** (1839), which attracted summer visitors including **Ralph Waldo Emerson, Henry Wadsworth Longfellow, John Greenleaf Whittier, Mark Twain, Sarah Orne Jewett, Childe Hassam,** and **William Morris Hunt**. They encouraged her to write about seacoast nature, and when she moved to Newtonville, Massachusetts (1856–80), with her husband, Levi Thaxter, she published verse and prose in the *Atlantic Monthly, Scribner's,* and *Harper's* magazines. Her Newtonville home was a literary salon frequented by **Annie Adams Fields** and other literary lions. Thaxter moved to Kittery, Maine (1880), and when she died on the Isles of Shoals, she was one of the best-known female poets in the nation.

THAYER, ELI (1819–1899). Congressman from Massachusetts. Born in Mendon, Massachusetts, on June 11, 1819, Thayer graduated from Brown University (1845). He was a teacher and lawyer but did not practice law. Elected to the state legislature (1853–55) by the Free Soil Party, Thayer founded the **New England Emigrant Aid Company** (1854) to send antislavery settlers to Kansas. He was a Republican in the House of Representatives (1857–61), wrote *A History of the Kansas Crusade* (1889), moved to Oregon, engaged in **railroad** construction, and died in **Worcester** on April 15, 1899.

THAYER, POLLY (1904–). Artist. Born in **Boston** on November 8, 1904, Ethel Polly Thayer studied at the Boston **Museum of Fine Arts** (MFA) school (1923–25) and in France and New York City. She is best known as a member of the genteel Boston School of painting, but expanded her range with *Circles* (1928) and portraits of her husband, the Boston lawyer and yachtsman Donald Carter Starr (1933) and **May Sarton** (1936). She was the first Boston artist to have a painting, *My Childhood Trees,* collected by the MFA (1940).

THAYER, SYLVANUS (1785–1872). Soldier. Born in Braintree, Massachusetts, on June 9, 1785, Thayer graduated from Dartmouth College

(1807) and from West Point (1808). He was an engineer building fortifications (1808–15) and studied military education in Europe (1815–17) before serving as superintendent of the U.S. Military Academy at West Point (1817–33). Thayer, the father of West Point, transformed it into a major educational institution. General Thayer became the U.S. Army's chief engineer, building New England coastal fortifications (1833–63). He endowed the Thayer School of Engineering at Dartmouth (1867) and Thayer Academy (1877) in Braintree, where he died on September 7, 1872.

THEROUX, PAUL (1941–). Writer. Born in Medford, Massachusetts, on April 10, 1941, Theroux graduated from the University of Massachusetts (1963). He served in the Peace Corps in Africa (1963–65) and taught English in Italy, Uganda, and Singapore while publishing short stories and novels, including *Waldo* (1967) and *Saint Jack* (1973). His popular and critically acclaimed nonfiction travel books include *The Great Railway Bazaar: By Train through Asia* (1975), *The Old Patagonian Express: By Train through the Americas* (1979), and *Riding the Iron Rooster: By Train through China* (1989). Theroux is one of modern **literature**'s most admired chroniclers of the expatriate, postimperialist life in exotic locales. *See also* LITERATURE.

THOMAS, ISAIAH (1749–1831). Journalist, editor, and publisher. Born in **Boston** on January 19, 1749, Thomas published the weekly *Massachusetts Spy* (1770) in support of the patriot cause and was a leader of the **Sons of Liberty**. British occupation of Boston in 1775 compelled Thomas to move his newspaper to **Worcester**, where he became the postmaster. He published his newspaper as well as the *Massachusetts Magazine* (1789–96), **almanacs**, and books with his own paper mill and bookbindery, producing over 1,000 titles. He retired in 1802, but he established the first bank in Worcester, wrote the *History of Printing in America* (1810), and founded the **American Antiquarian Society** (1812) by donating his extensive collection of Americana. Thomas died in Worcester on April 4, 1831.

THOMAS, SETH (1785–1859). Businessman. Born in Wolcott, Connecticut, on August 19, 1785, Thomas, the son of a **Scottish** immigrant, apprenticed with a carpenter. After joining Eli Terry and Silas Hoadley (1807) in a clock-manufacturing firm, Thomas opened his own factory in Plymouth Hollow (1812). He produced large numbers of inexpensive shelf clocks with wooden works, and by 1838 he opened a brass mill to make clock works. The Seth Thomas Clock Company (1853) pioneered in mass production of brass clocks at Thomaston (formerly Plymouth Hollow), Connecticut. After he died on January 29, 1859, his son Seth Thomas, Jr., expanded the firm. *See also* WATERBURY.

THOMPSON, BENJAMIN (1753–1814). Scientist. Born in Woburn, Massachusetts, on March 26, 1753, Thompson was apprenticed to a **Salem** merchant and studied medicine in **Boston**. Commissioned a major by the governor of New Hampshire (1772), Thompson fled to London (1776) and became undersecretary of state for the colonies (1780). He served as a colonel with the British army in South Carolina and New York (1781–83). Thompson spent 11 years in the Bavarian army and civil service, where he was knighted (1784) and named **Count Rumford** (the former name for **Concord**, New Hampshire) of the Holy Roman Empire (1791). His studies of artillery, diet, insulation, and physics established his scientific reputation. He founded the Royal Institute in London (1800) and settled in France, where his research led to practical inventions in the kitchen stove, fireplace, chimney, coffeepot (1806), cooking, oil lamp, gunpowder, and steam heat. His estate endowed the Rumford professorship at **Harvard** College after Count Rumford died in France on August 21, 1814. A statue of Count Rumford was placed in his hometown, Woburn (1899). *See also* LOYALISTS.

THOMPSON, BENJAMIN C. (1918–2002). Architect. Born in St. Paul, Minnesota, in 1918, Thompson graduated from Yale University (1941) and served in the U.S. Navy (1941–45). He joined Walter Gropius in founding The Architects Collaborative (TAC) in Boston (1946–66) and was chairman of the department of **architecture** at the Harvard Graduate School of Design (1963–67). Best known for his design of the marketplace at **Faneuil Hall** and Quincy Market (1971–76), Thompson won the highest American award for lifetime achievement in architecture, the Gold Medal of the American Institute of Architects (1992). His other works include the Gutman Library at **Harvard University**, buildings at Brandeis University, Colby College, and Amherst College, and renovations of Union Station in Washington, D.C. Ben Thompson died in Cambridge, Massachusetts, on August 17, 2002.

THOMPSON, JENNY (1973–). Athlete. Born in Georgetown, Massachusetts, on February 26, 1973, and raised in Dover, New Hampshire,

Jenny Thompson graduated from Stanford University (1994). She won 19 National Collegiate Athletic Association (NCAA) titles in college and two gold medals in the Olympic Games (1992). Thompson won two more gold medals at the 1996 Olympic Games and was named Swimmer of the Year (1993, 1998). New England's most victorious Olympic athlete, with six Olympic medals, continues to compete and to study at Columbia University Medical School.

THOMSON, MELDRIM, JR. (1912–2001). Governor of New Hampshire. Born in Wilkinson, Pennsylvania, on March 8, 1912, Thomson graduated from Washington & Jefferson College (1934) and the University of Georgia Law School (1935). After working for a New York City publisher (1936–51), he founded a publishing company (1951) in Orford, New Hampshire, near his family farm. Active in local and state Republican politics, Thomson was the only governor to serve three consecutive terms (1973–79). His ardently conservative policies and vehement opposition to the civil rights movement and liberals were supported by **William Loeb**, publisher of the *Manchester Union Leader*. Thompson's program to avoid sales or personal income taxes proved popular until he founded the Constitution Party (1979). Defeated in two campaigns for a fourth term, Thomson retired to his farm (1980) in Orford, where he died on April 19, 2001.

THOREAU, HENRY DAVID (1817–1862). Writer. Born in Concord, Massachusetts, on July 12, 1817, Thoreau graduated from **Harvard** College (1837) and published poems and essays in the **Transcendentalist** magazine *The Dial* while living in Concord with **Ralph Waldo Emerson**. After living alone in a small cabin on Walden Pond in Concord (1845–47), Thoreau published *A Week on the Concord and Merrimack Rivers* (1849). He is best known for his influential book *Walden* (1854) as well as *Maine* (1864) and *Cape Cod* (1865). Thoreau was the first environmental writer in America but also wrote on civil disobedience, passive resistance, and self-reliance. Thoreau died in Concord on May 6, 1862.

THORNTON, MATTHEW (1714–1803). Congressman from New Hampshire. Born in Ireland in 1714, Thornton immigrated with his family to Wiscasset, Maine (1716), and then to **Worcester**, Massachusetts. He practiced medicine in the **Scotch-Irish** community of Londonderry, New Hampshire (1740–76). Thornton served in the legislature (1758,

1760–61, 1776, 1783–85) and signed the Declaration of Independence as a member of Congress (1776–77). He was a New Hampshire **militia** colonel during the **American Revolution** and a state judge. Thornton retired to Merrimack (1789) and died in Newburyport, Massachusetts, on June 24, 1803.

THREAD CITY. A nickname for Willimantic, Connecticut. Chartered in 1893, Willimantic was home to several thread manufacturers (1820–1985) and other industries. Julian Alden Weir depicted the town in his painting *U.S. Thread Company Mills, Willimantic, Connecticut* (1897).

TICKNOR, GEORGE (1791–1871). Educator. Born in **Boston** on August 1, 1791, Ticknor graduated from Dartmouth College (1807) and became a lawyer (1813). After study in Europe, he taught literature and modern languages at **Harvard** College (1819–35). Ticknor wrote the scholarly *History of Spanish Literature* (1849) and *Life of William Hickling Prescott* (1864) and was a founder of the **Boston Public Library** (1852). Like many **Boston Brahmins**, he was a philanthropic gentleman scholar who made two Grand Tours of Europe (1815–19, 1835–37). Ticknor died in Boston on January 26, 1871.

TICKNOR, WILLIAM DAVIS (1810–1864). Editor and publisher. Born in Lebanon, New Hampshire, on August 6, 1810, Ticknor founded Ticknor and Fields publishing company in **Boston** (1832) and published the *Atlantic Monthly* (1857–64) magazine and the *North American Review* (1863) at his **Old Corner Book Store** (1832–64). The firm and bookstore at the corner of Washington and School Streets became a mecca for literary figures of the era. The first American publisher to deal honorably with authors, Ticknor died in Philadelphia on April 10, 1864. Ticknor and Fields later merged with Houghton-Mifflin Company. *See also* FIELDS, JAMES T.; LITERATURE.

TIFFANY, CHARLES LEWIS (1812–1902). Businessman. Born in Killingly, Connecticut, on February 15, 1812, Tiffany opened a jewelry shop in New York City (1837). Known for superior glass and porcelain, he manufactured his own fine jewelry (1848) with branches in Paris (1850), London, and Geneva (1868). During the **Civil War** Tiffany & Company became the most prominent source for jewelry, china, silverware, swords, and medals. Tiffany created unique **art** for the **Mark**

Twain House in **Hartford** before he died in New York on February 18, 1902. His son, Louis Comfort Tiffany, expanded the business.

TITHINGMAN. A town officer annually elected by the New England **town meeting** as a petty constable responsible for moral policing, especially violation of the Sabbath, disorderly **taverns**, drunkenness, gambling, and the unlicensed sale of alcoholic beverages. Common in England by 1070, in Massachusetts these sworn officers were elected by the 1680s and charged to admonish, report, or arrest lawbreakers with the constable. The officer, known by his long staff, could fine, whip, and place in the stocks or pillory minor lawbreakers or vagrants. Some towns had as many as four tithingmen. The office disappeared in the 1730s as the **Puritan** influence waned, but was revived in **Boston** in 1770 as part of the **blue law** tradition. Boston last used the pillory in 1803, and Vermont abolished the office of tithingman in 1840.

TOBACCO. A New England crop grown by **Native Americans** in the **Connecticut River** valley and by Massachusetts and Connecticut farmers in the colonial era. By 1801 South Windsor, Connecticut, manufactured the first cigars in the nation. New England shade-grown tobacco is still used for cigar wrapping.

TOBEY, CHARLES WILLIAM (1880–1953). Senator from New Hampshire. Born in Roxbury, Massachusetts, on July 22, 1880, Tobey moved to a farm in Temple, New Hampshire (1902). He operated an **insurance** business, was president of the F. M. Hoyt Shoe Company, and served as a Republican state legislator (1915–17, 1919–21, 1923–25), speaker of the house (1919–20), and state senator (1924–26). Elected governor (1929–31), Tobey continued the progressive policies of **John G. Winant** and introduced the practice of snowplows on state roads to expand the New Hampshire economy. He was elected to the House of Representatives (1933–39) and to the U.S. Senate (1939–53) and was a delegate to the International Monetary Conference at **Bretton Woods**, New Hampshire (1944). Tobey died in Maryland on July 24, 1953.

TOBIN, MAURICE J. (1901–1953). Governor of Massachusetts. Born in **Boston** on May 5, 1901, Tobin attended Boston College and was a manager of the New England Telephone Company. He served as a Democrat in the state legislature (1926–37) and was a protégé of **James Michael Curley**, whom he twice defeated for mayor of Boston (1937 and 1941).

The Curley-Tobin feud inspired **Edwin O'Connor**'s novel *The Last Hurrah*. Tobin was elected governor (1945–47) and served as secretary of labor (1948–53). He died in Boston on July 19, 1953, and was honored by a statue on the Charles River **Esplanade**. The Mystic River Bridge was renamed in his memory.

TOLL HOUSE COOKIE. Invented by Ruth Graves Wakefield (1908–77) at her Toll House Inn in Whitman, Massachusetts (1930). When she added pieces of semi-sweet chocolate to the traditional New England recipe for butter drop cookies, the result proved quite popular. The **tavern**, established in 1709 on the toll road from **Boston** to **New Bedford**, became renowned for these homemade cookies when Mrs. Wakefield wrote a cookbook, *Toll House Tried and True Recipes* (1948). The Massachusetts legislature declared the Toll House Cookie as the official state cookie (1997) despite much support for the **Fig Newton**.

TONIC. The name for any carbonated soft drink in **Boston** and Maine. It may derive from **Moxie**, a popular soft drink invented in **Lowell** (1884) by a doctor who claimed it had medicinal value.

TORIES. *See* LOYALISTS.

TORREY, CHARLES TURNER (1813–1846). Reformer. Born in Scituate, Massachusetts, on November 21, 1813, Torrey graduated from Yale College (1833). Ordained a **Congregational** minister in **Providence**, Rhode Island (1836), but unsuited for the pulpit, he broke with **William Lloyd Garrison** and founded the more conservative Massachusetts Abolitionist Society (1838). Torrey was an **abolitionist** editor known as the father of the **Underground Railroad** (1842). Arrested helping slaves escape to Canada, he died in the Maryland State Penitentiary on May 6, 1846. Following his public funeral in **Boston**, his grave at **Mount Auburn Cemetery** became a shrine in the antislavery movement.

TOUCEY, ISAAC (1792–1869). Senator from Connecticut. Born in Newtown, Connecticut, on November 15, 1792, Toucey practiced law in **Hartford** (1818–22) and was county prosecuting attorney (1822–35). He was elected as a Democrat to the House of Representatives (1835–39) and as governor (1846–47). Toucey served as the U.S. attorney general (1848–49) and U.S. senator (1852–57) and as secretary of the navy (1857–61). He returned to his law practice in Hartford, where he died on July 30, 1869.

TOURISM. A feature of New England society as early as 1760 when wealthy visitors from Philadelphia and southern plantations spent summers enjoying the cool wind and ocean in **Newport**, Rhode Island. Stafford Springs in Connecticut was a spa town in the European tradition, and Jabez Ricker rented rooms to summer visitors in Poland Springs, Maine (1794), where the soothing waters healed invalids. Passenger ships carried vacationers from **Boston** to **Portland** (1824), as did the Boston to Bangor packet boats (1845). Other resort towns with therapeutic waters were Williamstown, Massachusetts, and Clarendon Springs, Middletown Springs, and Brunswick Springs in Vermont. Most of these health spas had been used by Native Americans and attracted wealthy invalids to the resort hotel mineral baths until 1900.

Sandy **beaches** at Old Orchard, Kennebunk, Wells, Ogunquit, and York attracted summer visitors on **railroads** by 1836, and the Boston and Maine line (1873) made tourism an important industry on the **Downeast** seashore, lakes, mountains, and woods. Methodists enjoyed summer vacations at Oak Bluff on **Martha's Vineyard** (1835) but emphasized healthy recuperation and recovery more than recreation.

In New Hampshire **Mount Washington**'s refreshing air attracted summer visitors such as the ailing Rutherford B. Hayes (1847). After the **Civil War** the **Isles of Shoals** attracted artists and literary figures **Ralph Waldo Emerson**, **Nathaniel Hawthorne**, **Oliver Wendell Holmes**, and **Mark Twain** as the word "vacation" came into popular use. Influential clergymen like **Horace Bushnell**, **William Ellery Channing**, and **Thomas Wentworth Higginson** by the 1850s advocated healthy exercise and leisure for muscular Christianity, making the vacationing tourists good Christians. Middle-class tourists enjoyed the cool breezes and invigorating salt air of **Nantucket** and **Martha's Vineyard** (1835) and at the Watch Hill **temperance** resort (1870) in Rhode Island.

Grand tourist hotels opened on New Hampshire's seacoast and in the **White Mountains** (1852). **Railroads** carried urban hay fever sufferers to 34 hotels in Bethlehem, New Hampshire (1880). Governor Frank W. Rollins promoted tourism with **Old Home Week** in New Hampshire towns (1899) as well as improved roads, an annual state guidebook for tourists (1902), and protection of state forests. Vermont attracted visitors for hunting and fishing by 1850, and Brattleboro was a popular heath resort in the antebellum era. As tourism and recreation replaced farming, Vermont also established the first state publicity bureau in the nation (1890). Summer camps for children spread rapidly by 1920.

New England's seacoast was also attractive to summer visitors, especially elite families who built elaborate cottages in **Newport** and **Bar Harbor**. When middle-class summer visitors followed this pattern, the summer tourist season and growing interest in landscape and wildlife conservation formed a major industry with powerful political advocates. Magazines and guidebooks advertised historic sites in **New Haven** and **Cape Ann** as ideal tourist destinations (1880), creating another reason for travel. Urban growth combined with more interest in health and recreation in open space, as well as improved steamship, rail, and automobile travel spurred growth of hotels, motels, restaurants, state parks, campgrounds, and historic preservation. Massachusetts designated the **Mohawk Trail**, a scenic tourist route (1914), to promote the tourist industry and as a route to the growing **ski** industry in the 1930s. The Tercentennial celebration (1920) made **Plymouth** a popular site for Americans interested in the **Pilgrims**, and by 1999 over 4,000 visitors arrived there annually. Tourism, the third largest industry in Massachusetts, contributed $13 billion and 147,000 jobs to the **economy** from 28 million visitors, most (70 percent) in the summer (2001). Renovation of **Faneuil Hall** and the Quincy Market district in downtown Boston (1976), profitable private ventures, demonstrates the important role tourism plays in the regional **economy** and was an example followed by other cities.

Vermont Life magazine (1946), with the slogan "Vermont is a way of life" and an elaborate pictorial format, made **Green Mountains** recreation popular. Construction of the interstate highways (1957–82) opened the state to visitors, and Vermont banned highway billboards (1968) to protect its $4.2 billion tourist industry (2000). The New England Culinary Institute (1978) in **Montpelier** trained professional chefs for hotels, resorts, and restaurants. Tourism is a cornerstone of the Vermont economy, the state's second largest industry, supporting 75,000 jobs catering to 12 million visitors (2000).

New Hampshire earned $1.5 billion from 10 million tourists (2001). As *Down East* magazine (1954) and **L. L. Bean** shaped national images of Maine, the state dubbed Vacation Land reported $8 billion in tourism revenues by 1998. In recognition of the important role of tourism, the Maine Publicity Bureau (1922) was renamed the Maine Tourist Association (1999). **Acadia National Park** (1929) and **Cape Cod National Seashore** (1961) are major tourist attractions, as are the other national and state parks and historic places in the region. New England's distinct seasons, beautiful scenery, varied geography, and many art, cultural, and historic sites continue to attract visitors and generate revenues year round. Tourism created an American identity and national culture.

TOWN MEETING. A tradition of direct democracy developed soon after settlers arrived in New England. The first recorded town meeting was in Dorchester, Massachusetts (1633), and Charlestown elected the first board of **selectmen** (1634). The **Puritans'** desire for religious liberty gave birth to democracy in New England as townsmen created this annual forum to settle local disputes without recourse to the colonial or state legislature. This practice became common throughout New England. Vermont held its first town meeting in Bennington in 1762. Town meeting day, often the first Tuesday in March, is still the most important event of the year in many communities. The moderator, a respected local leader, chairs the meeting and the annual election of the **selectmen**, school board, and town officers. New England county government is concerned with courts, sheriffs, deeds, and roads, so town government exercises much autonomy over **public schools**, taxes, ordinances, and expenditures. Dubbed democracy in action, it may be the region's greatest gift to the nation. Colonial town selectmen exercised much autonomy in calling these meetings and permitting most adult male residents to vote and fining those absent. The Massachusetts Government Act (1774) that banned town meetings not called by the governor was one of the **Intolerable Acts** leading to the **American Revolution**.

Since **Boston** adopted city government (1822), some larger towns in New England replaced the open town meeting, in which every citizen could participate, with a representative assembly meeting several times a year as the town's legislative body. By 2001 about 49 of the 351 Massachusetts communities were cities and many towns hired professional town managers and finance directors. However, town meeting government remains a cherished **Yankee** tradition. *See also* OVERSEERS OF THE POOR; TITHINGMAN.

TOWN, ITHIEL (1784–1844). Architect. Born in Thompson, Connecticut, on October 3, 1784, Town studied in **Boston** with **Asher Benjamin**. He assisted in building the Center Congregational Church (1812) and designed Trinity Church (1814) and the new Greek Revival state house in **New Haven** (1828). Town was best known for more than 50 **covered bridges** in New England using his patented (1820) Town lattice truss. Practicing in New York City, he built the New York Custom House (1842) and the **Wadsworth Atheneum** in **Hartford** (1842). Town traveled to Europe with **Samuel F. B. Morse** (1829–30) and died in New Haven on June 13, 1844.

TOWNSHEND ACTS. Written by Charles Townshend and passed by the British Parliament (1767) after the repeal of the **Stamp Act**. Aroused by **James Otis** and **Samuel Adams**, New England merchants protested these **writs of assistance** and new customs duties by boycotting English goods, which led to the **Boston Massacre**. The laws were repealed (1770) when British trade declined, but the unpopular tea tax was retained.

TRAINING DAY. A colonial New England custom of scheduled military exercises by the town **militia**. The church service with solemn prayer, psalm singing, and a special sermon reminded the militiamen of their duty as spiritual warriors and demonized the **Native Americans** and other foes. The armed men mustered for drills and target practice on the town common four to eight times a year. By 1700 training day became a secular holiday with parades and pageantry in many towns. The painting *Salem Common on Training Day* (1808) by folk artist George Ropes, Jr., depicts this traditional event.

TRANSCENDENTALISM. A philosophy based on the superiority of imagination to reason, it was advocated by a group of writers and romantic reformers in antebellum Massachusetts, including **Bronson Alcott**, **Ralph Waldo Emerson**, **Margaret Fuller**, **Henry David Thoreau**, and **George Ripley**. They abandoned **Congregationalism** for the rational **Unitarian** religion organized by **William Ellery Channing** in **Boston** (1825) and admired the work of Immanuel Kant, Samuel Taylor Coleridge, and Thomas Carlyle. The **China trade** also introduced Asian philosophy and theology to the Transcendentalists. The Transcendental Club in **Concord** and Boston (1836) published an influential magazine, *The Dial* (1840–44), and many members lived at **Brook Farm**, a West Roxbury commune, or at **Fruitlands** in Harvard, Massachusetts. Rising from the discontent with religious, social, and economic issues, this intellectual movement supported many reforms and challenged the complacency of the established churches while offering Americans a vision of the universe in harmony.

TREATY OF PORTSMOUTH. Ended the Russo-Japanese War. It was mediated by President Theodore Roosevelt and signed at the

Portsmouth Naval Shipyard in New Hampshire on September 5, 1905. Roosevelt won the Nobel Peace Prize (1906) as a result.

TRIANGULAR TRADE. An international system of trade from New England to West Africa to the West Indies usually exchanging New England salt **codfish**, **lumber**, and **rum** for slaves, who were sold in the **West Indies trade** for sugar or **molasses** used to make rum. When the Royal African Company ended its monopoly of the slave trade (1697), rum distilleries expanded in Massachusetts, Connecticut, and Rhode Island. Prohibition of the foreign slave trade (1808) and the campaign by **abolitionists** diminished the notorious triangular trade. *See also* SLAVERY.

TRIMOUNTAIN. The name for three hills on the **Shawmut** peninsula that became **Boston** in 1630. The hills, called Pemberton (or Cotton), Beacon (or Sentry), and Mount Vernon, were leveled (1799) to fill adjacent marshes. Tremont Street alongside the **Boston Common** recalls the old name.

TRINITY CHURCH. Designed by **Henry Hobson Richardson** in **Boston**'s Copley Square (1877) is considered New England's greatest building and the most significant example of Romanesque **architecture** in the nation. Using pale granite and red sandstone, Richardson created a lavish monument for the wealthy Episcopalians of Gilded Age Boston, parishioners rich from **railroad**, mining, and **textile** investments and eager to celebrate the robust era. **John La Farge** created the murals, **Daniel Chester French** and **Augustus Saint-Gaudens** provided sculpture, and Charles McKim was one of Richardson's young architects. **Phillips Brooks** was the first pastor of the new church. Trinity Church was renovated and expanded in 2002.

TRIPLE-DECKERS. Three-story, wooden-framed houses with six-room apartments on each floor built in working-class neighborhoods of **Boston**, Springfield, **Worcester**, and other New England cities in 1890–1930. With small yards at the front, rear, and sides, the triple-decker was an economical solution to urban housing needs. The homeowner often lived in one apartment and used the rental income from the other two apartments to pay the mortgage and taxes. In some cases, all three apartments were occupied by extended family members. Although some were built in an inexpensive, box-like style, others were more elaborate in the Italianate, Mansard, Early Queen Anne, Late Queen Anne, Early Classical Revival, Gambrel, and Late Classical Revival styles. Many examples survive: 4,000 in Worcester and 16,000 in Boston. *See also* ARCHITECTURE.

TROTTER, WILLIAM MONROE (1872–1934). Journalist. Born in Ohio on April 7, 1872, Trotter's family came to **Boston** (1872) where he was the first **African-American** student to be elected to Phi Beta Kappa at **Harvard University** (1895). Trotter founded the *Boston Guardian* (1901–34), a national weekly newspaper famous for vocal opposition to Booker T. Washington. Trotter allied with **W. E. B. Du Bois** in the Niagara Movement (1905) but was too militant to join him in the National Association for the Advancement of Colored People (NAACP) in 1909. Trotter was a pioneer who anticipated the civil rights movement by 60 years and engaged in a public dispute with President Woodrow Wilson (1914) at a White House conference on segregation. Trotter died in Boston on April 7, 1934.

TROUSE. A jocular term for a house built around a trailer or mobile home by thrifty **Yankees** in northern New England. It is usually located on marginal land called **puckerbrush** and inhabited by people described as a **swamp Yankee** or **woodchuck**.

TRUMBULL, JOHN (1750–1831). Poet and lawyer. Born in Westbury, Connecticut, on April 24, 1750, Trumbull graduated from Yale College (1767) and studied law with **John Adams**. He practiced law in **Hartford**, where he was one of the **Hartford Wits**, a group of **Federalist** literary men. His major poem was *M'Fingal* (1776–82), a mock epic satirizing the **Loyalists** and British in the **American Revolution**. Trumbull abandoned writing for the law by 1785 and served in the state legislature, as state superior court judge, and on the state supreme court. He died in Detroit, Michigan, on May 11, 1831.

TRUMBULL, JOHN (1756–1843). Artist. Born in Lebanon, Connecticut, on June 6, 1756, Trumbull, the son of **Jonathan Trumbull**, graduated from **Harvard** College (1773). While serving in the Continental Army (1775–78) he studied **art** in **Boston** (1777–78) and was influenced by the work of **John Smibert** and **John Singleton Copley**. He trained in London with Benjamin West (1780) until he was arrested as a spy. Colonel Trumbull made the **American Revolution** his life's work, painting the first portrait of *George Washington* (1781) and *Jeremiah and Daniel Wadsworth* (1784) as well as *The Death of General Warren at the Battle of Bunker Hill* (1786) and *Declaration of Independence* (1787). His four Revolutionary War paintings were hung in the rotunda in the U.S. Capitol (1826). Impoverished in his old age, Trumbull donated his paintings to Yale College, establishing the first art gallery at an American college (1831). Trumbull, never fully recognized or acclaimed, died in New York City on November 10, 1843.

TRUMBULL, JONATHAN (1710–1785). Governor of Connecticut. Born in Lebanon, Connecticut, on October 12, 1710, Trumbull graduated from **Harvard** College (1727) and became a merchant. He served in the colonial legislature and governor's council (1740–66) and as chief justice of the superior court (1766–69). Elected governor by the legislature (1769–84) to replace **Loyalist** governor **Thomas Fitch**, he was the only governor to support independence from Britain. He signed the legislature's acts confiscating the property and authorizing imprisonment or death of Loyalists in the colony. George Washington noted he was the most generous governor, sending supplies and cattle to the Continental Army at Valley Forge (1777–78) and at Morristown, New Jersey (1779–80). Trumbull was the original **Brother Jonathan**, a term for **Yankee** Americans. He died in Lebanon on August 17, 1785.

TRUMBULL, JONATHAN, JR. (1740–1809). Speaker of the House. Born in Lebanon, Connecticut, on March 26, 1740, he was the son of **Jonathan Trumbull** and brother of the artist **John Trumbull**. After graduating from **Harvard** College (1759), he served in the state legislature (1774–75, 1779–80, 1788). Trumbull was paymaster of the Continental Army and comptroller of the Treasury and secretary to George Washington (1781). Elected to the House of Representatives (1789–95), he was the **Federalist** Speaker of the House in the Second Congress (1791–93) and served in the Senate (1795–96). Trumbull was lieutenant governor (1796–97) and governor of Connecticut (1797–1809) for 11 consecutive terms until he died in Lebanon on August 7, 1809.

TRUMBULL, JOSEPH (1782–1861). Governor of Connecticut. Born in Lebanon, Connecticut, on December 7, 1782, Trumbull graduated from Yale College (1801), studied law, and practiced in Windham and **Hartford**. He was president of the Hartford Bank and of the Providence, Hartford & Fishkill Railroad and was a state representative (1832). Elected to the House of Representatives as a Whig (1834–35, 1839–43), he returned to the state legislature (1848), was elected governor (1849–51), and returned to the state legislature (1851). Trumbull died in Hartford on August 4, 1861.

TRUSTEES OF RESERVATIONS. The first private, nonprofit, statewide conservation and preservation organization in the nation. It was founded in **Boston** by **Charles Eliot** (1891) and manages more than 34,000 acres of publicly accessible Massachusetts land and buildings of historic, scenic, or ecological value. The trustees and 25,000 members host 1 million visitors to its 80 reservations each year.

TSONGAS, PAUL E. (1941–1997). Senator from Massachusetts. Born in **Lowell** on February 14, 1941, Paul Efthemios Tsongas graduated from Dartmouth College (1962) and served in the Peace Corps in Ethiopia (1962–64) and the West Indies (1967–68). He graduated from Yale University Law School (1967) and practiced law in Lowell and **Boston**, where he was a deputy assistant attorney general (1969–71), city councilor (1969–72), and county commissioner (1973–74). Elected as a Democrat to the House of Representatives (1975–79) and to the Senate (1979–85), Tsongas was an unsuccessful candidate for the 1972 Democratic presidential nomination. He died in Boston on January 18, 1997.

TUCKER, SOPHIE (1884–1966). Singer. Born in Russia on January 13, 1884, Sonia Abuza Kalish grew up in the **North End** of **Boston** and **Hartford**. She launched her show-business career as Sophie Tucker in New York City (1906) **vaudeville** and burlesque theaters. The Ziegfeld Follies dubbed her the "Last of the Red-hot Mamas" (1909). Considered the "Queen of Vaudeville" in the 1920s, Tucker extended her career as a blues and jazz singer in nightclubs, radio, television, and movies. The Sophie Tucker Foundation (1945) endowed Hartford **Jewish** charities and a chair at Brandeis University (1955). The Broadway musical *Sophie* (1963) was based on her career, and she died in New York City on February 9, 1966.

TUCKERMAN, JOSEPH (1778–1840). Clergyman. Born in **Boston** on January 18, 1778, Tuckerman graduated from **Harvard** College (1798) and was a **Congregational** minister in Chelsea (1801–26). Moving to the **Unitarian** church (1825), he became a pioneer charity worker as the American Unitarian Association minister-at-large to the poor of Boston

(1826–36). He founded the Boston Society for the Prevention of Pauperism (1833) and the Boston Farm School on Thompson Island (1835) for delinquent boys. Tuckerman died in Cuba on April 20, 1840, honored as the father of American social work.

TUDOR, FREDERIC (1783–1864). Businessman. Born in **Boston** on September 4, 1783, Tudor was the first to ship blocks of ice packed in sawdust in Massachusetts ships. He sold ice to southern and West Indies ports (1805) and later to Cuba (1816) and India (1833). The lucrative New England ice trade to Latin America and the Far East (1805–60) made Tudor the Ice King. His supply of ice changed eating habits and introduced butter, cheese, milk, meat, and fruit to tropical consumers. Ice from the Kennebec River in Maine was sold in New York and Philadelphia (1861), and 5,000 New Englanders harvested ice from ponds and lakes (1880). Tudor, who built the first **railroad** in Boston (1830), died in Boston on February 6, 1864. His elegantly landscaped estate became the Nahant Country Club.

TUNXIS. An **Algonquin** people living on the Farmington River in central Connecticut when Governor **John Haynes** purchased land from the *sachem* Sequassen (1640). Relations with the colonists were usually harmonious, but the declining Tunxis joined the Oneida people in New York (1774). The last Tunxis people in Farmington died in 1830.

20TH MAINE INFANTRY REGIMENT. The most famous of the 31 infantry regiments from Maine. Mustered into service at **Portland** (1862–65), the 20th Maine is best known for repulsing Confederate attacks at the Battle of Gettysburg (1863). Four men, including Colonel **Joshua L. Chamberlain**, received the Medal of Honor. The regiment lost 293 of its 1,425 men in the **Civil War**, and from 73,000 Mainers who served in the Union Army and Union Navy there were 18,000 casualties.

20TH MASSACHUSETTS INFANTRY REGIMENT. Known as the **Harvard Regiment** because so many of its officers were Harvard graduates, including **Oliver Wendell Holmes, Jr.**, and Paul Revere, Jr. This unit fought many major **Civil War** battles (1861–65), suffering the highest number of casualties among New England regiments and ranked fifth in casualties among 2,000 Union Army regiments. It was dubbed the "Copperhead Regiment" because of the anti-abolitionist views of many officers in contrast to two of its companies of abolitionist German **immigrants**.

TYLER, ROYALL (1757–1826). Writer and lawyer. Born in **Boston** on July 18, 1757, Tyler graduated from Harvard College (1776). He was an officer in the **American Revolution** and in **Shays's Rebellion** (1787). Tyler practiced law in Maine and Massachusetts (1780–91) before settling in Vermont, where he was chief justice of the state supreme court (1807–13) and a professor of law at the University of Vermont (1811–14). Tyler is best known as the first American playwright, writing *The Contrast* (1787) and a novel, *The Algerine Captive* (1797), and Federalist satires in prose and verse. Tyler died in Brattleboro on August 26, 1826.

– U –

UNCLE SAM. The character symbolizing the United States of America, based on Samuel Wilson. Born in Arlington, Massachusetts, on September 13, 1766, Wilson (1766–1854) served in the **American Revolution** and sold salted meat in Troy, New York, to the U.S. Army. During the War of 1812 Wilson stamped U.S. on the barrels, and soldiers claimed the initials stood for "Uncle Sam" Wilson. In time Uncle Sam personified the federal government and cartoons depicted him as a lanky **Yankee** wearing a tall hat and star-spangled suit with a long white beard (1832). Congress later adopted Uncle Sam, derived from **Brother Jonathan**, as the national symbol (1961).

UNDERGROUND RAILROAD. A secret network of escape routes and safe houses for runaway slaves fleeing from slave states to New England and Canada (1800–63). The National Park Service identified more than 60 sites in New England operated by **abolitionist** "conductors" as Underground Railroad "stations" in Connecticut (13), Maine (7), Massachusetts (21), New Hampshire (7), Rhode Island (6), and Vermont (9). In the **Shadrach Case** (1851), an escaped slave was freed from the **Boston** courthouse by an abolitionist mob and sent to Montreal on the Underground Railroad. Many New England **Quakers** were active in this movement, like the farm of Rowland Thomas in Ferrisburg, Vermont. The **Touro Synagogue** in **Newport**, Rhode Island, also concealed **African Americans** escaping slave catchers. *See also* SLAVERY; TORREY, CHARLES TURNER.

UNION CLUB. A private club for gentlemen established (1863) on the site of **Boston**'s first house of correction at 7 Park Street. **Edward Everett**,

Charles Eliot Norton, **John Murray Forbes**, **Oliver Wendell Holmes**, and other patriotic **Boston Brahmins** founded the Union Club when their fellow members of the Somerset Club expressed **Cotton Whig** or pro-Confederate sentiments. The building, designed by **Charles Bulfinch** (1801), was the former home of **Abbott Lawrence** overlooking **Boston Common**. Some of the members also formed the New England Loyal Publication Society to write and distribute propaganda supporting the **Civil War**.

UNITARIANS. A religious sect in **Boston** (1825) under the leadership of the popular **Congregational** minister **William Ellery Channing** and **Transcendentalists** such as **Ralph Waldo Emerson** and **Theodore Parker**. This influential movement developed when liberal Congregationalists in New England questioned the Calvinist doctrines of predestination, original sin, the Trinity, and the infallibility of the Bible. The Unitarians preach no doctrine or dogma and welcome all to a universal brotherhood of God and human beings. They merged with the **Universalist** church to form the Unitarian Universalist Association in Boston in 1961.

UNITED FRUIT COMPANY. Established (1899) in **Boston** by a **Cape Cod** sea captain, Lorenzo Dow Baker (1840–1908), with Andrew Preston, Minor Keith, and Thomas Jefferson Coolidge, Jr. The company imported fruit from Jamaica and Central America to New England. When Baker introduced bananas (1870), the exotic fruit soon became a popular and profitable luxury dessert throughout the country. The influential company directors made Latin America an important issue in national politics. James Drummond Dole (1877–1958), who was born in Boston and studied agriculture at **Harvard University**, founded the pineapple industry in Hawaii in 1901.

UNIVERSALISM. A liberal New England sect founded at **John Murray**'s church in Gloucester, Massachusetts (1779). **Hosea Ballou** was its most influential leader. The Universalists, who played a role in the **Second Great Awakening**, merged later with the **Unitarians** to form the Unitarian Universalist Association (1961) in **Boston**.

UPDIKE, JOHN (1932–). Writer. Born in Shillington, Pennsylvania, on March 18, 1932, Updike graduated from **Harvard University** (1954).

He contributed poetry, essays, stories, and criticism to the *New Yorker* and won the Pulitzer Prize for two novels, *Rabbit Is Rich* (1981) and *Rabbit at Rest* (1990). After Updike moved to Ipswich, Massachusetts (1960), most of his later fiction is set in New England, including *Couples* (1968) and *The Witches of Eastwick* (1984). His subject is often middle-class New Englanders facing the issues of religion and responsibility.

URSULINE CONVENT. A Catholic boarding school for elite girls in Charlestown (now Somerville), Massachusetts, conducted by the Ursuline Sisters (1826–34). An anti-Catholic mob, incited by the incendiary sermons of **Lyman Beecher** and unrestrained by officials, police, or firemen, burned the convent to the ground on August 11, 1834. Unfounded rumors claimed that one of the sisters was kept in the convent against her will. The sisters and 50 students escaped, but this incident and the virulent **anti-Catholicism** that it represented led to the acquittal of 12 rioters on arson and burglary charges. Many **Boston Brahmins** were sympathetic, but the state legislature refused to indemnify the Ursuline Sisters or the Catholic diocese for their losses. *See also* ANTI-CATHOLICISM.

– V –

VALLEE, RUDY (1901–1986). Singer and actor. Born on July 28, 1901, at Island Pond, Vermont, in a **French-Canadian** family, Hubert Prior Vallee attended the University of Maine (1921–22) and graduated from Yale University (1927). He became a popular singer in nightclubs and an actor on Broadway, in movies, and on television. Vallee was best known for arranging and singing the University of Maine's *Stein Song* (1930). Rudy Vallee died in Hollywood on July 3, 1986.

VANE, SIR HENRY (1613–1662). Governor of Massachusetts. Born in England, Vane became a **Puritan** and emigrated to **Boston** (1635). Elected governor of the Massachusetts colony (1636), his support of **Anne Hutchinson** led to friction with **John Winthrop**. Vane founded **Harvard** College (1636) and authorized the **Pequot War** (1637). Returning to London (1637), he was treasurer of the Royal Navy (1639) and a moderate in the English Civil War. Vane was executed for treason in 1662.

VAUDEVILLE. The name for American musical theater coined by **B. F. Keith** in **Boston** (1885). Unlike burlesque, Keith offered the respectable public a more refined but popular form of entertainment that cynical performers dubbed the "Sunday School" show. The Keith-Albee theaters censored all acts to avoid the **banned in Boston** label, creating popular variety shows for the American family. Vaudeville was the most popular entertainment in the nation until 1930.

VAULT, THE. The name for a private group of **Boston** business leaders who met in the Boston Safe Deposit and Trust Company vault room (1959–97) to advise city and state leaders. As the Republican Party and the **Boston Brahmins** lost power in Boston and retreated from the city to the suburbs, **Ralph Lowell** and Mayor John Collins created this influential group, the Coordinating Committee or the Vault, to shape the urban renewal and economic redevelopment of Boston. This commitment to the New England tradition of civic leadership declined when many corporations relocated their headquarters outside the region.

VARNUM, JOSEPH BRADLEY (1750–1821). Speaker of the House. Born in Dracut, Massachusetts, on January 29, 1750, Varnum served as a **militia** general in the **American Revolution**, as an Anti-Federalist legislator (1781–95, 1817–21), and as a judge. Elected to the House of Representatives as a Jeffersonian Democrat (1795–1811), he was the Speaker of the House (1805–07, 1809–11) and served in the Senate (1811–17). Varnum was an early critic of the slave trade and supported the unpopular Embargo of 1807 and War of 1812. He again served in the state senate (1817–21) and founded the Massachusetts Peace Society (1819) before he died on September 21, 1821, on the Dracut farm where he was born.

VERMONT HISTORICAL SOCIETY. Founded in **Montpelier** in 1838 as a private not-for-profit, membership-supported organization to preserve and interpret the history of the state. It operates a research library and museum and offers educational and publishing programs on the prehistory and history of the **Green Mountain State**.

VERRAZANO, GIOVANNI DA (1485–1528). Explorer. Born near Florence, Italy, Verrazano explored the North American coast for France on the *Dauphine*, visiting the Hudson River, **Block Island,** and Maine (1524). He claimed this land for Francis I while seeking a western sea route to Asia. Verrazano was killed by **Native Americans** on a second voyage to Brazil. **Italian Americans** placed a statue in his honor on the Hudson River (1910), and a bridge in New York harbor (1964) was named for Verrazano.

VIKINGS. Established Vinland as a colony in Newfoundland (A.D. 1000). Led by Leif Eriksson (970–1020), the Norsemen or Vikings may have sailed from Vinland to New England, perhaps landing in Maine or Massachusetts. Eben Norton Horsford wrote *Discovery of the Ancient City of Norumbega* (1889), claiming Vikings landed on the Charles River in Cambridge, Watertown, and **Waltham**. He built a stone tower in Newton on the site of their settlement, Norumbega, although geologists, archaeologists, and historians found no evidence of Viking explorers. Similar claims were made for a stonewall in **Provincetown**, the rocky coast of Hyannisport, **Dighton Rock** in southeastern Massachusetts, a stone tower in **Newport**, Rhode Island, and sites in Maine. Still there was no proof, but Horsford donated a statue of *Leif Eriksson* by Anne Whitney on Commonwealth Avenue in **Boston** (1887), arousing public interest in these unverified claims for pre-Columbian Viking exploration of New England. **Longfellow**'s poem *The Skeleton in Armor* (1841) celebrates the Norse stone tower in Newport and inspired a **Newport mansion** called Vinland (1883). But a silver coin discovered in Blue Hill, Maine (1957), identified as a Viking penny from A.D. 1065–80 and the oldest European artifact in North America, is the only firm evidence that Vikings may have explored New England.

VOLPE, JOHN A. (1908–1994). Governor of Massachusetts. Born in **Boston** on December 8, 1908, John Anthony Volpe graduated from Wentworth Institute of Technology (1930) and was a building contractor in Massachusetts (1933–69) and federal highway administrator (1956–57). Elected Republican governor (1961–63, 1965–69), Volpe served as secretary of transportation (1969–73) and ambassador to Italy (1973–76). He died in Boston on November 11, 1994.

– W –

WADSWORTH ATHENEUM. America's oldest public **art** museum, founded by Daniel Wadsworth (1771–1848) in **Hartford**, Connecticut (1842). The collections include more than 45,000 works of art including

Egyptian, Greek, Roman, Renaissance, and baroque paintings, European decorative arts, 17th- and 18th-century American furniture and art, French and American impressionist paintings, as well as **African-American** and 19th-century American Hudson River School landscapes and contemporary art. The **Wallace Nutting** collection of **Pilgrim** century furniture and decorative art is especially comprehensive. **John Trumbull**'s portrait of Daniel Wadsworth and his father Jeremiah (1784) hangs in the Atheneum. The original building, designed in the Gothic Revival style by **Ithiel Town**, opened in 1842.

WAITE, MORRISON R. (1816–1888). Chief Justice of the U.S. Supreme Court. Born in Lyme, Connecticut, on November 29, 1816, Waite graduated from Yale College (1837) and practiced law in Ohio (1839–50). He served as a Republican in the state legislature and was a successful railroad and corporate attorney in Toledo (1850–71). President Ulysses S. Grant appointed him U.S. counsel in the *Alabama* claims arbitration in Geneva (1871–73) and as chief justice (1874–88). His decisions struck down the Civil Rights Acts of 1875 and gave states authority over public accommodations for **African Americans** (1883) and the regulation of business corporations that were legal persons. Waite died in Washington, D.C., on March 23, 1888.

WALDEN POND. Located in Concord, Massachusetts, 18 miles northwest of **Boston**. Formed as a kettle hole by the melting Wisconsin glacier 12,000 years ago, the 61-acre pond is the centerpiece of a state park (since 1922) and most famous as the site where **Henry David Thoreau** lived and wrote *Walden* in 1845–47.

WALKER, DAVID (1785–1830). Abolitionist. Born in Wilmington, North Carolina, on September 28, 1785, Walker was the son of a slave father and a free mother. He grew up free and was well educated when he opened a mariner's clothing store (1827) in **Boston**. He distributed his antislavery tract, *Appeal to the Colored Citizens of the World* (1829), among the many **African-American** seamen in New England ports. Despite warnings that his life was in danger, Walker continued his antislavery campaign until he died in Boston on June 28, 1830. His militant opposition to **slavery** was rejected by most Americans, but his *Appeal* was widely reprinted. His son, Edwin Garrison Walker, was elected to the Massachusetts legislature (1866), the first African-American legislator in the nation.

WALKER, FRANCIS A. (1840–1897). Educator. Born in **Boston** on July 2, 1840, Francis Amasa Walker graduated from Amherst College (1860) and was a general in the **Civil War** (1861–65). He was an editorial writer for the *Springfield Republican* (1868–69), director of the U.S. Census (1870), and U.S. Commissioner of Indian Affairs (1871–73). While a professor of economics at Yale University (1873–81), he directed the highly regarded census of 1880. As president of the Massachusetts Institute of Technology (MIT) in 1881–97, Walker increased the number of students and facilities. He was president of the American Statistical Association (1883–97), and a founder of the **Immigration Restriction League**. Walker died in Boston on January 5, 1897.

WALKER, QUOCK. Abolitionist. Born a slave in **Worcester**, Massachusetts, in 1754, Walker sued for his freedom under the new Massachusetts state constitution (1780). **William Cushing**, chief justice of the state supreme judicial court, ruled in *Commonwealth v. Jennison* (1783) that Walker was free because the constitution implicitly abolished slavery. Despite long-established custom and the 1641 slave law, slavery was not legal and contrary to natural rights. Although **African-American** men voted in **Boston** elections (1800), a state law prohibited interracial marriage (1786) and another law (1788) forbade any African Americans who were not legal residents from tarrying longer than two months in the state. Quock Walker won his freedom, but segregation and racial prejudice continued in New England long after this court decision. *See also* ABOLITIONISM.

WALSH, DAVID I. (1872–1947). Senator from Massachusetts. Born in Leominster, Massachusetts, on November 11, 1872, David Ignatius Walsh graduated from Holy Cross College (1893) and Boston University Law School (1897). While practicing law in Fitchburg, he was elected as a Democrat to the state legislature (1900–01). Walsh was lieutenant governor (1913–14) and the first Catholic Democrat elected governor (1914–16) and became the first **Irish** Catholic senator from Massachusetts (1919–25, 1926–47). Walsh supported woman's suffrage and Irish independence and opposed American aid to Great Britain in World War

II (1939–41). He died in **Boston** on June 11, 1947, and is honored by a statue by Joseph A. Coletti (1954) on the Charles River **Esplanade**.

WALTHAM. Part of Watertown, Massachusetts, in 1634 and founded in 1738 and incorporated as a city in 1884. The Charles River provided waterpower for the cotton factory **Francis Cabot Lowell** built in 1813 and for the Waltham Watch Company in 1854–1957. Known as the **Watch City**, Waltham is home to Bentley College (1917) and Brandeis University (1948), with a population of 58,000 in 2000.

WALTHAM SYSTEM. The factory management method **Francis Cabot Lowell** devised for his first cotton **textile** factory in **Waltham**, Massachusetts (1814–17). Sometimes referred to as the American or Lowell System, it used unskilled men, women, and children, but most often young rural girls, to mass produce machine-made cloth. The paternalistic owners housed the **mill girls** in supervised boardinghouses until 1845.

WAMPANOAG. The **Algonquian**-speaking **Native American** people living in southeastern Massachusetts and Rhode Island. The name means "Eastern People," and they numbered 100,000 people in 67 villages in 1600. Contact with European **fishing** boats introduced devastating epidemics (1616–18). The *sachem* **Massasoit** made peace with the **Pilgrims** (1621), but the **Puritans** found only 1,000 people in 1630 and fewer than 400 Wampanoags survived in 1675. Their cultural contributions to the European settlers include beans, **corn**, maize, wild rice, squash, pumpkins, artichokes, groundnuts, gourds, **maple syrup**, shellfish, **tobacco**, moccasins, snowshoes, toboggans, and turkey. Massasoit's son, **Metacom** (or Philip), organized a confederacy to drive out the English, but **King Philip's War** (1675–76) almost exterminated the Wampanoag. About 5,000 modern members of the tribe live in seven groups on **Cape Cod** and have revived their language, Wopanaak (1999). They are only one of two tribes in Massachusetts recognized by the federal government today.

WAMPUM. An **Algonquin** word for small white or dark purple/black beads fashioned by **Native Americans** from clam, quahog, or periwinkle shells collected on the southern New England coast. By 2500 B.C. the **Narragansett**, **Niantic**, and **Quinnipiac** tribes ground and polished these shells into small cylindrical tubes and wore them on strings, belts, capes, necklaces, and other items. They were traded to other tribes as far west as the Dakotas and used as gifts or tribute payments. **Henry Hudson** obtained wampum from Indians (1609), and **Pilgrims** at **Plymouth** saw **Massasoit** and other **Wampanoags** wearing these "beads" in 1620. Wampum formed a basis of trade as legal tender by Massachusetts colonists with Native Americans in 1620–60, but wampum had more symbolic or spiritual value than money.

WANG, AN (1920–1990). Scientist. Born in Shanghai, Wang came to **Boston** (1945) and earned a Ph.D. in physics at **Harvard University** (1948). He worked with **Howard H. Aiken** at Harvard and founded Wang Laboratories (1951) in Boston and in **Lowell**, where he obtained 35 patents. His major contributions to **computer** technology made magnetic core memory practical. Wang introduced an electronic calculator and a desktop computer (1965), manufacturing a series of workstations for laboratories and schools. His firm employed 30,000 workers (1986), but the company declined by 1989. Dr. Wang was a prominent philanthropist in Boston when he died on March 24, 1990.

WAPPINGER. A confederacy of **Algonquian**-speaking **Native Americans** living in western Connecticut (1600) and New York. Epidemics (1633) and wars with the Dutch (1640–45) decimated the tribe, and most of the survivors (1760) merged with the **Machican** and Delaware. Many Wappinger people fought for the Americans in the Revolution, but they were forced to move from **Stockbridge** to Oneida, New York (1786), and later (1822) to Wisconsin.

WARD, ARTEMUS (1834–1867). Writer. Born in Waterford, Maine, on April 26, 1834, Charles Farrar Browne adopted this nom de plume (1858) for his humorous character. Browne was a printer in Maine and **Boston** who became a national figure when he created Artemus Ward, the manager of a sideshow who commented on public issues in newspapers, books, and lectures. His droll **Yankee** character used puns, misspellings, and a deadpan expression to satirize American foibles. Browne wrote *Artemus Ward: His Book* (1862), *Artemus Ward: His Travels* (1865), and *Artemus Ward in London* (1867). Browne died in England on March 6, 1867.

WARNER, CHARLES DUDLEY (1829–1900). Writer. Born in Plainfield, Massachusetts, on September 12, 1829, Warner graduated from Hamilton College (1851) and the University of Pennsylvania Law School (1858). He practiced law in Chicago and was editor-publisher of the *Hartford Courant*. His travel articles were published in *Harper's Magazine*, but he is most famous for collaborating with Mark Twain on *The Gilded Age* (1873), a satirical novel that gave the name to the 1865–90 era. Warner died in **Hartford**, Connecticut, on October 20, 1900.

WARNER, SETH (1743–1784). Soldier. Born in Woodbury (now Roxbury), Connecticut, on May 6, 1743, Warner was a woodsman who moved to Bennington, Vermont, with his family (1763). Embroiled in the dispute between New York and New Hampshire over Vermont land titles, he was a captain in the **Green Mountain Boys** militia organized by **Ethan Allen** (1771). He fought in the capture of Fort Ticonderoga and Fort Crown Point on Lake Champlain (1775) and was elected lieutenant colonel when Congress and the New York legislature incorporated the Green Mountain regiment into the Continental Army. Warner played a key role in the invasion of Canada (1776) and General **John Stark**'s victory in the **Battle of Bennington** (1777). General Warner retired (1781) and died in Woodbury, Vermont, on December 26, 1784. *See also* AMERICAN REVOLUTION.

WARNING OUT. An English Poor Law practice common in colonial New England in which the town constable or **tithingman** ordered non-native paupers, tramps, or vagabonds to leave the town. The **selectmen** serving as the **overseers of the poor** refused public welfare services to those not born or legally resident in that town and ordered them to return to their birthplace. This reduced the financial burden on taxpayers and maintained the closed compact Christian nature of each New England community. The nonresident poor were sometimes removed by the constable from the town and whipped if they returned or merely ordered each year to leave town. During the **American Revolution** some towns warned out **Tories**. The practice of warning out to limit town welfare services persisted until the late 20th century.

WARREN, JOHN COLLINS (1778–1856). Physician. Born in **Boston** on August 1, 1778, Warren studied surgery with his father, John Warren (1753–1815), and in Europe. He practiced in Boston (1802–56) and taught at **Harvard** Medical School (1809–47). He was a founder of the **Hasty Pudding** Club, the *New England Journal of Medicine* (1812), and **Massachusetts General Hospital** (1821), where he performed the first operation using ether as anesthesia with **William T. G. Morton** (1846). A pioneer in surgery, he wrote *Surgical Observations on Tumours* (1837) and supported physical education, **temperance**, and the Massachusetts Agricultural Society before he died in Boston on May 4, 1856.

WARREN, JOSEPH (1741–1775). Hero. Born in Roxbury, Massachusetts, on June 10, 1741, Warren graduated from **Harvard** College (1759). He practiced medicine in **Boston** (1764–75) until the **Stamp Act** made him a leader of the patriots. Warren wrote the **Suffolk Resolves** (1774) protesting the **Intolerable Acts** and dispatched **Paul Revere** and **William Dawes** on their April 18, 1775, ride. After Dr. Warren died at the **Battle of Bunker Hill** on June 17, 1775, **Paul Revere** identified his body by the silver wire he produced for Warren's dentures.

WARREN, MERCY OTIS (1728–1814). Writer. Born in Barnstable, Massachusetts, on September 25, 1728, Mercy Otis was the sister of the patriot leader **James Otis**. She wrote poetry, pamphlets, and plays satirizing the **Loyalists** and Governor **Thomas Hutchinson**. Her *History of the Rise, Progress, and Termination of the American Revolution* (1805), reflecting her Jeffersonian views, was the first history published by an American woman. She married James Warren, a **Plymouth** farmer and merchant (1754), and they hosted George Washington, Alexander Hamilton, and **John Adams** at their home. She died in Plymouth on October 19, 1814. Her portrait by **John Singleton Copley** hangs in the **Museum of Fine Arts** in **Boston**.

WASHBURN, ICHABOD (1798–1868). Businessman. Born in Kingston, Massachusetts, on August 11, 1798, Washburn apprenticed with a Leicester blacksmith (1807). He manufactured lead pipes in **Worcester** (1820), as well as wire for pianos (1850), hoop skirts (1859), barbed wire (1876), and nails (1889). Washburn invented several tools and machines for his important wire company, Washburn & Moen, before he died in Worcester, Massachusetts, on December 30, 1868.

WATCH AND WARD SOCIETY. A private antivice organization founded in **Boston** (1878) by Bishop **William Lawrence**, the Reverend **Phillips Brooks**, and the influential **prep school** headmaster **Endicott**

Peabody. Inspired by **Anthony Comstock**, the Boston industrialist Godfrey Lowell Cabot (1861–1962) directed the society, censoring theaters, magazines, and books by Walt Whitman, Theodore Dreiser, Sinclair Lewis, and Ernest Hemingway. Lowell made the phrase **banned in Boston** a national joke. H. L. Mencken was arrested for selling a copy of *American Mercury* magazine to J. Frank Chase, secretary of the society (1926). The Boston Police Commissioners, district attorneys, and courts cooperated with the Watch and Ward until 1950 with some support from Boston's conservative **Irish** Catholics. By 1960 the society expanded from the search for the morally offensive to criminology. The group reorganized as the Crime and Justice Foundation, advocating and researching law and correctional issues.

WATCH CITY. A nickname for **Waltham**, Massachusetts (1634), the home of the Waltham Watch Company (1854–1956). Aaron L. Dennison (1812–95) was the first to use mass production methods in Waltham to manufacture inexpensive but reliable pocket watches.

WATERBURY. An industrial city in western Connecticut on the Naugatuck River known as the **Brass City**. Settled in 1674, **Yankee** entrepreneurs recruited English craftsmen (1820) to produce a variety of brass materials made from an alloy of copper and zinc. Israel Coe first manufactured brassware by the battery process in 1834. **Irish** immigrants were the labor force by 1850 until other **immigrants**, women, and **African-American** workers replaced them (1870–1920). Connecticut manufacturers, like **Seth Thomas** (1785–1859), who made clocks in his Thomaston factory (1838), used Waterbury brass for machine products. The Chase Brass and Copper Company (1876–1945) was famous for **Colonial Revival** replicas of candlesnuffers, candlesticks, and housewares. Incorporated as a city in 1853, Waterbury still produces clocks, watches, instruments, tools, electronic parts, plastics, and chemicals with a population of 108,961. The Timex Watch Museum attracts many visitors to the birthplace of the popular wristwatch (1917).

WATERHOUSE, BENJAMIN (1754–1846). Physician. Born in **Newport**, Rhode Island, on March 4, 1754, Waterhouse apprenticed with a Newport doctor and studied medicine in London, Edinburgh, and Holland (1775–82). He was a professor at **Harvard** Medical School (1783–1812) and medical superintendent of New England military bases (1812–20). He is best remembered for introducing medical smallpox inoculation (1799), winning public support by testing it on his own family. Waterhouse died in Cambridge on October 2, 1846. *See also* BOYLSTON, ZABDIEL.

WATSON, THOMAS A. (1854–1934). Inventor. Born in **Salem**, Massachusetts, on January 18, 1854, Watson was a bookkeeper, carpenter, and machinist. Hired as an assistant by **Alexander Graham Bell** (1874), he is best known as the co-inventor of the telephone in **Boston** (1876). Watson obtained a patent for the first telephone ringer (1878) but sought new challenges. After studying geology at MIT, he prospected for gold in Alaska, founded the largest **shipyard** in America at Fall River, Massachusetts (1890), and became a Shakespearean actor (1910). Watson died in Florida on December 13, 1934.

WAYLAND, FRANCIS (1796–1865). Educator. Born in New York City on March 11, 1796, Wayland graduated from Union College (1813). He studied at Andover Theological Seminary and was pastor of the First Baptist Church in **Boston** (1821–26). As president of Brown University (1826–55), he introduced economics, ethics, and philosophy to the reformed curriculum based on his own published works. He opposed the **Dorr Rebellion** (1842) and promoted public libraries, prison reform, and moderate **abolitionism**. Wayland died in **Providence**, Rhode Island, on September 30, 1865.

WAYMOUTH, GEORGE (ca. 1570–1607). Explorer. Captain Waymouth investigated the New England coast in 1602 and met **Native Americans** in Maine sailing a Basque boat and wearing European clothing. On his second voyage for **Sir Ferdinando Gorges** in the *Archangel* (1605), he kidnapped five **Abenaki** men in Maine and brought them to England. They learned English and provided valuable information for **Plymouth Company** colonization. One of the captives was **Squanto**, who later assisted the **Pilgrims** (1621–22). **Gorges** and Sir **John Popham** sent the Native Americans back to New England, and Squanto traveled with **John Smith** (1614). Waymouth's report on the **codfish** and whales he found at **Cape Cod** encouraged the **Popham colony** (1614), and persuaded **Henry Hudson** to explore Hudson Bay (1610). Waymouth disappeared from records in 1607.

WAYSIDE, THE. Nathaniel Hawthorne's home in Concord, Massachusetts (1852–64). It had been the home (1845–48) of the **Transcendentalist**

philosopher **Bronson Alcott**, who called it "Hillside." His daughter, **Louisa May Alcott**, used it as the setting for *Little Women* (1868). Now part of the Minute Man National Historical Park, the house was preserved by children's writer **Margaret Sidney**, author of *The Five Little Peppers*. The Wayside is the only national historic landmark that was home to three literary families.

WAYSIDE INN. Built in Sudbury, Massachusetts (1686), by Samuel Howe on the **Boston Post Road**, the main highway from **Boston** to New York City. **Henry Wadsworth Longfellow** immortalized the nation's oldest operating **tavern** in *Tales of the Wayside Inn* (1863), and the innkeeper is the narrator in Longfellow's poem, *The Midnight Ride of Paul Revere* (1860). Restored by Henry Ford (1922–46), the inn's famous guests included George Washington and the Marquis de Lafayette, as well as countless **tourists** seeking authentic **Yankee** cuisine.

WEARE, MESHECH (1713–1786). Governor of New Hampshire. Born in Hampton Falls, New Hampshire, on June 16, 1713, Weare graduated from **Harvard** College (1735). He served in the colonial legislature, was a delegate to the Albany Congress (1754), and played a key role in framing the state constitution (1776). As chairman of the **Committee of Safety**, he replaced the governor as the New Hampshire chief executive. Weare was chief justice of the Superior Court (1776–82) and presided over the legislature's upper house, the Council. On adoption of the state's second constitution (1784), he was elected governor (or president) for the first one-year term. Weare died in Hampton Falls on January 14, 1786.

WEBSTER, DANIEL (1782–1852). Senator from Massachusetts. Born in Salisbury, New Hampshire, on January 18, 1782, Webster graduated from Dartmouth College (1801). He practiced law in **Portsmouth**, New Hampshire, and was elected to the House of Representatives as a **Federalist** (1813–17). While practicing law in **Boston**, he achieved fame defending his alma mater in the ***Dartmouth College v. Woodward* case** (1819) before the U.S. Supreme Court. As a Massachusetts congressman (1823–27), senator (1827–33), and then as a Whig senator (1833–41), his speeches highlighted the golden age of American oratory. Webster was secretary of state (1841–43, 1850–52) and a Whig candidate for president (1836, 1852) and served in the Senate (1845–50). He championed the interests of New England and nationalism but was a conservative, widely criticized by New England **abolitionists** for supporting the Compromise of 1850. Webster died at his Marshfield, Massachusetts, home on October 24, 1852. **Hiram Powers**'s statue (1859) of Webster sits on the Massachusetts State House lawn. *See also* STORY, JOSEPH.

WEBSTER, JOHN WHITE (1792–1850). Criminal. Webster, a professor of chemistry at **Harvard** Medical School, was hanged for the murder of George Parkman, a physician who loaned him $400. Both men were members of **Boston Brahmin** families, and the sensational crime earned national publicity, attracting 60,000 onlookers to the 12-day trial. Dr. Parkman was killed during an argument about the debt in Professor Webster's office on November 23, 1849. Because his body was dismembered and burned, this was the first trial in New England to use dental evidence by **William T. G. Morton**. Webster confessed shortly before his execution on August 30, 1850, in **Boston**.

WEBSTER, NOAH (1758–1843). Editor and lexicographer. Born in West Hartford, Connecticut, on October 16, 1758, Webster graduated from Yale College (1778). He was a schoolteacher and practiced law (1781–1810), until he published his best-selling speller (1783), grammar (1784), and reader (1785) that made the national language independent of its English heritage. Webster edited **Federalist** newspapers and lobbied for a copyright law. His *Compendious Dictionary of the English Language* (1806) and his *American Dictionary of the English Language* (1828) were not scholarly but defined vernacular as well as literary words. He helped found Amherst College (1821) and died in **New Haven**, Connecticut, on May 28, 1843. Chauncey Allen Goodrich (1790–1860), Webster's son-in-law and a Yale professor, edited an enlarged edition of Webster's dictionary (1847), the first in a continuing series by G. & C. Merriam.

WEBSTER-ASHBURTON TREATY (1842). Established the northeastern Maine-Canada boundary and settled disputes between Great Britain and the United States that led to the bloodless **Aroostook War** (1839). Secretary of State **Daniel Webster** and Great Britain's Alexander Baring, Lord Ashburton, replaced provisions of the Treaty of 1783 by new terms concerning 12,000 square miles of territory. The United States received 7,000 square miles of the disputed land. Maine and Massachusetts each received $150,000 from Great Britain and reimbursement from the United States. The treaty also adjusted the Vermont and New York borders and gave the United States navigation rights on the St. John, St. Lawrence, St. Clair and Detroit rivers and gave the United States the Mesabi iron deposits in Michigan.

WEEKS, JOHN WINGATE (1860–1926). Senator from Massachusetts. Born in Lancaster, New Hampshire, on April 11, 1860, Weeks graduated from the U.S. Naval Academy (1881), served in the U.S. Navy (1881–83), and was a banker in **Boston** (1888–1914). He returned to the navy in the Spanish-American War (1898–99), was mayor of Newton (1902–03), and a Republican in the House of Representatives (1905–13) and the Senate (1913–19). Weeks, who opposed prohibition and women's suffrage, was the secretary of war (1921–25) and died in Lancaster on July 12, 1926.

WEEKS, SINCLAIR (1893–1972). Senator from Massachusetts. Born in West Newton, Massachusetts, on June 15, 1893, Weeks, the son of **John Wingate Weeks**, graduated from **Harvard University** (1914). He was a banker in **Boston** (1914–23) and served in the U.S. Army (1916–19) and as mayor of Newton (1930–35). Weeks was a Republican senator (1944) and secretary of commerce (1953–58) and died in **Concord**, Massachusetts, on February 7, 1972.

WEICKER, LOWELL P. (1931–). Senator from Connecticut. Born in Paris on May 16, 1931, Lowell Palmer Weicker, Jr., graduated from Yale University (1953) and the University of Virginia Law School (1958). He served in the U.S. Army (1953–55), the state legislature (1962–68), and as a Republican in the House of Representatives (1969–71) and the Senate (1971–89). Weicker taught at George Washington University Law School (1988–90) and was elected governor as an independent (1990–95). He was a candidate for the Republican nomination for president (1980) and an independent candidate in 1996.

WELD, THEODORE DWIGHT (1803–1895). Reformer. Born in Hampton, Connecticut, on November 23, 1803, Weld attended Andover Seminary and became an evangelical Presbyterian minister (1826) devoted to **temperance** and **abolitionism** (1830). He studied at Lane Theological Seminary (1832–34) in Cincinnati under **Lyman Beecher** but was dismissed for his extreme antislavery efforts. Weld founded schools in New Jersey and Massachusetts, assisted **John Quincy Adams** in opposing the gag rule (1844) in Congress, and recruited many leading abolitionists. He avoided public notice, but his book *American Slavery as It Is* (1839) inspired **Harriet Beecher Stowe** to write *Uncle Tom's Cabin*. Weld, who married the abolitionist and feminist Angelina Grimke (1838), continued as a reform leader until he died in **Boston** on February 3, 1895.

WELD, WILLIAM F. (1945–). Governor of Massachusetts. Born in Smithfield, New York, on July 31, 1945, in a **Boston Brahmin** family, Weld graduated from **Harvard University** (1966), Oxford University (1967), and Harvard Law School (1970). He practiced law in **Boston** and served as associate minority counsel to the U.S. House Judiciary Committee during the Watergate hearings. Weld also served as U.S. attorney for Massachusetts (1981–86) and as assistant attorney general (1986–88). He joined a **Boston** law firm until elected Republican governor (1991–97). Weld was reelected (1994) but resigned when President **George H. W. Bush** nominated him as ambassador to Mexico (1997). He withdrew his name when Senate confirmation was delayed. Weld then worked as an investment banker in New York City and as a novelist.

WELLES, GIDEON (1802–1878). Public official. Born in Glastonbury, Connecticut, on July 1, 1802, Welles studied at the American Academy (now Norwich University) in Vermont, and practiced law in **Hartford** (1826–35). He was an owner and editor of the *Hartford Times* (1826–36) and a Democratic state legislator (1826–35), served as state comptroller (1835–44), and was postmaster of Hartford (1836–41). He organized the state Republican Party and founded the *Hartford Evening Press* (1854). As secretary of the navy (1861–69), Welles rebuilt the small and outmoded U.S. Navy and performed admirably in the **Civil War**, supporting a lenient Reconstruction policy and President Andrew Johnson. He wrote the *Diary of Gideon Welles* (1911) and died in Hartford on February 11, 1878.

WELLES, THOMAS (ca. 1590–1660). Governor of Connecticut. Born in Warwickshire, England, about 1590, Welles came to **Boston** (1635) and moved to **Hartford** with **Thomas Hooker** (1636). He is the only man in Connecticut history to serve in all of the highest offices, as a member of the first Court of Magistrates (1637–54), as the colony's first treasurer (1639), as the secretary of the colony (1640–49), as deputy governor (1654, 1656–57, 1659), and as governor (1655, 1658). Welles was a commissioner to the **New England Confederation** (1649, 1654) and died in Wethersfield on January 14, 1660.

WELLS, HENRY (1805–1878). Businessman. Born in Thetford, Vermont, on December 12, 1805, Wells worked for a shipping firm on the Erie Canal (1835–41) and for an Albany-to-Buffalo express service. He and William G. Fargo founded Wells, Fargo & Company (1844) as a freight service to Chicago and St. Louis, which became the American Express Company (1850). The California gold rush created high demand for the firm, reorganized (1852) in New York City to carry mail, passengers, parcels, and gold on the famous **Concord Stage Coach** and by Pony Express. Wells built the first commercial telegraph lines and retired (1872) to travel and engage in philanthropies. He founded Wells College (1868) in New York and died in Scotland on December 10, 1878.

WELLS, WILLIAM (1837–1892). Soldier. Born in Waterbury, Vermont, on December 14, 1837, Wells was a surveyor and merchant in Waterbury. In the **Civil War** he served (1861–66) in the **1st Vermont Cavalry Regiment**, mounting his troopers on **Morgan horses**. He was promoted to brevet major general and received the Congressional Medal of Honor for his role in the Battle of Gettysburg. After the war, Wells was a state legislator, collector of customs for Vermont, and a leading businessman in Burlington until he died in New York City on April 29, 1892. Remembered by General Philip Sheridan as the ideal of a cavalry officer, a statue of Wells was erected at Gettysburg (1913).

WELSH. Immigrants who arrived in Massachusetts by 1667 and founded Swansea. Many other early settlers from Wales migrated to the **Appalachian Mountains** in New York, Maine, and Vermont (1790–1820). The Vermont **slate** and **quarry** industries attracted skilled workers from Wales in the 1850s to settle in Guilford, Poultney, Fair Haven, Northfield, and Thetford.

WENTWORTH, BENNING (1696–1770). Governor of New Hampshire. Born in **Portsmouth**, Wentworth graduated from **Harvard** (1715) and was a leading Portsmouth merchant who served in the colonial legislature. As the first royal governor (1741–67), he made 135 land grants in Vermont by 1749 (called the **New Hampshire Grants**), although New York also claimed that area. When settlers in Vermont violently resisted New York officers at Windsor (1770), Bennington (1771), and Westminster (1775), Governor Wentworth supported them. The British revoked the land grants for Vermont towns in 1764 but had not settled the boundary dispute over Vermont when the **American Revolution** began. Bennington, Vermont (1747), was named in his honor. He resigned (1767) and was succeeded by his nephew, **John Wentworth**, and died in England on October 14, 1770.

WENTWORTH, SIR JOHN (1737–1820). Governor of New Hampshire. Born in **Portsmouth** on August 14, 1737, John Wentworth graduated from **Harvard** College (1755). He joined his father as a leading member of the Portsmouth mercantile aristocracy; and after visiting London, he succeeded his uncle, **Benning Wentworth**, as the last royal governor of New Hampshire (1767–75). Although he opposed the **Stamp Act**, Wentworth supported parliamentary control of the colony. He granted a charter to Dartmouth College (1769) and remained popular until his strict administration of the Crown's policy of reserving white **pine trees** for the Royal Navy and blocking the nonimportation agreements aroused the patriots. His support for the **Coercive Acts** (1774), and General **Thomas Gage** in **Boston**, led the legislature to meet without his consent in Exeter. When the patriots raided Fort William and Mary in Portsmouth (June 1775), Wentworth fled New Hampshire forever on a British warship (August 1775). He was knighted, and Sir John Wentworth served as governor of Nova Scotia (1792–1808), where he died on April 8, 1820.

WENTWORTH, JOHN (1745–1787). Congressman from New Hampshire. Born in Salmon Falls, New Hampshire, on July 17, 1745, Wentworth graduated from **Harvard** College (1768). He practiced law in Dover and served on the **Committee of Correspondence** and in the state legislature (1776–80). Elected to Congress (1778), he signed the Articles of Confederation and served as a state senator (1784–86). Wentworth died in Dover on January 10, 1787.

WESSON, DANIEL BAIRD (1825–1906). Inventor. Born in **Worcester**, Massachusetts, on May 18, 1825, Wesson was a gunsmith in Norwich, Connecticut, in partnership with Horace Smith (1852). He invented a repeating pistol (1854) and sold his patents to **Oliver Winchester** for use in the repeating rifle. Smith and Wesson manufactured a series of popular revolvers in Springfield, Massachusetts (1856). When Wesson died in Springfield on August 4, 1906, the Smith & Wesson Company was one of several leading New England arms manufacturers.

WEST, DOROTHY (1907-1998). Writer. Born in **Boston** on June 2, 1907, Dorothy West was the daughter of an emancipated slave. After studying at Boston University, she became a writer in the Harlem Renaissance. She published *The Living Is Easy* (1948) and wrote for the *Vineyard Gazette* on **Martha's Vineyard** (1945–98). Her last book, *The Wedding* (1995), edited by **Jacqueline Onassis Kennedy**, was the basis for a film by the same title. Miss West died on August 16, 1998, in the Oak Bluff, Massachusetts, **African-American** summer community over which she had long presided.

WEST END. Marshy, low-lying western corner of the **Shawmut** peninsula. It was avoided by the **Puritans** until **Boston** became crowded. The New Fields, used only for pastures and **blueberries**, attracted ropewalks, distilleries, and mills (1720), and house lots and streets appeared once a new bridge (1793) crossed the Charles River to Cambridge. **Charles Bulfinch** built his own house there and a mansion for the wealthy gentleman **Harrison Gray Otis** (1796). Industry attracted rural migrants and **immigrants** by the 1840s, changing the district to a working-class neighborhood, first for the **Irish** then **Italian**, **Polish**, Ukrainian, **Albanian**, Lithuanian, and Russian **Jewish** immigrants. **Martin Lomasney** was the Democratic ward boss for West Enders until 1933. Herbert J. Gans arrived in 1957 to write his classic study *The Urban Villagers* (1962) before a controversial urban renewal plan eliminated the multiethnic, polyglot community of 12,000 Bostonians in 1959. The **Massachusetts General Hospital** (1821) is the major feature of Boston's West End today.

WEST INDIES TRADE. An important part of New England's maritime **economy** because mercantile laws permitted British colonies to trade freely with other British ports. The **triangular trade** saw New England ships bringing slaves from West Africa to the West Indies, exchanging slaves for **molasses** and bringing the molasses home, and taking **rum** back to Africa for more slaves. After the **American Revolution**, New England merchants were denied access to the British West Indies but found new ports in the Caribbean, Latin America, and Asia. When the slave trade ended (1808), New England ships diverted from Africa to Caribbean ports. The monoculture of sugar cane meant New England could provide food, **lumber**, barrel staves, onions, horses, livestock, **rum**, beer, and cider in exchange for West Indies molasses until the **Embargo Act of 1807** and the War of 1812 disrupted this commercial prosperity. *See also* CANDY; SLAVERY.

WGBH. The first educational radio station in New England (1951), founded by **Ralph Lowell**. The new FM station of the WGBH Educational Foundation first broadcast a live performance of the **Boston Symphony Orchestra**, and the WGBH public television station was added (1955) with a new studio in **Boston** (1965). WGBH became the flagship of the Public Broadcasting System (PBS), created by Congress (1967), offering innovative programs with **Julia Child**, **James Crockett**, and **Arthur Fiedler** and dramatic series from the BBC in London. *See also* BOSTON POPS.

WHALING. Began in New England more than 2,000 years ago when **Native Americans** hunted whales for food long before the Europeans arrived. **George Waymouth** (1605) recorded their techniques and use of drifting dead or beached whales. By 1540 Spanish whaling ships hunted the waters off Canada and New England, and Massachusetts and Connecticut ships hunted whales (1640) near the shore using traditional English techniques and turned to deep sea whaling by 1746. In 1774 at least 350 whaling vessels sailed from New England, and after the **American Revolution** the whaling fleet numbered 700 ships from 23 ports. **Nantucket**, Fairhaven, **Martha's Vineyard**, and **New Bedford**, Massachusetts, and New London and Mystic, Connecticut, and Bristol, Rhode Island, were major ports. The New Bedford shipwright George Claghorn (1748–1824) launched the *Rebecca* in 1785, the first American ship to round Cape Horn into the Pacific and return.

Sperm whales, exhausted by the **Yankee** fleet by 1800, provided leather, glue, lamp oil, soap, paint, lubricants, **scrimshaw**, candles, and perfume. Right whales were hunted almost to extinction by 1840. William A. Martin, an **African American** born in Edgartown in 1830, was captain of a whaling ship from **Martha's Vineyard** with a multiracial crew; by 1840 about one-sixth of the whalers were black men and many were hired in the Azores or **Cape Verde**. New Bedford continued long after other ports left the whaling industry, reaching a peak in 1845, with 329 ships employing 10,000 men.

Voyages lasted as long as four years, ranging across the Atlantic and Pacific to the Arctic. Two Connecticut whalers were the first explorers of Antarctica, Captain **Nathaniel Palmer** from Stonington sailed there (1820), and Captain **John Davis** of **New Haven** was the first man to land on this southernmost continent on February 7, 1821. **Herman Melville**'s masterpiece *Moby Dick* (1851) is based on a **Nantucket** ship sunk by a whale in the Pacific Ocean (1819). **Portsmouth**, New Hampshire, also operated a whaling fleet (1832–48).

The discovery of petroleum (1859), Confederate Navy raids (1861–65), the invention of electric lamps (1879), and the decreasing populations of whales ended the New England whaling industry. Photographs by Clifford Ashley (1881–1947), a Massachusetts artist, documented the work on a **New Bedford** whaler in 1904. The last whaler sailed from New Bedford in 1925, and America's last surviving wooden whaler, the *Charles W. Morgan* (1841), is preserved at **Mystic Seaport**. Since 1976 educational whale-watching tours from several New England ports to **Stellwagen Bank** off **Cape Cod** have become popular for **tourists** each summer.

WHEATLEY, PHILLIS (1753–1784). Poet. Born in Senegambia, West Africa, in 1753, Phillis Wheatley was brought to **Boston** as a slave (1761) and sold to John and Susannah Wheatley, who educated and encouraged her. Her poetry was published in England, *Poems on Various Subjects, Religious and Moral* (1773). Later she was freed and attracted much acclaim on a visit to England. She married (1778) John Peters, a free **African American**, but she worked as a Boston servant and died in poverty on December 5, 1784. Phillis Wheatley was the first important African-American poet, and a building at the University of Massachusetts in Boston was named in her honor.

WHEELOCK, ELEAZAR (1711–1779). Educator. Born in Windham, Connecticut, on April 22, 1711, Wheelock was a **Congregational** minister in Lebanon, Connecticut. He founded a school to train **Native Americans** (1754) as missionaries to New England Indians. With a charter and land grant from Governor **John Wentworth** (1769), he moved the school to Hanover, New Hampshire, and renamed it Dartmouth College (1770). The small college produced many white and Native American missionaries for the New England frontier before Wheelock died in Hanover on April 24, 1779. Dartmouth's most distinguished graduate, **Daniel Webster**, defended the college in the *Dartmouth v. Woodward* case (1819), and Dartmouth became a prestigious member of the **Ivy League** in 1956.

WHEELOCK, LUCY (1857–1946). Educator. Born in Cambridge, Vermont, on February 1, 1857, Lucy Wheelock graduated from **Elizabeth Peabody**'s Kindergarten Training School (1879). She trained teachers at Chauncy Hall School and founded her own school in **Boston** (1896). Active in the progressive **kindergarten** movement until she died in Boston on October 2, 1946, her school became Wheelock College (1939).

WHIGS. American opponents of the royal governors (1711) in contrast to the **Loyalists** or **Tories**. Whigs were called Patriots by 1775 and numbered 66 to 80 percent of the 2.5 million colonists in the **American Revolution**. Later the Whig political party, unrelated to Whigs in the **American Revolution**, was popular in antebellum New England until replaced by the Republican Party in 1854. *See also* CONSCIENCE WHIGS; COTTON WHIGS.

WHIPPLE, ABRAHAM (1733–1819). Naval commander. Born in **Providence**, Rhode Island, on September 26, 1733, Whipple captured several prizes as a privateer (1759–60) in the **French and Indian War**. He was a leader of the patriots who burned the *Gaspee* off Warwick (1772). Whipple commanded Rhode Island's small fleet and fought the Continental Navy's first sea battle of the war on the *Columbus* (1776). In Jamaica he captured 11 British ships (1779) but became a prisoner of war when Charleston fell (1780). Commander Whipple died in Ohio on May 27, 1819.

WHIPPLE, WILLIAM (1730–1785). Congressman from New Hampshire. Born on January 14, 1730 in Kittery, Maine, Whipple was a sea captain in the slave trade (1750–59) and a leading **Portsmouth**, New Hampshire merchant. He served in the **Committee of Correspondence** (1775); and as a member of the Continental Congress (1776–79) he signed the Declaration of Independence. After serving as a general in the Continental Army, Whipple was a state legislator (1780–84) and a state superior court judge (1782–85) when he died in Portsmouth on November 28, 1785.

WHISTLER, JAMES ABBOTT MCNEIL (1834–1903). Painter. Born in **Lowell**, Massachusetts, on July 11, 1834, Whistler lived in Europe as a boy, attended West Point (1851–53), then studied cartography and etching. In 1855 he left America, never to return, studied **art** in Paris, and by 1863 was prominent in London art and literary circles. His portraits emphasized aesthetic qualities by tonal effects and color harmony, especially *Thomas Carlyle* (1873), *Miss Cicely Alexander* (1873) and *Arrangement in Grey and Black No. I,* known as *Whistler's Mother* (1871). Whistler died in London on July 17, 1903, the most famous of the expatriate American artists.

WHITAKER, EDWARD WASHBURN (1841–1922). Soldier. Born in Killingly, Connecticut, on June 15, 1841, Whitaker was a captain in the

1st Connecticut Cavalry in the **Civil War** (1861–65). He earned the Congressional Medal of Honor for carrying dispatches at the Reams Station battle in Virginia (1864) and was chief of staff to General George Custer. Bearing the flag of truce to General Robert E. Lee at Appomattox, Whitaker announced the end of the war to the Union troops. He was promoted to brevet brigadier general, the youngest general in the Union Army, shortly before his discharge. Whitaker was postmaster of **Hartford**, Connecticut (1869), and a patent attorney in Washington, D.C., when he died on July 30, 1922. *See also* CIVIL WAR.

WHITE, E. B. (1899–1985). Writer. Born in Mount Vernon, New York, on July 11, 1899, Elwyn Brooks White graduated from Cornell University (1921). He established his reputation as a humorist while writing for the new magazine the *New Yorker* (1925–85) and for a monthly column in *Harper's* magazine (1940–43). Andy White is best remembered for his essays and short stories about life on a small farm in North Brooklin, Maine (1957–85). He also wrote the children's classics *Stuart Little* (1945) and *Charlotte's Web* (1952) and won the Pulitzer Prize (1978) for his body of work. E. B. White died on his **down east** farm in Maine on October 1, 1985.

WHITE, PAUL DUDLEY (1886–1973). Physician. Born in **Boston** on June 6, 1886, Paul Dudley White graduated from **Harvard University** (1908) and Harvard Medical School (1911). He trained at the **Massachusetts General Hospital** and in England and served in the U.S. Army (1917–19) in World War I. White introduced the electrocardiogram in Boston (1914) and became the father of modern American cardiology. He taught at Harvard Medical School and Massachusetts General Hospital (1911–70) and is best known for treating President Dwight D. Eisenhower for heart disease (1955). An early advocate of preventing heart disease by dieting and daily exercise (walking, bicycling, and golf), White died in Boston on October 31, 1973, and a bicycle path along the Charles River **Esplanade** was named for him (1960).

WHITE, THEODORE HAROLD (1915–1986). Writer. Born in **Boston** on May 6, 1915, Theodore H. White graduated from **Boston Latin School** (1932) and **Harvard University** (1938). He is best remembered as *Time* magazine's first foreign correspondent in Asia (1939–45) and for his chronicle of **John F. Kennedy**'s campaign, *The Making of the President, 1960* (1961), which won the Pulitzer Prize. Teddy White died in New York City on May 15, 1986.

WHITE MOUNTAINS. New Hampshire's most distinctive topographical feature. They comprise the northernmost section of the **Appalachian Mountains** with the highest elevations in New England. This area (1,300 sq mi/ 3,370 sq km) extends 87 miles (140 km) across north-central New Hampshire and western Maine, with 86 of the highest peaks in the northeastern states. Eleven of 86 **Presidential Range** peaks reach 1 mi/1.6 km in the White Mountain National Forest established by Congress in 1911 and designated a wilderness area in 1984. Its 781,000 acres, capped by **Mount Washington**, have three climates, the eastern deciduous forest on the foothills and lower slopes, the coniferous forest on the colder upper slopes, and the alpine flora around the summits. The White Mountains have been a **tourist** area since the 1820s, with bridle paths (1843), hotels (1852), 1,000 miles of hiking trails, and many **ski** slopes. By 1910 the Boston & Maine Railroad guidebooks described the White Mountains as the "heart of the nation's playground." Scenic locations attract 7 million visitors annually, especially to Franconia Notch with the **Old Man of the Mountain** or the Great Stone Face.

WHITNEY, ANNE (1821–1915). Artist. Born in Watertown, Massachusetts, on September 2, 1821, Whitney studied **art** in Philadelphia (1860) and **Boston** (1862–64). After study in Europe, she moved to Boston (1876), where she became the leading New England sculptor. Whitney is best known for statues of *Samuel Adams* (1873), *William Lloyd Garrison* (1880), *Leif Eriksson* (1887) on the **Back Bay** mall, and *Charles Sumner* (1902) at **Harvard University**. Whitney also made portrait busts of *Harriet Beecher Stowe* (1892) and *Lucy Stone*. She died in Boston on January 23, 1915.

WHITNEY, ELI (1765–1825). Inventor. Whitney was born in Westboro, Massachusetts, on December 8, 1765, and graduated from Yale College (1792). Visiting General **Nathanael Greene**'s plantation in Georgia, Whitney invented a machine to clean raw cotton. His cotton gin (1793) revolutionized cotton agriculture, revived the institution of **slavery**, and stimulated New England's **textile** industry. Patent infringements prevented his financial benefit, but he manufactured muskets for the U.S. Army (1798) in Hamden, Connecticut, using his new mass production method. With interchangeable, standardized parts, unskilled workers produced prefabricated guns in the "American System." Whitney died in **New Haven**, Connecticut, on January 8, 1825.

WHITTIER, JOHN GREENLEAF (1807–1892). Poet. Born in Haverhill, Massachusetts, on December 17, 1807, Whittier was a **Quaker** farmer's son with a limited education. When he published poems (1826) in **William Lloyd Garrison**'s newspaper, they became allies in the **abolitionist** crusade. Whittier was an editor in **Boston**, Haverhill, **Hartford**, and Philadelphia and served a term in the Massachusetts legislature (1835). Breaking with Garrison (1843), he published verse, prose, and 100 hymns while living in Amesbury, Massachusetts, including *The Barefoot Boy* (1856), *Barbara Frietchie* (1863), and *Snow Bound* (1866). Whittier, one of America's finest religious poets, died in Hampton Falls, Massachusetts, on September 7, 1892.

WHYDAH. The flagship of the Massachusetts pirate captain **Samuel Bellamy** (1689–1717) sunk in a storm off **Cape Cod** in 1717. Six of Bellamy's crew sailing in a captured ship, *Mary Anne*, survived shipwreck at Orleans and were hanged in **Boston** on November 15, 1717. The wreck was discovered in 1985, and some of its 10,000 artifacts, coins, and cannon are exhibited at the Whydah Museum in Brewster, Massachusetts. *See also* PIRACY.

WIFFLEBALL. Popular backyard baseball game invented in Fairfield, Connecticut (1953), by David N. Mullany. His small company in Shelton, Connecticut, still manufactures wiffle balls and bats used throughout the nation today. The World Wiffleball Association tournament is held each September at Hanover, Massachusetts.

WIGGLESWORTH, MICHAEL (1631–1705). Clergyman. Born in England on October 18, 1631, Wigglesworth came to **New Haven**, Connecticut, as a child (1638) and graduated from **Harvard** College (1651). As the pastor in Malden (1656–1705), he was famous for vivid sermons such as *The Day of Doom* (1662). His poetry *God's Controversy with New England* (1662) and *Meat out of the Eater* (1669) were popular with conservative Calvinists. Wigglesworth also practiced medicine in Malden, Massachusetts, until his death on June 10, 1705.

WIGWAM. An **Algonquian** word for the round or oblong dome-shaped huts built on a sapling frame and covered with woven reed mats or bark. Usually 12 to 15 feet in diameter, they varied somewhat; in northern New England the **Native Americans** used bark and straight poles, but

southern people built conical wigwams like those **Giovanni da Ver-**
razano saw at Narragansett Bay in 1524.

WILBOUR, ISAAC (1763–1837). Congressman from Rhode Island. Born
in Little Compton, Rhode Island, on April 25, 1763, Wilbour practiced
law in Little Compton (1793–1806) and served in the state legislature
(1800–06). He was lieutenant governor (1806–07, 1810–11) and acting
governor (1806) until elected as a Democratic-Republican to the House
of Representatives (1807–09). Wilbour was an associate justice of the
state supreme court (1818–19) and chief justice (1819–27). He died in
Little Compton on October 4, 1837.

WILDLIFE. Includes the bat, beaver, black bear, bobcat, chipmunk, cottontail rabbit (Eastern and New England), catamount, copperhead, coyote,
deer, dolphin, ermine, fisher, flying squirrel, frogs, gray fox, gray squirrel,
hare, lynx, mink, mole, **moose**, muskrat, newt, opossum, otter, porcupine,
porpoise, rabbits, raccoon, rat, rattlesnake, red fox, red squirrel, salaman-
ders, seals, shrew, snakes, striped skunk, toads, turkey, turtles, weasel,
whales, white-tailed deer, **woodchuck**, and wolf. The numerous birds in
New England include the American crow, American woodcock, bobwhite,
brown-headed cowbird, Canada goose, ducks, eagle, Eastern bluebird, fal-
con, grouse, hawks, loon, mallard, mute sparrows, swan, osprey, owls,
ring-necked pheasant, rock dove, ruffed grouse, terns, turkey, turkey vul-
ture, warblers, and wood duck. Some of this wildlife is not native to the region (Eastern cottontail and coyote), especially the flocks of feral green
parrots in Milford, Connecticut. Some animals are now rare (catamount,
fisher, and wolf). Suburbanization has led to conflict between wildlife and
people, and Massachusetts had 5,000 highway accidents with deer in 2001.
Motorists hit 136 moose on Vermont highways in 2001. Rural depopulation and conservation in recent decades have increased habitat for much
wildlife, but plans by environmental and wildlife organizations in 1999 to
reintroduce the Eastern timber wolf in northern New England forests
provoked public controversy. *See also* MASSACHUSETTS AUDUBON
SOCIETY.

WILLARD, EMMA (1787–1870). Educator. Born in Berlin, Connecticut,
on February 23, 1787, Emma Hart Willard became a teacher in 1803. After working as the principal of the Female Academy in Middlebury, Vermont (1807–09), she founded her own boarding school for girls in that
town (1814). With support from New York governor DeWitt Clinton, in

Waterford, New York, she opened (1819) the first school in the nation to offer a college-level education for women. This became the Troy Female Seminary (renamed the Emma Willard School in 1895), which she operated from 1821 to 1838. Emma Hart Willard was a pioneer in higher **education** for women. She wrote several textbooks and a volume of poetry before her death on April 15, 1870.

WILLIAMS, JOHN J. (1822–1907). Bishop. Born in Boston on February 12, 1822, John Joseph Williams was educated at the cathedral school in **Boston** and in a Montreal seminary and ordained in Paris (1845). He served as pastor in Boston and at an early age was vicar general for Bishop **John Fitzpatrick**. He became the fourth bishop of Boston (1866) and the first archbishop (1875). Bishop Williams organized new dioceses in Springfield (1870), **Providence** (1872), Manchester (1884), and Fall River (1905) and built the second Cathedral of the Holy Cross (1875), a seminary (1884), Boston College (1863), hospitals, charitable asylums, and orphanages and new ethnic parishes for **German**, **French-Canadian**, **Polish**, Lithuanian, **Syrian**, **Italian**, and **Portuguese** immigrants. Archbishop Williams died in Boston on August 30, 1907.

WILLIAMS, NATHANIEL (1675–1738). Physician. Born in **Boston** on August 25, 1675, Williams graduated from **Harvard** College (1693), earned his master's degree (1698), and was a minister in Barbados (1698–1700). Returning to Boston, he was a master at **Boston Latin School** (1703–08) and headmaster (1708–33). Williams studied medicine with his uncle in Cambridge and quickly had a large practice of elite Bostonians as well as **Native Americans** and the city's poor. He formed the Club of Physicians (1721) during the smallpox epidemic (1721–22), arguing for the new inoculation method. During the scarlet fever epidemic (1735), he founded the first Boston Medical Society to regulate his profession. Williams wrote *The Method of Practice in the Small Pox* (1752), published after his death in Boston on January 10, 1738.

WILLIAMS, ROGER (1603–1683). Governor of Rhode Island. Born in 1603 in London, Williams graduated from Cambridge University (1627) and was ordained (1628). He migrated to **Boston** (1631) and was a pastor in **Plymouth** (1632–33) and **Salem** (1633–35), until banished for nonconformist views by the Massachusetts **General Court** (1635). After he wintered with **Massasoit**, Williams purchased land from the **Narragansett** *sachem* **Canonicus** to found the Rhode Island colony at **Provi-**

dence (1636) with religious tolerance for all sects. In London he obtained a charter for his colony and published *The Bloudy Tenent of Persecution* (1644), defending religious liberty against the criticism of **John Cotton** and the Massachusetts **Puritans**. When England granted Williams a royal charter (1644), he united four Rhode Island colonies as a haven for **Quakers, Jews,** Anabaptists, and dissenters from the Puritans. When **William Coddington** had the charter annulled, Williams was able to restore (1651) and renew it (1663). Williams maintained peaceful relations with the **Native Americans** and wrote a dictionary of the **Algonquin** language (1643), until he fought the **Narragansetts** in **King Philip's War** (1675–76). He remained in political office until his death in Providence in April 1683. Even after statehood, his colony was known as Rhode Island and **Providence Plantations** until 1790.

WILLIAMS, TED (1918–2002). Athlete. Born in San Diego, California, on August 31, 1918, Theodore Samuel Williams was an outstanding outfielder for the **Boston Red Sox** (1939–60). He hit 521 home runs and had a lifetime batting average of .344, sixth highest in major league baseball. His career total number of walks (2,019) is second only to Babe Ruth. In 1941 Williams hit .406, a record not surpassed in 50 years. Considered the finest hitter in baseball history, his career was limited by active duty as a Marine Corps pilot in World War II and the Korean War. He later managed the Washington Senators (1969–71) and the Texas Rangers (1972) before retiring to Florida. The "Splendid Splinter" was elected to the Baseball Hall of Fame (1966), and his lifelong work for the **Jimmy Fund** and other charities has made Ted Williams the most beloved sports hero in New England. The **Big Dig** highway tunnel from **Boston** to Logan Airport is named in his honor (1999). Ted Williams, who became known as an inveterate sports fisherman in Maine, died in Florida on July 5, 2002.

WILLIAMS, WILLIAM (1731–1811). Congressman from Connecticut. Born in Lebanon, Connecticut, on March 29, 1731, Williams graduated from **Harvard** College (1751). He was a merchant in Lebanon and was elected to the colonial legislature (1757–62, 1763–76, 1780–84), and as a member of Congress (1776–77) he signed the Declaration of Independence. Williams was a judge (1776–1808) and state legislator for 24 years. He died in Lebanon on August 2, 1811.

WILSON, HENRY (1812–1875). Vice-president of the United States. Born in Farmington, New Hampshire, on February 16, 1812, Jeremiah

Jones Colbaith legally changed his name at age 21. Wilson had little formal education but became a successful shoemaker, employing a hundred workers by 1847 in Natick, Massachusetts. He joined the **abolitionist** crusade and entered politics as a Whig state legislator (1841–46, 1850–52) and then joined the Free Soil Party and the **Know Nothing Party**. Elected to the Senate (1855–73), Wilson joined the new Republican Party and was elected vice-president with President Ulysses S. Grant (1873–75), dying in office on November 22, 1875.

WILSON, SAMUEL. *See* UNCLE SAM.

WINANT, JOHN G. (1889–1947). Governor of New Hampshire. Born in New York City, Winant graduated from St. Paul's School in **Concord**, New Hampshire, and Princeton University (1910). He served as a Republican state legislator (1916–17) and taught at St. Paul's School (1913–17). After serving in the U.S. Army in World War I, he returned to St. Paul's and was elected as a progressive Republican state legislator (1920–24). Winant was the first governor to serve three terms (1924–27, 1931–35), and he signed more than 30 progressive laws supporting the New Deal. President Franklin Roosevelt appointed him to the International Labour Organisation in Geneva, Switzerland (1935) and as director of the Social Security Administration (1936–37). He succeeded **Joseph P. Kennedy** as ambassador to Great Britain (1940–46) and died in Concord on November 3, 1947.

WINCHESTER, OLIVER FISHER (1810–1880). Businessman. Born in **Boston** on November 30, 1810, Winchester was a shirt manufacturer when he purchased a **New Haven**, Connecticut, firearms company (1855) and reorganized it as the Winchester Repeating Arms Company in Windsor, Vermont (1866). The Henry rifle (1860) and Winchester model 73 were popular weapons in the Wild West. Winchester's firm was one of the leading arms manufacturers in New England when he died in New Haven on December 11, 1880.

WINDJAMMER. A nickname for a two-masted schooner built in the late 19th century to carry bricks, lumber, coal, oysters, and other New England cargo. Often more economical than steamships, thousands of these ships sailed along the Eastern coast. The last 14 restored windjammers in Maine now take **tourists** for short cruises on Penobscot Bay from May to October. The *Stephen Taber* (1871), the oldest sailing vessel in continuous service in the nation, and six other windjammers have been designated national historic landmarks.

WINGATE, PAINE (1739–1838). Senator from New Hampshire. Born in Amesbury, Massachusetts, on May 14, 1739, Wingate graduated from **Harvard** College (1759). He was ordained a **Congregational** minister in Hampton Falls, New Hampshire (1763–76). Moving to Stratham as a farmer, he served in the state legislature (1783) and the Continental Congress (1788) and as an Anti-Federalist in the U.S. Senate (1789–93) and again in the House of Representatives (1793–95). Wingate was a state legislator (1795) and state superior court judge (1798–1809). He died in Stratham on March 7, 1838, the last survivor of the Continental Congress.

WINSHIP, THOMAS (1920–2002). Editor. Born in Cambridge, Massachusetts, on July 1, 1920, Thomas Winship graduated from **Harvard University** (1942) and served in the U.S. Coast Guard in World War II. After working as a reporter for the *Washington Post* and as press secretary for Senator **Leverett Saltonstall**, he joined the *Boston Globe* staff (1956–84). As managing editor, Tom Winship transformed the staid and parochial *Globe* into one of the best big city newspapers in the nation. The investigative reporters and columnists he recruited won 12 Pulitzer prizes (1972–84) as the paper's reputation and circulation quickly increased. Winship, the self-described **swamp Yankee** newspaperman, died in **Boston** on March 14, 2002.

WINSLOW, EDWARD (1595–1655). Governor of **Plymouth Colony**. Born in England on October 18, 1595, Winslow was a **Pilgrim** leader in England and Holland. He arrived on the *Mayflower*, negotiated a treaty with **Massasoit**, and established the **fur trade** with Native Americans in Maine (1625) to raise revenue for the colony. On a voyage to England as a colonial agent (1623–24 and 1635), he was imprisoned (1635), but he returned to serve as governor (1633–34, 1636–37, 1644–45) and organized the **New England Confederation**. Winslow went to England on his third diplomatic mission (1646) but never returned, serving in Oliver Cromwell's government until his death at sea on May 8, 1655.

WINSOR, JUSTIN (1831–1897). Historian. Born in **Boston** on January 2, 1831, Winsor studied at **Harvard** College (1849–52), traveled in Europe, and began a literary career in Boston. He was the director of the

Boston Public Library (1867–77), founded the American Library Association (1876), and was director of the Harvard College Library (1877–97). He is best known for his *Memorial History of Boston* (1881). Winsor died in Cambridge on October 22, 1897.

WINTHROP, FITZ-JOHN (1638–1707). Governor of Connecticut. Born in Ipswich, Massachusetts, on March 14, 1638, the son of **John Winthrop, Jr.**, he served in the Parliamentary Army in England. He commanded Connecticut troops in the war with the Dutch and in **King Phillip's War**. After serving in the Connecticut legislature, and in Governor **Edmund Andros**'s council, he was the colonial agent who convinced William III to confirm the Connecticut charter. Fitz-John Winthrop served as governor (1698–1707) and died in **Boston** on November 27, 1707.

WINTHROP, JOHN (1588–1649). Governor of Massachusetts. Winthrop was born in England on January 12, 1588, and studied at Trinity College in Cambridge (1603–05). He practiced law in London, but his **Puritan** faith prompted him to settle in New England. As the organizer of the **Massachusetts Bay Company** (1628), he sailed with the Puritans on the *Arbella* in March 1630 to found **Massachusetts Bay Colony**. Winthrop was the major influence on the colony as its governor for 12 terms (1629–49). Although he opposed dissidents such as **Roger Williams** and **Anne Hutchinson** and dominated the colony to maintain its Puritan character, his life-long *Journal* (1630–47) and *The History of New England from 1630 to 1649* (1826) reveal he was a moderate on most issues. Winthrop died in **Boston** on March 26, 1649.

WINTHROP, JOHN JR. (1606–1676). Governor of Connecticut. Born in England on February 12, 1606, Winthrop, the son of **John Winthrop**, was educated at Trinity College in Dublin. He came to **Boston** as a lawyer (1631), served on the governor's council (1635, 1640, 1641, 1644–49), and founded the town of Ipswich (1633). He established the **Saugus Iron Works** (1644), practiced medicine, and was the first American elected to the Royal Society in London (1663). Winthrop founded Saybrook (1635) and New London (1646) and was deputy governor (1658) and governor in **New Haven** (1657, 1659–76). He obtained the royal charter (1662) uniting the **New Haven** and Connecticut colonies. Winthrop continued colonial New England's foremost political dynasty and died in Boston on April 5, 1676.

WINTHROP, JOHN (1714–1779). Astronomer. Born in **Boston** on December 8, 1714, Winthrop graduated from **Harvard** College (1732). The great-great grandson of **John Winthrop**, he taught natural philosophy and mathematics at Harvard (1739–79). Winthrop was the first astronomer in North America to study weather, sunspots, comets, and the earthquake that shook New England in 1755. He was elected to the Royal Society (1766), founded the **American Academy of Arts and Sciences** (1769), and was the first person to receive an honorary doctorate from Harvard College (1774). He died in Cambridge on May 3, 1779.

WINTHROP, ROBERT CHARLES (1809–1894). Speaker of the House. Born in **Boston** on May 12, 1809, Winthrop graduated from **Harvard** College (1828). He studied law with **Daniel Webster**, practicing in Boston (1831–40) and was a Whig state legislator (1835–40). Elected to the House of Representatives (1840–50), he was Speaker of the House (1847–49), but his moderate position on the abolition of **slavery** ended his political career in the Senate (1850–51). Winthrop was a prominent orator who made popular the term "manifest destiny" (1846). He was a noted philanthropist in Boston and for 30 years president of the **Massachusetts Historical Society**. Winthrop died in Boston on November 16, 1894.

WOLCOTT FAMILY. The most distinguished family in early Connecticut public service. **Roger Wolcott** (1679–1767) was second in command of the military force that captured Louisbourg (1745) and was governor of Connecticut (1750–54). His son, **Oliver Wolcott** (1726–97), graduated from Yale College (1747), and served in the **militia**. Wolcott, an assistant in the legislature and a judge, was elected to Congress (1775–78, 1780–84), signed the Declaration of Independence, and defended New York in the **American Revolution** (1776). He served as governor (1796–97) until he died in office on December 1, 1797. His son, **Oliver Wolcott, Jr.** (1760–1833), was the state comptroller (1791–95) and state auditor (1789–91), the first comptroller of the federal treasury (1791–95), and the second secretary of the treasury (1795–1800). He was also elected governor as a **Federalist** (1817–27).

WOODBURY, LEVI (1789–1851). U.S. Supreme Court justice. Born in Francestown, New Hampshire, on December 22, 1789, Woodbury graduated from Dartmouth College (1809), practiced law (1813–16), and was a superior court judge (1816–23). Elected Democratic-Republican governor (1823–24), he was a U.S. senator (1825–31) and then secretary of the navy (1831–34) and secretary of the treasury (1834–41). Woodbury was returned to the Senate (1841–45) until appointed to the U.S. Supreme Court (1845–51), where he served until his death in **Portsmouth** on September 4, 1851.

WOODCHUCK. A small marmot *(Marmot monax)* or groundhog common in New England and Canada. The name, derived from an **Algonquin** word, has become a jocular term for rural residents, people sometimes called **Swamp Yankees**, who often live in a **trouse** in the **puckerbrush**. *See also* YANKEE.

WOODHOUSE, CHASE GOING (1890–1984). Congresswoman from Connecticut. Born in British Columbia, Canada on March 3, 1890, Chase Going graduated from McGill University (1912) and studied at the University of Berlin and University of Chicago. She married Edward Woodhouse, a professor of government and the mayor of Northampton, Massachusetts. She taught economics at Smith College (1918–25) and Connecticut College (1934–46). The first woman elected secretary of state in Connecticut (1941–43), she served as a Democrat in the House of Representatives (1945–47, 1949–51). Woodhouse was a member of the state constitutional convention (1965) and died in New Canaan on December 12, 1984.

WOODS HOLE OCEANOGRAPHIC INSTITUTION (WHOI). Located in the village of Woods Hole in Falmouth, Massachusetts. It is a leading independent marine science research laboratory. Secretary of the Navy **Charles Francis Adams** (1930) founded this **Cape Cod** research center with funds donated by the Rockefeller Foundation. The WHOI conducted defense-related research during World War II and is recognized for deep-sea exploration and research. The nearby Marine Biological Laboratory (1888), the oldest private marine laboratory in North America, conducts important biomedical research, teaching, and summer institutes.

WORCESTER. The second largest city in Massachusetts and third largest in New England. It was settled by **Puritans** (1673), who displaced the **Nipmuc** people. The central Massachusetts city became a manufacturing center after the **American Revolution** and flourished when the **Blackstone canal** (1828) connected Worcester with **Providence**, Rhode Island. **Railroad** links (1834) stimulated the city's machine tool, wire, casting, die, printing, textile, and clothing firms employing **Irish, French-Canadian, Swedish, Italian, Jewish,** and **Polish immigrants.** Known as a center of antebellum women's rights and antislavery reform, Worcester is the home of the **American Antiquarian Society** and eight colleges. Today metropolitan Worcester has a population of 436,000 residents.

WRIGHT, CARROLL D. (1840–1909). Public official. Born in Dunbarton, New Hampshire, on July 25, 1840, Carroll Davidson Wright served as a colonel in the **Civil War** (1862–65). After practicing law in Reading, Massachusetts, and serving in the state senate (1872–73), he was director of the Massachusetts Bureau of the Statistics of Labor (1873–85), the first such agency in the nation. Wright was the first U.S. commissioner of labor (1885–1905) and director of the U.S. Census (1893). He was a pioneer in the science of statistics, using data to research labor issues and was president of the American Statistical Association (1897–1909). Wright was president of Clark College in **Worcester** (1902–09) and wrote *The Industrial Evolution of the United States* (1887) and *Battles of Labor* (1906) before he died in Worcester, Massachusetts, on February 20, 1909.

WRIGHT, ELIZUR (1804–1885). Reformer. Born in South Canaan, Connecticut, on February 12, 1804, Wright graduated from Yale College (1826) and became an **abolitionist** editor for the American Anti-Slavery Society (1834–52). By 1852 he was an actuary for Massachusetts **insurance** companies and state commissioner of insurance (1858–66), so instrumental in the reform and regulation of the industry that he was known as the father of life insurance. Wright died in Medford, Massachusetts, on November 21, 1885.

WRIGHT, HENRY CLARKE (1797–1870). Reformer. Born in Sharon, Connecticut, on August 29, 1797, Wright studied at Andover Seminary (1819–22) and was a **Congregational** minister in West Newbury, Massachusetts (1826–32). Abandoning pastoral work, he was a fund-raiser for Amherst College and an agent for the American Sunday School Union in **Boston.** By 1836 he became an agent for the American Peace Society before working for the American Anti-Slavery Society in Maine, Newburyport, and Philadelphia. Too radical for the pulpit or most **abolitionists,** Wright joined the radical, pacifist New England Non-Resistance

Society, lecturing in Britain (1842–47) on abolitionism and writing on health, marriage, and child rearing until his death in Pawtucket, Rhode Island, on August 16, 1870.

WRITS OF ASSISTANCE. Search warrants authorizing British customs officers to search houses or buildings for smuggled goods (1751). **James Otis** resigned as advocate general of the vice-admiralty court (1760) to defend **Boston** merchants against these unpopular writs. His stirring speech on the common law right to be free from unreasonable search and seizure led Chief Justice **Thomas Hutchinson** to delay action (1761). When the **Townshend Acts** (1767) revived the writs, New England courts refused to cooperate. These writs were listed as a grievance in the Declaration of Independence, and the fourth amendment (1791) in the Constitution's Bill of Rights banned writs of assistance.

WYETH, N. C. (1882–1945). Artist. Born in Needham, Massachusetts, on October 22, 1882, Newell Convers Wyeth studied **art** in **Boston** and Delaware before becoming an illustrator for the *Saturday Evening Post* and other magazines as well as books, including *The Last of the Mochicans*, *The Courtship of Myles Standish,* and *The Deerslayer.* He moved to Port Clyde, Maine (1920), painting the Maine seacoast in *The Harbor at Herring Gut* (1925). Wyeth died on October 19, 1945, but his son, Andrew Wyeth (1917–), and grandson, James Wyeth (1946–), became major artists in Maine. The Farnsworth Museum in Rockland, Maine, includes a major Wyeth collection (1997).

WYZANSKI, CHARLES EDWARD, JR. (1906–1986). Lawyer and judge. Born in **Boston** on May 27, 1906, Wyzanski graduated from **Harvard University** (1927) and Harvard Law School (1930). He practiced law in Boston, the only **Jew** in the **Boston Brahmin** firm Ropes and Gray (1930–33). **Felix Frankfurter** suggested that President Franklin D. Roosevelt appoint him solicitor to Secretary of Labor **Frances Perkins** (1933–35) and assistant attorney general in the Office of the U.S. Solicitor General (1933–37). Wyzanski defended the Wagner Act (1935) before the U.S. Supreme Court, and he was one of the architects of the New Deal. Roosevelt named him a judge on the U.S. District Court of Massachusetts (1941–65), and he became chief judge of that court (1965–71). Wyzanski taught at Harvard, MIT, Stanford University, and Columbia University and died in Boston on September 3, 1986.

– Y –

YALE, ELIHU (1649–1721). Merchant. Born in **Boston** on April 5, 1649, Yale was raised in England and made his fortune as governor of Madras for the East India Company (1687–92). He was a diamond merchant in London, who, at the request of Jeremiah Dummer, the Connecticut agent, donated (1714) books to the Collegiate School founded in Saybrook (1701). At the request of **Cotton Mather**, Yale contributed more books and goods (1718) to the Collegiate School relocated in **New Haven**, Connecticut (1717), which was named in his honor. Yale died in Wales on July 8, 1721, never having returned to New England.

YALE, LINUS (1821–1868). Inventor. Born in Salisbury, New York, on April 4, 1821, Yale learned the locksmith trade from his father. He opened a lock factory in Shelburne, Massachusetts (1840) and patented (1861) the first cylinder lock operated by a key, the basic door lock used today. Yale established the Yale Lock Manufacturing Company in Stamford, Connecticut (1868), and died in New York City on December 25, 1868.

YANKEE. The term for the descendants of the 17th-century New England **Puritans** derived from a disparaging Dutch term, Jan Kees (John Cheese), in the 1650s, or from a **Native American** mispronunciation of English. By the 1660s the Dutch in New Amsterdam applied it to English settlers in New England. British soldiers used the term derisively by 1758 for colonists known earlier as **Brother Jonathan**. Southerners applied the name to shrewd New England merchants, and the British army played a fife and drum march called *Yankee Doodle* (1750) to mock colonial troops, but by 1775 the colonials adopted the song and name proudly. It is the state song of Connecticut, perhaps based on the ragged troops led by Colonel Thomas Fitch of Norwalk (1758). The stage Yankee, a droll, simple, rustic, honest, and homespun character, was first seen in **Royall Tyler**'s plays *The Contrast* (1787) and *The Yankey in London* (1809). The term "Yankee peddler" was common by 1800 and "Damn Yankee" was introduced in the War of 1812. **Seba Smith**'s satires about Major Jack Downing (1829–50) made the Yankee wit a national favorite. **James Russell Lowell** used Yankee dialect for his characters in *The Biglow Papers* (1848), as did **Artemus Ward** in his books and lectures. During the **Civil War**, Southerners used this term for Union soldiers, but by 1917 it was applied to all American soldiers.

Yankees, as an ethnic group, are the descendents of **Congregational** British colonists but include **German**, Dutch, and **Huguenot** settlers in antebellum New England.

Yankees also assimilated **Scottish** and **Scotch-Irish immigrants** and spread their homogeneous, town-based culture and **Congregational** religion throughout the Northeast and then to the Midwest and the West Coast by 1850. The Yankee peddler, schoolteacher, tinker, and **Uncle Sam** were popular stereotypes by the antebellum era. By 1940 the **Fred Allen** radio comedy show featured a flinty Yankee character, Titus Moody, who later was a garter-sleeved storekeeper in **Pepperidge Farm** advertisements (1958–70).

Yankee cuisine includes a wide variety of seafood and native foods, such as beans, **corn**, **clam chowder**, squash, **blueberries**, pumpkins, and **cranberries**. Breakfast for rural New Englanders in the 19th century often consisted of leftover food from supper, including eggs, ham, beef, pork, veal, mutton, chicken, turkey, sausages, liver, kidneys, corned beef, fishcakes, hash, **baked beans**, potatoes, **brown bread**, cornbread, biscuits, and bread and **apple**, mince or **blueberry** pie. **Rum**, beer, ale, cider, coffee, and tea were beverages served at all meals. British visitors were astonished by the quantity and variety of breakfast foods consumed by traditional Yankees. One witty definition of a Yankee is someone who eats pie at breakfast. *See also* SWAMP YANKEE; WOODCHUCK.

YANKEE DIVISION. The U.S. Army 26th Division, a National Guard unit organized in **Boston** (1917). The Yankee Division included 32,000 men from every New England state and was the first fully formed American Expeditionary Force division in France. It had the longest and most sustained service with the highest casualty rate of any American unit in World War I. Some men had valuable experience when the **9th Massachusetts Regiment** ("Fighting Ninth"), having served in the Punitive Expedition on the Mexican Border (1916). The 26th Division served 210 days on the front lines in France with only 10 days of rest. They suffered 11,955 casualties with 1,739 men dead by November 11, 1918. Led by General Clarence R. Edwards and General Edward L. Logan, the doughboys won three Congressional Medals of Honor and more decorations than any other National Guard unit. Dubbed the "Sacrifice Division," the Yankee Division continues to serve the nation today. **Logan International Airport** was named in honor of General Logan (1923), a native Bostonian. *See also* CASS, THOMAS; GUINEY, PATRICK.

YANKEE INGENUITY. A reputation New Englanders developed by the 18th century for tinkering with a wide variety of practical inventions, devices, and gadgets. These include **Benjamin Franklin**'s lightning rod (1752), **David Bushnell**'s submarine (1776), **Eli Whitney**'s cotton gin (1793), **Benjamin Thompson**'s coffeepot (1806), **Thomas Blanchard**'s woodworking lathes (1819), and **Samuel Colt**'s revolver (1836). Other practical inventions were Thomas Davenport's power tools (1837), **Charles Goodyear**'s rubber (1843), **Samuel F. B. Morse**'s telegraph (1844), **Elias Howe**'s sewing machine (1846), **Elisha G. Otis**'s passenger elevator (1857), and Edwin T. Holmes's burglar alarm (1858). Versatile inventions also include James Plimpton's roller skates (1863), Moses Farmer's electric house lights (1868), **Chester Greenwood**'s earmuffs (1873), and **King Gillette**'s safety razor (1895). Mark Twain exploited this theme in *A Connecticut Yankee in King Arthur's Court* (1889), and explanations for Yankee inventiveness include the region's lack of natural resources, shortage of labor, and the **Puritan value** of frugality. The Yankee tradition of ingenuity and technology continued in the 20th century on a more scientific basis. *See also* COMPUTERS; ECONOMY.

YANKEE MAGAZINE. Founded in Dublin, New Hampshire (1935), by Robb Sagendorph (1900–70) to express and preserve New England culture. Monthly issues feature regional culture, history, fiction, poetry, humor, antiques, crafts, cooking, and gardening. One in five of the 600,000 subscribers live outside New England. The magazine also publishes the *Old Farmer's Almanac* founded in Massachusetts (1792) by Robert B. Thomas (1766–1846).

YAWKEY, THOMAS (1903–1976). Sportsman. Born in Detroit on February 21, 1903, Thomas Austin Yawkey was the owner of the **Boston Red Sox** (1933–76). He redesigned **Fenway Park** (1933) and spent lavishly on his team. The Red Sox won the American League pennant (1946, 1967, and 1975) but have not won the World Series since 1918. Tom Yawkey, a noted philanthropist who adopted the **Jimmy Fund** as the team's favorite charity (1953), died in **Boston** on July 9, 1976. He was the first executive elected to the Baseball Hall of Fame (1980). *See also* CURSE OF THE BAMBINO.

YOUNG, BRIGHAM (1801–1877). Clergyman. Born in Whitingham, Vermont, on June 1, 1801, Young settled in Mendon, New York, where he joined **Joseph Smith**'s new Church of Jesus Christ of the Latter Day

Saints (or Mormons) in 1832. He moved with the Mormons to Ohio and then Missouri and, despite Young's limited education, Smith named him one of the sect leaders in Illinois (1835). Young was a missionary in England (1839–41); and when Smith was assassinated (1844), Young succeeded him as the church leader (1845). He led the Mormon emigration to Salt Lake City, Utah (1846), where he was territorial governor of the cooperative theocratic community (1848–57) until replaced by President James Buchanan. Young's belief in polygamy delayed statehood for Utah (1896), but he governed the community as inspirational president of the church until his death in Salt Lake City on August 29, 1877.

– Z –

ZAKRZEWSKA, MARIE ELIZABETH (1829–1902). Physician. Born in Berlin, Germany, on September 6, 1829, Zakrzewska graduated from a Berlin school for midwives (1851) and from Cleveland Medical College (1856). After working at the New York Infirmary for Women and Children (1857–59), she was professor of obstetrics at the New England Female Medical College in **Boston** (1859–62). Dr. Zakrzewska founded the New England Hospital for Women and Children (1863) in Boston to provide women with medical care from competent physicians of their own sex and to train women as doctors and nurses. Supported by **William Lloyd Garrison**, **Wendell Phillips**, and **Theodore Parker**, she was a pioneer in medical education for women when she retired (1899) and died in Boston on May 12, 1902.

Appendix

State Symbols

CONNECTICUT

State Animal	Sperm Whale
State Bird	American Robin
State Capital	Hartford
State Composer	Charles Ives
State Flower	Mountain Laurel
State Folk Dance	Square Dancing
State Fossil	*Eubrontes giganteus*
State Hero	Nathan Hale
State Heroine	Prudence Crandall
State Insect	European Mantis
State Mineral	Garnet
State Motto	*Qui Transtulit Sustinet* (He Who Transplanted Still Sustains)
State Name	State of Connecticut
State Nickname	Constitution State, Nutmeg State
State Shellfish	Eastern Oyster
State Ship	USS *Nautilus*
State Song	*Yankee Doodle*
State Tree	Charter Oak

MAINE

State Animal	Moose
State Berry	Wild Blueberry
State Bird	Chickadee
State Capital	Augusta
State Cat	Maine Coon Cat
State Fish	Landlocked Salmon

State Flower	White Pine Cone
State Fossil	*Pertica Quadrifaria*
State Gemstone	Tourmaline
State Herb	Wintergreen
State Insect	Honeybee
State Motto	*Dirigo* (I Lead)
State Name	State of Maine
State Nickname	Pine Tree State
State Soil	Chesuncook Soil Serie
State Song	*State of Maine Song* by Roger Vinton Snow
State Tree	White Pine
State Vessel	Schooner *Bowdoin*

MASSACHUSETTS

State Beverage	Cranberry Juice
State Bird	Black-Capped Chickadee
State Capital	Boston
State Cat	Tabby Cat
State Children's Author	Theodor Geisel
State Children's Book	*Make Way for Ducklings* by Robert McCloskey
State Cookie	Chocolate Chip Cookie
State Dessert	Boston Cream Pie
State Dog	Boston Terrier
State Explorer Rock	Dighton Rock
State Fish	Cod
State Flower	Mayflower
State Folk Dance	Square Dancing
State Folk Hero	Johnny Appleseed
State Folk Song	*Massachusetts* by Arlo Guthrie
State Fossil	Dinosaur Tracks
State Game Bird	Wild Turkey
State Gem	Rhodonite
State Heroine	Deborah Samson
State Historical Rock	Plymouth Rock
State Horse	Morgan Horse

State Insect	Ladybug
State Marine Mammal	Right Whale
State Mineral	Babingtonite
State Motto	*Ense petit placidam sub libertate quietem* (By the sword we seek peace, but peace only under liberty)
State Muffin	Corn Muffin
State Name	Commonwealth of Massachusetts
State Nickname	Bay State
State Poem	*Blue Hills of Massachusetts* by Katherine E. Mullen
State Rock	Roxbury Puddingstone
State Shell	New England Neptune
State Soil	Paxton Soil Series
State Song	*All Hail to Massachusetts*
State Stone	Granite
State Tree	American Elm

NEW HAMPSHIRE

State Amphibian	Red-Spotted Newt
State Animal	White Tailed Deer
State Bird	Purple Finch
State Butterfly	Karner Blue
State Capital	Concord
State Emblem	Old Man of the Mountain
State Flower	Purple Lilac
State Freshwater Fish	Brook Trout
State Gem	Smokey Quartz
State Insect	Ladybug
State Mineral	Beryl
State Motto	Live Free or Die
State Name	State of New Hampshire
State Nickname	Granite State, White Mountain State
State Rock	Granite
State Saltwater Fish	Striped Bass
State Tree	White Birch
State Wildflower	Pink Ladyslipper

RHODE ISLAND

State Bird	Rhode Island Red Hen
State Capital	Providence
State Fish	Striped Bass
State Flower	Blue Violet
State Fruit	Rhode Island Greening Apple
State Mineral	Bowenite
State Motto	Hope
State Name	Rhode Island and Providence Plantations
State Nickname	Ocean State
State Rock	Cumberlandite
State Shell	Quahog
State Song	*Rhode Island's It for Me* by Charles Hall
State Tree	Red Maple
State Yacht	*Courageous*

VERMONT

State Animal	Morgan Horse
State Beverage	Milk
State Bird	Hermit Thrush
State Butterfly	Monarch Butterfly
State Capital	Montpelier
State Fish	Brook Trout and Walleye Pike
State Flower	Red Clover
State Fossil	White Whale
State Fruit	Apple
State Gem	Garnet
State Insect	Honeybee
State Mineral	Talc
State Motto	Freedom and Unity
State Name	State of Vermont
State Nickname	Green Mountain State
State Pie	Apple Pie
State Rocks	Granite, Marble, Slate
State Soil	Tunbridge Soil Series
State Song	*Hail Vermont* by Josephine Hovey Perry
State Tree	Sugar Maple

Selected Bibliography

CONTENTS

STATES

Connecticut

Baldwin, Peter C. *Domesticating the Street: The Reform of Public Space in Hartford, 1850–1930*. Columbus: Ohio State University Press, 1999.

Bushman, Richard L. *From Puritan to Yankee: Character and the Social Order in Connecticut, 1690–1765*. New York: W. W. Norton, 1970.

Collier, Christopher. *Roger Sherman's Connecticut*. Middletown, Conn.: Wesleyan University Press, 1971.

Cooke, Edward S., Jr. *Making Furniture in Preindustrial America: The Social Economy of Newtown and Woodbury, Connecticut*. Baltimore: John Hopkins University Press, 1996.

Daniels, Bruce Colin. *The Connecticut Town: Growth and Development, 1635–1790*. Middletown, Conn.: Wesleyan University Press, 1979.

Dayton, Cornelia Hughes. *Women Before the Bar: Gender, Law, and Society in Connecticut, 1639–1789*. Chapel Hill: University of North Carolina Press, 1995.

Gordon, Robert B. *A Landscape Transformed: The Ironmaking District of Salisbury, Connecticut*. New York: Oxford University Press, 2000.

Grant, Charles S. *Democracy in the Connecticut Frontier Town of Kent*. New York: Columbia University Press, 1961.

Lieberman, Joseph I. *The Legacy: Connecticut Politics, 1930–1980*. Hartford, Conn.: Spoonwood Press, 1981.

Lipson, Dorothy A. *Freemasonry in Federalist Connecticut*. Princeton, N.J.: Princeton University Press, 1977.

Osterweis, Rollin G. *Three Centuries of New Haven, 1638–1938*. New Haven, Conn.: Yale University Press, 1953.

Robertson, James Oliver, and Janet C. Robertson. *All Our Yesterdays: A Century of Family Life in an American Small Town*. New York: HarperCollins, 1995.

Roth, David M. *Connecticut: A Bicentennial History*. New York: W. W. Norton, 1979.

Sarna, Jonathan D., ed. *Jews in New Haven*. New Haven, Conn.: Jewish Historical Society of New Haven, 1978.

Siskind, Janet. *Rum and Axes: The Rise of a Connecticut Merchant Family, 1795–1850*. Ithaca, N.Y.: Cornell University Press, 2001.

Sklar, Kathryn Kish. *Catharine Beecher: A Study in Domesticity.* New Haven, Conn.: Yale University Press, 1973.

Van Dusen, Albert E. *Connecticut: An Illustrated History of the State from the Seventeenth Century.* New York: Random House, 1961.

Maine

Acheson, James M. *The Lobster Gangs of Maine.* Hanover, N.H.: University Press of New England, 1988.

Banks, Ronald F. *Maine Becomes a State: The Movement to Separate Maine from Massachusetts, 1785–1820.* Middletown, Conn.: Wesleyan University Press, 1970.

Clark, Charles E. *Maine: A History.* New York: W. W. Norton, 1977.

Coolidge, Philip T. *History of the Maine Woods.* Bangor, Maine: Furbush-Roberts, 1963.

Duncan, Roger F. *Coastal Maine, a Maritime History.* New York: W. W. Norton, 1992.

Federal Writers Project. *Maine: A Guide "Down East."* Boston: Houghton Mifflin, 1937.

Hunter, Julia A., and Earle G. Shettleworth, Jr. *Fly Rod Crosby: The Woman Who Marketed Maine.* Gardiner, Maine: Tilbury House, 2000.

Isaacson, Dorris A, ed. *Maine: A Guide Down East.* Rockland, Maine: Courier Gazette, 1970.

Judd, Richard W. *Aroostook: A Century of Logging in Northern Maine.* Orono: University of Maine Press, 1989.

——, Edwin A. Churchill, and Joel W. Eastman, eds. *Maine: The Pine Tree State from Prehistory to the Present.* Orono: University of Maine Press, 1995.

Kershaw, Gordon E. *The Kennebeck Proprietors, 1749–1775.* Somersworth, N.H.: New Hampshire Publishing Company, 1975.

Lee, William Storrs. *Maine, A Literary Chronicle.* New York: Funk and Wagnalls, 1968.

Malone, Joseph J. *Pine Trees and Politics.* Seattle: University of Washington Press, 1964.

Rich, Louise Dickinson. *State O'Maine.* New York: Harper and Row, 1964.

Rolde, Neil. *Maine: A Narrative History.* Gardiner, Maine: Harpswell Press, 1990.

Saltonstall, Richard. *Maine Pilgrimage: The Search for an American Way of Life.* Boston: Little, Brown, 1974.

Snow, Edward Rowe. *The Romance of Casco Bay.* New York: Dodd, Mead, 1975.

Taylor, Alan. *Liberty Men and the Great Proprietors: The Revolutionary Settlement on the Maine Frontier, 1760–1820.* Chapel Hill: University of North Carolina Press, 1990.

Ulrich, Laurel Thatcher. *A Midwife's Tale: The Life of Martha Ballard, Based on Her Diary, 1785–1812*. New York: Knopf, 1990.

Massachusetts

Bedford, Henry F. *Socialism and the Workers in Massachusetts, 1886–1912*. Amherst: University of Massachusetts Press, 1966.

Brown, Richard D. *Revolutionary Politics in Massachusetts: The Boston Committee of Correspondence and the Towns, 1772–1774*. Cambridge, Mass.: Harvard University Press, 1970.

Brown, Richard D., and Jack Tager. *Massachusetts: A Concise History*. Amherst: University of Massachusetts Press, 2000.

Conroy, David W. *In Public Houses: Drink and the Revolution of Authority in Colonial Massachusetts*. Chapel Hill: University of North Carolina Press, 1995.

Deutsch, Sarah. *Women and the City: Gender, Space, and Power in Boston, 1870–1940*. New York: Oxford University Press, 2000.

Duis, Perry R. *The Saloon: Public Drinking in Chicago and Boston, 1880–1920*. Urbana: University of Illinois Press, 1983.

Erskine, Margaret A. *Worcester: Heart of the Commonwealth*. Woodland Hills, Calif: Windsor Publications, 1981.

Frisch, Michael H. *Town into City: Springfield, Massachusetts, and the Meaning of Community, 1840–1880*. Cambridge: Harvard University Press, 1972.

Greven, Philip J., Jr. *Four Generations: Population, Land, and Family in Colonial Andover, Massachusetts*. Ithaca, N.Y.: Cornell University Press, 1970.

Handlin, Oscar. *Boston's Immigrants, 1790–1880: A Study in Acculturation*. Cambridge, Mass.: Harvard University Press, 1941.

Holloran, Peter C. *Boston's Wayward Children: Social Services for Homeless Children, 1830–1930*. Boston: Northeastern University Press, 1994.

Johnson, Richard A. *A Century of Boston Sports*. Boston: Northeastern University Press, 2000.

Jones, Douglas Lamar. *Village and Seaport: Migration and Society in Eighteenth-Century Massachusetts*. Hanover, N.H.: University Press of New England, 1981.

Kass, Amalie M. *Midwifery and Medicine in Boston, Walter Channing, M.D., 1786–1876*. Boston: Northeastern University Press, 2002.

Kenny, Herbert A. *Cape Ann: Cape America*. Philadelphia, Pa.: J. B. Lippincott Company, 1971.

Knights, Peter R. *The Plain People of Boston, 1830–1860: A Study of City Growth*. New York: Oxford University Press, 1971.

Lane, Roger. *Policing the City: Boston, 1822–1885*. Cambridge, Mass.: Harvard University Press, 1967.

Lawes, Carolyn J. *Women and Reform in a New England Community, 1815–1860*. Lexington: University Press of Kentucky, 2000.

Levy, Leonard W. *The Law of the Commonwealth and Chief Justice Shaw*. New York: Oxford University Press, 1987.

Lockridge, Kenneth A. *New England Town, First Hundred Years: Dedham, Massachusetts, 1636–1736*. New York: W. W. Norton, 1985.

Lyons, Louis. *Newspaper Story: One Hundred Years of the Boston Globe*. Cambridge: Belknap Press, 1971.

Morison, Samuel Eliot. *Harrison Gray Otis, 1765–1848: The Urbane Federalist*. Boston: Houghton Mifflin, 1969.

O'Connor, Thomas H. *The Hub: Boston Past and Present*. Boston: Northeastern University Press, 2001.

Rothenberg, Winifred B. *From Market-Places to a Market Economy: The Transformation of Rural Massachusetts, 1750–1850*. Chicago: University of Chicago Press, 1992.

Schneider, Eric C. *In the Web of Class: Delinquents and Reformers in Boston, 1810s–1930s*. New York: New York University Press, 1995.

Stout, Glenn. *Red Sox Century: One Hundred Years of Red Sox Baseball*. Boston: Houghton Mifflin, 2000.

Tager, Jack. *Boston Riots: Three Centuries of Social Violence*. Boston: Northeastern University Press, 2001.

Thernstrom, Stephen. *Poverty and Progress: Social Mobility in a Nineteenth-Century City*. Cambridge, Mass.: Harvard University Press, 1964.

Trout, Charles H. *Boston, the Great Depression and the New Deal*. New York: Oxford University Press, 1977.

von Hoffman, Alexander. *Local Attachments: The Making of an American Urban Neighborhood, 1850–1920*. Baltimore, Md.: Johns Hopkins University Press, 1995.

New Hampshire

Armstrong, John B. *Factory under the Elms: Harrisville, New Hampshire, 1774–1969*. Cambridge, Mass.: MIT Press, 1969.

Bedford, Henry F. *Seabrook Station: Citizen Politics and Nuclear Power*. Amherst: University of Massachusetts Press, 1990.

Cash, Kevin. *Who the Hell Is William Loeb*. Manchester, N.H.: Amoskeag Press, 1975.

Clark, Charles E. *The Meetinghouse Tragedy: An Episode in the Life of a New England Town*. Hanover, N.H.: University Press of New England, 1999.

Cole, Donald B. *Jacksonian Democracy in New Hampshire, 1800–1851*. Cambridge, Mass.: Harvard University Press, 1970.

Daniell, Jere R. *Experiment in Republicanism: New Hampshire Politics and the American Revolution, 1741–1794.* Cambridge, Mass.: Harvard University Press, 1970.

Hareven, Tamara K., and Randolph Langenbach. *Amoskeag: Life and Work in an American Factory-City.* New York: Pantheon Books, 1978.

Hill, Ralph Nading. *Yankee Kingdom: Vermont and New Hampshire.* New York: Harper and Row, 1973.

Howe, Nicholas S. *Not without Peril: 150 Years of Misadventure on the Presidential Range.* Boston: Appalachian Mountain Club, 2000.

Morison, Elizabeth Forbes, and Elting E. Morison. *New Hampshire.* New York: W. W. Norton, 1977.

Munyon, Paul Glenn. *A Reassessment of New England Agriculture in the Last Thirty Years of the Nineteenth Century: New Hampshire, A Case Study.* New York: Arno Press, 1978.

Nichols, Roy Franklin. *Franklin Pierce: Young Hickory of the Granite Hills.* Philadelphia: University of Pennsylvania Press, 1969.

Rudman, Warren. *Combat: Twelve Years in the U. S. Senate.* New York: Random House, 1996.

Sewell, Richard H. *John P. Hale and the Politics of Abolition.* Cambridge, Mass.: Harvard University Press, 1965.

Tolles, Bryant F., Jr. *Summer Cottages in the White Mountains: The Architecture of Leisure and Recreation, 1870 to 1930.* Hanover, N.H.: University Press of New England, 2000.

Veblen, Eric P. *The Manchester Union Leader in New Hampshire Elections.* Hanover, N.H.: University Press of New England, 1975.

Waterman, Laura and Guy. *Forest and Crag: A History of Hiking, Trail Blazing, and Adventure in the Northeast Mountains.* Boston: Appalachian Mountain Club, 1989.

Whittemore, Charles P. *A General of the Revolution: John Sullivan of New Hampshire.* New York: Columbia University Press, 1961.

Wright, James E. *The Progressive Yankees: Republican Reformers in New Hampshire, 1906–1916.* Hanover, N.H.: University Press of New England, 1987.

Rhode Island

Amory, Cleveland. *The Last Resorts.* New York: Harper & Row, 1948.

Buhle, Paul, Scott Molloy, and Gail Sansbury, eds. *A History of Rhode Island Working People.* Providence, R. I.: Regine Printing Company, 1983.

Chyet, Stanley F. *Lopez of Newport: Colonial American Merchant Prince.* Detroit, Mich.: Wayne State University Press, 1970.

Coleman, Peter J. *Transformation of Rhode Island, 1790–1860.* Providence, R.I.: Brown University Press, 1963.

Dennison, George M. *The Dorr War: Republicanism on Trial, 1831–1861.* Lexington: University Press of Kentucky, 1976.

Downing, A. F., and Vincent J. Scully. *The Architectural Heritage of Newport, Rhode Island, 1640–1915.* New York: C. N. Potter, 1967.

Fowler, William M. *William Ellery: A Rhode Island Politico and Lord of Admiralty.* Metuchen, N.J.: Scarecrow Press, 1973.

Gettleman, Marvin E. *The Dorr Rebellion: A Study in American Radicalism, 1833–1849.* New York: Random House, 1973.

Goodman, Jay S. *The Democrats and Labor in Rhode Island, 1952–1962.* Providence, R.I.: Brown University Press, 1967.

Herndon, Ruth Wallis. *Unwelcome Americans: Living on the Margin in Early New England.* Philadelphia: University of Pennsylvania Press, 2001.

James, Sydney V. *Colonial Rhode Island: A History.* New York: Scribner's, 1975.

Kellner, George H., and J. Stanley Lemons. *Rhode Island: The Independent State.* Woodland Hills, Calif.: Windsor Publications, 1982.

Lovejoy, David S. *Rhode Island Politics and American Revolution, 1760–1776.* Providence, R. I.: Brown University Press, 1958.

McLoughlin, William G. *Rhode Island: A Bicentennial History.* New York: W. W. Norton, 1978.

Polishook, Irwin H. *Rhode Island and Union, 1774–1795.* Evanston, Ill.: Northwestern University Press, 1969.

Schantz, Mark S. *Piety in Providence: Class Dimensions of Religious Experience in Antebellum Rhode Island.* Ithaca, N.Y.: Cornell University Press, 2000.

Thompson, Mack. *Moses Brown: Reluctant Reformer.* Chapel Hill: University of North Carolina Press, 1962.

Vermont

Albers, Jan. *Hands on the Land: A History of the Vermont Landscape.* Cambridge, Mass.: MIT Press, 1999.

Bailey, Consuelo Northrop. *Leaves Before the Wind: The Autobiography of Vermont's Own Daughter.* Burlington, Vt.: George Little Press, 1976.

Crockett, Walter Hill. *A History of Vermont,* 4 vols. Burlington, Vt.: Vermont Farm Bureau, 1938.

Fisher, Dorothy Canfield. *Memories of Arlington, Vermont.* New York: Duell, Sloan and Pearce, 1957.

Gallagher, Nancy. *Breeding Better Vermonters: The Eugenics Program in the Green Mountain State*. Hanover, N.H.: University Press of New England, 1999.

Hard, Walter, Jr., and J. Kevin Graffagnino, eds. *Vermont People*. Middlebury, Vt.: Vermont Books, 1981.

Hill, Ralph Nading. *Lake Champlain: Key to Liberty*. Woodstock, Vt.: Countryman Press, 1995.

Holbrook, Stewart H. *The Yankee Exodus: An Account of Migration from New England*. New York: Macmillan, 1950.

Jellison, Charles A. *Ethan Allen: Frontier Rebel*. Syracuse, N.Y.: Syracuse University Press, 1969.

Johnson, Charles W. *The Nature of Vermont: Introduction and Guide to a New England Environment*. Hanover, N.H.: University Press of New England, 1980.

Judd, Richard M. *The New Deal in Vermont: Its Impact and Aftermath*. New York: Garland, 1979.

Klyza, Christopher McGrory, and Stephen C. Trombulak. *The Story of Vermont: A Natural and Cultural History*. Hanover, N.H.: University of New England Press, 1999.

Ludlum, David M. *Social Ferment in Vermont, 1791–1850*. New York: Columbia University Press, 1939.

Miller, John M. *Deer Camp: Last Light in the Northeast Kingdom*. Cambridge, Mass.: MIT Press, 1992.

Miller, John M., and Howard Frank Mosher. *Granite and Cedar: The People and the Land of Vermont's Northeast Kingdom*. Middlebury, Vt.: Vermont Folklife Center, 2001.

Morrissey, Charles T. *Vermont: A History*. New York: W. W. Norton, 1981.

Roth, Randolph A. *The Democratic Dilemma: Religion, Reform, and the Social Order in the Connecticut River Valley of Vermont, 1791–1850*. New York: Cambridge University Press, 1987.

Sherman, Joe. *Fast Lane on a Dirt Road: Vermont Transformed: 1945–1990*. Woodstock, Vt.: Countryman Press, 1991.

Stilwell, Lewis D. *Migration from Vermont*. Montpelier, Vt.: Vermont Historical Society, 1948.

Van de Water, Frederic F. *The Reluctant Republic: Vermont 1724–1791*. New York: John Day Company, 1941.

Wilson, Harold F. *The Hill Country of Northern New England: Its Social and Economic History, 1790–1930*. New York: AMS Press, 1967.

Winks, Robin W. *Frederick Billings: A Life*. New York: Oxford University Press, 1991.

Yates, Elizabeth. *The Lady from Vermont: Dorothy Canfield Fisher's Life and World*. Brattleboro, Vt.: Stephen Greene Press, 1971.

POPULATION GROUPS

African Americans

Anthony, Billie C. *Hartford's Early Black History*. Hartford: Connecticut Historical Society, 1996.

Cottrol, Robert J. *The Afro-Yankees: Providence's Black Community in the Antebellum Era*. Westport, Conn.: Greenwood Press, 1982.

Coughtry, Jay. *The Notorious Triangle: Rhode Island and the African Slave Trade, 1700–1807*. Philadelphia: Temple University Press, 1981.

Cromwell, Adelaide M. *The Other Brahmins: Boston's Black Upper Class, 1750–1950*. Fayetteville: University of Arkansas Press, 1994.

Formisano, Ronald. *Boston against Busing: Race, Class, and Ethnicity in the 1960s and 1970s*. Chapel Hill: University of North Carolina Press, 1991.

Fox, Stephen R. *The Guardian of Boston: William Monroe Trotter*. New York: Atheneum, 1970.

Greene, Lorenzo J. *The Negro in Colonial New England, 1620–1776*. New York: Columbia University Press, 1942.

Grover, Kathryn. *The Fugitive's Gibraltar: Escaping Slaves and Abolitionism in New Bedford, Massachusetts*. Amherst: University of Massachusetts Press, 2001.

Hinks, Peter P. *To Awaken My Afflicted Brethren: David Walker and the Problem of Antebellum Slave Resistance*. University Park: Pennsylvania State University Press, 1996.

Horowitz, Helen Lefkowitz, and Kathy Peiss. *Love Across the Color Line: The Letters of Alice Hanley to Channing Lewis*. Amherst: University of Massachusetts Press, 1996.

Horton, James Oliver, and Lois E. Horton. *Black Bostonians: Family Life and Community Struggle in the Antebellum North*. New York: Holmes and Meier, 1979.

Jacobs, Donald M. *Courage and Conscience: Black and White Abolitionists in Boston*. Bloomington: Indiana University Press, 1993.

King, Mel. *Chain of Change: Struggles for Black Community Development*. Boston: South End Press, 1981.

Lewis, David Levering. *W.E.B. Du Bois: Biography of a Race, 1865–1919*. New York: Henry Holt, 1993.

Levy, Leonard W., and Douglas L. Jones, eds. *Jim Crow in Boston: The Origin of the Separate but Equal Doctrine*. New York: Da Capo Press, 1974.

Melish, Joanne Pope. *Disowning Slavery: Gradual Emancipation and Race in New England, 1780–1860*. Ithaca, N.Y.: Cornell University Press, 1998.

O'Toole, James M. *Passing for White: Race, Religion, and the Healy Family, 1820–1920*. Amherst: University of Massachusetts Press, 2002.

Piersen, William D. *Black Yankees: The Development of an Afro-American Subculture in Eighteenth-Century New England*. Amherst: University of Massachusetts Press, 1988.

Pleck, Elizabeth Hafkin. *Black Migration and Poverty, Boston 1865–1900*. New York: Academic Press, 1979.

Schneider, Mark. *Boston Confronts Jim Crow, 1890–1920*. Boston: Northeastern University Press, 1997.

Williams, Clarence G. *Technology and the Dream: Reflections on the Black Experience at MIT, 1941–1999*. Cambridge: MIT Press, 2001.

Boston Brahmins

Amory, Cleveland. *The Proper Bostonians*. New York: E. P. Dutton, 1947.

Daltzell, Robert F., Jr. *Enterprising Elite: The Boston Associates and the World They Made*. Cambridge, Mass.: Harvard University Press, 1987.

Duberman, Martin B. *Charles Francis Adams, 1807–1886*. Boston: Houghton Mifflin, 1961.

Galvin, John T. *The Gentleman Mr. Shattuck: A Biography of Henry Lee Shattuck, 1879–1971*. Boston: Tontine Press, 1996.

Gelfand, Mark I. *Trustee for a City: Ralph Lowell of Boston*. Boston: Northeastern University Press, 1998.

Linden-Ward, Blanche. *Silent City on a Hill: Landscapes of Memory and Boston's Mount Auburn Cemetery*. Columbus: Ohio State University Press, 1989.

Marquand, John P. *The Late George Apley*. Boston: Little, Brown, 1937.

Morison, Samuel Eliot. *One Boy's Boston, 1887–1901*. Boston: Houghton Mifflin, 1962.

Story, Ronald. *The Forging of an Aristocracy: Harvard and the Boston Upper Class, 1800–1870*. Middletown, Conn.: Wesleyan University Press, 1980.

Tyack, David. *George Ticknor and the Boston Brahmins*. Cambridge, Mass.: Harvard University Press, 1967.

Immigrants

Antin, Mary. *From Plotzk to Boston*. New York: M. Wiener, 1986.

Beattie, Betsy. *Obligation and Opportunity: Single Maritime Women in Boston, 1870–1930*. Montreal: McGill-Queen's University Press, 2000.

Blewett, Mary H. *The Last Generation: Work and Life in the Textile Mills of Lowell, Massachusetts, 1910–1960*. Amherst: University of Massachusetts Press, 1990.

Brault, Gerard J. *The French-Canadian Heritage in New England*. Hanover, N.H.: University Press of New England, 1986.

Burrill, Gary. *Away: Maritimers in Massachusetts, Ontario, and Alberta: An Oral History of Leaving Home*. Montreal: McGill-Queen's University Press, 1992.

De Marco, William M. *Ethnics and Enclaves: Boston's Italian North End*. Ann Arbor, Mich.: UMI Research Press, 1981.

Gans, Herbert J. *The Urban Villagers: Group and Class in the Life of Italian-Americans*. New York: Free Press, 1982.

Solomon, Barbara Miller. *Ancestors and Immigrants: A Changing New England Tradition*. Cambridge, Mass.: Harvard University Press, 1956.

Smith, Judith. *Family Connections: A History of Italian and Jewish Immigrant Lives in Providence, Rhode Island, 1900–1940*. Albany: State University of New York Press, 1985.

Stack, John F. *International Conflict in an American City: Boston's Irish, Italians, and Jews, 1935–1944*. Westport, Conn.: Greenwood Press, 1979.

Riccio, Anthony V. *Portrait of an Italian-American Neighborhood: The North End of Boston*. New York: Center for Migration Studies, 1998.

Tinory, Eugene P. *Journey from Ammeah: The Story of a Lebanese Immigrant*. Brattleboro, Vt.: Amana Books, 1986.

Woodham Smith, Cecil. *The Great Hunger: Ireland, 1845–1849*. New York: Harper and Row, 1962.

Whyte, William Foote. *Street Corner Society: The Social Structure of an Italian Slum*. Chicago: University of Chicago Press, 1943.

Irish

Ainley, Leslie G. *Boston Mahatma*. Boston: Bruce Humphries, 1949.

Beatty, Jack. *The Rascal King: The Life and Times of James Michael Curley (1874–1958)*. Boston: Addison-Wesley Publishing Company, 1992.

Curley, James Michael. *I'd Do It Again*. Englewood Cliffs, N. J.: Prentice Hall, 1957.

Dinneen, Joseph F. *The Purple Shamrock: James Michael Curley*. New York: W. W. Norton, 1949.

Goodwin, Doris Kearns. *The Fitzgeralds and the Kennedys*. New York: Simon and Schuster, 1987.

O'Connor, Edwin. *The Last Hurrah*. Boston: Little, Brown and Company, 1956.

O'Connor, Thomas H. *The Boston Irish: A Political History*. Boston: Northeastern University Press, 1995.

———. *South Boston, My Home Town: The History of an Ethnic Neighborhood*. Boston: Northeastern University Press, 1994.

O'Neill, Thomas P., Jr., and William Novak. *Man of the House: The Life and Political Memoirs of Speaker Tip O'Neill*. New York: Random House, 1987.

Mitchell, Brian C. *The Paddy Camps: The Irish of Lowell, 1821–61*. Urbana: University of Illinois Press, 1988.

Meagher, Timothy J. *Inventing Irish America: Generation, Class, and Ethnic Identity in a New England City, 1880–1928*. Notre Dame, Ind.: University of Notre Dame Press, 2001.

Ryan, Dennis P. *Beyond the Ballot: A Social History of the Boston Irish, 1845–1917.* Rutherford, N.J.: Fairleigh Dickinson University Press, 1983.

Native Americans

Bourne, Russell. *The Red King's Rebellion: Racial Politics in New England, 1675–1678.* New York: Atheneum, 1990.

Bourque, Bruce J. *Twelve Thousand Years: American Indians in Maine.* Lincoln: University of Nebraska Press, 2001.

Bragdon, Kathleen J. *Native People of Southern New England, 1500–1650.* Norman: University of Oklahoma Press, 1996.

Calloway, Colin G. *The Western Abenakis of Vermont, 1600–1800: War, Migration, and Survival of an Indian People.* Norman: University of Oklahoma Press, 1990.

——. *After King Philip's War: Presence and Persistence in Indian New England.* Hanover, N.H.: University Press of New England, 1997.

Cogley, Richard W. *John Eliot's Mission to the Indians before King Philip's War.* Cambridge, Mass.: Harvard University Press, 1999.

Demos, John P. *The Unredeemed Captive: A Family Story from Early America.* New York: Knopf, 1994.

Drake, James D. *King Philip's War: Civil War in New England, 1675–1676.* Amherst: University of Massachusetts Press, 1999.

Goddard, Ives, and Kathleen J. Bragdon. *Native Writings in Massachusett.* Philadelphia: American Philosophical Society, 1988.

Lepore, Jill. *The Name of War: King Philip's War and the Origins of American Identity.* New York: Knopf, 1998.

Plane, Ann Marie. *Colonial Intimacies: Indian Marriage in Early New England.* Ithaca, N.Y.: Cornell University Press, 2000.

Russell, Howard S. *Indian New England Before the Mayflower.* Hanover, N.H.: University Press of New England, 1980.

Salisbury, Neal. *Manitou and Providence: Indians, Europeans, and the Making of New England, 1500–1643.* New York: Oxford University Press, 1982.

Simmons, William S. *Spirit of the New England Tribes: Indian History and Folklore, 1620–1984.* Hanover, N.H.: University Press of New England, 1986.

Vaughan, Alden T., ed. *New England Encounters: Indians and Euroamericans, 1600–1850.* Boston: Northeastern University Press, 1999.

Puritans

Archer, Richard. *Fissures in the Rock: New England in the Seventeenth Century.* Hanover, N. H.: University Press of New England, 2001.

Baltzell, E. Digby. *Puritan Boston and Quaker Philadelphia: Two Protestant Ethics and the Spirit of Class, Authority and Leadership.* New York: Free Press, 1979.

Bradford, William. *Of Plymouth Plantation, 1620–1647.* ed. Samuel Eliot Morison. New York: Knopf, 1953.

Breen, Louise A. *Transgressing the Bonds: Subversive Enterprises among the Puritan Elite in Massachusetts, 1630–1692.* New York: Oxford University Press, 2001.

Bremer, Francis J. *The Puritan Experiment: New England Society from Bradford to Edwards.* Hanover, N. H.: University Press of New England, 1995.

Daniels, Bruce. *Puritans at Play.* New York: St. Martin's Press, 1995.

Demos, John P. *A Little Commonwealth: Family Life in Plymouth Colony.* New York: Oxford University Press, 1970.

Fowler, William M. *Samuel Adams: Radical Puritan.* New York: Longman, 1997.

Graham, Judith S. *Puritan Family Life: The Diary of Samuel Sewall.* Boston: Northeastern University Press, 2001.

Konig, David Thomas. *Law and Society in Puritan Massachusetts: Essex County, 1629–1692.* Chapel Hill: University of North Carolina Press, 1979.

Kupperman, Karen Ordahl. *Providence Island, 1630–1641: The Other Puritan Colony.* New York: Cambridge University Press, 1993.

Morgan, Edmund S. *The Puritan Dilemma: The Story of John Winthrop.* Boston: Little, Brown, 1958.

Rutman, Darrett B. *Winthrop's Boston: Portrait of a Puritan Town, 1630–1649.* Chapel Hill: University of North Carolina Press, 1965.

Silverman, Kenneth. *The Life and Times of Cotton Mather.* New York: Columbia University Press, 1984.

Stannard, David E. *The Puritan Way of Death: A Study of Religion, Culture, and Social Change.* New York: Oxford University Press, 1977.

Vaughan, Alden T. *The New England Frontier: Puritans and Indians, 1620–1675.* New York: W. W. Norton, 1979.

TIME PERIODS

Civil War Era

Blight, David W., ed. *When This Cruel War Is Over: The Civil War Letters of Charles Harvey Brewster.* Amherst: University of Massachusetts Press, 1992.

Burchard, Peter. *One Gallant Rush: Robert Gould Shaw and His Brave Black Regiment.* New York: St. Martin's Press, 1965.

Clifford, Deborah P. *Mine Eyes Have Seen the Glory: A Biography of Julia Ward Howe.* Boston: Little, Brown, 1979.

Desjardin, Thomas A. *Stand Firm Ye Boys from Maine: The 20th Maine and the Gettysburg Campaign*. New York: Oxford University Press, 2001.

Donald, David Herbert. *Charles Sumner and the Rights of Man*. New York: Knopf, 1970.

Duncan, Russell, ed. *Blue-Eyed Child of Fortune: The Civil War Letters of Colonel Robert Gould Shaw*. Athens: University of Georgia Press, 1992.

Hirshon, Stanley P. *Grenville M. Dodge: Soldier, Politician, Railroad Pioneer*. Bloomington: Indiana University Press, 1967.

Jellison, Charles. *Fessenden of Maine: Civil War Senator*. Syracuse, N.Y.: Syracuse University Press, 1962.

Kohl, Lawrence F., and Margaret Cosse Richard, eds. *Irish Green and Union Blue: The Civil War Letters of Peter Welsh, Color Sergeant, 28th Regiment, Massachusetts Volunteers*. New York: Fordham University Press, 1986.

Leonard, Elizabeth D. *Yankee Women: Gender Battles in the Civil War*. New York: W. W. Norton, 1994.

Marshall, Jeffrey D. *A War of the People: Vermont Civil War Letters*. Hanover, N.H.: University Press of New England, 1999.

Moorhead, James H. *American Apocalypse: Yankee Protestants and the Civil War, 1860–1869*. New Haven, Conn.: Yale University Press, 1978.

Niven, John. *Connecticut for the Union: The Role of the State in the Civil War*. New Haven, Conn.: Yale University Press, 1985.

Oates, Stephen B. *A Woman of Valor: Clara Barton and the Civil War*. New York: Free Press, 1994.

O'Connor, Thomas H. *Civil War Boston: Homefront and Battlefield*. Boston: Northeastern University Press, 1997.

Pride, Mike, and Mark Travis. *My Brave Boys: To War with Colonel Cross and the Fighting Fifth*. Hanover, N.H.: University Press of New England, 2001.

Silber, Nina, and Mary Beth Sievens, eds. *Yankee Correspondence: Civil War Letters between New England Soldiers and the Homefront*. Charlottesville: University Press of Virginia, 1996.

Smith, Mason Philip. *Confederates Downeast: Confederate Operations in and Around Maine*. Portland, Maine: Provincial Press, 1985.

Thomas, John L. *The Liberator, William Lloyd Garrison, a Biography*. Boston: Little, Brown, 1963.

Colonial Era

Anderson, Fred. *A People's Army: Massachusetts Soldiers and Sailors in the Seven Years' War*. Chapel Hill: University of North Carolina Press, 1984.

Bailyn, Bernard. *The New England Merchants in the Seventeenth Century*. Cambridge, Mass.: Harvard University Press, 1955.

Clark, Charles E. *The Eastern Frontier: The Settlement of Northern New England, 1610–1763.* New York: Knopf, 1970.

Daniell, Jere R. *Colonial New Hampshire: A History.* Millwood, N.Y.: KTO Press, 1981.

Deetz, James, and Patricia Scott Deetz. *The Times of Their Lives: Life, Love, and Death in Plymouth Colony.* New York: W. H. Freeman, 2000.

Demos, John. *Entertaining Satan: Witchcraft and the Culture of Early New England.* New York: Oxford University Press, 1982.

Dunn, Richard S. *Puritans and Yankees, The Winthrop Dynasty of New England, 1630–1717.* New York: W. W. Norton, 1971.

Fischer, David Hackett. *Albion's Seed: Four British Folkways in America.* New York: Oxford University Press, 1989.

Greven, Philip J., Jr. *Four Generations: Population, Land, and Family in Colonial Andover, Massachusetts.* Ithaca, N.Y.: Cornell University Press, 1970.

Hawke, David Freeman. *Everyday Life in Early America.* New York: Harper & Row, 1988.

James, Sydney V. *Colonial Rhode Island: A History.* New York: Charles Scribner's Sons, 1975.

Kupperman, Karen Ordahl. *Captain John Smith; A Select Edition of His Writings.* Chapel Hill: University of North Carolina Press, 1986.

Main, Gloria L. *Peoples of a Spacious Land: Families and Cultures in Colonial New England.* Cambridge, Mass.: Harvard University Press, 2001.

Morison, Samuel Eliot. *The European Discovery of America. The Northern Voyages AD 500–1600.* New York: Oxford University Press, 1971.

Norton, Mary Beth. *In the Devil's Snare: The Salem Witchcraft Crisis of 1692.* New York: Alfred A. Knopf, 2002.

Ulrich, Laurel Thatcher. *Goodwives: Image and Reality in the Lives of Women in Northern New England, 1650–1750.* New York: Oxford University Press, 1991.

Wilson, Lisa. *Ye Heart of a Man: The Domestic Life of Men in Colonial New England.* New Haven, Conn.: Yale University Press, 1999.

Zuckerman, Michael. *Peaceable Kingdom: New England Towns in the Eighteenth Century.* New York: Knopf, 1970.

Nineteenth Century

Abbott, Richard H. *Cotton and Capital: Boston Businessmen and Antislavery Reform, 1854–1868.* Amherst: University of Massachusetts Press, 1991.

Barron, Hal S. *Those Who Stayed Behind: Rural Society in Nineteenth-Century New England.* New York: Cambridge University Press, 1984.

Blanchard, Paula. *Margaret Fuller: From Transcendentalism to Revolution.* New York: Delacorte Press, 1978.

Blewett, Mary H. *Constant Turmoil: The Politics of Industrial Life in Nineteenth-Century New England.* Amherst: University of Massachusetts, Press, 2000.

Clifford, Deborah P. *Crusader for Freedom: A Life of Lydia Maria Child.* Boston: Beacon Press, 1992.

Cott, Nancy F. *The Bonds of Womanhood: "Woman's Sphere" in New England, 1780–1835.* New Haven, Conn.: Yale University Press, 1977.

Duberman, Martin. *James Russell Lowell.* Boston: Houghton Mifflin, 1966.

Dublin, Thomas. *Transforming Women's Work: New England Lives in the Industrial Revolution.* Ithaca, N.Y.: Cornell University Press, 1994.

Faler, Paul. *Mechanics and Manufacturers in Early Industrial Revolution—Lynn, Massachusetts, 1780–1860.* Albany: State University of New York Press, 1981.

Gollaher, David. *Voice for the Mad: The Life of Dorothea Dix.* New York: Free Press, 1995.

Hansen, Karen. *A Very Social Time: Crafting Community in Antebellum New England.* Berkeley: University of California Press, 1996.

Hartford, William F. *Money, Morals, and Politics: Massachusetts in the Age of the Boston Associates.* Boston: Northeastern University Press, 2001.

Kelly, Catherine E. *In the New England Fashion: Reshaping Women's Lives in the Nineteenth Century.* Ithaca, N.Y.: Cornell University Press, 1999.

Mann, Arthur. *Yankee Reformers in the Urban Age.* Cambridge, Mass.: Harvard University Press, 1954.

Nagel, Paul C. *John Quincy Adams: A Public Life, a Private Life.* Cambridge, Mass.: Harvard University Press, 1997.

Rivard, Paul E. *A New Order of Things: How the Textile Industry Transformed New England.* Hanover, N.H.: University Press of New England, 2002.

Ronda, Bruce A. *Elizabeth Palmer Peabody: A Reformer on Her Own Terms.* Cambridge, Mass.: Harvard University Press, 1999.

Rose, Anne C. *Transcendentalism as a Social Movement, 1830–1850.* New Haven, Conn.: Yale University Press, 1981.

Sears, John F. *Sacred Places: American Tourist Attractions in the Nineteenth Century.* New York: Oxford University Press, 1989.

Revolutionary Era

Bailyn, Bernard. *The Ordeal of Thomas Hutchinson.* Cambridge, Mass.: Harvard University Press, 1974.

Buel, Joy Day, and Richard Buel, Jr. *The Way of Duty: A Woman and Her Family in Revolutionary America.* New York: W. W. Norton, 1984.

Crane, Elaine Forman. *A Dependent People: Newport, Rhode Island in the Revolutionary Era.* New York: Fordham University Press, 1985.

Fischer, David Hackett. *Paul Revere's Ride*. New York: Oxford University Press, 1994.

Fowler, William M. *The Baron of Beacon Hill: A Biography of John Hancock*. Boston: Houghton Mifflin, 1980.

——. *Samuel Adams: Radical Puritan*. New York: Longman, 1997.

Frothingham, Richard. *History of the Siege of Boston and of the Battles of Lexington, Concord, and Bunker Hill*. New York: Da Capo Press, 1970.

Gross, Robert A. *The Minutemen and Their World*. New York: Hill and Wang, 1976.

Herndon, Ruth Wallis. *Unwelcome Americans: Living on the Margin in Early New England*. Philadelphia: University of Pennsylvania Press, 2001.

Kerber, Linda K. *Women of the Republic: Intellect and Ideology in Revolutionary America*. Chapel Hill: University of North Carolina Press, 1980.

Leamon, James S. *Revolution Downeast: The War for Independence in Maine*. Amherst: University of Massachusetts Press, 1993.

Lovejoy, David S. *Rhode Island Politics and the American Revolution, 1760–1776*. Providence, R.I.: Brown University Press, 1958.

Morgan, Edmund S., and Helen M. Morgan. *The Stamp Act Crisis, Prologue to Revolution*. Chapel Hill: University of North Carolina Press, 1953.

Purcell, Richard J. *Connecticut in Transition, 1775–1818*. Middletown, Conn.: Wesleyan University Press, 1963.

Richards, Leonard L. *Shays's Rebellion: The American Revolution's Final Battle*. Philadelphia: University of Pennsylvania Press, 2002.

Taylor, Robert J. *Western Massachusetts in the Revolution*. Providence, R. I.: Brown University Press, 1954.

Upton, Richard F. *Revolutionary New Hampshire: An Account of the Social and Political Forces Underlying the Transition from Royal Province to American Commonwealth*. New York: Octagon Books, 1971.

Wilderson, Paul W. *Governor John Wentworth and the American Revolution: The English Connection*. Hanover, N. H.: University Press of New England, 1994.

Young, Alfred F. *The Shoemaker and the Tea Party: Memory and the American Revolution*. Boston: Beacon Press, 1999.

Twentieth Century

Abrams, Richard M. *Conservatism in a Progressive Era: Massachusetts Politics, 1900–1912*. Cambridge, Mass.: Harvard University Press, 1964.

Albertine, Cornell. *The Yankee Doughboy*. Boston: Branden Press, 1968.

Bluestone, Barry, and Mary Huff Stevenson. *The Boston Renaissance: Race, Space, and Economic Change in an American Metropolis*. New York: Russell Sage, 2000.

Conforti, Joseph A. *Imagining New England: Explorations of Regional Identity from the Pilgrims to the Mid-Twentieth Century*. Chapel Hill: University of North Carolina Press, 2001.

Connolly, James J. *The Triumph of Ethnic Progressivism: Urban Political Culture in Boston, 1900–1925*. Cambridge, Mass.: Harvard University Press, 1998.

Hentoff, Nat. *Boston Boy*. New York: Knopf, 1986.

Higgins, George V. *Style versus Substance: Boston, Kevin White, and the Politics of Illusion*. New York: Macmillan, 1984.

Jeffries, John W. *Testing the Roosevelt Coalition: Connecticut Society and Politics in the Era of World War II*. Knoxville: University of Tennessee Press, 1979.

Juravich, Tom, et al. *Commonwealth of Toil: Chapters in the History of Massachusetts Workers and Their Unions*. Amherst: University of Massachusetts Press, 1996.

Kidder, Tracy. *The Soul of a New Machine*. Boston: Little Brown, 1981.

Kruh, David. *Always Something Doing: A History of Boston's Infamous Scollay Square*. Boston: Faber and Faber, 1990.

Lupo, Alan. *Liberty's Chosen Home: The Politics of Violence in Boston*. Boston: Little, Brown, 1977.

O'Connor, Thomas H. *Building a New Boston: Politics and Urban Renewal, 1950–1970*. Boston: Northeastern University Press, 1993.

Russell, Francis. *Sacco & Vanzetti: The Case Resolved*. New York: Harper and Row, 1986.

Thernstrom, Stephan. *The Other Bostonians: Poverty and Progress in the American Metropolis, 1880–1970*. Cambridge, Mass.: Harvard University Press, 1976.

Warner, Sam Bass, Jr. *Greater Boston: Adapting Regional Traditions to the Present*. Philadelphia: University of Pennsylvania Press, 2001.

Woods, Robert A. *The Neighborhood in Nation-Building: The Running Comment of Thirty Years at the South End House*. Boston: Houghton Mifflin, 1923.

OTHER CATEGORIES

Architecture and Arts

Bridenbaugh, Carl. *Peter Harrison, First American Architect*. Chapel Hill: University of North Carolina Press, 1949.

Brown, Elizabeth Mills. *New Haven: A Guide to Architecture and Urban Design*. New Haven, Conn.: Yale University Press, 1976.

Bunting, Bainbridge. *Houses of Boston's Back Bay: An Architectural History, 1840–1917*. Cambridge, Mass.: Harvard University Press, 1967.

Claridge, Laura P. *Norman Rockwell: A Life*. New York: Random House, 2001.

Congdon, Herbert Wheaton. *The Covered Bridge: An Old American Landmark*. Brattleboro, Vt.: Stephen Daye Press, 1941.

Conuel, Thomas. *Quabbin: The Accidental Wilderness*. Amherst: University of Massachusetts Press, 1990.

Cummings, Abbott Lowell. *The Framed Houses of Massachusetts Bay, 1625–1725*. Cambridge, Mass.: Harvard University Press, 1979.

Dickson, Harry Ellis. *Arthur Fiedler and the Boston Pops*. Boston: Houghton Mifflin, 1981.

Faxon, Alicia, and Sylvia Moore, eds. *Pilgrims and Pioneers: New England Women in the Arts.* New York: Midmarch Arts Press, 1987.

Fein, Albert. *Frederick Law Olmsted and the American Environmental Tradition*. New York: Braziller, 1972.

Fisher, Sean M., and Carolyn Hughes, eds. *The Last Tenement: Confronting Community and Urban Renewal in Boston's West End*. Boston: Bostonian Society, 1992.

Foster, David R. *Thoreau's Country: Journey through a Transformed Landscape*. Cambridge, Mass.: Harvard University Press, 1999.

Garvan, Anthony N. B. *Architecture and Town Planning in Colonial Connecticut*. New Haven, Conn.: Yale University Press, 1951.

Garvin, James L. *A Building History of Northern New England*. Hanover, N.H.: University Press of New England, 2001.

Gibbons, Gail. *From Path to Highway: The Story of the Boston Post Road*. New York: Thomas Y. Crowell, 1986.

Glassberg, David. *Sense of History: The Place of the Past in American Life*. Amherst: University of Massachusetts Press, 2001.

Holleran, Michael. *Boston's 'Changeful Times': Origins of Preservation and Planning in America*. Baltimore, Md.: Johns Hopkins University Press, 1998.

Hubka, Thomas C. *Big House, Little House, Back House, Barn: The Connected Farm Buildings of New England*. Hanover, N.H.: University Press of New England, 1984.

Kay, Jane Holtz. *Lost Boston*. Boston: Houghton Mifflin, 1999.

Kennedy, Lawrence W. *Planning the City upon a Hill*. Amherst: University of Massachusetts Press, 1992.

Kirker, Harold C. *Bulfinch's Boston, 1787–1817*. New York: Oxford University Press, 1964.

Kruh, Davis. *Always Something Doing: Boston's Infamous Scollay Square*. Boston: Northeastern University Press, 1999.

Lindgren, James Michael. *Preserving Historic New England*. New York: Oxford University Press, 1996.

Logue, Edward J. *Seven Years of Progress: A Final Report*. Boston: Boston Redevelopment Authority, 1967.

Lyndon, Donlyn. *The City Observed, Boston: A Guide to the Architecture of the City*. New York: Vintage Books, 1982.

McNichol, Dan. *The Big Dig*. New York: Silver Lining Books, 2000.

Mellon, Gertrud A., ed. *Maine and Its Role in American Art, 1740–1963*. New York: Viking Press, 1963.

Morgan, Keith, and Naomi Miller. *Boston Architecture: 1975–1990*. Munich: Prestel-Verlag, 1990.

Nylander, Jane C. *Windows on the Past: Four Centuries of New England Homes*. Boston: Bulfinch Press, 2000.

O'Gorman, James. *Living Architecture: A Biography of H. H. Richardson*. New York: Simon and Schuster, 1997.

St. George, Robert Blair. *Material Life in America*. Boston: Northeastern University Press, 1988.

Samuels, Ernest. *Bernard Berenson: The Making of a Connoisseur*. Cambridge, Mass: Belknap Press, 1979.

Shand-Tucci, Douglas. *Boston Bohemia, 1881–1909: Volume I of Ralph Adams Cram, Life and Architecture*. Amherst: University of Massachusetts Press, 1995.

——. *The Art of Scandal: The Life and Times of Isabella Stewart Gardner*. New York: HarperCollins, 1997.

——. *Built in Boston: City and Suburb, 1800–2000*. Amherst: University of Massachusetts Press, 1999.

Tawa, Nicholas E. *From Psalm to Symphony: A History of Music in New England*. Boston: Northeastern University Press, 2001.

Thorson, Robert M. *Stone by Stone: The Magnificent History of New England's Stone Walls*. New York: Walker and Company, 2002.

Tolles, Bryant F., Jr. *New Hampshire Architecture: An Illustrated Guide*. Hanover, N.H.: University Press of New England, 1979.

——. *The Grand Resort Hotels of the White Mountains: A Vanishing Architectural Legacy*. Boston: D. R. Godine, 1998.

Truettner, William H., and Roger B. Stein. *Picturing Old New England: Image and Memory*. New Haven, Conn.: Yale University Press, 1999.

Turner, James. *The Liberal Education of Charles Eliot Norton*. Baltimore, Md.: Johns Hopkins University Press, 1999.

Vogel, Morris J. *The Invention of the Modern Hospital: Boston, 1870–1930*. Chicago: University of Chicago Press, 1980.

Warner, Sam Bass. *Streetcar Suburbs: The Process of Growth in Boston, 1870–1900*. Cambridge, Mass.: Harvard University Press, 1962.

Whitehill, Walter Muir. *Boston Public Library, A Centennial History*. Cambridge, Mass.: Harvard University Press, 1956.

Whitehill, Walter Muir. *Boston Museum of Fine Arts: A Centennial History*. Cambridge, Mass.: Harvard University Press, 1970.

——, and Lawrence W. Kennedy. *Boston: A Topographical History.* Cambridge, Mass.: Harvard University Press, 2000.

Zaitzevsky, Cynthia. *Frederick Law Olmsted and the Boston Park System.* Cambridge, Mass.: Harvard University Press, 1982.

Ecology

Adam, Paul. *Saltmarsh Ecology.* New York: Cambridge University Press, 1990.

Anderson, Larry. *Benton MacKaye: Conservationist, Planner, and Creator of the Appalachian Trail.* Baltimore: Johns Hopkins University Press, 2002.

Aron, Cindy S. *Working at Play: A History of Vacations in the United States.* New York: Oxford University Press, 1999.

Beston, Henry. *The Outermost House: A Year of Life on the Great Beach of Cape Cod.* New York: Penguin Books, 1988.

Connor, Sheila. *New England Natives: A Celebration of People and Trees.* Cambridge, Mass.: Harvard University Press, 1994.

Cronon, William. *Changes in the Land: Indians, Colonists, and the Ecology of New England.* New York: Hill and Wang, 1983.

Cumbler, John T. *Reasonable Use: The People, the Environment, and the State, New England 1790–1930.* New York: Oxford University Press, 2001.

DeGraaf, Richard M., and Mariko Yamasaki. *New England Wildlife: Habitat, Natural History, and Distribution.* Hanover, N.H.: University Press of New England, 2001.

Forbush, Edward Howe. *Birds of Massachusetts and Other New England States.* Norwood, Mass.: Norwood Press, 1929.

Foster, David R. *Thoreau's Country: Journey through a Transformed Landscape.* Cambridge, Mass.: Harvard University Press, 1999.

Gordon, Nancy M. *Stepping Back to Look Forward: A History of the Massachusetts Forest.* Cambridge, Mass.: Harvard University Press, 1998.

Judd, Richard W. *Common Lands, Common People: The Origins of Conservation in Northern New England.* Cambridge: Harvard University Press, 1997.

Merchant, Carolyn. *Ecological Revolutions: Nature, Gender, and Science in New England.* Chapel Hill: University of North Carolina Press, 1989.

O'Connell, James C. *Becoming Cape Cod: Creating a Seaside Resort.* Hanover, N.H.: University Press of New England, 2003.

O'Gorman, James F. *Connecticut Valley Vernacular: The Vanishing Landscape and Architecture of the New England Tobacco Fields.* Philadelphia: University of Pennsylvania Press, 2002.

Raymo, Chet, and Maureen E. Raymo. *Written in Stone: A Geological and Natural History of the Northeastern United States.* Chester, Conn.: Globe Pequot Press, 1989.

Schneider, Paul. *The Enduring Shore: A History of Cape Cod, Martha's Vineyard, and Nantucket*. New York: Henry Holt, 2000.

Silver, Helenette. *A History of New Hampshire Game and Furbearers*. Concord, N.H.: Evans Printing Company, 1957.

Wilson, Harold Fisher. *The Hill Country of Northern New England: Its Social and Economic History, 1790–1930*. New York: Columbia University Press, 1936.

Worster, Donald. *Nature's Economy: A History of Ecological Ideas*. Cambridge, Mass.: Harvard University Press, 1985.

Economy

Black, John D. *The Rural Economy of New England*. Cambridge, Mass.: Harvard University Press, 1950.

Bright, A. A., ed. *The Economic State of New England: Report of the Committee of New England of the National Planning Association*, 2 vols. New Haven, Conn.: Yale University Press, 1954.

Brown, Dona. *Inventing New England: Regional Tourism in the Nineteenth Century*. Washington, D.C.: Smithsonian Institution Press, 1995.

Carroll, Charles F. *The Timber Economy of Puritan New England*. Providence, R. I.: Brown University Press, 1973.

Clark, Christopher. *The Roots of Rural Capitalism: Western Massachusetts, 1780–1860*. Ithaca, N.Y.: Cornell University Press, 1990.

Dalzell, Robert F., Jr. *Enterprising Elite: The Boston Associates and the World They Made*. Cambridge, Mass.: Harvard University Press, 1987.

Dawley, Alan. *Class and Community: The Industrial Revolution in Lynn*. Cambridge, Mass.: Harvard University Press, 1976.

Dolan, J. R. *The Yankee Peddlers of Early America*. New York: C. N. Potter, 1964.

Donahue, Brian. *Reclaiming the Commons: Community Farms & Forests in a New England Town*. New Haven, Conn.: Yale University Press, 1999.

Eisenmenger, Robert W. *The Dynamics of Growth in the New England Economy*. Middletown, Conn.: Wesleyan University Press, 1967.

Gregory, Frances W. *Nathan Appleton: Merchant and Entrepreneur, 1779–1861*. Charlottesville: University Press of Virginia, 1975.

Gross, Lawrence F. *The Course of Industrial Decline: The Boott Cotton Mills of Lowell, Massachusetts, 1835–1955*. Baltimore, Md.: Johns Hopkins University Press, 1993.

Hedges, James B. *The Browns of Providence*. Providence, R. I.: Brown University Press, 1968.

Hunter, Phyllis Whitman. *Purchasing Identity in the Atlantic World: Massachusetts Merchants, 1670–1780*. Ithaca, N.Y.: Cornell University Press, 2001.

Jacobson-Hardy, Michael. *The Changing Landscape of Labor: American Workers and Workplaces*. Amherst: University of Massachusetts Press, 1996.

Keyssar, Alexander. *Out of Work: The First Century of Unemployment in Massachusetts*. New York: Cambridge University Press, 1986.

Larson, John Lauritz. *Bonds of Enterprise: John Murray Forbes and Western Development in America's Railway Age*. Iowa City: University of Iowa Press, 2001.

Layton, Thomas. *The Voyage of the Frolic: New England Merchants and the Opium Trade*. Stanford, Calif.: Stanford University Press, 1999.

McGouldrick, Paul F. *New England Textiles in the Nineteenth Century*. Cambridge, Mass.: Harvard University Press, 1968.

Martin, John Frederick. *Profits in the Wilderness: Entrepreneurship and the Founding of New England Towns in the Seventeenth Century*. Chapel Hill: University of North Carolina Press, 1991.

Prude, Jonathan. *The Coming of Industrial Order: Town and Factory Life in Rural Massachusetts, 1810–1860*. Amherst: University of Massachusetts Press, 1999.

Roberts, Gwilym R. *New Lives in the Valley: Slate Quarries and Quarry Villages in North Wales, New York, and Vermont, 1850–1920*. Somersworth, N.H.: New Hampshire Printers, 1998.

Russell, Howard S. *A Long Deep Furrow: Three Centuries of Farming in New England*. Hanover, N.H.: University Press of New England, 1976.

Smith, David C. *A History of Lumbering in Maine, 1861–1960*. Orono: University of Maine Press, 1972.

Steinberg, Theodore. *Nature Incorporated: Industrialization and the Waters of New England*. New York: Cambridge University Press, 1991.

Temin, Peter, ed. *Engines of Enterprise: An Economic History of New England*. Cambridge, Mass.: Harvard University Press, 2000.

Wright, Conrad E., and Katheryn O. Viens. *Entrepreneurs: The Boston Business Community, 1700–1850*. Boston: Northeastern University Press, 1998.

Education

Ault, Warren Ortman. *Boston University: The College of Liberal Arts, 1873–1973*. Boston: Boston University, 1973.

Axtell, James. *The School Upon a Hill: Education and Society in Colonial New England*. New Haven, Conn.: Yale University Press, 1974.

Cary, Harold Whiting. *The University of Massachusetts: A History of One Hundred Years*. Amherst: University of Massachusetts Press, 1962.

Daniels, Robert V., ed. *The University of Vermont: The First Two Hundred Years*. Hanover, N.H.: University Press of New England, 1991.

Eschenbacher, Herman F. *The University of Rhode Island: A History of Land-Grant Education in Rhode Island*. New York: Appleton-Century-Crofts, 1967.

Freeland, Richard M. *Academia's Golden Age: Universities in Massachusetts, 1945–1970*. New York: Oxford University Press, 1992.

Horowitz, Helen Lefkowitz. *Alma Mater: Design and Experience in the Women's Colleges from Their Nineteenth-Century Beginnings to the 1930s*. Amherst: University of Massachusetts Press, 1995.

Katz, Michael B. *The Irony of Early School Reform: Educational Innovation in Mid-Nineteenth Century Massachusetts*. Cambridge, Mass.: Harvard University Press, 1968.

Kaufman, Polly Welts, ed. *The Search for Equity: Women at Brown University*. Providence, R.I.: Brown University Press, 1991.

Kozol, Jonathan. *Death at an Early Age*. New York: American Library, 1985.

Lazerson, Marvin. *The Origins of the Urban School: Public Education in Massachusetts, 1870–1915*. Cambridge, Mass.: Harvard University Press, 1971.

Lukas, J. Anthony. *Common Ground: A Turbulent Decade in the Lives of Three American Families*. New York: Knopf, 1985.

Marson, Philip. *Breeder of Democracy*. Cambridge, Mass.: Schenkman Publishing Company, 1963.

Messerli, Jonathan. *Horace Mann: A Biography*. New York: Knopf, 1972.

Morison, Samuel Eliot. *Three Centuries of Harvard, 1636–1936*. Cambridge, Mass.: Harvard University Press, 1981.

Schultz, Stanley K. *The Culture Factory: Boston Public Schools, 1789–1860*. New York: Oxford Universe Press, 1973.

Silverman, Kenneth. *Timothy Dwight*. New York: Twayne Publishers, 1969.

Smith, David C. *The First Century: A History of the University of Maine, 1865–1965*. Orono: University of Maine at Orono Press, 1979.

Solomon, Barbara Miller. *In the Company of Educated Women: A History of Women and Higher Education in America*. New Haven, Conn.: Yale University Press, 1985.

Story, Ronald, ed. *Five Colleges: Five Histories*. Amherst: University of Massachusetts Press, 1992.

Folklore

Bell, Michael E. *Food for the Dead: On the Trail of New England's Vampires*. New York: Carroll and Graf Publishers, 2001.

Earle, Alice Morse. *Child Life in Colonial Days*. New York: Macmillan, 1927.

Fischer, David Hackett. *Albion's Seed: Four British Folkways in America*. New York: Oxford University Press, 1989.

Hastings, Scott E. *The Last Yankees: Folkways in Eastern Vermont and the Border Country.* Hanover, N.H.: University Press of New England, 1990.

Mudge, John T. B. *The Old Man's Reader: History and Legends of Franconia Notch.* Etna, N.H.: Durand Press, 1995.

Neustadt, Kathy. *Clambake: A History and Celebration of an American Tradition.* Amherst: University of Massachusetts Press, 1992.

Nylander, Jane. *Our Own Snug Fireside: Images of the New England Home, 1760–1860.* New Haven, Conn.: Yale University Press, 1993.

Oliver, Sandy. *Saltwater Foodways: New Englanders and Their Food at Sea and Ashore in the Nineteenth Century.* Mystic, Conn.: Mystic Seaport Museum, 1995.

Ringel, Faye. *New England's Gothic Literature: History and Folklore of the Supernatural from the Seventeenth through the Twentieth Centuries.* New York: Mellen, 1996.

Rode, Neil. *So You Think You Know Maine.* Gardiner, Maine: Harpswell Press, 1984.

Seelye, John. *Memory's Nation: The Place of Plymouth Rock.* Chapel Hill: University of North Carolina Press, 1999.

Shaughnessy, Dan. *The Curse of the Bambino.* New York: Dutton, 1990.

Snow, Edward Rowe. *Pirates, Shipwrecks, and Historic Chronicles.* New York: Dodd, Mead, 1981.

Weston, George F., Jr. *Boston Ways: High, By and Folk.* Boston: Beacon Press, 1957.

Ulrich, Laurel Thatcher. *The Age of Homespun: Objects and Stories in the Creation of an American Myth.* New York: Knopf, 2001.

Labor

Blewett, Mary H. *Men, Women, and Work: Class, Gender, and Protest in the New England Shoe Industry, 1780–1910.* Urbana: University of Illinois Press, 1988.

Cameron, Ardis. *Radicals of the Worst Sort: Laboring Women in Lawrence, Massachusetts, 1860–1912.* Urbana: University of Illinois Press, 1993.

Dublin, Thomas. *Women at Work: The Transformation of Work and Community in Lowell, Massachusetts, 1826–1860.* New York: Columbia University Press, 1979.

Faler, Paul C. *Mechanics and Manufacturers in the Early Industrial Revolution, Lynn, Massachusetts, 1780–1860.* Albany: State University of New York Press, 1981.

Fones-Wolf, Kenneth, and Martin Kaufman, eds. *Labor in Massachusetts: Selected Essays.* Westfield, Mass.: Institute for Massachusetts Studies, 1990.

Gitelman, Howard M. *Workingmen of Waltham: Mobility in American Urban Industrial Development, 1850–1890.* Baltimore, Md.: Johns Hopkins University Press, 1974.

Green, James, and Hugh Donahue. *Boston's Workers: A Labor History.* Boston: Boston Public Library, 1979.

Gutman, Herbert G., and Donald H. Bell, eds. *The New England Working Class and the New Labor History.* Urbana: University of Illinois Press, 1987.

Hartford, William F. *Working People of Holyoke: Class and Ethnicity in a Massachusetts Mill Town, 1850–1960.* New Brunswick, N.J.: Rutgers University Press, 1990.

Juravich, Tom, William F. Hartford, and James R. Green. *Commonwealth of Toil: Chapters in the History of Massachusetts Workers and Their Unions.* Amherst: University of Massachusetts Press, 1996.

Rosenzweig, Roy. *Eight Hours for What We Will: Workers and Leisure in an Industrial City, 1870–1920.* New York: Cambridge University Press, 1983.

Russell, Francis. *A City in Terror: 1919, The Boston Police Strike.* New York: Viking Press, 1975.

Sanders, Michael S. *The Yard: Building a Destroyer at the Bath Iron Works.* New York: HarperCollins, 1999.

Wright, Carroll. *The Working Girls of Boston. Boston*: Wright and Potter, 1889; reprint New York: Arno, 1969.

Literature

Bellamy, Edward. *Looking Backward, 2000–1887.* Boston: Ticknor and Company, 1888.

Blanchard, Paula. *Sarah Orne Jewett: Her World and Her Work.* Reading, Mass.: Addison-Wesley, 1994.

Brooks, Van Wyck. *The Flowering of New England, 1815–1865.* New York: E. P. Dutton, 1936.

Brown, Dona. *A Tourist's New England: Travel Fiction, 1820–1920.* Hanover, N.H.: University Press of New England, 1999.

Delbanco, Andrew. *Writing New England: An Anthology from the Puritans to the Present.* Cambridge, Mass.: Harvard University Press, 2001.

Duhamel, P. Albert. *After Strange Fruit: Changing Literary Taste in Post–World War II Boston.* Boston: Boston Public Library, 1980.

Fairbanks, Henry G. *Louise Imogen Guiney: Laureate of the Lost.* Albany, N.Y.: Magi Books, 1973.

Glasser, Leah Blatt. *In a Closet Hidden: The Life and Work of Mary E. Wilkins Freeman.* Amherst: University of Massachusetts Press, 1996.

Howells, William Dean. *The Rise of Silas Lapham.* Boston: Houghton Mifflin, 1884.

McAleer, John. *Ralph Waldo Emerson: Days of Encounter*. Boston: Little, Brown, 1985.

MacFarlane, Lisa. *This World Is not Conclusion: Faith in Nineteenth-Century New England Fiction*. Hanover, N.H.: University Press of New England, 1999.

Niemi, Robert. *Russell Banks*. New York: Twayne Publishers, 1997.

O'Connell, Shaun. *Imagining Boston: A Literary Landscape*. Boston: Beacon Press, 1990.

Stern, Madeleine, ed. *L. M. Alcott: Signature of Reform*. Boston: Northeastern University Press, 2002.

Rowman, Judith A. *Annie Adams Fields: The Spirit of Charles Street*. Bloomington: Indiana University Press, 1990.

Tryon, Warren S. *Parnassus Corner: A Life of James T. Fields*. Boston: Houghton Mifflin, 1963.

Wagenknecht, Edward. *Henry Wadsworth Longfellow: Portrait of an American Humanist*. New York: Oxford University Press, 1966.

Maps

Conzen, Michael P., and George K. Lewis. *Boston: A Geographical Portrait*. Cambridge, Mass.: Ballinger Publishing, 1976.

Krieger, Alex, and David Cobb. *Mapping Boston*. Cambridge, Mass.: MIT Press, 1999.

Long, John H., ed. *Atlas of Historical County Boundaries: Connecticut, Maine, Massachusetts, Rhode Island*. New York: Simon and Schuster, 1994.

Meeks, Harold A. *The Geographic Regions of Vermont: A Study in Maps*. Hanover, N.H.: Geography Publications at Dartmouth, 1975.

Morris, Gerald F. ed. *Maine Bicentennial Atlas: An Historical Survey*. Portland: Maine Historical Society, 1976.

Wilkie, Richard W., and Jack Tager, eds. *Historical Atlas of Massachusetts*. Amherst: University of Massachusetts Press, 1991.

Wright, Marion I., and Robert J. Sullivan. *The Rhode Island Atlas*. Providence.: Rhode Island Publication Society, 1982.

Maritime

Bolster, W. Jeffrey. *Black Jacks: African-American Seamen in the Age of Sail*. Cambridge, Mass.: Harvard University Press, 1998.

Crane, Elaine Forman. *Ebb Tide in New England: Women, Seaports, and Social Change, 1630–1800*. Boston: Northeastern University Press, 1998.

Creighton, Margaret S., and Lisa Norling, eds. *Iron Men, Wooden Women: Gender and Seafaring in the Atlantic World, 1700–1920*. Baltimore: Johns Hopkins University Press, 1996.

Cutler, Carl. *Greyhounds of the Sea*. New York: Putnam, 1930.

Dana, Richard Henry. *Two Years Before the Mast*. New York: Harper and Brothers, 1840.

Davis, Lance E., Robert E. Gallman, and Karin Gleiter. *In Pursuit of Leviathan: Technology, Institutions, Productivity, and Profits in American Whaling, 1816–1906*. Chicago: University of Chicago Press, 1997.

Decker, Robert Owen. *Whaling Industry of New London*. York, Pa.: Liberty Cap Books, 1974.

Dewar, Margaret E. *An Industry in Trouble: The Federal Government and the New England Fisheries*. Philadelphia: Temple University Press, 1983.

Dow, George Francis. *Pirates of the New England Coast*. New York: Argosy-Antiquarian, 1968.

Dunne, W. M. P. *Thomas F. McManus and the American Fishing Schooners: An Irish-American Success Story*. Mystic, Conn.: Mystic Seaport, 1996.

Heffernan, Thomas Farel. *Stove by a Whale: Owen Chase and the Essex*. Middletown, Conn.: Wesleyan University Press, 1981.

Kurlansky, Mark. *Cod: A Biography of the Fish That Changed the World*. New York: Walker, 1997.

Morison, Samuel Eliot. *The Maritime History of Massachusetts, 1783–1860*. Boston: Houghton Mifflin, 1961.

Norling, Lisa. *Captain Ahab Had a Wife: New England Women and the Whalefishery, 1720–1870*. Chapel Hill: University of North Carolina Press, 2000.

Rowe, W. H. *The Maritime History of Maine*. New York: W. W. Norton, 1948.

Snow, Edward Rowe. *Pirates and Buccaneers of the Atlantic Coast*. Boston: Yankee Publishing, 1944.

Vickers, Daniel. *Farmers and Fishermen: Two Centuries of Work in Essex County, Massachusetts, 1630–1850*. Chapel Hill: University of North Carolina Press, 1994.

Politics

Abrams, Richard M. *Conservatism in a Progressive Era: Massachusetts Politics, 1900–1912*. Cambridge, Mass.: Harvard University Press, 1964.

Anbinder, Tyler. *Nativism and Slavery: The Northern Know-Nothings*. New York: Oxford University Press, 1992.

Banner, James M. *To the Hartford Convention: The Federalists and the Origins of Party Politics in Massachusetts, 1789–1815*. New York: Knopf, 1970.

Barbrook, Alec. *God Save the Commonwealth: An Electoral History of Massachusetts*. Amherst: University of Massachusetts Press, 1973.

Bernhard, Winfred E. A. *Fisher Ames: Federalist and Statesman, 1758–1808*. Chapel Hill: University of North Carolina Press, 1965.

Blodgett, Geoffrey. *The Gentle Reformers: Massachusetts Democrats in the Cleveland Era*. Cambridge, Mass.: Harvard University Press, 1966.

Brauer, Kinley J. *Cotton versus Conscience: Massachusetts Whig Politics and Southwestern Expansion, 1843–1848*. Lexington: University of Kentucky Press, 1967.

Bryan, Frank M. *Yankee Politics in Rural Vermont*. Hanover, N.H.: University Press of New England, 1974.

Bucki, Cecelia. *Bridgeport's Socialist New Deal, 1915–36*. Urbana: University of Illinois Press, 2001.

Clymer, Adam. *Edward M. Kennedy: A Biography*. New York: William Morrow, 1999.

Crocker, Matthew H. *The Magic of the Many: Josiah Quincy and the Rise of Mass Politics in Boston, 1800–1830*. Amherst: University of Massachusetts Press, 1999.

Dalton, Cornelius. *Leading the Way: A History of the Massachusetts General Court*. Boston: Office of the Massachusetts Secretary of State, 1984.

Eggert, Gerald G. *Richard Olney: Evolution of a Statesman*. University Park: Pennsylvania State University Press, 1974.

Farrell, John Aloysius. *Tip O'Neill and the Democratic Century*. Boston: Little, Brown and Company, 2001.

Formisano, Ronald P. *The Transformation of Political Culture: Massachusetts Parties, 1790s–1840s*. New York: Oxford University Press, 1983.

Goodwin, Doris Kearns. *The Fitzgeralds and the Kennedys: An American Saga*. New York: St. Martin's Press, 1987.

Hennessy, Michael E. *Four Decades of Massachusetts Politics, 1890–1935*. Norwood, Mass.: Norwood Press, 1935.

Hunt, H. Draper. *Hannibal Hamlin of Maine: Lincoln's First Vice-President*. Syracuse, N.Y.: Syracuse University Press, 1969.

Huthmacker, J. Joseph. *Massachusetts People and Politics, 1919–1933*. Cambridge, Mass.: Harvard University Press, 1959.

Kaufman, Polly Welts. *Boston Women and City School Politics, 1872–1905*. New York: Garland Publishing, 1994.

Kenney, Charles, and Robert Turner. *Dukakis: An American Odyssey*. Boston: Houghton Mifflin, 1988.

Kerber, Linda K. *Federalists in Dissent: Imagery and Ideology in Jeffersonian America*. Ithaca, N.Y.: Cornell University Press, 1980.

Lieberman, Joseph I. *The Power Broker: A Biography of John M. Bailey, Modern Political Boss*. Boston: Houghton Mifflin, 1966.

Lieberman, Joseph I., and Michael D'Orso. *In Praise of Public Life*. New York: Simon and Schuster, 2000.

Litt, Edgar. *The Political Cultures of Massachusetts*. Cambridge, Mass.: MIT Press, 1965.

Lockard, Duane. *New England State Politics*. Princeton, N.J.: Princeton University Press, 1959.

McCaughey, Robert A. *Josiah Quincy, 1772–1864: The Last Federalist*. Cambridge, Mass.: Harvard University Press, 1974.

Martin, Joseph W. *My First Fifty Years in Politics*. Westport, Conn.: Greenwood Press, 1975.

Nevin, David. *Muskie of Maine*. New York: Random House, 1972.

Newmyer, R. Kent. *Supreme Court Justice Joseph Story: Statesman of the Old Republic*. Chapel Hill: University of North Carolina Press, 1985.

Palmer, Niall A. *The New Hampshire Primary and the American Electoral Process*. Westport, Conn.: Praeger, 1997.

Peirce, Neal R. *The New England States: People, Politics and Power in the Six New England States*. New York: W. W. Norton, 1976.

Remini, Robert V. *Daniel Webster: The Man and His Time*. New York: W. W. Norton, 1997.

Strom, Sharon Hartman. *Political Woman: Florence Luscomb and the Legacy of Political Reform*. Philadelphia, Pa.: Temple University Press, 2001.

Sullivan, Edmund B., Barry Mushlin, and Robert E. Colt. *Campaigning with Curley*. Hanover, Mass.: Christopher Publishing, 2000.

Weicker, Lowell P., Jr., and Barry Sussman. *Maverick: A Life in Politics*. Boston: Little, Brown, 1995.

Whalen, Thomas J. *Kennedy versus Lodge: The 1952 Massachusetts Senate Race*. Boston: Northeastern University Press, 2000.

White, Theodore. *The Making of the President 1960*. New York: Atheneum, 1961.

Zimmerman, Joseph F. *The New England Town Meeting: Democracy in Action*. Westport, Conn.: Praeger, 1999.

Religion

Cole, Phyllis. *Mary Moody Emerson and the Origins of Transcendentalism: A Family History*. New York: Oxford University Press, 1996.

Conforti, Joseph A. *Jonathan Edwards: Religious Tradition, and American Culture*. Chapel Hill: University of North Carolina Press, 1995.

Conley, Patrick T., and Matthew J. Smith. *Catholicism in Rhode Island*. Providence, R.I.: Diocese of Rhode Island, 1976.

Cooper, James F. *Tenacious of Their Liberties: The Congregationalists in Colonial Massachusetts*. New York: Oxford University Press, 1999.

Dalin, David G., and Jonathan Rosenbaum. *Making a Life, Building a Community: A History of the Jews of Hartford*. New York: Holmes and Meier, 1997.

Dever, Joseph. *Cushing of Boston: A Candid Portrait*. Boston: Bruce Humphries, 1965.

Field, Peter S. *The Crisis of the Standing Order: Clerical Intellectuals and Cultural Authority in Massachusetts, 1780–1833*. Amherst: University of Massachusetts Press, 1998.

Gamm, Gerald H. *Urban Exodus: Why the Jews Left Boston and the Catholics Stayed.* Cambridge, Mass.: Harvard University Press, 1999.

Gaustad, Edwin Scott. *The Great Awakening in New England*. New York: Harper and Brothers, 1957.

Gill, Gillian. *Mary Baker Eddy*. Reading, Mass.: Perseus Books, 1998.

Hall, David D. *The Faithful Shepherd: A History of the New England Ministry in the Seventeenth Century*. Chapel Hill: University of North Carolina Press, 1972.

Hall, Michael Garibaldi. *The Last American Puritan: The Life of Increase Mather, 1639–1723*. Middletown, Conn.: Wesleyan University Press, 1988.

Jones, Mary J. A. *Congregational Commonwealth: Connecticut, 1636–1662*. Middletown, Conn.: Wesleyan University Press, 1968.

Levine, Hillel, and Lawrence Harmon. *The Death of an American Jewish Community: A Tragedy of Good Intentions*. New York: Free Press, 1992.

Lord, Robert H., John E. Sexton, and Edward T. Harrington. *History of the Archdiocese of Boston*. 3 vols. Boston: Pilot Publishing Company, 1945.

Merwick, Donna. *Boston Priests, 1848–1910: A Study of Social and Intellectual Change*. Cambridge, Mass.: Harvard University Press, 1973.

O'Connor, Thomas H. *Fitzpatrick's Boston, 1846–1866: John Bernard Fitzpatrick, Third Bishop of Boston*. Boston: Northeastern University Press, 1984.

——. *Boston Catholics: A History of the Church and Its People*. Boston: Northeastern University Press, 1998.

O'Toole, James M. *Militant and Triumphant: William Henry O'Connell and the Catholic Church in Boston, 1859–1944*. Notre Dame, Ind.: University of Notre Dame Press, 1992.

Putney, Clifford. *Muscular Christianity: Manhood and Sports in Protestant America, 1880–1920*. Cambridge, Mass.: Harvard University Press, 2001.

Sarna, Jonathan D., and Ellen Smith, eds. *The Jews of Boston*. Boston: Combined Jewish Philanthropies of Greater Boston, 1995.

Sassi. Jonathan D. *A Republic of Righteousness: The Public Christianity of the Post-Revolutionary New England Clergy*. New York: Oxford University Press, 2001.

Schultz, Nancy Lusignan. *Fire and Roses: The Burning of the Charlestown Convent, 1834*. New York: Free Press, 2000.

Stout, Harry S. *The New England Soul: Preaching and Religious Culture in Colonial New England*. New York: Oxford University Press, 1986.

Tracy, Patricia J. *Jonathan Edwards, Pastor: Religion and Society in Eighteenth-Century Northampton*. New York: Hill and Wang, 1980.

Weisman, Richard. *Witchcraft, Magic, and Religion in Seventeenth-Century Massachusetts.* Amherst: University of Massachusetts Press, 1984.

Weiss, Ellen. *City in the Woods: The Life and Design of an American Camp Meeting on Martha's Vineyard.* Boston: Northeastern University Press, 1998.

Williams, Selma R. *Divine Rebel: The Life of Anne Marbury Hutchinson.* New York: Holt, Rinehart and Winston, 1981.

About the Author

Peter C. Holloran is currently an assistant professor of history at Worcester State College in Worcester, Massachusetts. His interest in New England history comes from teaching Massachusetts history and being a native Bostonian. He has been executive secretary of the New England Historical Association and the Northeast Popular Culture/American Culture Association, and is an editor of the *Journal of Popular Culture*. His first publication was *Boston's Wayward Children: Social Services for Homeless Children, 1830–1930* (1989) and he has contributed to the *Encyclopedia of New England Culture, the American National Biography*, and the *Dictionary of American Biography*. He lives in Cambridge, Massachusetts, and summers in Maine and Vermont.